A Legal History of Money in the United States

1774-1970

A Legal History of Money
in the United States, 1774-1970

James Willard Hurst

UNIVERSITY OF NEBRASKA PRESS · LINCOLN

First printing 1973
Most recent printing shown by first digit below:
2   3   4   5   6   7   8   9   10

Contents

Preface

I am grateful to the faculty of law of the University of Nebraska for the invitation to deliver the Pound Lectures of 1970, from which this book derives. My appreciation goes also to Dean Henry Grether and Professor James A. Lake, Sr., and their colleagues for the hospitality with which they received me as guest to their campus.

This work deals with legal elements in the history of the system of money in the United States from about 1774 to 1970. The subject confronts a lawyer with a dauntingly large and intricate literature supplied by economists, economic historians, and bankers. Within the limits of my time and understanding I have explored this literature—enough, I hope, to locate those aspects of it most relevant to the operations of law upon money. In such a subject plainly a legal historian should not attempt independent judgments that call for expertness in other than legal matters. His task is, rather, to borrow the opinions of qualified specialists outside the law in order to provide a meaningful context in which to appraise what the law has done or failed to do. Thus I do not purport to write an economic history of money in the United States; I do undertake to tell the legal history of the country's system of money. I focus on the system of money, moreover, further to define the limits of this work. I do not deal with *money* as shorthand for economic, social, or political power held through command of economic assets; for example, I do not deal with money in politics—the influence that command of disposable economic

vii

assets has when men seek office or seek to influence officeholders. My concern here is money as a distinct institutional instrument, employed primarily in allocating scarce economic resources, mainly through governmental and market processes.

This volume has a place within themes concerning the history of law relative to the general history of the United States which I have pursued with past support from the Social Science Research Council, the Rockefeller Foundation, and the administration of the University of Wisconsin, and more recently with support from the trustees of the William F. Vilas Trust Estate, under whose auspices I hold a chair as Vilas Professor of Law in the University of Wisconsin. Of course, I do not purport to speak for any of these agencies, and I take sole responsibility for what I write.

James Willard Hurst

Analytical Table
of Contents

tions of comparative values of centralized and dispersed controls over the money supply.

a) Common law recognized a sphere of private contract for creating money.

b) Definition of the terms on which men might incorporate banks of issue were the first form of regulation of delegated power to create money.

(1) Prevailing opinion distrusted government-issued currency.

(2) Policy favored increasing reliance on commercial banks to provide currency.

(3) However, some states for a time curbed bank issues.

(4) From mid-nineteenth century prevailing policy accepted the monetary role of commercial banks, while subjecting them to ineffectively supervised regulation.

c) The two Banks of the United States, especially the second bank, undertook some management of the money supply, and under Biddle's direction the second bank moved toward a central-bank role.

(1) The second bank tended to provide a reliable national currency.

(2) Its lending policies tended to adjust regional and international trade balances.

(3) Its branches enabled it to exert broad influence.

(4) But the two banks became objects of political controversy because of the extent of power thus delegated to private control.

3. In this period all major branches of government shared in making monetary policy.

B. The years 1860-1908 moved toward more centralized regulation of money, but with a want of constructive policy.

1. Federal-state relations were not now the primary area of controversy; Congress made bolder use of its authority, but in practice left much scope for growth of deposit-check money by state-chartered commercial banks.

2. Most change and dispute in these years centered on the relative roles of legal and market processes, though with attention given disproportionately to govern-

A Legal History of Money in the United States

1774-1970

A Prelude to Policy
(1774-90)

Legal processes and the money supply have been involved with each other in ways of substantial importance in the social history of law in the United States. Public policy sanctioned diverse and increasing uses of law to affect the money supply; on the other hand, use of a money calculus in many aspects of social relations materially affected how law made public policy and implemented it. Beyond its immediate involvements with law, the abstract, impersonal character of money made it an instrument adaptable in a great variety and range of social adjustments. Thus its use entered into the operation not only of the market or of profit-seeking enterprises in general, but also of other social institutions wherever their affairs invited effort at rational reckoning of gains and costs. This is not to say that money was the best instrument for striking balances of gain or cost through the processes of law or of other social institutions outside the market, but simply that familiarity and utility—real or apparent—spread use of a money calculus to an extent that was of great general effect. Moreover, money was an instrument for effecting allocations of command over scarce resources; so long as there was a practically effective money supply, money was an instrument of power. Viewed in either aspect—as an instrument of social functions or of command—the money supply became of public policy concern in a legal order which emphasized the constitutional ideal that all social organizations should be legitimized by criteria of utility or justice not solely controlled by those most immediately interested.

The course of public policy on law and money does not fall into a neatly patterned story. To begin with, *money* was not a stable, sharply defined idea. What men thought of as money changed with shifts in business practice and invention and with changed expectations or demands laid upon the general economy; uses of law affecting the money supply changed with changed ideas of arrangements which served monetary functions. Uncertain definitions of money reflected not only objective changes in social behavior but over much of the time a considerable confusion of ideas about cause and effect in the currents of affairs in which money played a part. Poor theory was confusing in itself. It also gave great scope for developing public policy out of untutored practice and custom; a great part—perhaps the greater part—of public policy on money must thus be inferred from technical detail in legislative, executive, or administrative action, typically accompanied by little statement of general principles. Not least among factors which make it hard to tell a neatly patterned story on law-money relations is the close interweaving of problems of ends and means which marks the course of policy in this area. The legal history of the money supply in the United States centered on two main concerns: (1) determination of the legitimate purposes for which we might use law to affect the money supply; (2) allocation of legal authority affecting the money supply among different agencies, affected by varying appraisals of the impress which the structure, goals, and traditions of different agencies might have on the character and availability of money. These two centers of policy attention so stand out on the record as to demand separate consideration, and yet they cannot be sharply separated. Ideas about the proper purposes for which law might affect the money supply helped determine who should wield authority; ideas about the capabilities and limitations, the promises and the threats residing in different forms of legal processes contributed to shape decisions about the proper purposes of using law in this domain. The intertwining of these themes is not surprising; legal history teaches that ends and means tend to shape each other. But the mingling of concerns for goals and for apparatus means that there is inescapable overlap in the two parts which follow—the first examines the course of public policy defining the legitimate uses of law affecting the money supply, the second considers problems and effects connected with allocation of roles among legal agencies.

The legal history of money ramified from 1790 to 1970 into varied aspects of these two principal centers of concern, focused on purposes and on apparatus. Over these years public policy changed much in substantive content and in procedures. But the varied developments which took place rested on and in some measure were forecast and affected by experience and decisions taken in the formative generation of the United States. National existence began with legal actions which gave unusually sharp, formal definition to national legal order, first through the Articles of Confederation, then by the federal Constitution. Experience under the articles, and some basic choices of policy in the Constitution provided base lines from which to measure the later course of law affecting the money supply. The rest of this prelude examines some features of the law affecting money in the constitution-making years from 1774 to 1790.

In the first chapter of its national existence—as a loose alliance represented by the Continental Congress (1774-77) and then as a confederation under governing articles (1777-88)—the United States dealt with the money supply and public credit in ways which had counterparts over the next nearly two hundred years. At first legislators directly created money which had the form of debt; individual state legislatures, but especially the Continental Congress, issued paper currency in the form of bills of credit. Later, the central government delegated creation of credit and a paper currency to an institution—a bank—of mixed public and private character, subject to public inspection, whose notes should enjoy the protection of law against counterfeiters and the law's encouragement as instruments receivable in payments of duties and taxes. This early pattern of control reflected reality. The condition of the money supply so pervasively affected life that it must be a concern of the principal and most representative policy makers. On the other hand, an effective, responsible money policy called for focused, continuous, experienced attention which a legislature was poorly structured to provide. Another aspect of the matter reflected the fact that money was important to the conduct of both public and private business. From the outset of our national life, the market and the government vied for position in shaping the economy; it fit this sharing of power that a bank of mixed public and private character should help manage the money supply. And these beginnings included yet a third dimension of control over money, insofar as questions arose of the relative roles of central and state governments.

Legislative provision of paper money was the prime domestic means of financing the Revolution. The Congress had no authority to lay taxes, either before or under the Articles of Confederation. State legislatures lacked will to tax in any measure realistically responsive to the war needs. Thus legislative policy made no serious effort to transfer purchasing power from private to public hands, but instead allowed an increasing bulk of paper currency to compete unaided for goods and services. States ultimately issued some $210 million par value of bills of credit, and the Congress over $241 million of its own bills; as the United States moved into a crisis in public finance in 1781, bills of credit accounted probably for about 70 percent of the cost of the war to that time. Sharp depreciation set in from 1778, acknowledged by Congress in 1780 when it declared that it would accept its old bills in settlement of requisitions on the states at a ratio of one fortieth of their declared specie value. Fresh issues of bills at the new 1780 valuation in turn depreciated, as taxes continued at levels wholly inadequate to keep government currency in some balanced relation to the flow of real goods and services. Lacking was any machinery to set standards of fiscal and monetary responsibility, let alone to enforce them.[1]

Congress took a step in our political education in 1781 when it gave up the effort to run a national financial policy by legislative committee and turned to creating some part of the executive establishment which the situation called for. It named the country's leading merchant, Robert Morris, superintendent of finance.[2] Among other items, Morris promptly turned his attention to improving the money supply. In May 1781 Morris proposed and the Congress approved the organization of a corporation to accept deposits, issue notes intended to circulate as currency, and make loans. In December 1781 by special statute Congress incorporated the Bank of North America, which began business in January 1782. This was the country's first commercial bank of issue and deposit.[3] Its charter was a document simple to the point of being uninformative. Apart from conferring the rudiments of corporate status, it said nothing to define functions or powers beyond authorizing the bank "to do ... all ... things that to them shall or may appertain to do," and to "make ... and put in execution such ... regulations, as shall seem necessary and convenient to the government" of the corporation. Despite the brevity of the charter, some of its terms together with items in the prospectus which Morris put to the Congress showed that the bank was intended to fulfill public functions and to be under some related public regulation. Though the charter was silent on this important point, the prospectus contemplated that the bank would issue notes payable on demand and by law to be made receivable for the duties and taxes of every state and for requisitions made on the states by the United States. The bank in fact issued notes. By keeping its loans relatively liquid and holding its issues in conservative ratio to its assets, it won acceptance of its notes, so that although they suffered some discount the farther they circulated from Philadelphia, on the whole they supplied a reliable, useful addition to the currency.[4] Of equal importance in Morris's view to supplying acceptable currency was the bank's availability to assist in financing the government. In its first phase, in 1782 and 1783, the bank amply·met this expectation. It discounted private notes paid into the treasury for foreign bills of exchange so that the national government could obtain cash in the form of the bank's notes. More important, it loaned generously to the national treasury, tiding it over critical months.[5]

Such functions implied a public importance and influence which warranted public regulation. The charter limited the bank's property holdings of all kinds to $10 million "of Spanish silver milled dollars" and stipulated that its affairs be governed by a board of twelve directors. Morris's prospectus had said that the superintendent of finance should at all times have access to the bank's papers and should closely scrutinize its affairs; though the charter said nothing of this, during the period when the bank actively served the national treasury, Morris was in such close connection with its business as in fact to fulfill the promise of the prospectus.[6] Finally, the governing law was sensitive to the prerogatives of the states, and to the fact that James Madison and some other members felt that Congress had no authority to charter a corporation at all. Though the charter declared that in general it should "be construed . . . most favorably and beneficially for the . . . corporation," it specifically declared that nothing in it "shall be construed to authorize the [bank] . . . to exercise any powers, in any of the United States, repugnant to the laws or constitution of such State." Moreover, by separate resolution Congress recommended to the states to pass laws granting the bank status within their bounds; in Madison's view this action tacitly admitted Congress's want of power to issue a charter, and stood as a precedent against any further "usurpation."[7] In 1782, to resolve doubts of the bank's status, Massachusetts, New York, and Pennsylvania incorporated it. The bank regarded its Pennsylvania charter as its prime legal base; when local agrarian jealousy brought repeal of that charter in 1785, the bank obtained a corporate haven from Delaware, but bargained out a return to Pennsylvania incorporation in 1787.[8]

In the founding intention of Robert Morris and the Congress the Bank of North America was to be a *national* bank, because it would combine with pursuit of private business the service of the national treasury. The charter's preamble justified incorporation of the bank as assisting "the finances [and] . . . the exigencies of the United States," and the bank obtained the bulk of its original capital from the deposit there by the superintendent of finance of a shipment of specie loaned to the United States by France. In its preliminary resolution approving organization of a bank Congress expressed its intention to charter no other such institution during the war. In view of this declaration and the contemplated public-service functions of the bank, its creation might suggest the idea of a central bank. But in its brief span of public service it never played a central-bank role, for there was yet no banking system over which it could preside.[9] Its special function as aide to the treasury lasted only from 1782 to 1783; upon the peace the national government no longer depended on its loans. The bank's note issue was not large enough to constitute a national currency, and as the number of banks grew its notes became simply part of a diverse bank circulation.[10] Altogether, thus, the bank's distinctive role as a public institution was short-lived. But it set precedents: that private assets might be usefully mustered to support public credit and a general currency, that effective provision of money and credit called for continuous, skilled administration, and that—Madison's constitutional doubts to the contrary notwithstanding—there were legitimate national interests warranting national apparatus concerned with the supply of money and public loans.

Concern with law and the money supply fills a relatively small part of the record of the federal convention and the state ratifying conventions. Not that the constitution makers rated the matter simple or unimportant. They dealt rather shortly with it because throughout they felt that they grasped the full range of the problems and that they were in substantial agreement on what to do about them. They dealt in bold strokes because they felt that they knew the tangles into which loose handling here could bring affairs. The confident consensus which induced this short way with the subject was not altogether well-founded, and hence not without cost in ambiguities. Consequent difficulties fell in two important areas—federal and state authority over bank charters, and federal authority to issue paper money and to give it the character of legal tender. Part of the trouble was that the framers could not anticipate the growth in sophistication in the economy.[11] Part of the trouble was their failure fully to declare the substantive policies they sought; the record focuses mainly on government structure—the location and definition of power—and deals little in ideas about the functions of money and the legitimate uses of law concerning it.[12]

The clearest policy set in the federal Constitution showed strong distrust of allowing state legislatures to set money-supply policy. Thus the Constitution determined that ultimate control of the money supply should be a matter of national policy, in some respects fixed directly in the Constitution, and in others put under the authority of Congress.

The Constitution put no less than four direct limits on state dealings with the money supply. (1) It forbade the states to coin money—in sharp departure from the Articles of Confederation, which had recognized concurrent coinage authority in Congress and the states.[13] (2) In context with its grant to Congress of power not only to coin money but also to "regulate the value thereof, and of foreign coin," the Constitution implicitly forbade the states to attempt to define the value of the coinage—continuing the policy under the Articles of Confederation, which had made Congress the sole arbiter of the value of coin struck by authority either of Congress or of the states.[14] (3) The Constitution declared that "no state shall . . . emit bills of credit"—a complete departure from the Articles of Confederation, which had left to the states full discretion in issuing evidences of debt which might circulate as money.[15] (4) Further, the Constitution declared that "no state shall . . . make any thing but gold and silver coin a tender in payment of debts"—likewise a sharp change from the Articles of Confederation, which by silence left full powers in the matter to the states.[16] This ban concerned only state efforts to define the media of exchange which should be legally effective to settle transactions. The possibility remained that states might otherwise regulate creditors' rights, by setting procedural limits or delays on enforcing claims, for example, thus creating important—if secondary—effects on the utility of money. Well alert to this possibility, the framers put alongside the provisions limiting the states' direct dealings with money the prohibition on any law "impairing the obligation of contracts"—another significant change from the Articles of Confederation, which had no counterpart. The contract clause did not have the sharp finality of the bans on state coinage or emission of bills of credit; it declared more a standard than a rule, inevitably inviting case by case development of its content. But both the framers' intention and the kinds of economic and political situations most likely to invoke the new provision made the contract clause a complement to constitutional policy on the money supply.[17]

All the elements in this pattern of limits on the states appeared early and held steady in the process of framing the Constitution, supported in convention by spokesmen for large and small states alike.[18] The only major change that occurred attested the strength of the limiting policy, by tightening its expression. At a preliminary stage there were proposals that Congress might either permit or hold a veto over state laws creating bills of credit or defining legal tender. But the convention finally voted eight to one (with one state divided) for an absolute constitutional ban on state bills of credit, and eleven to zero for an absolute ban on state laws which would make anything but gold or silver legal tender.[19] Throughout, the explicit denial of state coinage and the implicit denial of state authority to fix money values stood in absolute form.[20] There is further testimony to the vigor of the policy limiting the states in the fact that no amendment or qualification of any part of the pattern—including the contract clause—was offered in the state ratifying conventions.[21] It would be wrong to read this record as establishing country-wide agreement. Outside the national and state conventions there was strong inflationary sentiment for leaving the states free to issue paper currency, and among small debtors fear and resentment that state law might not be able to ease hard times with relaxed legal-tender laws or stays on court enforcement of creditors' rights.[22] But these attitudes never showed significant force in the framing or ratification of the Constitution; there the clear, dominant view throughout put no trust in money policy made by state legislatures.

Negative judgments stand out more clearly than positive ones in this policy limiting state power. The constitution makers primarily wanted to standardize the money supply. This does not mean that they wanted to freeze a particular economic situation. They wanted to standardize money not to guard hoarded wealth, but to promote confident, vigorous action in market, including constructive use of credit. Dynamic rather than static, this market orientation sought money of stable value most clearly to foster a broader reach of trade at any given time; there was recurrent talk of maintaining the confidence of foreign traders and of traders dealing at a distance over state lines. There is no direct evidence of intent to regulate money in order to foster a greater reach of trade over time; the surest point we may make on this score is to say that the evidenced concern with stable money bore some implication of concern for encouraging men to lend in the reasonable expectation of repayment in money of comparable value to what they had put out.[23] To some extent governmental values figured, also. To put control of coinage and its value in the new federal government and to prohibit state bills of credit would assure that the new central government's taxing power would be economically effective and equitable and would help keep peace within the union. In contrast, free-wheeling state action on money would tend to drive specie out of circulation, bring only depreciated or worthless tokens into the federal treasury, allow the less responsible states to shirk their fair burden of federal expense, and promote rancor among those involved in trade among the states.[24]

But, although these market and political values were dynamic rather than static in purpose, they included little positive policy about managing the money supply for general economic growth.[25] What dominated contemporary talk was memory of the destructive depreciation that had marked recent issues of paper money by the states and by Congress.[26] Thus the most influential view among the constitution makers put more emphasis on defining limits of government power over money, than on setting substantive standards for an affirmative money policy. In particular, prevailing concern centered on distrust of the ability of legislatures to manage the money supply without falling captive to those who would persistently accept the risks and costs of inflation to get a boom.[27] Following the main direction of debate is the one important argument of substance pressed in behalf of state power over bills of credit and legal tender which sought to fulfill more a governmental than an economic function—to preserve full flexibility in the states to deal with temporary situations of extreme political or economic emergency for the safety and peace of the polity as a whole.[28] In response, the prevailing opinion in the federal and state conventions was, again, basically a political judgment: that state legal process had proved too vulnerable to focused inflationary pressures and could not be depended on to restrict use of such powers to closely defined emergencies. At basis, the framers' failure to avoid important ambiguities even in defining limits of government power probably stemmed from fear that to explore fuller definition would confront them with substantive issues of money management on which they might not be able to strike a working bargain. It seems indicative of such an attitude that the convention so decisively rejected the argument that concession be made to the paper money interest, by leaving the matter in the discretion of Congress, in order to reduce outside opposition to adopting the new Constitution.[29]

The constitution makers made no clear record on what experience proved to be a major area of state law affecting money. This was state chartering of private banks empowered to issue notes intended to circulate as currency. There is nothing directly in point on this matter in the work or discussion surrounding the making of the federal Constitution. The nearly unanimous condemnation of state-issued bills of credit was so strong and unqualified in the federal and state conventions that it might imply that the absolute ban on state bills of credit carried corollary condemnation of state franchises for issuing private bank notes.[30] Moreover, the pattern of limitations on state power suggested a general intention that the federal government enjoy a monopoly in making policy concerning the creation of money.[31] Two contemporary circumstances cloud these arguments. Though the constitution makers wrote a separate ban on state bills of credit, current criticism often characterized the evil as the issue of bills of credit to which state law gave the character of legal tender, and a substantial part of the criticism fastened on the legal-tender element as the root objection.[32] Clearly, the sweep of the Constitution's prohibition on the states against making anything but gold or silver legal tender barred giving this attribute to private bank notes.[33] It was by no means so clear that a prohibition that "no state" should emit bills of credit meant that the state might not permit circulating notes based solely on the credit of private franchise holders.[34] Given this ambiguity, and with the legal-tender problem otherwise disposed of, there was fair basis to argue—as did Madison, in 1831—that private bank notes lacking legal-tender quality did not present the historic problem to which the constitution makers intended response.[35] A second factor is that as of 1787 only two banks were operating in the United States under state franchises: the Bank of North America, in Pennsylvania, and the Massachusetts Bank, operating under state corporate charters since 1782 and 1784 respectively. These banks issued circulating notes. But they were only two, and their limited resources and the relative isolation of their operations did not add up to a situation likely to make the constitution makers perceive private bank notes as a significant expression of state law affecting the money supply.[36] Thus, with all due allowance for the hazards of memory over a span of more than forty years, in 1831 when Madison's recollection was that the ban on state bills of credit was written with no thought for the circulating notes of state-chartered banks, it is easy to believe him. As Madison observed, by 1831 experience had shown that depreciation of such bank notes could disturb the money supply with effects like those proceeding from state issues which had occasioned the constitutional prohibition.[37] But if the prohibition were to be read in the context of 1787, it did not speak to such problems as might arise from state franchising of private bank notes.

The array of limitations which the constitution makers put on the states might well imply intent to put in the federal government a monopoly of positive power concerning the money supply.[38] Moreover, the framers put into the Constitution not a single explicit limit on what the Congress might do about money, in sharp contrast to the prohibitions so prominently laid on the states; a fair inference might be that Congress should have as plenary authority over money as it had, for example, over commerce among the states.[39] However, the record as a whole left as much in question as it settled about federal power. The framers had some clearcut ideas about what they did not want the states to do. They did not show nearly as well defined a conception of what they wanted Congress to be able to do.

What the constitution makers made clear about the federal authority was a cluster of powers which most obviously served the function of standardizing the money supply. Congress had power "to coin money," and—in the context of the explicit ban on state coinage—held a monopoly in regulating that function.[40] The exclusive character of this power of Congress was underlined by contrast with the Articles of Confederation, which had given the old Congress only "the sole and exclusive right and power of regulating the alloy and value of coin struck by their own authority or by that of the respective states."[41] The framers had no doubt what they wanted on this score; the federal coinage authority stood the same, untouched and unquestioned, through all stages of shaping the constitutional text.[42] Continuing the precedent set by the Articles of Confederation, the Constitution further gave Congress power not only "to coin money," but also to "regulate the value thereof, and of foreign coin"; coupled with the ban on state coinage, this grant implied—as the Articles of Confederation had declared expressly—that Congress had exclusive power to fix the value of the coin for which it might provide.[43] Nothing in the record or in the Constitution elaborates what is meant by this power to "regulate the value" of coin. On the face of the language, the coupled grants were probably thought of as authorizing the manufacture of money tokens ("to coin money") with a metal content defined by law (thus "regulating the value").[44] Congress might in one sense regulate the value of money by making it legal tender. But there is no evidence that the framers thought of legal tender as a dimension of *value*; as we shall note shortly, when they spoke of legal tender it was as a separate subject, and one sharply distinct from—indeed, opposed to—dealings with coin.[45] Again, Congress might be thought to regulate the value in the sense of the purchasing power of money, if it used its monetary or fiscal powers to affect general price levels. But there is no hint of this sophistication in the convention's dealings with the *value* clause. Moreover, the times were against it; the debates are unanimous in condemning recent fluctuations in the market value of paper money issued by the old Congress and by the states before 1787, and the framers anticipated enough popular distrust of the extent of power proposed for the new central government so that it is unlikely that they would have meant to render their document more vulnerable in the ratifying conventions by overtly including an authority to manipulate prices.[46] The desire to insure that Congress could fully achieve formal standardization of the money system suffices to explain the value clause. As part of the same concern for standardization, the Constitution empowered Congress "to provide for the punishment of counterfeiting the securities and current coin of the United States." The Articles of Confederation had not spoken of any such authority in the old Congress; inclusion of the new item is part of the implied bias of the Constitution toward making the federal government the primary authority, if not the monopolist, in regulating the money supply.[47] Finally, there is implication of the importance attached to national standardization of the money supply in the fact that the convention rejected suggestions that Congress be empowered to consent to state issues of paper money, or be given a veto over the states' use of a retained power to issue paper money. It is significant that this one instance of what in effect was a plain constitutional limit on Congress's powers over the money supply should serve the values of national uniformity.[48]

These were all important matters concerning the role of the federal government in controlling the money supply that needed clarification. But other aspects in which constitutional policy on this score was left to arguable implication were to prove at least as critical in the later development of the national economy and of social and political controversy. Three major questions concerning Congress's authority stood without clear resolution in the constitution-making record: its power (1) to issue paper money, (2) to define legal tender, and (3) to charter national banks.

Continuing in effect a grant made to the old Congress under the Articles of Confederation, the Committee of Detail reported to the Philadelphia convention the proposal that the new Congress have power "to borrow Money, and emit Bills on the Credit of the United States."[49] In convention the framers voted nine to two to strike the reference to bills of credit, leaving simply the authorization to Congress "to borrow money on the credit of the United States."[50] The brief discussion recorded in connection with this action leaves two points quite clear. First, in striking the bills-of-credit reference there was no intent to limit the range of devices by which the government might exercise its borrowing authority. There was common concern that the government enjoy full flexibility of maneuver in obtaining credit, and agreement that the authorization "to borrow money" included by implication authority to issue such evidences of debt as would satisfy lenders.[51] The convention underlined the point when, later, it enlarged Congress's power to punish counterfeiting to protect not only "the current coin" but also "the securities" of the United States.[52] Second, in striking the bills-of-credit reference there was unanimity among those who spoke in the federal convention that the intent and effect were to deny Congress authority to issue government obligations designed primarily to furnish a circulating medium for the regular operations of the economy. Supporting Gouverneur Morris's motion to strike the bills-of-credit phrase, Oliver Ellsworth "thought this a favorable moment to shut and bar the door against paper money," James Wilson felt that "it will have a most salutary influence on the credit of the U. States to remove the possibility of paper money," while Madison—who at first questioned the Morris amendment as perhaps hampering the Treasury's borrowing capacity—explained in a postscript to his notes of the convention that he "became satisfied that striking out the words would not disable the Govt from the use of public notes as far as they could be safe & proper; & would only cut off the pretext for a paper currency and particularly for making the bills a tender either for public or private debts."[53] Thus at first appearance, the convention discussion seems to say that striking the express authorization of federal bills of credit totally barred Congress from creating a federal paper money. Even George Mason and Edmund Randolph, worried lest the Treasury's borrowing operations be unduly hampered, felt moved to declare their "mortal hatred" and "antipathy to paper money"; beyond recalling recent, unfortunate monetary history, the whole discussion did little to spell out detailed grounds of objection, but it was plain that almost all the speakers feared that if the government held broad power to issue paper money, it could not be trusted to avoid disastrous inflation or legislative disturbance of vested money claims.[54]

Despite this vigorous opposition to paper money, if we look closer at the concern expressed for fiscal flexibility we may infer that Congress still retained some authority to issue government paper on a scale likely to bring it into the money supply. Mason and Randolph made the strongest statements looking in this direction. Thus, "as [Mason] . . . could not foresee all emergences [*sic*], he was unwilling to tie the hands of the Legislature. He observed that the late war could not have been carried on, had such a prohibition existed" as he saw implied in striking the reference to bills of credit.[55] Madison cautioned that "promissory notes in that shape [i.e., as bills of credit] may in some emergencies be best" and explained that his final vote rested on his confidence that the abridged borrowing clause "would not disable the Govt from the use of public notes as far as they could be safe & proper; & would only cut off the pretext for a paper currency.[56] In the South Carolina convention Charles Pinckney—one of the framers—asserted confidently that "if paper should become necessary, the general government still possess the power of emitting it, and Continental paper, well funded, must ever answer the purpose better than state paper."[57] The proponents of striking the bills-of-credit reference did not disagree that Congress should have flexible authority to manage the national finances. But their comments do make it hard to strike a balance on the discussion, for they apparently believed that the government could readily borrow by issuing other securities than broadly held notes. In particular, Gouverneur Morris, on whose motion the bills-of-credit phrase was struck, felt that "if the United States had credit such bills would be unnecessary; if they had not [, the bills of credit would be] unjust and useless." In direct response to Madison's worry lest the government lose desirable flexibility, Morris (doubtless remembering his experience as aide to Robert Morris, who borrowed for the old Congress on his notes as superintendent of finance) was sure that "striking out the words will leave room still for notes of a *responsible* minister which will do all the good without the mischief."[58]

The sum of the brief convention discussion was clearly restrictive of federal authority to issue paper money. So far as the talk centered on monetary policy as such, it was overwhelmingly unfavorable to paper as a regular constituent of the money supply provided for the regular needs of the economy. Positive concern was not for the functions of money but for the general capacity of the national government to manage public finance so as to meet unusual conditions. In this aspect the record shows division, though not one neatly defined. Some, like Morris, so distrusted government's ability to use paper money without succumbing to pressures not produced by a justifying emergency, that they apparently would deny any authority to issue notes likely to be broadly held or circulating. Others, notably Madison, seem prepared to accept Congress's creation of such notes (whether by specific grant, or by implication from the authority to borrow money), where Congress might find the action reasonably necessary to deal with extraordinary conditions impinging on national welfare. These ambiguities in the constitution-making record forecast ambiguities in the later development of national policy.

The Constitution spoke sharply and definitely in barring the states from giving legal-tender character to anything but gold and silver. But the Constitution was silent on Congress's authority to define legal tender. The contrast might imply plenary power in Congress over the matter.[59] The force of this implication was reduced by the fact that the only explicit authorization on making money was "to coin" it; in the contemporary setting coinage meant mainly gold or silver, which were clearly acceptable as legal tender.[60] Legal-tender laws had become matters of recent controversy because they required acceptance of paper in settlement of money claims.[61] In their decisive vote to strike the proposed grant to Congress of power to emit bills of credit the framers apparently meant to deny Congress authority to issue government paper as part of the regular money supply for regular economic operations.[62] This step recommended itself to Pierce Butler and Madison as inherently removing the danger of unfair legal-tender laws, which they associated with paper money.[63] On the other hand, the record gives some support to the idea that Congress might still issue notes on a broad enough scale to bring them into common circulation, to enable government financing to meet conditions of (presumably temporary) national emergency or unusual impact on public welfare.[64] If such a power existed at all, it should be adequate to the purpose; hence it might well include authority to attach legal-tender character to such government notes, if this could be deemed materially helpful to meeting the nation's special need. Madison, indeed, indicated his view that authority to issue government notes implied authority to give them legal-tender force. In his first doubtful response against Morris's motion to strike the bills-of-credit authorization Madison asked, "Will it not be sufficient to prohibit making them a *tender?* This will remove the temptation to emit them with unjust views. And promissory notes in that shape may in some emergencies be best."[65] There is nothing else in the record to deny Congress authority to give legal-tender character to any paper which it was authorized to issue.

Grave doubt was felt by Madison and others, whether the old Congress under the Articles of Confederation had authority to charter a bank, though Wilson had argued that the authority existed wherever a matter fell beyond the competence of any one state. The point was left in doubt; on the one hand, Congress did charter the Bank of North America; on the other, it recommended that the states legislate to legitimate the bank's activities within their borders, and the bank itself took pains to operate under the umbrella of a state charter, also.[66] A substantial distinction existed, of course, between the earlier situation and that under the Constitution; the Constitution created a central government which clearly enjoyed sovereignty within the domain assigned it—including power to tax, borrow, and spend and to regulate commerce among the several states—and especially might make all laws necessary and proper for executing the powers vested in it.[67] Doubt arose less from the document itself (its silence on the subject of charters or banks, and its general character in creating a federal government of delegated powers) than from some brief and inconclusive events in the convention. Probably reflecting the disapproving view he had taken toward the old Congress's presumption in chartering the Bank of North America, Madison moved reference to the Committee of Detail of a proposal to authorize the new Congress "to grant charters of incorporation in cases where the Public good may require them, & the authority of a single State may be incompetent."[68] Later in the convention Madison moved to add his chartering proposal to Benjamin Franklin's proposition that Congress be empowered to provide for cutting canals where this might be deemed necessary in the national interest. Madison did not then say so, but probably he believed that there might at least be serious doubt whether Congress might charter any corporations without a specific grant of power to do so—though such a position seems hardly to give due weight to the necessary and proper clause. No one else clearly said that the specific authorization was needed.[69] Nor did Madison say anything to indicate that he had banks particularly in mind as creations of federal charters; the immediate context of his later motion was Franklin's canal proposal.[70] Those who spoke did indicate that they believed that if Congress held an otherwise unqualified authority to charter corporations, this authority would include banks. One brief exchange showed this and foretold future controversy over money supply. Rufus King opposed Madison's motion because "the States will be prejudiced and divided into parties by it—In Phila. & New York, It will be referred to the establishment of a Bank, which has been a subject of contention in those Cities. In other places it will be referred to mercantile monopolies." Wilson "mentioned the importance of facilitating by canals, the communication with the Western Settlements—As to Banks he did not think with Mr. King that the power in that point of view would excite the prejudices and parties apprehended. As to mercantile monopolies they are already included in the power to regulate trade." Mason concluded the short discussion by asserting that he "was for limiting the power [of incorporation] to the single case of Canals. He was afraid of monopolies of every sort, which he did not think were by any means already implied by the Constitution as supposed by Mr. Wilson."[71] Thereupon the convention voted to limit the whole proposal to canals and then defeated even the canal proposal by a record vote of eight to three. No more appears in the convention record on federal charters, for banks or other enterprises.

King's opposition to the proposed chartering clause, because it would authorize chartering banks, reads more as a counsel of political prudence—against making a possibly contentious issue explicit—than as an interpretation of the Constitution as it stood without the proposal. In 1791 Madison recalled the convention episode as flatly barring congressional authority to charter a bank, but this put a good deal more weight on the slender convention record than it should bear.[72] The record might better be argued to support the narrower point of opposition to chartered monopolies (*mercantile* monopolies, at that), but even here it offers little evidence of general feeling in the convention.[73] In sum, the convention left the matter of federal charters—including federal charters for banks—fairly open to development in the light of later experience.

Deliberation and the pull and haul of views and interests in Congress under the Confederation and in the federal convention provided some base lines for public policy about the money supply. But the net of this experience from about 1774 to 1789 was to leave the bulk of policy to grow out of later events. The two most abiding legacies from this first period of national life were a fear of government's likely excesses in issuing paper money and the laying of foundations for ultimate control of monetary policy in the central government. Beyond these matters, the early record left ill-defined and unresolved as many important questions as it answered.

This state of affairs was not unique to problems of law and money. Rather, it relates money policy to some broad characteristics of the place of law in the society. The lack of clarity and the gaps in the constitution-making record attest the novelty, pace, and often bewildering tangles of cause and effect in the growth of public policy in the United States. Legal processes here were always hardpressed by events. Further, compared to the range and variety of later developments, the limitations of the policy framework with which we began highlight how much our public policy was built by accretion of particular decisions, administrative routine, and occasional crisis. A narrowly pragmatic tone pervades the history of public policy in the country. Finally, the limitations of the developments from 1774 to 1789 point up the extent to which decision making even at a level of very competent constitutional deliberation proceeded under the immediacy of contemporary tensions. If it was to be functional to the continuing life of the country, the Constitution had to develop beyond much of its origins.

Notes

1. Morison and Commager, 1:207; Nevins and Commager, 81; Ver Steeg, 38, 39, 45, 63, 66. Robert Morris in 1781 put particular emphasis on the failure to levy adequate taxes as the root cause of the loss of public confidence in bills of credit. Ver Steeg, 63, 70, 71, 88, 98, 127. See the remarks of Rufus King in the Massachusetts ratifying convention. Jonathan Elliott, 2:56.

2. Ver Steeg, ch. 1.

3. For the charter, see Clarke and Hall, 12-13, and Hacker and Zahler (1), 1:215-17. On the charter as a first precedent, see Hacker and Zahler (1), 1:216; Lewis, 3; Morison and Commager, 1:208; Trescott, 1, 12, 16. Philadelphia merchants, including Morris, had considered organization of a commercial bank as early as 1763, but to no effect. Lewis, 3. In 1780 wealthy Philadelphians joined in subscription to a "Bank of Pennsylvania," which was, however, a pool of capital to buy supplies for the army rather than an organization to take deposits, make loans, or issue notes; this bank was wound up in 1784. Lewis, 17-23; Ver Steeg, 66.

4. Lewis, 28, 31, 42; Ver Steeg, 66, 67, 87, 88, 116.

5. Hacker and Zahler (1), 1:216; Lewis, 41, 47, 48, 61; Ver Steeg, 117. Cf. Farrand, 3:487 (James Madison, writing in 1830).

6. Lewis, 27-28; Redlich, 1:25; Ver Steeg, 66.

7. Hammond (1), 51; Hacker and Zahler (1), 1:216; Lewis, 3, 29, 36, 60, 61; Ver Steeg, 85, 86, 87. Cf. Farrand, 3:487-88 (Madison, writing in 1830). Proponents of the bank charter argued more on grounds of practical need than of the incidents of such sovereignty as the Articles of Confederation conferred. Ver Steeg, 85, 86. On Congress's recommendation of validating action by the states, see Clarke and Hall, 13-14; Lewis, 36, 60; Ver Steeg, 87. The issue of Congress's authority apart, the idea of the bank and its public functions met no apparent opposition; opinion was apparently ready for the activist role here assigned public policy. Cf. Ver Steeg, 67, 86, 87.

8. Hammond (1), 51, 54, 63; Lewis, 60, 61, 68, 73. In 1833 the advice of distinguished counsel—James S. Smith, Horace Binney, John Sergeant—was that the bank no longer derived corporate powers from any source other than its Pennsylvania charter, and hence might not rely on the original federal charter to warrant a material increase in capital stock. The opinion was ambiguous, whether this result derived from want of authority in Congress to issue the federal charter in the first place, or from a renunciation of the federal charter implied in acceptance of that of Pennsylvania. See Lewis, 94-95. See, id., 60, 61, for contrary arguments made in the 1785 debate over revocation of the Pennsylvania charter.

9. On the intended monopoly, see Clarke and Hall, 12; Lewis, 30. That the situation did not yet allow a central-bank role, compare Hammond (1), 65-66; Redlich, 1:97. Alexander Hamilton noted in 1790 that no public commitment to the Bank of North America barred chartering a Bank of the United States, since Congress had intended a monopoly for the former only during the war. Lewis, 77.

10. Hammond (1), 63, 64; Lewis, 3, 4; Ver Steeg, 66, 116, 120, 178. A factor which probably worked against a continued substantial role for the bank as a quasi-official agency of national money- and credit-supply policy arose when, under pressure of its financial needs, in late 1782 the government sold to private investors the majority interest in the bank's shares which the government had originally acquired by a loan from the bank. Hammond (1), 51, 63; Lewis, 32-33; Ver Steeg, 84, 85, 178. One of Hamilton's arguments for creating the first Bank of the United States was that the Bank of North America had developed into too-limited a Pennsylvania

commercial-banking role to serve the public functions at stake. Lewis, 76-79. His point was confirmed when the bank showed no favor to his suggestion that it might alter its structure to become the national bank. Id., 78, 79.

11. On the later developments in bank-note issue and in deposit-check money, see Trescott, 17-18, 21, 25-26, 268.

12. For examples of the typical focus on government apparatus rather than on money functions, see in the federal convention, Farrand, 1:42, 43, 134, 137 (George Mason and Charles Pinckney), 154-155 (Madison and Elbridge Gerry), 165 (Madison and Charles Pinckney), 288 (Hamilton); 3:52 (Gouverneur Morris), 616 (Roger Sherman). In state conventions, see Jonathan Elliott, 3:76 (Edmund Randolph, in Virginia), and 4:173 (William MacLaine, in North Carolina). Of like import are the references in note 31, infra, on the inclination to put a money-policy monopoly in the federal government.

13. *The Federalist,* no. 42, p. 264, and no. 44, pp. 277, 278; cf. *Journals of the Continental Congress,* 29:214.

14. *Journals of the Continental Congress,* 29:214.

15. *The Federalist,* no. 44, p. 278; cf. Farrand, 3:214 (Luther Martin).

16. *The Federalist,* no. 44, p. 279; cf. Farrand, 3:215 (Luther Martin).

17. For observations indicating that men linked stay laws and the like with paper money as parts of a pattern of state action affecting the integrity of money, see in the federal convention, Farrand, 1:288 (Hamilton), 2:76 (Gouverneur Morris), 3:100 (Sherman and Oliver Ellsworth), 215 (Luther Martin); and in the state conventions, Jonathan Elliott, 2:144 (Thomas Thacher, in Massachusetts), 486, 491-92 (James Wilson, in Pennsylvania), 3:66, 207 (Randolph, in Virginia), 4:157, 159 (William R. Davie, in North Carolina). Benjamin F. Wright, Jr., 5, noting the scant recorded debate on the contract clause, seems to question that the evidence suffices to link it to the money issue. But this seems too narrow a reading of the record, in light of the material here cited. Compare Charles A. Miller, 44, 45, suggesting that debtors and creditors alike saw the root problem in an unstable currency; if the character of money were improved, debtors would not need stay laws, and indeed might find that their threat choked off credit.

18. See, e.g., Farrand, 1:26 (Randolph), 3:616 (Sherman), and 2:136, 159, 3:106, 117-18, 607 (Charles Pinckney).

19. Randolph early urged that "Congress ought to possess a power to prevent emissions of bills of credit," Farrand, 1:26, and memoranda of Randolph and Wilson relating to work of the convention's committee of detail stipulated that no state might emit bills of credit without approval of the national legislature, though Randolph's notes showed proposal of an absolute ban on the states from making anything but specie legal tender, id., 2:169, 4:44. Other early proposals of Charles Pinckney and Sherman, however, suggested an absolute ban on state bills of credit. Id., 3:106, 117-18, 616. Ideas at this point were still fluid; the Sherman memorandum, in contrast to Randolph's early position, suggested that states might define legal tender "agreeable to the standard that shall be allowed by the legislature of the United States." Id., 3:616. The first report from the committee of detail made Congress the arbiter on both matters: "No State, without the consent of the Legislature of the United States, shall emit bills of credit, or make any thing but specie a tender in payment of debts." Id., 2:187. For the final votes see id., 2:435, 436, 439.

20. Farrand, 2:159 (Wilson notes of Pinckney plan), 187 (report of committee of detail), 3:117-18 (Charles Pinckney).

21. Warren (2), 550, 775, 776.

22. See Madison, in the convention, Farrand, 1:146-47, 154; in 1788, Warren (2), 775, note 1; and in 1831, Farrand, 3:495. Of like effect are other observations in the convention: Farrand, 1:154-55 (Gerry), 288, 289 (Hamilton), 2:76 and 3:150 (Gouverneur Morris), 3:214 (Luther Martin).

23. Talk in the national and state conventions did not draw well-defined lines among functions of money and in particular tended to blur consideration for the acceptability of money in current operations and over time. There is some arbitrariness in assigning particular remarks to one head or the other, therefore. Acknowledging this fact, one may find emphasis on protection of current trade in Farrand, 1:317-18 (Madison), 154-55 (Gerry), 2:26 (Gouverneur Morris), 3:100 (Sherman and Ellsworth), 150 (James McHenry); and in Jonathan Elliott, 1:369 (Madison, in Virginia), 2:491-92 (Wilson, in Pennsylvania), 3:566 (William Grayson, in Virginia), 4:20, 157 (Davie, in North Carolina); and in The Federalist, no. 44, pp. 278-79. Cf. Madison, in 1831, Farrand, 3:495. On protecting the acceptability of money over time, see Farrand, 3:616 (Sherman); Jonathan Elliott, 3:179 (Richard Henry Lee, in Virginia), 4:36 (Whitmill Hill, in North Carolina), 90 (Thomas Johnston, in North Carolina), 183-84 (Davie, in North Carolina), 306 (C. C. Pinckney, in South Carolina); Warren (1), 85.

24. On protection of the revenue, see Farrand, 3:106, 117-18 (Charles Pinckney); cf. Jonathan Elliott, 2:336 (M. Smith, in New York). On preventing interstate animosity, see Farrand, 1:317-18 (Madison); Jonathan Elliott, 3:76 (Randolph, in Virginia), 4:183 (Davie, in North Carolina); The Federalist, no. 44, p. 279.

25. The discussions show a few glancing suggestions of the importance of keeping the money supply in a good working adjustment to the volume of transactions. Thus Luther Martin criticized the limitations imposed on state creation of money as too rigid relative to trade needs. Farrand, 3:214, 215. Some support of the ban on state bills of credit invoked the Gresham's law argument, that experience showed that depreciated paper drove out specie and hence ultimately reduced the money supply to the detriment of commerce. See Farrand, 1:117-18 (Charles Pinckney); Jonathan Elliott, 4:90 (Johnston, in North Carolina); 4:334-35 (Charles Pinckney, in South Carolina); cf. Madison, in 1831, Farrand, 3:495.

26. Jonathan Elliott, 2:369 (Madison, in Virginia), 4:90 (Johnston, in North Carolina), 183-84 (Davie, in North Carolina); Warren (2), 550.

27. See note 12, supra.

28. Farrand, 3:150 (McHenry), 214, 215 (Luther Martin); Jonathan Elliott, 4:289 (Rawlins Lowndes, in South Carolina); cf. Jonathan Elliott, 3:290-91 (Grayson, in Virginia), 4:88 (Joseph M'Dowall, in North Carolina). In the South Carolina convention Robert Barnwell distinguished the past governmental utility of paper issues as having been found in issues by the Congress under the Articles of Confederation. Jonathan Elliott, 4:294.

29. Farrand, 2:439 (Nathaniel Gorham); cf. id., 3:495 (Madison, in 1831).

30. In particular, the fear expressed of state-issued paper money, that it would drive out specie and so weaken the quality and quantity of the money supply alike, might seem to imply a principle broad enough also to outlaw private bank notes issued under state franchise. See the statement of Charles Pinckney, Farrand, 3:117-18, with which compare Madison's analysis of this hazard as presented by private bank notes, in 1831, id., 3:495.

31. The sharp-cut federal monopolies on coining money and fixing its value, paired with the unqualified bans on state action in these two fields as well as in issuing state bills of credit or expanding the categories of legal tender beyond specie,

point toward a federal monopoly. Cf. *The Federalist,* no. 42, p. 264, and no. 44, pp. 277, 278. Of like import are the arguments made for the importance of a nationally uniform currency for the service both of trade, of government finance, and of domestic tranquillity. See notes 23, 24, supra. At an early point, even Luther Martin thought "that the United-States should also fix the Currency & determine what should be the circulating Medium, from New-Hampshire, to Georgia would meet but few or no Opponents within these Walls." Farrand, 4:23. The proposals, ultimately rejected, that state laws on bills of credit or legal tender be subject either to prior consent or to a veto of Congress point to a monopoly of money policy as implicit in the stronger flat prohibitions on state action finally put into the Constitution. See note 19, supra.

32. Farrand, 1:134, 137 (exchange between Mason and C. C. Pinckney), 288, 289 (Hamilton), Jonathan Elliott, 2:486 (Wilson, in Pennsylvania), 3:179 (Lee, in Virginia), 207 (Randolph, in Virginia), 4:20, 157 (Davie, in North Carolina); *The Federalist,* no. 44, p. 279.

33. This was Madison's interpretation in 1831. Farrand, 3:495.

34. Compare the recurrent, pointed concern with direct action of state legislatures in defining the evils feared from paper money. See note 12, supra. Note this focus particularly in a memorandum by Sherman, recommending "that the legislatures of the individual states ought not to possess a right to emit bills of credit for a currency." Farrand, 3:616.

35. Farrand, 3:495.

36. The brief charter of the Bank of North America as granted by the Congress and then by the Pennsylvania legislature did not expressly authorize note issues, but Morris's plan for the bank contemplated them and notes were issued. Hammond (1), 51; Lewis, 28, 31, 42. Likewise the short charter of the Massachusetts Bank (Mass. Stat. 1783, ch. 25—obviously copied in most respects from the charter of the Bank of North America) did not mention note issues, but the bank issued its notes, fulfilling the expectations of its promoters. Handlin and Handlin, 100, 101, 113-14; cf. Mass. Stat. 1791, ch. 65 (reflecting the bank's practice of note issue by setting new limitations on it). Blocked by competing interests from obtaining a state charter, the Bank of New York began operating in 1784 as an unincorporated joint stock company and did not obtain a charter until 1791. Broadus Mitchell, 351, 354. Hamilton's original plan for an incorporated bank envisaged its issue of circulating notes. Id., 352, 353. But, throughout the years of shaping the federal Constitution the New York bank enjoyed no franchise from the state; thus its existence was not calculated to press on the framers' attention the idea that their provision on state bills of credit should deal with bank notes issued by a delegate of the state. Had the framers given thought to circulating notes issued by private, chartered banks, the favor they showed for the protection of market processes in the contract clause might have led them to feel that the market should be trusted to regulate private bank notes. Compare the concern indicated to guard market autonomy in the Sherman memorandum's recommendation that state legislatures not have the right to make tender laws to discharge contracts "in any manner different from the agreement of the parties," save as Congress might define money. Farrand, 3:616.

37. Compare Charles Pinckney's fear of the Gresham's law impact of depreciated paper on specie in the money supply. Farrand, 3:117-18.

38. See the Sherman memorandum preparatory to the work of the Committee of Detail, recommending that the ultimate medium for settling transactions be "current money, agreeable to the standard that shall be allowed by the legislature of the

United States." Farrand, 3:616. Of like implication, note the remark attributed to Luther Martin early in the convention, "that the United-States should also fix the Currency & determine what should be the circulating Medium, from New-Hampshire, to Georgia would meet but few or no Opponents within these Walls." Id., 4:23. We should not put undue weight on these preliminary observations, but they convey a tone which seems carried on by the general character of what the framers later did. See note 31, supra.

39. Compare the tendency of argument in *The Federalist,* no. 15, to point to the desirability of recognizing the plenary character of the powers proposed for the central government within its sphere.

40. *The Federalist,* no. 44, p. 277; cf. Farrand, 4:23 (Luther Martin).

41. *The Federalist,* 278; see *Articles of Confederation,* Art. IX.

42. Farrand, 2:167, 168, 182.

43. The articles (Art. IX) had given Congress "the sole and exclusive right and power of regulating the alloy and value of coin" authorized by them or the states. The reference to alloy was continued in an early version of the comparable clause in the new Constitution but was apparently soon dropped. Farrand, 2:167, 168. It did not appear in the version reported from the Committee of Detail, but this may have been because, apparently following a suggestion of John Rutledge, the committee had suggested only giving Congress power "to regulate the value of foreign coin"–the alloy of which, of course, would already have been fixed by the foreign sovereign. Id., 2:182. When the final document continued the omission of *alloy,* while defining the power as that to regulate the value of both foreign and domestic coin, the likely inference is that it was thought either that power to determine alloy was implied in power to *coin* (as a technological matter) or in power to regulate *value* (considered as power to make legal definition of the metal content of the standard domestic coins, and to fix legally recognized translations of foreign money units into United States unit equivalents). There is nothing in the record to confirm or deny this reading. *The Federalist,* no. 44, p. 278, appears to differentiate coinage as a manufacturing process from the determination of either alloy or value, but this was said with reference to the situation under the Articles of Confederation, which recognized in some sense continued authority in the states to *strike* coins, alongside exclusive authority in the Congress to fix alloy and value. It is plain, on the other hand, that the contemporary view took for granted that the power to regulate the value of law-made money was exclusively in the new Congress. Cf. *The Federalist,* no. 44, p. 278.

44. Rutledge's suggestion–at first followed by the Committee of Detail–of limiting the value-regulating authority to foreign coin may mean that he and they felt that authority to define the metal content of the standard domestic money units inhered in the already given authority *to coin* money. If so, by contrast the language finally adopted suggests that the framers' more considered opinion was that to define a standard metal content was a different operation from manufacture of money tokens, and hence called for a separate authorization. Cf. Farrand, 2:167, 168, 182. Separate emphasis on, and provision for, standardizing the metal content of money units would fit the general tone of concern for facilitating reliable uniformity of transactions throughout the country. See note 38, supra.

45. Cf. Farrand, 2:309, 310 (Madison), 309 (Gorham). But see the Sherman memorandum, id., 3:616, which perhaps speaks of the money units as standardized by federal authority as inherently thereby regulating what the states may make legal tender.

46. On attitudes toward recent experience with the shifting market values of

paper money before the Constitution, as well as concern for animosities likely to be stirred by dealings with the money question in the proposed Constitution, see notes 26-29, supra.

47. Gouverneur Morris at one point suggested giving Congress broad authority to punish any counterfeiting, citing the importance of protecting the integrity of bills of exchange. Farrand, 2:315. His suggestion further evidences the contemporary concern with the values of assured standardization of instruments to effect business transactions. In light of later developments, the matter would fall well within the commerce power of Congress. There is nothing in the record responding to Morris's suggestion, which he apparently did not try to bring to issue by any motion.

48. See notes 19, 23, and 24, supra.

49. The articles (Art. IX) granted Congress "authority . . . to borrow money or emit bills on the credit of the United States, transmitting every half-year to the respective states an account of the sums of money so borrowed or emitted," and stipulated that Congress "shall never . . . coin money, nor regulate the value thereof . . . nor emit bills, nor borrow money on the credit of the United States . . . unless nine states assent to the same." That the articles referred to borrowing and emission of bills of credit in the alternative might argue that emission of bills was seen as an activity distinct from borrowing (and hence, perhaps, an authority to create a paper money supply as such). But the language seems also consistent with treating emission of bills as an alternative form of obtaining credit. Congress in fact issued the bulk of its bills of credit before the articles were adopted. These were originated as a form of obtaining credit to finance the war; this practical precedent thus suggests that contemporary experience would most naturally lead men to think of bills of credit as a form of borrowing rather than as a device to create a money supply. But, of course, the Continental bills were also used as money until they fell into hopeless depreciation, so that the record is ambiguous.

The phrasing reported by the Committee of Detail was the same as that set out in a preparatory memorandum by Wilson. Farrand, 2:167, 168, 182. Following separate authorizations to coin money and fix the value of the coin—i.e., following direct authorizations to create units of a money supply—and stated in immediate linkage to authority to borrow money, and in terms indicating the authorized bills as pledges of the government to pay in some other medium, the authorization to emit bills of credit seems on its face to be thought of more as an elaboration of modes of obtaining credit than as a power primarily designed to create an addition to the money supply as such.

50. Farrand, 2:303, 304. Maryland and New Jersey voted no. Compare the post-convention criticism of this vote by Luther Martin, addressing his Maryland constituents, id., 3:206, 214.

51. On general concern that the Treasury possess a full range of borrowing instruments, see Mason, in Farrand, 2:309, 310, and Randolph, in id., 310. On intent that the government have authority to issue some evidences of debt, see Morris, in id., 309, Gorham, in ibid., and Madison, in id., 310. Oddly, no one is recorded as invoking the necessary and proper clause, though this would seem to supply all the authority needed in aid of government borrowing. Rather, the speakers all seem to rely on what they find implied in the authorization of borrowing, as such. That Congress enjoyed broad auxiliary powers in aid of government financing was strongly affirmed in the South Carolina ratifying convention, by Barnwell and by Charles Pinckney, the latter a member of the federal convention. Jonathan Elliott, 4:294, 335.

52. Farrand, 2:312, 315, 4:52.

53. Id., 2:309 (Ellsworth), 310 (Wilson, Madison). Pierce Butler, seconding Morris's motion, spoke to similar effect, though he clouded his remarks by indicating that he felt the effect of the action was at least as much to bar creating legal-tender paper as to bar creating any form of paper money. Id., 310. George Read and John Langdon, also supporting elimination of the bills-of-credit phrase, spoke in rather veiled terms, but their attitudes implied desire wholly to deprive government of authority to issue paper money. Ibid. Mason and Randolph, and Madison in his first reaction to the Morris motion, incident to their concern over depriving the government of needed fiscal flexibility, in effect interpreted Morris's motion as depriving Congress of any authority to issue any kind of government paper, including of course paper money. Id., 309, 310. Mason, in particular, said that "congs. he thought would not have the power unless it were expressed." Id., 309. In general accord with these views was Luther Martin, later addressing his Maryland constituents. Id., 3:206, 214.

54. Mason, in id., 2:309; Randolph, in id., 310. Compare Wilson's observation that "this expedient [of bills of credit as money] can never succeed whilst its mischiefs are remembered." Ibid. On the remembered evils of past paper money, see Morris, in id. 309 (if United States lacks credit, bills of credit will be "unjust & useless"); Gorham, in ibid. (power to issue government paper will be "safe" only if limited to aid of borrowing); Ellsworth, in id., 309-10 ("the mischiefs" of recent money experiments "had excited the disgust of all the respectable part of America.") Cf. Read and Langdon, in id., 310, and 3:305. Writing in 1814, Morris said that in 1787 he opposed "propositions to countenance the issue of paper money, and the consequent violation of contracts." Id., 3:419. In effect there was further evidence of contemporary distaste for wide fluctuations in value seen as attending paper money in the fear of some that the ex post facto clause might result in requiring redemption at face of depreciated Continental currency. Warren (2), 502-3. Only John Mercer in the federal convention had a good word for government-issued paper money, but he put his view in such fashion as to indicate that he understood the Morris motion to reject government paper as a regular part of the money supply and that he interpreted the striking of the bills-of-credit phrase as having the legal effect of barring any authority in Congress to create such paper money. Farrand, 2:309. That the power given Congress to punish counterfeiting was extended to cover government "securities" as well as "current coin," but did not mention bills of exchange, may further imply that these were not seen as possibly constituting part of the regular money supply. Cf. McHenry's notes, in Farrand, 4:52, with the form given the counterfeiting clause. Id., 2:312, 315. For other indications of distrust of paper money for its fluctuations, see Grayson in the Virginia convention, Jonathan Elliott, 3:290-91, and Hill in the North Carolina convention, id., 4:36. Further, on distrust of legislative ability to withstand inflationary lobbies, compare Sherman, in Farrand, 3:616. But cf. Hill in the North Carolina convention, Jonathan Elliott, 4:36.

55. Farrand, 2:309, 310; cf. Randolph, in id., 310 ("notwithstanding his antipathy to paper money," he "could not agree to strike out the words, as he could not foresee all the occasions that might arise.") See also, Grayson, in the Virginia convention, Jonathan Elliott, 3:290, and M'Dowall, in the North Carolina convention, id., 4:88.

56. Farrand, 2:309, 310. Mercer opposed striking the bills-of-credit phrase because it "will stamp suspicion on the Government to deny it a discretion on this point." Id., 309. See also note 53, supra. But cf. Luther Martin, in id., 3:206.

57. Jonathan Elliott, 4:335. Barnwell, also speaking in the South Carolina convention, replying to Lowndes's praise of the utility of paper money in aiding revolu-

tionary finance, observed, "However, supposing that to be the clue that led us to our liberty, yet the gentleman must acknowledge it was not the state, but the Continental money that brought about the favorable termination of the war. If to strike off a paper medium becomes necessary, Congress, by the Constitution, still have that right, and may exercise it when they think proper." Barnwell cited no source for his opinion. Id., 294.

58. Farrand, 2:309. Compare Ellsworth, id., 310: "Paper money can in no case be necessary—Give the Government credit, and other resources will offer—The power may do harm, never good." And see Wilson, in ibid.: "This expedient [of paper money] can never succeed whilst its mischiefs are remembered. And as long as it can be resorted to, it will be a bar to other resources."

59. This pattern of the Constitution might be deemed to fulfill the policy suggested in a preparatory memorandum attributed to Sherman, recommending a ban on state legal-tender laws, so that the states might provide only for payments in current money "agreeable to the standard that shall be allowed by the legislature of the United States." Farrand, 3:616. The constitutional pattern, insofar as it be taken to imply congressional power to enact legal-tender laws, would be consistent, also, with indications of a general bias toward giving the federal government a monopoly of money policy; on the other hand, of course, part of that monopoly might lie simply in direct constitutional limitations on Congress as well as on the states. See note 38, supra.

60. There is nothing explicit in the record, however, to show that the authority "to coin money" was viewed inherently as also a power to confer legal-tender character on the coinage. Nor does the record show anything to suggest that the power given Congress to fix the "value" of coined money was thought of as including power to confer legal-tender character on such money. See note 45, supra.

61. *The Federalist,* no. 44, pp. 278, 279. Objections to state-issued paper money were often, though not invariably, linked to the fact that the laws made it legal tender. Warren (2), 551.

62. See notes 53 and 54, supra.

63. Seconding Morris's motion to strike the bills-of-credit reference, Butler commented that "paper was a legal tender in no Country in Europe. He was urgent for disarming the Government of such a power." Farrand, 2:310. In his retrospective note explaining his ultimate vote for the Morris motion, Madison explained that he "became satisfied that striking out the words would not disable the Govt from the use of public notes as far as they could be safe & proper; & would only cut off the pretext for a paper currency and particularly for making the bills a tender either for public or private debts." Ibid. It should be noted that not all objections to paper money focused only on the possibility that it would be made legal tender. Thus Gorham, in id., 309, "was for striking out [the bills-of-credit authorization], without inserting any prohibition [of legal-tender character, as Madison had first suggested]. If the words stand they may suggest and lead to the measure."

64. See notes 55, 56, and 57, supra.

65. Farrand, 2:309.

66. See notes 7 and 8, supra.

67. Cf., *The Federalist,* no. 15, pp. 86, 88, and no. 44, pp. 280-83.

68. Farrand, 2:321, 322, 325. Of like import but more general was the reference to the Committee of Detail of Charles Pinckney's proposal of authority "to grant charters of incorporation." Ibid. The committee brought out no positive response to either proposal.

69. Id., 615-16. Speaking apparently with reference to the combined Franklin-Madison proposal—focused as it was on canals—King "thought the power unnecessary," while Wilson felt that "it is necessary to prevent *a State* from obstructing the *general* welfare." Both men seem more likely to have meant *necessary* or not as a matter of wisdom or practicality in shaping public policy, rather than as an interpretation of the legal force of the Constitution's language.

70. All that Madison is recorded as saying of his proposed amendment to the Franklin proposal focused on the canal question: "His primary object was however to secure an easy communication between the States which the free intercourse now to be opened, seemed to call for—The political obstacles being removed, a removal of the natural ones as far as possible ought to follow." Id., 615.

71. Id., 616.

72. House, 2 February 1791, *Annals of Congress,* 1st Cong., 11:1896; Farrand, 3:362. Madison "had entertained this opinion [that Congress had no authority to charter a bank] from the date of the Constitution. . . . [H]e well recollected that a power to grant charters of incorporation had been proposed in the General Convention and rejected." Gerry questioned the wisdom of thus relying on memory of the convention proceedings, but also observed that "no motion was made in that Convention, and therefore none could be rejected for establishing a National Bank; and the measure which the gentleman has referred to was a proposition merely to enable Congress to erect commercial corporations, which was, and always ought to be, negatived." House, 7 February 1791, *Annals of Congress* 11:1952; Farrand, 3:362-63. Compare Jefferson in a letter of 15 February 1791, *Writings of Thomas Jefferson,* 5:286-87; Farrand, 3:363.

73. The suggestion was advanced in five state conventions that the Constitution should include a ban on Congress's creating any "company" or "company of merchants" "with exclusive advantages of commerce." See, e.g., Jonathan Elliott, 2:177 (Massachusetts), 407 (New York), 4:246 (North Carolina). The motion made in New York would also separately have banned congressional creation of monopolies as such. Id., 2:407. An effort to include such an amendment in the series recommended to the states by the First Congress failed. In the Second Congress, in 1793, the Senate tabled a like proposal and no more was heard of the idea. Ames, 255. The debate over chartering the first Bank of the United States produced no proposal to amend the Constitution in the matter. Ibid.

I. Functions of Law and Functions of Money

Money has a legal history in the United States because, first, law affected the system of money, and, second, the existence of a system of money affected the law. The interplay affected not just secondary details but basic institutional tasks of law and of money. Since interaction of the two institutions affected their reasons for being, it is realistic to center their common history first on questions of function. What were established as legitimate uses of law to affect the system of money? How did use of a system of money affect the operation of legal processes? These questions carry a basic ambiguity: they may refer to consciously contrived results or purposed action, or they may refer simply to effects of behavior, whether or not the effects were calculated. The ambiguity is in the record itself, and is no small part of the history.

In dealing with money public policy embodied custom and change, convention and creation. Law witnessed important changes in ideas about what money was—about what social devices should be treated as money and promoted or regulated so as to fulfill monetary functions. Thus the law variously recognized as money metal tokens standardized by public or private makers, paper declaring different commitments by governments or by private banks, and bank deposits on which depositors might draw checks. On the other hand, for a long time the law gave special status to money tokens made of, or resting on reserves of, precious metals the use of which was sanctioned at bottom by popular custom.[1] Defined by most immediately felt working effects, the functions of money were treated in public policy, most of the time, as being those customarily described by economists—to serve as a formal measure of economic values, to serve as a medium of exchange in economic transactions, to serve as a device to hold in suspension the ability to command more specific assets for specific economic uses (that is, to act as a store of value), and to serve as a standard of deferred payments.[2] Yet, both particular events and general trends in the country's growth generated pressures to use law to affect the money system for other purposes which did not fit neatly within the ordinary definitions.

The record shows clearly enough certain immediate points of impact of law on organization and operation of the system of money—as in defining standard units, authenticating source and legal effect, and requiring security or reserves to underpin currency, as well as other measures noted in the next section. The record is less clear in defining the range of large purposes which public policy accepted as legitimating these particular uses of law affecting money. Concern to decide what objectives would justify legal controls came only to partial—and often confused and misdirected—expression in open debate; objectives stood legitimized, or their legitimacy was qualified or denied, at least as much by practice as by proclamation. But, despite limits and ambiguities in its processes, what law did about money took on meaning through distinctions drawn among various ultimate objectives of its action. Concern attached to choices among three main types of goals for using law to affect the capacity of the money system: (1) to service a given, on-going economy, (2) to promote major increases or major adjustments in general economic performance, (3) to stabilize or change distributions of political, social, or economic power among classes or interest groups. The sum of events established the legitimacy of a broad range of legal actions under the first, with some wavering accepted a substantial role for law under the second, and rejected overt acceptance of legal action of the third category.

LAW AND MONEY IN A GIVEN, GOING ECONOMY

First in time and most continuously pursued was use of law to foster a system of money which would serve the current flow of resource allocations within an economy operated by broadly dispersed public and private decision making. Especially in the nineteenth century the market was to the fore in allocating resources. But it would distort matters to say that policy simply legitimated using law to help provide money in aid of market transactions. Serving the market was a high priority objective, pursued in many ways, in a society scarce of manpower and of fluid capital and hence desirous of encouraging institutions which would release productive private energies.[3] But at no point did public policy leave provision of money simply to market processes. That would have let money be governed by the cumulative play of exchanges too numerous, among too many dealers, to allow any effort at managing the large pattern of affairs. This middle-class culture trusted and valued the creative possibilities as well as the dignity residing in men's will, reason, and energy. With this outlook we had a managing attitude toward our experience, however much we disputed over particular ends or means.[4] Thus, law in the United States never resigned to the market the control of a system of money. Even while we made legal arrangements which dispersed power over the money supply—an approach dominant through the nineteenth century, and prominent, though to a less extent, into the twentieth—typically law embodied substantial controls on the money system. Prime symbol and potent expression of favor for dispersing control over money was the large role committed to privately owned banks in supplying money. Yet, public policy did not leave incorporated banks—and especially institutions of a central-bank character—to produce a faceless, impersonal, market-style determination of the money system. True, private bankers were numerous enough, and limited enough in immediate command of resources, so that their over-all impact on money was usually the product of accumulated decisions lacking firm, central direction.[5] Nonetheless, statutory franchises for banks gave them the discipline of corporate organization and special privileges to issue circulating currency and placed them under legal regulation of their finances unlike any imposed on the general run of business. This body of statute law constituted a substantial effort at promoting and legitimating the exercise of directed will on the money supply.[6]

If we were not content that money be governed by an impersonal market, we did expect that best results would come from interplay of a variety of economic interests, expressed mainly through bargained transactions, though partly through public fiscal measures. To this extent we set policy norms for a money system largely in marketlike terms. This viewpoint assumed that the prime, legitimate uses of law affecting money would be to make money serve the going course of an economy which, though it should foster productive growth, could usually be accepted as an established system, operating under a given set of functional imperatives. Law's ordinary job regarding money was not to regulate money to reshape the economy or other aspects of society, but to accept the current resource-allocations process as nonmonetary factors shaped it and to help it work by making money its handy instrument. In these terms, public policy saw law's proper relations with the money system as those through which law might help (1) make money a workable system of calculation or communication in current allocation of scarce resources, (2) contribute to the people's willingness to accept and use given money tokens, and (3) keep the supply of tokens in efficient relation to the demands of private and public transactions. We need to examine law's immediate points of impact on the money system under these categories, because main lines of public policy emerged out of such particulars. After this inventory, it will be more meaningful to note occasions when policy makers spelled out more explicitly the idea that to service the going economy was a legitimate function of legal controls on money.

Law and Money as a System of Notation

The simplest and most effective use of law affecting money was to help make a given system of money a workable instrument of notation and communication, by defining standard money units. By the act of 2 April 1792 Congress interpreted the constitutional grants of authority to coin money and to regulate its value to mean that by statute Congress might designate a basic money unit, which it called the dollar; define components of the basic unit, which it set up on a decimal basis; and assign a stated precious metals content to the basic unit, which it did on a bimetallic basis (so much fine gold or silver to the dollar).[7] Congress underlined the definition of the dollar as an act of sovereignty by making its own choice of a metal content for this unit different from that of the Spanish coin then most familiar among foreign pieces circulating in the country.[8] In important respects the pattern set in 1792 proved an enduring one. The dollar remained the basic unit, and the country adhered to the decimal style of designating subunits and larger units. Responding to varying judgments of utility, lawmakers from time to time added and dropped particular units, but throughout they kept the dollar, the quarter, the dime, and the cent.[9] Stability in any system of definition was necessary to realize the goal of making money a useful, because standardized, system of communication. Changes in denominations of units did not get in the way of this goal. But, frequent changes in definition of the precious metals content of the basic dollar unit would interfere with the communications function of money, apart from other possibly disturbing effects. Legislative practice was consistent with regard for money's communications function. Congress changed the fine gold content of the dollar in 1834. In 1934 it authorized the president to fix the weight of the gold dollar at any level between 50 and 60 percent of its prior legal weight, and under this authority the president devalued the gold dollar to 59.06 percent of its former weight. Congress never altered the fine silver content of the basic unit.[10] Acts of 1851 and 1853 not only changed the denominations of silver sub-units, but also reduced their silver content so that the metal in them was not proportionate to the metal in a coined silver dollar, and our policy thenceforth adhered to this device of providing lesser–"subsidiary"–coins defined in metal contents on a different measure than that of the dollar.[11] In 1873 a revised coinage statute omitted authorization of a silver dollar, but in 1878 Congress restored the silver dollar to the monetary pattern. Through years during and after the Civil War in which paper dollars fell in value compared with gold, Congress did not change the gold-content defi-nition of the dollar as fixed in 1834. Some debate attended creation of subsidiary coin, and high controversy surrounded the position of gold and silver in the dollar. But the moving force in the 1834 change in the dollar's gold content, in the 1851 and 1853 acts establishing a subsidiary coinage, in the mid-century adherence to the 1834 gold definition of the dollar, and in the late nineteenth-century shifts regarding silver was concern about the supply of money and not policy concerning money's function as a system of economic notation. The 1934 devaluation was designed to affect the general price level to stimulate economic growth, though the ban on private traffic in gold or gold coin did deal with an auxiliary issue of nota-tion. Thus the controversial aspects of these various measures belong to another story than that of policy on money as a notation system.

Legal provision for money as a notation pattern was noncontroversial through practically all the span from 1790 to 1970. The closest events came to an exception was some interest shown in the late nineteenth cen-tury that the United States join in establishing an international set of com-mon money units, but this idea foundered on opposition abroad and rela-tive indifference at home.[12] Not only was policy on money as a system of notation noncontroversial; it also was marked by striking absence of felt need for compulsion. Congress provided a pattern of money units, but did not require their use or declare unlawful the use of any other system of money-unit definitions. The utility of a commonly accepted notation was enough to obtain conformity to it, especially in a society which relied as much as this did on allocating resources through an energetic and expand-ing market for which a standardized money notation system rapidly be-came a functional imperative.[13] The one substantial issue of compulsion in using the law's standard money-notation scheme arose when private contracts provided for payment in agreed weights of gold or in coin or currency equal to the market value of the contracted weights of gold. The Supreme Court found nothing in congressional legislation to invalidate such payment stipulations under the statutes as they stood in the second half of the nineteenth century; in 1935 the Court found that Congress had rendered such stipulations illegal and unenforceable and that this statutory determination was within Congress's authority to regulate the value of money and to regulate the money supply in the interest of a properly functioning national economy.[14] The basic issue over the gold-or-gold-value payment clauses was not simply preserving a legally stipulated system of money notation, however, but, rather—as in the case of problems over the gold and silver content of the dollar and the provision of a subsidiary coinage—concerned regulation of the supply of money. Thus we shall come back to the matter in the context of supply issues as such.

The uncoerced, uncontested acceptance of the pattern of money notation set out in 1792 constituted the most continuously successful use of law to affect the money supply in the United States. Success reflected partly the fact that the pattern set in 1792 had definite, clearly understandable and calculable content, partly that these working virtues had quick appeal in contrast to the clumsy and uncertain condition of our previous dependence on a variety of foreign coin of unreliable content. Law was potent here in standardizing forms of behavior, because standardization was in fact functional to valued substance (a firm, readily useable scheme of money notation served the growth of the market), because public attitudes were receptive to this functional worth (common opinion in this country rated high devices which served economic productivity), and because substantial vested interests had not attached to earlier adopted forms (the act of 1792 became operative in an economy only on the threshold of development). It would be unrealistic to downgrade this success of law in affecting the money supply because it dealt only with the forms of money. Forms make possible contrivance of larger, more varied, and more effective ends and means of substance. They did so here. When law helps organize existence into meaningful (ends-and-means-oriented) experience, it is involved in the heart of the human enterprise. No such use of law is unimportant in the sum of social organization.

Law and the Practical Acceptability of Money

Money is an instrument for helping men create and manage some of their relationships. Money has no substantial meaning unless men will use it. That a design of money units is available for communication facilitates use. But a system of symbols, by itself arbitrary and abstract, offers only the minimum inducement of convenience to energize will and persuade individuals to commit themselves to action. To make a system of money have working effect, men must be willing to accept the money tokens and have confidence that others will accept them in effecting immediate exchanges, or as conferring future command over other assets, or as dependably measuring some deferred performance. So a central concern of public policy was how law could promote the practical acceptability of a given system of money.

Because money was an instrument in effecting relationships, how it worked was determined by interaction of factors in the relations of which it was a part. Law was almost always one of those factors, but only one. There is temptation to rate law a primary, if not indispensable factor—partly because the most visible forms of money (coin, paper currency) commonly bore the government's validating stamp or were issued under some franchise granted by law, partly because the commonly used money tokens existed always within some frame of legal promotion or regulation.[15] But the roles of private banks should caution against exaggerating law's direct contributions to the working money system. Bank deposits and checks drawn against them developed to provide the bulk of money. These developments first found sanction and support in the general law of contract and later in the more specialized growth of the law of commercial instruments, while the banks which created and administered this new kind of money were typically organized in forms set by corporation law. However, deposit-check money grew to its pre-eminence primarily on the initiative, invention, and energies of private dealers. Checks were in substantial use in principal commercial cities by the beginning of the nineteenth century. But the law's fumbling recognition that such drafts on deposits posed special problems concerning the money supply rather than merely problems of private contract lagged by about a generation behind emergence of this new monetary pattern. Not until mid-twentieth century did the law achieve reasonably effective accommodation to the problems which bank deposits and checks posed as the principal component of the money supply. Meantime, excessive shifts in credit balances matching excesses of business optimism or despair, recurrent liquidity crises, and the disastrous runs which banks suffered when they lost the confidence of depositors, all testified to how much deposit-check money depended on general economic and social factors apart from law.[16] We should assess law's roles with cautious skepticism, expecting that, though important, they will be specialized and relatively marginal among all factors which determined the practical acceptability of money.

Authenticity of Source and Form of Money

The most distinctive and effective use of law to promote acceptability of money was to give assurance that given tokens or symbols of money were produced by a responsible, identified issuer and were cast in such form that they would have some legal recognition as true elements in the money system. Thus the federal mint manufactured coin which bore the mint's guaranty of regularity of source and metal content; a federal printing agency produced authenticated paper notes of the United States, of nationally incorporated banks, and of the Federal Reserve System; state statutes provided franchises of incorporation to certify banks which in turn might issue circulating notes, and state statutes and judge-made law combined to standardize forms which would give reliable legal content to relations among banks, their customers, and third parties concerning checks drawn on bank deposits.[17] Authenticity of source and form served to make money units acceptable in two different ways. The law's certification guaranteed that coins contained specified standard metal content. The standard forms within which law guided the issue of paper money or checks guaranteed a designated issuer as responsible for the conditions on which the tokens were created and circulated, and as responsible to meet such promises of further performance (usually redemption or payment in coin or other money) as the tokens declared. Authenticity of source was obviously not an ultimate assurance that the people would in practice accept money; it contributed to acceptability because of further factors—the intrinsic value which the people felt to reside in given quantities of certain metals, or the people's confidence that particular issuers could be relied on to meet commitments which were valued more highly than the pieces of paper which symbolized them. But, though it was not an ultimate basis of acceptability, authenticity of source and form was a practical prerequisite to the operation of other factors and aided the everyday working of the money system. The law's modes of authentication raised presumptions of regularity which smoothed transactions and economized effort. That these were real contributions was evident in the continuous concern of the law with the threat which counterfeiters posed to the workability of the money supply, in early difficulties experienced with substandard foreign coins, and in the reference books which were common equipment in early nineteenth-century business firms to confirm the existence and reliability of note-issuing banks.[18]

The trend of public policy was to assure authenticity of source and form by unifying and centralizing authorized centers and forms of issue and by increasing the role of government in the process. In creating a national mint the federal act of 1792 used the offer of a government service rather than the imposition of compulsion to pursue the goal; this tack was emphasized both by the provision for coining either gold or silver and by the original absence of a fee for the coining. Service and compulsion were mingled when, in creating a national bank system in 1863 and 1864, government provided a facility to print national bank notes and required national banks to obtain their notes from this office.[19] Compulsion was the characteristic mark of the trend to unify and centralize sources and terms of creating money. The federal Constitution began this trend by giving the federal government a monopoly of official coinage and of direct creation of government paper money.[20] Nothing in the Constitution barred private manufacture of coin, and through the first half of the nineteenth century Congress did not act against private coinage. Though privately produced coin never made more than temporary and marginal contributions to the money stock, this phase of the matter highlights both the general favor for broad dispersion of decision making power in the economy and the ultimate vigor of the trend to monopolize final authority over money in government. Beginning in 1864 Congress barred private manufacture of metal tokens intended to circulate as money, and the courts accepted this claim of authority, apparently as a "necessary and proper" incident to the granted power to coin money.[21] General contract law allowed any contractor to issue his notes and circulate them so far as the market would take them. But, beginning with Massachusetts, New Hampshire, and New York legislation of 1799 and 1804, it became common policy in the states to declare that circulating paper might be lawfully issued only by banks duly incorporated under state statutes. This pattern of state policy seems to have begun in response to the desire of holders of early bank charters to enjoy legal protection against competition. But with increasing liberality the states chartered banks with note-issuing privileges, and in this context limitation of note issue to chartered institutions took on more the character of protecting authenticity.[22] In 1865 Congress imposed a prohibitive tax on circulating notes of state-chartered banks, and thus created a monopoly of note issue in the new national banks. This measure was taken largely to help finance the North's war effort (by helping create a market for federal bonds, which might be deposited as required security for note issues), but it was urged in part, also, as a means to create desirable uniformity in the form and sources of paper currency. There had been bewildering variation in the form of state bank notes, and in the discounts at which they were taken in trade, reflecting differences in popular faith in the soundness of the issuing banks. The new national bank issues—produced by a federal printing office in a format standard for the whole country, secured by deposit of government bonds, and issued by banks whose financial structures were under some uniform regulation—did provide paper money more readily identifiable and secure, and hence circulating free of discount. The movement for a uniform style of paper currency reached logical fulfillment when after 1935 Congress retired national bank notes in favor of the notes of the federal reserve banks.[23]

Deposit-check money did not lend itself to such rigorous uniformity as could be imposed on a paper currency, since deposit-check money was created by the activity of countless private negotiators. Here was no counterpart of the law's policy of forbidding private creation of coin or limiting private creation of general-circulation paper. Checks drawn on deposits fulfilled money functions because business practice accepted them so. However, the law of commercial instruments supported business practice by putting law's sanctions behind reliably defined claims of depositors on banks and of endorsees on makers and banks. Broader markets bred pressures for more assured uniformity in the legal character of deposit-check money. An early response to this pressure was in the courts; in *Swift* v. *Tyson* (1842) the United States Supreme Court asserted power in the interests of uniform administration of commercial law to declare its own doctrine on the effect of commercial instruments. More telling was the fact that the first nationally successful uniform act sponsored by the Commissioners on Uniform State Laws was the Negotiable Instruments Law, which created a standard pattern of obligations and claims affecting deposit-check money. In mid-twentieth century the new Uniform Commercial Code reinforced and enlarged this direction of policy. As use of checks spread over wider markets, banks became more and more involved in collecting or paying checks which had to be transmitted through one or more handling stages. Banks' imposition of charges for collection or payment in such circumstances inevitably qualified the money value which the face of checks indicated, and to that degree carried a threat to utility of deposit-check money. The first response was by private agreement; between 1900-12 banks in ninety-one cities agreed on uniform charges for handling checks. But, this kind of cooperation—especially as to regional arrangements—was exceptional, was mostly limited to large cities where many country banks kept balances, and in any event only regulated the amount of collection or payment charges but did not eliminate them. It was the competitive impact of the Federal Reserve System which at last largely eliminated payment charges and thus made the bulk of deposit-check money operative at its full declared value. If a bank and its depositors contracted for payment charges, the Federal Reserve Act did not forbid the agreement. But the Federal Reserve had and used the authority to refuse to accept for collection checks drawn on banks which deducted a fee for payment. The competitive convenience of Federal Reserve collection machinery was such that by mid-twentieth century about 88 percent of the country's commercial banks were paying checks at par through the Federal Reserve procedures.[24]

The law also acted to protect authenticity of the money supply against intentional private debasement. The Constitution expressly authorized

Congress to punish counterfeiting the coin or securities of the United States. An unsympathetic reading might have confined this authority to punishing only the manufacture of deceitful imitations. But the Supreme Court gave short answers to such literalism. The grant of authority to coin money, reinforced by the grant of powers necessary and proper to exercising the more specific authority, should be read to mean that Congress might punish passing as well as making counterfeit coin, or possessing counterfeiting tools with intent to make wrongful use of them. The power extended also to protecting the government's paper notes.[25] The ready liberality of this course of decision attested the gravity with which the judges estimated the threat of counterfeiting to an effective money supply, and the high importance assigned to assuring that money should gain all the acceptance which authentic issue could help give it. Congress was of like mind, and over the years steadily enlarged the reach of penalties against all varieties of counterfeiting action.[26] State law supplemented this policy by bans on forgery, which worked to safeguard the integrity of deposit-check money, as did like federal legislation against such frauds on national banks.[27] The pattern of liberal protection was filled out by the Supreme Court's readiness to find that uttering forged or counterfeit money tokens might be punished by both the United States and a state, as involving different offenses against each, without infringing the sovereignty of either or violating the constitutional policy against double jeopardy.[28]

In part by holding out useful service (the mint), in part by imposing standards within which men might exercise private options (styles of bank-note issue, legally defined claims and obligations concerning deposits and checks), law made itself felt on the money supply by attending to authenticity of source and form. Of course the law was effective in these respects because it drew on and supported common custom and prevailing business invention and practice: general trust in gold and silver as exchangeable goods, learned confidence in certain manners of transaction. Nonetheless, the pervasive use of forms defined in law and the absence of broad clashes of interest over measures taken to certify authenticity point to this use of law as that in which law had most clear-cut effect on the practical acceptability of money. Law had such successful impact in this area probably because, however important to good operations, arrangements to assure authenticity were of limited instrumental effect—not bringing into play a wide variety of more remote interests—and their prime utility (to foster reliability of communication through money) so plainly served a functional requisite of transactions as to evoke a ready sense of shared value among all those affected. Law has its clearest chance of effect when it not only serves functional requisites of social relations, but also is commonly perceived as doing so.

The Quality of Legal Tender

The idea that some money tokens should have a character called legal tender is as old as any item in national money policy. Legal tender is a quality of money wholly made by law, as much as the legally established or licensed forms which certify the authenticity of money. True, such operative effect as legal-tender status had outside the workings of legal process depended, like most aspects of money, on other factors besides the statutes, and particularly on public confidence or want of confidence in the general economy and the stability of government. Nonetheless, tokens had legal-tender effect only if the law said they should have it; likewise, law might legitimate the circulation of designated kinds of tokens as money without making them legal tender.[29]

The core idea of legal tender stood the same through the legal history of money in the United States: that certain law-designated tokens should, so far as the law was concerned, fully satisfy money claims recognized as legally enforceable. These might be claims of government on private persons for taxes, or claims of persons on government (as for repayment of money lent to the government on its notes or bonds), which the statutes declared might be discharged only in particular stated forms of money.[30] Or, the claims might be those of some private persons on other private persons, which the statutes said might be discharged by payment in particular tokens so designated by law.[31] The same tokens might not be legal tender for all purposes; some forms of money might be made receivable for debts owed the government, or to pay some obligations of government other than its bonds (as to pay salaries of public employees), which were not made binding means of payment among private persons.[32] One limitation inhered in all legal-tender laws: They operated only to determine what medium of payment must be accepted in law, and at what standard of value, to satisfy claims already reduced to fixed sums of money.[33] Law's authority to confer legal-tender status was not treated as authority to regulate the exchange value of money, so as thereby to regulate determination of the money worth of a claim (such as a claim for damages for personal injury) which had not already been set at a sum of money by contract, statute, or court judgment.[34]

On the whole the sanctions by which law enforced legal-tender status amounted to as stable a body of policy as the core definition of legal tender. Under stress of war the Continental Congress resolved in 1776 that anyone found guilty of refusing to receive its bills of credit in payment should be publicly declared "an enemy of his country and precluded from all trade or intercourse with the inhabitants of these Colonies."[35] The Congress did not claim authority in itself to declare or enforce legal-tender status for its notes, but under its urging legislatures in the rebelling colonies did so.[36] This early resort to positive penalties on those who would not honor the legal-tender quality of government paper proved to set no continuing precedent. After the revolutionary years and until mid-twentieth century government did not enact penal sanctions to implement legal-tender laws. The standard policy was to rely only on civil sanctions, and these of indirect operation. One approach was simply by persuasion, when statutes gave a limited legal-tender status to designated money by declaring that it would satisfy debts owed government; thus Congress declared national bank notes legal tender to pay taxes other than customs duties owing to the United States.[37] Conversely, limited legal-tender status might be given by limited compulsion. Thus generally in the nineteenth century the United States enacted that only gold or silver coin would discharge duties on imports.[38] And, in like character, Congress stipulated that any national bank must receive at par for any debt due it all notes issued by any lawfully organized national bank.[39] The sanctions in the law of legal tender affected the greatest range and variety of social relations insofar as they bore on settlement of private obligations which had been reduced to stated money sums. Where the law's definition of legal tender governed, it meant on the one hand that the claimant must accept payment offered in legal-tender tokens on pain, else, of being ruled in breach of contract or at least of being deprived of judicial remedy against his debtor, and that on the other hand the debtor must offer legal-tender tokens lest he become liable as defaulting on his contract.[40] Whether a court would hold that the legal-tender laws defined the only satisfactory performance in a given situation was decided in ways which showed the relative weight which public policy assigned to the market and to private governance of transactions on the one hand, and to official regulation of economic dealings on the other. Though early decisions were at some variance, the prevailing pattern favored full leeway to business custom. As it became customary to rely on all forms of legally legitimated currency and on bank checks to settle money debts, so the courts tended to presume that the parties intended to adopt such media where they merely provided for performance measured in money and had not stipulated for legal tender. Thus payment in currency that was not legal tender or by a good bank check constituted performance, unless the one to whom performance was due specifically objected.[41] Where the parties' agreement called for settlement in coin or dollars or lawful money, this was ready to require payment in legal-tender money, but without further specification by the parties, such terms would be satisfied by any legal-tender tokens which the law provided.[42]

In the second and third legal tender cases (1871, 1884), the Supreme Court ruled that Congress had authority reasonably to decide what definitions of legal tender would best serve public interest and that the public interest in an effective money supply warranted applying the statutory definitions of legal tender even to govern agreements for payment in legal-tender money made prior to the legislation.[43] However, the law's favor for freedom in private contract was dramatized by parallel decisions in which the Court interpreted the Civil War legal-tender legislation as not intended to bar enforcing, according to their terms, private contracts to pay debts in gold or in the gold value of existing legal-tender paper.[44] These decisions skirted the question of Congress's authority to restrict the competence of private contractors to settle the medium of exchange between themselves. In 1933 and 1934 Congress forbade private holding or dealing in gold, under penal sanctions, and barred enforcement of private contracts calling for payment of debts in gold or in paper currency valued in gold. In 1935 the Court ruled that Congress had authority to exert ultimate control in defining both lawful media of exchange and the media which in law would be treated as satisfying debts, even as to private contracts made prior to the legislation.[45]

Thus, again under urgent circumstances, in 1933-34 public policy returned to an approach which it had not employed since 1776—using positive regulation to compel persons to accept government paper as legal tender.[46] True, the 1930s policy did not go so far as that attempted in the Revolution. Congress did not compel persons to settle money transactions in government legal-tender notes; nothing that Congress did in 1933 and 1934 forbade individuals to settle their debts in deposit-check money, which by then was the principal type of money not of legal-tender status. However, in narrowing the range of legal-tender money by its general outlawry of use of gold or gold coin for all ordinary money transactions, the policy set in 1933-34 regulated the supply of money in a way which directly increased law's pressure to use a particular medium—government-sponsored notes—to satisfy money claims. The prime mover was regulation of the supply of money rather than of legal-tender status. But the effect was to add to law's sanctions for inducing men to honor the legal-tender status which law assigned given tokens, by drastically limiting options for settling money transactions.[47]

What we have considered to this point is what legal-tender status meant in legal definition and in legal sanctions. The content that public policy put into the term for the most part implied rather than expressed the purposes for which law conferred legal-tender status on some money tokens; we must infer purpose more often from function than find it declared. Some functions did not relate to the working of the money system as such. Thus, legal-tender status served the general interest in ready conduct of market transactions and in ready government allocation of economic resources, by making for more precise communication in contracts and by helping government and those subject to it to know the exact terms in which taxes and public debts might be satisfied.[48] Again, legal-tender status served the general interest in efficient operation of courts, by providing a specific measure of what would satisfy money judgments.[49] These were social functions of some importance, but they were not uses of the legal-tender device to serve the money system. However, in creating legal-tender status, Congress did seek to make two contributions to the operation of the money system as such. One purpose—embodied in the 1933-34 removal of gold from the category of legal tender—was that the definition of legal-tender tokens be auxiliary to determining the quantity of money; we shall take note of this matter again, in considering policy on money supply. A second purpose was to bestow legal-tender status to help promote the practical acceptance of given money tokens. This is the purpose of the legal-tender laws which presents their most distinctive, planned contribution to the money system.

Through most of the years there is little evidence that promotion of the acceptability of money was the dominant purpose in maintaining the legal-tender laws; most of the time it appears likely that the utility of legal-tender status lay in its service to the administration of contracts, of government finance, and of the courts. Crisis situations apart, there are two limited exceptions to this appraisal. In the first half of the nineteenth century, when the United States was markedly failing to match the supply of its own coin to the needs of the economy, Congress from time to time conferred legal-tender status on designated foreign coin, to enlarge the supply of currency by encouraging acceptance of such tokens.[50] Again, when Congress in 1851 and 1853 created silver coin in fractions of the dollar with silver content less than the formally declared value, it conferred legal-tender status on these subsidiary coins to limited amounts, seeking to encourage their acceptance both by the grant and by its limitations.[51] Of potentially greater public impact, however, was resort to the grant of legal-tender status to promote the acceptability of money tokens in periods of major economic stress, notably in war. The Continental Congress recommended—and legislatures in the rebelling colonies adopted—legal-tender status for the Congress's bills of credit, because lawmakers believed that the device would help support the financing of the war.[52] Policy makers did not lose sight of this potential of legal-tender status; it was proposed in aid of floating treasury notes to finance the War of 1812, became the subject of vigorous controversy, and in 1814 was rejected as an unfair use of government power.[53] Congress assigned legal-tender status to the United States notes (greenbacks) issued to help finance the North's war effort in 1862 and 1863, partly in the belief that legal-tender quality would help the government float them and keep them in circulation.[54] Incident to holding that Congress had constitutional authority not only to issue legal-tender paper but to make it effective to discharge private debts contracted before or after such currency was created, the Supreme Court recognized that promoting popular acceptance of the currency was one proper purpose for congressional action.[55]

Lawmakers might confer legal-tender status to make particular money more acceptable. Whether the device was effective to that purpose was something else again. Gold and silver were early declared legal tender because they had deep-rooted acceptance in popular custom, rather than the other way around. The federal Constitution implied acknowledgment of this state of affairs when it forbade the states to make any thing but gold or silver coin legal tender. Public policy also implicitly acknowledged the weight of popular practice by conspicuous absence of effort to limit currency to that which was declared legal tender. In the first half of the nineteenth century state bank notes supplied the bulk of money tokens. Their quality was uncertain enough to cause them often to circulate at a discount. Yet they circulated, and were allowed to do so without benefit of legal-tender status. Not until 1933 did Congress give legal-tender status to national bank notes or to federal reserve notes, circulating concurrently with legal-tender United States notes. In the late nineteenth century controversies over silver, men did not oppose giving legal-tender status to silver coin because it would force individuals to use a type of money token which in practice was unacceptable to them, but because the ratio proposed between gold and silver would overvalue silver relative to gold; the issue was not legal-tender status, but terms of supply. The two notable precedents for using legal-tender status to promote the acceptability of tokens suggested that the effectiveness of the device was at best marginal. The bills of credit of the American Revolution depreciated to worthlessness, for all their quality as legal tender and despite the threats by which Congress and local legislatures sought to compel their acceptance.[56] In the Civil War years the greenbacks soon depreciated substantially, relative to gold. Their legal-tender character notwithstanding, what determined the degree of the greenbacks' acceptability were other factors, especially the North's fluctuating fortunes in the war and market speculation. Against this background it appears that the prime purposes for which public policy maintained legal-tender money most of the time were those of the administrative regularity and convenience of the market and of government fiscal operations, and not to foster popular acceptance of particular money. The only domain within which legal-tender status clearly had practical effect was in the internal operations of legal processes themselves, and this simply because legal agencies could successfully set the terms of their own functioning; a court could effectively control its own judgments, so that in a proper case it might refuse to recognize that a debt had been satisfied save by the proffer of legal-tender money; so the tax collector might refuse to recognize that a claim for import duty might be discharged by any but the kind of money the statute stipulated. That legal-tender money had such undeniable effect in the operations of law itself might, indeed, indirectly persuade men to use the tokens in settling debts without pushing matters to formal confrontation through legal process. In time of stress sophisticated traders might invoke in market the background pressure of legal-tender laws; thus, recognition of the utility of legal-tender requirements generated substantial banker support for the act of 1862. But the record offers no basis for thinking that in ordinary times and among most men such responses were made under stronger compulsion than a sense of convenience; experience in the revolutionary and Civil War years showed that if circumstances brought crises of confidence in public finance legal-tender status could not be depended on to keep money acceptable in practice. In times of stress the significance of legal-tender status was auxiliary to the law's dealings with quite different problems, of the supply of money.[57]

Command of Other Assets: Liquidity

Ordinarily, in the going economy, men did not want money in order to hoard it. They wanted it because they believed that they could use it to obtain or command other assets, or to obtain reliable commitments of other assets in future. This belief rested on predicted willingness of holders of other assets to exchange them for money, resting in turn on confidence that the money would continue to be acceptable when the new holders wanted to exchange it for something else. There were some distinctively law-made factors contributing to the reliability of these ordinary expectations—the law's assurances of authenticity of the source and form of money tokens, and to a less degree its grant of legal-tender status. But the workability of money required a broader base than law's forms alone could establish. It required shared confidence that the economy was diversely and richly productive enough to supply a growing volume and variety of particular satisfactions. It required shared confidence that in a given state of the economy enough persons would accept particular money tokens in temporary substitution for other goods to make those tokens a reliable means to sustain differentiated roles in a society characterized by increasing division of labor. The kinds and extent of practical acceptability of money thus reflected and grew out of what the people sensed as the potentials of the whole economic and social context. It inheres in this estimate that law could make only limited contributions to the practical—as distinguished from the formal—acceptability of money. But this did not mean that law was not significantly involved. Law's principal business is with the good order of social relations, and the practical acceptability of money was both a product of and a moving factor in significant social relations.[58] The problem was not whether law should be involved in promoting the practical acceptability of money, but what should be the nature of its involvement.

Public policy dealt with the practical acceptability of money in two phases. The first phase—from early nineteenth century to the 1920s—took as law's goal the promotion of liquidity in the money system—a limited goal, involving quite limited uses of law. The later phase—which did not take form clearly until the 1930s—in effect identified achievement of the practical acceptability of money with achievement of efficient relations between the total supply of money and the working needs of the whole economy. In this second stage, policy continued some concern with liquidity. But preoccupation now was with managing the supply (the quantity and velocity) of money for the productive stability and growth of the economy; protection of the acceptability of money became a by-product, rather than the focus of policy.[59]

Liquidity of money tokens was an idea shaped in the first instance by business experience and not by law. It reflected hard realities in men's economic behavior, to which law had to respond if it was to promote needed enlargement of the money supply. From the early nineteenth century the growing volume and variety of economic exchanges and shared investments—brought to a focus on the money system especially by private search for profits in banking—produced a strong undertow of demand for growth in the volume and variety of forms of money. The response—a mingling of developments in business practice and in law—was extension of the kinds of money tokens which came into practical acceptance, from coin to bank notes, to deposit-check money, to government-issued circulating paper.[60] This growth was inhibited by recurring want of popular confidence that the newer tokens would in fact put in their holder the wide range of options that *money* should confer, to shift into other assets of more particularized use. Thus through the nineteenth century and into the 1930s a prime use of law affecting the money system was to foster the liquidity of money tokens. In this context liquidity meant the practical ability of the holder of one kind of money token to obtain for it on his demand another kind of token which he and most other persons regarded as of more assured acceptability for advancing or closing transactions. Specifically, up to the 1930s men wanted assurance that on demand they could obtain (1) gold or silver for paper currency (bank notes or, later, government-issued, circulating notes), and (2) paper currency for checks drawn on bank deposits.[61] This first, long phase of liquidity policy ended in 1933-34, when the law, eliminating the use of gold and silver as every-day money, decisively narrowed the liquidity issue to that of assuring that deposit-check money could be translated on demand into paper currency. At that point the public policy issue as to paper currency ceased to be one of liquidity and became wholly one of adjusting its supply to the transac-tional needs of the economy; the change was symbolized in 1963 when federal reserve notes ceased to carry the promise of redemption in lawful money of the United States and stood simply declared as legal tender for all public and private debts. Thus what for long was an area of money-system policy in which law accommodated itself to prevailing popular atti-tudes became one which the law substantially managed.[62] accommodated itself

The liquidity issue rested on the popular tradition that gold and silver coins were the norm of money, because the people were confident that everyone would always accept them. From the establishment of the na-tional mint (1792) to 1933 there was, thus, no liquidity issue about the gold dollar. In the late eighteenth century and the forepart of the nine-teenth silver figured prominently in common attitudes and practice as an ultimate measure of liquidity, when foreign silver coin circulated as a large part of the available money stock. But through much of the nineteenth century silver did not play this role, because the market price was too high to make it profitable to use silver as money.[63] There were acute issues of supply—of the provision of gold and silver coin in quantity to match trans-actional demands and in workable relation to each other.[64] In the last quarter of the nineteenth century growth in the quantity of silver brought to market and the pressure of particular interest groups for the first time created a liquidity—and not simply a supply—issue between the precious metals, as concern arose that silver would be so cheap relative to gold as to drive gold out of domestic circulation and thus make it not available at the option of holders of silver or paper-money tokens.[65] It was significant of the basic nature of all liquidity issues that the controversy over silver's rela-tion to gold created a liquidity issue out of imbalance in supply, where no liquidity issue had before been active. In any case, this was a problem of relation between gold and silver. Between both metals and the other prin-cipal types of money, there was never a liquidity issue; precious-metals coin enjoyed such popular confidence in their acceptability, compared with all other media, that they became the ultimate measure of liquidity. The framers reflected this norm of opinion when they forbade the states to make any thing but gold and silver coin a tender in payment of debts, as did Congress—until the issue of the Civil War greenbacks—when it limited the statutory definition of legal tender to the same coin.[66] One might question whether this popular exaltation of the precious metals is consistent with the successful creation (1851, 1853) of fractional silver coins which did not add up to the full quantity of silver in the dollar unit. Explanation of the ready popular acceptance of such subsidiary coins undoubtedly lies in a combination of the almost indispensable utility of the fractional coins, together with the fact that their limited denominations meant that users would never have large enough stakes in them to stimulate concern.[67] The functional problem about the subsidiary coinage was, thus, always one simply of adjusting supply efficiently to the needs of transactions. However, like the gold-silver ratio controversy of the late nineteenth century, the creation of subsidiary silver coins foreshadowed the eventual terms of resolving issues of the liquidity of full-dollar tokens, for establishment of a subsidiary coinage was a clear act of government management of the money system, and ultimate resolution of liquidity problems came only through government management of supply.

Public policy was slow to recognize that increasing the kinds of components of the money supply was likely to create a problem of liquidity, and as slow to recognize the working character of the problem. That legal provisions for liquidity were long grossly inefficient was partly because growth of the money system waited upon growth of business experience. But it was partly, also, because nineteenth-century legal processes and the habits and practices of nineteenth-century lawmakers were not geared to multidimensioned programming.[68] The liquidity problem and its resolution both derived from the fact that the money supply grew into a system of interdependent parts. To perceive and grapple with a system was just the kind of challenge to which our narrowly practical policy making was least adaptable. Want of business discipline and of economic knowledge helped make problems. Defects in the legal framework of money compounded the problems. There were two basic failures in legal arrangements. First, law legitimized different kinds of money tokens without providing means to assure them at least rough equality in public confidence. Law thus helped foster a practical hierarchy of tokens. In consequence, if some cause shook confidence in the economy the stress was not shared proportionately among all components of the money system but tended to fall disproportionately on the types of money which had been allowed to fall into second-class status.[69] Secondly, policy makers early and late failed to grasp the functional requisites to give money practical acceptability. Hence through much of the nineteenth century, law pursued an erroneous idea of liquidity, and naturally, therefore, failed to use appropriate means to achieve working liquidity. Money was too long treated as a debt, when it should have been treated as an instrument for flexible and reliable continuity in allocating resources.[70]

The first half of the nineteenth century saw rapid increase in the number of banks chartered by the states with the privilege of issuing circulating notes. State bank notes expanded not only because they served the profit of their issuers but because they were needed to supplement limited coin. Typically they promised redemption in gold or silver, but, also typically, they existed under no central supervision to enforce these promises, and their unregulated appearance thus introduced the problem of different orders of money tokens. That such bank notes were viewed under pressure as less reliable money than coin was attested by the range of substantial discounts under which they commonly circulated.[71] Save for discipline enforced in Massachusetts when Boston bankers insisted that country banks promptly redeem their notes on demand, the only effective central scrutiny kept over the liquidity of state bank notes was that administered by the second Bank of the United States under Nicholas Biddle in the late 1820s and early 1830s. Congress's refusal to recharter the national bank ended that discipline without replacement.[72] The national banking system created in 1863 and 1864 supplanted state bank notes, which Congress taxed out of existence in 1866, and the notes of the new national banks at least existed under uniform limitations imposed by statutory ceilings and requirements of deposited security.[73] However, Congress at the same time added a new problem of hierarchy in the money stock by helping finance the war by issuing $450 million of non-interest-bearing legal-tender United States notes designed to circulate as currency. That these in fact provided a fresh issue of liquidity was shown in the premium which gold commanded over them until in 1879, after years of controversy distracting to public affairs and disturbing to transactions, the federal government effectively made them redeemable in gold, as Congress had promised in 1875.[74] Overlapping the resolution of this issue came a new concern with hierarchy in the money supply. By accepting convertibility into gold as both the practical and in large measure the legal criterion of liquidity, public policy exposed the money system to the movements of the precious metals commodities market, and especially to the international market for gold. Law increased the potential for controversy insofar as it kept both gold and silver in the structure of money without providing a flexible formula to adjust the formally declared metal content of the dollar to the market ratio between the two metals. Through most of the nineteenth century silver was too high priced in market to enter the money stock, save as the mint provided a subsidiary, fractional silver coinage. However, from the middle 1870s a sharp decline in the market value of silver made its monetary use feasible and attractive to silver producers and to expansionist interests. Political battles raged over silver from the middle seventies to the Gold Standard Act of 1900. These controversies were part of the cost to the economy from muddled policy which kept alive the form of a bimetallic money system so poorly structured as to generate a liquidity issue between apparently superior and inferior units.[75] Resolution of the silver dispute did not end the liquidity issue over the currency so long as the law kept gold in the regular money system. Congress finally removed liquidity as a problem of the currency in 1934 when it banned private use of gold as money.[76]

Bank deposits against which checks might be drawn increased rapidly in volume from the first quarter of the nineteenth century. Especially important for the efficient conduct of transactions was the growth in bank-created demand deposits, reflecting extension of bank credit. Though bank notes exceeded deposits in circulation through the 1830s, from about mid-century deposits began to exceed bank notes, and in increasing proportion.[77] This development inherently created a new issue of liquidity. Men found bank deposits useful precisely because and to the degree that the banks' obligations were more readily acceptable than those of individuals or of particular business firms because the banks' pooled assets, by spreading risks, offered higher promise that claims would be honored and that currency would be forthcoming upon demand for withdrawal or for payment of checks, if currency was wanted.[78] This is to say that in prevailing attitudes liquidity was even more of the functional essence of deposit-check money than it was of currency. The superior utility of bank-deposit obligations over claims on other debtors lay in the size and quality of the ventures and commitments pooled through the banks' operations. This function of deposit-check money demanded for its efficient fulfillment that deposits, over-all, should stand in good working relation to the stock of coin and currency and to the volume and liveliness of productive transactions assisted by the whole money supply.[79] Both banking practice and theory and the law's provisions lagged badly behind the growth of bank credit in realizing that there was a major problem of keeping deposit-check money in working equality with coin and currency as part of the money supply. The banking community did not begin to attend to the system problems of deposit-check money until well into the mid-nineteenth century. With similar tardiness, law dealt only with the liquidity of bank notes substantially past the time when deposits had outstripped note circulation as banks' principal contribution to the money system. The first generation of regulation of bank-issued money required security or reserves only against bank notes, or—in the New York Safety Fund of 1829—included deposits by such inadvertence that the regulation was inadequate to the job. The outcome was that through the nineteenth and into the early twentieth century deposit-check money, which had become the bulk of the money stock, was allowed to exist in inferior status which exposed the economy to the costs and disorganization of recurrent liquidity crises.[80] There were two notable exceptions to this neglect. In the late 1820s and early 1830s, the second Bank of the United States was guided by Nicholas Biddle's vision of a central bank's responsibilities to exercise some supervision of the volume and quality of state banks' creation of deposits. And in the second half of the nineteenth century, by private co-operation, the New York clearinghouse and its imitators in some other key banking cities used clearing procedures to impose some discipline on their members' credit. These exceptional concerns with the liquidity of deposit-check money were important within their time and scope. Nonetheless, they were so limited, and so much the product of private action as to emphasize the general deficiency of public policy.[81]

Public policy thus fostered problems of liquidity by its tardiness in recognizing that all components of the money supply should be kept equally acceptable in popular practice by legal arrangements which treated them as interrelated parts of a system. Having helped create problems, the law compounded them by pursuing irrelevant solutions.

The growth in circulation of state bank notes first stirred policy makers to concern themselves with assuring liquidity (here, assurance of convertibility into coin) in order to make tokens acceptable. The law early favored freedom of contract in aid of the market energies which we relied on to expand productivity. It fit this bias of policy at first to accept a bank note as simply a kind of contract debt—a promissory note—and to conclude that its acceptability rested on the issuer's promise to pay and on law's readiness to enforce the promise.[82] From pioneer statutes of Massachusetts and New Hampshire (1799) and New York (1804) it became standard state policy to limit to banks chartered by the state the issue of notes intended to circulate as money. This legislation seems to have originated in the desire of some enterprisers to use law to restrict competition in a profitable kind of business, rather than in a view that special public interest required legal control on creating money tokens. The spread of such statutes later reflected more concern to assert public interest in the money supply.[83] But neither the earlier nor the later regulatory purpose affected the original view that bank notes were simply a kind of contract. Thus the first effort by law to promote their acceptability sought simply to strengthen the contract. Accordingly, by the mid-1830s statutory charters or general statutes commonly required that banks promise to redeem their notes in specie.[84] If further measures were needed, the logic of this approach led to stronger remedies to enforce the contract; these the law provided by stipulating that a bank might forfeit its charter for failure to redeem its notes on demand according to its promise, or at least might be compelled on that account to curtail its business.[85] This approach was in fact opposed to the practical problem, which was not to choke off the sources of needed components of the money supply, but to keep them in good working order. Both practice and declared policy came to acknowledge the dysfunctional character of a response wholly in terms of contract law and remedies. From time to time it became clear that a general public opinion, as well as the opinion of bankers, frowned upon those who pressed hard for redemption of bank notes in specie. Unofficial arrangements, and then the statutes, developed this view by recognizing that pressure to redeem bank notes was functional only if the pressure was used to maintain a working system of specie reserves against note issues.[86] Official action sometimes went even more directly to the point. Some state statutes forbade traffic in bank notes for less than their nominal value, or relieved banks of their obligation to redeem where notes were presented for redemption by persons who made a practice of receiving or buying notes at less than their nominal values, while other statutes relieved banks from penalties for failure to redeem notes during periods in which banks generally suspended redemption.[87] There was concession to functional reality— even if belated—also in the plain practice of public officers not to invoke the most severe penalties for suspension of specie payments during times of general distress.[88]

No less beside the point than reliance on contract forms and remedies to provide acceptability for bank notes was the law's next recourse, which was to various kinds of security. Building on the idea that a corporate charter was peculiarly the creation of the sovereign, states sought to bulwark bank notes by provisions written into the terms of incorporation of the chartered banks which alone, they stipulated, might issue circulating paper. Thus, statutes sometimes limited note issue to some percent of the bank's paid-in capital as well as conditioning the bank's entry on business upon some minimum of capital subscribed. Sometimes legislation limited dividend payments, and frequently imposed special liabilities on bank stockholders if the bank at any time failed to redeem its notes or left notes unpaid upon its dissolution.[89] These were hardly satisfactory devices to invigorate a going system of money. Stockholders' liability was but an analogue to stricter remedies in contract, when what transacting parties needed was a workable medium of exchange and not a lawsuit. Tying note issues to the bank's capital was no better; its capital was typically committed and not readily to be realized on; its capital base was fixed and not easily changed to match changes in the demands of business.[90] Somewhat better security was promised by the requirement which became standard with the adoption of general incorporation (free-banking) laws for banks, beginning with the statutes of Michigan in 1837 and New York in 1838, that bank notes be issued only against pledges of state or municipal bonds meeting standards of quality set by law. Analogous security stood back of notes of national banks chartered under the federal statutes of 1863 and 1864, which might issue only against deposit with the comptroller of the currency of specified United States bonds.[91] Such bond-deposit requirements were an indirect method of pledging the taxing power of various sovereigns to provide for ultimate redemption of the bank notes so secured, and they did underpin the bank notes with assets of some marketable character. However, the market value even of bonds of good quality proved likely to fall just when security was most needed, and the fall must be the greater if banks were driven to realize on the security. Moreover, bond deposits suffered the same functional irrelevance as all other kinds of security: what the community needed was not security for ultimate payment of debts represented in bank notes, but legal provisions which would maintain working continuity in the media used for exchange and for carrying forward business commitments.[92]

Beginning with a Virginia statute of 1837 and stretching over the years until a federal tax in 1866 ended state bank note issues, twelve states took a new tack by requiring that banks hold specie reserves (from a range of 5 percent to one-third) against their note issues.[93] The reserve requirement on bank notes never achieved the range of adoption of the requirement for deposit of government bonds which became a common incident of state free-banking laws.[94] The national bank system embodied both devices; the original legislation of 1863-64 required that national banks hold in their own vaults or with central city banks a 25 percent reserve in specie or lawful money against their notes and deposits; with confidence well established in the new bank notes, in 1874 Congress reduced the requirement for bank notes to that of keeping with the Treasury a redemption fund equal to 5 percent of the banks' outstanding circulation, designed simply to retire notes which became physically unsuitable for circulation.[95] The Federal Reserve Act in 1913 revived the idea of a substantial reserve against circulating paper, stipulating that federal reserve banks hold 40 percent of gold against their outstanding federal reserve notes. Congress eliminated the gold reserve requirement in 1968, in tardy recognition that it had lost meaning since Congress in 1934 forbade private monetary dealing in gold.

The idea of a legally required reserve moved policy a little closer to a functional answer to the liquidity problem, for it implied some recognition that the money supply as a whole was a system of interrelated components which should be kept in sound working relation to each other. But reserves as such were not the answer. The mere holding of reserves did not relate the money supply to the volume or velocity of transactions in the economy at large. Moreover, the rigidity of a statute-fixed reserve sharply limited its utility. True, it might be treated by bankers as a bench mark, so that approach to it should dictate restriction of credit, while a comfortable margin above it would invite expansion. But the reserve statutes typically provided no central scrutiny to generalize this use of the reserve requirement. Moreover, if the course of events brought banks to the reserve limit, the result was likely to be not a graduated response but severe dislocation. If public confidence fell away from paper currency under stress, demand for specie soon brought banks to the point where under the reserve requirement or as a matter of practice they might no longer redeem their notes, but must suspend specie payments, as they did in recurrent crises, or—an alternative as damaging to the economy—must by law stop lending until they restored the reserve ratio.[96] The real opportunity for effect in a reserves requirement lay not in the requirement itself but in continuous, close supervision by some agency outside the banks to keep their affairs in such order that noteholders' demands would not press against the reserves. However, through the mid-nineteenth century the state executive branch was too little developed to provide administration of such quality. Rather, the measure of what might be done was the success of privately organized and administered schemes of reserves discipline, in Massachusetts and in the country at large under the second Bank of the United States. In Massachusetts from 1818-24 the Suffolk Bank in Boston on its own, and from 1824-58 in association with six other Boston banks, in effect imposed a reserve system on Massachusetts country banks by presenting them with the alternatives either of facing regular demands for redemption at their own counters, or of maintaining balances in the Suffolk Bank to allow that agency to redeem their notes. This was a more ready and discreet device than the pressure which the second Bank of the United States applied in the Biddle regime by presenting state bank notes for redemption, for the Suffolk Bank had the administrative advantage of having the country banks' balances already in its hands. However, the heart of the generation-long success of the Suffolk Bank plan—as well as the good effects of the pressure applied over some years by the second Bank of the United States—was not in the *de facto* pressure thus applied to maintain reserves, but in the close supervision which tended to put some general discipline over the whole amount of liabilities which banks took on themselves.[97]

Public policy erred as much regarding deposit-check money as regarding bank notes in pursuing irrelevant solutions to the problem of liquidity. Policy was out of joint with reality, in the first place, because for a number of years it ignored the fact that deposits were an important component of the money supply. Thus various security measures adopted regarding bank operations—minimum paid-in capital, obligations limited to a stated percent of capital, special stockholder liability for the bank's debts—were either explicitly limited to bank notes or were ambiguous as to their coverage of deposit liabilities.[98] In 1829 New York launched an ambitious statutory Safety Fund for pooled assurance against defaults of banks theretofore specially chartered; the fund failed of continuing effect because its terms were inadvertently broad enough to cover deposits as well as bank notes—the draftsmen had obviously assumed that bank liabilities were practically synonymous with bank notes—but coverage of deposits had not been built into the reckoning, so that the fund could not stand up to underwriting the full range of bank-created money.[99] Requirement of deposit of government bonds to secure bank notes fast became a standard item under the free-banking laws which spread through the states in the 1840s and 1850s, but no comparable requirement was applied to deposit-check money.[100] Similarly, early statutes imposed specie reserve requirements only against bank notes.[101] That the law did not earlier show concern with liquidity of deposit-check money was not surprising, since until about mid-nineteenth century this aspect of liquidity did not appear a lively concern even within banking circles; partly from limits of available short-term commercial lending business, partly from competing attractions of medium and long-term lending opportunities (in lines of credit for industrial operations or in investment in railroads), banks were more often than not in a relatively frozen position at any given time. Moreover, it was not until the panic of 1857 that the country experienced a peacetime suspension of payments of currency because depositors lost confidence that they could on demand get currency for their deposits. However, though it may not be surprising that pressure did not emerge to develop legal requirements ahead of contemporary banking practice, the fact is no less significant as a caution against exaggerated expectations of the policy leadership to be had from legal process.[102] Even so, some states experimented. Louisiana in 1842 first required specie reserves against deposits as well as against bank notes, and at the unusually high figure of one-third. In the next generation another half a dozen states set reserve requirements on deposits. In creating the national bank system Congress, also, imposed reserve requirements for deposits. The Federal Reserve Act in 1913 brought the requirement into the new system.[103]

Reserves against deposits had the same functional irrelevance to the liquidity problem as reserves against bank notes. Both treated the matter as if the stake was to assure final settlement of a bank's debts, whereas the basic public interest was that there be a continuously available supply of tokens acceptable for moving the general run of economic transactions through their stages to resolution.[104] Again, policy makers failed to see that the problem was to treat the money supply as the system of interrelated components which it was. The few state reserve requirements and the requirement set by the national bank system fragmented reserves by leaving them tied simply to the administration of individual banks, or insofar as they allowed pooling—by counting in reserves balances held by central-city correspondent banks—they did not provide an ultimate source of credit to relieve the central-city banks when clients made massive demands on them.[105] Reserves against deposits, as reserves against bank notes, had potential for avoiding liquidity problems, where the legal requirement made a base for some central regulation of the whole money supply; indeed, in mid-twentieth century Congress at last allowed the Federal Reserve Board to vary required reserves as a means of controlling supply. But, through the nineteenth century the states lacked the executive vigor and experience to provide such administrative supervision. Under the national banking system the comptroller of the currency began as an officer charged primarily with the security of national bank notes. Gradually his office enlarged its role as bank examiner. But the focus of examination was on determining whether an individual bank's portfolio was sound, in the sense that loans were likely to be repaid; this was a supervision far removed from concern for adjusting the money stock as a whole to the economy as a whole. Through the money controversies of the last quarter of the nineteenth century and into the first generation of the Federal Reserve System in the twentieth, prevailing views in Congress and among top money administrators moved within the narrow confines of an effort to find in the gold standard an automatic regulator which was the antithesis of money management.[106]

In sum, liquidity was a problem in the money supply in part for a cause which by nature should have been more passing than it was. To serve a growing economy we needed to enlarge the kinds of money tokens. We did enlarge them: from coin to government-licensed and government-issued currency, to deposit-check money. Formal legal action could contribute to bringing new media into the system—by redefining the system of money notation, by assuring authenticity of source and legal incidents, for example—but, also, the people must be willing in fact to accept and use new types of money. Popular reactions to less familiar media meant that, while confidence was built, popular preferences would inevitably create ranks of superiority and inferiority among tokens. In stipulating contract terms and remedies, exacting security and requiring reserves, public policy made fumbling efforts to speed popular acceptance of the full range of money media on a parity with each other. These approaches shared the common defect, that implicitly they treated the problem as if it were one of collecting on debts represented by the money tokens themselves, whereas the true problem was to create and maintain a going money system which was never "collected," but which worked continuously as an instrument in allocating nonmonetary assets or conducting or resolving transactions the ultimate goals of which were to obtain goods or services other than money tokens.

Slowly we perceived that management of the supply of money was the only way to avoid, let alone get free of, crises of liquidity in the money system. Legal processes could produce no better public policy than the quality of our thinking allowed. The opportunistic bustle of nineteenth-century United States did not favor sure or rapid growth in sound theory about our problems, especially where the challenge was to recognize and provide for integration of many relations into a working system. However, our legislative process did have the potential for inviting innovation; creative leadership could write and press bills of any design for a wide range of purposes, and the existence of many states along with the Congress offered a diversity of legislative forums in which men could experiment. Though the main lines of nineteenth-century action were irrelevant to the real liquidity problem, policy did at last move through stages to more realistic solutions.

From the late 1820s into mid-century banking opinion and action under law moved toward maintaining liquidity of bank notes and deposit-check money by attending to the quality of bank credit. Under Biddle the second Bank of the United States not only policed bank-note issues by asking their redemption, but by making itself a regular creditor of state banks it was able to affect their lending. It could thus press them to settle their balances with it by turning over to it domestic and foreign bills of exchange which they had accepted. It could require that they shift to it balances from federal tax or land-sale collections which they had been allowed to hold for the time.[107] This was not discipline applied by direct command of law. But it was discipline which existed only by virtue of the law-given central monopoly of the Bank of the United States and its country-wide branch apparatus, and Biddle deliberately applied it.[108] Another item was added to a trend of policy when in 1842 Louisiana declared by statute that its banks might lawfully lend only for short-term, commercial ventures, except as they restricted long-term loans to the limits of their capital. Helped by the concentration of commerce in the port of New Orleans, the Louisiana mandate seems to have worked substantially up to the Civil War. It was indicative of a new attention to money as a total system, that at the same time the Louisiana legislation pioneered in requiring reserves against deposits as well as against bank notes.[109] Between 1853 and 1908 private organization, beginning in New York City, created clearinghouse associations in most metropolitan banking centers. Created simply to minimize coin or currency transfers by giving the participants a procedure to offset claims against each other, the clearinghouses grew to apply sharp discipline on their members' lending to insure that they would be able to settle their balances. The development showed that there were resources in the law of contract to allow some organized pursuit of liquidity through supervision of the quality of credit. But the clearinghouses functioned only in the central cities and without mandate or means adequate to managing the whole money stock in any but the short run.[110] Moreover, precisely as the clearinghouses came to meet liquidity needs of increasing public importance, policy makers decided that the job must be more directly and specifically regulated; thus the Aldrich-Vreeland Act of 1908 supplanted the clearinghouse function of overcoming liquidity crises in deposit-check money by handing the task over to special, federally sanctioned associations.[111]

Devices of legally required security (including the favored mid-nineteenth-century requirement of deposited government bonds) or reserves failed to solve the liquidity problem because they were too static and too fragmented. If this route were to be pursued, functional logic called for giving it strength by pooling under some central management. Again, the weakness of the nineteenth-century executive branch as well as the inexperience and narrowly practical thinking of policy makers worked against what might have seemed a rather obvious line of experiment. New York created a Safety Fund in 1829, intended to provide a base of public confidence in the notes of the banks the state had then chartered; the fund proved inadequate because in terms it included deposits, too, without financial provision sufficient to cover them; the fund had little practical impact after about 1842 and was ended in 1866. Five other states borrowed the idea before mid-century, but never put it to significant use.[112] Between 1907-18 eight states created programs for insuring bank deposits. At first successful in attracting depositors, the systems folded under the economic distress of the 1920s in the farm states, where the plans had been adopted. Pooling needed to be on a broader scale. But, more fundamental, the experience showed both that the insurance device for liquidity would not work without close and strong administrative policing of banks' lending policies, and that our policy tradition continued stubbornly opposed to acknowledging the extent of systematic organization which this prescription demanded.[113] Proposals for bank deposit insurance appeared on the national scene from time to time as early as 1886. But for years they floundered on bankers' opposition to regulation and fears that without the feared regulation weak banks would only drag down strong ones. At a later point the establishment of the Federal Reserve System bred a new opponent, which disliked the vision of a competitor agency. The extreme hardship of the liquidity crisis of the 1930s finally mustered the political force to bring a national deposit insurance program into being, under the Federal Deposit Insurance Corporation, which began operations on a temporary basis 1 January 1934 and became a permanent agency under the Banking Act of 1935.[114] That the plan responded to working reality, to the readiness of government to assume broader administrative responsibilities, and to widely felt public concern was attested by its rapid success in adoption. Within six months of the program's first effective date its membership included nearly 14,000 of 15,348 commercial banks in the United States, accounting for some 97 percent of all commercial bank deposits; by the early 1960s less than 400 commercial banks were outside the system, with deposits of less than one percent of total commercial bank deposits. Resistant because they thought the program should give more recognition to their lower risks, mutual savings banks were slower to enlist, but by the early 1960s insured mutual savings banks accounted for about 87 percent of all such deposits.[115] This rapid, massive adoption after so many years of inertia and opposition demonstrates how much functional need and imperfectly articulated public sentiment can be dangerously dammed up behind barriers of special interest, institutional frictions, and want of creative will for programming in the legislative and executive branches.

In its first generation federal insurance of bank deposits was not put under the test of such widespread loss of public confidence in the economy as marked the 1930s depression. Granted this reservation, both public acceptance and the operations of the Federal Deposit Insurance Corporation entitled the federal insurance to be rated a most successful device to meet the problem of liquidity of deposit-check money—indeed, perhaps, the single most successful money-management measure to emerge from the trials of the New Deal period.[116] But, however useful as a prestigious symbol, the label of insurance fell far short of explaining why public policy had at last apparently reached a workable solution to liquidity crises. Moreover, popular trust in the insurance label was likely to attach too much credit to the new federal program, and unrealistically to ignore the fact that if federal deposit insurance was as successful as it seemed, its success was due to a broader context of policy. National pooling offered such strength in an insurance fund as state experiments had fatally lacked. In addition, the broad scope of the program's coverage promised that infection of lost confidence would not readily spread from weak to strong banks.[117] But in a proper actuarial sense the liquidity of the money system as a whole could not be insured; if the money system as a whole fell into difficulties, these would arise in such a context of general economic distress as to swamp any insurance fund, considered as a fixed security.[118] The FDIC was successful because it was part of a pattern of federal policy which by mid-twentieth century had realistically come to grips with—and perhaps eliminated–the problem of liquidity in the money system by at last undertaking to manage the money supply. Whether we had enough knowledge or skill to manage money effectively remained in question. But public policy was now at least addressed to the reality, which was that a workable money system meant not provision of security for a debt represented by a money token, but provision of tokens acceptable because their supply stood in good working adjustment to the ongoing business of allocating resources.

Particular FDIC practice in effect emphasized that continuity of money supply was a prime goal. The corporation did not let a distressed bank fail, if it could fairly avoid that outcome; rather, it fostered a sound reorganization or merger, while it took responsibility for loss from depreciated assets. When a failure occurred, the corporation undertook forthwith to pay insured deposits, rather than paying out over time from what a receiver might collect. Its power to withhold desired insurance inherently carried a check over chartering new state banks, supplementing the authority which the comptroller of the currency and the Federal Reserve had over chartering national banks. The FDIC vigorously developed bank examination procedures, sometimes in conflict with the comptroller and the Federal Reserve.[119] Such particulars of policy were all helpful and relevant to maintaining liquidity of deposit-check money. But they did not reach the heart of the matter, which was to assure that there would be no liquidity crisis in the money system as a whole, because its components were brought into a situation of equality in law and in popular acceptance, and because there was an ultimate assured source of supply of as much money as the general economy required.

National pooling of risks through the FDIC contributed to the workability of the money system as a whole, but it could do so because it fit into the context of other supply policies which came to maturity between about 1930 and 1960. By forbidding private dealings in gold coin or gold, Congress in 1934 finally freed the money system from the chances of the precious-metals commodity market, released money from a rigid control which had no functional relation to general transactions, and removed the basic factor which had fostered superior and inferior grades among the components of the money system.[120] In 1945 Congress relaxed statutory limitations which had restricted issue of federal reserve notes by the system's gold reserve and its holdings of limited kinds of commercial paper, and thus armed the system to buy such securities as the Treasury might float to support operation of the Federal Deposit Insurance Corporation.[121] By mid-twentieth century Federal Reserve practice had developed, and Congress had ratified, flexible capacity in the system's central management to buy and sell federal securities in order to foster or restrict creation of deposit-check money by member banks.[122] Especially symbolic of the translation of the liquidity issue from unreal terms of security to real terms of assured supply was Congress's 1935 grant of authority to the Federal Reserve Board to make substantial cuts or increases within statutory bounds set on member bank reserves, so that reserve requirements might become an instrument of supply control.[123]

Provision for the Current Supply of Money

Policies designed to provide a standard notation scheme and to make given tokens practically acceptable affected the supply of money by helping bring particular forms of money into use. In this sense such policies regulated supply. However, notation and acceptability did not respond to the distinctive problem of supply, which was to make tokens available in quantity and timing adjusted to the flow of resource allocations; for example, in the interest of a uniform notation Congress banned private coinage, though this action limited the supply of tokens in fact usable; again, Congress sharply limited the time over which emergency currency might be outstanding under the Aldrich-Vreeland Act of 1908, because the prime object there was to maintain acceptability by weathering a liquidity crisis and not to furnish a regular component of the money stock.[124] To adjust money supply to transactions was a distinct undertaking; indeed, provisions about notation and acceptability sometimes got in the way of achieving it. Some civil-law doctrine asserted that money must be supplied exclusively by the sovereign. But in the North American setting conceivably we might have tried to leave the quantity and timing of money supply to the market. The economy of the North Atlantic coast was a relatively simple one into the 1820s. Scarcity of fluid capital and of manpower put a premium on the improvising ingenuity and energy of all who showed aptitude and ambition for trade and commercial production. Public policy reflected these pressures of the situation by accepting freedom of private contract as a norm. Thus it came easily to early nineteenth-century judges to say that, until the law spoke specifically to the contrary, anyone might launch into banking at his own initiative—contract to receive deposits, discount notes, deal in bills of exchange, and issue his own promises to pay designed to circulate as money. It fit this doctrine that, without restrictive regulation in the early nineteenth century, the law of contract provided a frame within which private arrangements built up the use of checks drawn on deposits as an increasingly important component of the money supply, while in the second half of the century private arrangements created clearinghouse procedures to facilitate use of depositcheck money and eventually even to exert some discipline on its creation.[125] So, too, there was no initial legal barrier to keep producers of precious metal from marketing their gold or silver by manufacturing it into tokens of standard weight and fineness capable of use as media of exchange, or to stop merchants, common carriers, or local public utilities from issuing metal pieces or paper certificates intended to facilitate settlements with their customers.[126] The federal Constitution specifically forbade the states to coin money or to issue their own paper obligations as currency, but it was silent on private creation of money tokens.[127] To mid-nineteenth century, public policy debate included some lively distrust of legal restraint on private contributions to the money stock, as likely to foster oppressive monopoly. There was objection on this ground when in 1741 Parliament extended the Bubble Act to the colonies, with the specific aim of forbidding a land bank.[128] The framers rejected a proposal to give Congress under the federal Constitution explicit authority to grant corporate charters; opponents feared that the authority would be used to create monopolies, and concern was also expressed that the grant would be taken to allow creating banks and that this, in turn, would stir added opposition to the proposed Constitution.[129] The Jacksonian attack which barred rechartering the second Bank of the United States in 1836 succeeded in part on objection to restricting dispersed creation of currency and credit by state-chartered banks through an institution to which Congress had given a monopoly of banking operations of national scope.[130] In 1839 in *Bank of Augusta* v. *Earle* the United States Supreme Court said that the presumption of policy favored free pursuit of ordinary banking transactions; thus, until a specific barrier was shown, the Court would assume that the law of a state as a matter of comity allowed a foreign banking corporation to sue there on a bill of exchange it had bought in the state.[131]

Nonetheless, the main line of public policy early and continuously established in practice the legitimacy of using law to control money supply. The federal Constitution boldly gave the central government a monopoly of official coinage and of whatever authority existed for government-issue paper currency.[132] The Constitution did not speak directly to the question whether states might charter banks with franchises to issue circulating notes and to accept or create deposits. Assuming without serious challenge powers earlier established in the crown and Parliament, state legislatures by special acts chartered banks in increasing numbers, and in 1837 the United States Supreme Court confirmed that nothing in the federal Constitution's ban on state bills of credit forbade the states to bestow note-issuing franchises on their chartered banks.[133] Meanwhile, beginning with statutes of 1799 in Massachusetts and New Hampshire and of 1804 in New York, state legislatures in effect asserted control of paper currency by declaring that circulating notes might be issued only by duly incorporated banks. Moreover, the common pattern of such legislation developed to limit all general banking business—receipt or creation of deposits as well as issue of circulating notes—to firms organized under and subject to their regulations set in state incorporation laws for banks. These limiting statutes probably originated in desire to limit competition among those who could get charters. But this aspect faded as legislatures proved liberal in grants. So, in the long run limitation of note issues and general deposit business to chartered banks implied primary concern for controlling the terms of money supply. State courts, and later the Supreme Court of the United States, held constitutional such statutory limits on entry into the banking business, because the regulations protected the integrity of the money supply; banking was a lawful activity at common law, but the legislature might supersede the common law by reasonable controls.[134]

Through the first half of the nineteenth century Congress acted variously to affect the money stock, though without developing a system of supply. It created a mint which, despite stretches of faulty administration, provided good enough service so that no large-scale private coinage arose in years when the law did not formally forbid it. Moreover, Congress provided terms on which owners of precious metal might have it converted at the mint into money tokens without charge, to encourage production of coin.[135] To the same end of encouraging a larger stock of coin, Congress at the outset established a bimetallic (gold and silver) standard of money units; the original purpose, to increase the money stock, was no less clear for all that the scheme failed because Congress did not enact the flexible procedure needed to keep the ratio of gold and silver in the dollar adjusted to the market ratio for the two commodities, so that market processes regularly drove one or the other metal out of circulation. Congress implicitly recognized this defect, and at the same time implicitly asserted the legitimacy of legislating to regulate the money supply, in 1834 when it reduced the fine gold weight of the dollar in order to encourage—as it did—importation and holding of gold in preference to silver.[136] In creating the first and second Banks of the United States (1791, 1816) Congress gave these institutions power to issue circulating notes, as well as broad authority to lend and thus to create deposit-check money and to augment the money stock by dealings in bills of exchange.[137] In 1851 and 1853 Congress again used its authority over money to increase the supply of standardized tokens, when it created a fractional silver coinage, of limited legal-tender status, containing less than proportionate amounts of silver, so to provide more tokens handy for exchange and to eliminate market pressure to export such coin simply for its precious-metal content.[138]

Civil War finance brought Congress to its boldest actions to that time in regulating current money supply. Between 1862 and 1864 Congress authorized the issue of $450 million of legal-tender United States notes, in part as a substitute for conventional borrowing at interest, but in part to furnish additional media of exchange to facilitate the government's war purchasing. As with the creation of a subsidiary fractional coinage in 1851-53, so in causing issue of the United States notes in 1862-64 Congress asserted the legitimacy of legislating to regulate money supply both by conferring legal-tender status and by increasing the quantity of money tokens.[139] In 1863 and 1864 it provided for incorporating national banks, with franchises both to issue bank notes and to conduct general deposit business; the intention was partly to help sell government bonds (under the inducement that by pledging them, the new banks would obtain authority to issue bank notes), but also to regulate the money stock so as to create a more uniform, discount-free currency.[140] Primarily to spur lagging organization of national banks (and a lagging market for government bonds), but with the inherent effect of asserting exclusive federal control of the currency supply, Congress in 1865 enacted a prohibitory tax on circulation of state bank notes. The device worked with dramatic speed to limit the currency stock to federal-issue (United States note) or federal-licensed (national bank note) currency. The Supreme Court thereafter upheld both the prohibitory tax on state bank notes and the issue of United States notes intended as currency, as reasonable measures to pursue what the Court recognized as a legitimate objective of federal law, to regulate the supply as well as the legal incidents of money.[141] For a generation after the war treatment of the greenbacks and then of silver agitated Congress and national politics. Though what emerged was a series of opportunistic bargains rather than an integrated policy—and measures of dubious impact at that—Congress further asserted its right to control money supply by enacting the Resumption Act of 1875, passing the Bland-Allison Act of 1878 which authorized silver purchase, supplanting it by the Sherman Silver Purchase Act of 1890, repealing the Sherman Act in 1893, and capping the record with the Gold Standard Act of 1900.[142]

Federal legislation did not touch the deposit business of state-chartered banks, which flourished and—with the deposit operations of national banks—soon grew to supply the principal component of the money supply. However, national banking legislation recognized legal controls on deposit business as part of the public policy toward money supply, both in the pains taken to define the business in which national banks might engage and, at a later point, in forbidding other federally chartered financial institutions to create deposit-check money. Before and after the national legislation the states commonly developed security and reserve requirements for bank notes and—less commonly—for deposits, and the national bank system adopted like devices. These requirements affected the supply of currency and deposit-check money. But their calculated objectives were, rather, to foster liquidity in order to promote acceptability of tokens; thus these measures count for less as precedents legitimizing legal adjustment of the quantity or timing of money supply to the flow of transactions. Both on the state and national scenes from mid-nineteenth century to early twentieth century there was a long and costly gap in policy attention to managing the supply of bank note and deposit-check currency. In the Aldrich-Vreeland Act of 1908 Congress provided for emergency, short-term issue of currency to overcome a liquidity crisis; again, the focus was not on continuing adjustment of the money stock to the movements of the economy.[143] Emphasis on short-run dealing with liquidity crises was strong in framing the Federal Reserve Act. But when Congress created the Federal Reserve System in 1913 it at least endowed the system with the potential for comprehensive, continuing control of the money supply. Slowly, with serious distortions wrought by three wars and a disastrous depression, the Federal Reserve Board established continuing regulation of the principal money stock—currency and deposit-check money alike—as legitimate business of federal law. The board built its control position partly by practice, partly by declared policy, and partly with the aid of strengthening amendments of its statute in 1935. En route to this outcome, Congress reduced the range of domestic money-supply problems and made its most drastic assertion of control of the money stock in 1933 and 1934 when it first restricted and then wholly banned private use of gold as money, as well as authorizing the president to cause the issue of up to $3 billion of United States notes.[144] The sum of this record, from 1790 to mid-twentieth century, was not a clearly articulated, comprehensive system of policy. But, it did establish beyond debate control of current supply as a legitimate use of law affecting the money system. Beyond this point lay questions of the legitimacy of regulating money for broader purposes—to foster economic growth or to affect general price levels. These issues belong to later stages of this book.

Dealings with bank notes and deposit-check money showed one continuing qualification on legal control of money supply. It was an aspect of policy which bore some analogy to the favor early expressed for free contract in banking and to the distrust early indicated of restrictive laws which might foster monopoly. This qualification was a disposition to prefer dispersed over central controls, and in doing so to favor a play of diverse or even competing controls which had some of the character of decisions reached in a market. Thus, while the states early limited issue of bank notes to banks which must satisfy the legislature's terms for incorporation, legislators proved liberal in multiplying banks even under special charters. In 1837 and 1838 Michigan and New York set a new trend emphasizing dispersion values, by substituting general incorporation acts (free-banking laws) for special charters. The change was made partly to eliminate occasions for corrupt manipulation in getting charters, partly from egalitarian dislike of special privilege. But it also reflected confidence typical of the times, that multiplying centers of decision making would provide more energy of productive action—in this case for a larger supply of currency and credit.[145] Consistent with the policy bias of the free-banking laws was the scope which law allowed to private provision of banking discipline, in the Suffolk Bank scheme to police note issues in New England (1824-55) and in the spread of city bank clearinghouses in the second half of the nineteenth century.[146] Federal policy accepted the line thus taken in state law when the Jacksonians allowed the second Bank of the United States to expire in 1836 and then underlined their policy bias by the Independent Treasury Act of 1846, which further reduced the central government's connection with the money supply by holding all federal funds in separate treasury offices. The national banking system launched in 1863 and 1864 carried on this favor for dispersed agencies to create money; the long absence of apparatus adequate for central control was the more conspicuous because the central government was the chartering authority. When Congress set up the Federal Reserve System there was, finally, the promise of central control, but it took forty years or more to realize the potential. Meanwhile various structural features of the new system evidenced the strong hold of the market analogy of shared power—continued acceptance of a dual system of national and state-chartered banks, care for the competitive position of the two kinds of banks relative to each other, creation of twelve federal reserve banks and ownership of their stock by their members, a Federal Reserve Board not at the outset in clear command, which had to build its authority by a generation of administrative practice and statutory amendment, and restriction of issues of federal reserve notes by tying them to a combined reserve in gold and in relatively short-term, self-liquidating commercial paper eligible for rediscounting by member banks at the federal reserve banks.[147]

A second qualification on legal control of money supply existed in proportion as law insisted that issuers stand ready to redeem paper currency in specie (meaning in practice, ordinarily, gold) as the norm of the money system. This policy did not deny the legitimacy of using law to control the money supply. Indeed, the law was regulating supply whether it required redemption of paper currency in precious metal, or authorized the issue of nonredeemable paper (the original greenbacks), or authorized temporary suspension of specie payments. Concern with relations between specie and other forms of money derived from popular custom. But this concern was strengthened and took on new expression because law incorporated it into the system.[148] Nonetheless, for law to put the money system under a specie standard was a strikingly limited, if not self-contradictory, assertion of legal control. So far as a specie standard worked, it subjected the money stock to the control of the market for one or two particular commodities, gold or silver, and to all the factors playing on that market—the chances of minerals discovery, the state of mining technology, the extent of industrial demand, the policies of other nations concerning the place of precious metals in their various money systems—however irrelevant these factors were to adjusting the money stock to the flow of resource allocations in the economy of the United States.[149] Nevertheless, from the time when the framers wrote into the Constitution their stringent bans on state bills of credit and on state laws making anything but gold or silver legal tender, until Congress removed gold from the domestic money supply in 1934, public policy resorted to a specie standard as the ultimate means to show distrust of money-supply decisions made by legal processes. The Constitution left broad capacity for control in Congress. But, as appeared in controversies over the second Bank of the United States, then over the greenbacks and silver, then over the emergence of the Federal Reserve System, we tended to treat this authority more as a regrettable necessity than as a desirable opportunity. To the extent that law tied the money stock to a specie base, it linked control to factors not determined by public officers. Until 1934 prevailing opinion accepted the social costs imposed from time to time by the irrelevance of specie commodity markets to general economic management, precisely in order to restrict the area of decision open to political process. Yet, this policy was always a qualification and not a denial of the legitimacy of ultimate legal control of the money supply, as the Gold Reserve Act of 1934 demonstrated.[150]

Though legislative practice and judicial acceptance established control of current supply of money as a legitimate objective of law, what most stands out from 1790 into the 1950s is fumbling and often inadequate, wasteful, and costly performance of law under this authority. The generally poor performance is striking in view of the functional importance of money supply to prime values of the society—notably to the society's reliance on the market, the confidence with which it pursued increase of material productivity, and its readiness to employ government subsidies, franchises, and regulation to invigorate private transactions and enlarge productive capacity. Some of this record can be explained by the warping influence of particular groups; an example is the impact of the competitive jealousy of certain political and financial interests in New York in helping bring down the promising beginnings of central-bank control of money supply under Nicholas Biddle.[151] But the costs of poor adjustment of money to the going operations of the economy were so widely felt—on farmers who could not move their crops at fair prices as well as on industrialists and merchants caught by credit contractions and liquidity crises— as to render unconvincing an explanation in terms of manipulation by special interests.[152] The record should give pause to those who would interpret the legal order as simply pursuing the profit and power of capitalists; capitalists were too often ill served by public policy on money supply.[153]

Detail of law's involvement with adjusting money supply to the current flow of the economy is the business of economic and not of legal history. Judgments on the over-all quality of money-supply performance involve such a range of economic data and theories as plainly to fall outside lawmen's competence. This is to say, also, that law's contributions were special and limited, however important within their scope, so that the story as a whole cannot be told within the history of legal processes.

However, one salient aspect of public policy relating money supply to the current needs of the economy has such relevance to law's functions as to require notice. Legal process can help, and often has helped bring choice of values into greater awareness, and, incident to this, has sharpened men's perception of relevant facts and relevant cause-effect relationships. Both a measure and a cause of the generally poor performance of public policy on current money supply was the failure to embody in law a workable definition of the money-supply problem. The basic defect was that law did not treat money as a system of interdependent parts, requiring continuing adjustment to each other relative to movement in the general economy. The result was that particular elements of public policy which might have contributed to a sensible total program got in the way of efficient supply because they stood in isolation. We have already noted aspects of this piecemeal approach. Policy makers wrote a bimetallic standard into their notation scheme, partly to encourage a larger coinage. But they provided no procedure to keep both metals in the working system by regularly adjusting the ratio of gold and silver in the dollar to the relative values of the metals in the commodity market; the rigidity of the notation scheme thus meant that one or the other of the metals was commonly undervalued and drawn out of the system. Legal requirements that state bank notes or United States notes be redeemable in specie subjected those important components of the money supply to influences that served no function in adjusting availability of money tokens to the whole flow of transactions. Measures to promote acceptability of money tokens did not take account of—and not surprisingly hence proved at odds with—adjusting money supply to the volume and timing of the business which money was supposed to facilitate. Legislators imposed security requirements—fixed ceilings or required deposits of government bonds as prerequisites of bank-note issues—of a rigidity inconsistent with sensible supply. They required that individual banks maintain reserves of currency or specie against deposit-check money. But, since they did not provide a central lender of ultimate resort, their reserve requirements fostered belated, abrupt contractions of credit and did not offer the assurance of cash needed to forestall runs on the banks. The issue of legal-tender United States notes as circulating media in 1862 and 1863 spawned years of unnecessary and distracting controversy, because Congress acted by simple fiat and declared no reassuring formula to relate the government's issues to the condition of the economy. Though the Federal Reserve System was set up to bring some integrated order into handling the money supply, this objective was stultified in large part for more than the first twenty years of the system's operation because—still not acknowledging the management role which was the justifying logic of its new creation—Congress sought to tie federal reserve credit and note issues to the presumably automatic working of the market for short-term, self-liquidating commercial paper.

Such elements of policy, defective or irrelevant from the standpoint of continuously adjusting the money stock to economic activity, shared a basic error. They all represented failure to treat the money supply as the product of a system, all of whose parts must be taken into account for effective legal control. Legislative practice and judicial acceptance did establish legal control of supply as a legitimate use of law affecting money. But, without a realistically comprehensive and bold concept of what the objective called for, the course of policy was condemned to costly contradictions and confusion. Ignorance, wrongheaded economic theory, and clashes of shortsighted special interest all entered into the failure to embody in law a properly systematic adjustment of money supply to economic needs. Also, lawmakers long failed to allocate decision-making power so as to respond to working needs of the money system. This aspect of the matter presents a distinctively legal influence on money history, which the next part explores.

Servicing the Going Economy as a
Legitimate Goal of Regulating Money

The legal regulations of money so far catalogued promised to serve the ordinary business of allocating resources through the market or through public finance. Varying judgments of economists, politicians, and men of affairs over how much effect law had caution us against exaggerating law's importance. Nonetheless, what policy makers believed law could do largely determined how they used law. Their usage—though it varied in detail according to experience and expediency—so consistently supported this function as to establish that to help money serve the ordinary operations of the economy was a legitimate purpose of legal regulation. Indeed, we took the social utility of this function so much for granted that we left its legitimacy more often implied than declared.[154]

However, the matter was too important to be left wholly to implication. The legitimacy of this current-operations goal found expression in attention to: (1) costs of a money system as social overhead costs, (2) the systematic coherence of money, and (3) deliberate adjustment of the supply of money tokens to the volume and timing of transactions.

First the framers of the federal Constitution included in the powers of Congress explicit authority to coin money. They did so without recorded discussion; provision of a current money supply was so clearly functional to the commonwealth as to be beyond debate.[155] In 1792 Congress affirmed this judgment by creating a mint. Its action the more strongly implied acknowledgment that the supply of money tokens was a proper overhead cost of society because the step was taken against opposition raised on grounds of economy.[156] Recommending a mint, Alexander Hamilton had recognized that a fair argument could be made that the mint should convert privately owned bullion into coin without charge to the owner tendering it for conversion, so as to "[make] . . . the expense of fabrication a general instead of partial tax." Hamilton recognized the validity of this approach by opposing any large fee for coinage, though he suggested a small charge; Congress, however, chose to treat the cost of coinage as a social charge, and in its 1792 statute authorized coinage "free of expense to the person . . . by whom the [bullion] . . . shall have been brought."[157]

Public policy also developed the idea that burdens from legal regulation of the current money stock must be borne by all, as proper overhead costs of society. Despite the high favor which public policy showed to freedom of contract, as part of the costs of maintaining a going economy all contractors must accept such inconvenience or risk as might be entailed when law prescribed the character of lawful money and of legal tender. Private contract would not be allowed to oust Congress of its ultimate control of the money system. So long as Congress acquiesced, private contractors might effectively stipulate to settle transactions in bullion or in paper adjusted to the market value of bullion. But at any point, and for past as well as future transactions, Congress might lawfully restrict the media of exchange to such tokens as it chose to recognize incident to its reasonable judgments as to the kind of money that would best service the going economy.[158]

Secondly, the legitimacy of using law to make money better serve the going economy came to expression in concern that money tokens should have such uniformity in definition and in authenticity and such liquidity as might make them harmonious parts of one system.

One reason which Hamilton advanced for creating a national mint was that "a nation ought not to suffer the value of the property of its citizens to fluctuate with the fluctuation of a foreign mint, and to change with the changes in the regulations of a foreign sovereign. This, nevertheless, is the condition of one which, having no coin of its own, adopts with implicit confidence those of other countries." [159]

In those years when the second Bank of the United States best functioned as a central bank, Biddle and his supporters asserted the legitimacy of using law-sanctioned regulation to keep state bank-note currency at more uniform discounts and to hold bills of exchange within narrower rates than loosely joined sectional or local markets provided, in the interest of a national money system. These efforts of the bank were clouded as public-policy precedent by the widespread attack on that institution, but in their time they added substance to the law's role affecting current money supply. [160]

The Supreme Court felt that an extensive interpretation of Congress's power to act against counterfeiting would best implement the Constitution's policy "of creating and maintaining a uniform and pure metallic standard of value throughout the Union." [161] Creation of a nationally uniform paper currency was taken by Congress as one justifying ground for establishing a national bank system, and it followed up this action by driving state bank notes out of circulation with a prohibitory tax. The Supreme Court upheld the action, for Congress had authority "in the exercise of undisputed constitutional powers . . . to provide a currency for the whole country," and to this end might wield exclusive authority to determine what paper might circulate, because "without this power . . . its attempts to secure a sound and uniform currency for the country must be futile." [162] Incident to removing gold from domestic money circulation and authorizing devaluation of the dollar in 1933 and 1934, Congress barred enforcement of private contracts which called for payment in gold coin or in currency measured by gold values. Congress here explicitly asserted the legitimacy of using law to maintain uniformity in the money system, noting that enforcement of gold clauses would "obstruct the power of the Congress to regulate the value of the money of the United States" and be "inconsistent with the declared policy of the Congress to maintain at all times the equal power of every dollar, coined or issued by the United States, in the markets and in the payment of debts." Upholding this determination, the Supreme Court recognized that legal control of money to service the going flow of transactions was a proper goal of policy: "It requires no acute analysis or profound economic inquiry to disclose the dislocation of the domestic economy which would be caused by such a disparity of conditions in which, it is insisted, those debtors under gold clauses should be required to pay one dollar and sixty-nine cents in currency while respectively receiving their taxes, rates, charges and prices on the basis of one dollar of that currency."[163]

Within the scope allowed it, state policy likewise affirmed the legitimacy of regulation designed to make money work as a going system. Because in their money-supply functions banks performed a service of broad public concern, they were properly regulated. Thus the Supreme Court of the United States supported sympathetic interpretation of a state statute to suppress unlicensed banking: "Its object was the protection of the people against the evils of an unauthorized currency—than which hardly any object of legislation is more important. The currency measures all values, and is the medium, directly or indirectly, of all exchanges. To keep it sound, and to guard it as far as possible from fluctuation, are among the most imperative duties and among the most difficult problems of government."[164] In 1829 New York launched a program requiring that note-issuing banks contribute to a safety fund to guaranty bank-note holders against loss; its proponent justified the program, because the banks "enjoy in common the exclusive right of making a paper currency for the people of the state and by the same rule should in common be answerable for that paper."[165] In the early twentieth century, recognizing the predominant importance which deposit-check money had assumed in the money supply, states experimented with bank-deposit insurance. The United States Supreme Court recognized that "enforcing the primary conditions of successful commerce" was a proper objective of legislation. "One of these conditions at the present time," the Court observed, "is the possibility of payment by checks drawn against bank deposits, to such an extent do checks replace currency in daily business." To require banks to contribute to a deposit-insurance fund was a reasonable regulation, not just for private benefit, but primarily "to make the currency of checks secure, and by the same stroke to make safe the almost compulsory resort of depositors to banks as the only available means for keeping money on hand."[166] Protection of the money system's capacity to service the current flow of transactions was the legitimating goal.

Thirdly, the propriety of this purpose of legal regulation was no more pointedly at stake than when policy makers specifically sought to adjust the supply of money tokens to the volume and timing of transactions. Most such efforts were manifest simply through action. But some declarations stand out, to convey the meaning of a great deal of unrationalized practice. Thus Hamilton recommended a bimetallic standard of money, to increase the quantity of circulating coin.[167] Similarly, he recommended that Congress sanction circulation of designated foreign coins as a temporary adjustment of supply until the mint should meet the domestic demand, and from time to time until 1857 the Treasury and the Congress acknowledged this policy in various legislation regulating use of foreign coin.[168] When Congress changed the gold content of the dollar in 1834 it acted without clear-cut debate or forthright explanation. But, in part at least, the move won support as a move to increase the quantity of gold in circulation, hopefully (in the minds of hard-money men) at the expense of silver and of the notes of the Bank of the United States.[169] Policy concerning paper money included declared concern to adjust supply to current demand. Hamilton urged chartering a Bank of the United States because "the institution of a bank has also a natural relation to the regulation of trade between the States, insofar as it is conducive to the creation of a convenient medium of *exchange* between them, and to the keeping up a full circulation, by preventing the frequent displacement of the metals in reciprocal remittances. Money is the very hinge on which commerce turns. And this does not merely mean gold and silver; many other things have served the purpose, with different degrees of utility. Paper has been extensively employed."[170] Both in keeping its own notes steady in relation to reserves and yet responsive to needs of trade, and in policing the redemption of state bank notes, the policies of the second Bank of the United States tended to fulfill Hamilton's prophecy.[171] Congress asserted its right to adjust the currency supply to transactional needs, within the over-all ceilings it set, by apportioning and reapportioning shares of national bank notes among banks in different sections of the country.[172] And when the Supreme Court in 1884 affirmed Congress's authority to issue United States notes, not simply under stress of war emergency, but in peacetime, the Court found that the Constitution empowered Congress "to provide a national currency" and to use its reasonable judgment whether there was "inadequacy of the supply of gold and silver coin to furnish the currency needed for the uses of the government and of the people."[173] On the borderline of policy between serving a going economy and helping move the economy into a new context, was the authorization of temporary, emergency currency to overcome a liquidity crisis, provided in the Aldrich-Vreeland Act of 1908. Though this legislation was used only once—in the crisis posed by the outbreak of World War I—it symbolized a prime concern which produced the Federal Reserve Act of 1913. The Federal Reserve System was to become significant for larger goals of economic growth and adjustment. But, the discussions surrounding its creation legitimized it in terms analogous to the thought behind the 1908 statute—that the law might properly provide for adjusting the supply of money to the immediate demand.[174]

REGULATION OF MONEY TO PROMOTE
MAJOR ECONOMIC OR POWER ADJUSTMENTS

Definition of the legitimate uses of law to affect the money system did not end in validating regulations which served the ordinary flow of transactions. Beyond this more limited objective, events reflected concern with two kinds of purpose of potentially broader impact: (1) Policy makers showed interest in regulating money to effect major readjustments in general economic performance, whether to keep or restore an equilibrium assailed by extraordinary pressures, or to promote multiple increase in productivity. (2) Some men desired, others feared, regulations of money which might bring large shifts in the distribution of wealth or income, to alter the structure of power among interests or classes. On balance the record legitimated legal regulation for the first of these two larger goals, and rejected the second.

Service of regular, current operations was a quite plain objective of most legal regulations of the money system, whether openly declared or implied in working effects. The evidence is much less clear on adoption or rejection of legal controls of money for purposes of major readjustment in economic functions or in distribution of place or power. Typically this society dealt with its affairs in narrowly pragmatic fashion, making a philosophy out of crossing bridges when it came to them; open discussion of the grander purposes of money policy was perhaps of no poorer, but also it was of no better quality, than the handling of most questions of broad reach. In these respects evidence from the implications of legal action was ambiguous. Most uses of law affecting the money system could be read plausibly as serving operation of the going economy. Given the typically limited horizons of policy making, plus the prevailing distrust of government intervention reflected in the enduring allegiance paid the gold standard, the safer implication from legal actions which might serve both immediate operations and purposes of larger effect was that the policy makers meant to validate only the more immediate purpose. True, legal regulations establishing a uniform notation scheme of money units, authenticating sources and legal incidents of money tokens, and promoting liquidity by requiring security or reserves, might all be viewed as fostering long-term economic growth by encouraging confident commitments. But the stronger implication is that policy makers adopted such regulations to serve current dealing. On the other hand, when regulation dealt directly with quantity and timing of money issues, whether for liquidity or for supply-demand adjustments, the actions could so readily serve goals of larger change that they must be counted more ambiguous. This is not an area of policy which should inspire dogmatic readings.

Goals of Major Adjustment in Economic Performance

From the late eighteenth into the middle twentieth century, the long-term bias of public policy favored using law to promote multiplied increase in productivity. This we took to be a self-evident good for individuals and for the commonwealth. This general bent of policy was manifest particularly in using government's fiscal powers (as by a protective tariff and subsidies for transport and communication), in government's power to grant franchises encouraging economic venture (in generous chartering of business corporations, and in special-action grants of authority to develop natural resources and lines of transport), and even in some regulations which carried penalties or imposed burdens or restrictions (as in limits which the Court held that the commerce clause put on state laws discriminating against interstate commerce). Within this general context, we might expect to find ready use of legal controls over money to promote increased productivity, or at least to assist major readjustments of economic relations to maintain or restore the economy's expansive capacities. On the whole, this did emerge as the prevailing attitude. But the record on legal regulation of money is less clear on this score than is the record of other types of legal action taken for economic promotion. I shall first inventory some policy measures, and then consider why legal regulation of money seems less clearly addressed to the larger goals than were other uses of law.

The story begins on a negative note. The federal Constitution gave Congress ultimate control of money policy and—with the important exception of its silence on state authority to charter banks—imposed strict limits on state action affecting the money system. Two purposes shaped this pattern. One was to foster such uniformity in the money system as would encourage broad markets among the states. This purpose might be interpreted as aimed at economic growth. But in 1787 this was not yet a clear direction of policy; the first emphasis seems simply on achieving such harmony in the money stock as would facilitate current trade.[175] However, the framers had a second goal which did concern relations of the law of money to major adjustments in the economy. When the Constitution forbade the states to issue bills of credit or to make any thing but gold or silver legal tender, the specific intent was to bar them from manipulating the money system to produce inflationary booms or to relieve debtors under extreme distress of depression. Plainly, the framers were aware that legal control of money might be used in efforts to move the economy from one level of growth (or, at least, of activity) to another. But they were critical of legislative favors which distressed debtors had obtained in years of disturbed markets following the Revolution. They did not show themselves minded to sanction legal regulations of money designed to assist large shifts in economic conditions.[176]

With hindsight it is tempting to read the breadth of the commerce clause as intended to warrant regulating money for economic growth. But the contemporary record is ambiguous. Principal attention focused on foreign and not on domestic commerce. Thus, the record tells little, to start with, about what the constitution makers regarded as legitimate goals of public policy in the home economy. Clearest was a purpose not then involved with regulating money, that is, to empower the central government to bar state discriminations against commerce among the states.[177] The framers' other plain intent was that the commerce power should assure Congress's authority to get revenue by some taxes on trade, and especially by laying tariffs on imports. Substantial opinion was that under this authority Congress should be able to lay tariffs for promotional purposes (as well as to give the United States bargaining counters in dealing with trade policies of foreign governments). Clearly, promotion of economic growth was accepted as legitimate in some contexts; the prevailing attitude was never one of dogmatic *laissez faire.* But this conclusion is too broad to settle the narrower question, whether power over the money system might properly be used to this end.[178] Indeed, since the framers included, along with the commerce clause, a specific grant to Congress of authority to coin money and regulate its value, and imposed specific limits on state authority over money, it might appear that they did not think of the commerce clause as a basis of legitimizing action on money matters.[179] When the Supreme Court much later invoked that clause as one item making up an aggregate authority of Congress over the money system, the Court could perhaps claim Alexander Hamilton for its argument.[180] But the most we can draw from the framers' discussion of the policy of the commerce clause is their highly general intent that the national government be empowered to act where the general interests of the Union were at stake, and the states were severally unable to deal with the matter. This conclusion, again, is of such sweep as to be of little help in answering the specific issue of the proper goals of regulating money.[181]

Through the nineteenth century there was only limited direct action by government to regulate money to foster economic growth or adjust the economy to major changes of circumstance. Most government action which looked in this direction delegated the promotional or adjustment roles to privately owned banks under private direction. This was the only field of money-system activity which the Constitution allowed to the states under a generation of legislative practice, ratified by the Court in 1837.[182] And it was the manner in which Congress chose to make its most sustained and broad-reaching promotional use of its money powers—first in chartering two Banks of the United States (1791, 1816), and then in providing (1864), and later liberalizing (1875) a general incorporation act for national banks.[183] Delegation to private hands of functions of public interest was a technique common in the nineteenth-century resort to law to foster economic growth; it was not an approach peculiar to legal control of money. The prime reasons for this way of proceeding lay in problems and policies concerning the structure of government relative to the structure of private power. Further consideration of this matter belongs in the next part.

Hamilton recommended to Congress that it create a single national bank on grounds which looked beyond serving government finances or current private transactions, to increasing the productive capacity of the whole economy. An advantage of such institutions, he argued, was

the augmentation of the active or productive capital of a country. Gold and silver, when they are employed merely as the instruments of exchange and alienation, have not been improperly denominated dead stock; but when deposited in banks, to become the basis of a paper circulation, which takes their character and place, as the signs or representatives of value, they then acquire life, or in other words, an active and productive quality. . . . [I] t is one of the properties of banks to increase the active capital of a country . . . . This additional employment given to money, and the faculty of a bank to lend and circulate a greater sum than the amount of its stock in coin, are, to all purposes of trade and industry, an absolute increase of capital.[184]

Chartering the first bank stirred sharp controversy in Congress. But the stakes were seen in sectional-political terms; the debate contributed nothing substantial to defining the legitimate economic goals of regulating money.[185] Nor did the career of the first bank develop firm precedent for a bold definition of goals. The bank served the government well as fiscal agent and assisted the going economy by adding reliable currency to the regular money stock. The bank pursued a conservative policy in holding its own issues in secure relation to its reserves and in using its position as lender to state banks to curb their speculative enthusiasm. Thus its practice tended to legitimize some effort at managing large movements in the money stock. The bank did not translate these activities into clear definition, however—perhaps out of prudent regard to the growing competitive jealousy of state-chartered banks which, along with some traditional agrarian distrust of concentrated financial power, brought Congress to refuse extension of the bank's charter in 1811.[186] Marked in its early years by poor management and then by limited conceptions of its possible role, the second bank in its first phase claimed no bold managing function over the money system. But, in the prime years of his governance (1823-30), while Nicholas Biddle devoted the bank primarily to the more efficient working of the going economy, especially in adjusting the money supply to seasonal and sectional trade differences, he also believed that the bank's responsibility extended to promoting sound growth in the general economy and to restraining inflationary speculation. It was the proper "business of the Bank of the U. States to guard ... [against the] ruinous consequences" of trade booms which outran sound marketing with the help of undisciplined lending by state-chartered banks. "The whole evil therefore lies in an overbanking which occasions an overtrading, and the whole remedy lies in preventing this overbanking."[187] Andrew Jackson's successful attack ended the bank's career as a central bank. But Jackson could not expunge the precedent which Biddle had added to Hamilton's prophecy of the possibilities in managing the money supply for large economic goals.

Overlapping the record of the two Banks of the United States was development of state policy toward banks. Except for a handful of banks in which a state held some ownership or to which a state gave a monopoly—banks which operated in too limited spheres to attempt managing roles as broad as Nicholas Biddle assumed—state-chartered banks carried built-in bias for economic expansion by expanding the money supply. As fragmented enterprises, they expressed their organizers' separate drives for profit, without central discipline. At the outset many saw their profit primarily in enlarging their issues of circulating notes. As they sought more loan business, they often found that the demand for short-term commercial credit was insufficient to sustain them or their ambitions; hence they responded the more readily to business demands that they supply medium and long-term capital.[188] In this context liberal chartering of banks—first by special acts, then under general (free-banking) incorporation statutes—meant much more than legitimizing legal provisions for a money supply simply to service the current flow of transactions. A few times legislatures openly showed their conviction that law might legitimately enlarge the money supply for economic development: Some statutes conditioned bank charters on the grantees' commitments to make a stated percent of their loans to agriculture or to industry; apparently it was taken for granted that banks would supply commerce.[189] Most of the time, however, the legitimacy of promoting multiplied economic growth by laws enlarging the sources of money was simply implied in practice, by liberality in chartering banks. This implication of policy was indirectly confirmed by the running fire of criticism the practice received from agrarian advocates of limiting the money stock to the precious metals. These hard-money men opposed banks less on arguments addressed to the more efficient operation of current transactions than from concern for the longer term effects of bank-made money on stability of prices and markets. This attitude was strong enough to bar banks altogether or sharply limit their creation in about a third of the states in the 1850s. But this reaction did not long prevail, and its significance is chiefly to point up the enthusiasm for promoting economic expansion which powered the prevailing practice.[190]

Congress enacted general incorporation laws for national banks in 1863 and 1864 avowedly for reasons of state, to help finance the North's war effort. Argument was also made for the new system on the ground that it would allow substituting a more uniform national currency for state bank notes, which were subject to varied discounts and to a good deal of counterfeiting. This was a secondary factor in the debates, though it was the primary goal of Secretary of the Treasury Salmon P. Chase, without whose stubborn persistence there probably would have been no national bank legislation. But so far as it figured, the focus seemed to be on servicing current market operations, and it was on this purpose that the Supreme Court centered when it upheld the prohibitive tax by which Congress finally drove state bank notes from the field.[191] Moreover, the rigid ceiling of $300 million which Congress put on national bank notes, the substantial minimum capitalizations on which it conditioned organization of national banks and conservative restrictions it put on their lending policies did not make the legislation a strong precedent for regulating the money supply to produce major expansion of economic activity.[192] In 1875 Congress removed the ceiling on national bank-note issues, thus making the national policy more truly one of free banking. This step was taken to conciliate expansionist sentiment, and to that extent affirmed the legitimacy of regulating the money supply for promotional purposes. But, the 1875 action was so much a product of political calculation, to serve the interests of Republican party unity, that its worth as a money policy precedent seems little.[193] As national banks matured they did in fact join state banks in producing large expansions in the money stock, mainly by enlarging deposit-check money. In this aspect, in the second half of the nineteenth century national free-banking laws, like state free-banking laws, worked to make the money supply a factor for economic growth. But the part of law in this course of events after 1864 was relatively remote; the business practice of bankers and the pressures of their clients were the moving elements.[194]

Once past the making of the federal Constitution, there is through most of the nineteenth century little sustained or well-defined direct action by the federal government to affirm or deny the legitimacy of regulating money to give long-term direction to the economy.[195] The one kind of bold action by Congress for direct manipulation of money for major economic adjustment—the issue of the Civil War greenbacks—was taken for purposes of the polity rather than of the economy and belongs in the next section. Indeed, nothing is more conspicuously lacking in the debates over the legal-tender act of 1862 than indication of awareness in Congress—or in the country—that the issue of United States notes involved a larger problem of meeting the dangers of inflation produced by competition between the civilian and the war economies. From time to time in the fore part of the century Congress authorized issues of Treasury notes, some of which apparently were used in circulation, but the purpose here was to finance government and not primarily to enlarge the stock of money.[196] Congress reduced the gold content of the dollar in 1834, but apparently to encourage entry of more gold coin and discourage current use of bank paper in the ordinary money supply, rather than for accomplishing any major economic readjustment.[197]

In the Specie Circular of 1836 the United States declared that it would accept only gold or silver coin in payment for public lands; this measure used government's fiscal rather than its monetary power (employing the government's command of public property, analogous to its purse power), but the circular had material impact on the money supply by tending to drain state banks of the gold which they needed to back up their circulating notes, and the consequent curb on speculation fostered by easy money was a purpose of the circular. Abrupt and rigid in effect, the action was not an efficient kind of regulation. Nonetheless, it implicitly asserted the legitimacy of using law to affect the money system for large adjustments in economic activity.[198] In 1846, by the Independent Treasury Act, Congress provided that government offices should hold all moneys paid to the United States and that all dues owed the United States should be paid in specie. The statute was a mixed expression of partisan politics, distrust of state banks as depositories and as issuers of paper money, and distaste for money management whether delegated to a central bank or attempted directly by the federal government. In effect, the act rejected an active money-managing role for the United States or any of its agencies. Yet, in doing so the statute embodied a decision on the large objectives of money management—in favor of an idea of long-term stability, which its supporters wanted to promote by discouraging use of paper currency and compelling note-issuing and lending banks to look more carefully to their specie reserves.[199] The 1846 requirement that payments to the United States be made only in specie never worked completely, but it operated enough to introduce dysfunctional changes in bank reserves according to tides of public receipts and spending. The act of 1864 allowed the United States to deposit its funds in the new national banks, and the 1846 scheme was practically abolished when Congress also allowed government deposits in the federal reserve banks created in 1913. In practice these relaxing laws allowed the Treasury to engage in some money management, by shifting government deposits when and where reserves were needed to support bank money. But to the end of the nineteenth century such Treasury action remained episodic and lacked governing principle. Thus these changes did no more than indicate that options remained open for the federal government to manage money to promote or accommodate large shifts in the economy.[200]

Of similarly ill-defined character as policy precedent was the other late nineteenth-century area of direct legal regulation of money—that involving disposition of the Civil War greenbacks and the analogous problem of silver. Though the United States notes were first issued for reasons of state, the postwar years brought a question of their continuance or withdrawal which was addressed largely to choice of national economic goals. In the spirit of the 1846 statute, some wanted to get government out of the dangerous business of supporting a paper circulation which, they feared, tempted to speculation that outran real production of goods and services. Opposed were expansionists who wanted a larger money supply to encourage greater market activity. The outcome was a shifting set of compromises, shaped at least as much by the play of partisan politics as by concern with money policy. Expansionists staved off sharp contraction of the greenbacks. Gold standard men won a commitment to resume specie payments in 1875 and saw this accomplished in 1879 and reinforced when the government borrowed through private bankers in 1895 to maintain its gold reserve. Fresh pull and haul followed the resumption battle. The stable money men struck the silver dollar from the national money pattern in 1873; from 1878 to 1900 they had to make limited concessions by resuming some silver coinage; then they battled through to formal declaration of the gold standard at the turn of the century.[201] To some men the gold standard spelled denial of the legitimacy of any legal regulation of money to manage the course of the economy. So interpreted, renunciation of an active role for law could be said to have lasted about a generation, until devaluation of the dollar in 1934.[202] But this is too simplistic a reading of events. There was considerable unreality about the gold-silver controversy all of its years, and the unreality did not lessen after 1900. For one thing, fresh discoveries and improved mining technology allowed gold to be a base for economic expansion after all; the decision for gold thus proved to be underwritten as much by chance and expediency as by principle. Furthermore, in increasing measure bank-created credit provided the bulk of the money supply. Gold reserves materially affected deposit-check money, but other influences played on the banks also, including actions of government. Meanwhile, the comparative lack of legal controls on creating deposit-check money helped allow economic expansion which tempered and made politically more palatable the anti-inflationary measures taken in the name of a gold-based money system.

At its enactment the Federal Reserve Act did not strengthen precedent for managing money for large economic objectives. In this respect Congress gave the Federal Reserve System a mandate vague almost to the point of lacking meaning—nothing more definite than that the federal reserve banks were authorized to use their powers for "the accommodation of commerce, industry, and agriculture."[203] The act tied the issue of federal reserve notes to a substantial gold reserve plus pledged security of commercial paper, and quite closely held down Federal Reserve lending to the short term, thus following a line indicated in the Aldrich-Vreeland (emergency currency) Act of 1908. The legislative history supports the implication of these provisions: Apart from servicing the ordinary currents of trade, the most ambitious managing role that the Congress had in mind for the system was to prevent or reduce the harm from such financial panics or liquidity crises as had occurred in 1907.[204] Restriction of system goals is not surprising. Prevailing opinion sought to limit, not enlarge, government's monetary intervention in the economy; this was the point of contemporary adherence to the gold standard, and of the faith which legislators put in the supposedly automatic controls imposed by limiting Federal Reserve lending and note issues to a base in short-term commercial paper.[205] Moreover, as the next part notes, creation of the system was surrounded with much distrust of its implications for the balance of power among political and economic interests; this was not an atmosphere favorable to large views of the system's title to manage money for major economic change or adjustment.

From the middle 1920s control of money to affect the general direction of the economy began to reach definition and gain legitimacy as a product largely of Federal Reserve practice, and partly of Federal Reserve doctrine, concerning open-market purchases and sales of federal securities by the federal reserve banks.[206] In the Banking Act of 1935 Congress implicitly legitimized this technique of money management by giving statutory status to a Federal Open Market Committee as part of the Federal Reserve organization. Moreover, Congress moved cautiously toward validating such money management for purposes beyond mere service of current transactions; open-market operations, it said, should be governed not only "with a view to accommodating commerce and business," but also "with regard to their bearing upon the general credit situation of the country."[207] In another aspect the 1935 act legitimized general economic management as an objective of money control, when it authorized the Federal Reserve Board to change reserve requirements for member banks within a wide range "in order to prevent injurious credit expansion or contraction."[208]

The Federal Reserve Board was too unsure of its statutory ground or its knowledge to make effectively bold use of its new open-market authority in the 1930s depression.[209] Demands of government finance interrupted progression along this line in World War II and its immediate aftermath and in the Korean War. But the Federal Reserve reasserted relative autonomy in money management in 1951, and in the next twenty years it consolidated its right to affect general economic growth or adjustments and the level of prices by open-market dealings. These matters came to sharper definition than they might otherwise, because the stakes were large in the competition of roles between the Treasury and the Federal Reserve; it was clear that much more was at issue than regulating the money supply merely to service a going flow of transactions.[210]

Federal Reserve legislation and administration were only one channel through which government might regulate money to attempt major economic adjustments. Two other direct precedents were set to this effect in the 1930s, and government also used its fiscal powers in ways which affected the roles of money. The Thomas Amendment to the Agricultural Adjustment Act of 1933 gave sweeping discretionary powers to the president to cause the secretary of the treasury to enter into agreement with the Federal Reserve System for direct purchase of Treasury obligations up to $3 billion, or alternatively—or in addition—to cause the Treasury to issue United States notes to that amount, as well as empowering the president to provide for free coinage of silver without limit or to reduce the gold content of the dollar by as much as 50 percent. These powers over money, the amendment declared, might be used to effect major adjustments in the economy, to overcome conditions in the international money market adverse to the nation's foreign commerce, or when "an economic emergency requires an expansion of credit, or an expansion of credit is necessary to secure by international agreement a stabilization at proper levels of the currencies of various governments." Unwilling to disclaim authority for vigorous action against the 1930s depression, President Franklin D. Roosevelt did not oppose the Thomas Amendment; probably he accepted it as a background threat that he could wield against a conservative Federal Reserve Board. However, he never used this delegated authority to issue United States notes, and he took only limited measures to enlarge currency based on silver. Given the sweep of the Thomas Amendment, this restraint implies continuing force in the fear of printing-press inflation which had had classic expression in the federal convention of 1787.[211] In addition to the authority conferred in 1933, Congress further empowered the president, by the Gold Reserve Act of 1934, to fix the gold weight of the dollar at any level between 50 and 60 percent of its prior legal weight, while also vesting title to all gold coin and bullion in the United States, discontinuing further circulation or manufacture of gold coins, and altogether removing gold from private use as money. In what proved to be a vain effort to raise commodity prices the president promptly exercised his authority by devaluing the dollar to 59.06 percent of its former weight.[212] In 1935 the Supreme Court held that Congress might constitutionally confer this power on the president. The point most immediately ruled on by the Court was to hold that Congress might also constitutionally ban enforcement of existing or future contracts calling for payment in gold according to the old weight of the dollar. But this ban on the gold clauses was relevant only because it was auxiliary to the change Congress had authorized in the gold content of the dollar. The Court indicated its awareness that at stake was the legitimacy of controlling money for major adjustments in the economy. For it took pointed care to ground Congress's power to fix the gold weight of the dollar not simply on Congress's authority to coin money and regulate its value, but

> in all the related powers conferred upon the Congress and appropriate to achieve "the great objects for which the government was framed"—"a national government, with sovereign powers". . . . The broad and comprehensive national authority over the subjects of revenue, finance and currency is derived from the aggregate of the powers granted to Congress, embracing the powers to lay and collect taxes, to borrow money, to regulate commerce with foreign nations and among the several States, to coin money, regulate the value thereof, and of foreign coin, and fix the standards of weights and measures, and the added express power "to make all laws which shall be necessary and proper for carrying into execution" the other enumerated powers.[213]

The Court's rationale was broad enough to validate the broad range of purposes for which the administration had sought to regulate the dollar—specifically, to affect commodity price levels (and hence the purchasing power of money), more generally, to promote economic growth.

The twentieth century also saw more deliberate uses of government's fiscal powers to regulate the money system, though most often in this domain the intent was to subordinate monetary to fiscal policy. Especially between 1898 and 1912 the Treasury engaged in calculated movement of government deposits in and out of commercial banks, to relieve sectional or seasonal deficiencies of the money supply which might have grown into crisis.[214] The 1934 legislation under which the president devalued the dollar put at the Treasury's disposal the bulk of the government's profit from the devaluation for use in market operations to stabilize terms of international trade, and also gave the Treasury broad powers to buy and sell gold. Under this latter authority, the Treasury sterilized gold imports in 1936-37 by withdrawing funds from the money stock by selling Treasury bills in market to pay for the gold, instead of issuing gold certificates to the federal reserve banks and drawing on the balances that might be so created; at later points the Treasury acted to relieve slackened business activity by putting some of its gold holdings into the federal reserve banks.[215] When Congress passed the Employment Act of 1946 it made another significant addition to the precedent validating regulation of money for purposes of major economic change or adjustment. Despite much dilution by compromise, out of the legislative bargaining from which this statute came there emerged a formal commitment of the federal government to use all its resources to promote maximum employment, production, and purchasing power. Fiscal and not monetary considerations dominated the maneuvers which produced the bill; proponents wanted prime reliance on government spending, which was precisely what the opposition most feared, and attention to public spending overshadowed the rather incidental references in the debates to roles of "banking and currency."[216] Nonetheless, the record included reference to monetary factors, and the breadth of the statute was such as to include them.[217] Shortly after the statute was passed, and with continuing emphasis, the Federal Reserve Board acknowledged that the act's policy was an authoritative guide for system decisions.[218]

Goals of Maintaining or
Changing the Distribution of Power

Money can be an instrument by which men wield power over assets and people. Conceivably, policy makers might regulate money not just in aid of economic performance, but in attempts to get or keep power. By the second half of the twentieth century public policy plainly legitimated legal controls on money both to service the going economy and to seek sustained or increased economic productivity. Policy put no comparably assured approval on regulating money to affect the distribution of power. To a significant extent the record denied the legitimacy of this purpose as an objective of legal controls on the money system.

There was never doubt that it was proper for government to regulate money to aid the ordinary life and operations of the state; indeed, we might fairly regard this use of law simply as a variant of regulating money to facilitate the ordinary business of resource allocations in general, whether by market process or by political process. A recognized purpose of granting Congress power to coin money and regulate its value was to assure reliable media through which government could effectively tax, borrow, and spend.[219] In Hamilton's conception, and according to their charters and their accepted practice, the two Banks of the United States issued their own circulating notes, extended their credit, and determined their policies toward state bank notes with a view to aiding federal taxing and borrowing operations; the Supreme Court took the second bank's utility as government fiscal agent as one ground of the constitutionality of the bank's charter.[220] The promotion of a more uniform currency which was one announced purpose of the national bank system created in 1863-64 and which the Court found to be a constitutionally sanctioned objective was partly in aid of the government's fiscal operations.[221] Though distrust and dispute surrounded other aspects of creating the Federal Reserve System, there was never disagreement that its operations should include serving as fiscal agent of the government and using its credit and deposit facilities to smooth adjustments between the market and public finance in the ordinary course of affairs.[222]

There was never doubt that government might regulate money to help finance a war. The federal Constitution forbade the states to issue bills of credit, reflecting the framers' revulsion against the depreciation of the currency which had attended resort to paper money by the states and the Continental Congress in the Revolution. Yet, they left the Constitution silent on the new Congress's authority to issue currency, and their discussion indicates that they did so in order that the federal government might command all the money resources it might need to deal with unusual circumstances. In the context of their times, that concern was most likely aimed at assuring Congress leeway to deal with wartime finance.[223] Financial difficulties in the War of 1812 helped convince Congress that it had been wrong not to extend the charter of the Bank of the United States in 1811 and that in 1816 it should create the second bank.[224] Congress issued United States notes and set up a national bank system to help finance the North's war effort in 1862-64, and in 1871 the Supreme Court held that Congress enjoyed a large discretion of judgment when it acted for this end.[225] In two world wars and in the Korean War the Federal Reserve subordinated its judgment on money control to the initiative of the Treasury, and when the Federal Reserve reasserted some autonomy in 1951, significantly it established its claim on the basis that a wartime emergency no longer warranted Treasury dominance.[226]

Practice and doctrine thus legitimized regulating money to support the ordinary of the wartime emergency needs of the state. The record looks quite different where questions arose about regulating money to affect distribution of power among private interests. Here interpretation is often difficult, because events usually mingled suspect, power-structuring purposes with goals of economic performance which prevailing opinion accepted as legitimate. So far as we can disentangle balance-of-power from economic-performance issues, the trend was to deny the legitimacy of using legal controls on money to advance specific social, political, or economic interests at the expense of others. This is not to say that particular interests never got what they wanted through manipulating the money system.[227] Indeed, the presumption of constitutionality which the Court attached to Congress's legislation inherently allowed scope for special interests to score gains within the sanction of presumed public-interest goals.[228] But gains made by those seeking particular advantage were precarious, because under the governing opinion they could not be claimed as of right.[229]

The federal convention revealed acute distrust of interest-group manipulation of the law on money. In banning state bills of credit and limiting state laws on legal tender the Constitution condemned recent state responses to pleas of distressed debtors. Moreover, the convention struck from the draft Constitution an explicit authorization to Congress to issue bills of credit; though members were unwilling flatly to prohibit Congress from increasing the money supply in emergency, they feared pressures to print money without limit, should the authority be given as a regular power.[230]

Both on the state and national scenes public policy toward banks responded to fears that bank notes and bank credit would become instruments of oppressive gain for a favored few at the expense of the many. In about a third of the states during the second quarter of the nineteenth century this attitude produced constitutional or statutory bans or limits on chartering banks. With more lasting effect, it was an attitude which helped develop the trend to free-banking (general incorporation) laws, launched by Michigan and New York in 1837 and 1838. In some regulatory aspects, as in setting substantial minimum capitalization requirements, the free-banking laws aimed at the economic goal of promoting acceptability of the money supply. But they also derived substantial impetus from desire to safeguard against legislative corruption and against overreaching in market by special interests. Whether expressed in restrictions or in more open access to charters, the indicated policy of the states was that promotion of particular interests was an illegitimate objective to govern the law on bank-created money.[231]

Opponents often raised the banner of the Constitution over their attacks on the first and second Banks of the United States. A good deal of this flag waving was a sanctimonious cover for partisan or commercial advantage. Also inspiring the fervor of attack, however, was a Jefferson-based, Jackson-renewed distrust of a banking monopoly seen as favoring limited financial and commercial interests at the expense of farmers, mechanics, and the raw-materials sectors of the economy generally. Creation of the two banks stood as weighty precedents legitimizing legal controls on money to promote general productivity; the refusals to extend their charters were clouded precedents for keeping jealous watch on regulating money in ways which might lend themselves readily to special gain; the net balance favored positive action, but legitimated such action only for goals of general economic performance.[232] Irony flavored both parts of the record. Hamilton argued for a Bank of the United States to promote general economic growth, but he tinged this argument with the supporting plea that the bank would be useful because it "links the interest of the State in an intimate connection with those of the rich individuals belonging to it; that it turns the wealth and influence of both into a commercial channel, for mutual benefit."[233] On the other hand, though the drive to end the second bank proclaimed concern for the industrious poor against a greedy and parasitic financial oligarchy, it drew decisive energy both from Jacksonian party zeal and from the self-seeking of some state-chartered banks which wanted to be rid of Nicholas Biddle's competition.[234]

The aftermath of Civil War public finance measures, and the silver controversy of late nineteenth century, brought continued condemnation of regulating money to allocate power or gain among classes or particular economic sectors. Though the national bank system was set up under a free-banking type of law, it did not escape this kind of criticism from those who saw it as putting a profitable monopoly of note issue in a privileged group of government bondholders. This attack was pressed hard by agrarian parties through the 1870s, and then fell off, perhaps because it became clear that note issues were neither a major source of profit nor the key element in the money system.[235] The span from the seventies through the nineties saw running battles over a commitment to make the Civil War greenbacks redeemable in gold, over conservatives' desire to see the notes retired and expansionists' desire to keep them outstanding or to enlarge them at expense of the national bank notes, and over increase of money from silver and silver-based paper. This thirty-year war presents a muddle of partisan maneuver, rhetoric of more passion than persuasion, and confusing crosscurrents of interest. So far as this period bestowed any positive legacy of policy, it strengthened precedent for regulating money for general economic growth or major economic adjustments.[236] But what infused these years with peculiar anger and excitement was the challenge hurled by each major combatant, that its opponent pursued an illegitimate objective of class or special-interest advantage. Claims, ambitions, and fears of particular groups—conservative bankers and merchants, more expansionist-minded industrialists, farm and labor partisans demanding bigger shares of power and wealth—energized the battles over greenbacks and silver. There is no simple reckoning of victories and defeats. The farm and labor interests lost their demands to supplant national bank notes with greenbacks and to get free coinage of silver. Conservatives won resumption of specie payments and the gold standard. On the other hand, the more growth-minded business interests succeeded in halting contraction of the greenbacks, got increased national bank facilities, and—with the farmers—found that they could live with the gold standard in a situation of increasing gold supply. However, though gain or loss might be calculated for any given interest, the contenders typically denied the legitimacy of regulating money primarily to allocate power or wealth. They claimed to act for the healthy growth of the whole economy, and they pressed their particular claims for power and gain with the argument that they sought only to redress unfair advantage won by opposing interests.[237] Of course, to control money in the name of just distribution inherently asserted the legitimacy of objectives other than those simply of economic function. But, it was significant for the use of political process that the late nineteenth century was so defensive about admitting this; the practical presumption was against regulating money for other than goals of general economic performance.

The background and terms of the Federal Reserve Act reflected sharp concern to repudiate special-interest manipulation of money. The act acknowledged the reality of diverse interests pressing on the money supply, in its vague admonitions that the system should act for "the accommodation of commerce, industry, and agriculture," and that appointments to the Federal Reserve Board should be made with "due regard to a fair representation of the different commercial, industrial and geographic divisions of the country," along with stipulations designed to make credit more readily available to farmers. But the legislative history shows that the overriding, legitimating purpose of the act was to promote better performance of the general economy, especially by preventing liquidity crises.[238] The prime symbol of this judgment was that the act put governance of the system in a board of public officials. Against bitter banker opposition President Woodrow Wilson made this constitution of the board an absolute condition of the legislation, because he saw it as the assurance that the system's objectives would be limited to those of general economic interest. The point was underlined by the administration's refusal in 1913 to accept the proposal of those who feared the bankers, that the Federal Reserve Board should include designated representatives of agriculture and labor.[239] A 1922 amendment gave ground on this matter by including "agricultural" along with "financial . . . industrial and commercial interests" as sectors of the economy entitled to "fair representation" on a board expanded from five to six appointed members.[240] But this change did not prove of material impact; over the years the board never took on the working character of a body representative of functional interests.

The gold devaluation of 1934 had an immediate purpose of raising prices for agricultural commodities. But, though the government acted to conciliate the farmers, it responded to their discontent out of concern for general social order, and in the hope that rising prices for farm production would stimulate the whole lagging economy.[241] So far as these New Deal monetary measures sought to relieve debtors from the pressures of deflation, in the general distress of the early 1930s this purpose could hardly be called one of special-interest advantage.[242] Senator Elmer Thomas indicated that his amendment to the Agricultural Adjustment Act of 1933 sought to use money regulations to redistribute wealth as well as social and political power, but it was not an administration measure. This legislation authorized the president to agree with the Federal Reserve Board for the issue of up to $3 billion of federal reserve notes, or—if such an agreement could not be had—to authorize the Treasury to issue up to $3 billion of United States notes. President Roosevelt chose not to use this greenback authority, but instead resorted to devaluing the dollar. Devaluation raised a storm of conservative outrage; turning to the printing presses would undoubtedly have stirred even more violent controversy, and the president probably concluded so and decided to enter no hotter a battle than he had to. In the context of the distrust of fiat money which reached back to the federal convention and had been sharpened in the greenback and silver controversies of the late nineteenth century, we may fairly read the failure to use the Thomas Amendment in the 1930s as another precedent against the legitimacy of regulating money for balance-of-power rather than economic-performance objectives.[243]

Grounds of money policy were often not well expressed, and action was by no means always consistent. We can see a bit better the limits which the main trends of policy put on proper objectives of monetary policy by contrasting accepted uses of law affecting money with accepted uses of government's taxing, spending, and general regulatory (police) powers. Law's dealings with money put a high premium on fulfilling expectations of stability in exchange relations. Of course, the law of property and contract also put a high value on fulfilling the reasonable expectations of men who committed assets to economic ventures. But contract and property law also accepted the legitimacy of doctrine which would help make orderly, fair, and flexible adjustments to change of circumstances; even the law of real property had its malleable doctrines of nuisance and waste, and contract law left courts considerable discretion in determining the existence and meaning of agreements by objective measures of intent, in determining the materiality of failures to perform and in defining what contracts should be held unenforceable as against public policy.[244] Law regulating nonconsensual relations—as tort law—or asserting general social interests in education, health, safety, or market dealings among parties of grossly unequal bargaining power (for example, law protecting workers, or consumers, and regulating public utilities) embodied a great range and particularity of legal intervention favorable to some specific interests and restrictive of others.[245] But, regulation of the money supply made itself felt among the people with a sharpness and breadth of impact which did not characterize uses of most fiscal or regulatory law. Money was part of the form and substance of almost all economic transactions and entered into the calculations and expectations by which men structured much of their lives and behavior outside the market. Thus, when particular interests sought to change the legal character of the money system to suit their own ends, they raised sharper concern over the legitimacy of law's roles than attended most specific uses of taxing, spending, and regulatory powers, which typically were felt only in more focused and limited contexts.[246] Our tradition insisted that law act within the frame of the constitutional ideal, that public power must be used in ways reasonably calculated to fulfill public interest. Within this frame, our practice—and, somewhat less clearly, our doctrine—accepted the legitimacy of using taxing, spending, and regulatory powers to affect the distribution of power, status, wealth, and income among different segments of the society and especially to enlarge and equalize life opportunities for otherwise disadvantaged groups. But prevailing opinion and practice denied, or at least erected a presumption against, the legitimacy of using law to affect the money system for such purposes. The only objective which prevailing policy clearly accepted as legitimate for laws regulating money was to promote the productive functioning and increased productive capacity of the economy as a whole.

INTERNATIONAL MONETARY RELATIONS
AS GOALS OF POLICY

Until the 1920s policy makers in the United States saw the range of legitimate uses of law in regulating money as bounded solely by national interest or by interests fixed within the country. Even, in the twentieth century, when monetary policy began to include some calculation of international concerns, its prime focus continued to be within the context of the United States economy. Lawmakers here, as lawmakers abroad, commonly regarded control of the system of money as an unquestionable prerogative of national sovereignty, to be used simply to serve national interests.[247] Hamilton early took this premise when he argued that Congress should define a distinctive United States money unit, because it was unbecoming that domestic transactions be conducted in money subject to the will of a foreign sovereign.[248] True, the United States long accepted international custom in defining money units in weights of gold and silver and in defining liquidity by the convertibility of bills of exchange or currency ultimately into gold and silver. But to rely on private markets in those metals to adjust international trade balances seemed consistent with a national orientation of monetary policy; impersonal markets, rather than competing national polities, would make the needed adjustments.[249]

Of course the nation was never prepared really to allow international markets in gold or silver to govern adjustment of trade balances, regardless of consequences for the domestic economy. Legislative, executive, and administrative practice legitimized using law—or power existing under delegation by law to bankers—to protect or energize the domestic economy by managing credit and monetary metal stocks to cushion the impact of foreign economic developments or to keep reserves deemed necessary for stable prices and convertibility of foreign exchange.[250] However, before the 1920s such measures were simply reactive and usually defensive; these activities did not involve positive efforts to determine the organization of international monetary relations, even to advance the national interest, let alone to advance world trade as such.

Thus, in 1834 when Congress reduced the gold content of the dollar, it did so to encourage importation of gold.[251] From time to time Nicholas Biddle used the credit of the second Bank of the United States to borrow abroad to build the lending base of his institution, or bought or sold bills of exchange abroad in order to sustain our foreign trade or to influence movement of gold in or out of the country; but his bank took all such actions only from the standpoint of the home economy.[252] After expiration of the second bank's charter in 1836 there was no central agency of money regulation in the United States except the Treasury.[253] Through the rest of the nineteenth century and into the early twentieth century the Treasury took little action of consequence addressed to the country's foreign monetary relations, except in early 1895 when through New York bankers it borrowed 3.5 million ounces of gold, on agreement that the bankers would obtain half of the gold abroad. Taken to shore up convertibility of the currency which had been formally resumed in 1879, this action was defensive and, again, aimed solely at the domestic economy.[254] The Federal Reserve Act (1913) might be taken to imply concern to maintain United States participation in an international gold standard when it required that federal reserve banks hold a gold reserve against deposits and federal reserve notes. But in its contemporary setting this limitation was primarily addressed to conservative fears that agrarian politicians would inflate the domestic money supply. In 1933-34 the Roosevelt administration removed gold as an active factor in the domestic money supply. This action paid some deference to continued use of gold as the ultimate means to adjust international trade balances, by providing that gold might be exported to foreign governments or their central banks under official license. But the administration's objective was only to make the system of money work more effectively at home. The limits of its concern became clear when in the summer of 1933 President Roosevelt aborted a London conference on international balance of payments problems by refusing to consider currency stabilization or further changes in the debts which foreign governments owed the United States growing out of World War I. In a logical, if belated, corollary to the 1930s policy which brought gold into a managed money supply rather than allowing domestic or international gold markets to govern, Congress in 1965 and 1968 eliminated the requirement that federal reserve banks hold gold reserves against deposits or federal reserve notes.[255]

The first recognition that a legitimate goal of public policy might be to join the force of United States law with that of other sovereigns to regulate the structure of an international money system came in the latter part of the nineteenth century. The United States then made ineffective gestures toward participating in international agreements on a bimetallic base for various monetary units including the United States dollar. But conferences in 1867, 1878, 1881, and 1892 came to nothing, stalemated by opposing interests within and among other countries. Thus the United States was not then called on to demonstrate in action what responsibility it would assume to help shape an international money structure. In any case, there was considerable indifference, and no showing of broad political backing for this country's participation in those efforts.[256] The first real action commitment to United States sharing in international monetary organization came between 1921 and 1927. In those years Governor Benjamin Strong of the Federal Reserve Bank of New York guided Federal Reserve effort to hold down interest rates at home, to discourage gold flows to the United States which would embarrass the efforts of England and several Continental countries to return to an effective gold standard. However, this activity was a precedent of uncertain content. Strong directly negotiated understandings with foreign central banks, while the Federal Reserve Board stood by passively. The White House and Treasury deliberately avoided involvement, on the ground that governments should not undertake to manage the international gold standard. True, the Federal Reserve Bank of New York was not a government office. But within the frame of the Federal Reserve Act the bank was clearly delegated functions of public interest and was immediately accountable to a public body, the Federal Reserve Board. In 1933 Congress amended the Federal Reserve Act to forbid any federal reserve bank to deal with a foreign government or central bank except with the consent and on the terms set by the board. The amendment reflected belated criticism of the initiative Governor Strong had exercised. In part the criticism had a nationalist cast, since it rested on the belief that, in holding down interest rates to help foreign central banks, Strong's efforts had contributed to the speculative credit boom that led into the 1929 crash. On the other hand, the 1933 amendment implicitly accepted the legitimacy of board-authorized dealings with foreign central banks or governments, though without defining the legitimate objectives of such dealings.[257] Also, the 1920s did see the White House (State Department) and Treasury involved in various international loans and agreements defining and redefining terms on which war reparations and war debts should be paid. These transactions had profound impact on the international balance of payments, and thus on the functional capacity of the systems of money through which international payments must be conducted. But they were not efforts at structuring or managing an international system of money as such.[258]

Between the 1920s and 1970 three factors worked slowly to develop the idea that a legitimate use of law was to share in creating international apparatus to manage money. First, the world's gold stock more and more fell short of sufficiency to maintain the liquidity of national currencies and bills of exchange as such paper expanded to reflect the growth in world trade.[259] Secondly, public and private practice responded to the gold shortage by supplementing inadequate gold reserves with reserves in certain national currencies—in the late nineteenth century the pound in particular, and after World War II in increasing measure the dollar. Bankers and businessmen as well as governments throughout the world felt that England and the United States held enough gold to assure convertibility of pounds or dollars, and that the size and continuing turnover of short-term, self-liquidating commercial paper in these national economies meant that paper drawn on these two money centers would always find a ready market and hence would supply convertibility practically as good as gold. The United States involvement in this second phase of international liquidity came about chiefly by passive acceptance of a role imposed on dollar credits by outsiders. Accustomed through the nineteenth century simply to react to English or European monetary events, policy makers here were slow to see that events might require that we take positive initiatives in using law not merely for domestic monetary goals but also for contributing to a workable system of money for world trade. Meanwhile, merely to drift into using the pound and the dollar as world reserve currencies spelled trouble. In the first place, the disruptions of two world wars and the costly 1930s depression so weakened other national economies as to thrust the English and United States financial markets into a degree of exposure they were not ready to bear. Between 1950 and 1970 new stresses arose. European and Japanese industry and trade burst into multiplied energy. Other nations, freed of colonial status, pressed for investment capital to enlarge their trade and industrial bases. The search for a balance of power with Russia and China, and the costly involvement of the United States in the Viet Nam war, added to the demand for dollars to buy goods and services abroad. Thus into the later twentieth century the volume of claims held throughout the world in pounds and dollars steadily mounted. These credits grew so large that the gold and the reliable, short-term collectible debts behind the pound and the dollar fell to levels so low relative to the volume of credit built on them as to breed doubts that other national economies could continue to rely on the convertibility of pound or dollar obligations to make such paper reliable reserves for their own systems of money.[260]

Finally, this postwar period saw rising expectations among masses of people in many nations. Aggressive new political movements appealed to these changed expectations, promising drastically to reorder power and advantage. The emergence of new nations increased situations of tension or overt clash among nationalist jealousies, fears, and ambitions. Over all this uneasy scene hung the threat that limited war might escalate into unprecedented catastrophe. In this context inefficient or inequitable monetary arrangements—with the consequences they might have in stagnant trade, in unemployment, and in public treasuries unable to respond to public demands—spelled no mere derangement of markets, but danger to all social order. Effective world monetary arrangements now took on a political urgency not felt in the nineteenth or early twentieth centuries. It was a situation which did not so much invite as demand that we enlarge our ideas to include the legitimacy of using legal processes to contribute our share to a more effective international system of money.[261]

The United States made its best defined commitment of this sort in 1946 when it subscribed to the Articles of Agreement of the International Monetary Fund.[262] Based on the Bretton Woods conference of July 1944, the articles were more than just a treaty for coordinated action of separate sovereigns. The articles set up a distinct legal and institutional entity, the fund, whose directorate was empowered to manage a pool of gold and national currencies provided by the member nations according to agreed quotas, to promote exchange stability, to maintain orderly adaptation of exchange to shifting conditions of trade, and to encourage the members to avoid competitive depreciation of the exchange value of their currencies, or restrictions on payments and transfers for current international transactions, or discriminatory currency arrangements, except within terms set by the agreement or approved by the fund.[263] The fund was structured strictly for current monetary management; the flow of investment capital internationally was the business of other institutions, especially the International Bank for Reconstruction and Development, which also grew out of the Bretton Woods conference. Thus the agreement defined the type of transaction for which the fund was constituted as typically "for the purpose of supplying a member, on the initiative of such member, with the currency of another member in exchange for gold or for the currency of the member desiring to make the purchase," provided that the purchaser must represent that the funds be "presently needed" for making payments in that currency of a sort consistent with the goals which the agreement posed for a freer international trade.[264]

Adherence to the IMF agreement was a precedent of some substance for directing United States monetary policy for international ends. For within the framework of the agreement the United States, like other fund members, accepted restrictions on its freedom of monetary action. Though no quota might be changed without the consent of the member concerned, on the other hand a four-fifths majority of the membership was also required for any change in quotas once pledged. By its participation the United States committed some of its money resources to this centralization of international reserves, paying 25 percent of its quota in gold and the balance in dollars; the United States contributed about 35 percent of the initial fund, paying $1.8 billion of its $2.75 billion subscription out of the "profits" it held from its 1934 devaluation. The United States assumed a greater risk than other participants—offset by intangibles of prestige— because the agreement stipulated that for determining quotas and for operations under the fund the par value of each member's currency should be expressed in gold or in the United States dollar of the weight and fineness in effect on 1 July 1944—thus tending to confirm the United States in the hazards as well as the gains of having its national currency treated as a key element in creating international reserves. Like other members, the United States agreed to buy or sell gold only within a range prescribed by the fund; to hold within a range of one percent of parity, or within such other margin as the fund considered reasonable, exchange transactions between the currencies of members taking place within its territory; not to change the par value of its currency wherever the change might affect the international transactions of fund members, except to correct a fundamental disequilibrium, and then only after consulting the fund and with the fund's concurrence; and not to impose exchange restrictions or discriminatory currency arrangements, except as allowed by the agreement or with the approval of the fund.[265]

We must not overestimate the legal or practical effect of the United States involvement in the International Monetary Fund. The nation's adherence to the IMF agreement was within its constitutional authority over money.[266] On the other hand, like any other treaty, so far as the law of the United States was concerned, the agreement might be overridden by a later act of Congress. The only sanction for such subsequent abrogation or inconsistent conduct by the Congress would be that, by the terms of the agreement, the United States would forfeit its right to enjoy the fund's benefits.[267] Moreover, in accepting and obeying the agreement the United States made quite limited surrender of its monetary sovereignty. It committed reserve assets to an international body only to the extent of its quota, which might not be changed without its consent. The fund was a pool of only a small amount of the world's liquid reserves, and the powers it enjoyed had only such practical force as that limited pool of assets conferred; the fund was a long way removed from the position of a world central bank with the resources of a lender of last resort.[268] In addition to these factors, Congress showed its jealous regard for domestic sovereignty in key terms of the statute by which it authorized United States adherence to the IMF. Congress—and not the president or the Treasury—must approve any change in the United States quota in the fund or in the par value of the dollar or other basic change under the IMF agreement, or any loan to the fund. Any federal reserve bank on request of the IMF should act as the fund's depository or fiscal agent, but under the supervision of the federal reserve board. Finally, Congress created a National Advisory Council on International Monetary and Financial Problems—including the secretary of the treasury (chairman), the secretary of state, the secretary of commerce, the chairman of the Federal Reserve Board, and the president of the Export-Import Bank—to coordinate policies and operations of the representatives of the United States on the IMF and of all relevant United States agencies. For all the emphasis on cooperative coordination, it was plain that an advisory council so broadly constituted was a body calculated, as well, to assure close scrutiny of fund developments which any domestic agency concerned with monetary policy might feel to encroach on national interest.[269] In addition to these legal and political limiting elements, an observer must note, too, the limits of operating experience under the fund. The fund did help the economically stronger countries of the "free world" to reduce restrictions on international trade through more stable exchange rates and readier relief for a country temporarily hardpressed in its balance of payments. But the fund lacked means or authority to correct sustained capital outflows, member countries proved to make rather limited use of the fund, and the fund's capital badly lagged behind the increase in world trade. Moreover, working as it naturally did mainly through its holdings in the world's stronger currencies, the fund was not equipped to render much service to the great number of countries which did not have strong and steady credits to bring their currencies into substantial demand in world markets.[270]

For all these qualifications, the Bretton Woods Agreement Act (1945) by which Congress authorized United States participation in the International Monetary Fund must be counted a significant development in monetary policy. More than any previous action, the statute enlarged the definition of the legitimate uses of law affecting money to include international as well as national goals. The concessions made at cost to traditional notions of national sovereignty in monetary policy were grudging and closely confined. But they pointed toward a world view of money and its relation to commonwealth values implicating all people.

INSTITUTIONAL IMPACTS OF THE
SYSTEM OF MONEY ON LEGAL ORDER

It is a proper job of legal processes to help define and resolve desirable or necessary choices among competing values of general concern. However, for this reason study of legal history has a built-in bias toward exaggerating goal-oriented attitudes and behavior. To put in a broader context the questions explored in the bulk of this part—dealing with ideas about the legitimate uses of law affecting money—we should take account of another dimension of law-money relationships. This is the dimension in which events went as they did because the system of money affected law in ways which typically involved less perception of goals than marked the uses of law to affect money. For the lines of cause and effect did not run all one way. If law helped determine the money supply, it was also true that the nature of the money supply influenced the operations of law. The point here is not that law and politics were materially affected because some men controlled much wealth and others less, though of course the distribution of wealth profoundly affected how and for whom legal order worked. The point here is, rather, that money as an institution—as a patterned instrument for conducting social operations—affected law as an institution. For realistic perspective on the uses of law affecting money we should briefly note that the existence of a system of money affected (1) the problems of social order put to law and law's general range of capacity to deal with them, and (2) the rationality or lack of rationality in public policy-making through law.

In proportion as public policy created an effective system of money in aid of an economy of national scope, it contributed to the faith and the fact that rising economic productivity, measured in market terms, helped keep the peace among contending interests.[271] Conversely, defects in the money supply helped create social disorganization, notably in the last quarter of the nineteenth century, raising the level of pressures on legal order to avoid violence and breakdown of social functions.[272] Looked at more from the instrumental aspect, the existence or growth of a workable money supply increased law's practical ability to serve a greater variety of public purposes, with more effect. Large-scale, flexible use of government's fiscal powers—to borrow money, and to tax and spend—waited primarily on developing a more productive economy, but it waited also on developing a more efficient system of money.[273]

Development of a more pervasive system of money had ambiguous implications for the rationality of private and public allocations of economic resources, relative to the full range of economic, political, and social values affected by such allocations. So far as law helped enlarge the availability and sophistication of money, it helped increase the capacity of private-market processes to allocate resources. Only in the second half of the twentieth century was there broad questioning, even among those who favored large scope for private decision making, as to whether a money calculus biased decisions toward exaggerating the short run, at the expense of the longer range vitality or productivity of the economy.[274] In governmental decision making, the record was at least equally clouded, if not more so. Law helped establish a money calculus as an instrument which men treated as normal, and indeed indispensable, to the more sophisticated public budgeting procedures which were necessary to realize the expanded fiscal capacity of government.[275] Yet, the more law helped accustom public decision makers to a money calculus, the more events showed that public policy-making and administration were vulnerable to monetary disturbances, or could be deflected from realistic perception and assessment of social gains and costs.[276] Because this aspect of the matter more immediately concerns the operations of legal processes, it warrants more extended comment here.

The existence and acceptance of a law-defined system of money helped legal processes work toward goals that were reducible to a money calculation. Conversely, changes in the system of money might affect the law's own operational capacities. Thus, judgments for damages in contract and tort, and the assessment of taxes, took on definition and could be the better implemented through the standardized money units set by law. This was so because the interests involved could be satisfied by money payments, as measuring the stakes for which the law could provide.[277] On the other hand, if the system of money broke down under extreme inflation or deflation, the breakdown could pose severe problems for the regular administration of legal order.

After the Civil War legislatures in southern states were impelled to enact formulas to translate into national (northern) money terms the values or damages at stake in suits arising out of executory, wartime transactions in the now totally destroyed Confederate currency. Most such state laws resolved the problem by abandoning ordinary rules of damages and awarding plaintiffs the fair value—in national money—of the bargained-for consideration as of the time the transaction was entered into. The United States Supreme Court ultimately found that this solution violated the contracts clause. But the Court's rulings came so late that the bulk of dealings had already been adjusted to the statutory formulas.[278]

In the catastrophic deflation of the 1930s litigants attempted to persuade courts to acknowledge the burdens which drastic change in the purchasing power of money laid on debtors; petitioners asked judges to scale down dollar claims to match the decline in price levels. Some state legislatures gave debtors the temporary relief of moratoria on enforcing mortgage debts, and the United States Supreme Court conceded that legislatures enjoyed a considerable discretion to make this kind of accommodation to drastic changes in the money supply.[279] But the courts found no authority to warrant them in their own discretion in altering ordinary rules of damages or of judgments to accommodate to the deflation.[280]

Taken together, the experiences under Civil War inflation and 1930s deflation showed that major disturbances of the system of money could subject the regular operations of law to great pressure. The stringent limits which the federal Constitution and congressional policy put on state dealings with the money supply meant that states could respond to pressures of money dislocation only indirectly, by changing procedures of enforcing money-measured claims. Legislative and judicial precedents of the late 1860s and 1870s, and of the 1930s, on the whole accepted the legitimacy of such procedural adjustments to drastic shifts in the practical (purchasing-power) value of money, where adjustment was on terms generalized in statute law rather than attempted through case-by-case judge-made policy. But even statutory adjustment was subject to supervision exerted by the United States Supreme Court under the contracts clause.

The existence of a workable system of money had deeper, subtler effects on policy making by law than those experienced in the ordinary administration of legal processes. The utility of a standardized money calculus in a broad range of affairs bred a bias toward thinking that relevant social interests could be defined as those interests that were measureable in money. Interests not readily translated into money terms were, therefore, the easier overlooked or denied as worthy or capable of the law's attention.

This attitude had material, limiting effects on public policy. (1) A money calculus was irrelevant where a satisfactory outcome in adjusting social relations required giving due weight to some utility or satisfaction which money could not command. To govern affairs simply by those factors which money could buy was to leave out of the reckoning such *real* gains or costs—such physical or psychological inputs or outputs in experience—as could not practically be induced or offset by tenders of money. This limitation in policy reckonings showed itself, notably, in unheeded destruction or waste of nonrenewable natural resources (like oil and gas) or in loss of potentially renewable natural resources (such as a prime-timber forest or a self-purifying stream).[281] (2) A money calculus might be not so much irrelevant as incapable of application, where chains of cause and effect, or experience of benefits or losses, were so diffuse as to defy close identification with particular actors. Such was often the case with activities which polluted air or water, or destroyed the beauty of landscape, or clogged channels of transport and communication within a sprawling city. These positive or negative impacts on life were no less real because they could not be counted in dollars. But through most of the nineteenth and twentieth centuries prevailing attitudes habituated to a money calculus treated such gains and costs as if they did not exist.[282] (3) The system of money made itself pervasively felt, especially in a market-oriented society of increasing division of labor and interdependence of economic activities. Hence men correctly believed that the terms on which money was available were of high practical importance. However, this weight of money in affairs tended to deflect an undue amount of attention to problems of money at the expense of other issues of social organization. So in the late nineteenth century the country spent on the questions of greenbacks and silver political energies which would more profitably have been put into shaping policy concerning big business. Undoubtedly deeper causes were at work. But wasteful preoccupation with monetary policy contributed to the failure to make timely response to revolutionary changes in the structure of power in the market.[283]

It was not accidental that these limiting aspects of a money calculus centered on the market—whether contributing to exaggerate the market's impact or to obscure factors which tended to subvert proper dispersion of power in market. The system of money had peculiarly close ties to the market, to whose operations money was for a long time more essential than it was to the operations of government. Through most of the country's history government and the market provided the principal processes for allocating scarce economic resources. One way to sum up the record is to say that the existence of the system of money profoundly affected the law by helping shape attitudes—and limitations of perspective—which worked first to extend the influence of market processes at the expense of governmental processes in resource allocation, and later to delay public policy responses to the increasing imperfection of market processes themselves.

Notes

1. Friedman and Schwartz, 168, 169, 195, 440; Hammond (1), 81, 378, 383, 557; Redlich, 1:91.

2. Cotter, 38; Schumpeter (2), 62-63, 297, 1087.

3. Cf. Hamilton, Report on the Subject of Manufactures (1791), in Morris, 280-83; Jefferson, letter to Benjamin Austin (1816), *Writings*, 6:521-23; Hurst (3), ch. I.

4. Cf. House, Ways and Means Committee, *Report on the Second Bank of the United States, Register of Debates,* 22d Cong., 1st Sess. (1830); 14 vols. (Washington: Gales and Seaton, 1833), 8:132-39, 142-43; reprinted in *The People Shall Judge* (Chicago: University of Chicago Press, 1949), 1:605-18; Hurst (3), ch. II.

5. Experiments in creating redemption centers or clearinghouses by private arrangement or discipline reflected concern over the tendencies to hazardous cumulation of uncoordinated action among private banks. See Hammond (1), 706; Redlich, 2:51, 54.

6. Cf. Chandler, 9, 10, 41; Hammond (1), 557-59; Primm, 21, 25.

7. 1 Stat. 246 (1792), Dunbar 226-29. The act followed recommendations made by Hamilton in his report of 28 January 1791. Hepburn 41, 43. That Congress's authority to offer a standard system of money notation derives from the constitutional grants of power to coin money and regulate its value seems implied in Bronson v. Rodes, 7 Wallace 229, 247 (U.S. 1869).

8. Hepburn, 41; Nussbaum, 53. The Congress under the Articles of Confederation had by resolution of 8 August 1786 given a distinctive definition in silver to the dollar it there designated as the basic unit. But this was an action of little immediate practical significance, since this Congress had not yet acted to issue any money and did not act to create a mint until September 1786. Even then there was production only of a small amount of copper coin. Cf. Hepburn, 38; Nussbaum, 47. Recommending a new national mint, in 1791, Hamilton stressed the issue of sovereignty, noting the depreciation of the Spanish dollar in weight and fineness and arguing that domestic transactions should not be thus at the mercy of another sovereign's decisions on the manufacture of money. See Taxay, 48.

9. Hepburn, 42; Nussbaum, 54, 59, 83, 84; Taxay, 305.

10. 4 Stat. 699 (1834), Dunbar, 234, slightly modified by 5 Stat. 136 (1837), Dunbar, 236; 48 Stat. 337, 342 (1934); Hepburn, 54-62; Nussbaum, 59, 77-78, 127, 182. That the 1834 change had unsettling effect on transactions already outstanding, see Maynard v. Newman, 1 Nev. 271, 290 (1865); Metropolitan Bank v. Van Dyck, 27 N.Y. 400, 426 (1863). Changes in the percent of alloy from time to time affected the full weight of coins, but the fine metal content was not thereby affected. Cf. Bronson v. Rodes, 7 Wallace 29, 248 (U.S. 1869); Nussbaum, 53, 77. A somewhat heavier silver dollar (the "trade dollar"), intended for use in settling trade balances with the Orient and not for circulation in the United States, was part of the money pattern and in limited domestic circulation between 1873 and 1887. Laughlin, 102-5, 256-58.

11. 9 Stat. 591 (1851); 10 Stat. 160 (1853), Dunbar, 238; cf. 11 Stat. 163 (1857), Dunbar, 240; Hepburn, 62, 64; Nussbaum, 83, 84. That the standard silver dollar was omitted in 17 Stat. 424 (1873), Dunbar, 242, only to declare a supposed intent of the 1853 act seems without support in the 1853 record and a disingenuous effort to cloud the later policy debate which arose over the 1873 action. See Nugent, 170. Copper was early treated differently from the more precious metals; 1 Stat. 299 (1793) reduced the copper content of the cent below full metal value. See Nussbaum, 54, 115. Cf. 13 Stat. 54 (1864), 517 (1865).

12. Nugent, 106, 114, 116. The 1873 act removing the silver dollar from our pattern of coin stemmed in part from our participation in the International Monetary Conference of 1867, which recommended the gold standard as the norm among nations. Id., 96. Unlike the situation in the United States, notation as such fell into controversy in France, where a split between those for and against the metric system contributed to block movement toward international unification of coinage. Id., 106.

13. Cotter, 37-38; North (2), 55; cf. Veazie Bank v. Fenno, 8 Wallace 533, 536, 549 (U.S. 1869). Following the Constitution there was a transition period, in some states extending even into the early nineteenth century, when public and private reckoning was in pounds, shillings, and pence, before the standard pattern of money units fixed by federal legislation became the norm of practice. Nussbaum, 56. There is no indication that this was more than a passing and marginal usage after 1790, however.

14. Bronson v. Rodes, 7 Wallace 229 (U.S. 1869); Butler v. Horwitz id. 258 (U.S. 1869); Norman v. Baltimore & Ohio Railroad, 294 U.S. 240 (1935). That the Court was not inclined to imply from federal legislation a ban on private agreements to measure transactions by commodity units other than those of the standard money system, see United States v. Van Auken, 96 U.S. 366, 368 (1877). In 16 Stat. 251 (1870) Congress to a limited extent directly sanctioned coexistence of specie and "lawful money" (paper) as components of the money stock by authorizing the comptroller of the currency to sanction issue of national bank notes promising payment in gold coin of the United States, up to a maximum of $1 million per bank. Cf. Nussbaum, 117.

15. The European civil law tradition took it for granted that coinage was the exclusive prerogative of the sovereign. Ederer, 105-6; Nussbaum, 86. For the first half of the nineteenth century United States law did not make this assertion. See note 21, infra; cf. Radin, 52-54.

16. Bruchey, 147-48; Chandler, 13-15; Friedman and Schwartz, 160-68, 171, 172; Hammond (1), 80, 81, 83, 595, 687; Redlich, 2:3, 4; Trescott, 151.

17. Joseph S. Davis, 2:102-3; Hepburn, 43; Nussbaum, 52-54, 109; Steffens, 78, 94-95; Tiffany, ch. 3; Trescott, 48, 49, 56; Triffin, 65; Williston, 4:3469-76;

Zollman, 6:1-2.

18. On the felt threat of counterfeiting, see United States v. Raynor, 302 U.S. 540 (1937); on variations in foreign coin, see Nussbaum, 10, 11, 12, 24-26; on variations in state bank notes and discount or validity tables used by merchants, see Friedman and Schwartz, 22-23; Hepburn, 102, 139, 145; Nussbaum, 65, 69; Robertson, 16, 31; Rodkey, 9.

19. Hepburn, 42; Nussbaum, 54, 55, 77; Taxay, 48, 50, 200; Trescott, 48, 49, 56.

20. U.S. Constitution, art. I, sec. 10; Prelude, supra, notes 13, 15. See Briscoe v. Bank of the Commonwealth of Kentucky, 11 Peters 257, 317, 318 (U.S. 1837); note 21, infra.

21. From 13 Stat. 55, 120 (1864), Rev. Stat. secs. 5461, 5462 (1878), 18 U.S.C.A. 486 (1966), Congress forbade production or passing of any metal coin "intended for use as current money, whether in the resemblance of coin of the United States or of foreign countries, or of original design." If privately produced tokens are intended for use as a general medium of exchange, the act is violated, but the statute does not forbid private tokens for use in limited transactions or tokens exchangeable only for merchandise or particular services. United States v. Roussopulous, 95 Fed. 977 (D. Minn. 1899); United States v. Gellman, 44 Fed. Supp. 360 (D. Minn. 1942); cf. United States v. Van Auken, 96 U.S. 366 (1877); Anchorage Centennial Development Co. v. Van Wormer & Rodriques, Inc., 443 Pac. (2d) 596 (Alaska, 1968). This, and analogous legislation, have the purpose and effect so "to provide against competition with the established national currency for circulation as money," as to assure the United States a monopoly of the coinage. See Hollister v. Zion's Co-operative Mercantile Institution, 111 U.S. 62, 65 (1884); United States v. Gellman, supra, 365; cf. in re Aldrich, 16 Fed. 369 (N.D. N.Y. 1883); United States v. White, 19 Fed. 723 (Cir. Ct. N.D. N.Y. 1886). See Curran v. Sanford, 145 Fed. (2d) 229, 230 (5th Cir. 1944). Compare 26 Stat. 742 (1891), 32 Stat. 1223 (1903), 18 U.S.C.A. sec. 489 (1966), and 35 Stat. 1120 (1909), 58 Stat. 149 (1944), 18 U.S.C.A. sec. 491 (1966), prohibiting likenesses of United States currency, apart from counterfeiting.

22. Cadman, 63, 64, 66; Hammond (1), 159, 192, 193, 578; Henderson, 45, 46; Livermore, 246-47, 251, 252.

23. 18 Stat. 311 (1865), with which compare Veazie Bank v. Fenno, 8 Wallace 533 (U.S. 1869); Friedman and Schwartz, 23, 442; Goldenweiser, 16; Nussbaum, 90, 109; Paris, 92, 94, 97. The 1853 legislation creating a subsidiary fractional silver coinage had in part the aim of driving out of circulational fractional-denomination paper. Hepburn, 62. A practical limitation on the authenticity of state bank notes might be said to have been constituted by the common practice of discounting them, according to recipients' fears or ignorance of the soundness of the issuing bank. See note 18, supra. Discounting reduced the hazards of such currency for the knowledgeable, but many were ignorant of the means of so protecting themselves. Cf. Hammond (1), 620. In any case the problem derived basically from issues of liquidity and supply, rather than authenticity. See text at note 71, infra.

24. Swift v. Tyson, 16 Peters 1 (U.S. 1842), with which compare Shulman, 1348; Ronald A. Anderson, 1:1-132; Bankers Manual, 26-69; Braucher and Sutherland, 60, 106, 107; Powell, 63-68, 71-72, 100-5; Tiffany, 97-98. There were old traditions of privately created exchange media established in Continental and English trade; even in the simpler years of our economy we drew on those business traditions in our foreign trade, through bills of exchange or the credits which our raw materials exporters built up with merchandising houses here and abroad. Cf. Hacker, 130-31;

Johnson and Krooss, 23, 305; Schumpeter (2), 296. The general law of contract left private bargainers free to choose and define consideration to their own satisfaction, for the exchange of commodities other than gold or silver, or for gold or silver as commodities apart from their embodiment in coin. Questions of forgery apart (note 27, infra), no issue of authenticity of source or form arose concerning such individualized, bargained-out items of exchange. If the bargains tended to create privately defined media of exchange, lawmakers might intervene, to prevent interference with the good functioning of the money system as such. In this case, however, the problem was likely one of the supply rather than the authenticity of money tokens. See note 14, supra, and accompanying text. On private agreements for uniform charges on collecting or paying checks, see Redlich, 2:236, 237, 239, 242, 257. American Bank & Trust Co. v. Federal Reserve Bank of Atlanta, 256 U.S. 350, 358-59 (1921) ruled that a federal reserve bank would exceed its lawful authority if, as a calculated means of pressure to conform, it accumulated checks drawn on a no-par-paying bank in order to make such an embarrassing demand for cash as to compel the bank to drop its payment charge. In a second stage of the same lawsuit the Court held, however, that in ordinary course of business a federal reserve bank might demand full payment of a check held by it for collection where the demand would not infringe any right otherwise established by law in the drawee bank. 262 U.S. 643, 648 (1923). Farmers and Merchants Bank of Monroe, North Carolina v. Federal Reserve Bank of Richmond, Virginia, 262 U.S. 649, 666-67 (1923) found that Congress had given the Federal Reserve System no mandate to establish par clearance of checks by all banks so as to override authorization of collection or payment charges under the law of the state which chartered a local bank; where state law sanctioned the arrangement, a bank might contract with its depositors for deduction of payment fees from the face of checks drawn on it, without infringing federal policy. Thus the Federal Reserve achieved substantial uniformity over the country in par collection of checks simply by competitive service, which the Court recognized as a lawful instrument of policy. 262 U.S. 643, 648 (1923). Cf. Pascagoula National Bank v. Federal Reserve Bank of Atlanta, 3 Fed. (2d) 465, 468 (N.D. Ga. 1924), aff'd, 11 Fed. (2d) 866 (5th Cir. 1926). See Land, 25, 32; Munn, 262; Waage, 228, 229, note 5. An analogous contribution to the full-face authenticity of deposit-check money was made by the various ways in which the Federal Reserve System worked to reduce costs of processing checks, by transporting them by air, by paying the costs of shipping them, and by maintaining leased wires by which funds might be transferred between member banks anywhere in the country within an hour. Waage, 227.

25. United States v. Marigold, 9 Howard 560 (U.S. 1850); Baender v. Barnett, 255 U.S. 224 (1921); see United States v. Howell, 11 Wallace 432 (U.S. 1870); Knox v. Lee, 12 Wallace 457, 536, 545 (U.S. 1871); Leib v. Halligan, 236 Fed. 82, 87 (9th Cir. 1916).

26. 18 U.S.C.A. ch. 25, especially secs. 471-77 (1966); see United States v. Raynor, 302 U.S. 540 (1937).

27. E.g., Wisconsin Statutes, 1967, secs. 403, 419, 943.38; see Daniel, 3:1902-09; Pratt, 54-55.

28. Cf. Fox v. State of Ohio, 5 Howard 410 (U.S. 1847); United States v. Marigold, 9 id. 560 (U.S. 1850); Cross v. North Carolina, 132 U.S. 131 (1889).

29. Juilliard v. Greenman, 110 U.S. 421, 445, 447, 449 (1884); Ling Su Fan v. United States, 218 U.S. 302, 310, 311 (1910); Dunne (2), 5, 8; Thayer, 84-87. Cf. Brown v. Welch, 26 Ind. 116, 118 (1866).

30. On legal tender for payment of customs duties: 4 Stat. 630 (1833), 9 Stat. 53

(1846), 12 Stat. 346 (1862), Rev. Stat. sec. 3009 (1878). This idea was foreshadowed in the prospectus for the Bank of North America, though its charter was silent on the point. Hammond (1), 48; Rowe, 10. On payments on United States notes and bonds: 12 Stat. 346 (1862), Rev. Stat. sec. 3694 (1878); cf. 16 Stat. 1 (1869), Rev. Stat. sec. 3693 (1878). The declaration that certain United States notes be receivable to discharge debts owed the United States is spoken of as a form of legal-tender status by Story, J., in Thorndike v. United States, 2 Mason 1, 18, 23 Fed. Cas. 1124, 1130 (Cir. Ct. D. Mass. 1819).

31. Juilliard v. Greenman, 110 U.S. 421 (1884); Hunt, ch. 3.

32. Hunt, 134, 135, 137. Cf. Lane County v. Oregon, 7 Wallace 71 (U.S. 1869), and note 57, infra.

33. Black, 1:216; Dawson, 670; Freeman, 1:163.

34. Dawson and Cooper, 861, 899, 904, 905.

35. *Journals of the Continental Congress,* 4:49, resolution of January 11, 1776. See Justice Joseph P. Bradley, concurring, in Knox v. Lee, 12 Wallace 457, 558 (U.S. 1871).

36. Dewey, 38; Shultz and Caine, 70; Studenski and Krooss, 28; cf. Hurst (1), 247-48.

37. Rev. Stat. sec. 5182 (1878). Analogous was the statutory commitment of the United States to pay interest on its notes or bonds in legal-tender coin. 12 Stat. 346 (1862), Rev. Stat. sec. 3694 (1878); cf. 16 Stat. 1 (1869), Rev. Stat. sec. 3693 (1878). See Lane County v. Oregon, 7 Wallace 71, 78 (U.S. 1869).

38. 4 Stat. 630 (1833), 9 Stat. 53 (1846), 12 Stat. 346 (1862), 19 Stat. 247 (1877), Rev. Stat. sec. 3009 (1878).

39. 13 Stat. 109 (1864), 16 Stat. 253 (1870), Rev. Stat. sec. 5196 (1878). Lane County v. Oregon, 7 Wallace 71 (U.S. 1869) interpreted the federal legal-tender statutes as not intended to include taxes levied by and due a state as "debts" for which United States notes were legal tender, thus leaving a state free to insist that its taxes be paid in gold or silver. The opinion implied that a contrary interpretation might call in question the validity of the federal statutes as infringing the constitutionally reserved tax powers of the states. 7 Wallace 71, 77. See Hagar v. Reclamation District No. 108, 111 U.S. 701, 706 (1884). The Lane County ruling might be taken as recognizing an authority over definition of legal tender left in the states by the U.S. Constitution, art. I, sec. 10, when it says that "no state shall . . . make anything but gold and silver coin a tender in payment of debts." However, the constitutional provision derived from concern about state action affecting private debts. See Prelude, supra, note 16. And, in any case, the focus in the Lane County opinion was on deference to state taxing authority and not on state authority to define legal tender. Cf. Veazie Bank v. Fenno, 8 Wallace 533, 541 (U.S. 1870); Sutherland, J., dissenting, in Missouri ex rel. Burnes National Bank of St. Joseph v. Duncan, 265 U.S. 17, 29 (1924).

40. Corbin, 5A:523-25, 528-29; Williston, 6:5139-40.

41. Corbin, 3A:511, 5A:523-25; Page, 5:5056; Parsons, 2:772, 774. Cf. Juilliard v. Greenman, 110 U.S. 421, 445, 449 (1884).

42. Williston, 6:5139-40; see Juilliard v. Greenman, 110 U.S. 421, 449 (1884); Vick v. Howard, 136 Va. 101, 116 S.E. 465 (1923).

43. Knox v. Lee, 12 Wallace 457 (U.S. 1871); Juilliard v. Greenman, 110 U.S. 421 (1884).

44. Bronson v. Rodes, 7 Wallace 229 (U.S. 1869); Butler v. Horwitz, id., 258 (U.S. 1869); cf. United States v. Van Auken, 96 U.S. 366, 368 (1877); Page, 5:4966. See Bradley, J., concurring, in Knox v. Lee, 12 Wallace 566, 567 (U.S. 1871), and

Trebilcock v. Wilson, 12 id. 687, and Bradley, J., dissenting, id., 699 (U.S. 1872).

45. Joint Resolution of June 5, 1933, 48 Stat. 112, and 48 Stat. 1, 51 (1933), 337 (1934); Norman v. Baltimore & Ohio Railroad, 294 U.S. 240 (1935).

46. Cf. notes 35, 36, supra.

47. Hart, 1062; Nussbaum, 197; cf. Corbin, 5A:523-25.

48. Even with its emphasis on serving government's need of a money supply with which to command resources in war, Knox v. Lee, 12 Wallace 457, 530 (U.S. 1871) also indicates the function of legal-tender status in promoting regularity of contract transactions. See Bradley, J., concurring, id., 562; Wesley C. Mitchell, 53. Cf. Pound (3), 3:175, 176. Concern with certainty and firm resolution of contract performance seems implicit in the rule that payment in legal-tender money was required in the absence of other definition by the agreement or the transactional context. See Page, 5:5056; Williston, 6:5133.

49. Cf. Black, 1:171-72, 216-17; Chafee and Simpson, 1:43-45; Dawson, 670; Freeman, 1:159-60, 2:235. The significance of the grant of legal-tender status to the operation of courts was peculiarly underlined by Wayman v. Southard, 10 Wheaton 1 (U.S. 1825). There the Court held constitutional the delegation by Congress to the federal courts of power to make rules to govern their procedure, under which the federal judges sitting in Kentucky adopted a rule that judgments in their courts might be discharged only by payment in gold and silver, notwithstanding Kentucky stay laws which undertook to postpone creditors' relief unless creditors would accept discharge of debts in notes of two banks chartered by the state. See Warren (3), 1:646.

50. 1 Stat. 300 (1793); 1 Stat. 539 (1798); 2 Stat. 374 (1806); 3 Stat. 322 (1816); 3 Stat. 779 (1823); 4 Stat. 681, 700 (1834); 5 Stat. 607 (1843). General legal-tender status for foreign coin was ended by 11 Stat. 163 (1857), Rev. Stat. sec. 3584 (1874). See Dunbar, 229-32, 233, 234, 236, 240, 244; Hepburn, 46-47, 51, 60, 66-67; Nussbaum, 56, 62, 63, 82, 84. Urging legal-tender status for certain foreign coin, the New York banks in May 1834 put as a reason for this measure the need to help provide a sufficient volume of legal-tender money to administer business. Hepburn, 57.

51. 9 Stat. 591 (1851); 10 Stat. 160 (1853); Rev. Stat. secs. 3586, 3587 (1874); Dunbar, 238, 244; Hepburn, 66; Nussbaum, 82, 83; Taxay, 220, 221. Cf. 5 Stat. 136 (1837), Dunbar, 236; People ex rel. Courtney v. Dubois, 18 Ill. 333, 336 (1857); The Bank of the State of Indiana v. Lockwood, 16 Ind. 306, 308 (1861).

52. See Prelude, supra, note 1; Nussbaum, 36; Hepburn, 13, 14, 72; Morison and Commager, 1:207.

53. Knox (1), 33. Cf. Dunbar, 63-80. Treasury notes of this period were given a limited legal-tender status when they were declared receivable for duties and taxes imposed by the United States. See Dunbar, 65, 69, 71, 76, 78; Nussbaum, 70. Argument was made for this limited legal-tender status on the ground that it would encourage circulation of the notes. Knox (1), 22, 24.

54. That there was need to confer legal-tender status to make the proposed United States notes acceptable in practice as circulating media of exchange—this, in turn, in aid of the government's borrowing and command of assets to meet its war procurement needs—was stated in the letter which Secretary of the Treasury Chase grudgingly supplied on 29 January 1862 to the chairman of the House Ways and Means Committee. *Congressional Globe*, 37th Cong., 2d Sess. (3 February 1862), 618. Though later as chief justice, Chase said that he felt that his judgment of this practical need for legal-tender status had been in error, he did not deny that it had been a ground urged in decision on Congress. See Chase, C.J., for the Court, in Hep-

burn v. Griswold, 8 Wallace 603, 620-621 (U.S. 1870); Chase, C.J., dissenting, in Knox v. Lee, 12 id. 457, 576-79 (U.S. 1871). Various grounds were urged in support of the grant of legal-tender status in Congressional discussion, often with considerable confusion of ideas. Among these grounds, and sharing the confusion, was the argument that this feature was necessary to promote circulation of the notes as media of exchange. Hammond (3), 171, 173, 176, 178, 184, 185-86, 191-92, 196, 201, 205-6, 212, 216-19, 223; Hepburn, 184, 186-89, 193; Wesley C. Mitchell, 54, 57, 62, 65, 71; Field, J., dissenting, in Juilliard v. Greenman, 110 U.S. 421, 455-57 (U.S. 1884). Cf. Dawson, 667; Dawson and Cooper, 899; Harrod, 29; Sharkey, 33, 34, 35, 44, 54, 55. See also Knox v. Lee, 12 Wallace 457, 541-43 (U.S. 1871). Compare, generally, Ederer, 48. Legal-tender status was not conferred on national bank notes or on federal reserve notes until by 48 Stat. 52, 113 (1933), and 79 Stat. 255 (1965). The Congress of the Confederate States never declared Confederate money to be legal tender for satisfying private debts. Dawson and Cooper, 714.

55. Knox v. Lee, 12 Wallace 457, 541, 542-43, 554 (U.S. 1871), and Bradley, J., concurring, id., 561, 562-63; Juilliard v. Greenman, 110 U.S. 421, 444-45, 447-48 (1884); cf. Field, J., dissenting, 110 U.S. at 461. Almost all of the state courts in which the question was raised before it was ruled on in the Supreme Court held the legal-tender laws constitutional, even as applied to debts contracted before the legislation. Several of these cases recognized as a proper purpose of the grant of legal-tender status the promotion of acceptance by the people of the United States notes as a circulating medium. See Breen v. Dewey, 16 Gilfillan 123, 128-219 (Minn. 1870); Carter v. Cox, 44 Miss. 148, 157 (1870); Maynard v. Newman, 1 Nev. 271, 292 (1865); Metropolitan Bank v. Van Dyck, 27 N.Y. 400, 435-36, 446, 479, 498, 522 (1863); O'Neil v. McKewn, 1 So. C. 147, 151 (1869).

56. Prelude, supra, note 1; Hepburn, 14-17, 19, 72; Nussbaum, 37-39. Cf. Field, J., dissenting, in Juilliard v. Greenman, 110 U.S. 421, 452 (1884).

57. That acceptability of the Civil War greenbacks—reflected in their varying discounts in contrast to gold—varied with the North's fortunes in war, rather than being stabilized by their legal-tender quality, see Hammond (3), 227-29; Wesley C. Mitchell, 99, 201, 203-8; cf. Hepburn, 197, 203; Morison and Commager, 1:711; Nugent, 10, 11; Nussbaum, 102-3; Unger, 15-16. Sharkey, 35, apparently judges that legal-tender status was necessary for acceptability of the United States notes, but he offers no evidence. Hammond (3), 185, 194, 196-98, 215, 217-18, 220, 232, shows substantial banker support for the 1862 act on the ground that its grant of legal-tender status would provide the banks with needed pressure on third parties to settle transactions in paper when gold was unavailable.

Various specific public policy measures centering on the greenbacks showed practical recognition of the weight of popular preference for specie over formal declarations of legal-tender status. The San Francisco mint continued making gold coins in the Civil War years, helping West Coast dealers to continue favoring contracts payable in gold. The California and Oregon legislatures declared that gold-payment clauses in private contracts were lawful, anticipating the Supreme Court's acceptance of such clauses as consistent with congressional policy. Bronson v. Rodes, 7 Wallace 229 U.S. 1869. In a decision based rather unconvincingly on deference to the constitutional independence of the states, the Court in Lane County v. Oregon, id., 71 (U.S. 1869), found that Congress did not intend to require that states accept United States notes in payment of state taxes, and indicated that Congress lacked authority to do so. In 16 Stat. 251 (1870) Congress gave limited authority to the comptroller of the currency to authorize issue of national bank notes promising payment in United States gold coin; the provision was implicitly addressed to, and used on, the West Coast. Nussbaum, 117, 123.

58. Because the functional meaning and workability of the money system both derive from and materially affect the general context of social relations, legal control of money is established within that legitimate concern of law with the good order of social relations, which has commonly been called the police power. Compare Norman v. Baltimore & Ohio Railroad, 294 U.S. 240, 307-11 (1935) with Proprietors of the Charles River Bridge Co. v. Proprietors of the Warren Bridge, 11 Peters 420, 548 (U.S. 1837), and Commonwealth v. Alger, 7 Cushing 53, 84-85 (Mass. 1851). On the interlock of law and the organization of transactions, see Berle and Pederson, 4-5, 11, 12, 18, 24, 31-32, 39, 60.

59. Triffin, 64, 65, 66, 71, discusses liquidity as relevant basically to providing a money supply adequate for economic growth. Symbolic of the shift in policy focus is the comparison between the emphasis on provisions to secure the issue of notes by the new national banks under 12 Stat. 665 (1863) and 13 Stat. 99 (1864), and on provisions to control gold in 48 Stat. 337 (1934). Overlap of the earlier concern with liquidity appears in creation of the Federal Deposit Insurance Corporation, 48 Stat. 168 (1933).

60. Berle and Pederson, 4, 6, 9, 11, 37, 52-55, 59, 66, 77-81, 117; Hammond (1), 624-26; Krooss (1), 236-45, 250-55, 259; Nussbaum, 64-69, 87-94, 100-4, 109-10, 159-60.

61. Berle and Pederson, 4, 23, 59, 92-93, 122-23; Chandler, 27-30; Friedman and Schwartz, 108-9, 123-24, 159-60, 166, 311, 407-8, 413, 440; Powell, 100, 125, 126, 130, 262, 270, 271, 274-75, 279, 330; Trescott, 20, 39, 150-51, 156-57.

62. See note 59, supra. On the symbolism of the events of 1933-34 as marking a shift from concern with liquidity to one with management of the money supply, compare Berle and Pederson, 12, 24, 122-23, 181, 186; Triffin, 32. The 1963 change in the form of federal reserve notes was made on direction of the secretary of the treasury under the authority given him in the original Federal Reserve Act to fix the "form and tenor" of such notes. 38 Stat. 267 (1913), 77 Stat. 54 (1963), 12 U.S.C. sec. 418. Consistent with the withdrawal of gold from domestic money circulation, Congress struck from the Federal Reserve Act the original pledge to redeem federal reserve notes in gold, leaving simply a pledge of their redemption in "lawful money." 38 Stat. 265 (1913), 48 Stat. 337 (1934). In addition, by 1963 national bank notes had been discontinued, and the United States had retired and withdrawn various forms of Treasury-issued currency. Thus, as a practical matter, the holder of a federal reserve note who presented it for redemption in "lawful money" was likely simply to receive in exchange other federal reserve notes. Hence the secretary used his discretion to alter the form of the notes to match the current realities and avoid misunderstanding. However, the Federal Reserve Act continues to declare federal reserve notes to be obligations of the United States, secured by collateral pledged by the issuing reserve bank and by "a first and paramount lien on all the assets of" the issuing reserve bank. 38 Stat. 265 (1913), 12 U.S.C. secs. 411, 412, 414. I am indebted to Howard H. Hackley, assistant to the Board of Governors of the Federal Reserve System, for material embodied in the foregoing summary. The end of the liquidity issue concerning currency was also implied when Congress removed the requirement of a gold reserve for federal reserve bank deposits and federal reserve notes. 79 Stat. 5 (1965), sec. 1; 82 Stat. 50 (1968), sec. 3.

63. Nussbaum, 62-64, 78, 82, 84. An argument against the issue of United States Treasury notes in 1812 was that they would not be accepted by banks or traders as

equal in value to gold or silver. Knox (1), 22. When 4 Stat. 699 (1834) and 5 Stat. 136 (1837) reduced the gold content of the dollar, the measure seems to have been directed at a problem of supply, to increase the quantity of gold available for the domestic money stock by correcting the previous undervaluation of gold which was seen as encouraging its export. Hepburn, 54, 57-60; Nussbaum, 61, 77.

64. See pp. 000-000, infra.

65. Nugent, 34-38, 98-101, 137-38, 144, 168-71; Unger, 330-31, 336-49.

66. U.S. Constitution, art. I, sec. 10; 5 Stat. 136 (1837); 9 stat. 397 (1849). Judicial opinions often reflect the popular acceptance of the precious metals as having intrinsic money value and being the measure by which all other money tokens should be appraised. See, e.g., United States v. Marigold, 9 Howard 560, 567-68 (U.S. 1850); Bronson v. Rodes, 7 Wallace 229, 249 (U.S. 1869); Bank of the Commonwealth v. Van Vleck, 49 Barbour 508, 520, 522 (N.Y. Sup. Ct. 1867); Warner v. Sauk County Bank, 20 Wis. 492, 495 (1866). Mid-nineteenth century agrarian distrust of banks and bank-issued money expressed a long-standing, dogmatic preference for *hard* coin. See Hammond (1), ch. 19.

67. Cf. Nussbaum, 82-83, 115-16; Taxay, 215, 219-21.

68. Cf. Hurst (4), 31, 59-60, 68-70, 91, 122-30, 184, 205, 207, 239.

69. See Culbertson, 159; Redlich, 2:10, 47; Norman v. Baltimore & Ohio Railroad, 294 U.S. 240, 303, 315 (1935).

70. See Hammond (1), 562; Redlich, 2:166, 167; Juilliard v. Greenman, 110 U.S. 421, 444-45 (1884).

71. Note 18, supra.

72. On the Suffolk bank system, in Massachusetts: Hammond (1), 551-55; Redlich, 2:77, 142; Timberlake, 95. On the second Bank of the United States: Hammond (1), 446, 447; W. B. Smith, 52, 62, 136, 242. The United States Treasury sought to exercise some police over state bank-note issues by a policy of refusing to accept or pay out such notes of small denominations, and Congress exerted some influence by statutory requirements that sums due the United States be paid in specie or in notes of the Bank of the United States. See W. B. Smith, 62, 103; cf. 9 Stat. 59 (1846). But there seems no evidence that these policies exerted substantial disciplinary effect on state bank-note issues.

73. 12 Stat. 665 (1863), 13 Stat. 99 (1864), 469 (1865), in Dunbar, 171, 178, 198; see Veazie Bank v. Fenno, 8 Wallace 533, 548, 549 (U.S. 1869); Friedman and Schwartz, 18, 23.

74. Nugent, 34-43, 159, 243-50, 258; Unger, 14, 18-19, 43, 94, 406.

75. Friedman and Schwartz, 119, 137; Hepburn, 67, 68; Knox (2), 150; Nugent, 12; Nussbaum, 61; Taxay, 194, 221, 260.

76. Note 45, supra. Cf. note 62, supra.

77. Hammond (1), 80, 81, 83, and (2), 4; Redlich, 2:3.

78. Cf. Gordon W. McKinley, 204, 210, 211.

79. Cf. Friedman and Schwartz, 168, 169, 170, 172; Redlich, 2:2, 3, 4, 7, 10; Tobin, 408, 411, 419.

80. Hammond (2), 4, 5; Redlich, 2:3, 4, 5, 7, 10. Cf. Culbertson, 151, 159. On the ignoring of deposits, see notes 98-106, infra.

81. On the second Bank of the United States: W. B. Smith, 52-53, 104, 134-36, 234, 253. On the clearing houses: Hammond (1), 706; Redlich, 2:47, 54; but cf. Redlich, 2:257, 270, 289.

82. Braucher and Sutherland, 60; note 24, supra.

83. Joseph S. Davis, 2:102-3; Dodd, 206, 214, 275, 280, 284; Hammond (1), 68, 159, 184, 578.

84. Friedman and Schwartz, 328, note 38; Redlich, 1:44, 2:79, 80. Adam Smith thought that public interest in safe issue of bank notes could be assured, without more, by the practical pressure of traders to insist on prompt performance of promises to redeem. Adam Smith, 1:293-94.

85. Dodd, 207, 208; Friedman and Schwartz, 328, note 38; Hammond (1), 180, 690, 691, 692. We are justified in looking skeptically at remedies by forfeiture of franchises; proceedings in the nature of *scire facias* or *quo warranto* were rigid in sanctions, and looked to consequences so severe as to make it unlikely that they would be invoked. Cf. Pound (1), 375-78. The New York court showed itself not disposed to give strict application to its forfeiture statute; though a bank had ceased operations for a substantial time, if it had successfully resumed and was meeting its note obligations when suit was brought to decision, the court denied forfeiture. People v. Bank of Niagara, 6 Cowen 196 (N.Y. Sup. Ct. 1826); People v. Washington & Warren Bank, id. 211 (N.Y. Sup. Ct. 1826). That relations between the bank and noteholders should be viewed as at basis contractual, with contract doctrine adequate to fulfill the public interest; see Livingston v. Bank of New York, 26 Barbour 304, 305 (N.Y. Sup. Ct. 1857).

86. On the weight of general and banking opinion against calculated pressures for redemption; see Hammond (1), 178-80, 691, 692. Pressures for a reserve system designed to foster continuity in the money supply came by private organization, in the Suffolk bank system in Massachusetts, about 1818-58, Hammond (1), 551-55; by the administrative practice of the second Bank of the United States for the currency at large, W. B. Smith, 52, 62, 242; and by statutory imposition of reserves on the national banks which alone provided bank notes after 1866, Hepburn, 309, 312, 317.

87. Friedman and Schwartz, 161, and 161, note 43; Hammond (1), 180, 691, 692. See Livingston v. Bank of New York, 26 Barbour 304, 308 (N.Y. Sup. Ct. 1857), where the court refused appointment of a receiver on a showing only of the bank's refusal to redeem during a general suspension.

88. Friedman and Schwartz, 161, note 43, 328, note 38; Hammond (1), 622.

89. Cadman, 91, 189-90, 369, 372; Dodd, 207, 212, 215, 280; Hammond (1), 696; Hartz, 256; Redlich, 1:44. The idea of tying a bank's note issue to its capital was not necessarily derived from resort to incorporation; in the late eighteenth century Sir James Stewart urged this as a matter of business policy. Redlich, 1:192, 199. Statutory terms of incorporation must always be read with the caution that their apparent effect might be diminished in interpretation. Thus the Massachusetts Supreme Judicial Court narrowly construed that state's statutory liability of bank stockholders for bank notes unpaid at dissolution, as limited to the nominal par value of the shares rather than extending to a proportionate part of the note indebtedness. Crease v. Babcock, 9 Metcalf 182 (Mass. 1845); see Dodd, 207-8. The practical weight of statutory liability for bank notes would of course also depend on the extent of note issues; Dodd, 209, points out that average note circulation of Boston banks, 1809-28, never exceeded 24 percent of their capital, and the average for "country" banks never exceeded 57 percent of capital.

90. Hammond (1), 696, 697, and (2), 11. Cf. note 102, infra.

91. Dodd, 285, 287; Hammond (1), 595, 596, and (2), 10; Hepburn, 308, 312, 334; Krooss (2), 10; Redlich, 1:44, 191, 194, 196-200, 2:2, 3, 8.

92. Cf. Friedman and Schwartz, 21; Hammond (1), 595, 596; Hepburn, 312, 313, 334; Redlich, 2:2, 3, 9, 44.

93. Hammond (1), 596, 696, 697; Redlich, 2:2, 9, 79, 80; Rodkey, 376. The requirement was considerably watered down where the bank was permitted to count

in its reserve balances held with correspondent banks. Rodkey, 377-79.

94. Thus in 1840 New York abolished the 12½ percent reserve required under its free-banking law of 1838. Connecticut adopted a 10 percent reserve requirement in 1848, but dropped it upon adopting a free-banking law in 1852. Hammond (1), 596; Redlich, 2:1, 2, 9. As hereafter noted, states commonly came to adopt requirements of reserves against deposits, but the issue became moot concerning bank notes when a federal tax made their issue unprofitable from 1866 on. Cf. Rodkey, ch. 5.

95. Friedman and Schwartz, 20, 21; Hammond (2), 11; Rodkey, 23. On the Federal Reserve: 38 Stat. 251 (1913), sec. 16; 59 Stat., 237 (1945), sec. 1 (a) (reduced to 25 percent); 82 Stat., 50 (1968), sec. 3. (requirement eliminated).

96. Rodkey, 4, 52-55; Trescott, 150-51, 157; see notes 87, 88, supra.

97. On the Suffolk bank system: Hammond (1), 551-55, 556, 562, 563; Redlich, 2:77, 142; Timberlake, 95. In New York for some years a combination of law-imposed requirements and private arrangements produced a pattern analogous to that in Massachusetts. New York statutes of 1840 and 1851 required banks there to redeem their bank notes at law-stated maximum discounts in New York City, Albany, or Troy, and two New York City and two Albany banks set up procedures to redeem notes from deposits which other banks kept with them. See Redlich, 2:79, 80; Rodkey, 17-18. On the supervisory action of the second Bank of the United States: Govan, 61, 64, 85; W. B. Smith, 52, 62, 242; Wilburn, 48, 52.

98. Cf. Cadman, 91, 189-90; Dodd, 207, 209, 211-12, 214-15; Hammond (2), 11.

99. Hammond (1), 557, 558, and (2), 5; Hepburn, 142-43; Robertson, 25-26. Inclusion of deposits as well as bank notes would have been functional in fact, if it had been properly planned for, since New York City banks were already more important to the money supply for their created deposits than for their circulating notes. Cf. Redlich, 1:93, 94.

100. Hammond (1), 555, 596.

101. Hammond (1), 596; Rodkey, 13, 19, and ch. 5.

102. Berle and Pederson, 18-19; Hammond (2), 1-3; Krooss (1), 238, 242-43; Redlich, 1:10, 44, 2:3, 5; Rodkey, 19. Further, on the tendency of nineteenth-century commercial banks to commit their resources to supplying working or investment capital, see Bruchey, 141, 143-44, 146-47; Cochran and Miller, 43, 45, 82; Cochran, 346; Hacker, 334; North (1), 181, 184, and (2), 79-80; Reynolds, 135; Rohrbough, 138, 221-22.

103. Friedman and Schwartz, 56, and 56, note 62, 118, note 44, 196; Goldenweiser, 288, 289; Hammond (1), 680-84, 696, and (2), 11; Redlich, 2:9, 10, 40. Rodkey, 30-35, counts six states with requirements of reserves against deposits up to 1879, and nine more by 1897. Symbolic of a relaxing attitude toward reserves was the liberalizing of collateral required against federal reserve banks' deposits, and elimination of the gold reserve originally required against deposits. 48 Stat. 337 (1934), sec. 2(b); 59 Stat. 237 (1945), sec. 1(a); 79 Stat. 5 (1965), sec. 1.

104. Cf. Clay J. Anderson, 54; Berle and Pederson, 131; Goldenweiser, 288, 289.

105. Barger, 249; Friedman and Schwartz, 57, note 62, 208; Krooss (1), 255; Rodkey, 23-24, 31, 36, 47; Trescott, 49, 149-50.

106. Cadman, 374; Cagan, 39-42; Dodd, 203, 205, 210, 212, 215, 275, 276, 278, 279, 282-83, 288; Friedman and Schwartz, 447; Hammond (1), 48, 559; Nugent, 36, 146, 147, 224, 272; Redlich, 2:92, 93, 95, 285; Robertson, 24-26, 47, 71-75, 81, 112; Sharkey, 293-302; Unger, 36, 37, note 76, 406.

107. Krooss (1), 240; W. B. Smith, 52-53, 104, 134-36, 234, 253; Trescott, 26-28; Wilburn, 47, 50, 51-52, 63, 65.

108. Barger, 20-22; W. B. Smith, 134, 135.

109. Hammond (1), 680, 684, 685; Hepburn, 149; Rodkey, 14; Trescott, 29, 34.

110. Hammond (1), 706; Redlich, 2:47, 54, 158, 161. Characteristic tardiness in developing administrative apparatus adequate to important management jobs appeared even in the course of the clearinghouses' informal role in promoting liquidity. The Chicago clearinghouse pioneered in creating a staff examiner to provide independent scrutiny of its members' accounts as late as 1905, whereupon the device was fast copied, by New York in 1911, and then to a total of twenty clearinghouses by 1913. Redlich, 2:286.

111. Friedman and Schwartz, 170, 172; Harrod, 37; Hepburn, 440; Redlich, 2:166, 167, 168.

112. Hammond (1), 557-62; Redlich, 1:93, 94, 2:ch. 5; Robertson, 25-26.

113. Friedman and Schwartz, 170, 172; Trescott, 108, 109, 161-62; cf. Redlich, 2:216; (Note) 36 *Colum. L. Rev.* 809 (1936). See Noble State Bank v. Haskell, 219 U.S. 104, 111, 113 (1911).

114. 48 Stat. 168 (1933), 969, 970 (1934), 49 Stat. 435, 684 (1935); Culbertson, 159; Friedman and Schwartz, 435; Harrod, 72; Trescott, 162, 207; (Notes) 36 *Colum. L. Rev.* 809 (1936), and 42 id. 1030 (1942).

115. Fischer, 209; Friedman and Schwartz, 437; Trescott, 207, 271.

116. Cotter, 64-65; Friedman and Schwartz, 123, 434, 440, 441; Rostow, 160.

117. Cf. Friedman and Schwartz, 436, note 14, 437, 440, 684. Courts tended to give a liberal interpretation to the scope of federal deposit insurance coverage, recognizing that the public interest lay in helping the system build public confidence in deposit-check money. See (Note) 42 *Colum. L. Rev.* 1030, 1033; (Recent Case Comment) 52 Harv. L. Rev. 523 (1939).

118. Cf. Timberlake, 96.

119. Fischer, 129, 138, 208, 209, 210; Friedman and Schwartz, 436, note 14, 440, 684; Robertson, 126, 134, 167. For reflections of the FDIC policy of acting to maintain the supply sources of bank-created money, see Lamberton v. FDIC, 141 Fed. (2d) 95 (3rd Cir. 1943); Brown v. New York Life Insurance Co., 152 Fed. (2d) 246 (9th Cir. 1945); FDIC v. Rectenwall, 97 Fed. Supp. 273 (N.D. Ind. 1951); Thomas B. Nichols & Son Co. v. National City Bank of Lynn, 313 Mass. 421, 48 N.E. (2d) 49 (1943), cert. den., 320 U.S. 742 (1943); FDIC v. Cloonan, 165 Kan. 68, 193 Pac. (2d) 656 (1948). See, also, *New York Times,* 28 October 1963, p. 41 col. 8. On FDIC examination procedures—which like their counterparts in other agencies centered on the repayable quality of individual bank portfolios—see Harl, 253; Randall, 696.

120. Note 45, supra; cf. Culbertson, 159; Harrod, 68-70; Krooss (1), 265.

121. 59 Stat. 237 (1945); cf. 49 Stat. 699 (1935).

122. Eccles, 168-74; Goldenweiser, 87-90; Youngdahl, 116-22.

123. 49 Stat. 706 (1935); see Friedman and Schwartz, 447; Trescott, 13, 207, 241, 245.

124. Notes 21 and 111, supra.

125. On the civil-law view: Vattel, 44, 45 (ch. 10, secs. 106, 107). Assertions of general power over money in the Congress, bulwarked by note that such authority was a common attribute of sovereignty, are not, of course, inconsistent with capacity to delegate aspects of money supply to private action. Cf. Knox v. Lee, 12 Wallace 457, 545 (U.S. 1871); Juilliard v. Greenman, 110 U.S. 421, 447 (1884). On freedom of contract, applied to banking: Savage, C.J., in New York Firemen Insurance Co. v. Ely, 2 Cowen 678, 710 (N.Y. Sup. Ct. 1824); Taney, C.J., in Bank of Augusta v.

Earle, 13 Peters 519, 595, 596 (U.S. 1839); Hammond (1), 10, 24, 27, 71, 159, 179, 185, 572, 573; Redlich, 1: ch. 7, and 187, 188, 292, note 7; id., 2:53, 163, 166. See, also, notes 17, 24, 81, 110, supra. In his veto of the bill to renew the charter of the second Bank of the United States, President Andrew Jackson took as one ground of opposition to the monopoly aspects of the charter the proposition that banking required no special license from law in the first instance. Richardson, 2:587, 590.

126. Nussbaum, 84-86, 113; Taxay, 209.

127. Cf. Prelude, supra notes 13, 40-42; supra, note 21. United States v. Gellman, 44 Fed. Supp. 360, 364 (D. Minn. 1942), intimates that the Constitution intends to put a monopoly of coinage in the United States, excluding private as well as state issues, but the opinion finds illegality to arise under statutes passed by Congress, implementing the grant of power to coin money. There seems to be no reported instance of federal government action against private coinage resting simply on a self-executing monopoly implied in grant of the coining power.

128. Joseph S. Davis, 1:5, 428, 439; Hammond (1), 24-25, 28.

129. Prelude, supra notes 68-73.

130. Hammond (1), 381, 405, 407, 410; Richardson, 2:578, 581.

131. Bank of Augusta v. Earle, 13 Peters 519, 595, 596 (U.S. 1839); Henderson, 47. Compare Osborn v. The Bank of the United States, 9 Wheaton 738, 861, 863, 864 (U.S. 1824), holding that Congress might give the bank general lending authority, as necessary and proper to implementing its roles as fiscal agent for the government and issuer of currency.

132. Prelude, supra, notes 13, 15, 19, 20, 39, 40, 42, 48, 49-58. See Knox v. Lee, 12 Wallace 457, 545 (U.S. 1871).

133. Id., notes 30-37; Briscoe v. Bank of the Commonwealth of Kentucky, 11 Peters 257, 313, 316, 317, 318, 348, 349 (U.S. 1837), with which compare Craig v. Missouri, 4 Peters 410, 432, 433, 435 (U.S. 1830). On the flow of special charters for banks and the implicit assertion of traditional chartering authority inherited from the crown and Parliament, see Hurst (6), 15, 17, 18, 37, 39, 115, 119; cf. Cadman, 206; Evans (1), 14-19; Handlin and Handlin, 113-22; Hartz, 53-55.

134. Joseph S. Davis, 2:102-3; Dodd, 205, 206, 214, 275, 280; Hammond (1), 68, 159, 184, 578; Hartz, 67, 68; Heath, 327; Henderson, 45, 46; Livermore, 246-48, 251-53; Redlich, 2:81, note 6. The first statutes of this type had the effect, and perhaps drew from the example, of the extension of the Bubble Act to the colonies in 1741. Hammond (1), 159, 578; note 128, supra. See, also, Redlich, 2:81, note 6, on a Virginia act of 1787, which, however, seems to have had no connection with the main line of policy beginning in 1799 and 1804. Interest in limiting authority to create money in order to protect a competitive position did not end with the pressures which probably produced the legislation of 1799 and 1804. See the pull and haul between national banks and federally chartered savings and loan associations reflected in material cited in note 143, infra. Part of the policy flavor of the 1799-1804 type of legislation was probably expression of generalized distrust of the social power and privilege which might be mustered under corporate charters. However, it is significant to our present topic that this generalized distrust should have come to so specific a focus on the subject of note-issuing banks. Cf. Hammond (1), 571, 578-79; Redlich, 2:61. The intertwining policies here are reflected in some New York developments after the original act. That act was extended in 1818 to forbid individual as well as associated banking activity other than in the corporate form. See Redlich, 2:61. That banking, with its peculiar relation to the money and credit supply, was the focus was underlined by rulings that the prohibition on banking

activity by "any person" applied to an individual keeping a regular banking office, but not to an individual lending his money without taking deposits. People v. Barstow, 6 Cowen 290 (N.Y. 1826); People v. Brewster, 4 Wendell 498 (N.Y. 1830). The focus on money supply was also emphasized as statutes of this type banned note issues by corporations other than incorporated banks, Hammond (1), 184, and limited to incorporated banks the taking of discounts and deposits as well as the issue of circulating notes. Redlich, 2:81, note 6. To the extent that legislators relaxed or limited these regulations by providing that individuals might engage in some banking operations, the variations underlined the implicit assertion of the legitimacy of legislative determination of the whole subject. Cf. Hammond (1), 580; Redlich, 2:70. The courts' acceptance of the legitimacy of legislation limiting access to deposit as well as note-issuing business to protect the public interest in the money system is exemplified in Myers v. Irwin, 2 Sergeant & Rawle 368, 370-71, 373 (Pa. 1816); Myers v. The Manhattan Bank, 20 Ohio Rep. 283, 303 (1851); Weed v. Bergh, 141 Wis. 569, 573, 124 N.W. 664, 665 (1910), and McLaren v. State, 141 Wis. 577, 124 N.W. 667 (1910); Noble State Bank v. Haskell, 219 U.S. 105, 113 (1911). See Morse, 1:155-58.

135. 1 Stat. 246 (1792), in Dunbar, 227; Nussbaum, 52. On absence of seigniorage as an encouragement of supply: Hepburn, 42; Nussbaum, 54, 77; Taxay, 48, 66, 200. A different basis for charging no seigniorage was suggested by Hamilton's intimation that the cost of coinage should be regarded as an overhead cost of society. Cf. Hepburn, 42; Taxay, 48, 66. For relatively indifferent adjustment of coinage to the movement of the economy through mid-nineteenth century, commentators divide responsibility among Congress (for not setting clear standards of performance), the White House (for confusion in allocating the mint to the State Department, and delay in correcting the error), and the mint administrators. See Hepburn, 43, 47, 48, 67, 68; Nussbaum, 56, 57, 62-63, 99; Taxay, 57, 123-26, 129, 130, 134, 136, 139; White (1), 139-42, 227. Awareness of the control-of-supply value at stake in the mint was shown by explicit opposition to contracting out production of coin to private manufacturers in the face of early complaints about the mint's performance. See Taxay, 134, 136, 139.

136. On the original purpose of establishing a bimetallic system in order to increase the circulating coin: Hepburn, 42, 45, 54; Nussbaum, 55; Taxay, 48, 50, 219, 261. To keep perspective, we must note that, despite this original decision, there was almost no further advocacy of bimetallism in the United States until after the act of 1873 struck the silver dollar from the roster of coins. Cf. Nugent, 33-34. On the impact of failure to provide an official formula to keep both gold and silver in the working money stock: Hepburn, 67, 68; Nussbaum, 61; Taxay, 194, 221. The practical result of this failure in creating a de facto monometallic system was in effect recognized by the 1873 legislation. See Knox (2), 150; Taxay, 260. The unreality of trying to operate without an official formula to keep gold and silver in working partnership in the money stock, or alternatively of formally adopting a monometallic standard, stood revealed when the Bryan agitation for silver was ended not so much by political process as because the bimetallic standard ceased to have political appeal when the general price level rose following a great increase after 1897 in the international stock of monetary gold; Bryan's final defeat and enactment of the Gold Standard Act of 1900 followed close on this change in the gold market. See Friedman and Schwartz, 119, 137.

Analogous to the original decision for a bimetallic standard to increase the supply of coin, as also constituting precedents for Congress's control of money supply, were the several acts through the fore part of the nineteenth century legitimizing and giving legal-tender status to specified foreign coins. Hamilton stated that increase of supply was the objective in recommending the first such legislation. Communication to the House of Representatives, "On the Establishment of a Mint," 28 January 1791, *Works,* 4:3, 54; Hepburn, 42, 46. Successive acts reinforced the policy, as the mint failed to furnish enough tokens for our needs. Hepburn, 47, 60, 67; Nussbaum, 82, 84; note 50, supra.

On the 1834 revaluation of the dollar: 4 Stat. 699 (1834), in Dunbar, 234; Hepburn, 54, 55, 59-60, 61; Nussbaum, 77, 78; Taxay, 193, 215. Taxay, 196, observes that another strand in the 1834 policy making was the assertion by Jacksonians opposed to the second Bank of the United States, that this overvaluation of gold was desirable to curb the paper currency put out by the bank and thus to diminish the bank's "monopoly" on media of exchange. Taxay finds the argument unreal in its time, in view of the continuing ready acceptability of the bank's notes in general circulation. See, in accord on this last point, W. B. Smith, 48, 131, 135-36, 144, 236-37. Though the 1834 act was a weighty precedent for the legitimacy of Congress's control of money supply, the backing and filling which preceded it over several years, and the haste in which the measure was finally taken, highlight the characteristic failure to take a systematic approach to money supply policy. Cf. Hepburn, 54-59; Taxay, 193-96. Whatever the frailties in the way Congress made its decision, the Supreme Court in later dicta accepted it as a constitutional exercise of authority over the money supply, even in its retroactive force. See Knox v. Lee, 12 Wallace 457, 548-49, 551-52 (U.S. 1871), and id., 565 (Bradley, J., concurring); Juilliard v. Greenman, 110 U.S. 421, 449 (1884); Norman v. Baltimore & Ohio Railroad, 294 U.S. 240, 303 (1935).

137. 1 Stat. 191, secs. 3, 7 (VIII-X) (1791); 3 Stat. 266, secs. 7, 11 (7th-9th) (1816); Dunbar, 22, 23, 25-26, 80, 83, 87-88. Osborn v. The Bank of the United States, 9 Wheaton 739 (U.S. 1825) confirmed that Congress had endowed the second bank with broad lending powers, and that this grant was within Congress's constitutional authority. The bank must be given the "faculty of lending and dealing in money" in order to be a useful fiscal agent of the United States (id., 861); these operations also "give its value to the currency in which all the transactions of the government are conducted" (id., 863); and "the currency which it circulates, by means of its trade with individuals, is believed to make it a more fit instrument for the purposes of government than it could otherwise be; and, if this be true, the capacity to carry on this trade is a faculty indispensable to the character and objects of the institution." (Id., 864). That authority to issue circulating paper was a prime goal in chartering the second bank was conceded by the hostile "Amphictyon" papers in 1819. Gunther, 73.

138. The 1853 law in particular was urged by the secretary of the treasury as a means to discourage export of silver and worked well to this end, as well as serving the more general purpose envisaged, of enlarging the whole stock of tokens. However, a notation purpose was also present, of driving out small-denomination paper. Hepburn, 62-64; Nussbaum, 82, 83. See Notes 11, 51, 67, supra. That creation of a subsidiary coinage is a legitimate supply-control measure by Congress is acknowledged, *obiter,* in Knox v. Lee, 12 Wallace 457, 547, 552 (U.S. 1871).

139. 12 Stat. 345 (1862), 532 (1862), 822 (1863), 709 (1863); Dunbar, 163, 167, 171, 173. The main focus of debate over issuing United States notes in 1862 was whether or not they should have legal-tender status. Knox (1), 122. But the basic concern of Congress and the administration was to increase the supply of circulating media available to facilitate the government's war purchases as well as to service the

general economy. Hammond (3), 176-77, 216, 218, 221; Nugent, 9; Sharkey, 33, 36-37. The main argument for legal-tender status was that it would help get the new currency into effective circulation; thus the underlying concern was with the supply of money. Cf. note 54, supra. The felt link of legal-tender status to effective provision of a money supply was reflected in rejection by both houses of Congress of amendments which would have authorized issue of United States notes, but stripped of legal-tender status. Hammond (3), 189, 194, 215, 221.

140. Inextricably mingled in provision for national bank notes were concerns for a more uniformly acceptable currency than what the state-chartered banks had supplied and for a currency stock therefore more functional to the national economy. Cf. Friedman and Schwartz, 18, 19; Hepburn, 306-7; Robertson, 36-45; Trescott, 47-48, 52. Thus the 1863 and 1864 legislation was not as clear-cut precedent for the legitimacy of supply as a policy objective as it would have been had the uniformity goal not been present. The underlying drive to control supply became clearer in light of the 1865 tax to drive state bank notes out of circulation. Note 141, infra.

141. On the 1865 tax: 13 Stat. 469, Dunbar, 198; Andersen, 51-52; Hammond (1), 107, 571, 734; Hepburn, 310-11; Robertson, 53-54; Trescott, 53. The question, whether Congress might legitimately seek to regulate the money supply as a whole by issuing circulating government paper, was not to the fore either in the suit over the 1865 tax or in the later litigation over the legal-tender notes. But creation of the tax and conferring of legal-tender status on the notes both had no justifying ground save as means in aiding the broader purpose of adjusting the money supply to national needs. Thus what the Court said in these cases supportive of broad power in Congress to regulate the money supply seems holding and not dictum. Veazie Bank v. Fenno, 8 Wallace 533, 536, 539, 548, 549 (U.S. 1869); Knox v. Lee, 12 Wallace 457, 540-41, 542, 545, 546 (U.S. 1871), and id., 562, 563-64 (Bradley, J., concurring); Juilliard v. Greenman, 110 U.S. 421, 439, 440, 443, 446, 448 (1884). The point becomes quite clear at 8 Wallace 548, and 12 id. 542, 562. Cf. Fairman (3), 713, 760.

142. 18 Stat. 296 (1875); 20 Stat. 25 (1878); 26 Stat. 485 (1890); 28 Stat. 4 (1893); 31 Stat. 45 (1900); Dunbar, 214, 246, 250; Friedman and Schwartz, 24, 48, 54-55, 81, 85, 108, 116, 119, 131-34, 148-49; Hepburn, 249, 302-4, 350, 356, 376, 475; Morison and Commager, 2:247, 251.

143. Chandler, 56; Friedman and Schwartz, 9, 170, 172; Harrod, 37; Hepburn, 440; Morison and Commager, 2:432; Nussbaum, 158, 163. Control of the supply of deposit-check money is made especially explicit in 48 Stat. 132 (1933), 82 Stat. 608 (1968), 12 U.S.C.A. sec. 1464(b), declaring that savings accounts in federal savings & loan associations "shall not be subject to check or to withdrawal or transfer on negotiable or transferable order or authorization to the association." See *New York Times,* 17 August 1970, p. 41, col. 8; id., 10 September 1970, p. 71, col. 7.

144. 38 Stat. 251, 264 (1913), 48 Stat. 168 (1933), 49 Stat. 684, 704, 705, 706 (1935), heading up especially to 12 U.S.C.A. sec. 263, creating the Federal Open Market Committee. Regulation of the current money supply was held within the statutory mission of the Federal Reserve System and the grant of this mission was held to raise no substantial constitutional question, in Raichle v. Federal Reserve Bank of New York, 34 Fed. (2d) 910, 913-14 (2nd Cir. 1929), citing particularly Juilliard v. Greenman, 110 U.S. 421 (1884). This objective and its legitimacy are recognized, *obiter,* in United States v. Philadelphia National Bank, 374 U.S. 321, 327-28 (1963). See, also, United States v. Manufacturers Hanover Trust Co., 240 Fed. Supp. 867, 892 (S.D.N.Y. 1965). Cf. Horne v. Federal Reserve Bank of Minneapolis, 344 Fed. (2d) 725 (8th Cir. 1965) (federal taxpayer and holder of foreign exchange lack stand-

ing to question constitutionality of Federal Reserve currency powers); Bryan v. Federal Open Market Committee, 235 Fed. Supp. 877 (D. Montana, 1964) (private holder of U.S. Treasury bill lacks standing to challenge legality of Federal Open Market Committee operations). From the 1950s Federal Reserve Board practice treated provision of appropriate long-term growth of the money supply as a legitimate objective in using the system's powers. Friedman and Schwartz, 628. 48 Stat. 52 (1933) authorized the issue of $3 billion additional United States notes, under the original greenback laws. The authority was not used. Friedman and Schwartz, 470, 518; Nussbaum, 182.

145. Hammond (1), 559, 562, 572; Krooss (2), 10; Redlich, 1:ch. 7; note 134, supra. There was, in the movement for free-banking laws, also some flavor of the general policy for freedom of contract, evidenced in the argument of a New York legislative committee recommending free-banking legislation in 1825, because every man had a "natural right . . . to employ his time and money in banking either individually or in association." Hammond (1), 572, quoting N.Y. Sen. Jour., 1825, p. 100.

146. Notes 72, 125, supra.

147. On the Independent Treasury Act: 9 Stat. 59 (1846); Friedman and Schwartz, 19, 127; Krooss (1), 245, 516; Nussbaum, 94-95, 170; Robertson, 21. See, also, Raichle v. Federal Reserve Bank of New York, 34 Fed.(2d) 910, 912 (2d Cir. 1929). On the free-banking aspect of the national bank legislation: Krooss (1), 254; Robertson, 45, 49; Trescott, 49; cf. National Bank v. Commonwealth, 9 Wallace 353, 362 (U.S. 1870); Mercantile Bank v. New York, 121 U.S. 138, 154 (1887). On dispersed power aspects of the Federal Reserve System: Chandler, 5, 9-11, 41, 42; David C. Elliott, 300; Mints, 281, 282; Rowe, 55, 87; Trescott, 159-60. Compare, generally, Barger, 257-67, 287-300, 330.

148. Cf. Barger, 213, 218; Friedman and Schwartz, 83; Unger, 263, 406.

149. Drucker, 60-62; Friedman and Schwartz, 8, 91, 133-34, 137, 188, 698; Hepburn, 40, 52, 68, 286, 304, 368, 385, 434; Johnson and Krooss, 295, 308; Nugent, 102-3, 158, 180; Nussbaum, 81-82, 84; Sutton, et al., 239-45; Unger, 329.

150. 48 Stat. 337 (1934).

151. Govan, 144-46, 152, 176; Hammond (1), 355-57, 392, 416. However, Wilburn, ch. 4, finds that the record does not show that local banking interests as a whole opposed continuation of the bank.

152. Nugent, ch. 6, introduces some skeptical realism into assessment of interest group alignment on money policy.

153. Cf. Pound (2), 367. See, generally, Friedman and Schwartz, 697-700.

154. On public policy practice as evidencing the legitimacy of legal action, see, e.g., McCulloch v. Maryland, 4 Wheaton 316, 401 (U.S. 1819); Proprietors of the Charles River Bridge Co. v. Proprietors of the Warren Bridge, 11 Peters 420, 551-52 (U.S. 1837); McGrain v. Daugherty, 273 U.S. 135, 157, 161-64 (1927).

155. Prelude, notes 40, 42. In the only comments on the matter in The Federalist, Madison finds that the one aspect of the authority over coin and currency given the Congress which warrants note as unusual is the policy indicated of giving the central government exclusive power, vis à vis the states. The Federalist, no. 42, p. 264, and no. 44, pp. 277-78.

156. 1 Stat. 246 (1792), in Dunbar, 227; Nussbaum, 52, 57, 85; Taxay, 61. Though the spokesmen for economy did not block creation of the mint, for some years it was denied adequate means to do a good job. Nussbaum, 57; White (1), 141.

157. 1 Stat. 246, sec. 14. Hamilton stated his view in his communication of 28 January 1791 to the House of Representatives, "On the Establishment of a Mint,"

Works, 4:3, 40, 41. Cf. Hepburn, 42. The 1792 act did, however, impose a small charge, if the bullion owner asked for immediate delivery of coin in exchange for his metal. Nussbaum, 54. Congress also authorized the holding of a bullion fund at the mint, to facilitate immediate exchange of coin for bullion. But for some time it failed to appropriate the money to maintain the fund. Taxay, 66, 84. Treatment of the costs of minting coin from regular bullion as social costs was further underlined by the distinction made in providing a special minting charge on coinage from debased metal. Id., 123. A wholly different purpose—that of combatting deflation—was involved when, turning seigniorage into a convenient fiction, Congress authorized the president in the early 1930s to buy domestically mined silver at a price about 50 percent lower than the nominal mint value; the difference was rationalized as a seigniorage charge. Friedman and Schwartz, 484; Nussbaum, 192.

Of analogous force, recognizing that social income and social cost factors were present in the supply of money, were arguments that because bank profits had the practical character of a tax on the people, the state should own any note-issuing bank, or at least should require bonuses to be used for public purposes as a condition of granting private bank franchises, in order to recoup income fairly owed the whole people. See Handlin and Handlin, 163; Hartz, 55, 56, 64, 245-46; Heath, 165-66; Primm, 21, 25; Walters, 44. Similarly, critics of the national bank system argued that currency issued by holders of "monopoly" franchises was illegitimate; all paper money should be issued by the government, because it should serve the profit simply of the whole community. Bogart, 683; Hepburn, 313, 321. Compare the argument in 1959-60 between the Joint Economic Committee of Congress and the chairman of the Federal Reserve Board, over whether expansion of bank reserves should not be by open-market operations rather than by reducing reserve requirements, so that government and not the commercial bank might reap the benefits of any increased earnings. Part Two, note 349.

158. Such appears to be the holding of Juilliard v. Greenman, 110 U.S. 421, 448, 450 (1884), in sustaining Congress's authority to continue the issue of circulating United States notes of legal-tender status, to meet current money-supply needs of a peacetime economy. Like concern to uphold Congress's authority over the money system as a part of social structure, as opposed to ordinary rights of contract, was manifest in the narrower context of war emergency and as applied to pre-existing contracts, in Knox v. Lee, 12 Wallace 457, 548, 549, 551 (U.S. 1871). Similar concern—but, again, in a more specific context than that indicated in Juilliard v. Greenman—produced the holding in Norman v. Baltimore & Ohio Railroad, 294 U.S. 240, 308 (1935), that private contracts must be deemed subject to Congress's authority to define the character of lawful money and of legal tender, incident to its aggregate powers to deal with the condition of the national economy and to try to rescue it from depression. Cf. note 14, supra. See, also, McLean, J., for the majority in Briscoe v. Bank of the Commonwealth of Kentucky, 11 Peters 257, 312 (U.S. 1837), that the breadth of the people's involvement makes money regulation a peculiarly sensitive area of policy.

159. *Works,* 4:3, 5. This policy yielded to passing expediency, though the yielding itself asserted the propriety of legal regulation to service the going economy (this time, for the immediate goal of supply), so long as Congress augmented the money stock by recognizing certain foreign coin as lawful money. See note 50, supra.

160. Barger, 20-21, 23; Hammond (1), 261, 279, 284; W. B. Smith, 43, 136, 239, 241; Wilburn, chs. 4, 5, and especially pp. 46, 51, 55, 64. Cf. *Register of Debates,* 22d Cong., 1st Sess., 8:132-39, 142-43. Even the "Amphictyon" papers of 1819, hos-

tile to the decision in McCulloch v. Maryland, had recognized that an important reason for chartering the second bank had been to provide a more regular currency than the state banks were supplying. Gunther, 73.

161. United States v. Marigold, 9 Howard 560, 567 (U.S. 1850). See notes 18, 25, 26, supra.

162. Veazie Bank v. Fenno, 8 Wallace 533, 549 (U.S. 1869); see Knox v. Lee, 12 id. 457, 545 (U.S. 1871); Juilliard v. Greenman, 110 U.S. 421, 446 (1884); Merchants National Bank of Baltimore v. United States, 214 U.S. 33, 44 (1909). Cf. Dorfman, 3:25; Hammond (1), 724-27; Hepburn, 193, 307; Robertson, 36-38, 42, 45; Trescott, 63. Judges who upheld Congress's authority to ban production of privately manufactured coin for circulation did so, likewise, on the ground that achieving a uniform, working system of money tokens for the nation was a legitimate goal of law. See note 21, supra. Promotion of a unified, systematic money supply was also urged in support of the legal-tender act of 1862, but the argument did not bulk large in that discussion. Hammond (3), 203, 205.

163. Joint Resolution of 5 June 1933, 48 Stat. 112 (1933); Norman v. Baltimore & Ohio Railroad Co., 294 U.S. 240, 312-13, 315 (1935). McReynolds, J., dissenting, seems not to deny the legitimacy of regulating money in the interests of servicing the going economy, but, rather, to find that in his judgment Congress was acting for the illegitimate purpose of shifting wealth among interests or classes in the population. See 294 U.S., 240, 374.

164. Davidson v. Lanier, 4 Wallace 447, 454 (U.S. 1867). See Shriver v. Woodbine Savings Bank, 285 U.S. 467, 476 (1932). On the existence of general authority in the state to treat banking as a limited-access franchise, see Noble State Bank v. Haskell, 219 U.S. 104, 112, 113 (1911), and Assaria State Bank v. Dolley, id., 121, 127 (1911).

165. Hammond (1), 557.

166. Noble State Bank v. Haskell, 219 U.S. 104, 111 (1911). Cf. Farmers and Merchants Bank of Monroe, North Carolina v. Federal Reserve Bank of Richmond, Virginia, 262 U.S. 649, 661 (1923); United States v. Rock Royal Co-operative, Inc., 307 U.S. 533, 573 (1939). That the validity of compulsory deposit insurance upheld in Noble State Bank v. Haskell rested on its character as a regulation in the general social interest and was not based on depositors' contract relations with banks so as to bring the issue under contract clause protection as against later modification, see Abie State Bank v. Bryan, 282 U.S. 765, 782 (1931). Cf. Veix v. Sixth Ward Building & Loan Association of Newark, 310 U.S. 32, 38 (1940); Frankfurter, J., concurring, in American Federation of Labor v. American Sash & Door Co., 335 U.S. 538, 553, note 10 (1949).

167. Works, 4:16. Hamilton coupled this recommendation on supply policy with recognition of need to establish a proportion between gold and silver in the formally defined money units which would be sufficiently aligned to the general markets for those commodities to keep both in circulation. However, his perception did not reach to clear acknowledgment of the need for some means for ready adjustment of the money ratio to changes in the market ratio. Id., 17.

168. Hamilton, Works, 4:3, 54. Cf. Hepburn, 42, 46, 51, 57, 67.

169. Govan, 139, 265-66, 269-70; Hepburn, 57-60; Nussbaum, 77; notes 10, 137, supra. See Bronson v. Rodes, 7 Wallace 229, 248 (U.S. 1869); Knox v. Lee, 12 id., 457, 552 (U.S. 1871).

170. Hamilton, Communication to President George Washington, Opinion as to the Constitutionality of a National Bank, 23 February 1791, Works, 3:445, 480.

171. W. B. Smith, 131, 236-37, 242. In 1819 the "Amphictyon" papers hostile to the decision in McCulloch v. Maryland, accepted as a prime moving factor in 1815 for chartering the second bank the desire to provide a more reliable currency than the state banks had been supplying. Gunther, 73.

172. 12 Stat. 665, sec. 17 (1863); 13 Stat. 99, sec. 22 (1864); 13 Stat. 498, sec. 21 (1865); 16 Stat. 251, sec. 6 (1870); 18 Stat. 123, sec. 9 (1874); Dunbar, 171, 178, 199, 202, 210. This kind of legislation on its face asserted control of current supply as a proper use of law affecting money. Thus the 1863 act provided that within an over-all ceiling of $300 million of national bank notes, $150 million "shall be apportioned to associations in the States, in the District of Columbia, and in the Territories, according to representative population, and the remainder shall be apportioned by the Secretary of the Treasury among associations formed in [those areas] ... having due regard to the existing banking capital, resources, and business, of such States, District, and Territories." The extent of supply control was underlined in the 1870 act, which increased the over-all ceiling by $54 million, stipulated that the increased amount of notes authorized "shall be furnished to banking associations organized or to be organized in those States and Territories having less than their proportion under the apportionment contemplated by" the act of 1865, and that if the increase were not fully taken up within one year the comptroller of the currency was authorized "to issue such circulation to banking associations applying for the same in other States or Territories having less than their proportion, giving the preference to such as have the greatest deficiency." Hepburn, 311, 313, 315, 319; Nugent, 59, 127, 138; Trescott, 57, 146. Legal control of supply was, finally, asserted by repeal of the over-all ceiling and of regional distribution provisions. 18 Stat. 296, sec. 3 (1875), and Stat. 302 (1875); Hepburn, 319. The discretionary character of the controls thus exercised was underlined when President Ulysses S. Grant vetoed an 1874 bill which would have increased the ceilings both for greenbacks and for national bank notes. Hepburn, 221; Nugent, 225. Trescott, 154.

173. See Juilliard v. Greenman, 110 U.S. 421, 448, 450 (1884). Compare Knox v. Lee, 12 Wallace 457, 540, 541-42, 546, and Bradley, J., concurring, 562, 564 (U.S. 1871), where, though the holding turns on Congress's power to regulate money in a situation deemed to require major readjustment of the economy—under stress of war—the opinions recognize, *obiter,* that provision of a money supply to meet the going flow of ordinary transactions is a legitimate goal of legal regulation of money.

174. Chandler, 13-14; Friedman and Schwartz, 163, 408; Hacker and Kendrick, 462; Hepburn, 388-95, 397, 415; Link, 200, 214, 223; Redlich, 2:166-68.

175. *The Federalist,* no. 42, pp. 258, 262, 264; cf. Prelude, supra, notes 13-16, 19, 23, 25-29. See Craig v. Missouri, 4 Peters 410, 432 (U.S. 1831).

176. Prelude, supra, notes 16, 17, 19, 22, 23, 25. Cf. Sturges v. Crowninshield, 4 Wheaton 117, 204 (U.S. 1819). As the next section of this part notes, by the limits they put on local legislatures the constitution makers also wanted to curb manipulations of money for reasons of state or of politics; however, this concerns a different objective than that of affecting the general condition of business.

177. Abel, 444, 458, 462, 465, 469, 470, 475, 478; Stern, 1344, 1345.

178. Abel, 450, 451; Warren (2), 397, 569, 572-74, 579, 585. Cf. Joseph Story, 2:432, 433, 434, 438, 520, 523, 525, 527, 532, 534-36.

179. Abel, 477, 481.

180. See Knox v. Lee, 12 Wallace 457, 534, 546 (U.S. 1871); Norman v. Baltimore & Ohio Railroad, 294 U.S. 240, 303 (1935); cf. Hamilton, Opinion on the Constitutionality of a National Bank, 23 February 1791, *Works,* 3:445, 489.

181. Stern, 1339, 1340.

182. Prelude, supra, notes 30-37; Briscoe v. Bank of the Commonwealth of Kentucky, 11 Peters 257, 316, 317, 318 (U.S. 1837); Bank of Augusta v. Earle, 13 id. 519, 595, 596 (U.S. 1839).

183. 1 Stat. 191 (1791); 3 Stat. 266 (1816); 13 Stat. 99 (1864); 18 Stat. 296 (1875); Dunbar, 22, 80, 178, 214; Fleckner v. The Bank of the United States, 8 Wheaton 338, 350 (U.S. 1824); Osborn v. The Bank of the United States, 9 id. 739, 860-64 (U.S. 1825); First National Bank of Bethel v. National Pahquioque Bank, 14 Wallace 383, 394 (U.S. 1872); Merchants National Bank of Baltimore v. United States, 214 U.S. 33, 42 (1909).

184. Hamilton, communication to the House of Representatives, 14 December 1790, On Establishing a National Bank, *Works*, 3:388, 390, 393; cf. id., 406. Hamilton foreshadowed his emphasis on the utility of a national bank for promoting economic growth in letters he wrote to Robert Morris in 1780 and 1781. *Works*, 3:319, 338, 341, 342, 361-62. In the opinion which he submitted to President Washington, upholding the constitutionality of a national bank, Hamilton was less ambitious in describing the contributions of banks to the economy; his observations here seem focused on servicing the going flow of transactions, though in resting the constitutionality of a bank charter partly on the commerce clause his opinion carries intimations of a broader role. See note 180, supra. Probably Hamilton felt that he should put the matter to the conservative president in more, rather than less, conservative terms. Cf. Crosskey, 1:217.

185. Hammond (1), 115, 116. Cf. Crosskey, 1:201.

186. Barger, 22; Bogart, 362; Bruchey, 113, 150; Faulkner, 227; Govan, 28-33, 132; Hammond (1), 200, 202, 206-7, 208, 210-25; Hepburn, 84, 85; Robertson, 19; Trescott, 26; Walters, 171-73, 237-40.

187. W. B. Smith, 143, quoting instructions by Biddle to one of his officers, 3 March 1828; see, generally, W. B. Smith, ch. 9. Barger, 23, thinks Biddle did not really do a central-bank job.

188. On bank chartering: see Bogart, 370; Cadman, 206, 207, 208; Evans (1), 14, 15, 20, 24, note 31, 26-29; Hammond (1), 617-18; Hartz, 38; Heath, 305-6. On state-owned banks or single banks given a monopoly position: see Hammond (1), 170, 243, 566, 612, 616, 618-19; Primm, ch. II; Trescott, 29. On profit sought from issue of circulating notes: see Bogart, 363; Hammond (1), 189, 364, 549-50, 689; Krooss (1), 238; Trescott, 17, 21. On pressures to supply medium and long-term capital via bank loans: see Bogart, 373; Hacker, 334; Rohrbough, 137, 222; notes 102, 103, 119, supra. Hammond (1), 627, observes that analogous pressures underlay some of the issue of circulating notes, which some issuing banks used to buy state internal improvement bonds.

189. Bruchey, 130, 145; Dodd, 203, 207, 215.

190. Hammond (1), 605-30; Krooss (1), 241-43; Schumpeter (1), 1:294-96.

191. Bogart, 488, 683; Faulkner, 627; Hammond (3), 325-28, 330, 333; Hepburn, 192, 193, 201, 307; Trescott, 48, 56; Veazie Bank v. Fenno, 8 Wallace 533, 549 (U.S. 1869).

192. Hepburn, 308, 313, 314-15, 317; Trescott, 49, 52, 57, 63; Unger, 115, 116. The incompatability of a statutory ceiling on note issue with a purpose of promoting large-scale economic growth was underlined by the cumbersomeness of the process by which Congress amended the ceiling in 1870 and unsuccessfully sought to do so in 1874. See note 172, supra.

193. Nugent, 46, 59, 127, 226; Unger, 235, 243, 245, 254, 256, 258, 260-63.

Nugent, 138, 213, 225, finds that there was support in 1870 and 1874 for raising the statutory ceiling and more generously distributing authorizations for issue of national bank notes, among manufacturers who then feared greenbacks and silver as inflationary, but still wanted a money supply which would serve economic expansion.

194. Friedman and Schwartz, 7, 56; Hepburn, 332, 338; Trescott, 51, 91-92, 107. That the prime factor in the last quarter of the nineteenth century in the national banking system was not government's action in removing the bank-note ceiling but the bankers' response to government fiscal policy and to demands for loans and their perception that their profit lay in deposit business, was indicated by the failure of note circulation to respond by material enlargement after 1875. Friedman and Schwartz, 21, 23, 128, 182, 781; Hepburn, 323; Robertson, 63.

195. The comprehensive, effective restrictions set by the federal Constitution remove any question of direct state action on money supply. Prelude, supra, notes 13-16.

196. On want of attention to the inflation issue in 1862: Hammond (3), 230-31. On other issues of Treasury notes: Hepburn, 90, 133, 135, 137, 172, 173; Knox (1), 20, 22, 24, 26, 34, 38; Nussbaum, 70, 71. Soon after the expiration of the charter of the second Bank of the United States, Congress argued over proposals for large issues of Treasury notes for currency, to make good the disappearance of the bank's notes. Such issues were opposed partly by proponents of a new Bank of the United States and partly by such hard-money men as Senator Thomas Hart Benton, who opposed the idea precisely because he did not want government-issue paper in the money stock. Hepburn, 137; Knox (1), 41, 42. There were issues of Treasury notes, nonetheless, in 1837 and 1838, but they were not clearly made for currency purposes. Cf. Knox (1), 44.

197. Note 169, supra.

198. Barger, 18, 24; Cochran and Miller, 45; Gates, 357, 358; Krooss (1), 32; Hammond (1), 455; Hibbard, 220; North (1), 199-200; Rohrbough, 248, 291, 301. The Specie Circular was tied to problems of the federal government in meeting Congress's determination that the federal surplus be distributed to the states—an aspect of the matter which underlines that we deal here in the impact of fiscal upon monetary policy. Cf. North (1), 199; Govan, 298, 301, 334.

199. 9 Stat. 59 (1846), Dunbar, 138. The statute relaxed the requirement on specie payments to the extent of allowing payments to the United States to be in Treasury notes as well as in gold or silver; it also directed the Treasury to pay out in gold or silver, or in Treasury notes if the creditor agreed. Id., secs. 18, 19. The act was preceded by an analogous statute passed at President Martin Van Buren's urging in 1840, which the Whigs repealed when they gained power in 1841. Hammond (1), 542-43; Hepburn, 133-37, 151. On the mingled factors in enactment of the 1846 measure: Bogart, 374; Faulkner, 231; Govan, 317, 334; Hammond (1), 542-43; Hepburn, 155. On the 1846 act as rejecting a money-managing role for the United States, though in fact regulating the money system see: Barger, 25-27; Hammond (1), 497, 499, 542, 544-45; Krooss (1), 245, 516; Robertson, 21; Trescott, 28; Augustus Hand, cir. j., in Raichle v. Federal Reserve Bank of New York, 34 Fed. (2d) 910, 912 (2d Cir. 1929).

200. On the dysfunctional operation of the requirements as to specie payments in and out of the national treasury: Friedman and Schwartz, 127; Krooss (1), 516; Trescott, 43. Cf. Chandler, 105; David C. Elliott, 297. Relaxation of the 1846 policy was by 13 Stat. 99, sec. 45 (1864); 38 Stat. 251, 265, sec. 15 (1913). The 1846 scheme was repealed by 41 Stat. 654 (1920), effective 1 July 1921. Hepburn, 198,

381, 468; Nussbaum, 95. On Treasury management of money supply by shifting deposits, to the end of the nineteenth century: Friedman and Schwartz, 19, 128; Hepburn, 468.

201. Nugent, 34, 41, 114, 137, 138, 142, 143, 166, 170, 171, 222-27, 243-50, 258; Nussbaum, 154-57; Sharkey, 60, 102, 103, 131-32, 135-40, 171; Unger, 252-63, 324, 328-64, 372-73, 403-6. Cf. note 193, supra.

202. Dorfman, 3:215, 230, 231; Hepburn, 58-59, 375, 378, 380; Nugent, 36, 37, 272; Nussbaum, 155-57. The contemporary naïveté which saw in gold coin a complete escape from government manipulation of money for government-determined goals seems reflected in Bronson v. Rodes, 7 Wallace 229, 250 (U.S. 1869), when the Court observes that the care taken to insure precise weight of precious metal in coin from the mint "recognizes the fact, accepted by all men throughout the world, that value is inherent in the precious metals; that gold and silver are in themselves values, and being such, and being in other respects best adapted to the purpose, are the only proper measures of value." On the other hand, no more than the politicians did the Court commit itself to a dogmatic renunciation of all government action on money save that of establishing a precious-metals standard. Juilliard v. Greenman, 110 U.S. 421 (1884) sustained Congress's power to keep government fiat paper in the money stock in peacetime. Its holding appears to be that Congress might do this to provide a money supply adequate to the ordinary flow of transactions. Note 173, supra. But also, *obiter*, the Court indicated that Congress might provide such paper currency to meet an "exigency" of the peacetime economy, though it did not go so far as to acknowledge authority to issue paper money simply to promote economic growth. Juilliard v. Greenman, supra at 450.

203. 38 Stat. 251, 254, sec. 4 (1913); cf. 38 Stat. 265, sec. 14(d). On the want of a definite mandate, including the lack of any clear-cut direction to manage the money supply for promoting major growth or adjustments in the economy: Attorney General's Committee (1), 3, 5, 19-20; Chandler, 4-6, 54; Clifford, 347; Eccles, 212, 228; Friedman and Schwartz, 193; Knipe, 4, 5; Mints, 283; Rowe, 67.

204. The title of the act pointed to these limited objectives as those most sharply in the intent of Congress, when it said that the system was created "to furnish an elastic currency, to afford means of rediscounting commercial paper, to establish a more effective supervision of banking in the United States, and for other purposes." 38 Stat. 251 (1913). That the only larger purpose in view at enactment and in the system's early years was to deal with liquidity crises: Barger, 46; Chandler, 14-15; Friedman and Schwartz, 189, 192, 193, 408; Goldenweiser, 109, 110; Knipe, 32. Cf. Attorney General's Committee (1), 3, 5. Mints, 281, 282, highlights the implication of this purpose in the statutory restrictions on lending and note issue by the federal reserve banks.

205. On reliance on a gold base to restrict need of government discretionary action regarding money: Friedman and Schwartz, 240; Sproul, 65, 66. On reliance on required ties to short-term commercial paper as of like effect (faith in the automaticity of holding operations to "real bills"): Clay J. Anderson, 169, 170; Eccles, 171, 172; Friedman and Schwartz, 191, 267; Knipe, 278.

206. Clay J. Anderson, 47, 48; Barger, 232, 242; Chandler, 208, 222-29, 233-34, 242; David C. Elliott, 310, 312, 313; Friedman and Schwartz, 251, 252, 552, 553, 689; Knipe, 32-33; Youngdahl, 120, 121. In the early years, the clearest use of open-market operations for goals of major economic adjustment was in support of re-establishing an international gold standard. Chandler, 313-14, 322, 328, 355, 377; David C. Elliott, 312, 313.

207. 49 Stat. 705, 706 (1935); Clifford, 131, 133; Goldenweiser, 280; Young-dahl, 121, 122. Treiber, 262, 263, particularly points out that this 1935 legislation recognized Federal Reserve practice.

208. 49 Stat. 706 (1935); Clay J. Anderson, 54; Friedman and Schwartz, 196; Jacoby, 218; Mints, 39, 40. The 1935 act made permanent and put wholly in the hands of the Federal Reserve Board an authority to alter reserve requirements, which had been given as an emergency power to be used only with permission of the president by the Thomas Amendment to the Agricultural Adjustment Act of 1933. 48 Stat. 54 (1933). That Congress in these measures changed the idea of legitimate goals of money regulation is made clearer by comparison with earlier reserve requirements, which had aimed, however ineffectually, at liquidity. Notes 104-6, supra. Cf. Golden-weiser, 39, 50; Jacoby, 213, 216, 218.

209. That the board made faltering use of its open-market powers partly from lack of congressional guidance as to proper purposes and out of doubts of the whole scope of its statutory authority: Clifford, 86; Friedman and Schwartz, 193; Golden-weiser, 123, 124; Wallich and Wallich, 334-37. That the board's hesitation was born partly of a felt lack of theory: Clay J. Anderson, 163-66; Friedman and Schwartz, 253, 254, 533.

210. On the strong development—especially in the 1950s—of practice and doc-trine legitimating open-market operations for large economic goals: Bogen, 346, 347; Clifford, 275-78; Dewald and Johnson, 187; Friedman and Schwartz, 628; Knipe, 5-7; Pritchard, 385. This is not to say that the power was used effectively or with clear results: Culbertson, 159, 164, 165; Knipe, 28, 31. On subordination of Federal Reserve controls to wartime finance needs of government: Bogen, 339, 342, 343; Clifford, 230, 231; David C. Elliott, 301-4; Hansen, 71-72.

211. 48 Stat. 51 (1933); Acheson, 167, 168, 249; Friedman and Schwartz, 465, 470, 483, 487, 518, note 13; Nussbaum, 181-82, 191, 192; Schlesinger, 41, 42, 197, 236; Stein (2), 41, 48; Taus, 337; Wish, 442. The Thomas Amendment authorization of additional United States notes was repealed by 59 Stat. 238 (1945), sec. 4; its authorization of devaluation of the dollar expired 30 June 1943, according to 55 Stat. 396 (1941), having meanwhile been amended by 48 Stat. 337, 342 (1934), sec. 12.

212. 48 Stat. 337, 342 (1934), sec. 12; Friedman and Schwartz, 469, 470; Nuss-baum, 184-88; Schlesinger, 234, 237-41, 250-52. This devaluation authority was allowed to expire 30 June 1943, according to 55 Stat. 396 (1941).

213. Norman v. Baltimore & Ohio Railroad, 294 U.S. 240, 303 (1935). The Court's quoted remarks were characterized by it as the grounds taken in the second and third legal-tender cases. The characterization seems accurate enough, taken in a general sense and addressed particularly to the concept of national sovereignty. But the quoted passage from 1935 relates the federal government's authority regarding money to economically oriented objectives more clearly than do the passages it cites from the decisions of 1871 and 1884. Cf. Knox v. Lee, 12 Wallace 457, 532, 536 (U.S. 1871); Juilliard v. Greenman, 110 U.S. 421, 438 (1884).

There are two levels of decision in the Norman case. In upholding that part of the government's monetary policy which barred enforcement of gold clauses, the Court invoked Congress's authority to maintain uniformity in the money system for fair conduct of the going economy. Note 163, supra. But regulation against gold clauses came in issue only because Congress authorized the president to change the gold weight of the dollar, and at stake in this underlying action was the objective not of promoting a given pattern of going operations, but of changing the level of operations altogether. Thus the Court's acceptance of the legitimacy of the broader objective seems a necessary basis for its more specific ruling upholding the ban on enforcing the gold clauses. Cf. Dawson, 666, 667; Dunne (2), 90. Two other aspects of the Norman opinion indicate the Court's awareness that it was upholding Congress's authority to pursue objectives of major economic change or adjustment, as well as servicing the current flow of transactions. First, the Court took care to quote the broad-purpose language of the Thomas Amendment, authorizing the president to fix the weight of the gold and silver dollars "at such amounts as he finds necessary from his investigation to stabilize domestic prices or to protect the foreign commerce against the adverse effect of depreciated foreign currencies." 294 U.S. 240, 296. Second, the Court notes that the gold clauses in suit before it were themselves designed to deal not with current-operations problems of money but with large changes in economic conditions, being "intended to afford a definite standard of measure of value and thus to protect against a depreciation of the currency and against the discharge of the obligation by a payment of lesser value than that prescribed." Id., 302. This end, of adjusting transactions to major economic change, had earlier been noted as the function which contractors intended by gold clauses, in Bronson v. Rodes, 7 Wallace 229, 246 (U.S. 1869), and Butler v. Horwitz, id., 258, 259, 260 (U.S. 1869), where the Court interpreted the current policy of Congress as not barring enforcement of the clauses. It is with reference to this major-adjustment goal of the contractors that the Court in the Norman opinion asserts that Congress may bar enforcement of their intention, for "parties cannot remove their transactions from the reach of dominant constitutional power by making contracts about them." Norman v. Baltimore & Ohio Railroad at 308. Implicit here it seems is the ruling that Congress may validly regulate money to affect the general direction or adjustment of economic conditions. Moreover, McReynolds, J., dissenting, based his objection on his finding that the whole pattern of action centering on devaluation of the dollar was for what he viewed as an illegitimate, long-term adjustment purpose, "to raise the nominal value of farm products by depleting the standard dollar." Id., 373, 374.

214. Friedman and Schwartz, 149-52; Taus, 86, 87, 93, 94, 104, 106, 110, 111, 115-19, 122-26; Timberlake, 168-71, 182.

215. Friedman and Schwartz, 471, 510-11, 519; Goldenweiser, 178, 263, 264; Taus, 207, 208, 225-28.

216. Bailey, 41, 44, 47-48, 51, 54, 60, 112, 113, 115, 118, 119, 120, 121-23, 130, 134, 135, 138, 145, 163, 165, 167, 171, 223, 224-25; Burkhead, 69, 76; Friedman and Schwartz, 596; Hansen, 33, 38; Lekachman, 171-73, 175; Nourse, 67, 79.

217. 60 Stat. 23 (1946); Bailey, 14, 47-48, 112, 122, 124, 134, 225, 230, 245. Cf. Burkhead, 68; Heller, 9, 13, 64, 75, 85-86, 100, 102; Lekachman, 189-90.

218. Clifford, 278; Knipe, 6, 196; Sproul, 65, 66. Treiber, 262, 263, emphasizes that in acknowledging the 1946 act's guidelines, the Federal Reserve was recognizing the legitimacy of kinds of action which the system had developed by its practice in prior years.

219. Prelude, supra, note 24; United States v. Marigold, 9 Howard 560, 568 (U.S. 1850); Knox v. Lee, 12 Wallace 457, 532-33 (U.S. 1871); Juilliard v. Greenman, 110 U.S. 421, 445, 447, 448, 449 (1884); Norman v. Baltimore & Ohio Railroad, 294 U.S. 240, 303, 315 (1935). Compare the policy implications of the Court's readiness to interpret Congress's legal-tender legislation as not intended to bar states from insisting on payment of taxes to them in coin, as well as the Court's intimation that contrary legislation by Congress might be an unconstitutional invasion of the state sovereignty recognized by the Tenth Amendment. Lane County v. Oregon, 7 Wallace

71, 77-78 (U.S. 1869); Hagar v. Reclamation District No. 108, 111 U.S. 701, 706 (1884). That government coinage was in part legitimated by its service to collection of dues owing the government was indicated by the requirement of the Independent Treasury Act of 1846 that all money owing the United States be paid in specie. By the same action, Congress in effect limited the utility of state bank notes. Note 199, supra.

220. Hamilton, *Works,* 3:388, 394, 445, 474 ff.; 1 Stat. 191, secs. 7 (XI), 9, 10, and 3 Stat. 266, secs. 11 (Tenth), 13, 14, Dunbar, 22, 26, 28, 29, 80, 88, 91; Bogart, 361, 364; Faulkner, 227, 229; Hammond (1), 208, 310-12; W. B. Smith, 237, 244-45; McCulloch v. Maryland, 4 Wheaton 316, 402, 407-9, 422 (U.S. 1819).

221. Note 162, supra. One argument in support of the legal-tender act of 1862 was that provision of the legal-tender United States notes would aid the collection of taxes, but this point did not figure prominently in that discussion. Hammond (3), 189, 193, 194; Redlich, 2:113.

222. 38 Stat. 251 (1913), sec. 15; Clifford, 204, 205, 295-97; David C. Elliott, 296-98; Hepburn, 399, 406; Taus, 135.

223. Prelude, supra, notes 15, 16, 26-28, 49-58; Bradley, J., concurring, in Knox v. Lee, 12 Wallace 457, 554, 558-59 (U.S. 1871); Juilliard v. Greenman, 110 U.S. 421, 443-44 (1884).

224. Bogart, 229; Faulkner, 364; Hacker, 330-31; Hammond (1), 227, 229, 231-32, 239; Hofstadter (1), 41.

225. Bogart, 625, 626; Faulkner, 673-74, 682-83; Hammond (3), ch. 6; Wesley C. Mitchell, 53-71; Thayer, 82, note 1, 94, 97; Knox v. Lee, 12 Wallace 457, 531, 540-43, and Bradley, J., concurring, 560, 562-63 (U.S. 1871).

226. Bogen, 339, 342, 343; Clifford, 164, 165, 180, 183, 186, 195; Eccles, 382; David C. Elliott, 301-4, 310, 312; Goldenweiser, 133, 134, 192, 195; Timberlake, 207; Youngdahl, 129-33.

227. Compare Nugent, 142, 143, evaluating the competition of interests between industrialists, merchants, and bankers, concerning contraction of the greenbacks in the early 1870s.

228. Veazie Bank v. Fenno, 8 Wallace 533, 548 (U.S. 1869); Juilliard v. Greenman, 110 U.S. 421, 450 (1884); cf. Daniel v. Family Security Life Insurance Co., 336 U.S. 220, 224 (1949); Williamson v. Lee Optical of Oklahoma, 348 U.S. 483, 486, 487-88 (1955).

229. One exception to the text proposition might be the destruction of the Confederacy's money system in the defeat of the South. Cf. Dawson and Cooper, 734, 735. The complete destruction of the Confederate currency by inflation proceeded substantially from defects of the Confederacy's own fiscal policy, but was also a product of the North's war effort, especially of the blockade. Morison and Commager, 2:13, 14; Lerner, 12, 14-15, 17, 22, 29, 32; Nussbaum, 123-26.

230. Prelude, supra, notes 15-17, 19, 26-28, 53, 54, 61, 63, 65. In his communication to the House of Representatives 14 December 1790, Hamilton argued for creating a national bank with the privilege of note issue, because he felt that this separate, privately managed agency would not be under the temptations of political expediency which would make Congress prefer to print money rather than to levy taxes. Hamilton, *Works,* 3:413.

231. On bans or limits on chartering banks: notes 134, 190, supra; Hammond (1), ch. 19. On free-banking laws: note 145, supra; Hammond (1), ch. 18. See, also, Andersen, 14-24; Benson, 97-98, 100-2, 104; Hofstader (1), 63; Meyers, 120-22; Trescott, 30-33. One explicit exception to the general trend to deny the legitimacy of

shaping the law on bank-created money to favor particular interests lay in occasional conditions attached to special charters, that the franchised bank make some stated part of its loans to agriculture or to industry. But, though these provisions apparently had some effect on lending policies, there is no reason to think that they were more than marginal in impact. In any case, such provisions can be interpreted as aimed at the goal of over-all economic performance, as readily as they can be read as favoring particular interest groups. See note 189, supra.

232. Notes 130, 160, supra; Coit, 261, 263, 264, 329, 331-32; Gouge, chs. 1, 9, 20; Hammond (1), 119, 211-14, 353, 386, 442-43; Hofstadter (1), 32, 35, 41, 50-51, 56-58, 63; Meyers, 6-9, 16, 80, 120; Peterson, 76-78; Unger, 18.

233. *Works,* 3:338. As early as his letters to Robert Morris, urging a national bank, in 1780 and 1781, Hamilton argued that an advantage would be to involve "the *immediate* interest of the moneyed men to co-operate with government" in supporting the currency. Id., 3:319, 332, 338.

234. Hammond (1), 353-58, 443; W. B. Smith, 235, 248, 250, 251; Walters, 357, 362; Wilburn, 81, 83, 85, 100, 115, 118, 120-25, 129. Biddle, too, played politics for the advantage of the second bank, but the most painstaking commentator on his management pleads in mitigation that Biddle acted only after Jackson forced him on the defensive, and finds that the record will not support a clear-cut verdict that Biddle manipulated a credit stringency to discredit the Jacksonians. W. B. Smith, 249, 252.

235. Dorfman, 3:114, 177, 225, 231; Friedman and Schwartz, 19, 23, 56, 182; Hammond (1), 34, 573, 725, 727, and (3), 332; Hepburn, 214, 215, 313, 318, 321, 323, 324, 328, 332, 378; Nugent, 42, 46, 59, 127; Nussbaum, 147; Trescott, 54, 63, 146, 148, 154; Unger, 74-75, 205, 208-10, 230, 236, 237. A slight thread of Populist-style thinking ran through the debates on the legal-tender act of 1862. Some supported the measure as calculated to supply a currency not controlled by or profiting bankers at the expense of the common people. Hammond (3), 191, 222, 223. One opponent, on the other hand, more realistically saw the measure as useful to the bankers, providing them reserves on which they might multiply their own notes and credits. Id., 220-21. These comments added up only to a minor theme in the discussion, however.

236. Notes 193, 194, 201, 202, supra; cf. notes 139-42, 172, 173, 183, 191, 192, supra.

237. Beer, 84-88; Dorfman, 3:4-20, 114-17, 223-31; Friedman and Schwartz, 48-49, 113-19; Hofstadter (2), 66, 73-77, 104-5; Nugent, 57, 131, 137, 138, 143, 155, 157, 166-71, 213, 225; Sharkey, 102, 103, 108, 131-40, 165, 171, 220, 293-302; Unger, 5, 45, 49, 54, 59, 73-76, 145, 149, 151, 195, 200-202, 232, 256-57, 260, 263, 286, 289, 324, 350, 403-5. Bradley, J., concurring in Knox v. Lee, 12 Wallace 457, 554, 561 (U.S. 1871), argued for the original, wartime issue of legal-tender notes partly as representing a proper judgment by the Congress in the interests of class equality in financing the war. To meet the war emergency Congress might—as an alternative to borrowing by selling its bonds to "capitalists"—authorize the president to take private property for the public use by eminent domain, giving government certificates for what was taken. "Can the poor man's cattle, and horses, and corn, be thus taken by the government when the public exigency requires it, and cannot the rich man's bonds and notes be in like manner taken to reach the same end? If the government enacts that the certificates of indebtedness which it gives to the farmer for his cattle and provender shall be receivable by the farmer's creditors in payment of his bonds and notes, is it anything more than transferring the government

loan from the hands of one man to the hands of another–perhaps far more able to advance it? Is it anything more than putting the securities of the capitalist on the same platform as the farmer's stock?" As the text observes, this argument is a defensive one, rather than a claim of the legitimacy of regulating money to cause positive shifts in class position. Cf. Boudin, 2:175, 176.

238. 38 Stat. 251, 254, sec. 4, 260, sec. 10, 263, sec. 13, 265, sec. 14(d), 273, sec. 24; notes 203, 204, supra. The principal aid to agriculture was expected to flow from the general service of the system in easy expansion of the currency when needed and ready movement of funds from one section of the country to another. But, in addition, the statute for the first time permitted national banks to lend on farm mortgages and allowed rediscounting at federal reserve banks of six-month agricultural paper, while holding discountable commercial paper to shorter maturities. 38 Stat. 251 (1913), secs. 13, 24; Bogart, 815; Faulkner, 460-61; Link, 219-20, 222.

239. Land, 20; Link, 204, 214, 216, 217, 220, 224-27, 229, 236, 238.

240. 42 Stat. 620 (1922); David C. Elliott, 311.

241. Acheson, 174-78, 191; Benedict, 293-99; Bogart, 831; Faulkner, 769, 770; Krooss (1), 265; Lekachman, 118; Nussbaum, 181-85; Paris, 23, 40, 106; Schlesinger, 234, 237-41, 250-52. But, compare McReynolds, J., dissenting, in Norman v. Baltimore & Ohio Railroad, 294 U.S. 240, 361, 369 (1935), that "under the guise of pursuing a monetary policy, Congress really has inaugurated a plan primarily designed to destroy private obligations, repudiate national debts and drive into the Treasury all gold within the country, in exchange for inconvertible promises to pay, of much less value."

242. Faulkner, 763; Hacker and Zahler (2), 383-85; Lekachman, 117, 118; Morison and Commager, 2:593-96. In one limited respect Congress provided, and the president used, monetary authority for the advantage of a sharply identified particular interest, that of the silver miners. But the silver acquired under power given by the Thomas Amendment to the Agricultural Adjustment Act of 1933, and in the Silver Purchase Act of 1934–48 Stat. 53 (1933), 1178 (1934)–apparently did not make a great net addition to the money stock. Friedman and Schwartz, 484-88; Nussbaum, 192-95; Paris, 43, 49, 51, 54, 79.

243. Lawrence H. Chamberlain, 336-38; Friedman and Schwartz, 465, 469, 470, 518, note 13; Nussbaum, 181, 182; Paris, 18, 103; Schumpeter (1), 2:997; Stein (2), 41, 48; Williams, 631.

244. Freund, ch. 2; Hurst (3), 11-13; 18-23.

245. Commonwealth v. Alger, 7 Cushing 53 (Mass. 1851); Nebbia v. New York, 291 U.S. 502 (1934); Freund, ch. 1; Hurst (3), 40, 76, 80, 85, 88-96, 98, 102.

246. Compare McLean, J., for the Court in Briscoe v. Bank of the Commonwealth of Kentucky, 11 Peters 257, 312 (U.S. 1837): "There is no principle on which the sensibilities of communities are so easily excited, as that which acts upon the currency; none of which States are so jealous, as that which is restrictive of the exercise of sovereign powers." Indicative of the sensed breadth of concern with the money system are those aspects of public policy which treat the costs of providing a money supply as part social overhead costs and which stress the need of treating the particular elements of money as parts of a system. Notes 155-66, supra. Compare twentieth-century pleas, partly from distrust of government abuse of power, partly for efficiency (by reducing sources of uncertainty in economic decision making), that public agencies be neutral in private contests over distribution of income, or that money supply be controlled by a nondiscretionary rule written into statute. See Auerbach, 223, 224, 243 (Council of Economic Advisers' pleas for neutrality of gov-

ernment in wage and price decisions, short of inflationary crises); Barger, 257-67, 287-300, 330, and Friedman, 51-55 (appraisals of worth of a nondiscretionary rule governing money supply).

247. Note 125, supra.

248. Note 159, supra.

249. Note 202, supra; Part Two, infra, notes 229-30.

250. Notes 4-6, supra. See, also, Friedman, 41; Myrdal, 73; Triffin, 29.

251. Notes 10, 136, 169, supra.

252. Part Two, infra, notes 141-43. See, especially, Govan, 87, 93, 95, 97-98, 205-6, 210; W. B. Smith, 242-43, 291-92, note 22.

253. Timberlake, 168-71; cf. Raichle v. Federal Reserve Bank of New York, 34 Fed. (2d) 910, 912 (2d Cir. 1929).

254. Faulkner, 634; Friedman and Schwartz, 111, note 35; Morison and Commager, 2:252; cf. Taus, 87, 93, 94, 98-100.

255. Acheson, 167-74; Myers, 336; Nussbaum, 183. 38 Stat. 251 (1913), sec. 16, imposed gold reserve requirements on federal reserve bank deposits and circulating note issues, at 35 and 40 percent, respectively; 59 Stat. 237 (1945), sec. 1, put both kinds of reserves at a reduced 25 percent; 79 Stat. 5 (1965), sec. 1, dropped the requirement as to deposits; 82 Stat. 50 (1968), sec. 3, ended the requirement as to federal reserve notes. See Barger, 298. Abrogation of the gold reserve requirement was hastened by fears that the gold outflow which accompanied a persistent, large deficit in the country's balance of payments would grow further as foreigners saw the United States gold stock drawn down closer to the statutory cover. Cf. Commission on Money and Credit (1), 234; *New York Times,* 24 September 1963, p. 57, col. 1. But, even in this light, the step was primarily defensive of the national economy, rather than a move toward reordering the international system of money. The same can be said of earlier Treasury interventions in gold movements, in the 1936 sterilization of gold imports, and in the 1961-64 actions to hold up short-term interest rates to discourage loss of gold. Part Two, infra, note 410.

256. Friedman and Schwartz, 49; Nugent, chs. 8, 21; Nussbaum, 149, 151-52; Unger, 398, note 133.

257. Chandler, chs. 7-11; note 293, supra.

258. Morison and Commager, 2:502-5; Myers, 293-95.

259. Commission on Money and Credit (1), 232; Rostow, 202; Triffin, 50-53, 70, 80-82.

260. Barger, 299; Commission on Money and Credit (1), 212-13, 222, 233; id. (2), 249, 250; Myers, 363, 404, 407-8; Myrdal, 72, 76-77; Nussbaum, 222; Trescott, 248; Triffin, 8, 9, 10, 12, 54, 57.

261. Commission on Money and Credit (1), 213, 214; Myers, 399-404; Myrdal, 81-83; Rostow, 339, 356. But compare cautions, that effective monetary arrangements are important preventives of crisis, but will not suffice to move the world economy into productive growth. See Commission on Money and Credit (1), 226-31; Myrdal, 76-80, 86-88.

262. 59 Stat. 512 (1945) (the Bretton Woods Agreement Act); 60 Stat. 1401 (1946) (Articles of Agreement of the International Monetary Fund, dated 27 December 1946). Within the basic limits of subtraction from national control of money indicated by the original act, Congress steadily reaffirmed adherence to the IMF by agreeing to increase in the country's quota, enlarging authority for lending to the fund, and agreeing to the Special Drawing Rights scheme. 73 Stat. 80 (1959); 76 Stat. 105 (1962); 77 Stat. 334 (1968); 79 Stat. 119 (1965); 82 Stat. 188 (1968).

263. The agreement declared the intention to create "a permanent institution which provides the machinery for consultation and collaboration on international monetary problems." 60 Stat. 1401 (1946), Art. I (i). Under the agreement, the fund had capacity to act as an entity through its board of governors—consisting of one governor named by each member in such manner as the member determined—and for current operations through a body of executive directors under delegation from the board. 60 Stat. 1401 (1946), Art. XII, secs. 2 and 3. The declared goals looked to an interlock of international and national gains, as Article I (ii) set forth the fund's central aims "to facilitate the expansion and balanced growth of international trade, and to contribute thereby to the promotion and maintenance of high levels of employment and real income and to the development of the productive resources of all members as primary objectives of economic policy." Cf. Evans (2), 359; Myers, 363, 399; Myrdal, 74; Nussbaum, 215.

264. 60 Stat. 1401 (1946), Art. V, secs. 2, 3 (a) (i). Article V, section 3 (b) further specified that a member should not be entitled, without the fund's permission, to use the fund's resources to acquire currency to hold against forward exchange transactions. Article VI, section 1 (a) underlined the emphasis on servicing current transactions, by stipulating that a member might not make net use of the fund's resources to meet a large or sustained outflow of capital, though subsection (b) left the door open to using fund resources for capital transactions of reasonable amount required to expand exports or in the ordinary course of business, or to effect capital movements met out of a member's own resources, so long as those movements be in accord with the purposes of the fund. Cf. Commission on Money and Credit (1), 237; Myers, 363, 399.

265. 60 Stat. 1401 (1946), Art. III, sec. 2 (quota changes), sec. 3 (quota commitment); Art. IV, sec. 1 (a) (U.S. dollar as par), sec. 2 (gold purchases and sales to be held within prescribed limits), sec. 3 (limits on exchange rate variations), sec. 4 (members must cooperate to maintain exchange limits), sec. 5 (limits on changes in par value of member currency), sec. 6 (sanctions of loss of fund rights for violation); Art. VII, secs. 2, 3, 4 (unless with fund approval, no member may impose restrictions or discriminations on exchange, or deny current exchange to a member within fund). That membership in the fund entails some commitments and restrictions on the full scope of discretion members would otherwise enjoy over their monetary policy is noted in Commission on Money and Credit (1), 212-13; Evans (2), 358, 363; Friedman and Schwartz, 509, note 8; Hacker and Zahler (2), 545; Harris (2), 179; Myers, 363; Myrdal, 74; Nussbaum, 216-18.

266. Kolovrat v. Oregon, 366 U.S. 187, 198 (1961).

267. If there is conflict, a subsequent statute prevails over a treaty in the courts of the United States. The Cherokee Tobacco Case, 11 Wallace 616, 621 (U.S. 1871); Head Money Cases, 112 U.S. 580, 597 (1884). However the courts will not lightly impute to Congress an intent to abrogate or modify a treaty. Pigeon River Improvement, Slide & Boom Co. v. Cox, 291 U.S. 138, 160 (1934). 60 Stat. 1401 (1946), Art. IV, sec. 6, specified loss of fund privileges as the sanction for breach of the IMF Agreement. Cf. Evans (2), 358, 363; Harris (2), 178; Triffin, 94, 96-98, 100-101, 102.

268. Cf. Evans (2), 363; Harris (2), 179.

269. 59 Stat. 512 (1945), sec. 4 (a) (National Advisory Council on international monetary and financial problems), 5 (Congress must approve any change in United States quota, or par value of United States dollar, or other basic change in IMF agreement), 6 (federal reserve banks as depositories or fiscal agents). Cf. Friedman and Schwartz, 509, note 8; Myers, 363.

270. Commission on Money and Credit (1), 223, 237, 238; Myers, 399, 403; Nussbaum, 218, 219; Trescott, 249. *New York Times,* 8 September 1964, p. 43, col. 4. On the limited significance of the IMF for developing countries, compare Evans (2), 363; Myrdal, 291; Triffin, 97, 100.

271. Cf. Beard and Beard, 1:751, 2:248-49, 426-29, 719-20; Hacker and Kendrick, 232-33, 722; Lynd and Lynd (1), 80, 89, and (2), 13, 34, 41, 408-10; Potter, 122-27. See Veazie Bank v. Fenno, 8 Wallace 533, 549 (U.S. 1869).

272. Bogart, 680-82, 688-93; Faulkner, 629-40; Hacker and Kendrick, 207-15. Prime symbols of the capacity of monetary issues to create or foster social dissension are William Jennings Bryan's "Cross of Gold" speech in 1896, Krooss (3), 3:2009, and the recitals of the relation of the legal base of the money supply to the country's economic distress in the 1930s, in Norman v. Baltimore & Ohio Railroad, 294 U.S. 240, 295-97, 312, 315-16 (1935).

273. The Whiskey Rebellion of 1794 early symbolized the dependence of smooth government fiscal operations on an abundant, flexible money supply. Beard and Beard, 1:357; Bogart, 329; Hurst (4), 308. On the modern situation, see, e.g., Burkhead, 64-67; Evans (2), 169-71; Lekachman, 104-5; Pfiffner and Presthus, 386-87, 431-37.

274. Cf. Berle (3), 78-80, 83-84; Hurst (6), 54, 105, 107, 153, 163; Sutton et al., 217-20, 263.

275. Burkhead, 358-64, 366-68; Hyneman, 147-50; Pfiffner and Presthus, 373-75.

276. See the differences among commentators over the influence of statutory gold reserve requirements as a block to desirably flexible Federal Reserve responses to the 1930s deflation, cited in Part Two, infra, note 337. Cf. Schumpeter (2), 277-78.

277. Notes 48, 49, supra.

278. Dawson and Cooper, 727, 734, 735, 739, 743, 748, 749. In adjustments to inflationary destruction of paper money values in both the American Revolution and in the southern states in the Civil War, generally by statute or judge-made law it was determined that there would be no revaluation of the consideration given in executed transactions. Id., 171, 719. Legislation scaling debt obligations by measurement in different money units than those prevailing before extreme deflation usually referred to adjustment simply of contract debts; however, courts commonly gave a liberal interpretation to such statutes, applying them to money obligations in general, such as to trustees' money obligations. Id., 722, 727. In all instances a first step toward adjustment was—by statute or by judge-made law—to decide that parol evidence might be introduced to show that when the parties to a southern-state contract had stipulated in *dollars,* they meant Confederate paper dollars; the scaling statutes would not apply if the contract specified a gold measure of payment, or on the other hand showed clearly that the parties meant to assume the risk of settlement in whatever money was current at the debt's maturity. Id., 715, 716, 720, 721.

279. Home Building & Loan Association v. Blaisdell, 290 U.S. 398 (1934); Dawson and Cooper, 899; Hale, 206-9.

280. Dawson and Cooper, 899, 913, 916; Skilton, 73-77.

281. Ciriacy-Wantrup, 54-55; 70; Clark, 141-42; Hurst (4), 89, 128, and (5), 35, 36, 44, 50, 94, 102, 111-12, 124, 135, 220-21, 262-63, 602-3.

282. Cf. Clark, 40-42, 58-60, 139-42; Kapp, 14, 232-35; Schumpeter (2), 278.

283. Notes 235-37, supra.

II. Allocations of Control over the System of Money

The locations of formal and practical decision-making power have been of prime concern to many types of legal order. At an elementary level these matters concern any legal system which seeks to assert an effective monopoly of force in its society. They have presented issues especially marked for attention in the United States, where the constitutional ideal made further demands—that public policy should measure the legitimacy of all public and private organized power by standards of utility or justice. Thus, who should control the money supply and who should decide how to use law to affect the system of money were questions as much the focus of public policy as those concerning proper objectives of legal action regulating money. Indeed, allocation of control at times stirred controversy which influenced events more than issues over objectives, even to the detriment of accepted social functions of money; such were the consequences, notably, of Jackson's veto of a renewed charter for the second Bank of the United States and later of differences over the extent of centralized authority entrusted to the Federal Reserve Board.

Three types of issues concerning allocation of controls over money marked the course of public policy: (1) the relative authority of the national government and of the states; (2) the roles of private commercial banks, vis à vis regulation embodied in statutes or delegated by law to central bankers or to public administrators; (3) apportionment of power among the principal branches of government, and between these agencies and central bankers. Division of labor among various authorities fell into three well-marked patterns in time. One course of policy emerged from 1787 through 1860, another from 1861 to about 1908, and the third from 1908 into the 1970s. The three types of allocation issues are not equally prominent in each of the three time periods. But each time period shows a sufficient character of its own to warrant taking them as the principal framework for analysis, and examining the relative treatment of allocations issues within each time division.

ALLOCATIONS OF CONTROL OVER MONEY: 1787-1860

National and State Authority over Money

The federal Constitution gave a strong nationalist lead to policy regarding money. It laid impressive restrictions on the states, explicitly forbidding them to coin money or regulate its value, to emit bills of credit, or to make any thing but gold or silver legal tender. Moreover, the contract clause limited the states' capacity to impose their own ideas of legal tender indirectly, by stay laws which might prevent creditors from enforcing claims to lawful money. Though the framers less sharply defined the authority they granted Congress, the Constitution indicated that the central government should have authority to assert full and exclusive control of the system of money, if it chose to do so. The Constitution explicitly authorized Congress to coin money, to regulate its value, and to punish counterfeiting, and in the setting of contemporary discussion it implied some authority to issue a paper currency and to create legal tender. Both the text and the debates ignored the authority either of Congress or the states over banks, as possible contributors to the money supply. The unhelpful silence on banks left room for the main developments of policy regarding allocation of power between the central government and the states over money in the next seventy years.[1]

In its first generation the nation realized much of the potential with which the Constitution clearly endowed the central government for controlling money policy. Under its authority to coin money Congress early created a mint.[2] The Constitution was so plain, that no state ever challenged the United States monopoly of official coinage within the federal system.[3] Under its authority to regulate the value of money Congress in 1792 also created a standard notation scheme, defining a dollar unit and the decimal pattern of calculation. Again, the Constitution was too plain for question; no state ever challenged that within the federal system it was Congress's exclusive prerogative to define money units.[4] Congress used its clear authority to punish counterfeiting, in laws which reached out to embrace related conduct, and the Court had no difficulty in sustaining this broader reach as necessary and proper to fulfill the core grant of power.[5] On the other hand, policy did not require treating the power to act against counterfeiters as resting solely in the federal government. True, the authorizations to coin money and regulate its value sought to achieve a standard of uniformity which required exclusive power in the nation. But, the interest of national uniformity could be served by state as well as by federal penalties on counterfeiting, and the Court sensibly ruled so.[6]

The law moved onto less sure ground where governments undertook directly or indirectly to create paper money or to promote and regulate the creation of private credit. The first issue of the federal balance of power of this type arose in 1791 when Congress chartered the first Bank of the United States, and further controversial developments attended creation of the second bank in 1816. The policy battles over these institutions were shaped so much by the growth of state-chartered banks that we can better examine the two Banks of the United States after considering some legal developments affecting the terms of state authority.

Meanwhile, we should note another thread of policy concerning direct action by the federal government—the issue of United States Treasury notes. Secretary of the Treasury Hamilton had thought that in its own actions Congress should observe the spirit of the Constitution's ban on state bills of credit:

> Though paper emissions, under a general authority, might have some advantages not applicable, and be free from some disadvantages which are applicable, to the like emissions by the States separately, yet they are of a nature so liable to abuse—and, it may even be affirmed, so certain of being abused—that the wisdom of the government will be shown in never trusting itself with the use of so seducing and dangerous an expedient. In times of tranquillity it might have no ill consequences—it might even perhaps be managed in a way to be productive of good; but in great and trying emergencies, there is almost a moral certainty of its becoming mischievous. The stamping of paper is an operation so much easier than the laying of taxes, that a government in the practice of paper emissions would rarely fail, in any such emergency, to indulge itself too far in the employment of that resource, to avoid, as much as possible, one less auspicious to present popularity.[7]

Hamilton's success in obtaining a national bank meant that for the time there was no occasion to press his warning. On the whole the first Bank of the United States met those fiscal needs of the federal government which the ordinary flow of revenue did not satisfy. Thus there was no issue of Treasury notes from 1789 to 1812. But, on the heels of Congress's refusal in 1811 to renew the bank's charter, the War of 1812 brought heavy financial demands on the government. The Treasury issued interest-bearing notes in 1812, 1813, and 1814. Some opposed the first of these issues, partly from expressed fear that the people and the banks would not accept them in place of specie, that the government would not command resources to redeem them, and that hence they would depreciate as had the bills of the Continental Congress. Proponents argued successfully that the notes would achieve currency because the law made them receivable for dues owed to the government, as well as paying interest on them, backed by such taxing authority in the new central government as the Congress had not enjoyed under the Articles of Confederation. Thus the debate showed sensitivity to relations of Treasury note issues to the general money supply. However, until a further issue in 1815 the notes were in denominations too large for general circulation, and the government would exchange the smaller as well as the larger notes for other securities of yields sufficiently attractive that even the smaller notes tended to be converted. The 1815 issue was of bearer notes without interest, in denominations from three, five, and ten dollars upward, receivable in payments to the United States without time limit. These apparently circulated to some extent, since the government repeatedly reissued the notes after their conversion into bonds.[8] Though these note issues occasioned some policy debate, they were so plainly tied to the government's need to borrow that they raised no substantial constitutional question. But, for the same reason they created only a limited precedent for Congress's power to provide a national currency.[9]

With the opportunism that so often marked arguments on the constitutionality of money laws, lawmakers in the late 1830s tangled the question of Treasury notes with that of a national bank. Advocates of a large issue of Treasury notes in 1837 argued that it was needed to supply more currency, after expiration of the charter of the second Bank of the United States. Such hard-money men as Senator Thomas Hart Benton opposed the issue precisely because the notes might be used as currency. On the other hand, advocates of a third Bank of the United States opposed fresh Treasury issues because they preferred notes of a new national bank. Congress authorized issues of Treasury notes in 1837 and in 1838, against objections that they were bills of credit and that Congress lacked authority to create such instruments.[10] Questions both of constitutional power and of policy were more sharply drawn in 1844, when the House Ways and Means Committee declared its belief that Treasury notes carrying a nominal interest and convertible into coin on demand were in effect bills of credit. The committee felt that there was not a true borrowing where the Treasury bound itself to repay in coin on demand; thus the committee found the notes to be *ultra vires,* since the statute on which they were based authorized only true borrowings. Beyond this, the committee thought that when the federal Convention struck out an explicit authorization to Congress to emit bills of credit, it meant to exclude the issue of federal government paper primarily for currency. The precedent effect of this episode was blurred, however. Some of the disputed notes were issued before the committee spoke, and the whole transaction went on within the distorting context of partisan maneuvers between Whigs and Democrats.[11] Treasury note issues in 1847 and 1857 seem to have been incident only to regular borrowing, and in any event their passage added nothing to the record on Congress's authority to create a national currency. Thus, up to 1860 legislative practice reinforced and perhaps somewhat extended the policy indicated in the federal Convention—that Congress might authorize circulating paper as an incident to borrowing—but gave scant basis for claiming an independent power to provide a government-issue currency.[12] The one proposal (1814) to give legal-tender status to any of these pre-1860 Treasury note issues was decisively voted down by the House.[13]

Back of the Constitution's declaration that "no state shall . . . emit bills of credit" were bitter memories of the destructive inflation which accompanied the issue of paper money by the states and the Continental Congress in the Revolution. Tangled with this distrust of government-issued circulating paper was an equal distaste for state laws that hindered regular enforcement of creditors' rights—displeasure expressed in the Constitution's linked command that "no state shall . . . make any thing but gold and silver coin a tender in payment of debts."[14] This is about all that the text of the Constitution and the contemporary record tell about the meaning of the ban on state bills of credit; what particular content the prohibition held, it must gain largely from future development.[15] From the outset the ban stood under considerable tension. It reflected conservative desires for stable economic calculations, which had been outraged by the revolutionary experience. But, also, it ran against the bias of an optimistically striving society, which sought to enlarge production, multiply transactions, and win such speculative capital gains as were promised by the rise of business and population. Whether they moved to promote economic growth or to combat economic distress, sizable interests wanted freedom to use law wherever the law promised to be a helpful tool. The legal instruments closest to hand were those in the gift of state legislatures. Thus, there was much impatience with limiting the power of states to deal with the economy. In the field of monetary policy this impatience was sharpened by distrust of such relatively remote, centralized authority as that represented by the second Bank of the United States.[16]

Within the federal system no state challenged the ban on bills of credit by directly issuing its own currency; however uncertain, the reach of the Constitution's prohibition plainly forbade this.[17] The growth of policy turned on questions of permissible specialization or delegation of roles under state law, affecting the money supply. When did a *state* create currency? Might creation of money tokens be so tied to particular, segregated assets as to remove the hazards of undisciplined sovereign will? Events moved along two lines of development: (1) resort by states to centralized, statutory agencies of economic promotion; (2) expansion of privately managed, commercial banking under state charters. The second of these proved to be the line of major, lasting effect, and concern for it determined, finally, how the law dealt with the first.

In 1821 Missouri's legislature tried to relieve debtor farmers by setting up state offices authorized to issue certificates to a maximum of $200,000, ranging in value from 50¢ to $10, which the state would lend to any one borrower on real estate security in amounts up to $1,000 and to one offering security in personal property in amounts up to $200. The program sought both to provide fresh credit for distressed debtors and a circulating medium for the general benefit of a lagging economy.[18] The plan was not a success. But, as an aftermath, it generated lawsuits, including an action by the state on promissory notes given for loan office certificates. The debtors resisted, arguing that the consideration for their notes was illegal, since it consisted in state bills of credit. In 1830, in *Craig* v. *Missouri*, the United States Supreme Court held for the debtors, in a four to three decision; Chief Justice John Marshall spoke for the majority.[19]

None of the justices in *Craig* disputed that the loan offices were official agencies of the state; this program was one of direct state action, and the legal challenge to it presented a square clash of federal and state authority affecting money.[20] Marshall put his rather fuzzy opinion on three findings. First, the loan office certificates were not true instruments of state borrowing, because they were not issued in return for money or services made available for the state's present use.[21] Second, the certificates showed the state's intent that they should circulate as money. They were issued in low denominations and were made receivable for dues owed to the state or to its local governments and in payment for salt purchased from lessees of state-owned salt lands.[22] Third, the certificates were declared redeemable at a future day, partly on the pledge of all debts then or later due to the state, but also on the general faith of the state.[23] The majority opinion and one of the dissenters agreed that the fact that the Missouri law did not declare the loan office certificates to be legal tender did not bring them outside the constitutional ban—a conclusion historically well based.[24]

The dissenters in *Craig* focused largely on concern that the decision improperly encroached on the states' conceded authority to borrow and to issue evidences of debt incident to borrowing. However we assess their difference with Marshall over what kinds of transactions truly were borrowings, this debate in itself casts little light on the scope which the Constitution might allow the states in affecting the money supply.[25] But, there was another interplay between majority and dissent which bore more directly on the federal allocation of power over money. Marshall felt that the Court should construe the ban on state bills of credit with a vigor sympathetic to the substance of the policy for which the ban stood. Back of the constitutional limitation had been fear of likely unchecked expansion in the quantity of currency that states might issue. "Such a medium," Marshall cautioned, "has been always liable to considerable fluctuation. Its value is continually changing; and these changes, often great and sudden, expose individuals to immense loss, are the sources of ruinous speculations, and destroy all confidence between man and man."[26] The dissenters countered, that the danger of uncontrolled, inflationary issues arose where the sovereign put out money simply on its general credit. Missouri's loan certificates did not raise the peril against which the bills-of-credit ban stood, because Missouri had provided a distinct fund for their redemption, pledging therefor especially all proceeds of the state's salt springs and all debts due or to become due to the state, while providing the functional equivalent of another redemption fund by making the certificates receivable for dues owed to the state.[27] To dissenting Justice Smith Thompson, "These are guards and checks against . . . depreciation [of the certificates] by insuring their ultimate redemption." The defect of the bills issued before the Constitution was that, since they were "not . . . bottomed upon any fund constituted for their redemption, but resting solely for that purpose upon the credit of the State issuing the same," it followed that "there was no check, therefore, upon excessive issues, and a great depreciation and loss to holders of such bills followed as matter of course. But when a fund is pledged, or ample provision made for the redemption of a bill or voucher, whatever it may be called, there is but little danger of a depreciation or loss."[28]

By attaching significance to a pledged redemption fund, the *Craig* dissenters made a constructive effort to put more functional content into the Constitution's ill-defined ban on state "bills of credit."[29] However, their reliance on the redemption fund is ultimately unconvincing, because the Missouri statute included no formula tying the amount of loan certificates to the amount of pledged assets. True, the statute set a $200,000 ceiling on the total issue. But nothing in Missouri law prevented the legis-

lature from raising the ceiling. Thus, though Marshall did not come squarely to grips with the dissenters' redemption-fund rationale, he seems warranted in finding that the Missouri loan certificates fell within the historic
fear of potentially unlimited issues.[30]

Contemporary with the Missouri legislation which eventually produced
Craig, in 1820 Kentucky sought to relieve its distressed debtors by chartering the Bank of the Commonwealth of Kentucky, authorized to issue
notes for circulation. As in *Craig,* a borrower from the Kentucky bank resisted enforcement of his debt, claiming that the instrument on which the
bank sued had been made in consideration of the bank's loan of its notes,
which were bills of credit emitted in violation of the federal Constitution.[31] Division within a Court reduced by illness postponed decision of
the Kentucky case from 1834 to 1837. In 1837, after Marshall's death, a
reconstituted Court decided *Briscoe* v. *Bank of the Commonwealth of
Kentucky,* in substance overruling *Craig* v. *Missouri.* There was a dissent by
Justice Joseph Story, only survivor of the *Craig* majority; he said that
Chief Justice Marshall would have joined him in dissent.[32]

Briscoe made an unconvincing attempt to establish that there was no
emission of bills by the state under the Kentucky statute. True, the Bank
of the Commonwealth was a distinct, corporate entity, whose charter gave
its president and directors no power formally to bind the state, but did
vest in them authority to decide the time and circumstances in which they
would issue the amount of notes the charter authorized. True, also, by its
charter the bank might be sued on its notes, while no action lay against the
state.[33] But Story's dissent devastated the majority's claim that *the state*
was not the acting party. So far as the bank held a capital stock, the capital was promised wholly by the state, mainly by grant of proceeds of sales
of the state's lands; indeed (in pointed, if implicit, criticism of the Bank of
the United States) the Kentucky charter stipulated that no individual or
corporation be permitted to own or pay for any part of the bank's capital.
As sole stockholder, the state was alone entitled to any earnings of the
bank, and the charter said that net interest earned on the bank's loans
should be deemed part of the state's revenues, subject to the legislature's
disposal. The legislature chose the president and directors by joint ballot
of both houses, and might remove them at its pleasure. The state might at
any time repeal the charter.[34]

So far as we can extract a workable formula from McLean's muddy
opinion, the saving factor for the bank's notes is ruled to be their tie to a
segregated redemption fund—the criterion which the dissenters had advanced in *Craig.* McLean found that the notes contained no pledge of the
faith of the state, but rather declared that they were issued on the credit
of the bank's funds.

The capital, it is true, was to be paid by the State; but in making loans, the bank was required to take good securities, and these constituted a fund to which the holders of the notes could look for payment, and which could be made legally responsible. In this respect the notes of this bank were essentially different from any class of bills of credit which are believed to have been issued. The notes were not only payable in gold and silver, on demand, but there was a fund, and in all probability, a sufficient fund, to redeem them. This fund was in possession of the bank, and under the control of the president and directors. But whether the fund was adequate to the redemption of the notes issued, or not, is immaterial to the present inquiry. It is enough that the fund existed, independent of the State, and was sufficient to give some degree of credit to the paper of the bank.[35]

That, by its charter, the bank might be sued on its notes was apparently taken as further evidence that the notes stood on the separate credit of the institution. In contrast to this pattern, in *Craig* assets of the state and the faith of the state were pledged to redeem the Missouri loan office certificates.[36]

McLean nowhere clearly explains why provision of a separate redemption fund should take the Kentucky bank notes out of the prohibition on bills of credit. Dissenting in *Craig,* Justice Thompson had indicated that the virtue of a pledged redemption fund was that legislation which authorized issue of notes against such a pledge did not invite the unbridled expansion which had been the downfall of the bills of credit on which the Constitution frowned.[37] In *Briscoe,* Justice John McLean intimated this reasoning when he said that to constitute the forbidden bills of credit, the issuers must act only as state agents, not incur any personal responsibility, "nor impart, as individuals, any credit to the paper." Cautious not to condition his ruling on the adequacy of the redemption fund, he emphasized that the crux was "that the fund existed, independently of the State."[38] Reliance upon a separate, pledged fund in *Briscoe* carried the same flaw as in *Craig*: No more than in Missouri did Kentucky law embody a formula to limit the quantity of circulating paper by the quantity of pledged assets, or to put any limit on the power of future legislatures to multiply issues. Appraised in light of this omission in the challenged Kentucky legislation, the decision in *Briscoe* substantially overruled *Craig* v. *Missouri.*[39] Despite the want of a binding limit on such issues of circulating paper, later decisions remained content with the separate-fund rationale.[40]

Relative to the system of money as a whole, the prime importance of the various opinions in *Craig* and *Briscoe* lay not in their rulings on paper issues of state-owned banks, but in their dicta upholding the legality of notes issued by private, commercial banks incorporated under state statutes. A number of states besides Kentucky chartered state-owned, note-issuing banks which—like Kentucky's bank—were in substance state agencies. Some of these banks operated responsibly, with benefit to local economies. But this type of institution proved too limited in assets and in reach of business to pre-empt the roles that bankers played in the money supply. Through the first quarter of the nineteenth century private commercial banks, empowered to issue circulating notes, figured heavily in the growing number of business corporations which state legislatures created by special charters. By the 1830s such banks numbered well over three hundred, and their circulating notes formed the largest component of the money stock.[41]

In this state of affairs the dissenters in *Craig* v. *Missouri* expressed concern that the breadth of Marshall's concept of the ban on state bills of credit would invalidate the circulating paper of all state-chartered banks. Though at one point Marshall spoke of bills issued "by a State government," he seemed to cast a wider net when he also defined the forbidden bills as "a paper medium, intended to circulate between individuals and between government and individuals, for the ordinary purposes of society."[42] The text of the Constitution was consistent with either a restrictive or an extensive construction. The Constitution's command was that "No State" should emit bills of credit. But a state could act only through agents; the constitutional language left scope for future federal lawmakers to decide how broadly or narrowly they would identify issuers of circulating paper as state agents. The contemporary context of the Constitution gave little help. Plainly, back of the ban on state bills of credit was deep fear of paper money inflation; himself steeped in the experience out of which the Constitution came, Marshall said in *Craig* that the intent of the bills-of-credit clause was "to cut up this mischief by the roots," with the implication that the Court should exert itself to insure full force to the prohibition.[43] On the other hand, the "mischief" which the framers had experienced was direct issue of paper currency by governments. When the Constitution was adopted, only two incorporated private banks were operating, and these of local influence and effect; that such institutions might become the principal suppliers of money was an idea which the framers had no basis for conceiving, and there is no evidence that they did.[44] All the historic examples of emission of bills of credit to which Marshall's opinion referred were direct actions by governments, the Missouri case itself involved action by a state office—as Marshall pointed out—and nothing in his *Craig* opinion plainly touched private banks.[45] Moreover, in his earlier opinion for the Court in *McCulloch* v. *Maryland* (1819) Marshall accepted the power to create corporations, including banking corporations, as a normal appurtenance of sovereignty, and observed that "the existence of state banks can have no possible influence on the question" of Congress's authority to create a national bank.[46] Nonetheless, the private bank question was obviously a sensitive one to Justices McLean and Thompson, who indicated that a material factor in their dissents in *Craig* was the fear that the majority decision would eventually have effect to bar all notes issued by any state-chartered banks.[47]

Speaking for the Court in *Briscoe,* McLean came close to justifying the decision in favor of the notes of the state-owned bank not so much on the merits of that institution as on the need to avoid casting doubt on the lawful note-issuing capacity of private banks chartered by the states. This was a possibility laden with such unsettlement to the economy that he felt it must be put to rest: The idea that the ban on state bills of credit might prohibit state bank notes generally "is startling, as it strikes a fatal blow against the State banks, which have a capital of nearly four hundred millions of dollars, and which supply almost the entire circulating medium of the country."[48] Though he thus made plain that his prime focus was on economic policy, McLean found two legal arguments for a calculated dictum upholding the validity of notes of state-chartered private banks. First, he could properly say that prevailing opinion and practice recognized that authority to create business corporations was part of the general legislative power which the states inherited upon the Revolution, with no exception drawn against chartering banks.[49] At the time, the issue of circulating notes was a familiar incident of banking; thus, authority to charter banks might fairly be taken, so far as state law was concerned, to include authority to sanction their note issues. More dubiously, McLean sought to read the intent of those who adopted the federal Constitution by appeal to banking practice before 1789. Since the Bank of North America and the Massachusetts Bank were then operating and issuing notes, McLean argued that the framers could not have thought that their ban on state bills of credit applied to the familiar paper of these existing banks. The argument is hardly convincing. There were but these two chartered banks then, their notes were of too-limited reach to have brought them into the framers' awareness as part of the problem at which the bills-of-credit clause was aimed, and there is no evidence that the operations of such private banks were then considered as part of that problem.[50] More relevant was official practice since the Constitution. By the time of *Craig* and *Briscoe* the states had incorporated many note-issuing private commercial banks; somewhat less than 100 such institutions were chartered before 1812, but the number doubled by 1815, and despite some slowing and many failures, by 1830 there were 329 of them.[51] McLean's *Briscoe* dictum gave weight to this record: "A uniform course of action, involving the right to the exercise of an important power by the State governments for half a century, and this almost without question, is no unsatisfactory evidence that the power is rightfully exercised."[52]

Justice Story dissented from the decision in *Briscoe,* but agreed with McLean's calculated dictum validating notes of state-chartered private banks. Story "utterly" denied that issues of all state-chartered banks must fall with those of Kentucky's state-owned, state-managed institution. The vigor with which he pressed this point suggests that he estimated his colleagues' decision to be at least as much moved by their concern for the private banks which were not parties to the lawsuit as for the state bank which was immediately under challenge.[53] But Story went as much out of his way as McLean to validate the notes of the privately owned and managed banks. To that end he adopted the separate-fund criterion which was the key reliance of McLean and Thompson. However, Story made still more explicit the dispersed-power rationale of the separate-fund test, as showing that the notes were not issued on the general credit of the state:

> When banks are created upon private capital, they stand upon that capital, and their credit is limited to the personal or corporate responsibility of the stockholders, as provided for in the charter. If the corporate stock, and that only, by the charter is made liable for the debts of the bank, and that capital stock is paid in, every holder of its bills must be presumed to trust exclusively to the fund thus provided, and the general credit of the corporation. And in such a case, a State owning a portion of the funds, and having paid in its share of the capital stock, is treated like every other stockholder, and is understood to incur no public responsibility whatsoever. . . . [But] in the present case, the Legislature expressly prohibited any partnership, or participation with other persons in this bank. It set it up, exclusively upon the capital of the State, as the exclusive property of the State and subject to the exclusive management of the State, through its exclusive agents.[54]

No more than his colleagues did Story explain why provision for funds back of bank notes should take such issues out of the evil aimed at by the federal ban on state bills of credit, where state laws did not tie the quantity of notes issues to the size of the funds. Perhaps his emphasis on "banks . . . created upon private capital" implied that he relied on a check by market forces to remove the hazards of excessive issues where the state was directly in control. Certainly Story did not mean to write off all curbs by the national government on state laws affecting the money supply. For he took pains to note that the authority of states to charter note-issuing private banks was "subject always to the control of Congress, whose powers extend to the entire regulation of the currency of the country."[55]

Briscoe seems wrong in holding that the notes of Kentucky's state-owned, and essentially state-managed bank did not fall within the ban on state bills of credit. Certainly the decision chose a restrictive rather than a sympathetic reading of the ban, and in temper if not in formal statement it overruled *Craig*. But, in light of the silence of the constitutional record and the validating force of a generation of legislative practice, the deliberate dicta legitimizing note issues of state-chartered private commercial banks were well grounded and stood thereafter unchallenged.[56] Other developments of policy built on this basis of state legislative authority, but also on Story's forecast of ultimate federal power.

Against this background of the growth and constitutional legitimizing of state-chartered, note-issuing banks, we can now better place the meaning of events concerning Congress's authority to charter national banks. The text and setting of the Constitution left the matter open.[57] In one of his boldest strokes of policy, Secretary of the Treasury Hamilton promptly undertook to establish this federal power by using it. Hamilton put to Congress the plan of a single national bank, defended its constitutionality against the objections of Secretary of State Thomas Jefferson in a memorandum requested by President George Washington, and saw the proposal through to enactment in 1791.[58] Given the stout objections raised on constitutional grounds, Congress's creation of the first Bank of the United States set a major legislative precedent for this scope of congressional power.[59] Congress's failure to extend the charter upon its expiration in 1811 occurred in the context of renewed argument that the central government lacked constitutional authority. But the 1811 decision was so colored by party strife, by the competitive jealousy of other banks, and by hostility to foreign ownership of some of the bank's stock, that it cannot realistically be read to repudiate the prior constitutional precedent.[60] The constitutional question seemed to be raised almost ritualistically when Congress chartered the second Bank of the United States in 1816; on the whole record, the action was taken without serious doubt of the national authority, and with the support of President Madison, who had been a prime challenger of Congress's power to set up the first bank.[61] The new-felt, practical power of the second bank, sharpened in impact by early mismanagement, produced renewed constitutional challenge. Opponents questioned Congress's power again in 1819, in an abortive effort to repeal the charter, and over the bank's first five years several states sought to use taxes or exclusionary laws to keep the bank from operating within their borders. The state laws produced the Court's decisions in *McCulloch* v.

Maryland (1819) and *Osborn* v. *Bank of the United States* (1824), affirming the power of Congress and striking down state taxes designed to interfere with the federal policy.[62] With better management and better times, the constitutional question faded through the 1820s, only to be revived sharply as Jackson's opposition to renewing the charter moved to climax in 1832. Jackson's veto put him on record as denying that Congress had constitutional authority to find that such an institution as Nicholas Biddle had shaped was necessary and proper to the execution of federal powers. But Jackson made no wholesale denial of Congress's authority to create some form of national bank; indeed, his message reserved wholesome discretion in Congress and the president to shape policy on that score. Moreover, the veto message so mixed arguments of policy and of constitutionality as to make impossible a plain demarcation of such constitutional precedent as the veto constituted.[63] In 1841 President John Tyler vetoed two attempts to charter a third national bank, set up on lines more restrictive than those of its predecessors, but still with capacity to play a role in the national economy. Tyler took the stand that he was protecting the federal balance; bank credit was a local matter, and a national institution might not be empowered to set up branches in the states without the positive consent of the states.[64]

Such is the skeletal story of legislative and judicial precedent regarding Congress's authority to create a national bank. But the substance of the matter lay in what the lawmakers did to define the purposes for which the authority might be used. At this point the course of policy is less clear. The record shows two areas of development, each marked by some ambiguity: (1) There was concern over the relative spheres of policy of the central government and of the states, as these might be affected by a national bank, but this concern was not throughout so plainly focused on monetary goals as hindsight might lead us to expect. (2) The Banks of the United States presented a lively issue between central banking power and dispersed banking power—and in that sense another issue of a "federal" character. But this issue tended to be drawn less as one of the relative authority of central and state governments than of the relative roles of money management and a banking market. Postponing this second matter to the next section, let us here take stock of the extent to which the issue of the federal balance of power was seen as one of authority over monetary policy.

Hamilton recommended a national bank to the Congress both as a useful fiscal agent of government programs, and also as an instrument to promote the national economy by activating capital and stimulating transactions, by creating currency and credit to augment specie. In his opinion to President Washington, focusing rather on constitutionality than on economic goals, he gave most of his attention to defining the general scope of national power and to demonstrating that Congress might create a fiscal agent as necessary and proper to its powers to tax, borrow, and maintain the armed services. However, he grounded his proposal, also, on the proposition that Congress might regulate (and enlarge) the money supply not only to aid its taxing power, but also to regulate commerce among the states, by creating a nationally useful medium of exchange, promoting "a full circulation by preventing the frequent displacement of the metals in reciprocal remittances," and adding a paper currency to the stock of coin.[65] What Hamilton argued in supporting the role of a national monetary agency in affecting the national economy was the more pointed because it responded to Jefferson's flat denial that this was a field of effort which might properly engage the national government at all; to Jefferson it then seemed that whether banks might contribute to the money supply was a matter wholly of the domestic economies of the states, to be regulated entirely by state law as was the ordinary law of contract or property.[66] Consistent with Hamilton's arguments, its charter endowed the bank with capacity to pursue a national monetary policy by creating currency and credit under a centralized direction, effecting its policy through a nationwide network of branches. Moreover, the charter's preamble contemplated that the bank's services would not only be to public finance, but should also "be productive of considerable advantages to trade and industry in general."[67] Thus the first legislative precedent might be read as asserting Congress's authority to create an instrument of national monetary policy in aid of an economy conceived as of national scope.

But this aspect of national power was less sharply defined in a good deal of later policy debate. Those who opposed renewing the first bank's charter in 1811 talked about invasion of states' rights, but the opposition seemed to stem more from partisan jousting and from the business jealousy of state-chartered banks than from concern that state policy makers should have a free hand to set monetary policy for state economies.[68] In 1816, discussion of chartering the second bank included some reference to need of national regulation of currency. But Congress—as was natural, given the recent difficulties of financing the War of 1812—focused mainly on restoring to the national government the fiscal agent it needed.[69] In sweeping terms *McCulloch* v. *Maryland* (1819) upheld Congress's authority to create a national bank and to empower it to effect its policies through branches, free of state taxes designed to bar its operations. But Marshall devoted himself to expounding the general character of national power and said nothing about regulating the system of money except as such regulation might serve the government's own operations.[70] Marshall's handling of *Osborn* v. *Bank of the United States* (1824) suggests that he did not grasp, or was not interested in Hamilton's perception that to regulate the general money supply might be a legitimizing function of a national bank. Marshall explained that Ohio might not tax the general business done by the bank, not because the bank was fulfilling a proper federal function in regulating the money supply as such, but because the bank's issue of currency and extension of credit to private persons were operations necessary and proper to the bank's existence as a fiscal agent of the United States.[71] Justice William Johnson dissented in *Osborn* on jurisdictional grounds, but was prepared in a proper case to uphold Congress's power to charter a national bank to promote a sound national economy by regulating the money supply. Johnson put the matter bluntly, as one of division of powers within the federal system over the control of money, and not merely as an issue of power to create a federal fiscal agent:

> Had [the Bank's] effects . . . and the views of its framers, been confined exclusively to its fiscal uses, it is more than probable that this suit, and the laws in which it originated, would never have had existence. But it is well known, that with that object was combined another, of a very general and not less important character. The expiration of the charter of the former bank, led to state creations of banks; each new bank increased the facilities of creating others; and the necessities of the general government, both to make use of the state banks for their deposits, and to borrow largely of all who would lend to them, produced that rage for multiplying banks, which, aided by the emoluments derived to the states in their creation, and the many individual incentives which they developed, soon inundated the country with a new description of bills of credit, against which it was obvious that the provisions of the constitution opposed no adequate inhibition. A specie-paying bank, with an overwhelming capital, and the whole aid of the government deposits, presented the only resource to which the government could resort, to restore that power over the currency of the country, which the framers of the constitution evidently intended to give to Congress alone. But this necessarily involved restraint upon individual cupidity, and the exercise of a state power; and, in the nature of things, it was hardly possible for the mighty effort necessary to put down an evil spread so wide and arrived to such maturity, to be made without embodying against it an immense moneyed combination, which could not fail of making its influence to be felt, wherever its claimances could reach, or its industry and wealth be brought to operate.[72]

In effect, Justice Johnson was recognizing the monetary-control functions which Nicholas Biddle's practice developed, in using the legal apparatus and economic power of the bank to affect the issue of currency and the creation of credit by state-chartered banks. Biddle's course might be taken to be a practical construction, evidencing Congress's constitutional authority to use a national bank for monetary goals. But the second bank's activity along this line was not sufficiently consistent, long-lived, or uncontested, to allow its conduct the weight which the Court has sometimes assigned to executive practice in interpreting the Constitution; moreover, as a private delegate of public-interest functions, the bank had questionable title to such deference as might be accorded the practice of official agencies. [73]

The taxes and regulations with which several states sought to exclude the second bank and some arguments made for repealing the charter in 1819, in effect asserted that within the federal system the regulation of that part of the money supply created by bank notes and bank credit was the business of the states, at least to the extent that state policy in that domain should be free of federal control. But, as Justice Johnson acutely observed in *Osborn,* the impetus of challenge here derived as much from the desire of one set of business competitors to rid themselves of another, as it did in claims of state policy makers to govern state economies in order to protect distressed local debtors and encourage local venture. The two interests were too much entwined to let us count these state actions or the arguments for states' rights as clear-cut assertions simply of an issue of federalism. [74]

Jackson's opposition to renewing the bank's charter brought only partly into focus the issue of federal-state roles in monetary policy. In December 1830 Jackson seemed ready to concede so much national monetary control as could be exerted by a national bank stripped of its power to issue currency or make loans, and able to discipline state banks only so far as it could do so by refusing to accept their notes in payments to the United States if the notes were not kept redeemable in specie. Jackson's expressed concern here was, in part, that "the states would be strengthened by having in their hands the means of furnishing the local paper currency through their own banks." [75] At sharp variance with the president, the House Ways and Means Committee in 1830 found that a prime justification for using federal power through the bank was precisely that the bank had promoted a more adequate, stable, uniform national money supply. [76] In an unpublished opinion in June 1831, Attorney General Roger B. Taney advised the president that the bank's power to open branches without the consent of the states and its large banking powers were not necessary and proper incidents to its service as fiscal agent of the United States. But Taney's objections here did not seem addressed to the federal balance of power affecting monetary policy. His prime concerns were, first, with the balance of power between a bank threatening monopoly as opposed to the general market for bank credit and currency, and, second, with political relations between a privately run government agency and the government which, though its creator, might be overawed by it.[77] These same emphases were strong in Jackson's 1832 veto message, which had relatively little reference to federal-state distribution of authority over monetary policy as such. The veto message cast doubt on Congress's authority to create a paper currency, but chose more firmly to deny that Congress had authority to delegate creation of currency to a private corporation—a matter, it would seem, less of the federal balance than of the separation of powers within the central government itself.[78] The same may be said of Jackson's argument that Congress and not the bank should decide on establishing branches; the most pointed concern here expressed for state power was not regarding the states' role in monetary policy, but regarding their capacity to raise revenue by taxing banking done within their borders.[79]

Altogether, the Jacksonian attack did not yield a well-defined issue over allocating federal-state power affecting the system of money. Nor was the issue much better drawn in Tyler's two muddled veto messages in 1841. In Tyler's view, experience showed that the national bank's "discount" (credit-creating) business had not been a necessary and proper incident either of regulating the currency or of assisting public finance. As had Jefferson in 1791—but with no warrant in the more nationally interlocked economy of the 1840s—Tyler claimed that banks' creation of credit was purely local in economic impact and policy relevance.[80] In any case, this was an appraisal of business fact more than of constitutional doctrine. Tyler drew the issue of federal-state power more sharply when he objected to creating a federal fiscal agent empowered to operate or create a branch inside a state without the state's continuing, positive consent. But his brief and cloudy statement fell short of asserting this position on behalf of state control of monetary policy and seemed rather to speak for some abstract idea of state sovereignty.[81]

In net balance, events between 1790 and 1841 established some constitutional authority in Congress to charter a national bank. Clearly Congress might do so to provide a fiscal agent for the national government. It was less plain whether Congress might do so as a means of regulating the system of money, by providing currency and credit in addition to coin, to promote the growth and efficiency of a national economy. Hamilton claimed that this function was a legitimizing basis for chartering the first bank. Marshall's Court did not clearly ratify Hamilton's position, but in effect it did so when it invalidated state taxes designed to negate a monetary-policy role for the second bank. Closely related to creating a valid monetary mission for the national bank was the grant to it of power to create branches which would arm it to make its policies nationally effective. *McCulloch* also upheld this branching authority, though, characteristically, the Court's opinion said nothing to tie the branching authority to the conduct of monetary policy. The two charters and the Court's decisions outweigh the contrary positions taken by Jackson and Tyler. Jackson's prime questions ran to the validity and wisdom of the terms on which Congress had organized and delegated powers to the bank, rather than to defining national as against state authority affecting the system of money. Tyler's attempt to deny that banking had national economic relevance was too unrealistic to deserve deference. Altogether, despite the failure to continue a national monetary agent such as Congress and Nicholas Biddle had shaped, events at mid-century left the national government a substantial potential for regulating banking as a means of effecting a national monetary policy.

Market Controls and Central-Bank
Controls on Bank-Created Money

The activities of banks in adding their note issues and credit to the money supply posed problems analogous to those of federalism. The coexistence of two Banks of the United States and of hundreds of banks chartered by states generated questions about apportioning responsibilities between centralized and dispersed decision makers. In particular, the structure and practices of the two Banks of the United States raised questions, whether these institutions should undertake central-bank managing responsibilities over the bank-made parts of the money system. However, other factors were involved in banking developments which were not simply analogues of federal values. The creation of national and state banks alike required decisions on the relative scope of official and private decision making in shaping banks' contributions to the money supply. Banking did not go on in a free market; legal regulation bulked large as soon as banks became prominent in the economy. Nonetheless, strong currents of interest and of policy inclined lawmakers to leave in private hands substantial areas of banking decisions affecting money policy. Thus there was tension between governance of banks' money functions by market-type discipline or by government-imposed discipline, and this theme interwove with problems of centralized decentralized controls. To put the matter another way: Part One centered on attitudes toward using law to help fulfill the subtantive economic and social purposes of money; this part needs to focus on values or effects which men felt to derive specially from the location of decision-making power over the money supply.

The period 1780-1860 left no more lasting legacy of policy and problems concerning money than the tradition it established of delegating to private management large discretion in determining the supply of money.[82] This delegation policy characterized the states, as with increasing generosity they chartered private commercial banks; it characterized the central government, as it created two Banks of the United States which, though created to serve public interest, were nonetheless put under private management. Delegating jobs of public concern to private associations was not unique to banking and money; the same years saw such delegation as the principal means of providing for public transportation, insurance, education, libraries, water supply, hospitals, and institutions to care for dependent persons. Back of such delegations were practical reasons which applied as well to the banking field as to others: the difficulty in a cash-scarce economy of raising tax money for direct government services, the lack of experience in public administration and the accompanying need to encourage volunteer talent, and in the background the want of legislative knowledge or tradition for broad policy making.[83] However, there were also interests and attitudes specially centered on banks and money which shaped the delegations in that field.

The first stage of specialized state policy on delegating money supply decisions to private hands centered on using the corporation for banking purposes. No issue was raised at common law over allocating power between public and private decision makers; it was taken for granted that the general freedom to contract under the common law extended to issuing notes and establishing credits by lending or discounting.[84] We may properly be skeptical of the strength of this asserted common-law freedom, because it was never really tested in the United States in regard to private rights to create circulating currency; as soon as bank notes became at all prominent in the economy, their issue went on within a statutory framework.[85] Indeed, in 1840 the Alabama court said, in effect, that public policy accepted the common-law freedom to do banking only on the assumption that the activity created no problems of community interest that ordinary market dealings could not handle: regulating the currency was "certainly one of the highest duties of the sovereign power, and if the notes of private bankers should so far enter into the circulation, as to become prejudicial to the community, it would doubtless be the duty of the Legislature, either to suppress private banking altogether, or to require adequate pledges for the redemption of the notes."[86] The common-law freedom to do banking business had working reality for another important operation besides issuing currency; deposit-check money grew to the dominant role in the money supply through the mid-nineteenth century, resting largely on business practice and contract law, without a substantial statutory base.[87] However, though men might conduct some banking operations as individuals or as partners without special legal license, if they wished to incorporate a bank, they must seek statutory authorization; only the legislature might grant corporate status.[88] This, again, was not a doctrine peculiar to banks.[89] But state policy early turned toward using incorporation as a regulatory device special to banking. Massachusetts in 1799, and New York in 1804, enacted laws, specifying that men might issue circulating notes or discount commercial paper only if they held corporate charters from the state. Over the next twenty-five years other states borrowed this approach to limit lawful access to banking operations.[90] Taken at face value such statutes might be read as showing legislative concern that delegating money functions to private management was of such public impact as to require close public licensing and scrutiny. In fact, the early restrictive laws seem to have responded to the desire of already chartered banks to limit fresh competition.[91] As late as 1839 a Supreme Court opinion read the intent of comparable legislation limiting note issues to incorporated banks as expressing "the interest and policy of the State . . . to protect its own banks from competition [of out-of-state banks] in . . . the issue of notes for circulation."[92]

However, state policy did not stay long in the simple posture of protecting bankers against competition. State law developed lines of policy the grounds of which were not well expressed and which presented confusing differences and sometimes diametrically opposed estimates of the public interest. But state legislation had one underlying unity, in a manifest concern with the special promises and hazards in delegating money supply decisions to private operators. Four kinds of value judgments found places in this story: (1) In the background was distrust of currency directly issued by government. (2) Preponderant opinion favored increasing delegation to private banks of capacity to create money. (3) This policy stood out the more, because for a time some states so completely rejected it, by banning or sharply restricting private banks, out of fear of the power the private bankers might wield over the public. (4) About 1840-60 there emerged as the dominant approach the continued delegation of money system functions to private banks, accompanied by a tempered distrust expressed in regulations which created a poorly defined and poorly implemented public utility status.

Delegation of currency issue to private bankers was never seriously challenged before 1860 by any effort to pre-empt the field with direct government issues. The text of the federal Constitution and contemporary debate showed keen distrust of the capacity of legislators to withstand the temptations to inflate an official currency. On the other hand, at that stage no one except Hamilton seems to have foreseen the role banks might play in providing circulating paper.[93] In 1790, recommending to the Congress the creation of a national bank under dominantly private management, Hamilton claimed as a virtue of this private delegate that it would not be subject to government's temptation to avoid unpopular taxes by printing money.[94] In 1837 the Court made the existence of separate funds of assets pledged to redeem circulating notes the criterion which saved issues of state-chartered banks against the federal Constitution's ban on state bills of credit. Thus, in effect the Court continued Hamilton's emphasis on trusting the creation of currency to private management, because it would be insulated by its separate, specialized operations from the pressures that beat upon public officials.[95] Particularly telling was the confidence which the conservative Justice Story put on the built-in limitations against abusive expansion of money which he found in the character of chartered commercial banks: "When banks are created upon private capital, they stand upon that capital, and their credit is limited to the personal or corporate responsibility of the stockholders, as provided for in the charter."[96]

Through the 1830s, while most states limited banks of issue and discount to those which could obtain special charters of incorporation, the practice grew to be one of generous chartering. In this context obviously the grounds of legislative action were other than that acquiescence in bankers' desire to limit competition which marked the first statutes. As it became apparent that almost any group which could show substantial promise of raising the pledged capital might have a charter, the implicit policy which emerged was one favoring delegation of money functions to private management, out of belief that liberal delegation would best muster the energy and resources to spur the economy.[97] This view became entwined with two others, to lead into a new stage of policy. There was concern that insisting on special charters invited corruption of legislatures, to obtain privileges that could not be had by some regular, generalized procedure.[98] There was, also, concern that because of their roles in creating money, if banks were limited in number, they would grow to hold oppressive power.[99] But a more positive factor dominated the direction of policy. The number and variety of business enterprises grew at headlong pace in the second quarter of the century. In this setting the governing temper favored using law to promote multiplied economic growth. If the economy benefited from generous grants of special charters for banks, expansionist-minded legislators were ready to be persuaded that they would better promote economic growth by yet broader delegation of money supply functions to private management.[100] There are confusing crosscurrents of party ideology here. More equal access to bank franchises had appeal to the egalitarian values preached by the Jackson Democrats, but at the same time, especially in rural areas, the Democrats spoke for distrust of all banks and for an economy operated only with hard money. More equal access to bank franchises had appeal to business-oriented Whigs, the more so as the proposition included minimum capital requirements which would limit access to banking opportunities to sound men, while at the same time it encouraged a wider capital market relatively free of legal regulation. Measured by practice more than by words, the Whig bias of policy was the prevailing one.[101] Thus, when Michigan in 1837 and New York in 1838 pioneered in enacting general incorporation laws for banks, their "free-banking" statutes were rapidly taken as models by other states, to become the norm by 1860.[102]

Though prevailing policy favored committing important monetary functions to chartered private banks, a short-lived period of strong dissent underlined the reality of the delegation issue. Before they turned to general incorporation acts, some states by their constitutions required a two-thirds vote of the legislature to enact special charters. Contemporary opinion showed that this restriction was imposed particularly from distrust of bank promoters.[103] The two-thirds vote barriers may have originated partly in the hope of established bankers to limit competition, but the barriers reflected, also, fear of the lobby pressures generated by the attractions of the power residing in banks' money roles.[104] In almost a third of the states between 1840-60 fear of private financial power produced outright constitutional bans on creating banks or special limitations on their operation.[105] The career of these constitutional provisions highlighted the comparative valuations put on governmental monopoly in contrast to a substantial role for private management of the money supply. Ambition for economic growth collided with fears of private power. In the surging expansion of the economy, favor for economic growth won out. Wisconsin's story dramatized the conflict. In the proposed constitution of 1846 agrarian zeal produced a flat ban on banks and on the circulation as well as issue of bank notes. When the document was submitted to the voters, opponents argued that the bans on banking and currency would imperil Wisconsin's economic development, especially in competition with free-banking states. The voters rejected the 1846 draft, largely because of the banking and currency clauses. A new draft constitution was approved by the voters in 1848, with a provision which—omitting any limitation on circulating bank notes—sought to balance fear and ambition by stipulating that the legislature might provide for chartering banks only if a popular referendum approved such legislation. In 1851 the Wisconsin legislature presented a general incorporation act for banks, and the voters resoundingly approved it.[106] The Wisconsin record forecast the trend elsewhere. By 1863 all but two of the eleven states which had adopted strict constitutional limits on banking had dropped them, in most cases in favor of free-banking laws.[107]

Through the 1830s some policy makers could be found who carried their arguments against limiting legal access to banking to the point of a laissez-faire position—that anyone should be able to do banking business without need of the law's license and without special regulation.[108] But the prevailing view was steadily to the contrary. Even among those who supported banking privileges, there was recognition that by their effect on the money supply note-issuing banks held such power in the economy as required special care for the terms on which the power was delegated. Thus the sponsor of New York's 1829 Safety Fund for insuring bank notes justified requiring all banks to participate in the fund, because the banks "enjoy in common the exclusive right of making a paper currency for the people of the state and by the same rule should in common be answerable for that paper."[109] At the outset legislatures sought to provide checks on the banks by elements built into corporate structure. Though such provisions appeared in charters for other kinds of enterprises, bank charters showed particularly consistent care to fix limits on corporate organization. Bank charters took pains to specify the sanctioned corporate purposes and sometimes explicitly barred ventures into trade or other business, as a barrier to concentrated power. Bank charters put ceilings on capitalization, while they also required minimum paid-in capital as prerequisite to launching into business. Commonly they imposed special liabilities on bank officers, directors, and stockholders to those injured if the bank did not meet its liabilities. Always they set a term of years on the bank's corporate life (commonly twenty years), if only as leverage for imposing new limiting conditions upon a charter's renewal.[110] However, after 1838, when Michigan and New York had launched their experiments with general incorporation laws for banks, state policy turned to the view that limits built into corporate structure did not focus closely enough on the peculiar functions of banks which involved the public interest in the money supply. Prime attention went to regulations affecting bank notes. Thus, Wisconsin's Chief Justice Edward G. Ryan observed that Wisconsin's free-banking act of 1852 "contains many safeguards to protect the paper currency which it authorizes, and no control over the banks to be established under it, in any other respect. The only concern of the state was to secure, as far as it could, a safe local paper currency. . . . The state had a public policy in the system, but no [proprietary] interest; no pecuniary connection with the banks; no interest in their currency, except as a possible holder of their bills, in common with other holders."[111] What emerged was a pattern of regulations which began to treat banks as a kind of public utility. One mark of this status was that law set its own limits on access to the banking business. However, the requirement of some stated minimum, paid-in capital was the only substantial limit on access to banking under the general incorporation laws. Otherwise the free-banking laws imposed no equivalent of a certificate of public convenience and necessity to relate the organization of banks to the general condition of state economies.[112] Controls took a more pointed character when they aimed at particular banking practices affecting money, first by requiring deposit of qualified public bonds to secure bank-note issues, and then by requiring specie reserves against such notes. However, most such regulations had decreasing relevance to the main direction of banks' money supply functions. At first the controls dealt only with bank notes, and not with bank credit, which was becoming the banks' principal contribution to the money supply. Further, both security and reserves requirements were static and addressed to the affairs only of individual banks; they did not include criteria or means for policing bank credit as a whole, or its quantity or quality relative to the movements of the economy. By contrast, Louisiana's act of 1842—which required reserves against deposits as well as against note issues, and which set liquidity standards for bank credit—highlighted the limited character of most regulation of the time.[113]

What state policy makers did not face up to through the first half of the nineteenth century was that to combine broad delegation of money supply functions to private management with effective external standards for the public interest required the will to create continuing, specialized official scrutiny of the banks' behavior. States took just enough action to reflect the reality of the problem, but not enough to meet the problem. Two kinds of state action were especially revealing of the generally defective treatment of delegation of money-supply jobs to private management. In 1829 New York set up its Safety Fund, to insure liabilities of specially chartered banks, and the state was realistic enough to create public commissioners to oversee the system. But, apparently without realizing the scope of its undertaking, the legislature blanketed deposits as well as bank notes under the fund, which was not financially set up to bear so broad a burden. The state did not revise the fund to include banks created after 1838 under the general incorporation act, so that the system was in any event doomed to dwindling significance. In 1843 the legislature abolished the office of the commissioners, despairing that such officers could curb improper banking practices, but without effort to improve their capacity to do so. The fund was ended in 1866.[114] Four other states adopted the New York plan, but none with material effect.[115] Free-banking laws borrowed from the New York Safety Fund the idea of providing specialized officials to enforce such regulations as the statutes put on banks' money functions. But, at the outset this was almost certainly only a gesture; there is little evidence that legislatures adequately armed these officials, or exacted significant performance from them.[116]

The second kind of state action which reveals the states' unreadiness to face up to the implications of their delegation policy was the common practice—by legislation, by deliberate executive inaction, or by judicial decision—of relieving banks of legal sanctions for failing to redeem their circulating notes in specie during times of general suspension of specie payments.[117] Commonly the governing statutes threatened forfeiture of bank charters, or put special liabilities on banks or their officers for failing to redeem notes. The public interest would not have benefited from wholesale application of such sanctions in times of general distress; although what judges or executive officers did to relieve the banks sometimes had dubious warrant in the statutes, the general pattern of official response was sensible. These determinations not to apply sanctions recognized that banks had grown to operate as interdependent systems in supplying currency and credit and that there was a high social interest in keeping the system in working order.[118] However, this realistic perception was not matched with realistic readiness to develop official apparatus which could regularly monitor the systems. Instead, official concern was typically shown after trouble had burst forth in full force, and then produced only *ad hoc* responses to trouble. In sum, at mid-nineteenth century state law recognized that the values sought by delegating substantial money-supply functions to private banks were bought at the cost of risks which called for public regulation, but the states gave only imperfect definition to this public utility status of banks and provided little continuing, specialized machinery to police that status.

Into the imperfect money market made by several hundred state-chartered banks in the first half of the nineteenth century, national policy introduced two Banks of the United States (1791-1811, 1816-36).[119] Their governing statutes contemplated that these would be institutions of more mixed public and private character than were the typical banks which held state charters. Each Bank of the United States existed under an exclusive federal franchise. Each charter contemplated a substantial, though minority, capital investment by the United States, and designation by the United States of a substantial minority of the board of directors. From each of these national banks Congress expected substantial service to national policy, as fiscal agents of the government and as suppliers of currency and of credit for national economic growth. This national bank legislation was like that of the states, in delegating functions of public interest to organizations predominantly private. The two men most influential in shaping these institutions shared a common faith that such delegation was wise. Hamilton felt that private control meant that the bank would give more careful attention to its public as well as to its private business and that its private organization would insulate it from the forces that pressed legislators to inflate the money stock.[120] A generation later Nicholas Biddle believed that "the great problem of American institutions was whether a general government with comparatively feeble means, could accomplish its purpose in so extensive an empire." For Biddle, as for Hamilton, the answer was to entrust public-interest jobs to private managers; the responsibilities assigned them would discipline the private managers to operate in the public interest, as well as for their own profit, while private organization would protect their functions against elected officials who might seek patronage or political power out of public institutions.[121] The choice between direct government action and delegation of money-supply functions was high-lighted in 1841 when President Tyler's vetoes of bills to create a third Bank of the United States resigned wholly to the Treasury such role as the national government would play regarding money for the rest of this half-century period.[122]

The two Banks of the United States—and especially the second bank, from about 1826-32—developed functions which made them in some measure managers of the country's money supply. Their operations had effect not only by their own lending and note issues, but through their impact on the currency and credit provided by state-chartered private banks. Such a central-bank role was not forecast in the charter of the first bank, nor was it a substantial objective in chartering the second. When Hamilton proposed, and Congress adopted, the first national bank act in 1790-91, there was no occasion to think of that agency directing or disciplining a money supply largely created by hundreds of state banks. In 1791 only four commercial banks were operating in the states, and their activities and influence did not reach beyond their localities.[123] Hamilton in 1790, and Secretary of the Treasury A. J. Dallas in 1814 and 1815, saw an important service of a national bank as that of supplying a reliable currency acceptable in national markets. So far they envisaged a monetary function for a national bank. But, they did not urge this service of supply as part of a general charge to regulate the money supply as a whole. By the end of its career the first bank, it is true, had stirred some resentment by pressing state banks to redeem their circulating notes in specie. However, reactions to this activity do not seem to have been a prime factor either in the decision not to renew the bank's charter in 1811, or in chartering the second bank in 1816.[124] Moreover, in important respects the two national bank charters were ill-adapted to developing a central-bank role, as later experience would define that role. The charters set a ceiling of 6 percent on the banks' lending rate, forbade the banks to trade in government securities, and forbade them to incur demand obligations (beyond claims for money actually deposited) greater than their capitalizations.[125] These were proper hedges about the working of an ordinary, private bank. But, they did not reflect a vision of the responsibilities, and the consequent desirable flexibility, of a lender of last resort for the whole money system. Obviously this idea did not enter into the making of these charters; indeed, the managers of the two banks—even the bold and ingenious Biddle—never indicated that they saw changes in the banks' lending rate or in their dealings in government securities as possible instruments for regulating the money supply.[126]

Though their charters had rigidities not consistent with fully effective money management, the banks' structures included elements which gave their managers scope to develop some central-bank functions. Congress stood pledged in the charters to create no other national banks; combining this monopoly of national banking privileges with the capacity for centralized direction given by its corporate organization, each Bank of the United States had the potential for decisive, disciplined action of broad effect.[127] Each bank could command impressive capital. Though the charters set ceilings, they authorized capitalizations large for the times—$10 million for the first bank, $35 million for the second.[128] Congress also put ceilings on the demand obligations that the banks might create, but within those limits the charters gave the banks broad discretion to decide the quantity, timing, and quality of note issues and loans; the impact which the second bank had by a conservative policy which kept state banks its debtors attested the practical importance of this lending discretion.[129] Both banks enjoyed great leverage on state banks and on the general economy by their charter authority to receive deposits of moneys paid to the federal government and to pay out federal funds. In this role the banks became the largest recipients and disbursers of money in the country. They also thus achieved a strategic position vis à vis the state banks, for the quantity of state bank notes taken in payments to the United States gave the national institutions the means of exerting pressure by demanding redemption of the notes in specie. In this respect the second bank's charter put it in a stronger position than the first bank had enjoyed. The first bank's charter merely authorized that institution to be a United States depository. But the act of 1816 directed that federal funds be deposited in the second bank, unless the Treasury assigned specific reasons for not doing so.[130] Finally, the charters of both banks authorized their directors to set up branches anywhere in the country without limitation of number, to appoint the branch directors and to make rules for the branches' administration. Thus, empowering each bank to create its own nationwide apparatus, Congress endowed these institutions with the potential for effecting throughout the country such monetary policies as its central management might adopt. In *McCulloch* v. *Maryland* (1819), the Court held that Congress was entitled to make a reasonable judgment that branches were necessary and proper instruments of the national purposes for which the bank was created, and that the branching authority given to the Bank directors was a valid delegation by Congress of "subordinate arrangements," guided by the statutory prescription of "the great duties of the bank." [131] However, it is further evidence how little forecast of a central-bank role was in men's minds, that in 1790-91 and in 1815-16 the opposition to chartering the banks did not emphasize the reach of control which the branching power might give over the private economy; such hostility as early appeared to the branches expressed tension between state and federal power, rather than between official and market control of money. [132]

When a legislature delegates power, it may introduce energies into public policy-making that might not otherwise come to focus and that may take directions quite different from any forecast. Though their charters did not declare this goal, by their own practice the managers of the two Banks of the United States began to move their institutions into the functions and responsibilities of a central bank. This process had only small beginnings in the first bank, which made its main public-interest impact as fiscal agent for the government. However, the first bank used its leverage as federal depository to exert some discipline over state bank notes, by presenting them to their issuers for redemption in specie. It could better apply pressure, because its generally conservative lending policy tended to keep state banks in its debt. Further, it attempted some mild money management by adjusting its own note issues to its estimate of general economic conditions. [133] The second bank got off to a poor start as a money-system manager. The administration of William Jones (1817 to early 1819) at first ran too much with the boom tide of the country to be counted a controlling influence, though the Philadelphia headquarters showed some grasp of the idea that the bank and its branches should work as an interlocking system. For the bank's own safety, Langdon Cheves (1819 into 1822) had to continue restrictive lending policies which Jones had belatedly adopted, while he stopped altogether the issue of circulating notes by some branches. Caution was reasonable in the circumstances, and the economy had turned sufficiently slack that the bank's negative tone probably did not add much restraint to that already created by general conditions. The bank's management provided no such balancing action as would have been appropriate to a central bank when, between 1818 and 1821, the government used revenue surpluses to make drastic reductions in Treasury notes outstanding since the War of 1812. Altogether, the bank's performance thus far did not add up to a strong directing influence on the money supply. [134]

Between 1824 and 1832, with bold will and imagination, Nicholas

Biddle used the bank's structure and powers to move the institution a good way into the role of a central bank. Three aspects of Biddle's administration had special importance concerning (1) the bank's own note issues, (2) its lending policies, geared to regional economic relations within the country as well as to foreign trade, and (3) the supervision of its branches, to fulfill its goals in providing currency and credit.

Even in the ups and downs of the Jones-Cheves years the bank maintained public confidence in its circulating notes, though—after injudicious lending at the outset—it did so with an abrupt conservatism which did not show the flexibility appropriate to a central bank.[135] Responding to the needs of growing markets, Biddle steadily expanded the quantity of the bank's notes, while in general he did a good job of preventing sharp contractions or expansions in its circulation in the face of business fluctuations.[136] To do this required a firm initiative in legal as well as in economic decisions. The charter stipulated that the bank's own notes be signed by its president and cashier. When this cumbersome procedure threatened to keep the bank from issuing the quantity of circulating paper appropriate to the economy, Biddle reacted with characteristic boldness, by permitting his branches to add to the circulation their own notes drawn on the parent. Although there is no evidence that those who adopted the charter in 1816 contemplated the issue of circulating paper by branches of the bank, the branch notes seem legally warranted as a necessary and proper instrument to fulfill the bank's responsibility to promote a national currency. The branch notes became a favorite target of the bank's opponents. But Biddle did not allow them to run into inflation, and a federal court ruled them to be issued within the lawful discretion of the bank's management.[137] Biddle's notable accomplishment in managing the bank's note issues was to build confidence in their convertibility, by maintaining a specie reserve which regularly dwarfed the specie holdings of state-chartered banks and which made the Bank of the United States the effective central reserve for the whole circulating paper of the country.[138] However, it was his imaginative development of the bank's lending policies which made this central-reserve function workable.

Biddle intended the second bank to be a profitable business, and he managed it accordingly.[139] Nonetheless, he also showed unusual awareness that bank credit and commodities and goods markets were developing sensitive interrelations as a system. Such system relationships, he felt, created the opportunity and the responsibility for the national bank to program its lending to manage the money supply. Thus the bank might promote economic growth, while its operations reduced costly gyrations in the flow of transactions.[140] From his insight into the emerging interplay of money and business, Biddle made a constructive link between currency and credit. He valued a sound specie reserve. But, he did not treat it as a mechanically sufficient measure of the proper supply of circulating paper. As depository of moneys paid to the federal government and as a lender operating through a nationwide organization, the bank was strategically positioned to discipline state banks by requiring that they provide means to redeem their notes which came into the bank's hands as federal fiscal agent or as creditor. However, Biddle did not demand redemption as his principal means to affect state bank issues. Nor did he measure his own bank's issues primarily by the bank's specie holdings. Rather, his rule was that both the bank and its branches, and the state banks, should issue their circulating paper only in secure proportion to the volume of commodities and goods moving currently to market. To this end Biddle employed the bank's resources in buying bills of exchange, to an extent which brought the bank almost to monopolize dealings in domestic bills, and to become the dominant dealer in foreign bills. As circulating paper of the state banks or of the Bank of the United States and its branches flowed from agricultural and industrial sectors of the economy toward the country's mercantile and financial centers, bills secured by commodities or goods were available at the points of settlement, maturing in timely order to provide means to pay off the bank notes. By pressing his own branches to lend their notes only in proportion as they bought bills of exchange, and by purchasing bills held by state banks, Biddle could thus exert some control on the quantity and timing of currency issues.[141] More basic was the influence which the second bank could win over the general volume of credit by its commanding dealings in bills of exchange; this influence had larger implications for the future than did regulating the currency, for even by the 1830s bank loans were creating the bulk of the money supply, though contemporary opinion was generally slow to appreciate the fact.[142] Yet another of Biddle's creative insights was his perception that the whole of bank-created money (currency and credit) should be managed so as to foster the national market, by promoting more efficient meshing of regional economies and of different functional sectors of the economy. The primacy that Biddle gave to dealings in bills of exchange, and his lively concern for proportioning credit to the flow of transactions, meant that the bank helped move short-term capital from commercial and financial centers to agricultural and industrial areas, while it helped farmers and manufacturers to satisfy their creditors by timely movement of goods and commodities to their ultimate markets. Notably between 1824 and 1832 the bank showed that a central money manager could materially help enlarge and facilitate the national market. The bank's beneficial effects were manifest in narrowing the spread and fluctuations of discounts on bills of exchange. Moreover, these accomplishments were reflected in the support which the bank obtained in its battle for a renewed charter, from traders and state banks in those parts of the country which most closely felt the benefits it gave in smoothing adjustments among different functional and sectional areas of the economy.[143]

Biddle pursued his innovations in money management by taking better advantage than his predecessors of the bank's capacity to extend its influence through its branches. Hamilton had included branching authority in the first bank's charter. But he had opposed using the branching power at the bank's beginning, because he feared that the parent office would lack the means and skill to achieve a "safe and orderly administration" of a dispersed organization. Nonetheless, the first bank's directorate began to use its branching authority in 1791, and when like power was included in the 1816 charter the second bank promptly acted on it.[145] Experience bore out Hamilton's misgivings. With its more ambitious activity, the second bank had particular difficulty in monitoring its branches, whether to enforce ordinary honesty and efficiency, or—more to our present concern—to control lending and note issues.[146] The abrupt retrenchment at the end of the Jones administration, and the continuing tight policy under Cheves, represented a caution needed to save the bank from its early imprudence. But the rigor of these changes also implicitly testified to earlier failures in supervising the branches.[147] Even Biddle did not wholly succeed in controlling the branches. But he created a far more disciplined organization than the bank had had before. He took special care in selecting branch cashiers, whom the parent office trained to be loyal agents of its policies; he supervised the selection of branch directors and presidents; he insisted on a steady flow of information to the center, and he sought to coordinate action throughout his organization by a steady flow of information and directives from the center. These measures had the more significance for tightening the organization, because Biddle mustered stockholders' proxies to give him a determining voice in selecting the parent board of directors, and he concentrated the board's power within a small executive committee which he dominated.[148] Thus he took advantage of the facilities offered by the corporate form of enterprise to combine central direction with a widespread, hierarchical organization. With such an apparatus he could with some effect undertake to adjust currency and credit to the federal government's fiscal operations and to the varied currents of transactions in different geographical and functional sectors of the economy. The reach of his organization particularly facilitated his key managing technique, of concentrating the bank's resources in dealings in domestic and foreign exchange. Its structure thus allowed the bank to attempt to give direction to the total money supply in ways beyond the capacities of the fragmented money market provided by the uncoordinated, provincial, jealously competitive activities of several hundred state-chartered banks.[149]

We must not exaggerate Biddle's accomplishment. He did not fully realize the implications of his vision of managing the money supply. Thus, he did not see the possible utility of rediscounting paper for other banks at varying rates, or of fixing reserve requirements, or of using regional or national clearinghouse procedures to manage the rising volume of deposit-check money. Nor did he grasp the possibilities of developing cooperative relations with state banks as his correspondents, instead of confronting them only as competitors or targets of regulation. His bank did not play the role of lender of last resort in crises. And, like twentieth-century central bankers, he sometimes misjudged the timing or the force of shifts in business activity relative to the money supply.[150] Even so, on balance from about 1824 to 1832 he used his centralized, wide-reaching organization to build constructive precedents for central-bank direction of the system of money.

The fact that the two banks of the United States grew to perform functions productive for the general welfare did not save them from sharp and ultimately successful opposition. Amid a confusing variety of charges, fears, and competing interests a common reason explains why Congress did not continue either of the banks. Here the favored early nineteenth-century technique of delegating public interest jobs to private direction was overextended. Congress put too much responsibility on agencies whose private character was bound to create ambiguities and distrust when their public functions called on them to run counter to other private interests with which they also stood in competition.

It is temptingly simple to explain that what ended the Banks of the United States was agrarian dislike of all banks. Such feeling seems to have been a factor when Congress refused to renew the first bank's charter in 1811, and Jefferson reflected the attitude when he said that, rather than trust to bank notes, he would issue Treasury notes to supply any needed supplement to coin.[151] In vetoing a new charter for the second bank in 1832, Jackson appealed to farmers' traditional faith in hard money and to their suspicion of bankers' paper and bankers' profits and power; consistent with this approach, so far as he indicated support for some kind of a national bank, it would only be a government fiscal agent, denied all power to lend or to issue circulating notes.[152] However, the agricultural areas did not show unremitting hostility to the two banks. In 1811 some congressmen from new states supported renewing the first bank's charter and expressed fear that eastern banking interests wanted the national bank out of the way so that they might better assert their financial supremacy.[153] From late 1818 into 1820 the second bank tightened its lending and pressed hard on its debtors, when for its own safety it sought to repair its earlier unwise expansion of credit. In the debtor West and South this period, it is true, left a legacy of fear and anger toward what the people saw as a grasping institution, distant in sympathy from those who risked and labored to produce tangible wealth. The discriminatory taxes which several states then laid on the bank's branches pointedly expressed this resentment. But, when Biddle undertook to muster support for renewing his charter, he evoked substantial response from the South, Southwest, and West; apparently those agrarian regions felt growing appreciation of the money management which from 1826-32 had helped move credit in timely fashion to debtor areas and had created more stable lending rates on the bills of exchange which financed the movement of crops to market.[154] In these later years of the second bank such dissatisfaction as appeared in debtor sections of the country seemed less over what the bank did to regulate the stability of currency and exchanges than over the fact that it did not find means for more credit to meet the almost insatiable demands of growing markets. Certainly these regions had no ground to complain that the bank discriminated against them. For, even while Biddle's bank sought to keep a sound balance between the money supply and the flow of transactions, the bulk of its own note issues and of its dealings in bills of exchange was concentrated in the South, Southwest, and West.[155] On the whole, agrarian hostility does not suffice to explain why Congress did not override Jackson's veto.

An immediate cause of Congress's failures to renew the charters of the two banks was the political influence wielded by some state-chartered banks in financial and mercantile centers, or in settled areas not experiencing acute shortages of credit. Against such influence the national banks paid a high price for their private character. These state bank opponents did not react particularly against the central-bank-style operations which the Banks of the United States undertook in the public interest. Rather, they resented the banks as direct competitors for profitable business. So, too, they objected to the national bank's range of influence less from concern for states' rights, than because that influence spelled rivalry to their own ambitions to build their own empires of correspondent banks.[156]

Nevertheless, though the hostility of some state banks was narrowly based in their competition for business, their opposition was potent, because they could ally themselves with others—such as Andrew Jackson and Roger Taney—who feared the national banks on grounds of political principle. To Jackson and those for whom he spoke, an institution privately owned and privately managed, which enjoyed the privileges and powers of the second bank, threatened to upset a healthy balance of power between public and private interest. This was the area of controversy in which the bank was vulnerable precisely because it was a private delegate of functions of broad public impact and concern.

On the one hand, there was concern about the scale of economic power which the bank could wield—because it held large moneys as the depository of federal funds; because with the advantages of limited legal-tender status for its notes and a widespread organization to issue them, it could produce a substantial national currency; and because under Biddle it combined a strong central leadership with a branching apparatus that could make its policies felt throughout the country. This fear of the bank's potential power commonly produced condemnation of the bank as a *monopoly*. The fear might have been no less, had comparable functions and resources been committed to an official agency of the federal government. But, in a relatively simple society, in which for the most part power was broadly dispersed, the private character of the bank accented concern about its centralized control and its concentrated means.[157]

In part, criticism ran not just to the quantity of power put in the Banks of the United States, but also to the fact that the banks had potential capacity to affect the economy by calculated decisions. Such power was seen to be a dangerous subtraction from the controls that might be imposed by a banking market created by the cumulated activities of hundreds of commercial banks.[158] Conservative men trusted such market controls because they were thought to be more impersonal and objective than regulations imposed through the pressures exerted on legislatures. At its peak of size and influence the second bank was never in fact a monopoly and never able of itself to determine the state of the economy. It accounted at most for 20 percent of all bank loans, 20 percent of all note circulation, a third of bank deposits, and a third of the country's specie (though, indeed, its specie holdings far outstripped those of any state banks); it won its dominant position in the markets for domestic and foreign bills of exchange by continuing competition; and its only clear-cut economic monopoly—admittedly an important one—was as the depository of federal funds.[159] But fears about the concentrated power of the two national banks focused not just on advantages that were economically valuable or economically measureable; they were fears of injustice and abuse in the structure of political and social power, and as such they had their own impact which mere economic argument could not remove.

Jefferson, Jackson, and Taney distrusted the Banks of the United States not just because they held power, but because that power was under private and not official direction, in institutions which the critics saw as structured to produce conflicts of interest between the general welfare and the hunger for power or profit of the private managers. Jefferson and Madison thought that the first bank would be primarily an instrument to subsidize private speculation with public money; the bank was in the business of lending for profit, yet the federal government was to subscribe a fifth of its capital, and private subscribers might pay up to three-fourths of their capital contributions in United States securities, while the institution would also gain working capital by holding the government deposits.[160] Advising Jackson in 1832, Taney thought that the bonus which the second bank would pay for a renewed charter betrayed the primacy of the private profit motive in the institution; to him such a dynamic was inconsistent with responsibility for regulating the money supply in the public interest.[161] Jackson reached a similar estimate. The most concession he made to the idea of a national bank was to say that he might support an institution which had no lending or note-issuing powers (that is, one without the prime means to seek banking profit), but only authority to act as depository of government funds; and eventually he decided that there would be too much hazard of conflicts of interest even in so limited an institution, if it were in private management.[162] That foreigners as stockholders might share in the profits was another count brought against the banks, and not the less so though both charters in effect denied foreign stockholders any voice in selecting the directors (by limiting proxy voting to resident stockholders) and stipulated that only stockholders who were United States citizens might be directors.[163]

What most worried those who feared the effects of the banks on the general alignment of power in the country was that the institutions might use their position to build political influence through patronage and favors.[164] In 1791 the Jeffersonians saw the first bank as a nest of Federalist job-holders and speculators. At its inception the second bank fell under less suspicion, because the Jefferson party then dominated the situation and launched the bank under men of its own choosing.[165] But by 1832 serious charges of abuse were made against the second bank. For the most part these charges seem ill-founded. The second bank did not create branches or choose branch managements to curry local favor, but set them up and administered them as it deemed that regular business and its fiscal-agent duties required.[166] The bank made loans to congressmen and other political figures. However, it did not conspicuously play favorites, lending to political foes as well as to friends; such transactions were a very small part of its total loans; they generally met the business standards of the times, without political strings attached; and the bank administered them as loans and did not make them into covert gifts.[167] When charter renewal came into serious question, Biddle exerted himself to obtain favorable memorials to Congress and caused the printing and wide distribution of materials to support the bank's cause. But he was entitled to plead the case for a publicly useful institution, especially against ill-founded complaints, and he did not spend the bank's money corruptly.[168] Taney made it a count in his indictment of the bank that it pressed for a new charter on the eve of a presidential election to embarrass Jackson. Biddle did choose his time, and probably erred tactically in his choice, but Jackson's 1829 message had warned of the president's likely opposition, and by 1831 there was ample evidence that the bank needed to look to its protection.[169] The most serious charge of abuse of power was that, to make the public feel the need of the bank, Biddle fostered a boom in 1832 and then tightened credit to produce a recession in 1834-35. Later judgment has substantially acquitted the bank, or at least had found that it made mistakes in economic forecasts rather than engaging in power plays, and that other causes than the bank's decisions were chiefly responsible for movement in the economy.[170]

In the contemporary setting the charges and the distrust they manifested took on special urgency and conviction for the critics because of one overshadowing factor—the evident domination of the bank by one man, who was not accountable as a public officer to the president or to congress. Biddle built his control on the opportunities afforded by the bank's corporate structure, in ways more familiar to the twentieth than to the early nineteenth century. The bank's voting arrangements invited management domination, limiting the votes of large stockholders, barring the vote to foreign investors, and holding directors to a four-year tenure while allowing the president an unlimited term of office. Biddle won proxies, to obtain a cooperative board of directors, and found that the complexity of the bank's operations meant that his directors—and a fortiori, his stockholders—were content to leave most decisions to him. He was ex officio a member of all committees and named all committees except one charged with general review of operations. The bylaws sanctioned a committee on bills of exchange, which in practice became the executive committee of the board, dominated by Biddle. He tied his branches to him, carefully selecting branch cashiers trained at the parent office to be faithful agents of policy made at the center and exercising close supervision over choices of branch directors and presidents. In all of these aspects there was little that was intrinsically sinister. Biddle did not invent most of his opportunities; he built on structure and procedures already present or developing, and the tight central control at which he aimed was functional for operating so widespread an organization and for achieving its potential and desirable role of a manager of the general system of money.[171] But he was a vastly self-confident, and somewhat vain man. He fostered fear of his power by injudiciously showing how well aware he was of it. It is not surprising that, in retrospect, Taney justified the decision against renewing the bank on the ground that "it made the existence of the state institutions dependent upon the will of a single individual" and that individual a man of "aspiring views and gigantic plans."[172]

On net balance both Banks of the United States proved to be institutions which served the public interest at least as well as their own profit. In the prime years of Biddle management (1826-32) the second bank was developing central-bank functions which the country needed, if it was to have a system of money adequate to a national economy. The general welfare suffered when this promising effort was cut short, the more so since the resulting functional deficiencies were not made good for nearly another one hundred years. The causes of this failure of public policy were diverse. Two linked factors were peculiarly failures in using legal processes and as such belong especially to legal history.

First, in the area of monetary policy the fortunes of politics denied Hamilton's vision of using the positive as well as the regulatory potentials of law to accommodate market processes to the public good. Partly by the drift of their practice, partly with the silent acquiescence of Congress and the explicit sanction of the Supreme Court, the states developed a bumbling money market out of the uncoordinated activities of several hundred state-chartered banks. The volume and variety of production and transactions grew, involving an increasing proportion of the population in general market dealings. An unreliable currency, and shortages and costly fluctuations in current credit, showed the need of legitimating some responsible direction of the money supply beyond what the contemporary money market could give. Jackson's veto defaulted on this responsibility of the federal government. Refusing to recognize an obligation to take an affirmative leadership, Jackson—and the opinion for which he spoke—took the simplistic position that it was enough to get rid of what was seen as a danger to a healthy polity. But the frustrations of the next seventy-five years taught that when market processes do not fulfill social needs, policy makers must be prepared to use law affirmatively to structure the situation to achieve chosen goals, with such commitment to continuing public administration as this kind of effort may require.

The second—and related—failure in using legal processes to shape monetary policy was in delegating too broad public responsibilities and too much legal and practical power to an agency primarily private in ownership and management. This kind of delegation seemed wise and workable in many areas of public concern in the late eighteenth and early nineteenth centuries. This readiness to delegate derived partly from contemporary limitations of governmental means and skill. It was also a favored approach because resort to private action appealed to the practical sense of a society which relied as much as this then did on the market to allocate scarce resources. But, the course of public policy concerning the Banks of the

United States, and especially the decision not to renew the second bank, showed that delegation of public-interest jobs to private hands would not be accepted for long, if the private delegate's activity affected a great range of other people's interests without reasonably clear and effective, externally imposed standards to hold the delegate to act for the general welfare and not primarily for his own gain or power. The Jacksonian attack on the bank was wrong, because it was wholly negative. Yet, it stood for an important limiting principle, which would find later expression in the law of public utilities and in the antitrust laws.

The Jackson administration delivered a further blow to central money management in 1833 when it removed the government deposits from the second bank and turned over to selected state banks the holding of government moneys. Federal funds bulked large enough to give considerable leverage for money management to whoever held them. The 1833 change was not necessarily inconsistent with using that leverage, were the Treasury ready to wield effective control over its agents to relate government fiscal policy to the condition of the money supply. However, the attitudes and interests which brought down the second bank were not consistent with quickly committing such a leading role to the Treasury, and the Treasury did not show itself administratively capable of carrying out such a role. Some state bank depositories soon abused their positions for their own interests, no central policy emerged from the Treasury, and in the 1840s Congress took another tack, which in effect confirmed the judgment that there should be no central money direction.[173]

Congress failed to override Tyler's vetoes of two bills to establish a third national bank.[174] Instead, in statutes of 1840 and 1846 Congress committed to the Treasury all federal government action affecting the money supply. Moreover, this legislation—especially the 1846 act—set limits on the Treasury so rigid as to withdraw the federal government from a money management role. The Treasury was to make no banker's use of the moneys it collected for the United States; all officials receiving federal funds were "required to keep safely, without loaning, using, depositing in banks, or exchanging for other funds than [gold or silver] . . . all the public money collected by them, or otherwise at any time placed in their possession and custody." Further, all sums due to the United States for taxes or other payments "shall be paid in gold and silver coin only, or in treasury notes issued under the authority of the United States," and all payments by the United States should be made in the same media. Up to 1846 Treasury notes had been issued almost wholly as instruments of government borrowing; there was such scant practice of issuing them in quantity or on terms calculated to make them a substantial currency, that the statute's reference could hardly be taken to intend a money-supply function for the Treasury. What was left was not only just a depository function, but a depository function so restricted as to deny the Treasury even the power to administer the government's fiscal operations so that they would not unnecessarily disturb the general money supply.[175] Thus, for the time being the central government had resigned the general control of money which the Constitution makers probably envisaged in 1789, leaving the major components of the money supply to the un-coordinated activities of many state-chartered, private, commercial banks. Federal policy on money would shortly take on new vigor under the pressures of war. However, even the changes wrought between 1861-65 would not much alter the directionless situation left by the disappearance of the second Bank of the United States.

Roles of Major Legal Agencies

This opening period of monetary policy involved leading contributions by all the principal branches of government. The makers of the federal Constitution set the ground for leadership by the United States. They closely confined the states in those aspects of policy they foresaw, but their foresight did not include the part which the states might yet play by incorporating banks.[176] State constitutions typically spelled out few specifics on legislative power, and the stream of state banking statutes—first, special charters, then free-banking (general incorporation) acts—poured forth simply under the "legislative power" which state constitutions vested in their principal elected assemblies. In several states between about 1840-60 constitutional provisions laid particular bans or limitations on chartering banks, but this proved to be a passing phase of policy.[177]

Within constitutional bounds legislation set the main content of money supply policy. This outcome was constitutionally dictated in the central government, where both executive and judge-made law must depend on congressional initiative.[178] In the states statute law on monetary policy was important in the one area which the federal Constitution left open to state action. Promoters wanted to incorporate their banks, and only the legislatures might give corporate status; in the earlier, special-charter years and later under general incorporation acts, state law on bank-created money began as a specialty of the statute law of corporations.[179] Not only was it true that the legislature alone might confer corporate status, but also the legislature alone had authority and means to generalize broad new requirements of conduct and to create new official apparatus to implement the standards of conduct it laid down. So the record included such innovations as the New York Safety Fund of 1829, and the Louisiana Bank Standards

Act of 1842.[180] However, though federal and state statute law set the principal content of public policy on money, the contributions made through the legislative process were limited. Legislation typically lacked broad pattern, and legislative intervention usually was *ad hoc* and sporadic. The First Congress was the notable exception, when it created a money notation system, a mint, and a national bank. Later, Congress simply stood by, while—without plan or discipline—state bank charters brought into being the principal components of the money supply. Such exercise as Congress made of the federal power over money was abrupt and restricted, as when Congress authorized Treasury notes to meet particular exigencies, and in its 1834 act suddenly changed the gold content of the dollar.[181] State legislation showed only two examples of broad policies affecting money—the statutes limiting note issue and general discounting or lending to incorporated banks, and the general incorporation (free-banking) acts. However, this legislation spread by imitation as much as by considered examination of policy; the shallowness of its roots was betrayed by the typical failure of legislatures to investigate its operation or provide machinery sufficient to implement it.[182]

Legislatures' failures to create adequate administrative means for helping make and carry out monetary policy were a prime aspect of the relatively crude record of the legislative process in this field. However, the contemporary condition of the executive branch itself had great effect on legislative performance. It is significant that Congress made its most coherent approach to a monetary policy under the programming lead given by Secretary of the Treasury Hamilton and that it chartered the second Bank of the United States largely under the initiative of Secretary of the Treasury Albert Gallatin. Likewise, it is significant that the only other broad consideration that Congress gave to the system of money responded largely to Jackson's determination to end the second bank. When—as most of the time—the Treasury was under uninspired leadership, the federal executive establishment gave no positive lead to Congress on regulating the system of money, and Congress itself took no lead, except in 1846, when it formally denied the Treasury any rightful guidance of monetary policy.[183] The unsystematic character of bank-created money in the states reflected want of direction within legislative processes, but it reflected, also, the typical want of policy programming from state chief executives. It was not until the end of the nineteenth century, and for the most part only after about 1905 that governors began to emerge in the states who found the skills and the means to make themselves felt in shaping legislative approaches to broadly defined public problems; the timing was not right for a stronger lead in monetary policy in the first half of the nineteenth century.[184]

If legislatures were at fault for not inventing means of generating their own programs, or administrative machinery capable of continuous and reasonably effective supervision of monetary policy, their fault is mitigated by the lack of contemporary models for strong policy leadership or strong public administration. A realistic, contemporary measure of the situation in these respects is the readiness with which both Congress and state legislatures delegated public-interest functions of money supply to private organizations. This delegation technique was the broadest common pattern of policy affecting the system of money up to 1860. Its prevalence attests to the pervasive impact that want of executive and administrative experience and precedent had. Early nineteenth-century policy makers were largely prisoners of their institutional inheritance, as policy makers continue to be. Traditions bred of the parliamentary revolution in England, by the years of tension between the colonies and the crown, and by the leading roles which legislative bodies played in fighting the war for independence, all inclined the people to a lively distrust of executive power. This distrust was reflected in the calculated weakness of the executive that became a pattern from early state constitutions and in the cautious brevity and generality with which the framers of the federal Constitution provided the potential for a strong office of the president.[185] Lawmakers lacked experience, and all worked with scant resources of money or managerial talent to meet the sharply focused, immediate demands generated by a society experiencing headlong growth. When these limiting circumstances were joined with the pressure of inherited suspicion of executive leadership in programming policy and of inherited distrust of sustained and strong administration in carrying out policy, it is understandable that legislators fumbled the job of providing for a comprehensive monetary policy.

In the years before 1860 the principal part played by the courts was to legitimize experiments in developing the money supply through legislation and through market processes. In *McCulloch* and in *Osborn* the Supreme Court unreservedly acknowledged that Congress had constitutional warrant to take affirmative leadership in monetary policy, free of state interference. The calculated dicta in *Briscoe* put the circulating notes of state-chartered commercial banks outside the constitutional ban on state bills of credit, and thus sanctioned the growth of the main element in the early nineteenth-century currency. Fateful as this action was, it was not inconsistent with the dominant authority of Congress as this was recognized in *McCulloch*. That currency and credit created by state-chartered banks became the bulk of the money stock, within such limits only as were set by the states—or, over some years, by the Banks of the United States—was the result of congressional default and not of the Court's requirement.[186]

State courts played less conspicuous, but still significant, parts in building public policy affecting the system of money. The sharp limits which the federal Constitution set to state power in this field meant that, as with the legislative branch, the state judiciary must make its principal contribution in matters touching bank-created money. State judges recognized the functional importance of bank notes to growth and continuity in transactions, by relaxing strict legal penalties when banks generally suspended redemption of notes in times of general financial crisis, and in more ordinary times by recognizing business customs of accepting currency that was not legal tender in discharging contract debts.[187] As bills of exchange and created deposits bulked larger than coin or currency in the total money supply state courts made their greatest impact by elaborating the judge-made law of commercial instruments which promoted the acceptability of deposit-check money by standardizing its legal incidents.[188] The functional limits of the judicial process meant that out of their own distinctive powers courts contributed primarily to making the system of money serve the needs of conducting particular transactions; this was the law which lent itself to development in the context of lawsuits, focused on the particular concerns of particular actors.[189] Overall, the law which helped shape and regulate money as a total system had to derive from legislative and executive or administrative action.

ALLOCATIONS OF CONTROL OVER MONEY: 1861-1908

The span from 1861 to 1908 was a period of recurrent, high controversy over law affecting the system of money. In the preceding period questions of banks' part in the money supply generated substantial issues in state as well as in national politics. The last half of the nineteenth century saw conflict mainly focused on the activity of the Congress. The contrast points to the main trend of policy, which moved in halting fashion toward that central-government leadership in monetary policy which the federal Constitution contemplated. However, the net product of about fifty years of agitation and combat did not represent much accomplishment over the situation that existed in 1860. Especially did this later period fail to add constructive policy dealing with the bank-created instruments—currency and checks drawn on deposits—which now provided the bulk of the money supply. Thus, despite the extensive political maneuvers over money through these years, the story of the law's impact on the system of money can be told rather shortly.

To say that developments in the 1860-1908 period centered on the actions or defaults of Congress should not be read as saying that the issues of this period centered on the federal-state balance of power. Indeed, the contrary was the fact. Controversy rose and fell about the place of Treasury notes in the money supply, about legal tender, about circulating paper of national banks, and about the ties of the money stock to gold or silver. Most of the conflict on these matters was not over federal as compared with state authority, but over the relative controls which law and market processes should have on the system of money. This distribution of issues fit the structural realities of the situation. Whatever the ambiguities concerning Congress's powers, the federal Constitution put such close and definite bounds on state action affecting money as to limit sharply the possible area of federal-state conflict. In the last half of the nineteenth century the rapid growth of an interdependent, national economy added pressures of fact to those of law, in reducing the possible roles of state policy affecting money. Moreover, from the seventies on the country experienced unprecedented developments in large-scale private economic organization, new styles of focused, private-interest pressures on political and lawmaking processes, and the emergence of more diffuse, unstable, yet occasionally effective groupings of farmers, workers, and middle-class reformers who sought to offset the political power of more concentrated private interests. This outpouring of private organizational energies made the relations of public and private power matters of increasing concern in the late nineteenth and early twentieth centuries, in contrast to older issues of the federal balance of power. In this context it is not surprising that allocations of roles between legal and market processes provided more of the substance of controversey over monetary policy than did allocations of functions between the central government and the states.

National and State Authority over Money

Between 1862 and 1864 Congress provided for issuing nearly $450 million of Treasury notes designed for circulation as currency. There could be no claim that it thereby invaded a reserved power of the states. The Constitution's ban on state bills of credit raised an unchallenged bar to comparable state issues of paper money. *Briscoe* had offered an avenue to states to provide currency backed by segregated funds. But the option which the court there allowed the states contained nothing which denied Congress the authority to provide a national currency. Moreover, a generation after *Briscoe* the states generally had shown no initiative, nor did they seem under effective political pressure, to use such opportunity as the Court had allowed them to set up state counterparts of the Banks of the United States.[190] Congress also declared that its $450 million of Treasury notes should enjoy legal-tender status. In this respect, too, no substantial question could be raised that its action encroached on state prerogative. Even more sharp-cut than the Constitution's ban on state bills of credit was its declaration that no state should make anything but gold and silver coin a tender in payment of debts. In contrast to its action in *Briscoe,* the Court opened no path of escape from this sweeping prohibition. Any doubt created by the Constitution's silence on Congress's authority to define legal tender bore not on Congress's obligation to respect state authority, but on such obligation as it might be under to respect private contract and property.[191] The Constitution matched its ban on state coinage with a grant to Congress not only of power to coin money, but also "to regulate the value thereof." Plainly, the existence of the states put no limit on Congress's power to fix the gold or silver content of the dollar; again, the issues that might be raised were not of federal-state power over money, but of the proper scope of federal money regulation relative to whatever constitutional principle might protect market processes.[192]

Given the limits set by the Constitution at the outset, together with later developments in legislative practice and judicial doctrine, the one area of substantial overlap of federal and state action affecting money involved banking. Between 1861 and 1869 the main current of federal action seemed set to drive state-chartered banks altogether from the field of monetary policy. That state banks survived to play a major role in supplying money was the result of a hodge-podge of factors. These included inept administration of the Treasury, unrealistic ideas about the nature of money, the want of a Hamilton to present a coherent program and press it with energy and skill, and—within the opportunity created by these elements of disorganization—the play of jealous private interests narrowly focused on local money markets.

Lacking such a fiscal agent as the second Bank of the United States, upon the onset of the Civil War the Treasury met its earliest needs by borrowing from eastern commercial banks. The scale of the war would have driven the government at last to other means of finance. But by sticking to the letter of its governing statutes the Treasury exhausted the utility of bank borrowing sooner than it need have done. The secretary of the treasury insisted on obeying the full, literal reach of the Independent Treasury Act of 1846, rejecting the flexibility possible under an amendment which, in August 1861, ambiguously "suspended" the 1848 statute in order to assist the government's unusual borrowings. The secretary insisted, thus, that the banks must make their loans available not by checks drawn against the government's loan-created deposits, but in gold. Publicly, the secretary justified his position as fulfilling the intent of Congress. But huge commercial bank loans to the United States were devices outside the experience and hence hardly within the intention of the Congress in 1846 or before. The terms of the 1846 act reflected this fact, for they were awkwardly applied to dealing with government receipts and disbursements under such bank credits; the credits did not readily fit the description of those "sums of money accruing or becoming due to the United States" which the 1846 act said should be paid to the United States in specie, nor was a commercial bank lender plainly an "officer or agent engaged in making disbursements on account of the United States" so as to be under the statutory duty to make payments for the United States, on its drafts, only in specie.[193] In addition, however ambiguous the 1861 amendment to the 1846 act, the fact that in the summer of 1861 Congress authorized the Treasury to borrow so great a sum as $250 million showed the felt urgency of the government's need, and fairly implied Congress's wish that the machinery of borrowing be adapted to meeting the need.[194] Off the record, the secretary claimed that if he had not demanded gold, the government's demands would have produced a dangerous expansion in state bank-note issues. The explanation lacks conviction. The scale of the government's war purchases would almost certainly have generated such administrative pressures as to force greater use of checks. As it was, by hampering the banks' capacity to help, Chase created the need for a different kind of inflationary paper money, in the shape of Treasury notes.[195] In any event, the pressure resulting from his insistence on gold led the banks to suspend specie payments by December 1861.[196]

The Treasury did not formulate, so much as it backed into, a policy of supplying a national currency under the prodding of wartime urgencies. Through 1861-63 the immediately effective pressure was the need to finance the war. Thus when in 1861 Congress authorized $50 million of small-denomination Treasury notes, declared payable in specie on demand, the step was taken to aid the government's borrowings from the eastern banks.[197] It was primarily the need to borrow beyond what could be had from the banks which produced the acts of 1862 and 1863 authorizing $450 million of Treasury notes, designed for circulation as currency and declared legal tender in payment for all public and private debts. That fiscal rather than monetary considerations were decisive was clear in Congress's discussion and in the support which Secretary Chase grudgingly gave despite his fear of the inflationary possibilities of government paper.[198] When in 1871 the Court finally held constitutional the legislation conferring legal-tender status on this government currency, the justices relied on Congress's power to take such measures as it reasonably found necessary to enable the government to borrow to meet its war bills.[199] In 1863 and 1864 Congress provided for chartering national banks which should have the privilege of issuing circulating paper secured by deposit of United States bonds. The action was taken against the background of pleas by the president, the secretary of the treasury, and influential men in and out of Congress, that the legislation was needed further to create a market for government bonds to help finance the war. At this point in time the need may have been less urgent than was the pressure which produced the 1862-63 legal-tender notes, but this does not negate the fact that proponents justified the national bank laws largely by the aid they might give to the government's fiscal program.[200]

The sum of these events was that by 1864 the United States had gone further than ever before in providing a money supply under national law, but had done so primarily to serve its own fiscal needs rather than to regulate the system of money. From this perspective the actions of 1861-64 raised no necessary challenge to continuation of the states' role in providing money through state-chartered banks.[201] Indeed, though the legal-tender laws of 1862-63 were enacted primarily to enable the government to borrow money more effectively, they had a secondary effect in support of state-chartered banks, which produced strong pressure for the laws from that quarter. Faced with the shortage of gold which led to the general suspension of specie payments at the end of 1861, the banks were much concerned that they be provided legal-tender paper with which they could lawfully discharge their debts and satisfy not only their more importunate creditors, but also those state statutes which required that state bank notes be redeemable in lawful money. Congress would not have passed such controversial legislation merely to bulwark the legal and business position of state banks, but the leadership showed some fear that the government notes would fail of general acceptance if the banks refused them. In any case, since the rigidity with which the Treasury enforced the 1846 statute was immediately responsible for the banks' shortage of gold, it was not inequitable that the legal-tender acts gave the banks this much balancing benefit.[202]

Nevertheless, there was an undercurrent of policy in these events of the early sixties which looked toward a national money supply which would not supplement but would supplant money created by state-chartered banks. Before and after he became Secretary of the Treasury, Chase believed strongly that state bank notes invaded what the Constitution had meant to be a sphere of policy exclusively for the central government and were so dysfunctional to a national economy that the country should rid itself of them. Fearing lack of discipline in direct government issues, he gave his sustained effort to obtain legislation for a national currency provided by delegation to privately owned and managed national banks. Thus Chase reluctantly accepted Congress's creation of the legal-tender United States notes because it was the only measure he could get at the time. But he stubbornly persisted in urging his national bank scheme, though it had dubious relevance to the government's fiscal need.[203] Some supporters of the legal-tender laws of 1862 and 1863 thought that the United States notes would be a welcome step toward a uniform national currency in place of the variable and unreliable notes of state banks.[204] The like argument was made in support of the national bank laws of 1863 and 1864.[205] But Congressional policy did not turn decisively toward realigning federal-state roles in the money supply until 1865. Chase and some congressmen had thought that the privilege of issuing national bank notes would speedily induce most bankers to switch from state to federal charters. The results quickly disappointed their impatience. So, in 1865, Congress moved decisively—as it thought—to end the states' role regarding bank-created money, by laying a tax on every national or state bank of 10 percent on the amount of notes of any state bank paid out after 1 July 1866.[206]

Measured by the expectations of its proponents, the 1865 tax was the most drastic pre-emption of monetary policy by the national government over the states since the framing of the Constitution. The tax was intended to and, in fact speedily, did end the issue of currency by state-chartered banks. Thus, together with the laws authorizing the issue of United States notes, the 1865 act established a central government monopoly in providing circulating paper.[207] Taking this as the purpose of the 1865 tax, in *Veazie Bank* v. *Fenno* (1869) the Court held that the tax did not violate the constitutionally reserved powers of the states; rather, the tax was within Congress's authority to adopt reasonable means to carry out what the Court ruled to be the constitutional prerogative of Congress "to supply a currency for the entire country." The functional justification for such action was to service the national economy. The allowable means must match the desired national impact. "To this end . . . Congress may restrain, by suitable enactments, the circulation as money of any notes not issued under its own authority. Without this power, indeed, its attempts to secure a sound and uniform currency for the country must be futile."[208]

The policy intention of the 1865 tax was broader than a ban on state bank notes as such. Though an increasing proportion of transactions were being settled by drawing on bank credits, most policy makers did not yet grasp that checks were becoming the bulk of the money supply. Because the proponents of the 1865 act identified the money-supply role of banks with the issue of bank notes, they thought that they were wholly removing the state banks from influence on the money supply when they made the use of state bank notes unprofitable. In fact, deposit-check money rather than bank notes was becoming the principal instrument of bank lending and bank profits. Experience taught this lesson quickly; by the early 1880s state-chartered banks were again increasing, and checks drawn on deposits created by bank lending provided a large part of the money stock. Thus the course of business frustrated the federal monopoly of monetary policy which Congress thought it was achieving in 1865.[209]

These developments strengthened the interests vested in state-chartered banks. Congress showed little heart for inviting battle by seeking to put all bank lending as well as all bank-note issues under national law, though such an effort would have pursued the substance of the policy set in 1865. The vigor with which *Veazie Bank* v. *Fenno* sanctioned a federal monopoly of currency might seem to warrant federal control of bank lending that materially affected the money supply. But, it is unlikely that in the 1870s the Court, any more than prevailing opinion in the Congress or in the country, was ready to perceive deposit-check money based on bank lending as the critical element in the system of money.[210] In any event, Congress did not take such action as would have put the issue to the Court. In 1863 and 1864 Congress made no effort to end the state banks by national fiat. Its manifest policy was to set up a competing system, with considerable expectation that the national banks' competition would drive the state banks out of existence. True, in substance the 1865 tax was viewed as a death blow to state banking. However, when business practice preserved the state banks, Congress took no further measures of outlawry, but reverted to its original stance of letting competition determine the outcome. Later legislation, into the twentieth century, confirmed the position; Congress exerted itself simply to assure that national banks should not suffer competitive disadvantage for want of legal powers to enter the same markets and offer like services as would match the activity of state-chartered banks.[211] Thus the creation of a dual banking system, with all of its implications for regulating the money supply, was determined more by the cumulative weight of unplanned business practice and the local interests which grew by accretion upon that base, than by a calculated policy of preserving a state sphere in making monetary policy. From the late sixties to 1908 the states showed little interest or capacity in making monetary policy. Like the contemporary federal legislation on national banks, state banking law focused on the individual soundness of banks as single entities in market. State law showed little concern for—or, indeed, conception of—banks as parts of a total money system under some public direction. Until past the turn of the century prime attention in making public policy affecting money was on allocating roles between official and market power, rather than on achieving some desired adjustment of roles between the national and the state governments.

Market Controls and Treasury Influence on Bank-Created Money

Most controversy over monetary policy in this period centered on defining the relative roles of legal processes and market processes. The most

striking feature of the record is how lopsided was the distribution of controversy—lopsided to an extent that was unrealistic and dysfunctional.
Most attention went to coin and currency. Little attention went to controls on credit, though the related deposit-check money became the bulk
of the money supply. Moreover, the effort invested in shaping policy on
coin and currency almost all went into futile search for rigid controls on
official power, in a field in which only flexible formulae could work. In
both aspects the record adds up to as inept a course of policy making as
United States legal history shows. Contending special interests thrashed
about, affecting what was done or was not done. But events developed at
least as much out of men's ignorance as out of their interest. The one central concern that emerged with some clarity was the preoccupation with
relations of governmental and market power over the money supply. Past
that point we must be careful not to impose artificial order on a course of
policy making which showed little coherent perception either of goals or
of cause and effect.

No conservative element was older in United States monetary policy
than distrust of government as direct issuer of paper money. Events of the
later nineteenth century confirmed this attitude as a policy, but rejected it
as a constitutional limitation on the Congress. Their legal-tender quality
apart, the United States notes for which Congress provided in 1862 and
1863 represented some development, but no revolution, in constitutional
doctrine. The framers had stricken from the draft Constitution an explicit
authorization to Congress to emit bills of credit. But the contemporary
record shows that they intended that Congress should have authority,
especially in time of emergency, to issue such paper as it might find necessary and proper to implement its authority to borrow money.[212] Before
1860 there was legislative precedent, stretching back to 1812, for the existence of this authority. However, the legislative precedent was thin for
including—as an incident of borrowing—the issue of paper designed to be
useful as circulating money.[213] In 1862 after more extensive debate than
ever before, and on a scale which elevated its actions to greater force as
precedent, Congress firmly claimed its authority to issue circulating paper
to help the national government to deal with a national, political emergency. In this framework the 1862-63 legislation had strong title in the
record of the federal Convention. The focus of opposition in 1862 was to
granting legal-tender quality; significantly, leading opponents of the 1862
measure conceded Congress's authority to issue circulating paper in aid of
its borrowings, and urged that the Treasury rely on such instruments, without attaching legal-tender status to them.[214] In *Veazie Bank* v. *Fenno*
(1869) the Supreme Court validated the position by holding that—as it
deemed was "settled by the uniform practice of the government and by
repeated decisions" (presumably referring to state courts which had al-

ready ruled the Civil War paper to be lawful currency)–"Congress may constitutionally authorize the emission of bills of credit." The Court carefully reaffirmed this ruling in 1870 when it held the grant of legal-tender quality to be beyond Congress's power; and the new majority which in 1871 reversed that decision and held the legal-tender notes constitutionally issued likewise affirmed Congress's authority to issue circulating treasury notes that were not made legal tender.[215]

The years 1878 and 1884 brought the truly drastic change affecting the distribution of power between the government and the market over the place of money in the economy. In 1878 Congress forbade the Treasury to retire any more of the United States legal-tender notes and directed that any such notes paid in to the Treasury should be reissued and paid out again and kept in circulation; the effect of the statute was to keep $347 million of the greenbacks in circulation. The measure had its roots in a typical legislative bargain, rather than in constitutional principle; continuation of the circulating notes was a price paid for preventing repeal of Congress's pledge of 1875 to make the government's paper redeemable in specie. The 1878 action produced no great addition to constitutional literature. Nonetheless, implicitly it asserted a major extension of Congress's power. In keeping the notes in circulation Congress responded to those who feared that severe retirement of the government paper would bring deflation which would bear harshly on both business and farmer debtors. In other words, the 1878 statute claimed authority in Congress to determine the issue of government circulating paper in order to regulate the on-going condition of the peacetime economy.[216] In 1884 the Supreme Court validated this claim. The Court found that the debate in the federal Convention was too inconclusive to bar Congress from deciding that the issue of paper money would serve the national interest in a smoothly functioning economy. Congress's power to issue money could not fairly be tied only to its power to borrow, though that power itself was broad enough to validate a wide discretion in choice of means. Building on *McCulloch* and *Veazie Bank* v. *Fenno,* the Court found in Congress authority to provide a currency for the whole country for the service of the economy, and it found this authority "fortified" by Congress's power to regulate foreign and interstate commerce. Within so generous an endowment Congress must have discretion to judge the wisdom and expediency of issuing paper money, "whether . . . in war or in peace," and whether "by reason of unusual and pressing demands on the resources of the government or the inadequacy of the supply of gold and silver coin to furnish the currency needed for the uses of the government and of the people."[217]

So far I have stressed the firm establishment by Congress and the Court of Congress's authority directly to create paper money, apart from the matter of legal tender. This emphasis does not match the emphasis of the policy makers of 1862-71, who generally did not contest this power of Congress, but fought rather over granting legal-tender status. However, my focus is true to the longer span of law-and-money history. Even by the years 1873-78, in which contending interests fought over contracting or expanding the greenbacks, the lasting issues were emerging as questions of who or what processes should determine the definition of lawful money (whether legal tender or not), and the quantity and timing of the provision of money. Measured by the longer course of policy, the grant or withholding of legal-tender status proved much less an object of concern than the other attributes of government control of the system of money. In this longer perspective, the most important impact of the legislation of 1862, 1863, 1865, and 1878, and the Court cases which grew out of these statutes, was to confirm in the broadest terms Congress's authority to create currency as well as coin.[218]

The fact remains, that in 1787 and in 1862 policy makers expressed their sharpest fear of government paper money when the law made it legal tender. The main object of fear was not the effect which money had peculiarly from legal-tender status. True, there was concern when given tokens were made legal tender retroactively, upsetting prior expectations. But retroactivity posed transitional problems; one way or another men would work through their older deals, and bargainers could adjust future transactions to legal-tender money. The more deeply disturbing aspects of legal-tender status were in what it symbolized and in the working effects it might have to make the symbol real. In the most unreconcilable fashion it symbolized the assertion that legal process should prevail over market process in determining what should be effective money, in practice as well as in law. More than assertion was at stake. Some who spoke against legal-tender paper in 1787 and in 1862 believed that legal-tender status would make given tokens so much more acceptable in practice—even if under compulsion—as to encourage larger issues of government paper than might otherwise circulate. To print money would be politically easier than paying higher and higher borrowing costs or raising more and more taxes. Legislators would soon press their resort to legal-tender currency into destructive inflation, subverting such controls as ordinary market dealing might otherwise create to hold the money supply in realistic relation to the flow of goods and services.[219]

The federal Convention let the Constitution stand silent on whether Congress had authority to confer legal-tender status on money; the record and the constitutional text fairly implied that Congress might do so as to coin, but it did no more than show the framers' distaste for legal tender as an incident of paper, without finally resolving what authority the Constitution gave.[220] In 1861-62 influential voices in and out of Congress sharpened the issue by asserting that the government should seek the funds it needed by going into the market to borrow, at whatever rates the market would demand by taking the government's bonds below par. Thus, in 1862 when Congress elected to issue circulating, legal-tender notes instead, clearly it sought to reject market governance, though the premium which gold commanded over the government's notes quickly showed that legal-tender status did not negate market influence and that the basic issue was not legal tender but the quantity and timing of the money supply relative to the general flow of resource allocations.[221] To the extent that Congress gave legal-tender status to the 1862 notes because it thought that this feature would make them in practice more acceptable as currency, mistaken or not, it acted within its constitutional discretion to choose means necessary and proper to carry out its other powers. In its 1870 decision invalidating the legal-tender act the Court invaded the legislative sphere in substituting its judgment on this point for that of Congress. The Court betrayed unease on this score, when it also put its decision on "another view, which seems . . . decisive, to whatever express power the supposed implied power in question may be referred." This "decisive" objection was the retroactive operation of the statute, which the Court found to offend "the spirit of the Constitution" symbolized in the contract clause limiting the states and in the due process clause limiting Congress. The essence of this objection was the drastic supplanting of market-established expectations in regard to the money value of contracts previously made.[222] Overruling the first decision, in 1871 a new majority of the Court held that Congress had authority to authorize legal-tender notes with both retroactive and prospective effect. The Court now ruled that market processes, as they operated through the law of contract, must yield to legislative decision concerning what tokens must be accepted as legally satisfying obligations to pay money. "[G]eneral power over the currency . . . has always been an acknowledged attribute of sovereignty." In view of the sweep of monetary powers given the Congress in contrast to the limitations put on the states, this kind of sovereign power should not be denied the United States. Congress could reasonably believe that legal-tender status would make the notes more acceptable in practice, whereas the ordinary course of market dealings would bring only steady depreciation of nonredeemable paper that was not legal tender; since such a judgment was within bounds of reason, Congress was entitled to make it, and thus to use law to give money an ingredient the market could not supply. The function of constitutional language—to arm government to deal with a changing future—precluded restricting Congress to lawful money based only on precious metals, for the market for those particular commodities "might prove inadequate to the necessities of the government and the demands of the people." Nor was there a "spirit" of the Constitution which exalted private contracts over the law's ultimate control of the system of money, even regarding contracts made before a given legal regulation was enacted. Like other aspects of life, contract and the market must be subject to government's proper concern with the good order of social relations generally. "Every contract for the payment of money, simply, is necessarily subject to the constitutional power of the government over the currency, whatever that power may be, and the obligation of the parties is, therefore, assumed with reference to that power."[223] When in 1884 the Court extended its earlier ruling by holding constitutional the reissue of legal-tender notes to serve the peacetime economy, it greatly extended Congress's authority to impose its own monetary policy on the market. The scope of this power, the Court re-emphasized, was "not defeated or restricted by the fact that its exercise may affect the value of private contracts. . . . [I]t is no constitutional objection to [the] . . . existence or . . . exercise" of a power of Congress "that the property or the contracts of individuals may be incidentally affected."[224]

Along with these assertions of sovereign prerogative over the system of money went a continuing, lively distrust of government's capacity to use this power fairly or efficiently. The Congress and the Court were ultimately unwilling to find substantial constitutional limits on Congress's control of money. But their policy—poorly articulated—was to use the law in ways calculated to foster and protect considerable scope for market, or marketlike, processes to affect the quantity, quality, and timing of the money supply. This policy took such shape as it achieved out of the cumulation of four kinds of policy decisions.

First, Congress consistently put statutory ceilings on new components of the money stock. It did so in the original laws of 1862 and 1863, which finally held the total United States notes authorized to $450 million, and it did so in effect in the 1878 act which continued the greenbacks then in circulation to a maximum of the then outstanding total of $347 million. It set an ultimate limit on the quantity of circulating notes which might be issued by the national banks provided under statutes of 1863 and 1864, by basing them on eligible government bonds, available only in limited supply, and within this outer limit for some years it imposed particular dollar limits. When it made concessions to those who wanted the coinage of silver and the issue of paper based on silver, it put ceilings on government purchases of silver and on the issue of silver-based paper. Consistent with this pattern, at the end of the period we are examining, when the Aldrich-Vreeland Act of 1908 authorized temporary associations of national banks to issue currency to meet financial crises, Congress carefully limited the length of time for which the emergency currency might be outstanding and imposed an over-all limit on the total amount of such currency which all national banks might provide.[225] In this course of legislation Congress never seriously entertained the idea of delegating to any executive agency or to any organization of national banks continuing authority to decide— within statutory guidelines—what quantity of currency would best serve changing economic conditions. The absence of any such deliberate delegation was highlighted by occasional, but episodic, exercise of discretion by the Treasury to use such questionable power as it might have under the statutes to adjust the money stock to the economy.[226] Congress's general approach was consistent with traditional distrust of executive power and with other kinds of limits (for example, on corporate capitalization) familiarly imposed on private delegates of public-interest jobs. But, in the context of continuing public controversy over the inflationary dangers of paper money, there was more than a separation-of-powers value embodied in the consistent jealousy with which Congress held these matters within its own particular decisions. All law-sanctioned paper money implied more dependence on the fairness and self-discipline of Congress itself than prevailing opinion usually liked. Back of the precise finality of these statutory limits was a dream of the comforting supervision of an impersonal, objective money market.

Secondly, the Court early contributed to this pro-market pattern of policy, by a questionable reading of the legal-tender acts as not intended to bar enforcement of contracts which called for settlement not in money but in specified quantities of gold or silver. This interpretation tended to defeat the uniformity in media of exchange which has always been a prime object of law. This defect of the ruling is so striking as to suggest the presence of a powerfully felt counter value. That counter value was the Court's obvious distaste for reading the federal statutes as encroaching any further than their terms strictly required, upon contract determinations as to what should be the operative means of exchange.[227]

Thirdly, between 1870 and 1900 recurrent controversy over the place of gold and silver in the money supply expressed a continuing search for the illusory certainty and objectivity of a commodities-market control rather than overt legal control of the money stock. Controversy moved through two phases. The first phase grew out of conservative demands that the United States notes be made legally and effectively redeemable in gold. In 1875 Congress made a commitment to resume gold payments in 1879, and by the latter year the Treasury succeeded in accumulating a sufficient specie reserve to make good the commitment.[228] Along the road to this conclusion, in the immediate aftermath of the war, the Treasury launched a program of retiring the greenbacks. But this policy stirred fears of deflation among debtor farmers and businessmen—industrialists, especially—who wanted an expanding economy and hence wanted an expanding money supply. Responding to this pressure, in 1866 Congress put the brakes on the Treasury's contraction efforts; in 1868 it "suspended" the Treasury's authority to reduce the currency; in 1874 Congress authorized a small increase in greenbacks (from $356 million to $382 million, though with a firm ceiling at $382 million); in 1875 it provided that the Treasury should retire $4 of its circulating notes for every $5 increase in national bank notes, and then finally in 1878 Congress again suspended retirement, to leave outstanding $347 million of greenbacks.[229] Despite the difference in their goals, there was a significant likeness in the attitudes held by many of the opponents in the fight over retiring the greenbacks. Those who wanted to reduce, and ultimately eliminate, the government notes sought to make the market supply of gold provide the base of the money supply, and thereby reduce the influence of political processes. Many who opposed retiring the greenbacks argued that the government notes should be left as they were, while the increase of business activity caused the economy to "grow up to them." Some conservative financial opinion opposed the 1875 act promising resumption of specie payments, because many bankers and businessmen distrusted any central, money management, and saw this statute as a move in that direction. On both sides, thus, there was underlying desire to increase the role of market processes, and reduce the role of government in regulating money.[230]

The second phase of controversy over a specie base for the money supply concerned the relative roles of gold and silver. A bewildering variety of ideas and interests played over this issue from the late seventies to 1900. The most stable element in the controversy—one not focused on monetary policy—was the straightforward industrial interest of the silver miners. Some paper-money men who at bottom wanted no restriction of the money stock to any specie base supported free coinage of silver because they saw this as a measure which in practice would lead to greater paper issues. But many of the gold men, the silver men, and the practical politicians who bargained between them, had a good deal in common from a separation-of-powers point of view. All of these wanted some specie base, because it would reduce the continuing intervention of lawmakers in determining the money supply. Justice Stephen J. Field spoke the basic article of faith shared by many such opponents: To him it was "the fact, accepted by all men throughout the world, that value is inherent in the precious metals; that gold and silver are in themselves values, and being such, and being in other respects best adapted to the purpose, are the only proper measures of value."[231] Secretary of the Treasury Hugh McCulloch translated this sentiment into a prescription for a separation of powers between the law and the market: "Coin being the circulating medium of the world, flows from one country to another in obedience to the law of trade, which prevents it from becoming anywhere, for any considerable period, excessive in amount; when this law is not interfered with by legislation, the evils of an excessive currency are corrected by the law itself."[232] Beyond this point, supporters of a gold base relied on the limits of gold supply to prevent an inflationary increase in the money stock and hold money to a value which was real because it was intrinsic. Their fears had confirmation in the support which some paper-money men gave to silver precisely because they thought either that silver would usefully supplement paper, or because of its inconvenience would facilitate further issues of paper.[233] On the other hand, silver spokesmen saw gold to be in such limited supply that a legally imposed gold standard spelled an artificial, law-created monopoly of money in the hands of those who controlled credit. In contrast, silver had come into easy supply, so that a silver base insured that financial men could not use the legal framework of money to their peculiar advantage.[234] We must not exaggerate the amount of such thinking which went into the twenty-five-years combat over the gold-silver ratio; emotion, myth, political ambitions, and the silver miners' search for a guaranteed market gave more impetus to the confused controversy than did ideas about cause and effect in the workings of money. Nonetheless, among the factors shaping policy the record includes a continuing desire to use some kind of specie market to regulate the money supply in order to limit the influence of law.

Finally, in creating a national bank system in 1863 and 1864 Congress further showed its preference for marketlike rather than government regulation of money. Proponents argued for the new national banks as potential buyers of government war bonds. But there was never convincing enthusiasm for this rationale; at best this new bond market promised to develop more slowly than the government's needs. It was a monetary goal—to provide a uniform and reliable national currency—that sustained Secretary Chase's stubborn persistence in getting his national bank legislation. Chase did not want government directly to issue paper money and with great reluctance accepted the authorization of the legal-tender notes. Like Hamilton, he feared that Congress would always yield to political pressures to inflate government-issued currency; like Hamilton, he had confidence that private bank management, within general limits set by statute, could resist such pressures. Some opponents of the national bank system highlighted this market-government, separation-of-powers value issue by objecting that the creation of money should be viewed as a function of government which it might not properly delegate.[235] On the other hand, Chase differed from Hamilton—and from Biddle—in readily favoring a dispersed rather than a centralized private-banking system, thus further electing a market-type rather than an administered discipline of money. Neither Chase nor his supporters sought to achieve a uniform national currency through a third Bank of the United States. Chase lacked the understanding of money and credit which might have inclined him to want a central bank. But the prime reason why he did not take this tack was undoubtedly that no practical politician would see profit in rekindling the controversy which had attended the end of the second bank. State-chartered banks had now had twenty more years in which to increase their number and the interests vested in them. State bankers mustered enough opposition to the new national banks to suggest the towering hostility that would have met a proposal for a federal central bank with a branching apparatus to extend its influence throughout the country. Thus the supporters of the 1863-64 legislation were content to rely on *McCulloch* v. *Maryland* to warrant Congress's authority to charter banks for national purposes, without trying to re-create Biddle's bank.[236] Instead, they borrowed from New York the pattern of a free-banking law, inviting the creation of many separate, private banks. The statutory regulations they imposed—minimum capitalization, required reserves against deposits and bank notes, United States bonds deposited as security for bank notes, periodic reports of condition—were relevant more to the business soundness of individual banks and their individual note issues, than to the efficiency of the national banks as a money-supply system.[237] The national bank acts created a national supervisory office, that of the comptroller of the currency. However, the functions of that office, like the underlying pattern of the statutes, looked simply to the regularity and security of issues of bank notes and the maintenance of required reserves by individual member banks of the system. Congress imposed, and charged the comptroller to enforce, some outside limits on national bank note issues, and Congress asserted control of authorized total issues by specific statutory ceilings and regional distributions. These regulations were static rather than dynamic. Rather than locating and legitimizing responsibility for bringing the national banks' contribution to the money supply into functional relation to the economy, Congress mainly set fixed outer limits of policy which introduced dysfunctional rigidities. As with contemporary state banking laws, the emphasis of the national acts was on securing the currency as if it were a debt to be paid, rather than managing it to serve the economy.[238] The outcome was partly the product of ignorance and want of vision. It was partly, also, the product of a preference, so taken for granted that policy makers did not feel need to expound it, for letting the volume and timing of national bank-note currency be determined by the cumulative impact of profit-seeking by individual banks, as a kind of money market, rather than by any deliberate management.

Contests over public and private controls on money between 1860 and 1908 were misdirected in proportion as they fastened on coin and currency and neglected bank lending, which had become the principal source of the money supply.[239] In the free-banking laws which became the norm in the states and were taken as the pattern for the national bank system, law contributed to creating the problem, joining calculated, permissive public policy to the driving energies of businessmen. Having thus fostered private agencies for expanding deposit-check money, legislators left this principal component of the money stock substantially alone through two generations of unsettling fluctuations in credit, punctuated by costly financial crises. The law's one major attention to bank deposits was to require that the individual bank hold a legally fixed coin or currency reserve against deposits. Established in only a handful of states before 1880, a law-imposed reserve existed in some fifteen states by the turn of the century and was a feature borrowed from the pioneering state legislation in the national bank acts in 1863 and 1864.[240] However, neither in conception nor in effect were these reserve requirements instruments for regulating the over-all supply of deposit-check money. Their original purpose was to protect depositors as contract claimants of the banks. They were fixed requirements, which made no claim and created no means for any legal agency to relax or tighten the required reserves in order to induce increase or decrease in bank lending relative to the condition of the economy. Standing alone, reserve requirements created no resources in law for a credit pool by which government might affect private banks' lending. Nor did the legal reserve requirements provide means to relate the stock of coin and currency to the condition of deposit-check money; the neglect of the deposit component bore fruit in recurrent runs on banks, when the law's very success in building confidence in the currency led fearful depositors to clamor for currency in preference to deposits. Moreover, in effect the reserve requirements abdicated legal responsibility for the over-all condition of bank lending, while they fostered private, centralized power which the law in nowise made publicly accountable. The statutes did so by authorizing local banks to keep substantial parts of their required reserves as deposits with other banks in key cities. This portion of the required reserve tended to move especially to New York City, and there to be lent largely on call in supporting stock market transactions. The outcome was to focus the pressures of fearful depositors or nervous local banks on one or a few private money markets, typically at times when general business conditions were disturbed, and with no publicly responsible agency available to furnish either added credit, or currency, or supervision, if the demands made exceeded the capacity of the private banks.[241]

Conceivably, the law's limited attention to deposit-check money reflected a conscious separation-of-powers judgment comparable to that which led Hamilton and Chase to prefer currency issued by privately managed banks over currency issued by government. By this reading, legislators left deposit-check money to be managed mostly by the play of private credit markets, because they distrusted government's capacity to act with wisdom and skill to adjust contending interests for the general good. However, the record does not support so rational an interpretation. Through the nineteenth century there was no substantial effort to create legal supervision of the volume, timing, and quality of bank credit as a whole. Had such an effort been made—with energy comparable to that invested, say, in the gold-silver controversy of the last quarter of the century—probably a sharp issue would have been drawn over the relative weight of market and government controls. The bitter contest waged in 1912-13 over banker control compared with public control of a new central-bank apparatus suggests how lines of combat would have been drawn, had the matter been put to decision earlier. However, since the question was not pressed to issue in the nineteenth century, it is at most a plausible hypothesis that strong but latent attitudes and interests supported the reliance on market controls of deposit-check money which was the principal policy de facto before 1908.[242] The terms in which the battle was waged over the Federal Reserve System suggests a second, more basic difficulty in the nineteenth-century policy record. As late as 1912-13, in a climate then favorable to extending legal controls over money, debate still centered largely on currency and on reserves against currency and deposits and contributed little to ideas about managing over-all bank credit. It is not surprising, therefore, that prevailing opinion through the nineteenth century identified money with coin and currency and simply did not perceive bank-created deposits as part of the problem. True, more sophisticated observers appeared, who reckoned deposits and checks in the active money supply. But common attitudes treated bank lending as part of the realm of private contract and of relevance in public policy only as that policy favored free contract and protected obligations among the contracting parties themselves. No issue was pressed between government and market controls on deposit-check money largely because prevailing perception did not include deposits as a component—let alone the principal component—in the system of money.[243]

Two developments in the second half of the nineteenth century showed that the growth of deposit-check money was creating new problems in organizing the money supply. In a fumbling way these developments acknowledged that the money system needed control apparatus more deliberately managed than markets operating only through the cumulative impact of thousands of private transactions. One of these developments was the expansion of clearinghouse procedures created by private agreement of large-city banks. The other was the tendency of the United States Treasury to play a central banker's role with the leverage afforded by the public moneys.

Several New York City banks established the first clearinghouse in 1853. Set up at first simply as an exchange convenience, the device had such utility for the systems relationships of its participants that its functions steadily expanded. In short order clearinghouses moved into regulating the solvency of their member banks and policing their members' liquidity under the effective discipline of required daily settlement of balances. Assuming to a limited extent the role of lenders of last resort, they created interest-bearing, clearinghouse certificates based on deposited liquid securities. By 1860 they had added agreed pooling of specie held by trustee committees. After 1873 the issue of clearinghouse certificates became a regular response to currency crises. Slowly, in the early 1900s clearinghouses began to establish uniform collection charges, or par collection, for out-of-town checks. The growth of correspondent relations between country banks and central-city banks in effect extended the impact of clearinghouse operations in the large cities.[244]

The clearinghouse developments showed that there was considerable potential for using private agreements to impose organized controls on otherwise unplanned credit markets. Yet, the experience also showed serious limitations in this contract-style response to the needs of the money supply as a system. The growth of systems cooperation through such localized and diverse channels was slow, hampered by competitive jealousy and parochialism; as late as 1893 resort to clearinghouse certificates in crisis was limited to a few big cities, and regulation of collection charges lagged far behind the increased use of checks. In the continuity and day-to-day closeness of their scrutiny, the clearinghouses applied a discipline to their members' lending practices which was far superior to the clumsy, static limits indicated by fixed legal-reserve requirements. But dependence on private volunteer effort limited the geographical scope and the financial resources which clearinghouses could command. The law's legislative processes were slow and clumsy, too, and they also tended to respond to parochial interests. Nonetheless, Congress provided a single arena of decision for problems that made themselves felt nationwide, and Congress could provide standards and apparatus reaching throughout the whole country, and financial resources to match the pressures of country-wide problems.[245] The ultimate defect in private organization of controls through the clearinghouses arose from their very progress—as had been the case with the second Bank of the United States. In the financial crisis of 1907 clearinghouse certificates were issued by fifty-one clearinghouses, and by some in denominations small enough to allow the certificates to function as a circulating medium. At this point, privately organized power once again touched so broad a range of public interests as to generate calls for public regulation. Already, in 1895, 1898, and 1902, Congressmen had introduced bills to legitimize the terms of issuing clearinghouse certificates. In 1908 Congress enacted the Aldrich-Vreeland Act, authorizing agreements among groups of national banks to provide currency backed by a wide range of security, including short-term commercial paper, but under a statutory ceiling and subject to taxes designed to compel rapid retirement of the issues.[246]

The Treasury provided the other groping response to the need for some central management of money derived from bank lending. Thanks to the public revenues, the Treasury often held great potential power to grant or withhold liquid assets on which banks could base their lending. The first half of the nineteenth century saw scattered incidents in which the Treasury used this power—restrictively, for example in the Specie Circular of 1836; expansively, in shifting public deposits from the second Bank of the United States to selected state institutions. The Independent Treasury Act of 1846 formally divorced the Treasury from money-management relations with banks, and Secretary Chase so rigidly applied the (amended) 1846 act as to thrust the government into creating a fiat currency. But the acts of 1863-64 gave the Treasury authority to use the new national banks as depositories of public money. Other statutes providing for qualified retirement of the greenbacks in effect put further discretion in the Treasury to affect the money supply by temporary variations in the quantity of those notes available. Within this framework, in the last quarter of the century by administrative practice the Treasury developed several modes of enlarging or contracting the reserves available as a base for bank lending. On occasion it released or reissued greenbacks to relieve a seasonal shortage of currency. To prevent the deflationary effect of accumulating revenues, it used its surplus to redeem government debt or to prepay interest on the debt, and it deposited internal revenue proceeds in national banks, sometimes placing such deposits to relieve seasonally tight money in agricultural areas, sometimes to add to central-city reserves. Through the end of the nineteenth century these Treasury actions were sporadic, *ad hoc* responses to particular urgencies. The Treasury was reaching toward central-bank functions, but without contributing to the economy the confidence which could rest only on a responsible definition of mission and an assured continuity of resources. Secretary of the Treasury Leslie M. Shaw (1902-6) sensed that desirable impact was lost for want of more formal assignment of jobs and the means of doing them. At the end of several years of the most conscious and active Treasury efforts at money management, Shaw recommended that Congress provide a $100 million fund for deposit or withdrawal from banks as the Treasury might find expedient to adjust the money supply to the movements of the economy, plus power to vary banks' reserve requirements against deposits as well as to change the conditions for national bank-note issues to enlarge or contract the circulation as the Treasury found desirable. In effect, Shaw would have put the Treasury directly into the role later given to the Federal Reserve System. The close contest and compromises out of which the Federal Reserve emerged ten years later indicates that Shaw's proposals were politically impracticable. That he made the proposals at all, however, was significant of the tardy movement of public policy toward legal controls which would recognize the reality of bank lending as the critical component of the money supply.[247]

Roles of Major Legal Agencies

The years just after the war witnessed extraordinary activity in amending the federal Constitution. But, though men fought hard over the legitimacy of various legal actions on money between 1860 and 1912, they did not bring formal constitution-making processes into play on these questions. This is not surprising, for with one exception the matters in contest did not reach beyond the bounds of established legislative and judicial procedures. Within the standards set by the Constitution's language and the records left by those who framed and adopted that language, and within the scope which seventy-five years of political practice allowed for developing constitutional doctrine by legislative, executive, and judicial precedent, no formal change was required to accommodate the direct issue of government currency in national emergency, the chartering of national banks as agents of national governmental and economic goals, the preemption of the role of state-chartered banks in issuing currency, the resolution of the place of gold and silver in national patterns of money notation and value, or the subjection of past or future market transactions to the sovereign's power to fix the terms of a money system which was a necessary constituent of any market. The possible exception, where fair argument can be made that change should have been by constitutional amendment, consists in the 1878 statute authorizing continuation and reissue of United States notes in peacetime, to serve the regular needs of the economy, and the Court's validation of that statute in 1884. There is substantial question whether the 1878 act had warrant in the Constitution's terms, read in the context of sharp contemporary differences over government-issued currency and the caution and distrust manifest toward such issues in the federal Convention. Taken in that setting, the matter did not lie in the realm of debatable fact and judgment familiar to questions under the necessary and proper clause—a realm in which our practice firmly legitimates growth by legislative and judicial precedent. Rather, at issue was a more naked question—whether the 1878 statute fell under any basic head of Congress's authority at all. What the Congress and the Court did here pressed our informal practice of constitutional amendment to its limit. On the whole, it seems fair to judge that their actions did not go beyond the limit, in light of the indicated constitutional intent that the national government fully control the system of money and that it enjoy broad authority to promote a truly national economy.[248]

Congress was the primary forum in which basic decisions were taken on the law of money in this period. The federal executive supplied some initiative in programming policy, but either the goal of its activity was legislation (as in the national bank laws) or its action (such as the Treasury's episodic ventures in money management) could go on only within a statutory framework. The Court made itself felt in this field almost entirely by responding to questions posed by legislation—ruling on the constitutionality or the interpretation of what Congress had done. Functional logic dictated that Congress should provide the main content of the law on the money supply. After 1860 there was fresh need to generalize monetary policy for national goals; generalization is the special job of legislation; generalization of national policy is the special job of the national legislature. Challenges of war and then of peacetime economic growth called for new organization of the money supply; to provide government apparatus (as in the office of the comptroller of the currency) or franchises to serve public interest (as in the national banks), or broad standards or rules to govern conduct (as in defining legal tender or the relation of gold and silver in the money base), was to take legal action of such character as our tradition assigned to the legislative branch. In a time of increased public revenues and spending, government fiscal policy could not but affect the supply of money available in private channels; no job was more firmly set as the exclusive prerogative of the legislature than control of the public purse. So far as Congress allowed, legislatures likewise made the states' most important contribution to monetary policy, when they used their franchise powers to spread the free-banking laws and so to help multiply agencies to create deposit-check money.[249]

The executive in the federal government—more the Treasury than the president—gave some direction to monetary policy in the war years, though its action was uneven and often faltering, whatever its errors or shortcomings. After the war federal executive policy leadership lacked insight or sustained creativity. The country might fairly ask from the Treasury more sophistication in money matters than could be expected from general opinion. But the Treasury did nothing to educate Congress or the country in the significance of bank lending as the principal source of the money supply. Indeed, this deficiency was thrown into sharper relief by the Treasury's spasmodic ventures in manipulating the public debt or the public deposits to affect bank reserves. The most costly default in executive leadership was that successive presidents and their financial advisers uncritically accepted and merely reacted to the common opinion which held that the specie base of money was the key issue in monetary policy, first in the contest over providing specie payments on United States notes, then in the sterile controversy over free silver.[250]

Tradition and practice have assigned to the Congress and the presidency large responsibility for mediating the conflict of major interests in the national society. Hopefully these agencies may help resolve conflicts in workable peace and rationality, in ways calculated to serve the public interest. So measured, the legislative and executive efforts put into making monetary policy between 1870 and 1908 appears either feeble or largely wasted; about the best that can be claimed for the performance is that it had the negative virtue of rejecting extremes of inflationary or deflationary policy urged on government by zealots of soft- and hard-money persuasions. Again, what dominates the record is the unrealistic concentration upon the specie basis of the money system: unrealistic because it sought an impossibly impersonal and automatic governor for the money supply and because it omitted concern for the general condition of bank lending which produced the bulk of the money supply. Within this unprofitable frame of reference Congress proceeded to fail the public interest—by allowing the silver mining industry to wield absurdly disproportionate influence on policy, by warping monetary issues to serve narrow and short-term partisan advantage, and by allowing policy direction to be lost amid the confused and fragmented estimates which a variety of special interests (merchants, bankers, industrialists, labor organizers, farmers) made from time to time of what they could gain or lose by one device or another. Probably the greatest social cost of all this shuffling lay not in the peculiar profit which any of the special interests won for itself, but in the fact that their interplay—undisciplined by any strong policy leadership generated through legal process—added to the misdirection of effort which subjected the country to the costs of an inefficient system of money.[251]

The most convincing plea in mitigation of this poor legislative-executive performance is that men lacked knowledge to better adapt the system of money to the rapidly expanding market society of the late nineteenth century, and lacked tradition or experience in providing the administrative skill and organization which more ambitious money management required. These are valid points. They remind us with what grinding force ignorance and inertia constrain public policy making. But it is precisely because ignorance and inertia weigh so heavily on life that, in a fairly open society, we properly measure policy makers by their capacity to use the resources of legal process to add more meaning to experience. By this test the Congress and the presidency, most charitably judged, did a mediocre job in shaping monetary policy in the last quarter of the nineteenth century.[252]

The Supreme Court's contribution to monetary policy between 1860 and 1908 was chiefly to give Congress the scope to do better than Congress did. The Court began with a major blunder in 1870, when it ruled that Congress had exceeded its constitutional authority in giving legal-tender status to the United States notes authorized by Congress in 1862. There was some ground to question Congress's authority to issue any paper money at all, although notes issued—as these were—to help meet a national war emergency were clearly within the powers which those who spoke in the federal Convention showed that they meant Congress to have. Quite a different issue was posed, however, by the grant of legal-tender status. If legal-tender quality was warranted, plainly it was on the ground that it was a necessary and proper incident to fulfilling Congress's authority to issue an effective currency, or to borrow money in order to deal with emergency war financing. What Congress might reasonably deem a necessary and proper means for exercising its basic authority presented questions of fact and of judgment on facts, regarding which by traditional doctrine Congress's action was entitled to the benefit of a strong presumption of constitutionality.[253] The utility of legal-tender status to effectuating Congress's scheme for financing the war was at least in the realm of reasonable debate, and hence must be upheld. When the Court first held invalid the legal-tender acts, it flagrantly invaded the sphere of legislative prerogative; in a contemporary criticism Oliver Wendell Holmes, Jr., put the matter accurately when he said that the decision "presented the curious spectacle of the Supreme Court reversing the determination of Congress on a point of political economy."[254] In 1871, reversing itself to uphold the legal-tender acts, the Court corrected its error, and properly relied on the presumption of constitutionality to do so. Considerable ink has been spilled over the fact that this reversal was by the votes of two recent appointees, Justices Bradley and Strong, with the inference drawn that President Ulysses S. Grant packed the Court to get the decision. Responsible later appraisals have found no basis for the charge; the already formed and declared views of the two appointees, that the legal-tender acts were within Congress's constitutional authority, were known to Grant, but there is no evidence that the appointments were conditioned on any pledge of future votes, nor was there any departure from regular practice when a president nominated men with whom he felt a community of values on matters of broad public policy. In any case, the first legal-tender decision was so clearly an improper exercise of judicial policy making, and the second decision so clearly a proper exercise of judicial self-restraint, that the innuendos over the Bradley-Strong appointments have the importance only of gossip.[255] The third legal-tender decision, in 1884—upholding the continuation of government note issues to serve the regular, peacetime economy—perhaps pressed to the limits of the Court's proper authority to shape the Constitution to changing concepts of public policy. But the decision had reasonable warrant in the general monetary policy indicated by the Constitution as well as in the commerce power, and it did not involve the vice of the 1870 decision, of identifying the justices' views of economic wisdom with the Constitution.[256]

ALLOCATIONS OF CONTROL OVER MONEY: 1908-70

When we look at the latest period in monetary policy there is temptation to find that lawmakers have resolved all problems and achieved a settled pattern of values. The urge to discover comforting order is understandable, but lacks realism. The years after 1970 would probably find monetary policy still in lively and often confused controversy, still bedeviled by want of knowledge and of will and by clash of interests. This state of things should not be surprising. The system of money was an effective instrument of power and was functionally tied to allocating resources and distributing costs and benefits in this high division-of-labor, high capital-investment society; public policy here could not become fixed so long as men contested over economic power and bumbled their way toward new apportionments of gains and losses in their common living. Nonetheless, the years 1908-70 hang together as a chapter in the allocation of power over money, and some matters of policy do in those years fall into a settled condition. Questions of the federal balance now appear resolved in favor of centralizing major money-policy decision making. Jurisdictional questions between official and private power now stand firmly resolved in favor of official controls; what here remains in question is whether government can command or acquire the skills and discipline to make its controls meaningful. It was regarding the separation of powers among official agencies that this period showed the most unsettled basic issue, concerning the relative roles of the Treasury and the new Federal Reserve System.

National and State Authority over Money: Regional Federalism

These twentieth-century years showed that there remained no substantial question arising from the existence of the states, as to the plenary power of Congress over the system of money, when Congress chose to use that power. When Congress authorized change in the gold content of the dollar in 1934, the Court treated as the only serious constitutional question the claim on behalf of private right against retroactive application of the change; no issue of federalism troubled the justices.[257] Creation of the Federal Reserve System in 1913 and of the Federal Deposit Insurance Corporation in 1933-34 might be thought to raise more colorable issues that Congress was invading spheres of public policy which the Tenth Amendment left to the states. By regulating rediscount rates and by affecting terms of credit through open-market buying and selling of government securities the Federal Reserve Board and its regional banks injected potent federal regulation into creditor-debtor relations whose general incidents were typically governed by state law; bank deposit insurance, some said, was just a matter of creditor security, which was the normal business of state law. Perhaps because the bases of federal authority were so well established in this realm, the Supreme Court was not required to rule on the constitutionality of the Federal Reserve System or the FDIC.[258] Judges in lower federal courts found no difficulty in upholding Congress's authority, in the rare instances where litigants pressed the Tenth Amendment issue. Congress was well within the area of discretion which the necessary and proper clause gave it, in deciding that the Federal Reserve and the FDIC were agencies reasonably calculated to promote and protect the good working of a national system of money. If the ordinary operation of state law of contract or property, or the conduct of transactions ordinarily governed by state law, had material effect upon the national money system, Congress might to such extent supersede state law. This was made plain by Supreme Court decisions reaching from *McCulloch* v. *Maryland* to *Juilliard* v. *Greenman,* and by cases upholding broad statutory protections for the federal functions of national banks created under the act of 1864. The conclusion was so clear, thought the federal Second Circuit Court of Appeals, that it "would [not] . . . seem even reasonable to argue" that there was not federal power to warrant Federal Reserve open-market operations undertaken to regulate terms of bank credit.[259]

That Congress had authority to set its own goals and create its own agencies of monetary policy did not necessarily challenge the continued existence of state-chartered banks as contributors to the money supply. Under the Constitution and congressional and judicial precedent, banking was the only field left in which state lawmakers might help shape the system of money. Here the twentieth-century years consolidated positions already well set. However, in those years the central government asserted greatly increased general power over the national economy. This development naturally suggests the question, whether Congress might validly eliminate state-chartered commercial banks or require all state-chartered financial institutions to submit their deposit business to federal regulation, as measures necessary and proper to federal control of a money supply now provided mostly by checks drawn against deposits.[260] The question remained without direct answer, because Congress never directly posed it. Unlike its gesture of 1865, in the twentieth century Congress never acted to abolish state banks, nor even to impose uniform reserve requirements on them. When it created the Federal Reserve System in 1913 and in 1933 and 1934 set up a system to insure bank deposits, it took deliberate decisions to leave optional with state-chartered banks whether they would enter these arrangements or, having entered, withdraw, though it conditioned their entry on terms set by federal statute or by federal administrators under statutory delegation.[261] This policy could be taken to mean that the continued co-existence of state-chartered banks created some check on restrictive regulations imposed by Congress or the Federal Reserve Board on member banks, lest the latter find it to their interest to leave the system and operate apart under state charters. However, the record did not show that members of the system overtly used this threat.[262] Because all bank lending affected the money supply, Congress might have been brought seriously to consider pre-empting regulation of commercial banking, had states shown a disposition to attempt some positive money management through the terms they set on state bank operations. But, with one exception, the states held their regulations within closer confines; their principal declared goals were to restrict the chartering of banks to numbers sufficient to serve the ordinary business needs of localities and to supervise banks to assure their integrity as going businesses for the benefit of their creditors.[263] In this context, twentieth-century state banking law—more sharply than its counterpart in the first half of the nineteenth century—spoke simply for local interests involved in local economies, and did not enter the area of monetary policy where Congress might assert paramount control.[264] The one exception to this limited pattern was instructive. Between 1907 and 1918 a handful of states created statutory schemes of deposit insurance for their own chartered banks. Such measures touched monetary policy, because they helped support deposit-check money. Under the impact of agricultural depression in the 1920s, these plans collapsed; individual state economies offered too narrow an asset base for a secure insurance scheme. Thus the states' one positive innovation in banking law directly affecting the system of money failed in a way which pointed up the functional pressures toward central-government control. In any event, in their time these state deposit-insurance plans were not seen as challenging paramount federal power.[265] Had Congress been brought squarely to pre-empt the whole field of commercial banking, as an action necessary and proper to providing a suitable national money supply, probably the Court would have sustained the legislation.[266]

In the national bank acts of 1863 and 1864 Congress had set a policy of competitive coexistence of nationally chartered and state-chartered banks. After experience showed the limited impact of the 1865 federal tax on circulating state bank notes, federal legislation held to the coexistence policy. Congress made some effort to arm national banks with powers enabling them to compete in offering services to customers and with protections against state taxes or regulations which might impair their ability to fulfill federal policy; on the other hand, so far as consistent with fulfillment of their federal functions, national banks were held to compliance with state laws. This continued to be Congress's declared policy on relations of federal and state banking law in the twentieth century. But the policy was not as settled as it might appear to be. Both sides in the relationship were unhappy. National banks complained that Congress did not truly equalize their competitive position vis à vis state-chartered banks. In the early 1960s a vigorous comptroller of the currency, James J. Saxon, criticized federal administrators for not having used the discretion he found in the statutes to allow national banks to be more competitively innovative. In turn, state bankers and bank regulators were stirred to fear and controversy by the comptroller's liberality in chartering new national banks and enlarging the business privileges of national banks; concern appeared that state banks might begin to convert to federal charters to get more flexibility for action. However, through 1970 neither party had mustered enough strength or concern to obtain a restructuring of the coexistence policy from Congress.[267]

Coexistence was plainly a kind of policy Congress was constitutionally authorized to make in an area of concurrent national and state powers. It was a policy which could be pursued without prejudice to such further authority as Congress might have, if it chose to assert it, to supersede state laws in order to achieve a paramount federal purpose.[268] The debatable issue over the competitive coexistence policy was of its wisdom and not of its constitutionality. There is little in the record to show that competitive coexistence continued and took further root in the twentieth century for reasons better than institutional inertia (the familiarity of state-chartered banks, plus a generalized bias in our political tradition favoring dispersed power) reinforced by the vested interests of state banks and state administrators. The unreality of a federal balance-of-power rationale for a dual banking system is suggested by the absence of concrete evidence that the option to hold a state charter and stay apart from the Federal Reserve System was used by member banks of the system to check its power.[269] The reality of the interests vested in state banking systems was attested in the process of shaping the Federal Reserve Act and, again, in the 1930s.

The suggestion was made in 1913 of requiring Federal Reserve membership by all banks accepting deposits on which checks might be drawn. The idea met political opposition too formidable to be overcome, from state banking commissions, from state bankers resisting both federal jurisdiction and the threat of regulations more restrictive than those of the states, and from big city banks which feared the loss of correspondent accounts. The banking acts of 1933 and 1935 in substance limited the new federal deposit insurance to banks which became members of the Federal Reserve, but Congress removed the requirement in 1939.[270] Yet, only with difficulty could the coexistence policy be justified in functional terms. Functionally, money should be a single system for the national economy. Since all banks were implicated in creating money, functional values pointed to banks under one system of law. The dual banking pattern was dysfunctional insofar as it allowed diverse reserve requirements, varying standards of bank examination, and uneven controls on the quality of bank-created credit. There was plausible functional argument for the existence of numerous independent banks rather than a few institutions with many branches. But the advantages of unit banks as facilities responsive to local need were advantages of maintaining a kind of widely dispersed credit market, and not of maintaining dual legal regulation.[271]

The federal policy of competitive coexistence did not preclude federal regulation of state bank operations in particular respects which the central government found to bear upon an effective national money supply. Thus President Roosevelt's bank "holiday" proclamation of 6 March 1933 closed all state as well as national banks at a moment of nationwide financial crisis.[272] "For the purpose of preventing the excessive use of credit for the purchase or carrying of securities," the Securities and Exchange Act of 1934 empowered the Federal Reserve Board to regulate the amount of credit that might be extended or maintained on any federally regulated securities by state or national banks.[273] The federal Bank Holding Company Act of 1956, as amended in 1966, provided federal standards for creation of bank holding companies and approval of their acquisitions, applicable to "any institution that accepts deposits that the depositor has a legal right to withdraw on demand." This statute thus set a federally determined floor for regulating holding company activity involving state as well as national banks; the act reserved to the states the right to adopt more restrictive legislation, if they chose to do so.[274] Resolving doubts as to applicability of the Sherman and Clayton acts to banks, federal legislation on bank mergers in 1960 and 1966 applied to state as well as to national banks.[275]

In the second half of the twentieth century the impact of federal regulation on the monetary role of state banks could not be measured simply by explicit supersession of state by federal law. In 1864 Congress had adopted the policy of competitive coexistence to avoid a divisive clash of interests. But such nationalists as Secretary of the Treasury Chase had accepted this pattern in confidence that the attractions of national charters would drive state banks from the field; competition would end coexistence. By the 1880s it was plain that the national bank system had not won such a victory, and into the twentieth century state-chartered banks grew to far out-number national banks.[276] However, by mid-twentieth century the Federal Reserve System and the deposit insurance administered by the FDIC had indirectly accomplished in the monetary field the victory envisaged by the nationalists in 1864. By 1964 though only 18 percent of state banks had elected to become members of the Federal Reserve System, the member banks of the system—national and state banks together—accounted for about 85 percent of the bank deposits in the country. By 30 June 1964 of 13,668 commercial banks in the United States, 13,394 were FDIC-insured.[277] These membership figures meant that substantial federal regulation entered into the conduct of most state-chartered banks, and especially into the operations of those state banks of most consequence for the money supply. Federal Reserve membership meant that the member bank was subject to terms of operation set by the Federal Reserve Act and by board action under the act affecting reserves, the rediscount rate for borrowing at the federal reserve banks, and examination of books. Moreover, the member bank came under the discipline of its regional bank through the strictness with which the federal reserve banks typically scrutinized members' requests for rediscounting their paper. State banks which were not members of the Federal Reserve System but which elected to take FDIC insurance—numerically, the bulk of state banks—thereby came under a uniform procedure of examination of their affairs by the federal corporation.[278]

In addition to the reach of such overt regulations, all state banks came under pressures of Federal Reserve policy enforced by fact; when the bulk of bank deposits were held in federal reserve member banks, and the services offered by the system attracted into its processes the handling of a great part of deposit-check money, nonmember state banks inevitably found their scope of operation bounded by what the system did. The costs of clearing checks presented an early example. Many nonmember state banks, especially the smaller, country banks, charged an exchange fee for remitting the sums due under checks drawn on them and deposited by the recipient at some distant point. An amendment to the Federal Reserve Act forbade federal reserve banks to pay exchange fees for clearing checks. Moreover, it was system policy to promote par clearance of checks across the country as a contribution to uniformity and full value in the system of deposit-check money. In early years the system put pressure on nonmember banks to abandon exchange charges by presenting checks on the fee-charging banks at their counters, where by law they must pay in full in cash; the threat of presentation over the counter required the banks to hold more cash reserves than otherwise, and so cut doubly into their profits, both by loss of exchange fees and by loss of profit on the money they might have loaned out had they not had to hold it in reserve. State banks resisted, by litigation and by obtaining protective statutes from their state legislatures. The Supreme Court drew a line which in effect distinguished between duress and pressure produced by function. The Court found no warrant in the Federal Reserve Act for federal reserve banks deliberately to accumulate checks drawn on banks which charged exchange fees in order to present at the counter for cash an embarrassing quantity of such checks. But the act did authorize the federal reserve banks to provide clearing facilities. If the banks drew to themselves increasing quantities of checks for clearance, because their clearing service was efficient and cheap, they were legally entitled to present at the counter for cash such checks as came to them in the normal course of business, drawn on banks which otherwise insisted on an exchange fee for remitting the proceeds to distant points. Business loss to the local banks caused by competition in service was not a legal injury.[279]

Of far greater weight was the impact of the system's open-market buying and selling of government securities. At the outset the Federal Reserve Act empowered the federal reserve banks to engage in such transactions, administrative practice developed these dealings as an instrument to ease or tighten bank credit generally, and in the Banking Act of 1935 Congress ratified the new type of control. Given considerable fluidity of credit and substantial competition in seeking and offering it, such open-market operations tended to make themselves felt wherever money was loaned. The critical scrutiny which bankers generally gave to Federal Reserve open-market dealings attested the reality of this pervasive pressure, which the courts declared to be within the constitutional authority of the federal government to create in order to make effective its control of the national money supply.[280]

The continued separate existence of state-chartered banks was important for the organization, staffing, and everyday administration of individual institutions. But by 1970 the competitive attractions of the Federal Reserve System and the Federal Deposit Insurance Corporation meant that the federal government had in fact nationalized banking in the respects most directly affecting banks' contributions to the money supply.

The creation of the Federal Reserve System brought into being a statutory analogue to the constitutional allocation of authority in a federal system in the shape of an assignment of powers between the Federal Reserve Board and the federal reserve banks. The federal analogy was not complete. Here the units offsetting central power were not states, but rather geographical regions, defined partly by political expediency but also by reference to shared economic concerns. Moreover, the regional federalism of the Federal Reserve System was not compounded simply of a distribution of power among official agencies; part of the balance was seen as between a central board named by government and regional bank directorates named preponderantly by private constituencies.

Among the various interests concerned with national monetary policy in the shaping years 1908-13, there was never a move with any political substance back of it to set up a single central bank with branches, in the style of the two Banks of the United States. Both the left and the right feared that a single agency would fall captive to the enemy; Bryan Democrats believed that a central bank would become the creature of Wall Street; some big-city bankers wanted a central bank if they could run it, but otherwise feared a central control point as likely to become the obedient servant of populist politicians with an insatiable appetite for inflation. No acceptable new form of money control could be found which did not promise some sharing of power among different centers.[281]

There was considerable sentiment both on the left and on the right for placing money control among several financial institutions of equal stature and considerable autonomy, though there were differences as to the desirable number of such agencies and the character of any central supervision that might be put over them; conservative bankers wanted relative centralization, in three of five institutions; those distrustful of banker power usually wanted a wider sharing. This approach might have yielded an analogy to a confederation rather than to a federal system.[282] But President Wilson insisted that there must be a strong, central, supervising board as the "capstone" of a workable organization which must involve enough decentralization to allay the fears of those who saw centralized power as inevitably falling into the hands of the bankers. Thus the final bargain was for a system combining a central body with separate banks operating in different districts, which the statute allowed to be as few as eight or as many as twelve.[283] The act contemplated functional distinctions between central and dispersed authority in the system, but in no mechanical analogy to the nation-state division; the districts, it directed, "shall be apportioned with due regard to the convenience and customary course of business and shall not necessarily be coterminus with any State or States." However, the Federal Reserve Act did not draw sharp lines demarcating the roles of the Federal Reserve Board and the regional banks; what should be the working content of their relations was left largely to practice and experience.

What emerged by mid-twentieth century was a system which in real measure was a regional federalism with areas of significantly differentiated functions for the board and the banks, but a system in which the banks had much more restricted roles than most lawmakers contemplated in 1913.

The original act gave the regional banks considerable autonomy in organization vis à vis the center. Events confirmed this pattern, and Congress did not disturb it. The pull of local interest was shown when the organizing committee empowered by the 1913 statute to set up the system saw fit to create the maximum allowed districts, twelve. That there was significant weight of policy back of the district pattern was confirmed in 1915. As the act allowed, the Federal Reserve Board then modified some district lines. But four of the appointive members of the board believed, further, that experience already showed that eight or nine regional banks would more efficiently reflect the functional needs of the economy than twelve. Before they could effectively press their view, Secretary of the Treasury William G. McAdoo out-maneuvered them by obtaining an opinion from the attorney general that the board lacked authority to make any reduction in the number of districts from the twelve set up by the original organization committee under the statute. Congress, said the attorney general, expected that the federal reserve banks "would extend their roots deep; that upon them as a foundation permanent banking arrangements better than any we have ever known would be constructed; and that they would become interwoven with the business fabric of the country." In 1916 the attorney general reaffirmed his position, while ruling also that the board had no statutory authority to change the location of banks remained as these had been fixed at the outset.[284] In addition, the banks remained the distinct corporate entities which they were at the beginning, with their own stockholders (their member banks), their own boards of directors, and their own employees (who were not under Civil Service). Their organizations were not without ties to the center; one third of their directors were appointed by the central board, and from this number that board also named the chairman and deputy chairman of the bank directorate; moreover, though the bank directors appointed the president and first vice president of their own organization, these appointments were subject to the central board's approval. Events worked to reduce to little practical effect the ownership of the banks' capital stock by their member banks. By mid-twentieth century the capital thus provided was less than one-half of one percent of the regional banks' total resources, so that the members lost such entitlement as their capital contributions might have given them to exercise surveillance over the banks' operations. Yet, although this development itself symbolized relative independence in the banks' directorates vis à vis their immediate constituencies, the member banks' stock ownership still conferred on the banks a title as decision-making entities, the legitimacy of which did not depend on officials in Washington.[285]

What counted more in distributing power within the system was the allocation of jobs between the central board and the banks. The basic statute was not clear-cut in job allocations, for this was a key area in which typical legislative bargaining compromise had been made, with each bargainer hoping to get his desired outcome from language that was deliberately vague. But the statute did declare as one of its general purposes the intent "to establish a more effective supervision of banking in the United States." As applied to the affairs of individual member banks this function invited decentralized supervision such as the regional banks were positioned to provide. In practice the banks developed a substantial content for this supervisory role. They advised member banks on the quality of their lending and on their capital positions, made information and opinion available to them on the conduct of lending operations, and by advice and admonition as well as judicious denial of credit fostered their members' traditional reluctance to go into debt and discouraged continuous borrowing from the Federal Reserve. Of particular importance, the banks rejected the idea which some bankers at first pressed on them, that the banks were legally bound to rediscount eligible paper whenever a member tendered it. Judges recognized this to be a valid stand; the Federal Reserve Act authorized, but did not command rediscounting. In the Banking Act of 1933 Congress confirmed the position by declaring explicitly that in deciding whether to grant or refuse accommodation to its members a federal reserve bank should give consideration to the general character and amount of the loans and investments of its member banks with a view to preventing unsound conditions of credit.[286]

Though the federal reserve banks thus consolidated a distinctive role within this regional federalism, the consistent trend of practice and legislation strengthened the capacity of the central board to determine general monetary policy for the system. One part of this trend was to eliminate competing organs of decision dominated by regional bank officers. Administrative practice early created the office of governor as chief executive of each bank. A few years showed that, in the hands of men of will and imagination, such as Benjamin Strong (first governor of the Federal Reserve Bank of New York), this office could become the principal seat of power in the system, overshadowing the central board.[287] Out of a meeting called by the board in October 1914 to consider problems of the system grew a governors' conference which took the lead in co-ordinating the regional banks' operations in buying or selling government securities and promised to become the forum for deciding general policy. However, early in 1923 the board dissolved the governors' conference, substituting a committee composed in fact of the same officers, but named by the board and under its direction.[288] The Banking Act of 1935 supplanted the office of governor with that of president in each regional bank and gave the board a veto over the regional bank's designation of its president. At the same time it symbolized the centralizing of power by renaming the Federal Reserve Board, the Board of Governors of the system, with longer terms and higher pay.[289] The 1935 act also made a basic change to centralize general monetary policy in the board. It legitimized the board action of 1923 which had set up a continuing committee to manage the banks' buying and selling of government securities in open market—the device which became the system's most powerful instrument to control general monetary policy. But the 1935 act constituted this statutory Federal Open Market Committee out of the board (seven members) plus five voting presidents of regional banks. Moreover, the act—translating into an allocation of power what practice had established as a counsel of prudence—declared that the regional banks might no longer buy and sell government securities in market for their own account, but might deal only with the explicit approval or direction of the FOMC. The 1935 act bore specially on the New York bank's role. Advantaged by its seat at the country's financial center, by its power as the Treasury's prime fiscal agent, and by vigorous leadership, the New York bank early tended to shape system policy. But the 1935 act gave the board a clearer title to leadership, which it developed further under strong chairmen.[290] The constitution of the FOMC allowed the possibility that its action might be decided by a majority made up of bank presidents and some board members; thus, even in this centralizing move Congress adhered to the idea that there should be some sharing of power between the center and the parts within the system. In practice the board members of the FOMC usually came to its meetings prepared to vote as a bloc, and thus to control it.[291] Further the FOMC reinforced centralization when its bylaws declared that the regional bank officers sitting on it should not serve as representatives of, or be instructed by, their banks, or inform their regional boards of the committee's actions.[292] Congress took note of another problem of competing centers of general policy making within the system, in legislation of 1917 and 1933. In 1917 Congress specified that the board's general supervisory authority over the regional banks included the terms of their dealings in foreign exchange. But in the 1920s under the vigorous leadership of Governor Benjamin Strong, the Federal Reserve Bank of New York in effect made policy for the system in dealings with foreign governments and their central banks on stabilizing exchange rates in aid of postwar efforts to return to an international gold standard. The Banking Act of 1933 amended the Federal

Reserve Act to make a very tight declaration of the board's exclusive control in this field. The 1933 amendment was more stringent in its terms than was consistent with practical conduct of operations, and because of its position at the country's center of financial dealing the New York bank continued to play a distinctive role affecting foreign exchange. Nonetheless, the principle had been reaffirmed, that the board and not the regional banks should control general monetary policy.[293]

The Federal Reserve Board became the decisive agency for fixing general monetary policy within the system principally by increase of its substantive powers, not only relative to the regional banks but also directly over the member banks. Two changes were critical in removing the capacity of the regional banks to determine general monetary policy. In 1913 the expectation had been that each regional bank would fix its own rate for lending to its member banks; that there might be different rediscount rates among the districts was accepted as a normal reflection of differing business conditions among the districts; in this view the central board would intervene only to correct a regional bank which set a lending rate which unreasonably eased or restricted credit. It was a reading of the board's role which could find support in the authority which the 1913 statute gave to the regional banks to set rediscount rates "subject to review and determination of the Federal Reserve Board."[294] However, in practice the board began to initiate rate suggestions and to aim for substantial uniformity throughout the country. In December 1919 the New York bank challenged the board's leading role and threatened to raise the rediscount rate in the New York district despite the board's opposition. Secretary of the Treasury Carter Glass obtained the opinion of the attorney general that the board not only had the authority to review rediscount rates, but also the authority to direct specific changes in rates. An issue was made again, in 1927, when the board ordered the Chicago bank to reduce its rate, contrary to the bank's wish; the Chicago bank finally yielded, and thereafter there was no serious challenge to the board's right in substance to determine rediscount rates for the country according to its own judgment.[295] The Banking Act of 1935 in effect supported the board's controlling position by requiring the banks to fix rediscount rates every fourteen days or oftener if the board deemed it necessary, thus legitimizing a situation in which the board would have frequent title to act, if it disagreed with bank decisions on lending rates.[296] A second respect in which administrative practice and legislation limited the substantive powers of regional banks and enhanced the power of the central board concerned open-market dealings in government securities. The 1913 act authorized each bank to deal on its own, subject to board regulations. But the informal creation of co-ordinating machinery—first in the governors' conference,

then in the board-appointed committee of bank representatives—
acknowledged that individual bank action was not efficient or productive
of good direction of monetary policy. When in 1935 Congress legitimized
central governance of open-market operations, it not only created a Federal Open Market Committee on which the board held the majority vote,
but in addition it abolished the former statutory power of each bank to
buy or sell government securities for its own account, and forbade future
such dealings save with explicit approval and direction of the FOMC.[297]

Administrative practice and legislation most enhanced the board's control in the system by increasing the board's legal and practical capacities to
act directly upon the lending operations of member banks. The development of open-market operations in government securities under board
direction furnished a means of control which reached pervasively and flexibly into the whole credit market.[298] When Congress created other, new
forms of money supply control over member banks, it put these powers
directly in the board and not in the regional banks. These controls included power to increase or decrease the required reserves of member
banks, within wide limits, in order to affect the money supply;[299] to limit
banks' lending on corporate securities otherwise under federal regulation;[300] to limit interest paid by member banks on savings and time deposits;[301] to limit banks' supply of consumer credit;[302] and to regulate all
banks' dealings in foreign exchange.[303] The consistent policy implicit in
this legislation was to center the making of general monetary policy within
the system firmly in the board. It was a trend which fitted the working
realities of a national economy. However monetary policy making might
be divided at the center, experience taught that somewhere there must be
effective power to co-ordinate that policy for the country as a whole. At
least within the Federal Reserve System, the board was the obvious agent
for such co-ordination and needed to develop positive powers accordingly.[304]

Market Controls and Public Controls on Money Supply

Throughout our national history public policy established that to regulate the money supply was a legitimate use of law; at no time was the
country willing to commit the supply of money wholly to the operation of
private markets. This outcome—which the previous part examined—
amounted in itself both to a determination of the legitimate functions of
law regarding money and to an allocation of power over money between
official and private decision makers. This second aspect of the matter demands more detailed appraisal. For, to say that public policy consistently
accorded the law a title superior to that of the market in controlling

money did not at all mean that policy gave no role to the market. To the contrary, the record also showed steady distrust of the likely abuse of official power in this field. Hence through the years lawmakers provided substantial scope for private decisions affecting money. The period opening in 1908 was no exception. But these years also witnessed decisive enlargement of law's roles. This bias of policy was reflected in the fact that beginning in the middle 1920s, but especially from 1933 on, the more acute issues became ones of allocating power among official agencies (the subject of the next section of this analysis) rather than of allocating power between government and the market.

In the years 1908-70 public policy concerning the balance between public and private power over money dealt both with (1) government's direct structuring of the system of money, and (2) its indirect regulation, through the terms it set on those to whom it delegated capacity to affect the money supply. First, the 1930s depression spurred direct government intervention by drastic changes in the use of gold in the system of money. Secondly, the impact of two declared and two undeclared wars, as well as of the 1930s depression, brought major reassessments of the proper scope of power delegated to private decision makers affecting monetary policy. Under the pressure of these events the federal government had to deal with delegation of power in two spheres—delegation to the general market and to the specialized credit market provided by bankers. Concern with the general market focused on price control and the purchasing power of the dollar. Concern with banks centered on relations of official and private power within the structure of the Federal Reserve System and under federal insurance of bank deposits.

The sharpest imposition of government monetary authority on private markets was by federal legislation of 1933-34, capped by the Gold Reserve Act of 1934. In this series of actions Congress barred private dealings in gold, denied legal effect to existing or future contracts providing for settlement in gold or in gold values, and authorized the president to fix the gold content of the dollar anywhere between 50 and 60 percent of its former weight as this had stood since 1834. The president exercised his authority to fix the gold content of the dollar at about 59 percent of its former weight. In 1933 in the Thomas Amendment to the Agricultural Adjustment Act, in addition to empowering the president to reduce the gold content of the dollar, Congress had authorized the president to arrange for the Federal Reserve System to issue federal reserve notes up to $3 billion for direct purchase of Treasury obligations, or alternatively or in addition to cause the Treasury to issue United States notes to that amount designed for circulation. Both sets of measures affirmed that the market must operate within such a system and quantity of money units as Congress might provide; there could be no more clear-cut subordination of the private market to public monetary policy. The president chose not to use the Thomas Amendment, though he made no public record of his reasons for not using it. The fact that he preferred to act within gold-measured criteria instead of cutting wholly free of reference to gold paid implicit tribute to traditional distrust of a money supply measured solely by official fiat. Drastic as was the departure from limits on the money supply set by the market for gold, still under the 1934 statute, as contrasted with the Thomas Amendment, it was change measureable by reference to quantities of gold, subject to such discipline as intergovernmental dealings in gold might impose in reflection of conditions of international trade, and change to that extent rendered more accountable to critics outside the Congress and the federal executive and administrative establishment.[305]

As in the legal tender cases, the serious challenge to the 1933-34 legislation on behalf of market autonomy went not to Congress's authority to change the gold content of the dollar or to limit what might lawfully pass as money, but to Congress's authority to give these measures retroactive effect. Retroactivity posed an issue on which large private stakes depended. In holding that existing as well as future contracts were subject to Congress's continuing power to fix the pattern of money, the Court confirmed a substantial, additional dimension to the primacy of legal over market processes. Yet, in its effects the issue of retroactivity was a passing one. What had most weight was the reaffirmation, without substantial contest, that in its discretion Congress might fix the character and amount of money, at least so long as what it did could be deemed to serve socially useful economic functions.[306] The last qualification must be made, because it was in fact integral to what the government did on gold in 1933-34. In the core values it sought to implement Franklin Roosevelt's was a conservative administration. It did not take its gold measures in order to change political and social power among social or economic classes, but rather to forestall change in the basic existing structure of power. The 1933-34 gold legislation was another device tried in order to renew the health of an economy viewed as largely oriented to market allocation of resources and as operating within a given pattern of middle-class values and upper middle-class political control. Thus, the Court's ruling in 1935 did not settle—because the Court was not presented with—the question of Congress's authority to upset market expectations regarding the system of money in order to realign the power of particular political groups or social classes.[307] In any case, this was a matter which the Court probably would never need to decide. The variety of interests and ideas which swirled about the 1930s is suggestive. Within the presumption of constitutionality there would always be enough plausible economic basis for Congress's actions to sustain its revisions of the system of money. In such a posture of affairs, the Court would probably rule that it could not properly invalidate legislation because it suspected the presence of an illegitimate, political or social "motive" for changing monetary policy.[308] Thus, if private markets kept some check on official monetary policy, they would have such effect out of functional pressures and legislative and executive traditions, rather than by judicial precedent.

Law might define the formal value of money. But money had operating value defined by its purchasing power. Public policy left this aspect of money mainly to determination by the market between 1790 and 1915. During the American Revolution the Congress recommended, and some states adopted, statutes which set ceilings on prices for key commodities and services. Given the lack of means or experience for administrative enforcement, it is not surprising that these regulations were ineffective; their want of effect, as well as the absence of even token price control in other states, were reflected in the disastrous depreciation of the currency issued by Congress and by the states. The result testified as much to the incapacity of the market, as to the incapacity of law, to hold steady the practical value of money under such stress.[309] Substantial depreciation of the currency attended the War of 1812, helped by the government's loss of its fiscal agent when Congress allowed the charter of the First Bank of the United States to expire in 1811. No attempt was made at price control in this period.[310] In the Civil War neither the Treasury nor the Congress showed understanding of the effect that the government's competition for goods and services would have upon the purchasing power of money. Tax policy was not geared to restrict competing claims on resources. There was no move directly to control prices or ration goods or services except through the market. Again, the market produced inflation which profited a few and was costly to the many by unsettling the practical value of money.[311] Policy makers had gained a little more sophistication by World War I, when the federal government embarked on some effort at price control, limited both in coverage and in administrative investment. The effort was not enough, and not skillful enough, to prevent damaging inflation. But at least it set legislative and executive precedent which, in a war situation, legitimized legal intervention in market processes to steady the purchasing-power value of money.[312] By World War II the lesson had been better learned. Congress put control of prices and the rationing of goods and services under the control of various specialized administrative agencies with sufficient authority and means to offer substantial curbs on market responses to the extraordinary competition for resources between the private and public sectors. There was still substantial open and concealed inflation, but it was allowed less scope than in previous war experiences. Moreover, the forthrightness and scale of the price control and rationing efforts set firmer legislative and executive precedent than before to extend the range of government's responsibility to protect the purchasing-power value of money.[313]

These precedents of the two world wars enlarged the federal government's monetary policy authority beyond anything forecast in the record of the Philadelphia convention. True, the Constitution authorizes Congress "to coin money, regulate the value thereof, and of foreign coin, and fix the standard of weights and measures." However, the context suggests that the framers were thinking here of *value* simply as the formal definition of money units. And, duly allowing for the abortive price-control gestures of the Revolution, nothing in the record suggests that the framers had in mind that "regulating the value" of money meant regulating the market in order to control the purchasing power of money. Indeed, in view of their plain distrust of legislation creating paper money and limiting creditors' rights, it is more likely that they would have elected to trust to the market to determine general price levels, had they plainly confronted the point.[314] Precedent really begins, thus, with the World War I price-control efforts. The precedent is not necessarily the worse for that. The Constitution plainly meant that Congress should have full and superior authority to provide a national money supply. Within such a broad mandate our tradition accepts that the particular content of constitutional authority may grow with experience, by responsible action of the top branches of the national government. However, it reflected the want of clear precedent, when the solicitor general argued to the Supreme Court the validity of World War I price control, that the closest Court precedent he found to invoke were cases upholding regulation of prices charged by public utilities—a type of regulation concerned with the fair balance of power in specialized markets, unrelated to monetary policy.[315] The Court ruled that a World War I statute was invalid, because it was so vague as to violate due process of law by not giving fair warning to the regulated class of the standard of conduct the law required of them; the decision thus did not examine the substance of Congress's power over the system of money.[316] By the time World War II price control was litigated, counsel as well as the Court apparently felt that the lessons of experience and of a more sophisticated economics had been too well learned to leave a substantial issue of substantive power. Upholding the Emergency Price Control Act of 1942, the Court noted that the substantive validity of the act had not been disputed, and indicated that in the Court's view it was unquestionably within Congress's authority to adopt general price control as a means reasonably deemed necessary to carrying on a war.[317]

Plain as this record was, it was just as plain that it was limited to allowing price controls in a war emergency.[318] *Knox* v. *Lee* (1871) had validated

United States notes issued as a war measure; *Juilliard* v. *Greenman* (1884) had pressed further, to validate such notes when they were kept in circulation to serve a peacetime economy. As of 1970 the Court had not confronted in a clear-cut way the question, whether it would accept an analogous expansion of Congress's authority to protect the purchasing power of money, from a power in aid of war to a power in aid of a healthy peacetime economy. The National Recovery Administration delegated to private controllers authority to control prices in order to combat a nationwide depression in which deflation was destroying the practical utility of money. The Court held the National Industrial Recovery Act unconstitutional. It did so in part on the ground that, as applied, the act exceeded Congress's power under the commerce clause. This was not a ruling in favor of the market against government, but in support of the balance of power between the nation and the states. Nonetheless, its implications might be taken as hostile to recognizing peacetime price control as a reasonable incident of Congress's monetary authority. However, the Court also held the statute unconstitutional as an invalid delegation of legislative power, and this aspect so strongly colors the decision as to render doubtful the force of the commerce clause ground.[319] NRA died soon after the decision, without a successor. It was an effort so hastily and opportunistically contrived, as to rob it of weight as a policy precedent, quite apart from the reading one may give to the Court's decision.

Somewhat firmer precedent for government intervention in the market in the interests of price stability began to emerge in the 1950s and 1960s through efforts of the Treasury and the Council of Economic Advisers on the one hand, and of the Federal Reserve Board on the other—all, though with differing emphases, claiming warrant under the policy mandated by the Employment Act of 1946. That statute declared the responsibility of the federal government through all its agencies to seek conditions which would provide employment for all who were able, willing, and seeking to work, and which would "promote maximum employment, production, and purchasing power."[320] The act was born out of concern that, for want of effective mass purchasing power in market, the economy converting to peace after World War II would be marked by great unemployment. In this context the focus was on the fiscal policy of the federal government—its spending—and not on monetary policy. It is not surprising, then, that the 1946 act said nothing explicitly about prices, and in particular said nothing about promoting full employment only so far as might be consistent with maintaining price stability.[321] This silence matched like silence under the Federal Reserve legislation, though different reasons explained why price stabilization was not among the declared goals or responsibilities of the Federal Reserve System. In 1913 attention focused mainly on averting financial crises produced by lack of concentrated credit facilities, and prevailing economic theory did not include the idea that monetary policy might be shaped to regulate the general price level. The middle 1920s saw the first perception among policy makers of the use of legal controls on credit to protect the purchasing power of money. But a 1926-28 effort to write this goal into the Federal Reserve Act failed, not because there was opposition to the legitimacy of the purpose, but because there was no agreement on means of achieving the goal and because the system opposed the imposition on it of a responsibility which it felt—quite realistically—that it could not alone fulfill. Despite the want of product, the 1926-28 effort is not without meaning for the growth of policy; it is significant that opposition to a broader range of government responsibility in this area was not made in the name of market autonomy as such. The fact that nothing further developed on these lines within the next twenty-five years seems the result of the failure of policy inventiveness and leadership in the Federal Reserve Board, together with the limiting circumstances, first of depression and then of war, rather than of active concern to protect market control of the general price level.[322] In the 1950s the Federal Reserve Board asserted its "independence" of the Treasury in fixing monetary policy, in a context which the next section of this part examines. Relevant at this point is the fact that a prime goal of this independence was to use Federal Reserve instruments to protect the purchasing power of the dollar, and implicitly to keep the system of money a more neutral factor in the economy and thereby to foster the capacity of the market as resource allocator. To legitimize this kind of effort, the Federal Reserve Board turned to the Employment Act of 1946, in which—despite the want of explicit declaration—it found a mandate to hold measures for economic growth within bounds consistent with maintaining price stability.[323] Beginning in 1962 the Council of Economic Advisers added particular emphasis to the claim that the 1946 act warranted official action to discourage inflationary erosion of the purchasing power of money. The council's interest in this theme seems to have had a different bias of policy than that which marked the concern of the Federal Reserve Board. Where the board feared that expansionist programs of the Treasury and the Congress would upset private expectations regarding the value of money and private commitments made in reliance on the stability of the dollar, the council feared that the private power in market wielded by corporate management and labor unions would interfere with accomplishing the objects of public fiscal policy.[324]

Coupled with these differently based official concerns with price levels was another thread of policy which recalled familiar distrust of government intervention in market processes. Congress, the White House, the

Council of Economic Advisers—and, for that matter, the Federal Reserve Board and bankers generally—showed little enthusiasm for translating care for price stability into formal price controls comparable to those of World War II. The council, in particular, in some years supported officially pronounced wage-price guidelines, but guidelines to be enforced mainly by persuasion and publicity. In part policy makers shied away from the administrative complexity, costs, and uncertain results of broad-scale, compulsory price controls. But, also, their caution spoke for a continuing tradition which, while conceding that law had superior title to regulate money, wanted to leave great scope for market processes, both for their flexibility and for their utility as a check on official power.[325] Up to 1970 Congress never adopted direct peacetime price controls to protect the purchasing-power value of money, and of course, therefore, the Court had had no occasion to declare itself in the matter. The dominant tone of the record, however, was not one of abstaining from such regulation out of serious doubt of authority, but rather out of choice among what were deemed permissible alternative lines of action. Moreover, the Court had upheld sweeping exercise by Congress of its powers to shape monetary policy, and it sustained broad programs of price regulation by the states and by Congress undertaken to restore vitality to large sectors of an ailing general economy.[326] In this perspective, it seemed likely that the Court would sustain peacetime federal price controls, so long as Congress could claim reasonable ground therefor in supporting an efficient money supply and a productive economy.

As with policy on delegation of money controls to the general market, so with policy on delegation to specialized credit markets, the regulation of bank-made money through the Federal Reserve System showed significant concern with the balance of official and private power. Fears of banker control shaped Federal Reserve structure. President Wilson insisted that the central board which he demanded as the unifying element in the system's regional federalism should be composed wholly of men selected by the government—originally, the secretary of the treasury and the comptroller of the currency, ex officio, and five other members designated by the president with the consent of the Senate. No less than this, Wilson thought, could legitimize the system as an agent of public interest, accountable to public authority. The presence of a distinct issue over public and private power was highlighted by the contrast with the principal alternative program—the Aldrich Plan—which would also have had a central governing body, but one whose selection would be dominated by banker members of the system. Of the same bias of policy as Wilson's insistence on a "public" board was the provision that a third of the directors of each regional bank be named by the Federal Reserve Board (to include the chairman of each bank board) and—under the Banking Act of 1935—that the chief executive (president) of each bank, though named by its board, be subject to the approval of the Federal Reserve Board.[327]

However, Federal Reserve legislation included countervailing provisions designed to mitigate bankers' fear of "political" control. At the base of the system were the private commercial banks which were system members. National banks must join. But those who pressed for some central-bank-style reform in 1912-13 early concluded that the combined opposition of state bankers and state regulators made it impossible to require membership of all banks providing deposit-check money. Thus membership was left optional for state-chartered banks, providing a potential curb on the system not only because a state-bank member might leave, but because a national-bank member by resigning its national franchise for a state charter might take itself out of the apparatus.[328] Moreover, the member banks owned the capital stock of the federal reserve banks, as their title to select two-thirds of the directors of the regional banks, of whom one-half should be of banking experience and the other one-half nonbankers of general experience of affairs.[329] An additional gesture of assurance to private power in the system was the provision for an all-banker Advisory Council to the Federal Reserve Board.[330] Of related policy implication was the compromise struck in creating the Federal Open Market Committee under the Banking Act of 1935, by which in addition to the seven members of the Federal Reserve Board the FOMC included five presidents of regional banks. Partly a tribute to the value put on regional federalism in the system, the 1935 act also measured the need to conciliate those who were concerned to keep within the top policy-making procedures of the system some men who did not owe their position wholly to official appointment.[331]

Nonetheless, the main currents of economic function and political values ran against the effectiveness of these provisions to build some nongovernment influence into Federal Reserve structure. Member bank capital contributions dwindled to a minor part in the growth of Federal Reserve assets, and the directorates of the regional banks developed traditions of regulatory independence vis à vis their member-bank constituencies. Of particular shaping importance was the early role of the Federal Reserve Bank of New York. Its position in the country's financial center, plus the vigorous will and imagination of its first governor, Benjamin Strong, led that bank to produce a striking range and degree of policy leadership in the 1920s which fostered the growth of a separate institutional character in the Federal Reserve apparatus. Altogether, the member banks never played a significant role in system policy making.[332] Though the country's commercial banks thus won no definable influence on system decision making, federal regulation won increased influence over the banks. State-chartered banks continued to hold the election to join or not to join the system. But the principal state banks found that membership offered services which created impelling inducements to join. Later, the creation of federal deposit insurance created a demand by bank customers which spelled practical compulsion on almost all banks to come under that new form of federal supervision. Law and experience thus materially reduced the independence of the private banking sector as a check on federal monetary controls.[333] Beyond these factors, the shift of general monetary policy making to the Federal Reserve Board meant that the banker-businessman predominance in regional bank directorates lost the broad policy impact which framers of the 1913 act had envisaged.[334] Within the Federal Open Market Committee, wielding what proved to be the system's most effective instrument of money supply control, the tendency was for the Federal Reserve Board members to reach agreement on policy among themselves, and so by its majority to reduce such banker-businessman influence as had been designed for the five regional bank presidents who sat there.[335]

Development of the Federal Reserve Board's instruments of monetary control was still more potent than features of organizational structure in enhancing public over private regulation of the money supply. This was no less true, for all that the board's control instruments owed the range and depth of their effect largely to a key feature of organization—the centralization of decision making, of reserves, and of maneuverable assets in the system. In particular, by centralizing reserves the law itself created an underlying functional need—and, eventually, demand—for more public intervention in the bank credit market. The money supply thus became more subject to leverage effects. A much greater bulk of deposit-check money could be erected on centralized reserves; on the other hand, by the same token any decrease in reserves was calculated to produce a more drastic reduction in the money stock than before. In this context there could be less tolerance of ungoverned market impacts on banks' reserve positions.[336]

In 1913 policy makers relied chiefly on control of the interest charged by the system on loans to member banks to endow the federal reserve banks and the board with all the influence they would need over bank-created money. At the same time in the standard set for Federal Reserve lending the 1913 act reflected conservative dislike of broad-scale public intervention in private credit markets. Member banks might borrow from the system only on short-term paper "arising out of actual commercial transactions" or out of actual trade in agricultural commodities. Federal reserve banks might issue federal reserve notes (vehicles for loans to member banks) only against the pledge of eligible rediscounted paper—originally in amount equal to the amount of notes issued, reduced in 1917 to 60 percent plus continuation of the 40 percent gold reserve also required by the 1913 statute. In effect this statutory standard followed the *real-bills* doctrine then and for years to come favored by many bankers and economists. According to this formula, the banking system would respond in almost automatic precision to the economy's changing needs of money, if credit and currency came into being and expired with the launching and completion of trading in current goods. Thus the money supply would adjust to demands for money without requiring or warranting exercise of discretionary judgments by public officers. It took the harsh impact of the 1930s depression to drive home that this was not a formula for regulating the money supply to foster the productivity of the economy, but a rationalization of passive responses to ungoverned swings of the market. Fearing drastic decline in commercial dealings and the hazard thus that the requisite commercial paper would not be available to underpin Federal Reserve lending or the issue of federal reserve notes, with consequent pressure on Federal Reserve gold holdings, in 1932 Congress gave federal reserve banks broad, though temporary, authority to lend at short term and on penalty interest to member banks on any security satisfactory to the lenders and to issue federal reserve notes backed by pledge of government securities. In 1935 and 1945 Congress made permanent these two new grants of authority. Thus policy moved to accept the need of broad official discretion in Federal Reserve lending and note issue.[337]

Within both the original and the enlarged frames of lending authority, moreover, there were developments which strengthened Federal Reserve lending as a control instrument. Backed by judicial opinion, the system established that a proper reading of the Federal Reserve Act gave member banks no statutory right to obtain loans from the federal reserve banks. From this base administrative practice and formal regulations established as a norm of policy that, rather than putting the discount rate regularly at *penalty* points above going market rates, the federal reserve banks would control member borrowing by being sparing in loans and lending typically only on a short-term basis. Private bankers' custom then developed a matching tradition of reluctance to go into debt to the Federal Reserve, particularly by discounting customers' paper. This pattern meant that the level of member-bank reserves, rather than the discount rate, tended to create the prime disciplinary influence of the system as lender of last resort. In this context discount rate changes proved a cumbersome and dubiously effective device, valuable more to indicate policy otherwise implemented, than as a distinct means of controlling bank credit. That this outcome was not inherent in the instrument was indicated by a Federal Reserve committee report in 1968. The committee suggested amending the regulations to allow members to obtain lines of credit for several-month periods at the federal reserve banks, substantially on a no-questions-asked basis, under discount rates frequently adjusted to market rates. Such an approach might convert Federal Reserve lending into almost as flexible a regulatory device as open-market operations.[338]

Legal reserve requirements could have committed monetary control substantially to government, had they required commercial banks to hold a 100 percent cash reserve against all deposits. That Federal Reserve legislation continued to require only fractional reserves after the time when policy makers ceased to regard reserve requirements as relevant simply to liquidity and saw them as an instrument of controlling the money supply was a factor which implicitly reaffirmed the policy of delegating substantial discretion to the private credit market in affecting the stock of money.[339] However, the Banking Act of 1935 armed the Federal Reserve Board with an instrument of sharper and more immediate impact than regulation of the discount rate, when it authorized the board to change member bank reserve requirements between the minima set in 1917 and twice those amounts. But the formality of such action, its applicability under the existing law to all banks and all banking credit regardless of differentiating factors of credit uses or bank conditions, and the quick and heavy effect of substantial changes were elements which made this a device more suitable for special intervention than for continuing flexible management.[340]

What most effectively enlarged the board's capacity to affect bank-created money was the development of Federal Reserve trading in government securities in open market. Here is a prime example of the dynamic policy making that can be set in motion by statutory delegation to administrators. The 1913 act authorized the Federal Reserve Banks to trade in government securities in open market, without defining the goals or uses of such trading. The framers, and for some time Federal Reserve officials also, saw such trading possibly as auxiliary to the discount rate, but mainly as a means for the regional banks to earn money to meet their operating budgets. Moreover, administrative innovation had to wait upon favorable circumstances; it was not until after World War I that the federal government had a sufficient volume of its securities outstanding to allow trading to have much weight.[341] But then experience taught that the trading might affect the reserve position of member banks. In 1923 the Federal Reserve Board declared that open-market operations offered a proper means of regulating the supply of bank-created money. Successive administrative and statutory steps centralized direction of the system's open-market trading, ultimately in the Federal Open Market Committee as this was established by the Banking Act of 1935.[342] Despite these developments, this potent technique lay largely unused, or ineffectively used, from its administrative recognition in 1923 past its statutory validation in 1935, until the 1950s. There were varied causes for this indifferent record—uncertainty as to the specific uses of the new tool, lack of strong leadership in the board in fashioning criteria of monetary policy, and the constraining circumstances of depression and war.[343] When the board did resume independent and more vigorous use of open-market operations after 1951, from 1953 to 1961, it subjected the technique to a severe limitation of the board's own making, by restricting almost all dealings to short-term government bills. Resting in part on arguments of administrative efficiency, the bills-only policy contained a declared bias in favor of minimizing the extent of government influence on money markets; in particular it meant that the board would not try to fix the structure of interest rates as between short-term and long-term obligations. In effect the policy committed management of United States debt maturities to the Treasury. But this separation-of-powers point tended to be lost in the general reaction, that bills-only was a strategic decision in regulating the money supply. The latter aspect of the matter seemed emphasized when the board abandoned the bills-only restriction in 1961, for it did so in a context which asserted a broader money management role; the board might now vary the maturities of the government securities it dealt in, to encourage higher short-term interest rates in order to prevent the flow of gold abroad and to encourage lower long-term rates to promote investment in the face of business recession at home. Indications were that the broad-range policy would be permanent, confirming open-market operations as the principal means of Federal Reserve influence over bank-created money.[344]

As they were defined by statute and administrative policy and practice, adjustments in the discount rate, reserve requirements, and open-market trading in United States securities were instruments for regulating the over-all, total position of bank-created money. They were not devices to regulate bank credit according to the particular uses to which borrowers might put it. The real-bills theory—embodied before 1932 in the statutory requirement that Federal Reserve lending and Federal Reserve notes be secured by pledge of short-term commercial paper—might seem to legitimize a qualitative control on bank credit. But the appearance was illusion, for the requirement put no limit on the end uses of credit based on eligible paper.[345] The caution with which Congress and the Federal Reserve Board approached regulation of particular uses of bank credit implicitly testified to the continued high value put on substantial autonomy for private markets. In 1920-21 the Treasury urged the system to press its member banks to deny credit for use in stock market speculation. But the fledgling

Federal Reserve Board then took a relatively passive attitude toward its role in regulating the money supply; it neither claimed nor asked authority to embark on such qualitative control. In 1929 the board, now more ambitious, wanted the regional banks to discipline their members against speculative credit. The regional banks disagreed; they held that the proper way to check security speculation was to raise the discount rate, and that it was the business prerogative of any member bank to determine for itself the make-up of its lending portfolio. Amid this controversy no strong action was taken.[346] One aftermath of the stock market crash was great public disenchantment with that arena of private credit maneuver; thus in 1934 Congress authorized the Federal Reserve Board to fix margins for lending on regulated securities.[347] World War II rationing and price controls for the time removed occasion for considering further qualitative regulation of credit. In 1950 the Korean War brought new danger of inflation. Indicating continuing distrust of the reach of qualitative controls, Congress now extended them only into limited fields of consumer and real estate credit, and held these authorizations to limited times. The board used its rule-making powers under these specialized authorizations. But the areas so regulated were so limited in extent that this Federal Reserve activity had little demonstrable effect on the money supply as a whole.[348]

The prevailing trend of policy legitimated an increasing range and impact of public controls on the money supply. But the course of policy also reflected continuing concern to maintain substantial areas of private market influence on the system of money. At the inception of the Federal Reserve System even its promoters envisaged for it a relatively narrow regulatory role, falling far short of responsibility for general management of the money supply. The prime object was to overcome such monetary crises as that of 1907 To do this all the active regulatory power that was needed was the capacity to respond with speed and sufficiency when the market showed a panicky preference for currency over deposits. Hence the original emphasis was on the federal reserve banks' authority to rediscount their members' commercial paper and to use the rediscount rate as the instrument of control. The real-bills criterion for handling the money supply accepted this emergency-response function as substantially fulfilling the Federal Reserve's management responsibilities. This pattern shows the most subtle influence of the market orientation in shaping the system; the initial definition of the system's role stood this way less as the outcome of overt contest between promarket and public-management partisans, than because a broad spectrum of contemporary opinion took it for granted that market controls were the norm and public intervention the exception. Even then, however, a deliberate balance-of-power calculation entered to reinforce the pattern, and this element tended to become more self-conscious as public controls increased. Policy makers' distaste for peace-time general price controls reflected preference for market administration of the economy. The same preference was implicit in the Federal Reserve Board's delayed recognition of the regulatory potential of open-market operations, as well as in the board's policy (observed into the 1950s) of confining open-market operations to short-term Treasury bills, and in the fact that the board made hesitant use of the instrument even within that limitation. Despite the outlawry in 1933 and 1934 of private resort to gold or gold-measured obligations to settle transactions, policy makers clung to an ill-defined gold standard rather than assign to government a clear-cut responsibility to manage money. Corollary to this attitude, Congress was tardy and reluctant in freeing Federal Reserve lending and note issues from market-oriented requirements that deposits and notes be backed by re-serves of short-term commercial paper and gold. It was as part of this pat-tern that Congress took twenty years to move from treating bank deposit reserve requirements as a creditors' security device, to legitimating them as a means of variable controls on the money supply, and that Congress was late and grudging in giving the Federal Reserve Board some authority to impose qualitative controls on credit.[349]

The law earliest showed its favor for the market in the scope which the law of contract, property, and corporations afforded for businessmen's invention of ways of dealing. At the beginning of the nineteenth century courts applied this policy in the monetary field when they declared that individuals might create money tokens by private contract until a legisla-ture should forbid the practice.[350] The same attitude found expression in the twentieth century; absent positive limitations otherwise set by law, contract, property, and corporation law sanctioned business invention of new media of exchange and new forms of credit security, and thus allowed new ways of increasing the liquidity of assets. These twentieth-century years saw the development of nonbanking institutions which created a wide variety of new financial instruments of substantial liquidity. Life insurance companies, factoring houses, stock brokers, savings and loan associations, and mutual funds were leading creators of claims which were not used directly as money but were readily convertible into money and affected the demand for money and the volume of transactions which could be erected on given stocks of money. Banks and nonbanking com-panies contrived the consumer credit card; by 1967 the Federal Reserve estimated that credit granted by all sources on credit cards exceeded $11 billion. Corporations specializing in financing consumer installment credit sold great amounts of their short-term paper. Nonfinancial corporations with idle funds seeking short-term investment became substantial elements in the market for government securities, in lending to dealers in government securities, and in buying the notes of finance companies dealing in consumer installment purchase contracts. Industrial corporations enlarged the short-term commercial paper market by offering their own notes, as borrowers. Private lenders who were neither regulated brokers nor regulated banks made funds available for margin trading in stocks. The variety and scale of this flowering of new forms of short-term credit attested to how much room public policy still left at mid-twentieth century for private innovations fulfilling some functions of money and affecting operations of the legally regulated money supply.[351]

Most of this development went on without direct check from monetary regulations. The new creators of liquidity were indirectly affected by legal controls on bank-created money, for these financial intermediaries held their own fractional reserves in the form of bank deposits, and thus might feel pressure when the Federal Reserve tightened bank credit.[352] On the other hand, by banning interest on demand deposits and setting interest ceilings and reserve requirements on time deposits, the law regulating commercial banks spurred the entry into the credit market of nonbanking corporations which were free to pay such interest, and operate on such margins, as they deemed to fit their self-interest.[353] Given the scale to which such operations mounted by the 1960s, the absence of controls on the liquidity of these new creators of short-term credit meant that they could be a dangerously unsettling influence on the money market, if big industrial corporations suddenly switched funds from short-term notes to investment in inventories or equipment, or suddenly lost confidence in private short-term borrowers. The quick, massive action which the Federal Reserve System felt called on to make in the spring of 1971 when the Penn Central Railroad defaulted on its short-term paper demonstrated the relevance of the new commercial paper market to the general money supply.[354]

Despite this relationship, however, there was no move within or outside the Federal Reserve System to authorize it to regulate creation of liquid assets by all types of financial intermediaries. The administrative load would be heavy. Regulation would be difficult because of the great differences in working character among the different types of financial assets created by nonbanking institutions. But, such considerations apart, in the perspective of decades of monetary policy, it is fair to conclude that the basic reason that no movement developed for broad regulation was continuing belief that it was socially useful to maintain a broad realm for flexible, private decision making.[355]

This implication of policy is sharpened by the fact that positive response to these developments fell only within the established area of Federal Reserve regulation of member banks. Convinced that banks' competitive bidding for lendable funds had contributed materially to the stock market crash in 1929 and the ensuing depression, Congress, in the Banking Acts of 1933 and 1935, forbade payment of interest on demand deposits in member banks or in nonmember banks insured by the FDIC and required that interest on time deposits be held within limits set by the Federal Reserve Board or the Federal Deposit Insurance Corporation. For years market rates were too low for the legal ceiling on interest for time deposits to be of practical effect. But, as privately bargained rates moved higher, the ceilings became a regular target of bankers who found them a particularly objectionable symbol of government constraints upon market flexibility. Congress did not yield to pleas that the interest ceiling had originated in a mistaken diagnosis of the 1929 troubles and that in any case the regulation should be put on a stand-by basis and the banks freed to compete for funds in the market so long as no emergency appeared.[356] Seeking to overcome the competitive limits put on their time-deposit business, both by the interest ceiling and by reserve requirements, banks sought to hold their own in the expanding short-term credit market by selling their own short-term notes to obtain more lendable funds. Amid some controversy, the Federal Reserve Board amended its rules, to treat such bank borrowings as "deposits" subject to regulations on interest and reserves. When bank holding companies undertook to sell their notes to provide funds for the banks they controlled, Congress in 1969 resolved challenge to the board's authority by amending the Federal Reserve Act to give the board sweeping power "to determine what types of obligations, whether issued directly by a member bank or indirectly by an affiliate of a member bank or by any other means, shall be deemed deposits."[357] Movement in legal regulation thus acknowledged the impact of contract innovations in liquidity affecting the money supply, but the response was significantly limited in field.

At no time from 1780 on was public policy prepared to commit the money supply to the governance of the market. Moreover, the years between 1908 and 1970 witnessed marked relative decline in the scope of influence conceded to the market. Nonetheless, concern that private innovation and private decision making remain as significant balance-of-power factors obviously persisted as living elements in the course of monetary policy.

Roles of Major Legal Agencies

Federal executive and administrative officers dominated twentieth-century monetary policy. State agencies simply maintained familiar patterns of state-chartered banking, and, with local bankers, mounted jealous watch against federal incursions on the dual banking system.[358] Within the central government Congress played only a limited role, and the Court almost no part at all.

In the Federal Reserve Act of 1913 Congress made specific, durable, and indispensable contributions to monetary policy by creating a new structure for regulating money. To do so its processes had to resolve stubborn differences among private interests and overcome profound mutual distrust among those who feared politics and those who feared Wall Street. Patience, bargaining, and skillful management of symbols and of political and economic power went into this outcome. These qualities showed the pragmatic strength of the legislative process, even as prices paid for accommodation—in the continued acceptance of dual banking, for example, or the calculated ambiguities in allocating power between the board and the regional banks—showed characteristic limitations. The two houses did not operate alone. President Wilson's insistence on a bill, his adroit conciliation of the Bryan Democrats, and his determination that the Federal Reserve Board be a body of public officers, were critical to the result. Of course Congress and the president did not create the new organization simply on their own initiative. Events had been pressing policy makers toward inventing some centralized direction of monetary affairs, and the crisis of 1907 precipitated this sentiment into the Aldrich-Vreeland Act, with its creation of a National Monetary Commission. But events do not of themselves fix responsibility for decision making, or arm decision makers with authority and instruments; only Congress, with its power to create apparatus and to provide working resources, could do this.[359]

But Congress's principal—indeed, practically its only—contribution was to create and set in motion a new organization for making monetary policy. The 1913 act made no helpful definition of goals of monetary policy, let alone attempting to rank goals. To the contrary, the act stated objectives in terms so vague as to lack meaning. This outcome reflected one of the most enduring characteristics of legislative process—that it normally operates only on and within the problem that most closely presses on it. The policy makers were immediately moved by their reactions to the liquidity crisis of 1907, their prime concern was to underpin deposit-check money with flexibly available cash, and insofar as they had a general theory it was that if the statute provided for Federal Reserve lending and federal reserve notes backed by short-term commercial paper and gold, this much apparatus would service the economy in the most needful respect and at the same time hold to a desired minimum government intervention in money markets. The preamble of the 1913 statute pointed to this concept as much as anything when it declared that Congress acted "to furnish an elastic currency, to afford means of discounting commercial paper, to establish a more effective supervision of banking in the United States, and for other purposes." The body of the statute did no better in spelling out the objectives of the new system than when it said that the federal reserve banks should use their discounting authority "to accommodate commerce and business."

Perhaps more could not fairly be expected. Neither bankers, businessmen, or economists, let alone lawmakers, then saw control of the money supply as a means to promote economic growth or to keep the general price level in constructive relation to general costs and profits. Too, the country lacked experience in using a central bank. Arguably, the constraints of the situation made it wise to say little of the objectives and techniques of the new system and to wait on time.[360]

But with experience Congress did not move to bolder definitions of monetary policy. Between 1913 and 1970 Congress took only four actions of major substance relevant to regulating the system of money—in the gold legislation of 1933-34, in the Banking Acts of 1933 and 1935, and in the Employment Act of 1946.[361] These actions invited broader-range management of money; none of them produced more definite guide lines for the job. The gold legislation had basic importance. For the long run it released the system of money from the fortuitously "automatic" constraints of the gold standard; for a limited time it empowered the president to cause a large increase in the issue of currency. But it declared no new standards for using this enlarged room for maneuver.[362] So far as concerned over-all management of the money supply, the Banking Act of 1933 was a way station en route to the act of 1935. True, the 1933 statute made a basic contribution to the liquidity of deposit-check money by launching federal deposit insurance. But, significant as this step was for removing the old threat of liquidity crises, in itself it contributed no guidance on using monetary regulation for economic growth or price stabilization.[363] The Banking Act of 1935 provided the only major addition to the Federal Reserve's own structure between 1913 and 1970, in legitimizing and firmly centralizing control of the money supply through open-market operations. The bill which became the 1935 act proposed a mandate that the system use its powers to promote business stability and to mitigate influences disturbing the general course of production, trade, prices, and employment. But, caught between those who would extend and those who feared Federal Reserve initiatives, Congress rejected any such venture into further definition of goals. Instead it simply enacted that open-market operations "be governed with a view to accommodate commerce and business and with regard to their bearing upon the general credit situation of the country." The 1935 act also gave the board the potent new control instrument to vary member-bank reserve requirements within wide limits. But Congress said only that this enlarged authority should be used "in order to prevent injurious credit expansion or contraction." Thus in its statement of goals the 1935 act moved little if any beyond the empty generalities of 1913.[364] Hedged with overlapping and ambiguous qualifications born of hard legislative bargains, the Employment Act of 1946 did commit the United States to use all its powers and agencies to foster employment and economic growth. But, again, the legislature showed its characteristic inclination to focus on one concern at a time; in 1946 Congress was thinking primarily of using its taxing and spending powers for economic development and was silent on the place of monetary policy. Members of the Joint Economic Committee of Congress, along with the Council of Economic Advisers, and finally the Federal Reserve Board, all eventually drew on the 1946 act to legitimize varying priorities in monetary policy. But these developments owed little to what Congress did in enacting the Employment Act itself.[365]

Anyone who would regulate money for more ambitious ends than servicing the going economy confronted hard choices among competing interests and values—notably, among the goals of business expansion, price stability, and high employment. Decisions were the harder because economic theory was divided or in flux, and operational skill and knowledge were lacking. Congress betrayed unease over the discretion it was committing to the Federal Reserve Board, but also showed its willingness to shift responsibility, when it set criteria for board membership. The 1913 act said that the five appointive members should be named with "due regard to a fair representation of the different commercial, industrial and geographical divisions of the country" and should include "at least two . . . experienced in banking or finance." Following sharp (and probably unfair) criticism from farm interests, that the board had so tightened credit as to cause a farm recession in 1919-20, in 1922 Congress added a sixth appointive member and—dropping the earlier reference to banking and financial experience—now directed that appointments be made with due regard for "a fair representation of the financial, agricultural, industrial and commercial interests, and geographical divisions of the country." The legislation thus threatened to build group pressures into the official apparatus. Fortunately the stipulations proved vague enough to let the board develop its own character in practice, while presidential appointments fell into no rigid interest representation. However, this outcome does not disguise Congress's confession and avoidance of difficult problems of interest adjustment inherent in money regulation.[366] In later years the failure of various bills aiming to give more precise directives to the Federal Reserve System showed the practical difficulties that Congress met, insofar as it considered a bolder policy-making role. Meanwhile, the Federal Reserve Board took no strong lead to develop more explicit conceptions of its mission for Congress's consideration, but most of the time seemed content for Congress to leave the subject alone.[367]

Sympathy with Congress's problems cannot remove the effects of Congress's defaults. Measured by the generous criteria which the Court has set, Congress did not make unconstitutional delegations of power to the Federal Reserve.[368] However, that Congress did not behave unconstitutionally does not prove that it behaved wisely. With their broader representative base and their clear-cut authority to innovate and experiment on the frontiers of public policy, legislators have more assured legitimacy than administrators to establish bold value judgments. They should not ask administrators to take the principal heat of battles of interests; such is the practical wisdom back of the formal doctrine that a legislature may delegate power to administrators so long as it does so within declared, intelligible standards. The stipulations in 1913 and 1922 for "fair" representation of "divisions" or "interests" affected by money only threw into sharper relief the load put on the board by the unhelpful generality with which the legislation spoke of its goals.[369] In servicing the going economy the Federal Reserve System did reasonably well most of the time—with the major exception when it stumbled in the banks' liquidity crisis of 1930-33. Significantly, this current-operations-service area of Federal Reserve action was within the most readily discernible area of policy embodied in the 1913 statute. When events invited or pressed the system to regulate money for broader goals of economic growth or stability, Federal Reserve action was most tardy and uncertain in concept and in execution—that is, just in those areas in which Congress had done least to legitimize the system's activity.[370]

Congress affected the system of money by what it did in other areas of law. Thus, we must not ignore two fields of congressional action and inaction which set particularly important—if unplanned—boundaries to monetary policy.

Congress shaped and proposed the sweeping terms of the Sixteenth Amendment, empowering the United States to tax "incomes, from whatever source derived, without apportionment among the several States, and without regard to any census or enumeration." Ratification of the amendment proved to add great reach to the federal government's practical as well as legal capacity to affect the economy—including the availability of money—through fiscal policy. The amendment thus provided the base for what emerged as the principal competitor to Federal Reserve control of bank credit in determining the condition of the money supply. This outcome had not been a goal—indeed, had not been foreseen—in the pressures which produced the amendment. Those who worked for the amendment wanted to allow Congress to put on the wealthy a fairer share of the costs of government and incident to that end to encourage lower tariffs. Conservatives supported the amendment to stave off the more immediate threat of a new income tax statute, which would give the Court an opportunity to overrule the *Pollock* decision, which had invalidated a federal income tax not apportioned by population. As in creating the Federal Reserve System, so in promoting the Sixteenth Amendment, Congress again demonstrated the impact that the legislative process can have by loosing new currents of policy which may run far beyond the vision of those who open the spillways.[371]

In contrast, congressional default was the weighty factor in the other field of nonmonetary policy which bore particularly on the system of money. The Sherman Act (1890) and the Clayton and Federal Trade Commission acts (1914) declared a strong national interest in maintaining competitive markets. For long years antitrust policy paid little heed to investment and commercial banking or to the integration of antitrust law with law more specifically affecting the banking industry. In addition, for decades Congress failed across the board to develop sanctions to match the increasing sophistication of private business techniques of concentration, or to provide enforcement resources remotely commensurate to the growth in private power. It was consistent with the over-all pattern of neglect that Congress thrust antitrust responsibilities on a Federal Reserve Board, already heavily burdened with responsibilities more directly focused on the money supply. However important, the story is too complicated and too indirect in bearing to elaborate here. It suffices to note that the relative ineffectiveness of antitrust policy against big-city concentration in commercial and investment banking created a significant limiting factor on the Federal Reserve's control of the money supply in relation to general economic conditions, especially before the Banking Act of 1935 confirmed and enlarged the board's powers over open-market operations and member bank reserves.[372]

Such major legislation as there was after 1913 directly relevant to money was the product of the bargaining of interests within the congressional arena more than of executive leadership. The exception was the treatment of gold in 1933-34, which President Roosevelt finally determined. The earlier Thomas Amendment to the Agricultural Adjustment Act (1933) was forced on a reluctant president by congressmen moved partly by business expansionists, but also by traditional farmer favor for easy money; the president's prime decision here was simply not to use the authority Congress had put in his hands.[373] The White House was indifferent or even hostile to the Banking Act of 1933 and wavered in confusion over the act's most important feature of deposit insurance.[374] Executive influence was important in producing the Banking Act of 1935, when Marriner Eccles conditioned his acceptance of appointment to head the Federal Reserve Board on administration efforts to obtain increase in the board's powers. But the sustained effort to get a bill through was within the Congress, where—ironically—Congressmen T. Alan Goldsborough and Henry B. Steagall had to battle Senator Carter Glass to strengthen his creation of 1913.[375] President Harry S. Truman lent his support to obtaining some kind of full employment act in 1946. But there was division among his own advisers, and he lacked sufficient leverage in the country and in his own party to determine the outcome among the large forces battling before Congress.[376]

The intricacy of the subject, the unsettled state of ideas about it, and the diversity of major interests affected made definition of goals and priorities in monetary policy an area that invited leadership from the White House. However, Wilson's involvement in the 1913 act was the only highly calculated example of that leadership; Roosevelt's actions on gold indeed brought changes of lasting importance, but his entry into the monetary field was an opportunistic episode in his calculations. For better or worse, patient, applied work by individual congressmen and congressional committees and by administrators charged with long-term responsibility seems the practical way to build policy that calls for combining skilled bargaining with knowledgeable handling of evolving theory and difficult technique. The president's most effective role is likely to be that of Wilson in 1913—to intervene at a late stage with decisive will, to bring the long work of others to some resolution.

If Congress was not moved, or able, to spell out goals and priorities in monetary policy, conceivably it could still make continuing impress on the Federal Reserve System by using its two most distinctive (and related) powers—those of (1) controlling the public purse and (2) investigating the conduct of government agencies. Congress finally chose not to use the purse power to supervise the system. It made limited, but gradually increasing use of its power of investigation.

Changing the prior legislation, as it had been construed by the attorney general, the Banking Act of 1933 declared that funds paid to the board by the regional banks should not be construed to be government funds or appropriated moneys so as to bring them under external audit, but that the board should govern its own receipts and expenses; committees of both houses said that the intent was to give the board "the determination of its own management policies." The board's accounts had been audited by the Treasury from 1912 to 1921, and by the comptroller of the currency from 1921 to 1933. The federal reserve banks were never audited by a government agency outside of the system. Recurrent efforts or suggestions that the system be subjected to audit by Congress's agency, the General Accounting Office, failed in the face of appeals for Federal Reserve independence. To conciliate distrustful congressmen, the board and the regional banks under board supervision created their own internal auditing procedures, eventually including participation by qualified independent private accountants chosen by the board. That the system not have to depend on congressional appropriations for its operating funds was a substantial safeguard against its use for political patronage. Probably budget or external audit controls would have proved at once too cumbersome and too drastic to be effective instruments for congressional influence on particular monetary policy. However, we should not put much weight on the system's freedom from purse-power surveillance. Congress's investigations, and the fiscal discretion it committed to the Treasury, provided ample means for officials outside the system to pass judgments on Federal Reserve performance.[377]

Congress made no significant effort to use its investigative power to influence Federal Reserve policy making before 1950.[378] Between 1950 and 1970 on some ten occasions congressmen or senators used the committee process, or such analogous devices as proposed sense-of-Congress resolutions, to rally criticism over the system's current monetary policy. There is no convincing evidence that these activities materially shaped the subsequent course taken by the Federal Reserve Board or the FOMC. At most some coincidences in timing suggest that congressional activity produced occasional tactical response from the system. The congressional critics usually distrusted Federal Reserve restraints on credit, which they saw as holding back desirable economic growth and high employment; through most of the 1950s and 1960s the Federal Reserve authorities were indeed more concerned than their critics with limiting price rises, but felt it prudent to avoid plain statement of their price-stabilization goal lest they draw too damaging fire. Even so, there is no convincing case that congressional criticism substantially affected the system's strategy as distinguished from its occasional tactical concessions, or that the board of the FOMC were intimidated.[379] Close to the over-all character of the relationship was Speaker Sam Rayburn's exasperated complaint in 1959, that the Federal Reserve authorities "consider themselves immune to any direction or suggestion by the Congress, let alone a simple expression of the sense of Congress." Reacting to the board's successful opposition to a policy directive proposed by the Democrats on the House Ways and Means Committee, Rayburn observed, "It appears that the fault of the suggested committee bill was not that the language itself was wrong, but that the Congress dared even to speak to the Federal Reserve, a creature of Congress."[380]

Realism suggests that we not accept the Speaker's acrid comments as the whole of the matter. The board and the FOMC did, indeed, show that they were likely to hold to their own long-term judgments where congressional pressure stayed at the level of committee action. Most of the time the Congress as a whole proved wary or indifferent about committing itself on monetary policy. But the Thomas Amendment of 1933 and the Gold Reserve Act of 1934 should remind us that Congress as a whole could change the frame of policy reference, if events or a resolute president applied pressure broadly felt through the congressional ranks.

In proportion as the Federal Reserve Board successfully maintained independence in decision, experience of mistakes in timing and of actions taken on poor prophecies of cause and effect showed the need for informed appraisal from outside critics to whom the board must pay attention. Ill adapted to shaping specific monetary decisions, Congress's investigative authority might play a constructive role if it were properly institutionalized rather than treated as a basis for episodic indictments. The Banking Act of 1935 looked in this direction when it enlarged the reporting duties of the board and stipulated that the new Federal Open Market Committee keep a full record of all its actions. But, left alone, the reporting agency could and did report tardily and with calculated ambiguity or unhelpful generality.[381] Though in terms ignoring the Federal Reserve System, the Employment Act of 1946 for the first time created machinery for sustained legislative scrutiny of Federal Reserve decision making through interplay of the president's annual economic report (and the work of his Council of Economic Advisers) and a new Joint Economic Committee of Congress charged to review the report and the course of the economy. Scoring at best minor tactical successes over the 1950-70 years, some members armed with the legitimacy conferred by the mission of the Joint Economic Committee began slowly to build the grounds of more informed congressional interaction with the board and the Council of Economic Advisers on the one hand and economists, bankers, and other affected economic interests on the other.[382]

Over the 1908-70 span courts had little part in fashioning the system of money. Of course federal and state courts handled many lawsuits over the day-to-day administration of deposit-check money—involving, for example, the effectiveness of deposits or endorsements, or the incidence of loss from forgery or business failure.[383] Such matters were important to operating the system of money. Yet, they did not call for examining the goals or structure of the system. Almost no suitors presented such basic questions, and without lawsuits courts cannot share in making policy. The exception was the litigation over the constitutionality of the federal statutes which rendered unenforcible gold clauses in public and private contracts. Yet, the Supreme Court's decisions upholding this legislation were of secondary importance for monetary policy. The seriously fought issue was application of the laws to contracts made before the laws were passed; on authority stretching from *McCulloch* v. *Maryland* to *Juilliard* v. *Greenman* none of the justices saw a substantial question of Congress's authority to fix the place of gold or paper currency in affecting future transactions. However large the immediate stakes, the retroactive force of the laws posed an issue of passing effect. Moreover, the Court's decisions fell easily within the limits of the judges' role as marked by the presumption of constitutionality. In this light, in upholding the gold legislation the Court itself added little to the content of national monetary policy. Reasonable men could find that a national economic emergency existed in fact and that it would serve public interest to subordinate ordinary rules of contract law to Congress's authority to prescribe the system of money without which contract could not function in a modern economy. In this context the Court must uphold what Congress had done.[384]

Apart from the gold cases, only a scattering of court rulings touched the bases of the money system. Up to 1970 no case had required the Supreme Court to pass on the constitutionality of Federal Reserve authority to manage the money supply.[385] On familiar precedent the Court readily disposed of Tenth Amendment challenges to statutes designed to keep national banks on a competitive footing with state-chartered banks, so that national policy might be fulfilled. Similarly, after clarifying the Federal Reserve's statutory powers, the Court had no trouble in ruling that the system might validly insist that all checks cleared through its procedures clear at par, whatever competitive pressure this policy put on state banks.[386] In any event, these were matters relevant mainly to current operations. A handful of speculators raised deeper issues, by challenging the legality of Federal Reserve management of the money supply through open-market operations or the issue of federal reserve notes. The Second Circuit Court of Appeals summarily dismissed a challenge based on claims that such money management violated traders' rights, protected by the Fifth Amendment, to seek market profits. The Federal Reserve's money management authority was so clearly relevant to reasonably defined public interest as to present no substantial constitutional question. Moreover, judicial review plainly was too slow and cumbersome to oversee regulation of the shifting currents of money markets.[387] Without moving into such intricacies, conceivably judges might have found the 1913 and 1935 statutes unconstitutionally vague in the sweep of powers they delegated to Federal Reserve administrators. Granted, the delegations were very broad and expressed no adequately comprehensive pattern of monetary goals. But, again, the presumption of constitutionality gave Congress wide scope in building law to deal with problems bristling with complex and unknown factors. Thus it is not surprising that such lower courts as touched the matter of delegation of powers saw no barrier to the legislation.[388]

Probably the Eighth Circuit Court of Appeals came to the heart of the reasons why judges had so little opportunity to make law in this field. That court ruled that suitors lacked standing—whether as citizens, taxpayers, or investors in government securities—to challenge the constitutionality of Federal Reserve money management authority. The system of money is one of the most pervasively effective of legal institutions. Reaching the broadest range of transactions, providing operationally critical instruments for the existence of markets of all sorts, money bears on many individuals in many diverse ways, and yet—allowing for their individual circumstances—with weight not so peculiar to any of them as to create the focused kind of adversary interests requisite to justiciable cases or controversies. As the economy developed within the law after 1913, the functional character of a managed system of money excluded judges from the ranks of principal policy contributors in this area.[389]

The sum of these factors is that executive and administrative processes provided practically all the impetus for making substantive monetary policy. Moreover, we can bring the story to sharper focus than this. Administrators on the Federal Reserve Board and the Federal Open Market Committee shared policy making with a top-executive cluster including the president, the Treasury Department, and the president's Council of Economic Advisers. Other agencies—notably the comptroller of the currency, the Reconstruction Finance Corporation, and the Federal Deposit Insurance Corporation—had missions materially affecting the system of money. But their activities provided support for a situation in which money management might be undertaken; they did not enter directly into the active management of the money supply, which is the prime concern of this volume.

The comptroller of the currency and the FDIC influenced the number and location of commercial banks that created deposit-check money; the comptroller played this role directly, since his office had authority to grant or deny applications for national bank charters; the FDIC played the role informally, because state-chartered banks must satisfy the corporation's requirements in order to become insured banks and without deposit insurance it was in practice nearly impossible for a bank to operate.[390] All three agencies were actively concerned to foster the solvency of individual banks. In the 1930s depression the Reconstruction Finance Corporation kept some banks in existence, by replenishing their capital through investing in their preferred stock or their capital notes and by making them secured loans to relieve them of peril when their ordinary commercial assets were found to be frozen.[391] The comptroller (for national banks) and the FDIC (for insured banks not members of the Federal Reserve) shared with the Federal Reserve (for state-chartered member banks) authority to conduct periodic examination of the finances of banks. This examination function had the substantial effect of policing individual banks' working integrity.[392]

These agency activities affecting the creation and the continuing vitality of commercial banks were basic contributions to the deposit-check "currency" which was the bulk of the money supply. But such activities did not enter directly into regulating the quantity, timing, or velocity of money supply. FDIC insurance was a major invention to keep deposit-check money in operation by removing old fears over the liquidity of deposits in terms of cash. Of course this result had direct impact on the going money supply. However, the FDIC performed this function by enforcing the statutory qualifications for insurance and examining insured banks; its money-supply function did not make it a competitor with the Federal Reserve Board and the FOMC in continuing regulation of the size or movements of the stock of money.[393] Cautiously conservative, the RFC never used its resources for such open-market operations in government securities as might have made it the prime supporter of the banking system at a time when the Federal Reserve System was failing to realize its role as lender of last resort.[394] Terms set formally by the comptroller or informally by the FDIC for chartering new banks bore on the state of competition in local banking markets rather than on over-all money movements.[395] Examination of the financial condition of individual banks was an instrument not adapted to shaping or enforcing general money policy; criteria for monetary policy referred to factors of too great sweep to be translated into details of individual banks' portfolios, and a broadscale attempt to do so was likely to imperil the function of examinations, to protect the functional capacity of the individual institutions. Congress was jealous of creating selective credit controls and held these to quite limited categories. The examining agencies thus properly rejected use of the examining function as a tool of monetary policy.[396] The notable exception highlights the reason of this rejection, because it concerned a point both capable of ready generalization and helpful to Federal Reserve use of open-market operations; this was the agreement obtained by the Federal Reserve Board with the comptroller and the FDIC in 1938 that banks' holdings of securities might be valued at cost instead of at market, to protect banks otherwise basically sound from collapse under the pressure of sharply falling securities markets and to make them more ready to sell in response to Federal Reserve pressure.[397] In another aspect events reflected the judgment that concern with individual banks' solvency involved goals other than those of general monetary policy. Critics complained of the overlaps and duplications of effort, as bank examining fell within the authority of three federal agencies. It is significant that the criticism ran mainly in terms of administrative costs and efficiency and that strong argument was made for the Federal Reserve Board to be relieved of examining banks, as well as of other regulatory tasks not immediately related to money, precisely in order that it might better focus its energies on managing the money supply.[398]

Between 1836 and 1913 the only central agency in position to attempt some direct management of the national money supply was the Treasury. Over those years competing initiatives in monetary policy came from the Treasury or from diffuse private or partisan interests pressing on Congress. Within that context the bargains struck in the act of 1913 reflected lively, but ill-defined concern on right and left that the new Federal Reserve Board be "independent." In one aspect the statute sought to protect the board against private—meaning, primarily, banker—influence. The act created a board wholly of public officers named by government and subjected to the board's over-all regulation the regional reserve banks, into whose structure some private check and balance factors were included. Administrative practice, ratified and tightened by the Banking Act of 1935, strengthened the independence of the board against the private factors in the system. Dominant policy was thus clear, that the Federal Reserve Board should have substantial autonomy apart from the market. This course of events ran against the conservative concern in 1913 to bulwark monetary policy against "politics"—which, so far as the fear had shape, was fear of populist or agrarian inflation. However, creation of the Federal Reserve System also tended to bring this conflict into a sharper focus than it had had before. The system spelled the potential of a new competition among central official agencies—between the governors of the system on the one hand, and the White House and Treasury on the other. Thus a new issue was born—defining the "independence" of the Federal Reserve authorities within the executive and administrative apparatus of the national government.

Within the central government Federal Reserve independence in setting general monetary policy always existed only within three limiting factors, one of them legal, the other two factual.

First the Federal Reserve System had no basis for claiming policy independence of Congress, whose creation it was. Its officers could, and did, hold to their own policy positions in sparring with particular congressmen or senators or with particular congressional committees, even a committee with so broad a mandate as the Joint Economic Committee under the Employment Act of 1946. But Congress's rightful command of legislation was something again. Congress might change any feature of the system's organization or powers, and in fact it made some changes, though few of basic importance. Thus, in the interests of the Federal Reserve Board's independence, in 1935 Congress removed from the board the secretary of the treasury and the comptroller of the currency, who had been ex officio members since 1913. There is little evidence that the board had been substantially constrained by the presence of either officer. But in itself the change showed favor for putting considerable autonomy in the board. Congress might also enact policy directives. True, it left vague its statements of monetary goals and priorities. But this record reflected practical difficulties stemming from sharp conflicts among interests and from want of reliable knowledge and did not rest on doubt of Congress's authority. Finally, at the base of policy was Congress's constitutional authority to determine the character of the system of money within which both the Treasury and the Federal Reserve must work; thus Congress provided a new frame of reference for monetary policy in 1933-34 when it took gold out of the domestic money structure.[399]

Secondly, it was a political fact that the Federal Reserve System, including the Federal Reserve Board and the FOMC, belonged to a working national government. If a sufficiently determined president with congressional support, or a sufficiently determined Congress on its own, fixed a national economic policy for the times, the Federal Reserve authorities must in practice fit their actions into that policy.[400] The Banking Act of 1935 reflected a felt need to strike workable accommodations in this respect. It increased to fourteen years the terms of Federal Reserve Board members. On the other hand, it forbade two full consecutive terms for a member, and it limited the term of a member as chairman of the board to four years, in the expectation that this arrangement would permit each president to name from within the board a chairman of his choice.[401] Subordination to White House leadership was clearest when the nation was at war. Without serious demur during the most active periods of World War I (1917-18), World War II (1942-46), and the Korean War (1950), the Federal Reserve Board subordinated its policy judgments to those of the Treasury.[402] If the imperative to follow top executive leadership was less clear in peacetime, it was because ordinarily there was more practical leeway for indecision and conflicts of views within the office of president and within the Congress.[403]

Thirdly, throughout its life from 1913 to 1970 the Federal Reserve Board's practical independence was confined by the poor and disputed state of theory and of operational knowledge about central-bank roles and the desirable and practicable uses of monetary policy to affect the general economy. Operational knowledge had to be bought by trial and error, for want of anything better. Theories about the ends and means of monetary policy continued in sharp debate within and without the system. It was hard steadfastly to assert the independence of Federal Reserve management when most of the time there were so many conflicting voices on what independence should be used for, or how it should be used. Indicative is the fact that in the spring of 1951, when the board made its most dramatic bid for independence of the Treasury, board officials declined to support a joint resolution tendered in Congress which would have declared that the board had primary power and responsibility for regulating the over-all supply of credit and that the Treasury should conform its actions concerning the federal finances to the monetary policies set by the Federal Reserve. The proposed resolution offered the board more responsibility than it was ready to assume. Instead, board officials took the position that they wanted simply recognition that the board enjoyed equality with the Treasury in considering policy affecting money, leaving high-level differences to be bargained out among equals.[404]

Offsetting these limiting factors were some functional facts which in practice worked to give the Federal Reserve Board and the Federal Open Market Committee substantial freedom of decision in the week-in-week-out handling of the money supply. Executive and congressional budget-making and fiscal decision processes involved the need to bargain in immediate confrontation with many private, partisan, and bureaucratic interests. Thus they were typically slower than the more sharply focused Federal Reserve decision-making operations, and not so well adapted to close and continuing development of policy by trial and error, or to close and continuing management of a policy once adopted. Moreover, if the Federal Reserve Board was limited in bold use of its potential by want of tried and accepted theory and operating knowledge, this want was still more felt in development of fiscal policy by the White House and the Congress. For in the Congress and even in the White House the problem was typically not divergence among relatively sophisticated ideas for action, but the time-costly need to overcome quite unsophisticated notions about economic and social priorities and the chains of cause and effect involved in economic processes. Furthermore, in working with bank-created money the Federal Reserve Board had the advantage over legislative measures of bringing to its aid the useful flexibility of which the market was capable. If created deposits exceeded public preferences for spending, bank deposits tended to decline, else banks would lose income. Thus, through bank-created money the burden of adapting the money supply to the over-all state of the economy could be put largely on the private banking sector. But if money were created by legislative fiat in excess of what was healthily needed to promote real transactions, built-in vested partisan and politically potent economic interests probably would operate to leave no recourse but to wait—as the country did in the last quarter of the nineteenth century—for the economy to grow into adjustment to the government-made money.[405]

The net result of assessing the legal and practical factors limiting Federal Reserve autonomy, and the functional factors favoring it, is to induce caution lest we inject more drama into the question of Federal Reserve independence than the record warrants. Because functional factors reinforced the substantially separate organization which the Federal Reserve act had created, the Federal Reserve board and the Federal Open Market Committee in regular course did most managing of the money supply. That this was so was not, however, the result of a regular succession of battles over Federal Reserve autonomy. Indeed, the net result of the legal and practical limitations was that Federal Reserve independence was an active issue during relatively little of the system's life from 1913 to 1970. From 1914-16 the new organization was busy setting up shop. In 1917-18 there was no question that the system must loyally support the financing of the war. The first instance of controverted Treasury pressure came in 1919 when the system reluctantly kept credit easy to help float the last war loan, though the war emergency was over and inflation threatened; the Federal Reserve shortly asserted itself by tightening credit, and thence came under farm-area criticism when commodity prices fell in 1919-20. As the later 1920s boom mounted to the 1929 crash disputes over credit policy were more within the system, between some of the regional banks and the board, than with the administration. In the mid-1920s, with a degree of initiative it did not often show before the 1950s, the board learned to use open-market operations for regulating the money supply. That it could develop this device was an unplanned consequence of Treasury action; extensive open-market operations in government securities would not have been possible with the small, firmly held supply of such securities before 1917. On the other hand, the board met no Treasury opposition to its new control instrument; rather, it had Treasury approval of deliberate and coordinated management of such dealings, because this approach avoided disturbing the market for Treasury flotations. In the lean years from 1930 to 1940, however, the board itself took a relatively passive attitude toward its responsibilities to counter the downswing of business. Symptomatic was an episode of the spring of 1937. Following the board's use of its new (1935) statutory power to raise reserve requirements, the Treasury protested at the White House that investment values were in peril because banks were selling government bonds to build up their reserves; under Treasury and White House pressure the board then engaged in its first large open-market purchases in over three years. This was primarily a defensive use of open-market operations, and one which in effect conceded Federal Reserve responsibility to stabilize the government bond market. In part from concern for the statutory requirements on its own reserves, the board was timid in using open-market purchases positively to stimulate business; here the limitations of the board's own outlook, rather than pressure from the Treasury or the White House, kept it from a positive role. From 1941-45 war finance as determined by the president and the Treasury again dominated the scene; plainly the reserve's duties as government fiscal agent were to carry out the government's policy and at most to advocate taxing more and borrowing less to meet war costs.[406]

The span from 1946 into the spring of 1951 brought the first sustained period when either the pressure of the federal debt or the specific pressure of the Treasury were felt as serious constraints on the Federal Reserve's freedom to make peacetime monetary policy. Between 1946 and 1947 the Federal Reserve Board successfully asserted its powers to allow short-term government borrowing rates to rise. But the system continued to support the long-term government bond market at the low rate set in wartime. It did this until 1950 primarily because the board shared Treasury fears that the fall in bond prices which would accompany a rise in interest rates would endanger economic stability, given the large outstanding investment in long-term, wartime issues. However, the board felt more and more concern that by continuing to buy bonds at prices pegged to hold down interest rates it was feeding an inflation danger serious enough to offset the hazard of falling bond prices. Moreover, from the early fifties outside support for Federal Reserve independence tended to become identified with those who saw the board as a bulwark for stable prices and a steady purchasing power of the dollar and feared that the Treasury had a built-in bias for inflationary low interest rates which might ease its job of managing the large federal debt. In 1950 the board asserted a greater independence, by selling in the open market to raise interest rates. But when the Treasury insisted on floating low-interest bonds to meet Korean War expenses, the board reluctantly resumed buying the Treasury's issues to keep them from failing. However, the board was now so moved by its fear of inflation that in March 1951 it pressed for and got an agreement with the Treasury allowing the Federal Reserve to assume more control. The Treasury would cooperate by offering to exchange nonmarketable bonds convertible into five-year marketable notes for outstanding, marketable bonds, while the system eased the adjustment by continuing some purchases on a reduced scale. But the FOMC would also cut back open-market operations in short-term government securities in order to put member banks under pressure to borrow at the federal reserve banks. In 1953 the FOMC tightened its independent stance by announcing that it would deal only in short-term government securities and that it would direct its dealings only at monetary goals. It was then that the board refused to support the proposal of a number of senators that Congress should give the board full authority to regulate the money supply and declare that Treasury financing must be subordinated to Federal Reserve monetary goals. Thus the board in 1951 settled for recognition as an equal bargainer with the White House (acting primarily through the Council of Economic Advisers) and the Treasury in setting monetary policy.[407]

Between 1951 and 1970 there were sometimes sharp disagreements between the board on the one hand and the White House (or the Council of Economic Advisers) or the Treasury on the other, over domestic policy. The tendency was for the board and the outside advocates of its independence to be concerned with price stability and inflation, and the White House and the Council of Economic Advisers with unemployment rates and the vigor of business activity, while the Treasury was likely to be more engrossed in cutting budgets and in low-cost debt management.[408] But despite these differences, there were no overt efforts to manipulate specific policies of the board by pressure on appointments, by competing uses of Treasury balances, or other techniques that might be open to the executive. Thus after some twenty years, administrative and executive practice—characteristically, without being codified or ratified by an explicit declaration from the Congress—had given Federal Reserve independence approximately the meaning for which the board had settled in 1951: that it be treated as an equal consultant and bargainer when there was contention at high levels over adapting monetary policy to the situation of the domestic economy.[409]

This proposition must be stated with reference to domestic policy, because two precedents implied that the Federal Reserve Board conceded leadership to the Treasury when the prime issue was the international balance of payments. By the mid-1930s, moved largely by fears of war or major political upsets abroad, gold was flowing into the United States in such quantity as threatened to push bank reserves to heights which could spell dangerous inflation. The Federal Reserve Board used to the statutory limit its new (1935) authority to increase member bank reserves, but the gold was still coming. At this juncture, in 1936 the Treasury took the initiative in sterilizing much of the gold inflow, by borrowing in order to buy gold—to this extent exerting downward pressure on the availability of credit at home—and then holding the gold in its vaults. Conceivably the Federal Reserve Board could have acted to like effect by bold open-market sales of government securities. But it lacked will for such action, and it did not make an issue when the Treasury now used its borrowing power for this monetary goal. With so large a gold stock as its purchases were building, the Treasury inherently acquired capacity to control bank reserves by its own decisions to hold or release gold. In 1937 the board in effect acknowledged this monetary capacity of the Treasury when, faced with recession, the board asked and obtained the Treasury's cooperation in releasing some of its gold to increase bank reserves. The second precedent for this type of Treasury leadership grew out of concern in the 1960s over gold outflow rather than gold inflow. Between early 1961 and the fall of 1964 the Treasury took the initiative in acting to keep up short-term interest rates to discourage the export of dollars seeking higher returns, while it sought to promote low long-term rates to encourage investment at home. It did this by operations peculiarly within its control, investing heavily in long-term securities for government trust funds which it managed—thus tending to lower the yields on long maturities—while selling in the public market an unusually high proportion of obligations of less than one year, through such supply pressure on the short end of the market pushing yields there to levels relatively higher than normal. In this 1961-64 period the Federal Reserve Board cooperated in a subordinate role by simply continuing to hold a little over 50 percent of under-one-year maturities in its portfolio; thus it lent support to a high level of short-term rates by not buying heavily in that range to ease domestic credit. In both the 1936 and the 1961-64 episodes the record lacks any clear declaration of policy on Treasury-Federal Reserve division of labor. But the implication common to both is that, confronted by Treasury initiative, the board was prepared to concede Treasury leadership in using Treasury borrowing power for monetary goals involving international movements of high-powered (reserve-creating) assets.[410]

Further definition of Federal Reserve independence emerged from the context of key statutory powers and working practices of the Treasury and the Council of Economic Advisers. The Federal Reserve Act declared that it should not be interpreted to subtract from authority otherwise given to the secretary of the treasury. Whatever else lurked in this Delphic reservation, at least it meant that within the executive and administrative establishments the Treasury was empowered to fix the terms of contracting or refunding federal debt and managing the current flow of federal receipts and disbursements.[411] Practice made plain that secretaries would not concede a Federal Reserve veto over the exercise of these prerogatives. The Treasury's exercise of discretion in managing federal debt could have significant impact on the general money supply. However, aside from the actions taken in 1936 and in 1961-64 reacting to international gold flows, the Treasury typically seemed moved by considerations of debt management as such, rather than by desire to achieve monetary goals. So, the success and cost of its flotations and maintaining confidence in the investment stability of government bonds were apparently the Treasury's prime concerns in 1919 when it influenced the Federal Reserve Board to support the last of the World War I bond drives; in 1937 when it pressed the board into open-market purchases in order to cushion the impact of increases in required reserves of member banks; and between 1946 and 1951 when it persuaded an increasingly reluctant board to continue pegging long-term bonds at prices which would keep the rate of return set on their original issue. On the other hand, where it did not feel under special constraint of circumstances, the Treasury ordinarily cooperated with the board to keep federal debt management from disturbing the general money market. In any case, the experience of both routine and extraordinary operations showed that, within the frame of domestic economic policy, it was the Treasury as manager of federal debt, rather than the Treasury as would-be manager of the money supply, which posed issues of Federal Reserve autonomy. In 1956 the Federal Reserve Board recommended to the Senate Banking and Currency Committee that the reservation of powers of the secretary of the treasury be dropped from the Federal Reserve Act as a provision which "so far as is known . . . has never had any significant effect on any of the operations or authority" of either the system or the secretary. At the same time, with implications somewhat inconsistent with denying significance to the reservation clause, the board recommended that the Federal Reserve Act be amended to declare that all activities of federal reserve banks as fiscal agents of the United States "should be made specifically subject to supervision and regulation by the Board." Congress did not respond to the suggestions.[412]

The Federal Reserve act specifically obliged the federal reserve banks to render service as fiscal agent when the Treasury required it. Congress authorized the Treasury to keep government moneys on deposit with the federal reserve banks, though it did not command that the funds be kept there; Congress did, however, in 1921 end the subtreasury depositories which had existed since 1846, thus leaving the federal reserve banks as the only quasi-official agencies of deposit. At first the Treasury continued to keep some government deposits in commercial banks. But rather soon it turned to using the federal reserve banks as its principal, regular depositories. Late nineteenth- and early twentieth-century experience had shown that by shifting government deposits among different depositories the Treasury could play a central-bank role, affecting the reserves against which banks might lend. Conceivably the Treasury might have continued to manipulate its deposits in this manner. Instead it chose to keep its balances predictably patterned simply to suit its own operating needs, and thus by its own self-restraint to make the government deposits a relatively neutral factor in regulation of the money supply.[413]

The other prime competition with the Federal Reserve Board in making monetary policy was likely to come from the president, aided by his Council of Economic Advisers and by his secretary of the treasury acting as a top political-economic counselor rather than as head of a body of debt managers. The Employment Act of 1946 made this combination a more likely source of intervention than the presidency alone had theretofore proved to be. In creating the Council of Economic Advisers the 1946 act set up a body which could contribute a continuity of knowledgeable attention to money affairs previously lacking in the White House establishment. Before 1950 White House intervention in monetary policy was only crisis intervention; the White House led in the actions on gold in 1933-34, but otherwise showed no clear-cut leadership. After the Council of Economic Advisers was created and after it abandoned the posture of detached commentator and assumed that of an involved agency of the administration in power, there was a marked growth in administration scrutiny of Federal Reserve money management and in discussion and sometimes controversy between the board (through its chairman, typically) and the administration. Between 1950 and 1970, in tune with the accord of 1951, this new relationship emerged generally as one of exchange among peers. However, the presence of the Council of Economic Advisers meant that the president was now potentially closer to the flow of monetary policy than he had been and that the independence of the board was to this extent potentially more constrained than it had been.[414]

Appraisal of Federal Reserve Board independence within the official apparatus of the national government should be kept in careful perspective to experience. Newsmen, and even scholars, thrive on the drama of controversy. They may thus be biased toward putting more weight than they should on the Treasury-Federal Reserve accord of 1951. Most of the time outsiders were content to leave to the specialized apparatus of the board and the FOMC the intricate, technical, time-taking, week-in-week-out operations of managing the system of money. This was an independence conceded in the ordinary run of affairs, partly from outsiders' indifference, partly from their respect for technical mysteries, partly from the practical need that all men are under to live by some division of labor. It was not an independence to be counted on under stress. Moreover, where stress existed, through most years of its life to 1970, the board did not assert bold enough leadership to produce showdown issues over defining the extent of its practical freedom. Through most of its life, pressures put on the board—whether by congressional committees or by the activity of particular congressmen, or by the White House establishment—were applied in an atmosphere more of bargain than of command, and there is little except occasional tactical concessions by the board to evidence that such pressures had impact. Finally, we must not forget the limiting conditions noted at the start of this discussion: the unquestioned legal supremacy of Congress over controlling money, the practical force of a president with reliable congressional support in pursuing an administration monetary policy, and the hesitations of will introduced by want of firmly set theory or operating knowledge affecting the big questions. By 1970 *independence* had a firm place in the vocabulary of discussion over the Federal Reserve Board's place in the federal government, but there was little record test of how much strain the idea would bear.

Notes

1. Prelude, supra, notes 13-17 (limits on states), 30-36 (state-chartered banks), 31, 38, 39 (potential federal monopoly), 40-47 (authority of Congress), 50-58 (federal paper money), 59-65 (federal legal tender), 67-71 (national banks). On the indicated policy for control of the system of money ultimately by the national government, see Johnson, J., dissenting, in Osborn v. The Bank of the United States, 9 Wheaton 738, 871, 873 (U.S. 1824); United States v. Marigold, 9 Howard 560, 567 (U.S. 1850).

2. 1 Stat. 246 (1792), Dunbar, 227. The constitutionality of the mint act was in effect acknowledged in McCulloch v. Maryland, 4 Wheaton 316, 432-33 (U.S. 1819). In its first years the mint operated with less than desirable efficiency, partly because of the mistake in originally putting control of it in the Department of State instead of in the Treasury, where functional interest might have insured closer attention to it. See Part One, supra, note 135.

3. See Briscoe v. Bank of the Commonwealth of Kentucky, 11 Peters 257, 317, 318 (U.S. 1837). Private manufacture of coin raised no issue of the federal balance of power, unless one deemed use of private coin to be sanctioned by the states' law of contract and property. However, no one seems to have raised this view of the matter. Private coin never contributed more than marginally to the stock of money; this is probably why Congress was silent on the matter until it outlawed private coinage in 1864, asserting for itself an exclusive prerogative which the courts had no difficulty in accepting. Part One, supra, notes 21, 127.

4. 1 Stat. 246 (1792). See United States v. Marigold, 9 Howard 560, 567 (U.S. 1850). Private contracts stipulating for settlement by other measures than the units of value defined in law did not raise an issue of the federal balance of power, unless one treated such stipulations as deriving their force from the states' law of contract. When question was first raised about the enforceability of such contracts, no one seems to have cast the matter as raising a colorable question of the relative roles of federal and state law; instead, without question, the Supreme Court ruled that federal legislation governed, and when the Court in 1869 held that contract clauses for settlement in gold bullion or in the gold value of currency were enforceable, it ruled so on the basis of its interpretation of the intent of Congress. Part One, supra, note 14. On obedience to the constitutional limit on state legal-tender laws, see note 14, infra.

5. United States v. Marigold, 9 Howard (U.S. 1850); Part One, supra, notes 25, 26.

6. Part One, supra, notes 27, 28.

7. Hamilton, *Works,* 3:388, 413; cf. Knox (1), 19.

8. Dewey, 135-37; Knox (2), 22, 23, 24, 26, 30, 34, 38; Nussbaum, 70, 71. See 2 Stat. 766 (1812), 801 (1813); 3 Stat. 100, 161 (1814), 213 (1815); Dunbar, 63, 68, 70, 76.

9. It indicates the limited precedent constituted by the War of 1812 Treasury note issues that, despite his general aversion to circulating paper, in 1814 Jefferson favored meeting the needs of the national economy by issuing large-denomination Treasury notes for circulation, while providing small-denomination money in coin. Apparently he found authority for such paper issues in Congress's constitutional authority to borrow. Letter to Thomas Cooper, 10 September 1814, *Works,* 6:375; cf. Henry Adams, 8:246; Dewey, 136. That arch exponent of hard-money faith, Senator Benton, arguing for the state in Craig v. Missouri, 4 Peters 410, 423 (U.S. 1830), conceded the validity of the 1812-15 Treasury notes: "They were freely circulated throughout the United States without objections, and they were most useful instruments in the financial operations of the government during the last war." In addition to tying these issues thus to government borrowing, Benton stressed the absence of legal-tender status as a reason why these notes were not of the genus "bills of credit." Ibid. His point on this latter score seems irrelevant, in light of the historical background of the ban on state bills of credit, which included bills with and without legal-tender status. See Marshall, C. J., id., 434. But Benton's obvious desire to narrow the 1812-15 precedents is significant of the sensitivity of hard-money men to the possible implications of these issues for national power over currency.

10. Dewey, 232, 234; Knox (1), 41, 42, 44; see 5 Stat. 201 (1837), 228 (1838), 323 (1839), 370 (1840), 411 (1841), 469 and 473 (1842), in Dunbar, 118, 122, 124, 125, 130, 132.

11. 5 Stat. 614 (1843), in Dunbar, 136; House, Committee on Ways and Means, Reports of Committees, 1st Sess., 28 March 1844, Vol. 2, Rept. no. 379; cf. Knox (1), 49, 52, 53-61; Nussbaum, 86-87. One tastes a partisan flavor in the Ways and Means report, in its key doctrinal observation that "it was thought that it was too late to undertake to revive the exploded Federal doctrine of claiming power because it had not been expressly forbidden." Committee on Ways and Means, Rept. no. 379, p. 7.

12. 9 Stat. 118 (1847), 11 Stat. 257 (1857), in Dunbar, 142, 149; Dewey, 255; Hepburn, 27; Knox (1), 20, 70, 71; Nussbaum, 87. The issues of 1837, 1843, 1847, and 1857 might be deemed to extend congressional claims beyond those established under stress of war finance needs in 1812-15. Cf. Nussbaum, 70, 71. Before 1860 the Supreme Court had no occasion to speak directly to the authority of Congress to issue currency. Indicative of the cloudiness of early attitudes on the matter, however, are some glancing references in Craig v. Missouri, 4 Peters 410 (U.S. 1830). In his majority opinion, Marshall, C. J., observes that "treasury notes" were known to serve as money in colonial Virginia. Id., 435. Johnson, J., dissenting, id., 442, seems to feel that the ban on state bills of credit reflected a hard-money policy which might preclude federal paper issues: "The whole was intended to exclude everything from use as a circulating medium except gold and silver, and to give the United States the exclusive control over the coining and valuing of the metallic medium. That the real dollar may represent property, and not the shadow of it." On the other hand, Thompson and McLean, JJ., in their separate dissents, seem to accept that Congress

may issue currency incident to its borrowing power; their observations thus seem to hold the situation in the posture in which the federal convention discussion left it. Id., 447-48, 461.

13. Knox (1), 33. Opposed to the idea of legal-tender status for paper, Secretary of the Treasury A. J. Dallas in 1814 did not deny Congress's authority to create it, but thought it a step to be taken only with great caution: ". . . whether the issues of a paper currency proceed from the national Treasury or from a national Bank, the acceptance of the paper in a course of payments and receipts must be forever optional with the citizens. The extremity of that day cannot be anticipated when any honest and enlightened statesman will again venture upon the desperate expedient of a tender-law." Henry Adams, 8:249.

14. Prelude, supra, notes 15, 16, 26. Probably because the Constitution's limit on state legal-tender laws was so clear-cut, the Court never dealt with a direct collision between this limitation and state legislation. In its debtor-relief legislation of the 1820s, Kentucky attempted to give something like legal-tender status—in a roundabout way—to notes of the state-chartered, state-owned Bank of the Commonwealth of Kentucky, by stipulating that a creditor who would not accept the bank's notes in discharge of his claim must submit to certain stays in enforcing his rights. The Court upheld an indirect curb on this device of state policy when it found statutory and constitutional authority in the federal courts to enact rules of practice which forbade erecting this block to an action which the creditor was entitled to bring within federal jurisdiction. Wayman v. Southard, 10 Wheaton 1 (U.S. 1825). See Warren (3), 1:648-49. Briscoe v. Bank of the Commonwealth of Kentucky, 11 Peters 257, 316 (U.S. 1837), found it unnecessary to decide whether, in its reference to the bank's notes, the Kentucky statute was in substance a legal-tender act, since the question would arise only on execution, and did not arise in the present suit presenting a question of the legality of promissory notes given for a loan effected in the bank's notes. Dunne (2), 60, note 55, is ingenious, but seems to press this aspect of Briscoe beyond what the Court's observation warrants, when he interprets the Briscoe analysis to suggest that a statute-imposed procedural delay in enforcement would not be deemed subject to the constitutional limit on state laws declaring legal-tender status. Nussbaum, 48, thinks that the terms of the constitutional limitation on state legal-tender laws may imply that, apart from the declared limitation, power over legal tender remained in the states, but says that "that loophole proved innocuous." Apart from the question of legal-tender status for notes of state-chartered banks, there seems to be no significant "loophole."

15. Marshall, C. J., for the Court in Craig v. Missouri, 4 Peters 410, 432 (U.S. 1830), and Story, J., dissenting, in Briscoe v. Bank of the Commonwealth of Kentucky, 11 Peters 257, 330, 332 (U.S. 1837), claimed to find no great difficulty in deriving a definition of *bills of credit* from circumstances and usage of the time of making the Constitution. Their claim seems to stand up, however, only so long as one assumes the most clear-cut direct action by the state, in issuing obligations solely on its credit, to circulate as money. When legislation presented a less straightforward arrangement—as in charters for private, note-issuing banks, or perhaps even in charters for state-owned, separate-fund institutions—the dissenters in Craig v. Missouri and McLean, J., for the Court in Briscoe seem more realistic in finding the Constitution's ban to lack clear definition either from the text or from history. See Johnson, J., dissenting, id., 4 Peters 438, 442; Thompson, J., dissenting, id., 445, 447, 448, 452; McLean, J., dissenting, id., 450, 453; McLean, J., for the Court, 11 id., 257, 312, 318. A like judgment is expressed in Billis ads. The State, 2 McCord 12, 15 (S. C. 1822).

16. Warren (3), 1:725-27, notes the relevance of these general currents of interest and opinion to problems of the federal balance affecting control of money.

17. See Marshall, C.J., in Craig v. Missouri, 4 Peters 410, 432 (U.S. 1830), and Johnson, J., dissenting, but agreeing on this point, id., 443; cf. Marshall, C.J., in Sturges v. Crowninshield, 4 Wheaton 192, 203-4 (U.S. 1819) (the ban a sharp break from previous state authority); Beveridge, 4:217. States of the Confederacy issued their own currency, which after the war courts held of no lawful effect, partly because the issues were direct violations of the Constitution's ban on state bills of credit, partly because they were instruments of rebellion. Given the sweep of the break with the Union, however, these instances do not seem exceptions to the principal proposition in the text. See Bank of Tennessee v. Union Bank of Louisiana, 2 Fed. Cas. 678, 679 (No. 899) (C.C.D. La. 1872); Hale v. Huston, Sims & Co., 44 Ala. 134, 137, 139 (1870); Thornburg v. Harris, 43 Tenn. 157, 160, 161, 165, 172 (1866). A scattering of other cases involved the validity of state evidences of debt, challenged as being bills of credit. Where the state paper showed a limited purpose, so that the court was convinced it was not intended for general circulation, it was upheld. Lasseter v. State, 67 Fla. 240, 64 So. 847 (1914); Pagaud v. State, 13 Miss. 491 (1845). Where the court was convinced that the paper was issued against a separate fund of assets, it was upheld, though issued by the state, or ultimately backed by the faith of the state, following the Briscoe case. See note 40, infra. Some decisions invalidated state paper, where the court found an intent that it was available for general circulation and where it was issued simply on the general credit of a public body emitting it. City National Bank v. Mahan, 21 La. Ann. 751 (1869); State ex rel. Shiver v. Comptroller General, 4 S.C. 185, 229, 233 (1872), and Auditor v. Treasurer, id. 311 (1872); Wesley v. Eells, 90 Fed. 151 (C.C. N.D. Ohio, 1898), decree affirmed, 177 U.S. 370 (1900); Robinson v. Lee, 122 Fed. 1012 (C.C.D.S.C. 1903), affirmed on other grounds, 196 U.S. 64 (1904). All of these cases add up to a minor element in the whole picture of money-system policy.

18. Primm, 5; cf. McLean, J., dissenting, in Craig v. Missouri, 4 Peters 410, 457 (U.S. 1830).

19. Craig v. Missouri, 4 Peters 410 (U.S. 1830). The decision was applied, without further elucidation, in Byrne v. Missouri, 8 Peters 40 (U.S. 1834). See note 17, supra.

20. Marshall, C.J., Craig v. Missouri, 4 Peters 410, 433 (U.S. 1830); cf. Johnson, J., dissenting, but acknowledging this point, id., 439; Primm, 5. Benton's argument for Missouri in Craig expressed sharp displeasure that the sovereign state was thus "summoned" before the Court. 4 Peters 410, 419-20. Marshall took note of this temper of the case. Id., 437; cf. McLean, J., dissenting, id., 458, 464. See Warren (3), 1:725.

21. Craig v. Missouri, 4 Peters 410, 432 (U.S. 1830). Marshall drew on common usage of words, plus judicial notice of the history preceding adoption of the Constitution, to conclude that the prohibition on the states to *emit* their bills did not describe the issue of evidences of debt incurred for the present receipt of money or services. Id., 432. He might well have cited in support *The Federalist,* no. 44, p. 278, where the idea of emission of bills of credit is clearly equated to action of states "to substitute a paper medium in the place of coin."

The Court later fulfilled the indications of Marshall's opinion, that the forbidden bills of credit did not include state instruments—specifically, interest coupons on state bonds, declared receivable, when due, to pay taxes or other sums owed to the state—which were created incident to receipt by the state of advances from lenders, in a context where no purpose appeared other than that auxiliary to the state's borrowing. Poindexter v. Greenhow, 114 U.S. 270, 284, 285 (1885); cf. Houston & Texas Central Railroad Co. v. Texas, 177 U.S. 66, 89 (1900). Poindexter seems consistent with Craig. The Texas decisions extended the concept somewhat, in a direction threatening encroachment on the bills-of-credit ban, since it upheld legislation which made state treasury instruments receivable for debt payments due by the railroad to the state, on condition that the railroad receive such instruments in payment for transportation services. But this feature of the Texas treasury paper was specifically auxiliary to a particular program of state financial aid to railroads, and thus a long way from creating general exchange media. 177 U.S. at 89. But cf. Brown, J., dissenting on this score, id., 102. The Court there also re-emphasized the importance of not trenching upon the states' acknowledged borrowing papers: "The decisions of this court have shown great reluctance under this provision as to bills of credit, to interfere with or reduce the very important and necessary power of the states to pay their debts by delivering to their creditors their written promises to pay them on demand, and in the meantime to receive the paper as payment of debts due the state for taxes and other like matters." Ibid. Wesley v. Eells, 90 Fed. 151 (C.C.N.D. Ohio, 1898), decree affirmed, 177 U.S. 370 (1900), distinguished Poindexter, in finding that South Carolina "revenue bond scrip" constituted forbidden bills of credit, where the scrip was not payable at any particular time, but was to be retired one-fourth per year under a special tax levied therefor, was receivable to pay dues owed to the state anytime from issue (and not just at a fixed maturity date), and might be reissued by the state treasury as often as received, except for paying interest on state debt. Moreover, the scrip was reissued in low denominations convenient for circulation, bore no interest, and was issued in what the court deemed a great volume relative to the state's economy.

22. Craig v. Missouri, 4 Peters 410, 433 (U.S. 1830). Marshall found other, subsidiary evidence of intent that the certificates should have such character "as would give them currency," in the statute's stipulation that the loan officers "are required to issue" them, and that the officials be under duty "to withdraw annually from circulation" a tenth of the total issue—so that, Marshall observed, "the law speaks of them in this character" of circulating media. Id., 430, 431, 433.

23. Id., 433.

24. Marshall, id., 434, 435, pointed to the fact that the paper issues which generated the fears of the Constitution makers were not all of legal-tender status and argued from the text, which does not limit the bills-of-credit ban to legal-tender money and which contains a separate limiting stipulation on state power to define legal tender. Johnson, J., id., 442, agreed with Marshall, though he observed that the certificates might be deemed legal tender to the extent that the law declared them payable to meet salaries of public employees. Thompson, J., id., 448-49, agreed with Marshall's history and acknowledged that the constitutional language was broad enough to make it embarrassing to hold it down to issue of legal-tender paper. But he felt that the grant of legal-tender status was the historic source of the main injustices and fears producing the bills of credit ban and that hence the want of legal-tender quality in the Missouri certificates should be deemed at least a partial reason for excluding them from the ban. McLean, J., id., 454, 457, flatly assigned the want of general legal-tender status as reason enough to rule these emissions not bills of credit, but he provided no convincing basis to answer Marshall. In his opinion for the Court in Briscoe v. Bank of the Commonwealth of Kentucky, 11 Peters 257, 313-14 (U.S. 1837), McLean, J., in effect conceded that his Craig dissent was in error in insisting

that legal-tender status was necessary to constitute a bill of credit. Concurring, Thompson, J., did not mention legal-tender status. Story, J., dissenting, reasserted Marshall's reading of history. Id., 333-37. Further, that pre-1787 bills of credit were not limited to legal-tender instruments, see Juilliard v. Greenman, 110 U.S. 421, 448 (1884); Billis ads. The State, 2 McCord 12, 17 (S.C. 1822). The grant of legal-tender status was taken as strong evidence of intent that paper be a circulating medium, in Bragg v. Tuffts, 49 Ark. 554, 6 S.W. 158 (1887).

25. Of course Marshall conceded the states' authority to borrow money. Craig v. Missouri, 4 Peters 410, 431-32 (U.S. 1830). Concern for encroachment on this authority was stated by Johnson, J., id., 443, Thompson, J., id., 447, and McLean, J., id., 455. McLean, J., id., 455, thought that the small denominations of state paper should not be taken to negate its character as borrowing instruments; small denominations might be necessary to attract lenders. The point seems inapt for the Missouri loan certificates, which were loans by, rather than to, the state. Johnson, id., 443, felt that if borrowing were a form of tax anticipation—as indicated where instruments were made receivable for taxes—small denominations might be necessary if the paper were to be useful to the taxpayer for this purpose. Johnson, id., 443, 444, thought that the specificity with which the Missouri statute provided a pledged fund (notably, by pledge of all debts due to the state) indicated a true debt. He felt, also, that though the state received no present consideration for the loaned certificates, it could realize its immediate cash needs by discounting the notes it received for its paper, and thus treat the transactions as in effect borrowings. That the loan certificates provided on their face for interest payments by the state, Johnson thought deprived them of the uniformity of value necessary for an effective medium of exchange. Id., 443, 444.

That the prevailing opinions in Briscoe v. Bank of the Commonwealth of Kentucky, 11 Peters 257 (U.S. 1837), did not discuss the maintenance of the state's capacity to borrow was perhaps because the decision there upheld the state program. In his dissent, Story, J., did not touch the question of state debt, perhaps because he saw the Kentucky institution as so clearly a device for issuing money. Id., 343-46.

26. Craig v. Missouri, 4 Peters 410, 432 (U.S. 1830). In our colonial experience, Marshall further observed, "paper money . . . whether made a tender or not, was productive of evils in proportion to the quantity emitted." Id., 435. And the exigencies of the Revolution had induced use of paper money "to a most fearful extent." Id., 432. Thompson, J., dissenting, id., 448, conceded the general evil of overissue demonstrated by past experience, though he found the Missouri program distinguishable. That the governing policy back of the bills-of-credit ban was experience of the evils of "unrestrained issues, by the Colonial and State governments, of paper money, based alone upon credit," was reasserted in Poindexter v. Greenhow, 114 U.S. 270, 283 (1885). See, accord, Houston & Texas Central Railroad Co. v. Texas, 177 U.S. 66, 87-88 (1900). All of these observations might have claimed the authority of Madison, in The Federalist, no. 44, p. 278: "The extension of the prohibition to bills of credit must give pleasure to every citizen, in proportion to his love of justice and his knowledge of the true springs of public prosperity. The loss which America has sustained since the peace, from the pestilent effects of paper money on the necessary confidence between man and man, on the necessary confidence in the public councils, on the industry and morals of the people, and on the character of republican government, constitutes an enormous debt against the States chargeable with this unadvised measure, which must long remain unsatisfied; or rather an accumulation of guilt, which can be expiated no otherwise than by a voluntary sacrifice on the altar of justice, of the power which has been the instrument of it."

27. Missouri Laws, Special Session, 1821, p. 11, sec. 23. The statute also pledged all interest accruing to the state and all security realized under pledges given by borrowers of the loan certificates.

28. Craig v. Missouri, 4 Peters 410, 448 (U.S. 1830). Thompson, J., further spelled out his criterion of the constitutional limitation: "The natural and literal meaning of the term [bills of credit] import a bill drawn on credit merely, and not bottomed upon any real or substantial fund for its redemption. There is a material and well-known distinction between a bill drawn upon a fund and one drawn upon credit only." Id., 447. To the same effect, Johnson, J., dissenting, id., 444, emphasized the provision of the Missouri statute which made the loan office certificates receivable for all dues owed to the state: ". . . the objection to a mere paper medium is that its value depends upon mere national faith. But this [Missouri paper] certainly has a better dependence; the public debtor who purchases it may tender it in payments," with the added security that the federal Constitution's contract clause binds the state to honor its commitment to accept the certificates. "This approximates them to bills on a fund, and a fund not to be withdrawn by a law of the State." McLean, J., did not make the fund point as sharply as his fellow dissenters, but he seems to intend it when he says that to be a forbidden bill of credit an instrument "must contain a promise of payment by the State generally, when no fund has been appropriated to enable the holder to convert it into money." Id., 454.

29. On the want of clear meaning in the bills-of-credit ban, see note 15, supra.

30. The dissenters in Craig declared no reliance on the statute's $200,000 ceiling, nor did they mention the want of any legal formula limiting the quantity of certificates by the quantity of pledged assets. Marshall took note of the statutory pledge of assets, and of the related provisions making the certificates receivable for dues owed to the state, but only because he saw these provisions as relevant to establishing the state's intent that the certificates circulate as money. 4 Peters 410, 433 (U.S. 1830). One element in one of his definitions of the forbidden bills of credit seems to be the idea of an indefinite promise of redemption: "To 'emit bills of credit' conveys to the mind the idea of issuing paper intended to circulate through the community for its ordinary purposes, as money, which paper is redeemable at a future day." Id., 432. In reciting the history out of which the bills-of-credit ban emerged, he recurred to the emphasis that "paper money . . . whether made a tender or not, was productive of evils in proportion to the quantity emitted." Id., 435.

31. The bank's charter—Laws of Kentucky, Act of 25 December 1820, p. 183—was one of a set of Kentucky statutes for relief of debtors, one of which stayed levy of execution for two years, unless the creditor would accept notes of the Kentucky bank in payment of his judgment. This approach to a legal-tender law was denied effect concerning actions brought in federal courts, by Wayman v. Southard, 10 Wheaton 1 (U.S. 1825), note 14, supra. Cf. Warren (3), 1:644, 648.

32. Briscoe v. Bank of the Commonwealth of Kentucky, 11 Peters 257, 309, 328 (U.S. 1837). Perhaps reflecting sharp criticism of Green v. Biddle, 8 Wheaton 1 (U.S. 1823), where it was claimed that less than a majority of the justices had decided against the constitutionality of another Kentucky debtor-relief measure (the occupying claimant law), Marshall explained in 1834 that the Court's policy was not to give judgment on a constitutional question unless a majority of the whole Court concurred. 8 Peters 122 (U.S. 1834); 9 id. 85 (U.S. 1835); Beveridge, 4:583; Warren (3), 1:790, note 1. Story declared that on the first argument of Briscoe a majority of the sitting justices, including Marshall, were of opinion that the bank's note issues were forbidden bills of credit. 11 Peters 328, 350. Johnson, J., was absent, and Duval, J.,

aligned himself with Marshall, C.J., and Story, J., in disagreement with Thompson, McLean, and Baldwin, JJ. Beveridge, 4:583. Once Briscoe was heard for final disposition, it was determined speedily, within ten days of completed argument. Warren (3), 2:27.

33. McLean, J., 11 Peters 257, 320, 321 (U.S. 1837). McLean found that the fact that the bank might be sued was a factor particularly relevant to distinguish the bank's notes from the instruments historically established as bills of credit: "It is believed that there is no case where a suit has been brought, at any time, on bills of credit against a State, and it is certain that no suit could have been maintained, on this ground, prior to the Constitution." Id., 321-22. Since a sovereign may consent to be sued in any context it sets, McLean's point seems of little weight, save insofar as it may be deemed a facet of the separate-fund formula, next considered. This seems in essence the relevance of the bank's liability to suit, as it is viewed by Thompson, J., concurring in Briscoe, id., 328.

34. Id., 257, 343, 344. The promised capital for the bank also included so much of the capital stock owned by the state in the defunct Bank of Kentucky as might come to the state after that institution's affairs were settled, together with many profits on that stock not previously appropriated or pledged by law. Story emphasized that control of the state's capital contributions was in the state, since the charter did not itself convey to the bank any state lands or any other state funds (though it was made the statutory duty of the state treasurer to pay over to the bank the public lands proceeds or the Bank of Kentucky residues, as he might receive such items). Concurring in Briscoe, Thompson, J., yet declared that, if he found the bank's notes otherwise bills of credit, he could not agree that they were not emitted by the state: "The State is the sole owner of the stock of the bank, and all private interest in it is expressly excluded. The State has the sole and exclusive management and direction of all its concerns. The corporation is the mere creature of the State, and entirely subject to its control." Id., 328. McLean's majority opinion had to concede (id., 319) that the preamble of the bank's charter gave "much plausibility" to the idea that the institution was "a mere instrument of the State to issue bills," since the preamble recited that it would be "expedient and beneficial to the State and the citizens thereof to establish a bank on the funds of the State, for the . . . relief of the distresses of the community." In the context of the rest of his opinion, McLean brushed aside this declaration, apparently because he felt that the text of the bank's charter did not fulfill the preamble's indication. He also rejected the idea that the bank was identical with the state because the state was its sole stockholder; invoking Bank of the United States v. The Planters' Bank of Georgia, 9 Wheaton 904 (U.S. 1824), he ruled that in becoming party to a business venture, the state, for transactions of that venture, divested itself of sovereign character, as evidenced by the stipulation of its charter that the bank might be sued on its notes. Id., 324, 326, 327. An argument thus drawn with regard to the policy of the Eleventh Amendment seems irrelevant to the quite distinct and different policy represented in the bills-of-credit ban. Such functional point as there is in McLean's argument on this score seems less in establishing that the state did not "emit" the bank's bills, than in arguing that insofar as there was a separate fund of assets back of the bills, they did not run counter to the policy of the prohibition of bills of credit.

35. 11 Peters 257, 320 (U.S. 1837). The bank demurred generally to defendant's plea alleging that the bank never received from the state any of the capital promised by the charter. The state's principal promised contribution was the proceeds of sales of state lands. McLean seems to say that, nonetheless, in substance the state lands

backed the notes, because the charter made the notes receivable by the state in payment for its lands, and when the state treasurer paid over these proceeds of land sales
to the bank, his actions "would lessen the demand against it." As McLean went on to
indicate, this meant in effect that the continuing fund behind the bank's notes would
be, not state lands proceeds, but security taken on credit extended by the bank. Id.,
310, 315-16, 320. The further inference might be that thus the bank notes were
guarded by segregated assets not supplied by the state, and hence were not issued on
the credit of the state; but it is typical of the blurred character of the majority
opinion that it does not make this point clearly. However, this estimate of the whole
matter seems the reason that in his key statement on the redemption fund, McLean
identifies that fund simply with the "good securities" which the charter required the
bank to take on the credit it extended in the general course of its business.

Briscoe v. Bank of the Commonwealth, 11 Peters 257, 321-22, 327 (U.S. 1837).
Similar grounds appeared in the concurring opinions of Thompson, J., id., 328, and
Baldwin, J., 11 Peters, Appendix, 127. Story, J., dissenting, thought it immaterial
that the state might not be sued on the bank's notes; the bodies issuing bills of credit
before 1787 were not liable to suit, either; in any case, a state was not open to suit,
but "in equity and in justice" the bank's notes should be treated as those of the state
as true principal—apparently harking back to his finding that the bank was wholly an
instrument of the state. Id., 347. Story found it historically irrelevant that the bank's
charter provided a fund to redeem its notes, since like provision had been made for
many of the bills of credit whose abuse provoked the constitutional ban. Id., 345.
Provision of a redemption fund did not suffice to prove that noteholders took the
bank's notes in sole reliance on the fund; with dubious relevance, Story invoked the
proposition that "it is at the common law held incumbent on those who insist that
there has been any exclusive credit given to a fund, to establish that fact, by clear and
irresistible proofs." Id., 346. More to the point, it would seem, was whether such link
as there was of the notes to a fund could be held to obviate the danger of overissue,
which was the prime evil against which the constitutional ban was aimed.

37. Note 28, supra.

38. 11 Peters 257, 318, 321 (U.S. 1837). Less cautious than McLean, Thompson,
J., concurring in Briscoe still focused on the fund; the bank's notes escaped the
constitutional ban because "there is an ample fund provided for their redemption,"
plus the fact that the bank might be sued on its notes. Id., 328. Story, J., dissenting,
id., 339, though arguing that historically the availability of a fund created by borrowers' security did not keep instruments from being bills of credit, came close to
averring that a secure, separate fund in specie would save issues from falling within
the forbidden category, though issued by the sovereign.

39. Though the majority opinion carefully avoided explicit repudiation of Craig,
Story, J., saw Briscoe as overruling Marshall's decision. 11 Peters 257, 328, 350 (U.S.
1837). Kent thought that the 1837 decision "essentially" overruled Craig. James
Kent, 1:408, note (a). Accord: McFarland v. State Bank, 4 Ark. 44, 48, 51 (1842).
Cf. Beveridge, 4:509; Boudin, 1:380, 384. Warren (3), 2:27 unconvincingly sides
with the Briscoe majority, that Craig could be distinguished, but he commits himself
to no specification of a satisfactory distinction.

40. Speaking for the Court, McLean, J., reaffirmed Briscoe in Woodruff v. Trap-
nall, 10 Howard 190, 205 (U.S. 1850), and Darrington v. Branch of the Bank of the
State of Alabama at Mobile, 13 id. 12, 16 (U.S. 1851). In these opinions he did not
appreciably clarify the rationale of Briscoe, but his intent seems, again, to emphasize
that separate funds of assets were provided for redemption, under separate management.

The importance of a segregated redemption fund, as providing a more limited base for note issues than the general credit of the state, was put with somewhat more clarity by Curtis, J., for the Court, in Curran v. Arkansas, 15 Howard 304 (U.S. 1853). Under the charter of the State Bank of Arkansas, of which the state was sole stockholder, the state had transferred state bonds to the bank. Interpreting the transfer provision as not intended to allow the state later to withdraw the bonds from the bank's assets and apply them to other debts of the state, the Court said that, if it did not so interpret the charter, the bank would have "had no proper capital which was bound by its contracts," and in such light the bank's bills would probably be forbidden bills of credit. Id., 318. The legal separateness of a redemption fund was thus critical: "But if the charter of the Bank has not provided any fund, effectually chargeable with the redemption of its bills, if what is called its capital is liable to be withdrawn at the pleasure of the State, though no means of redeeming the bills should remain, then the bills rest wholly upon the faith of the State and not upon the credit of the Corporation, founded on its property." Ibid.

For sometimes rather expansive applications of the separate-redemption-fund rationale, to maintain the validity of issues of paper by state-authorized institutions, see Central Bank of Georgia v. Little, 11 Ga. 346, 351 (1852); Smith v. City of New Orleans, 23 La. Ann. 5 (1871); Western & Atlantic Railroad Co. v. Taylor, 53 Tenn. 408, 415 (1871); Gowen v. Shute, 63 Tenn. 57, 62 (1874). The want of a tie to a pledged fund was found objectionable in Bragg v. Tuffts, 49 Ark. 554, 6 S.W. 158 (1887).

41. Note 51, supra.

42. 4 Peters 410, 432 (U.S. 1830). In another broad definition he said that "to 'emit bills of credit' conveys to the mind the idea of issuing paper intended to circulate through the community for its ordinary purposes, as money, which paper is redeemable at a future day." Ibid. One might feel warranted in interpreting Marshall as intending the broader, rather than the narrower, reach of his definitions in view of his accompanying emphasis that the Court should recognize the Constitution's ban as designed "to cut up this mischief by the roots." Ibid. Broad, too, was the implication of that part of his analysis which denied significance to the fact that the Missouri paper had the form of loan certificates of the state, and not of money; the Constitution was not to be evaded by labels. Id., 433. So, also, rejecting the argument that the instruments were not bills of credit because they were not legal tender, he said that "the prohibition is general. It extends to all bills of credit, not to bills of a particular description." Id., 434.

43. 4 Peters 410, 432 (U.S. 1830). On the blurred edges of the concept of bills of credit as of 1787-89, see note 15, supra.

44. The two incorporated banks operating as of 1789 were the Bank of North America, chartered in Pennsylvania in 1781, and the Massachusetts Bank, chartered in 1784. The Bank of New York opened in 1784 without incorporation and did not obtain a charter until 1791. Though efforts to organize a bank in Maryland began as early as 1782, capital could not be raised, and the Bank of Maryland was not chartered until 1790, and finally opened in 1791. Hammond (1), 65, 66, 167. Each of these early banks operated almost solely in its immediate locality. Id., 87. Nelson and Davis, JJ., dissenting in Veazie Bank v. Fenno, 8 Wallace 533, 551 (U.S. 1869), claim that four state banks were in existence and in operation when the Constitution was framed, and that in this light the bills-of-credit ban must be deemed to have been written with acceptance of the validity of such institutions. But, as has been noted, the Maryland bank was not yet then in existence, let alone operating. And, as posing

clear questions of *state* action, only the two incorporated banks seem relevant, with their relevance most questionable in view of their almost exclusively local impact. The only reference to banks in the recorded discussions of the federal Convention was a glancing one, related not to the system of money but to possible creation of monopolies in trade. See Prelude, supra, notes 69-71.

45. Cf. Craig v. Missouri, 4 Peters 410, 433, 434-35 (U.S. 1830).

46. 4 Wheaton 316, 409, 410, 424 (U.S. 1819). See Nelson and Davis, JJ., dissenting, in Veazie Bank v. Fenno, 8 Wallace 533, 551 (U.S. 1869).

47. Thompson, J., thought that bank notes were "more emphatically" bills of credit than the Missouri loan office certificates, if the test were that the instruments should serve as a "substitute for money." So broad a criterion must apply against notes not only of banks directly under state management, but also of banks "established under the authority of a State. . . . For the States cannot certainly do that indirectly which they cannot do directly." He felt that "this prohibition in the Constitution could not have been intended to take from the States all power whatever over a local circulating medium, and to suppress all paper currency of every description." 4 Peters 410, 449. Though Thompson did not clearly make this link, the majority's rejection of significance in a separate pledged fund as taking paper out of the bills of credit category might be taken to be the ground of his belief that bank notes could not survive the Craig decision. Cf. id., 448. On the other hand, his appeal to the Constitution makers' likely intent ignores the fact that the framers simply gave no evidence of foreseeing the rise of note issues by state-chartered private banks. Like Thompson, McLean, J., argued that bank notes must fall under Craig, because a state might not do indirectly "by an act of incorporation" what the Constitution forbade it to do directly. However, his language seems narrower than Thompson's, since McLean seems to refer only to state laws authorizing notes issued "on the capital of the State," that is, apparently, by state-owned banks. Id., 455. In the argument of Craig, counsel on both sides recognized the existence of a possible question as to the legality of notes of state-chartered banks. Id., 419 (Sheffey, arguing against Missouri), 422 (Benton arguing for the state). Johnson, J., the third dissenter in Craig, did not mention banks, but he stated the underlying purpose of the bills-of-credit ban so broadly, and in so rigorously a hard-money sense, as to suggest that the clause would forbid all state bank notes: "The whole [of the ban] was intended to exclude everything from use as a circulating medium except gold and silver, and to give to the United States the exclusive control over the coining and valuing of the metallic medium. That the real dollar may represent property, and not the shadow of it." Id., 442-43. In the same year as Craig, the House Ways and Means Committee expressed doubt that the United States had authority to forbid states to charter banks. Mints, 126.

48. 11 Peters 257, 316 (U.S. 1837). So, id., 313, he had already indicated that the broadest of Marshall's Craig definitions of bills of credit must be rejected for this reason. McLean noted that the printed brief against the legality of the Kentucky bank's issues had argued against the legality of any state bank notes, but that the contention was dropped in oral argument. For the bank, Harden held out this horrendous possibility, should the decision go against his client. Id., 285. But Southard, in oral argument for the defendants below, disavowed a broad antibank position. Id., 293. Though he had evinced concern on this matter in his Craig dissent, Thompson, J., concurring in Briscoe, said nothing about implications for state bank notes generally, perhaps because he was satisfied with what McLean set out. In the weight that McLean assigned to the possible effects of a contrary decision on a broad range of

interests not immediately involved in Briscoe his opinion bears striking resemblance to the contemporary decision in Proprietors of the Charles River Bridge v. Proprietors of the Warren Bridge, 11 Peters 420, 552, 553 (U.S. 1837), where Taney, C.J., in effect said that the Court was deciding the bridge case less from concern for the bridge interests than for the railroad interests which were not before the Court, but which might be grievously affected by a decision for the older bridge proprietors.

49. 11 Peters 257, 417 (U.S. 1837): "But a State may grant acts of incorporation for the attainment of those objects which are essential to the interests of society. This power is inherent to sovereignty; and there is no limitation in the Federal Constitution, on its exercise by the States, in respect to the incorporation of banks." On this point McLean was supported by the doctrinal record. Hurst (6), 15, 17, 119-20. Story, J., agreed that state legislative authority included power to create business corporations in general, and banking corporations in particular. 11 Peters 257, 349.

50. Prelude, supra, notes 35, 36. McLean, 11 Peters 257, 318, strained the record by noting that as of 1787-89 the Bank of North America and the Massachusetts Bank "and some others" were in operation. The two named institutions were the only incorporated banks then operating. It runs past belief that the Constitution makers would think of unincorporated private bankers, operating under the general law of contract, as conceivably agents of the state. Cf. Part One, supra, notes 125-31. Story, J., dissenting in Briscoe, but in effect concurring in the Briscoe dictum favorable to the legality of note issues of state-chartered private banks, said that at the time of the Constitution private banking operations had furnished no examples "of a durable or widely extended public mischief" such as occasioned the bills-of-credit ban. Id., 348. This seems a more relevant resort to contemporary history than McLean's, because Story may be read as simply noting the absence of awareness of a private-bank problem, without pressing on to the notion—for which there is no evidence—that the framers had a focused intent to accept the legality of private issues.

51. Bureau of the Census, Historical Statistics, 261; Evans (1), 14, 15, 17, 18, 24; Hammond (1), 227, 418; Krooss (1), 239; Trescott, 16, 17, 30.

52. 11 Peters 257, 318 (U.S. 1837). The Court's reliance on a generation of generally accepted state practice in chartering note-issuing banks seems the convincing answer to the assertions made from time to time in congressional debates by proponents of the two Banks of the United States, that such bank notes violated the substance of the bills-of-credit ban. Cf. Hammond (1), 564, 565. These were typically observations made for the opportunistic ends of debate. More sober evidence of Congress's estimate of the situation seems 3 Stat. 343 (1816), in Dunbar, 95, authorizing the Treasury to accept notes of specie-paying state banks, following the practice set by Hamilton at the outset of the government.

53. 11 Peters 257, 348 (U.S. 1837).

54. Id., 349.

55. Ibid. Another foreshadowing of later exertion of federal power superseding state banking policy affecting the money supply may be found in the 1855 suggestion of Secretary of the Treasury James Guthrie, that Congress might find it necessary to tax note issues of state-chartered banks and "thus render the authority to issue and circulate them valueless." Mints, 127, citing Senate, Report on State of the Finances, 34th Cong., 1st and 2nd sess., Senate Documents, 1855-56, 5:22-23.

56. In 1814, reflecting on financial problems of the central government connected with the war, Jefferson was prepared to see the nation's money supply provided by Treasury notes for larger denominations and coins for the smaller, with the disappearance of state bank notes. He then said that he would rely on state legislators

to "relinquish the right of establishing banks of discount" from "patriotic principles," but he also implied that Congress might, if necessary, limit state action in this field, when he said that "the noncomplying [states] may be crowded into concurrence by legitimate devices." Letter to Thomas Cooper, 10 September 1814, *Works,* 6:375; see Henry Adams, 8:246. One must weigh these sentiments, also, in light of Jefferson's general distaste for banks. Still, his remarks seem to accept the legality of operations of state-chartered banks, absent superseding action by Congress.

Hammond (1), 137, thinks that the state bank note currency as of the fore part of the nineteenth century "had in its favor, besides vested interest, the weak decision of a Jacksonian court" in Briscoe. This judgment seems to confuse the holding in Briscoe—which does seem shaky—with its dicta on the status of notes of private banks, which seem much more solidly grounded. Hammond's comment, moreover, overlooks that on this latter count Story agreed with the "Jacksonian court."

On the acceptance of the authority of states to charter money-creating banks, see Nathan v. Louisiana, 8 Howard 73, 81 (U.S. 1850); Nelson and Davis, JJ., dissenting, in Veazie Bank v. Fenno, 8 Wallace 533, 549, 550, 552, 553 (U.S. 1869); Joseph Story, 3:19, 20; James Kent, 1:408, 409, note (a). The prevailing acceptance of note-issuing state banks was reflected in the fact that nothing came of several proposals between 1836 and 1838 to limit or forbid such circulating paper by constitutional amendment. Cf. Ames, 257-58. The pattern of events and policy was identified with special acuity by Johnson, J., dissenting, in Osborn v. The Bank of the United States, 9 Wheaton 738, 871, 873 (U.S. 1824). Johnson pointed out that "the provisions of the constitution opposed no adequate inhibition" to the multiplication of note-issuing private banks chartered by the states, and that in this situation "a specie-paying bank, with an overwhelming capital, and the whole aid of the government deposits, presented the only resource to which the government could resort, to restore that power over the currency of the country, which the framers of the constitution evidently intended to give to Congress alone."

57. Prelude, supra, notes 63-77.

58. Hamilton, *Works,* 3:388 (Communication to the House of Representatives, 14 December 1790); id. 445 (Opinion to President Washington, 23 February 1791); 1 Stat. 191 (1791). Cf. Jefferson, *Writings,* 7:555 (Opinion to President Washington, 15 February 1791).

59. McCulloch v. Maryland, 4 Wheaton 316, 401-2 (1819) recognized the enactment as a weighty precedent in construing the Constitution. The legislative precedent takes on the more weight from the fact that, despite the vigorous controversy attending the charter, there was no contemporary proposal to amend the Constitution in the matter. Cf. Ames, 255.

60. Henry Adams, 5:207, 327-28, 330, 332, 335; Beveridge, 4:172-74; Mayo (1), 375-77; Warren (3), 1:502. The charter passed the House in 1791 on a vote of thirty-nine to twenty; the Senate vote is not recorded. In contrast, the bank failed of renewal in 1811 by one vote in the House, and by the casting vote of Vice President George Clinton in the Senate. Cf. Beveridge, 4:176; Hammond (1), 116, 117. Jackson's message accompanying his 1832 veto of a renewed charter for the second bank, in assessing the legislative precedents, asserted that in 1811 Congress "decided against" a national bank, that "One Congress, in 1815, decided against a bank; another, in 1816, decided in its favor," and concluded that "prior to the present Congress, therefore, the precedents drawn from that source were equal." Richardson, 2:576, 582. This argument had been anticipated by Judge Spencer Roane in his "Hampden" papers attacking McCulloch v. Maryland in 1819. Gunther, 137. Ap-

praised against the whole record, this seems a debater's point, rather than a realistic judgment; like Jackson's own message, Congress's handling of the matter turned on disputes over policy more than over constitutional power, and except for Jackson's veto and the 1841 vetoes by President John Tyler, actions taken through the legislative process added up to a preponderant assertion of authority.

61. Henry Adams, 9:106, 107, 111; Bruchey, 122; Coit, 111; Gunther, 4, 5; Hammond (1), 232-34; Morison and Commager, 1:432, 434; Rowe, 16. Madison had vetoed a new bank bill in January 1815 on policy rather than constitutional grounds; he felt that, as set up, the new bank lacked the means or the obligation to fulfill the needs of government finance. A later bill in 1815 came to nothing, but the constitutional issue does not seem to have figured in the outcome. Hammond (1), 232. The legislative precedent set by chartering the second bank was the more striking, not only because it had the support of the Madison administration, but because in the interim years, 1811-15, nothing had come of three proposals to amend the Constitution explicitly to empower Congress to create a national bank. Cf. Ames, 255.

62. On the 1819 repeal effort: Beveridge, 4:288, 289; Gunther, 3, 4; Hammond (1), 259; Warren (3), 1:509, 521, 523. On the hostile state laws: Beveridge, 4:206-8; Hammond (1), 266; W. B. Smith, 112; Warren (3), 1:505, 536. The McCulloch decision is reported in 4 Wheaton 316 (U.S. 1819), and that in Osborn in 9 id. 738 (U.S. 1824). The Court gave further support to the institution in Bank of the United States v. The Planters' Bank of Georgia, id., 904 (U.S. 1824), recognizing the second bank's full-fledged, statutory right to sue in a federal court and to collect what was owing it from a state-chartered bank in which the state was a stockholder. Four states memorialized Congress in favor of, and eight states memorialized Congress in opposition to, a resolution of the Pennsylvania legislature in 1820, urging a constitutional amendment to forbid creation of any national bank to operate outside the District of Columbia. Congress took no action on the matter. Ames, 256.

63. Jackson, Veto Message of 10 July 1832, in Richardson, 2:576. Some authority in Congress to create "a bank of the United States" is recognized, id., 576, 583 (proper discretion exists under necessary and proper clause), 589 (chief executive would supply a plan for a bank, if called on to do so). Stress on points of policy difference over the organization and powers of the proposed, renewed institution appears especially, id., 577 (inadequate public return for monopoly given), 579-80 (foreign stockholding unwise), 584 (monopoly not necessary), 585 (foreign stockholding not necessary; capital excessive; branching should not be left to private decision), 586 (bonus reflects undue private advantage from charter). Cf. Govan, 201; Hammond (1), 405; Hockett, 2:85; Hofstadter (1), 60; McLaughlin, 415-16; Meyers, 18, 19; Morison and Commager, 1:487. Significantly, there grew out of the controversy no movement to amend the Constitution to forbid Congress to charter national banks. Ames, 257.

64. Veto Messages of 16 August 1841 (regarding a bill "to incorporate the subscribers to the Fiscal Bank of the United States"), in Richardson, 4:63; and of 9 September 1841 (regarding a bill "to provide for the better collection, safe-keeping, and disbursement of the public revenue by means of a corporation to be styled the Fiscal Corporation of the United States"), id., 68. Cf. Hammond (1), 543; Hepburn, 151-53; Wiltse, 176-77. See, also, Ames, 257.

65. Hamilton, Communication to the House of Representatives, 14 December 1790, *Works,* 3:388 (referring to fiscal-agent roles), 389, 394, 414 (to service of the general economy), 389, 390, 393, 399, 402, 405; Opinion rendered to President Washington, 23 February 1791, id., 445, emphasizing the general character of the

central government's constitutional powers, 447, 448 (corporations), 449, 466 (general scope), 453, 458 (necessary and proper powers), 489 (aggregate powers), its authority to create a fiscal agent, 474, 478, 482, and its authority to pursue monetary policies not as auxiliary to its other powers, 474, 475, and in exercising its authority over commerce, 480.

66. Jefferson told President Washington that the emission of bank notes, no more than the harvesting of wheat or the mining of ore was a subject of regulating commerce, for "to make a thing which may be bought and sold, is not to prescribe regulations for buying and selling." Moreover, such a regulation of commerce "would be void, as extending as much to the internal commerce of every State, as to its external." Jefferson, *Writings,* 7:555, 556-57. To these points Hamilton replied with emphasis on Congress's proper care for the national economy as such: The immediate regulation of buying and selling would not be the regulation of interstate commerce, as Jefferson seemed to say, but rather proper business for state law; on the other hand, the "care [of the general government] . . . must have presumed to have been intended to be directed to those general political arrangements concerning trade, on which its aggregate interests depend, rather than to the details of buying and selling." And if a true national interest existed in such matters, it might properly be followed wherever it led, into the internal trade of the states. Hamilton, *Works,* 3:481, 482; cf. id., 485.

67. 1 Stat. 191 (1791), secs. 3 (general powers), 4 (president and directors), 7 (IX and X—credit, XIII—notes; XV—branches), 10 (notes receivable for dues owed to the United States), 12 (national monopoly). The charter of the second bank was comparable. 3 Stat. 266 (1816), notably secs. 7, 8, 11 (subsecs. 8, 12, 14, 17), 14, 16, 18, 19, 21.

68. Govan, 29, 34; Hammond (1), 212, 213; Warren (3), 1:502. Hammond (1), 216, 217, observes the presence of some support for rechartering the first bank from interests which otherwise might have been expected to voice agrarian objections to it, but which valued a fresh source of loan capital against what they saw as the selfishly restrictive credit policies of banks in the older, wealthier states. So far as it existed, such sentiment might be read as a form of support for an agency promoting a national monetary policy.

69. Henry Adams, 7:386, 8:214-15, 244, 249, 257, 9:106, 107, 111, 116-18; Hammond (1), 234. John C. Calhoun argued that the federal government had proper concern with the structure of banking, since bank paper had become the chief component of the money stock; he confessed that in his 1811 opposition to renewing the first bank's charter he had not foreseen the impact of state banks on the currency. Barger, 19, 23; Coit, 111-12; Hammond (1), 236, 237. The "Amphictryon" papers, attacking McCulloch v. Maryland in 1819, portrayed the desire for a more reliable currency, than the depreciated paper of state banks, as a leading motive for chartering the second bank. Gunther, 73. In 1834, attacking the removal of the government deposits from the second bank, Calhoun recognized that the federal government's constitutional responsibility for the national money supply should include concern with bank credits and deposits, as money. Coit, 264; Hammond (1), 367, 368.

70. For the Court's validation of Congress's authority both to create a national bank and to empower it to establish branches, see 4 Wheaton 316, 424-25 (U.S. 1819). The absence of attention to monetary policy as a distinct field of national government authority is highlighted by the specificity with which Marshall mentions the services which an effective money supply could render to government fiscal operations. Id., 409, 422. In contrast, the opinion made only glancing reference to the

commerce power, which had figured so distinctly in Hamilton's opinion to the president, upholding the first bank charter. Id., 407. Moreover, Marshall's reliance on the aggregate powers of Congress implicitly suggests that he perceived the bank mainly as a government fiscal agent and did not visualize its possible role in monetary policy as a substantial, independent ground of legitimacy. Id., 408. Gunther, 4, 5, 7, plausibly argues that Marshall slighted the monetary-powers issue because legislative and executive precedent by 1819 left little of substance in controversy on that score and observes that the leading contemporary attacks on the decision, especially that by Judge Spencer Roane, likewise paid scant attention to the bank question as such. The central government's powers to deal with internal improvements and with slavery, he suggests, appeared to these few farsighted men as the critical relevance of the decision. Hammond (1), 265, suggests that Marshall did not single out Congress's authority over monetary policy partly because he wished to establish the national government's capacity to protect itself against state attack with reference to any national functions, and partly because the bank's performance before 1819 in affecting the general money supply had been poor and hence embarrassing as a ground of reliance. It seems equally plausible that Marshall ignored the monetary-policy aspect because of the attitudes hereafter noted as manifest in his opinion in Osborn. Bank of the United States v. Deveaux, 5 Cranch 61 (U.S. 1809) had involved efforts of Georgia to tax a branch of the first bank, but the court did not reach the question of Congress's authority to create the bank, deciding the case on a point of the jurisdiction of federal courts. Without citing evidence, Boudin, 1:265-66, suggests that the Court took a strained position on its jurisdiction here in order to avoid passing on the constitutionality of the bank at a time when unfriendly debate was brewing over renewal of the charter, and it seemed likely that President Madison would veto a renewal bill, were one passed. However, in light of the Court's continuing difficulties with the jurisdictional point first encountered in the Deveaux case, it seems fair to take the Court's handling of that case at its face value. See Osborn v. The Bank of the United States, 9 Wheaton 738, 817-18 (U.S. 1824); Pacific Railroad Removal Cases, 115 U.S. 1 (1885); Henderson, ch. 4.

71. 9 Wheaton 738, 859-63 (U.S. 1824). See, especially, page 863: "The [general business] operations of the bank are believed not only to yield the compensation for its services to the government, but to be essential to the performance of those services. Those operations give its value to the currency in which all the transactions of the government are conducted. They are, therefore, inseparably connected with those transactions. They enable the bank to render those services to the nation for which it was created, and are, therefore, of the very essence of its character, as national instruments. The business of the bank constitutes its capacity to perform its functions, as a machine for the money transactions of the government." See, also, id., 864, 865, 867. In contrast, the later view of the second bank commonly rated it a national instrumentality as much for its currency function as for its service as government fiscal agent. See Thurgood Marshall, J., dissenting, in First Agricultural National Bank v. State Tax Commission, 392 U.S. 339, 348, 355 (1968).

72. Osborn v. The Bank of the United States, 9 Wheaton, 738, 871, 873 (U.S. 1824). Johnson, J., of course, also found a legitimizing basis for the bank in its role as United States fiscal agent. Id., 872. Johnson's past familiarity with Charlestown business may have inclined him to sympathy for a national monetary power. Cf., Morgan, 105, 164-65. Compare his emphasis on the importance of national authority sufficient to prevent "conflict of commercial regulations, destructive to the harmony of the States," in his concurring opinion in Gibbons v. Ogden, 9 Wheaton 1, 222,

224, 229, 231 (U.S. 1824). Note, especially, his broad conception of the *commerce* which Congress might regulate, as including money: "Commerce, in its simplest significations, means an exchange of goods; but in the advancement of society, labor, transportation, intelligence, care, and various mediums of exchange, become commodities, and enter into commerce; the subject, the vehicle, the agent, and their various operations, become the objects of commercial regulation." Id., 229-30.

73. On Biddle's pursuit of general monetary policies, see Part One, supra, notes 107, 108. On practical construction, see United States v. Midwest Oil Co., 236 U.S. 459, 472-473 (1915); Inland Waterways Corporation v. Young, 309 U.S. 517, 522, 524 (1939).

74. On state actions: Beveridge, 4:206-8; Cochran and Miller, 43, 50; Hammond (1), 259, 263, 266; Hepburn, 99-100; Warren (3), 1:505-6, 525-26, 528, 531. On the 1819 repeal effort: Beveridge, 4:288, 289; Hammond (1), 258, 259; Warren (3), 1:509, 521, 523. The main contemporary reactions to McCulloch seemed to be determined by concern with the general political balance of power between nation and states rather than by attention to the federal distribution of authority over monetary policy as such. Cf. Beveridge, 4:309-12, 314-17, 323, 325, 331, 332, 334, 336; Warren (3), 1:514, 516, 518, 524-25, 534-36. Feeling in the states subsided rapidly as the bank was better managed and pressure on debtors relaxed with better times, so that when Osborn was decided in 1824 there were no substantial political repercussions from the decision. This pattern of events further suggests that the heat of earlier years was generated by creditor-debtor tensions and competitive jealousy among bankers rather than by interests primarily concerned with state prerogative. Cf. Hammond (1), 268; W. B. Smith, 4; Warren (3), 1:538. Of like import was the distressed-debtor base of the animus against the second bank, roused by its resort to federal courts to enforce its claims free of procedural curbs set by state law on creditors' actions in state courts. See Wayman v. Southard, 10 Wheaton 1 (U.S. 1825), and Warren (3), 1:646-48.

75. Richardson, 2:529; cf. Govan, 135-36; Swisher, 173. In his first efforts to shape a policy on a national bank, in 1829, Jackson indicated his desire to limit such an institution to roles befitting a government fiscal agent, coupling this position with (unwarranted) criticism of the bank's failure to establish a sound, uniform currency. However, at this point, as at later ones, it is difficult to untangle Jackson's distrust of all banks from his distrust of the second bank. Cf. Govan, 123-24, 126-27; W. B. Smith, 5, 149, 242. Biddle interpreted Jackson's remarks in his 1830 message as aimed at "inviting the state governments to strengthen themselves by usurping the whole circulating medium of the country." Swisher, 173.

76. House, Ways and Means Committee, *Report on the Second Bank of the United States, Register of Debates,* 22nd Cong., 1st sess. (1830); 8:132-39, 142-43. Cf. Govan, 128-29; W. B. Smith, 149.

77. Swisher, 191, 192. Taney had expressed opposition to branching in 1831. Id., 173.

78. Richardson, 2:576, 586. Prime concern with the extent of power delegated to a privately run agency emerged also in a memorandum by Jackson to his cabinet and advisers in March 1833 where he said he might approve a bank in the District of Columbia (with branching authority contingent on state consent and state-set terms), if the government named the bank's president and a controlling number of its directors, and reserved power to amend or repeal its charter at any time. Swisher, 217, 218.

79. Richardson, 2:585, 578, 586-88.

80. Id., 4:63, 64-65, and 68, 71.

81. Id., 66-67. It befits the cloudy fashion in which Tyler drew issues over a national bank that his actions provoked no proposals for a constitutional amendment on the matter, one way or the other. Cf. Ames, 257.

82. Cf. Briscoe v. Bank of the Commonwealth of Kentucky, 11 Peters 257, 317 (U.S. 1837); Bank of Augusta v. Earle, 13 id. 519, 590, 591, 593-94 (U.S. 1839).

83. Hurst (3), 63-65; (4), 114; (5), 92-93, 147, 175, 251, 459, 535.

84. See Osborn v. Bank of the United States, 9 Wheaton 738, 860 (U.S. 1824); Bank of Augusta v. Earle, 13 Peters 519, 596 (U.S. 1839); Attorney General v. The Utica Insurance Co., 2 Johnson Chancery 371, 377 (N.Y. 1817); People v. Utica Insurance Co., 15 Johnson 353, 8 American Decisions 243, 250 (N.Y. 1818); New York Firemen Insurance Co. v. Ely, 2 Cowen 678, 710 (N.Y. Sup. Ct. 1824); Bradish, Pres., in Warner & Ray v. Beers, 23 Wendell 103, 185 (N.Y. Ct. Err. 1840); Bronson, C.J., in DeBow v. People, 1 Denio 9, 12 (N.Y. Sup. Ct. 1845). Cf. Jackson's Veto Message, 10 July 1832, Richardson, 2:576, 590. See, also, Nussbaum, 17; Part One, supra note 125.

85. The Bank of New York, originally balked of a charter by politically powerful competitors, probably issued circulating notes while it operated as an unincorporated association. Hammond (1), 65; Nussbaum, 45. But, if so, this was exceptional; in contrast to the European tradition, in which banks of issue originated in purely private enterprises, banks of issue in this country were chartered by governments, though under private management. Rowe, 10.

86. Nance v. Hemphill, 1 Ala. 551, 556 (1840). The court went on to observe that "until this is done [i.e., until such legislative intervention], it is not easy to perceive how such a transaction [as a loan of circulating notes] can be considered illegal." Ibid. If this last statement is to be read as disclaiming resources in the common law to provide redress, should private banking behavior amount to a public nuisance, it seems an unduly restrictive estimate. The common law developed various doctrines as to the obligations of "common" callings. See Munn v. Illinois, 94 U.S. 113, 126 (1876). The Fourteenth Amendment introduced no principle limiting the law's capacity to make reasonable adjustments to developing community needs, that the common law had allowed free access to banking activity did not mean that the law must always stand so. Cf. Noble State Bank v. Haskell, 219 U.S. 104, 113 (1911); Adler, 135; Pound (2), 369.

87. The general contract-law framework of deposit-check money receives varied recognition in Merchants' National Bank of Boston v. State National Bank of Boston, 10 Wallace 604, 647, 648 (U.S. 1871); Oulton v. German Savings & Loan Society, 17 id. 109, 118 (U.S. 1873); Central National Bank of Baltimore v. Connecticut Mutual Life Insurance Co., 104 U.S. 54, 63-64 (1881); Armstrong v. American Exchange National Bank of Chicago, 133 U.S. 433, 466 (1890); Auten v. United States National Bank of New York, 174 U.S. 125, 142, 143 (1899). See, also, Part One, supra note 24.

88. Hurst (6), 14-17, 119-20; cf. Rowe, 10.

89. Our English inheritance taught that corporate status for any purpose was so distinctive a concession of potential power and legal capacities to private persons as to require the special and deliberate attention of the sovereign. Hurst (6), 3, 9, 19. The fact that, in the early years, corporate charters were in practice sought only for enterprises obviously of broad potential social impact reinforced the inherited image of the corporation as so specially important as to require particular legal sanction. Id., 16-18.

90. Massachusetts Acts and Resolves (1798-99), ch. 32, p. 372 (reprint 1897); New York Laws, 27th sess. (1804), ch. 117. No serious challenge seems ever to have been raised that a ban on unincorporated banking was not within legislative power as this stood before the Fourteenth Amendment. Indicative of the ready acceptance of this as a proper exercise of legislative power was the assertion of the authority by Tilghman, C.J., in Myers v. Irwin, 2 Sergeant & Rawle 368, 370 (Pa. 1816), "the issuing of bank paper being a subject so immediately and deeply interesting to the public that it necessarily falls under the legislative control." Cf. People v. Utica Insurance Co., 15 Johnson 353, 8 American Decisions 243 (N.Y. 1818). See, generally, Cadman, 63, 64, 66; Joseph S. Davis, 2:102-3; Dodd, 205, 206; Heath, 327; Henderson, 44, 45; Livermore, 248, 251, 252. The first New York act was interpreted not to ban individual banking, but only the banking activities of unincorporated associations; an 1818 amendment covered individuals; in 1837 advocates of free banking succeeded in amending the legislation again, to allow individuals to receive deposits and make discounts. Hammond (1), 577, 580; Redlich, 2:61. The restrictive laws did not bar activity that avoided note issues or discounting. Hammond (1), 192, 193; Redlich, 2:63, 70.

91. Dodd, 206, sees this restraint-of-trade pressure as important in producing the 1799 Massachusetts act, and Hammond (1), 28, 159, 578, so reads the background of the 1804 law in New York. Dodd, 264, notes that there were recurrent charges that existing Boston banks wielded undue influence over the grant or refusal of new charters whenever the Whigs controlled the legislature, as they did most of the time in the fore part of the century.

92. Bank of Augusta v. Earle, 13 Peters 519, 594, 595 (U.S. 1839). The focus here on protection against out-of-state banking competition, rather than competition of unincorporated against incorporated bankers, and thus might be read as presenting primarily an issue of federalism and national, as compared with local, money markets. The contest was also tinged with fears of corporate power as such, apart from banking and money issues. Nonetheless, it is pertinent to our present concern, that sophisticated contemporaries in the Supreme Court did not see this kind of state restriction as grounded primarily on considerations of controlling the scope of private power over the money supply as such. Cf. Henderson, 37, 45-46, 48; Swisher, 380-85; Warren (3), 2:50, 52-54, 58, 60, 61.

93. Prelude, supra notes 15, 27, 49-58; Part One, supra, note 230. Some of the discussion attending issues of Treasury notes after 1812 raised the spectre of government's tendency to inflate issues of its own circulating paper, but the discussions did not develop a clear-cut rationale in favor of privately managed currency issues. Cf. notes 7, 11, 12, supra.

94. Hamilton communication to House of Representatives, 14 December 1790, *Works,* 3:388, 413; cf. id., 420-21, 427. See note 7, supra.

95. Cf. notes 28, 35-38, 49, 53, 54, supra.

96. Note 54, supra. In comparison to this line of development, the favor which Jefferson expressed in 1814 for issuing Treasury notes to supplant all bank notes seems simply out of the main stream of policy. See note 9, supra.

97. Dodd, 214, notes that in 1834 the Massachusetts Senate Committee on Banks and Banking said that the practice was to approve any charter where there was reason to believe that the capital would be subscribed. Cf. id., 275, 280. See Briscoe v. Bank of the Commonwealth of Kentucky, 11 Peters 257, 317 (U.S. 1837), reflecting approval of the multiplication of organized assets and economic energy which liberal bank chartering had yielded.

98. In Warner & Ray v. Beers, 23 Wendell 103 (N.Y. Ct. Err. 1840), see opinions of Senator Verplanck, id., 163, and President Bradish, id., 185. Cf. Hepburn, 143; Redlich, 1:187, 197.

99. Hepburn, 143; Livermore, 246-47; Redlich, 1:189. A variant of this concern appeared in early charter provisions limiting the number of votes which might be cast by large stockholders in the internal governance of banking corporations. Dodd, 268.

100. In his opinion in Warner & Ray v. Beers, 23 Wendell 103, 139 (N.Y. Ct. Err. 1840)—the decisions finally upholding the validity of New York's free-banking act of 1838—Senator Verplanck expressed the boom attitudes which provided much of the enthusiasm for broader delegation of money supply to an expanding bank market: "Strong public opinion and the requirements of trade were thought, by a large majority of the legislature of 1838, to demand some legislation whereby the business of banking could be thrown open, under proper restraints, to all who might choose to engage in it, and this without dependence upon political patronage. Capital could not be brought into such an employment under general unlimited responsibility imposed by our law of partnership, even if the restraining act [against unincorporated banks] were repealed." The strength of the favor for freer access to banking privileges in the interests of economic boom may be measured by comparing the attitude taken in Warner & Ray v. Beers, supra, with the plausible position to the contrary outlined in a lower court, in Thomas v. Dakin, 22 Wendell 9, 75, 103, 111 (N.Y. Sup. Ct. 1840), and in the dissent by Senator Hand in Gifford v. Livingston, 2 Denio 380, 389, 400 (N.Y. Ct. Err. 1845). On economic growth, 1820-60, see North (1), 189, 192, 194, 197, 199, 204-5, 207, 209-11. On the implications for policy toward banking, see Hammond (1), 83, 564, 620, 627-29; Redlich, 1:66.

101. Benson, 97-103; Dodd, 283, 284; Hammond (1), 572, 582, 592. The confusing crosscurrents of ideology appear in a comparison of developments in New York (1838) and in Wisconsin (1846-52). The Wisconsin Democrats began by opposing all banks and ended by grudging concessions that it might be safe to enact a general banking act, provided the people were wise enough to install Democrats in office to police its use; the Wisconsin Whigs throughout supported legal authority to create banks and pressed for a free-banking act after the 1848 constitution empowered the legislature to seek popular referendum approval for such legislation. The Jacksonians in New York spoke against legal limitations on access to banking with a sweep which seemed to envisage a completely laissez-faire policy; so far as it reduced the special privilege character of banking, a free-banking law suited their views, but the more doctrinaire Democrats opposed such limitations as the 1838 act imposed, while their more business-oriented fellows favored the legislation. The Whigs in New York likewise mingled somewhat opposing views in the law which they pushed—on the one hand, they sought a wider free market for capital and credit, on the other, they wanted a market dominated by men sound by their concepts. Cf. Andersen, 15-21 (Wisconsin); Benson, 97-103 (New York).

102. A general incorporation act for banks was "unknown in the history of legislation, either in this state or any other state or country," the Michigan court observed in Green v. Graves, 1 Douglas 351, 355 (Mich. 1844). See Hammond (1), ch. 18; Hepburn, 143, 145, 157; Krooss (2), 10; Trescott, 30.

103. See Falconer v. Campbell, 8 Federal Cases 963, 965 (No. 4620) (D. Mich. 1840); Green v. Graves, 1 Douglas 351, 363 (Mich. 1844). Cf. Hammond (1), 603; Redlich, 1:187, 197.

104. Green v. Graves, 1 Douglas 351 (Mich. 1844) held that Michigan's general incorporation law for banks was invalid for failure to comply with the two-thirds

vote requirement, either in passing that act or in creating particular corporations under it. The Michigan court felt that the constitutional voting requirement should be strictly enforced, because it bespoke a strong community feeling distrustful of corporations, "and especially in respect to those possessing banking powers," out of concern for the practical power such institutions could wield. Id., 363. The kind and extent of power thus delegated to private manager was to the fore when the New York court confronted the same challenge to its comparable banking statute. The New York court found that the two-thirds voting requirement did not apply, because it was aimed at the dangers of creating a limited number of institutions holding potent, exclusive privileges, and this danger, the court felt, was obviated by the nature of a general incorporation act. Warner & Ray v. Beers, 23 Wendell 103, 127, 139, 163, 178, 183, 188 (N.Y. Ct. Err. 1840), reaffirmed in Gifford v. Livingston, 2 Denio 380 (N.Y. Ct. Err. 1845). This analysis, focusing on the extent of power delegated to private institutions, seems more realistic and more relevant to the interests that were in fact moving policy, than the effort also made in some of the judges' opinions to demonstrate that banking associations were not the kind of corporate bodies at which the constitutional voting requirement aimed. On original, restraint-of-competition pressures, see Hammond (1), 578-79. Hammond (1), 585-92, details the conflict between New York's lower and highest court on the application of the two-thirds vote requirement to the 1838 statute.

105. Freund, 160, 163-64; Hammond (1), 605, 615, 616. A related type of restriction was that put into some state constitutions, requiring submission of banking laws to popular referendum. This measure not only undesirably blurred legislative responsibility, but also tended to freeze policy. See Porter v. State, 46 Wis. 375, 1 N.W. 78 (1879) (banking law validated by popular referendum may not be amended without popular referendum). After 1875 no state constitution adopted this requirement. Freund, 162.

106. Andersen, 14-24. The constitution proposed in 1846 was defeated at the polls by a vote of about 20,000 to 14,000; that proposed in 1848 was adopted by a vote of 16,799 to 6,384. Raney, 128. In November 1851 a referendum proposal that the legislature enact a banking law carried by 21,219 to 9,216, in an outcome sharply contrasted with a close vote between Democratic and Whig candidates for governor. Andersen, 21. The result was comparably clear-cut when in 1852 the legislature submitted to the people a proposed free-banking law, which the voters approved, 32,826 to 8,711. Id., 23. Cf. Brown, 1949 Wis. L. Rev. 648, 676-81, 692-93; 1952 id., 23, 48-51, 62. The pull of inconsistent attitudes—between fear of banking power and ambition for economic growth—became especially apparent in the second constitutional convention, as both Democrats and Whigs, in the report of a contemporary, "had arisen and declared their utter hostility to banks, and in the same breath had gone on to present propositions by which they might be created." 1952 id., 49.

107. Freund, 162-64; Hammond (1), 605.

108. Barger, 247-50; Benson, 94-97; Hammond (1), 338, 498; Trescott, 18, 38.

109. Hammond (1), 557; cf. Redlich, 1:90, 95 (similar argument by Governor Van Buren). That bank corporations should be viewed as agents of public policy regarding the supply of money, see Green v. Graves, 1 Douglas 351, 357 (Mich. 1844). Strictly applying the requirement of Michigan's constitution that a two-thirds vote be mustered by the legislature to enact corporate charters, the Michigan court held the 1837 free-banking statute improperly adopted for want of such a vote; in delegating creation of banks as much as it did to private initiative, the general incorporation act was deemed to violate the underlying objective of the constitutional

requirement, to maintain a case-by-case scrutiny of such delegations of power as corporate charters allowed. Falconer v. Campbell, 8 Federal Cases 963 (No. 4620) (D. Mich. 1840), had held to the contrary, but Nesmith v. Sheldon, 7 Howard 812 (U.S. 1848) followed familiar doctrine in ruling that the federal courts must follow the Michigan court's interpretation of that state's constitution. For recognition in later years that states might impose a public utility status on banks, see Part One, supra, notes 164, 166.

110. Cadman, 91, 364, 367, 368; Dodd, 202, 210, 213, 216, 274, 280; Hartz, 254, 255, 256; Hurst (6), 39, 40, 45, 46.

111. Porter v. State, 46 Wis. 375, 379, 1 N.W. 78, 79 (1879).

112. Holding Michigan's first free-banking act unconstitutional for want of a constitutionally required two-thirds vote of the legislature in passing it, the Michigan court justified its strict enforcement of the constitutional requirement in part by its concern that the multiplication of banks under the general act threatened to outstrip the economy. Green v. Graves, 1 Douglas 351, 366, 372 (Mich. 1844). Banks multiplied fast after enactment of various free-banking laws. Hammond (1), 596, 601; Krooss (1), 242; Trescott, 30, 31. With relatively uncontrolled increase there went waves of failures when times turned hard; of more than eighty banks first organized under New York's general act, over twenty failed to survive their first three years, and in Michigan within two years of the free-banking statute forty banks were in receivership; other states witnessed similar mortality of banks under free-banking laws before 1860. Cochran and Miller, 84-86; Hacker, 333-34; Hammond (1), 586, 601, 619; Krooss (1), 242. For recognition in later years, that states might constitutionally impose a limited-access, public utility status on banks, see Part One, supra, notes 164, 166.

113. Andersen, 7, 22, 37, 38; Barger, 249; Dodd, 290, 291; Hammond (1), 680-84, and (2), 1, 3, 10; Kuehnl, 122; Redlich, 2:9, 10. Various provisions written first into special charters and then into general incorporation laws for banks, stipulating protections and remedies of bank creditors, represented a type of regulation midway between reliance on corporate structure and on external regulation of business standards, as a means to control banks. Cf. Dodd, 207, 209, 212, 280, 285.

114. Benson, 47, 92, 96, 102; Hammond (1), 557-62; Hepburn, 105, 142-43; Redlich, 1:90, 95; Robertson, 25, 26.

115. Safety fund plans were adopted by Vermont in 1831, Michigan in 1837, Ohio in 1845, and Iowa in 1858. Indiana imposed a mutual guaranty on its banks, without a fund. Robertson, 25.

116. Andersen, 37; Dodd, 212, 270, 273, 276-79, 280-83; Hammond (1), 593; Handlin and Handlin, 219, 222; Hartz, 266, 267; Heath, 188; Hepburn, 103, 142. 162; Robertson, 24, 26; Trescott, 29, 30.

117. On legislation relieving banks during general suspension of specie payments, see Atchafalaya Bank v. Dawson, 13 La. 497, 501, 503, 510 (1839); Bank of Missouri v. Bredow, 31 Mo. 523, 529 (1862); State v. Bank of Charleston, 2 McMullen 439, 452 (So. C. 1843); cf. Long v. Farmers' Bank, 2 Pa. Law Journal 230, 233, 237, 238 (Pa. 1842). For judicial action, see Livingston v. Bank of New York, 26 Barbour 304, 308 (N.Y. Sup. Ct. 1857), interpreting penalty legislation as allowing the court discretion to refuse appointment of a receiver, on the ground that suspension of specie payments did not show the bank was "insolvent," when the bank acted so during a condition of general suspension. For a reflection of executive decision not to enforce penalty legislation, see Martin, J., in Atchafalaya Bank v. Dawson, supra, 510 (La. 1839). See, generally, Friedman and Schwartz, 328, note 38; Hammond (1), 691,

692; Hepburn, 170. Of analogous policy import was legislation which forbade traffic in bank notes for less than their nominal value, or relieved banks of the obligation to redeem their notes where these were presented by dealers engaged in the practice of receiving or buying bank notes at less than their nominal value. Hammond (1), 180; Nussbaum, 66. Arguments were made in Congress without success in 1827, in 1837 following a special message by President Van Buren, and in 1840 to deal with the problem of suspending banks by enacting either a bankruptcy law solely for banks or a general bankruptcy law including banks. The efforts foundered on a variety of opposing claims. One persistent thread was the assertion that it exceeded the bankruptcy power of Congress to apply it against state-chartered corporations, and especially against state-chartered banks, because this would infringe a Tenth Amendment reserved authority of the states over their corporate creations. Some argued that bankruptcy was an inept instrument for effectuating monetary policy. Probably decisive in exclusion of all corporations from the short-lived bankruptcy act passed in 1840 was the practical fear of southerners that bankruptcy proceedings would bear heaviest on the weak banks of their region. Warren (1), 43-44, 56-59, 60, 65-67; cf. Barger, 248-49. Thornhill v. Bank of Louisiana, 23 Federal Cases 1135 (No. 13,990) (D.La. 1870) held the 1867 bankruptcy act properly applicable to a state-chartered bank. See, also, Sweatt v. Boston, H. & E. Railroad Co., id. 530, 533 (No. 13,684) (Cir. Ct. D. Mass. 1871).

118. Eustis, J., in Atchafalaya Bank v. Dawson, 13 La. 497, 501 (1839), observed that "the connection of the banks with each other, is immediate and inseparable, under the system which has existed by law in this state. It is requiring too much from human credulity to suppose that it was the intention of the legislature to subject the currency of the country to the caprice of a debtor; to render the charter of one bank null and void, for an act which other banks could do with impunity, and when the inevitable consequence would be bankruptcy to all of them, and prostration of the credit of the states." So, Rost, J., id., 507, stressed "the mutual connection and quasi solidarity of all our banking institutions, as well as the vital interest which the state has in those who have raised their capital upon its bonds" (and who might press the state to pay those bonds, held as security for the banks' note issues, should the banks' charters be forfeited). The need to respect the continuity of what had emerged as an interlocked system of bank-created money was recognized also in the denial of a receivership in the context of a general suspension, in Livingston v. Bank of New York, 26 Barbour 304, 308 (N.Y. Sup. Ct. 1857), where the court said that the governing statute must be read in light of the realities of banking business, which included the fact that "in the very organization of such institutions . . . in case of a panic or sudden rush, the banks, although amply able and clearly solvent, may not have specie enough on hand immediately to satisfy all claims."

119. 1 Stat. 191 (1791), 3 Stat. 266 (1816); Dunbar, 22, 80.

120. Hamilton, *Works,* 3:388, 413; cf. id., 420-21, 427. See Dunne (2), 20; Knox (1), 19; Rowe, 8, 9, 12-14; Schachner, 269. In 1814 Secretary of the Treasury Dallas urged the utility of a new national bank to supply a national currency, as both more reliable and as relieving the government of need to pay interest on the Treasury notes which might provide an alternative circulating paper; moreover, the bank would maintain the public services it supplied out of its own profit. Henry Adams, 8:249, 253; Knox (1), 31.

121. Govan, 103, presents Biddle's views, as declared in his 1828 speech on the opening of the Chesapeake and Delaware Canal. Compare Redlich, 1:88, emphasizing the extent to which Biddle's actions in the second bank represented exercise of an essentially private discretion.

122. Timberlake, 167-71. The fuzzily stated grounds of Tyler's vetoes seem to emphasize an issue of federalism—concern that the national bank's branches not be set up in states without their consent—but the objective impact of the vetoes was to force the choice between delegated and direct official action on the money supply. See note 64, supra; Hepburn, 152-54; Nussbaum, 94-95.

123. Hammond (1), 65-66, 126, 128, 197; cf. Redlich, 1:96-97. In his communication to Congress, recommending a national bank, Hamilton observed that in creating such an institution Congress would in nowise prevent the states from creating as many banks as they pleased; the tone of his remarks showed that he regarded the existence of state-chartered banks as in a different realm of policy altogether from the aims he was pursuing, and he showed no concern (or, for that matter, perception) regarding the effects state-created banks might have on the money system. Cf. Hamilton, *Works*, 3:388, 445, 452, 461, 490. When he argued that Congress had constitutional power to set up a national bank, from its commerce-clause authority to care for the aggregate interests of trade in the country, the argument had the seed of action by the central government to establish central-bank-style control of the money system. But, there is no evidence that Hamilton foresaw this form of national policy. Cf., id., 481.

124. Cf. Henry Adams, 5:329, 8:249; Hamilton, *Works*, 3:388, 480; Redlich, 1:103, 104; Timberlake, 163, 164.

125. On the 6 percent limit: 1 Stat. 191 (1791), sec. 7 (X), 3 Stat. 266 (1816), sec. 11 (Ninth), Dunbar, 26, 88; cf. Catterall, 449; Redlich, 1:140; W. B. Smith, 56, 253, 254. For the ban on trading in government securities: 1 Stat. 191 (1791), sec. 7 (X), 3 Stat. 266, sec. 11 (Ninth), in Dunbar, 26, 88; cf. Catterall, 268, 271; W. B. Smith, 53, 254. For the limit on demand obligations: 1 Stat. 191 (1791), sec. 7 (IX), 3 Stat. 266 (1816), sec. 11 (Eighth), in Dunbar, 25, 87; cf. Hammond (1), 259.

126. Mints, 176; Redlich, 1:141; W. B. Smith, 253. Even Biddle seemed to regard changes in the bank's lending rate as relevant only to its competition for business with other banks. Redlich, 1:141.

127. The monopoly of national banking franchises was given by 1 Stat. 191 (1791), sec. 12, and 3 Stat. 266 (1816), sec. 21, in Dunbar, 29, 93. On the advantages of corporate status for firm, central direction, see Catterall, 274, 279-84; Govan, 230-32; Redlich, 1:59, 113-17; W. B. Smith, 248.

128. 1 Stat. 191 (1791), sec. 1; 3 Stat. 266 (1816), sec. 1, in Dunbar, 23, 80. Hamilton rejected using the existing Bank of North America as the national bank, because he deemed its capital too small (as it had been reduced since its founding). Rowe, 12. In an unpublished opinion rendered to President Jackson in June 1832, Attorney General Taney found the $35 million capitalization of the second bank excessive for its job as fiscal agent, at a time when it appeared that the federal government would sharply reduce its taxes and its spending; obviously, he feared the leverage which the bank's capital might give it on affairs in general. Cf. Swisher, 191, 192; Timberlake, 164, 166.

129. 1 Stat. 191 (1791), secs. 6, 7 (IX, X, XIII), 10; 3 Stat. 266 (1816), secs. 7, 11 (Eighth, Twelfth, Seventeenth), 14, 17; Dunbar, 23, 25, 26, 29, 83, 87, 88, 91, 92. Cf. Redlich, 1:99. Giving some indication of the kind of national bank he might approve, President Jackson in his second message to Congress, in 1830, specified that he would deny such an institution authority to issue circulating notes or to lend money. He did not then ignore the utility of some check on state bank notes, but indicated that he would effect that check through a national bank in its role simply as depository of federal funds. Richardson, 2:529; cf. Swisher, 173, 217, 218. In his

unpublished opinion to Jackson against the second bank, in June 1832, Attorney General Taney specifically criticized the bank's lending powers as unnecessary to its fiscal-agent functions and as constituting a significant addition to the feared general power of the institution. Swisher, 191, 192.

130. 1 Stat. 191 (1791), sec. 7 (IX); 3 Stat. 266 (1816), sec. 16; Dunbar, 25, 91. Cf. Hammond (1), 312; Redlich, 1:102, 103; W. B. Smith, 234, 244; Timberlake, 164, 166. Redlich, 1:98, 99, noting that the first bank did not hold a monopoly of collections for the United States, doubted the importance of its depository function as a basis for a central-bank role; Hammond (1), 198, nonetheless estimated that the first bank's receipt of state bank notes incident to receiving payments for the United States, did permit the bank to exert some pressure on state bank note issues.

131. 1 Stat. 191 (1791), sec. 7 (XV); 3 Stat. 266 (1816), sec. 11 (Fourteenth); Dunbar, 27, 89; McCulloch v. Maryland, 4 Wheaton 316, 424 (U.S. 1819). See, also, Baldwin, circuit justice, in United States v. Shellmire, 27 Federal Cases 1051, 1052, 1053 (No. 16,271) (E.D.Pa. 1831).

132. Cf. Bank of the United States v. Deveaux, 5 Cranch 61 (U.S. 1809); Warren (3), 1:391. After the second bank had made clearer demonstration of the reach and effect of a nationwide organization, the branching power became a substantial object of attack. See note 154, infra.

133. Hammond (1), 198, 199, 200, 208, 209; Redlich, 1:99, 106; Rowe, 16; Timberlake, 160.

134. On the Jones period: Hammond (1), 256, 259, 260; Redlich, 1:105, 106, 108, W. B. Smith, 105, 106-7, 113; Wilburn, 62, 63. These students of the bank's performance agree on the whole that the Jones administration built no strong precedents for the bank's leadership in money policy. They differ somewhat, in criticizing the bank's management for want of defined standards or strength of will, or in excusing it because the fledgling institution was caught up in a country-wide boom spirit. On the Cheves administration: Redlich, 1:108, 109; W. B. Smith, 119, 120, 121, 124, 129; Timberlake, 164.

135. Hammond (1), 259; W. B. Smith, 113; Wilburn, 62, 63.

136. W. B. Smith, 235, 236.

137. 3 Stat. 266 (1816), sec. 11 (Twelfth), continuing 1 Stat. 191 (1791), sec. 7 (XIII), in Dunbar, 27, 89, set the procedure for issuing the bank's own notes. Recognizing that the branch notes "form a very important item in the currency of the country and the operation of the branches," Baldwin, Circuit Justice, held them authorized as necessary and proper auxiliaries to the parent bank's power to issue its own notes and conduct a widespread organization. Observing that the charter contained no explicit prohibition of such branch paper, Baldwin was also prepared to give weight to the several years of administrative practice of the bank in sanctioning their issue. United States v. Shellmire, 27 Federal Cases 1051, 1052, 1053, 1054 (No. 16,271) (E.D.Pa. 1831). That the branch notes were an invention not contemplated by the charter, but were functionally justifiable for the operation of the bank as a nationwide organization, see Catterall, 123; W. B. Smith, 239, 240; cf. Swisher, 181. Smith, ibid., finds that critics erred in charging that the bank allowed the branch notes to be issued in excessive quantity.

138. Hammond (1), 255, 446, 447; Redlich, 1:104, 140; W. B. Smith, 110, 111; Timberlake, 163-68.

139. Catterall, 96, 97, points out that the bank's discipline over state bank notes was partly for the bank's own profit, since it needed this restraint in order to allow it safetly to increase the lending of its own notes. Biddle generally did not treat the

bank's lending rate as a device to regulate the money supply, but rather as a device to be handled to meet the competition of state banks. Cf. Redlich, 1:141.

140. Cf. Hammond (1), 295, 297, 324; W. B. Smith, 57, 70, 124, 253, 254; Timberlake, 163-68.

141. Catterall, 112, 114, 115, 117, 130; Govan, 86; Hammond (1), 297, 305, 378, 384; Redlich, 1:129, 130, 131; Timberlake, 164, 166; Wilburn, 63.

142. Catterall, 98, 100, 112, 130, 132, 139, 140; Mints, 205, 206; Redlich, 1:132, 133, 135; W. B. Smith, 124, 253, 254.

143. Govan, 86; Redlich, 1:132, 133, 179; W. B. Smith, 236, 238, 241; Wilburn, 45, 63, 64, 85, 118. Smith credits Biddle with improving the quantity and distribution of credit to the South, Southwest, and West. He finds that the evidence does not clearly establish that the bank's operations lowered interest rates generally, though he finds that the dominant position the bank won in domestic and foreign exchange in the face of competition from those who had previously pre-empted those fields indicates that it gave lower cost service. W. B. Smith, 236.

144. Hamilton, *Works,* 3:388, 425; cf. Rowe, 15.

145. The first bank opened branches partly on the advice of Oliver Wolcott, comptroller in the Treasury. Redlich, 1:99. Though some opposition had been voiced to branching authority—out of jealousy for states' rights, primarily—in early consideration of creating a second national bank, the 1816 charter more pointedly contemplated the creation of branches than had the act of 1791. 1 Stat. 191 (1791), sec. 7 (XV); 3 Stat. 266 (1816), sec. 11 (Fourteenth); cf. Catterall, 10; Redlich, 1:105, 106.

146. Hammond (1), 256, 260; Redlich, 1:106; W. B. Smith, 105, 106-7, 120; Wilburn, 62.

147. Cf. Catterall, 53, 54, 63, 64, 70, 73; Hammond (1), 259; W. B. Smith, 113; Wilburn, 62, 63.

148. Biddle, too, had his failures in disciplining the branches. Catterall, 152-63. However, compared with his predecessors, he achieved notable success at the endeavor. Catterall, 101, 102, 103, 152-63, 274, 279-84, 377-78; Govan, 230, 232; Redlich, 1:59, 113-17, 118, 119-21; W. B. Smith, 248.

149. Catterall, 141, 376, 422-23, 436; Hammond (1), 295, 297, 305; W. B. Smith, 57, 70, 124, 253, 254; Timberlake, 164.

150. Cf. Barger, 23; Catterall, 433; Redlich, 1:138, 140, 142.

151. Henry Adams, 8:246; Hammond (1), 212.

152. Richardson, 2:576, 578, 583, 589; Redlich, 1:169, 180. Cf. Gouge, 17.

153. Henry Adams, 5:335; Hammond (1), 216, 217, 219. But cf. Redlich, 1:100.

154. On the impact of the tight policy of 1818-20: Catterall, 53, 58, 60, 61, 63, 77, 81, 84; Hammond (1), 259, 268; W. B. Smith, 240, 241; Warren (3), 1:646-48. On state taxes as reflecting reaction to the 1818-20 policy of the bank: Beveridge, 4:206-8; Warren (3), 1:505-6. Wilburn, 46, 48, 51, 54-55, 63-65, presents evidence of gratitude in the South and West for the bank's aid in those areas' development and in evening out the flow of capital and exchange rates between the older and the newer parts of the country.

155. W. B. Smith, 240, 241; cf. Hammond (1), 287, 443.

156. Beveridge, 4:173, 174; Catterall, 95-97, 112, 131, 132, 140, 166, 451; Hammond (1), 212, 216, 217, 242, 279, 284, 287, 322, 380, 390, 391; Mayo (1), 375-77; Wilburn, 45, 63, 64, 85, 118. A shrewd, detached observer, Johnson, J., dissenting in Osborn v. Bank of the United States, 9 Wheaton 738, 873 (U.S. 1824), found that contemporary antagonism to the second bank sprang alike from objec-

tions to "a restraint upon individual cupidity, and the exercise of a state power." That the pressure of competition for business spurred state banks' opposition, more than concern for states' rights, may be inferred from the fact that there was a rapid decrease in antibank agitation when business improved in the early 1820s, so that by the time the Osborn decision came down, it roused no great interest. Warren (3), 1:536. Commenting to Story on Jackson's veto, in 1832, Marshall thought that the impetus to the gathering storm over the bank came largely from the competitive ambitions of eastern financial interests: "[New York] . . . has sagacity enough to see her interest in putting down the present bank. Her mercantile position gives her a control, a commanding control, over the currency and the exchanges of the country, if there be no Bank of the United States." Beveridge, 4:533.

157. Concern about the extent of power concentrated in the first bank may be seen in Jefferson's characterization of it as an institution "of the most deadly hostility existing against the principles and form of our Constitution. . . . An institution like this, penetrating by its branches every part of the Union, acting by command and in phalanx, may, in a critical moment, upset the government." Jefferson, *Works,* 10:57 (letter to Albert Gallatin, 13 December 1803); cf. Beveridge, 4:172, 173 (like fear expressed in 1809). Even Hamilton was not without some such concern, witnessed in the charter provisions he included limiting the size of individual stock subscriptions (other than by the United States), holding any individual stockholder to a maximum of thirty votes, and stipulating for a moderate par value and wide subscription opportunities, as well as limiting directors' tenure and setting ceilings on capitalization, on assets held, and on loans to governments. 1 Stat. 191 (1791), secs. 1, 2, 7 (I, II, VIII, IX, X, XI), 8, 9. Cf. Rowe, 12-14, 17, 18. The scale of the "monopoly" power, practical as well as legal, in the second bank was a common target of attack. Beveridge, 4:336; C. W. Smith, 67-78; Warren (3), 1:521, 523. Fear of the extent of concentrated power in the bank's "monopoly" position had specially potent expression in Jackson's veto of a new charter. Richardson, 2:576, 577 (inadequate return via the proposed bonus, for privileges given), 584 (generalized warning against monopoly), 585 (excessive capitalization), 590 (such an institution is calculated to be the agent of the rich and powerful). Taney put his influence behind like warnings (1831, 1832), preceding the veto. Swisher, 176, 191, 192 (a fifteen-year monopoly unnecessary and dangerous in view of experience of the evils of moneyed monopolies). Taney returned with conviction to this theme in retrospect (1849). Id., 166-71. In considering the various expressions of fear over the power concentrated in the banks, it is useful to recall Henry Adams's observation on the first bank, that "in a society and government so little developed as those of America, a National Bank was out of keeping with other institutions." Henry Adams, 5:329.

158. This pro-market flavor appeared in Clay's attack on renewing the first bank's charter in 1811, when he argued that "it is a mockery, worse than usurpation, to establish [this Bank] . . . for the ostensible purpose of aiding in the collection of the revenue, and, whilst engaged in this, the most inferior and subordinate of all its functions, [to allow it] . . . to diffuse itself throughout society, and to influence all the great operations of credit, circulation, and commerce." Mayo (1), 376. Cf. Beveridge, 4:288, 289; Catterall, 167, 175, 184, 205; Warren (3), 1:509, 521, 523.

159. W. B. Smith, 234, 236, 244. True, it enjoyed legal monopolies; it was assured the only federal banking franchise, and its notes had limited legal-tender status, since they were receivable in settlement of debts owed to the United States. But, at least, it offset these legal privileges by public services rendered.

160. Beard and Beard, 1:347, 353; Bowers, 75, 78, 87-90; Malone, 339-40. Cf. 1 Stat. 191 (1791), secs. 2, 7 (IX), 11.

161. Swisher, 191, 192, 196, 197.

162. Redlich, 1:169, 180; Swisher, 217, 218. Confirmation of the position to which men of the Jacksonian persuasion came on this point of avoiding conflict of interest in an agency handling the public funds may be seen in the creation of the independent Treasury system, following the end of the second bank. 5 Stat. 385 (1840), 9 Stat. 59 (1846), in Dunbar, 125, 138.

163. 1 Stat. 191 (1791), secs. 2, 7 (I, III); 3 Stat. 266 (1816), secs. 3, 11 (First, Third); Dunbar, 23, 24, 81, 86. The limiting terms of the 1791 charter reflected Hamilton's concern over allowing power to foreign stockholders; he rejected the idea of using the Bank of North America as the national bank in part because its charter allowed foreigners to vote by proxy and to be directors. Rowe, 12-14. Objection to English stockholders figured in the nonrenewal of the first bank's charter in 1811. Henry Adams, 5:328, 329. However, in the 1811 debate some Congressmen from newer states favored foreign investment in the bank, because it encouraged entry of needed capital. Hammond (1), 219. Senator Benton put demagogic stress on the foreign stockholders as profiting from the second bank, ignoring the facts that they lacked a practical voting share in the institution's affairs and that they contributed capital to it. W. B. Smith, 248. With no more ground than Benton's arguments provided, Jackson's veto continued this kind of criticism. Richardson, 2:576, 577, 579-80. On the eve of the renewal battle only 466 of 4,145 stockholders were foreigners. Catterall, 168, 181, 201.

164. Taney conveyed the tone of this fear of the bank as an engine of patronage in his retrospective manuscript on the "Bank War," in 1849. Swisher, 166, 169.

165. On the first bank: Henry Adams, 5:328, 329; Beveridge, 4:172, 173; Warren (3), 1:504. On the second bank, at its inception: Beveridge, 4:180. On this score note the implications of a proposed amendment to the Constitution, offered in 1793, to exclude from Congress officers or stockholders of the bank; the proposal was amended to limit it to bank officers, and was then rejoiced, twelve to thirteen. Ames, 30.

166. Compare Taney's complaint on this score, in 1832, Swisher, 191, 192, with the counter appraisal of Catterall, 101-3, 176-78, 377-78. Late in 1829 Biddle sought to conciliate Jackson by naming to some branch positions men friendly to the administration, but these appointments were of a quality consistent with good operations. Catterall, 182, 189.

167. Hammond (1), 424, 425; W. B. Smith, 249.

168. Hammond (1), 378, 410, 426; W. B. Smith, 250. Some of Biddle's efforts of this kind were probably tactically unwise, but to say so is a long way from finding them true grounds for the opposition's attacks.

169. W. B. Smith, 250; cf. Swisher, 172-73, 183-84.

170. Redlich, 1:138, 141; W. B. Smith, 167, 252.

171. Catterall, 274, 279-84; Govan, 230-32; Redlich, 1:59, 113-17, 121; W. B. Smith, 248.

172. Swisher, 169, 170, quoting Taney's 1849 manuscript on the "Bank War."

173. Hammond (1), 438; Hepburn, 115, 116; W. B. Smith, 160.

174. Hepburn, 151, 152.

175. 5 Stat. 385 (1840), secs. 6, 19; 9 Stat. 59 (1846), secs. 6, 18, 19; Dunbar, 127, 128, 140, 141, 142; Inland Waterways Corporation v. Young, 309 U.S. 517, 520-24 (1940). The 1840 act—which was repealed by 5 Stat. 439 (1842)—provided for a transition to required specie payments of dues owing to the United States, one-quarter at a time annually. On the use of Treasury notes mostly in aid of borrowing,

up to 1846, see notes 8, 9, supra. Cf. Part One, supra, notes 199, 200. The Specie Circular of 1836 had provided a forecast of the Jacksonians' want of perception that, if the United States were going to manage its own finances in ways bound to have substantial monetary effects, it should be prepared to take on some close management of the resulting monetary impact. The Specie Circular was not issued primarily as a regulation of money supply; its abrupt action was designed to curb unwise speculation in the public lands; the relevance of the episode to the law's treatment of the system of money lies in what it implies as to current policy makers' willingness to take *ad hoc* action on public finance in part for monetary effect, but without assigning major weight to money-system values. Cf. Part One, supra, note 198.

176. Prelude, supra, notes 13-16, 30-34, 39-48.

177. Notes 97-107, supra.

178. Hurst (2), 189, 190, 397, and (6), 115-21.

179. Hurst (6), 15, 17, 37, 39.

180. Notes 109, 113, supra.

181. Part One, supra, notes 7, 10, 17, 135-37; notes 2, 4, 5, 8-12, 18-55, supra.

182. Notes 90-92, 97-102, 111-16, supra.

183. White (1), 117, 126, 223, (2), 134-37, (3), 163-65. Cf. Morison and Commager, 1:332-34; Walters, 260.

184. Hurst (2), 402-4.

185. Id., 382-84.

186. Notes 41-55, 62, 70-73, supra. One should recall, also, that the Supreme Court gave an extensive interpretation to Congress's constitutional power to act against counterfeiting. Note 5, supra.

187. On courts' recognition of business custom in determining what was *money* under contracts: Part One, supra, notes 41, 42. On court decisions relaxing redemption requirements: Part One, supra, notes 84, 85, 87, 88; notes 117, 118, supra.

188. Part One, supra, note 24, and note 87, supra.

189. Hurst (2), 180, 181, 185.

190. Prelude, supra, notes 15, 19, 22; notes 17, 19, 20, 36-41, supra. So clear was the Constitution's prohibition on the states to coin money that no issue was ever raised on this head. Prelude, supra, notes 13, 20, 21. It is significant of the line drawn in the text, between issues of federalism and issues of legal compared with market processes, that the only area of ambiguous policy concerning the coinage arose out of Congress's silent tolerance for some years of private manufacture of coin. Part One, supra, notes 126, 127, 132.

191. Prelude, supra, notes 16, 19, 22, 29. In Briscoe v. Bank of the Commonwealth of Kentucky, 11 Peters 257, 316 (U.S. 1837), the Court said, *obiter,* that it would be unconstitutional for a state to confer legal-tender status on notes of a state-chartered bank. See, accord, Miller, J., dissenting, in Hepburn v. Griswold, 8 Wallace 603, 627 (U.S. 1870). The Court showed its want of sympathy for state stay laws when used to enhance the acceptability of circulating paper of a state-owned bank, in Wayman v. Southard, 10 Wheaton 1 (U.S. 1825); notes 14, 31, supra. Lane County v. Oregon, 7 Wallace 71 (U.S. 1869), provided one narrow exception, in which concern for the federal balance figured in a decision concerning Congress's definition of legal-tender status for greenbacks. There, interpreting the federal statutes as not intended to require a state to accept United States notes rather than specie in payment of taxes due the state, the Court intimated that a contrary result might raise a substantial question whether the federal legislation infringed the constitutionally reserved tax powers of the states. Nussbaum, 123, finds the ruling ques-

tionable, and it does seem that the tax power—working as it must, practically, through the system of money—should be deemed inherently subject to federal control of money.

192. Prelude, supra, notes 13, 14, 20, 22, 40-46; Part One, supra, notes 7-11. See, generally on the matter involved at notes 190-92, Knox v. Lee, 12 Wallace 457, 545 (U.S. 1871).

193. Loans or equivalent financial accommodations by previous institutions of a central-bank character formed no precedent against which the 1846 act could fairly be construed. The special legal status of the Bank of North America, and of the two Banks of the United States, expressed an intended character as public fiscal agents alien to the character of the commercial banks from which the United States was borrowing in 1861. Cf. Prelude, supra, notes 4, 5; notes 65, 69, supra. Moreover, the Bank of North America was a lender to the central government for only a time. Prelude, supra, notes 5, 9, 10. Substantial parts of the original capital of the two Banks of the United States consisted of government securities received in payment for the banks' stock, but these were transfers of outstanding securities and not the creation by the banks of loans to the government. The two banks lent substantial sums to the government, but the second bank's loans were typically for limited terms and often were designed to adjust the government's finances—especially the retirement of government debt—to the general current state of the general economy. Cf. Hepburn, 83; W. B. Smith, 66-69, 244-45. Borrowing for expenses of the Mexican War was by notes or long-term bonds of the Treasury, involving fresh issues of $33 million, which the public bid in for more than twice the amount and at or above par. 9 Stat. 39 (1846), 118 (1847), in Dunbar, 137, 142; Myers, 136; Redlich, 2:95.

9 Stat. 59 (1846), sec. 18, required that "all duties, taxes, sales of public lands, debts, and sums of money accruing or becoming due to the United States . . . shall be paid in gold and silver coin only, or in treasury notes issued under the authority of the United States." Section 19 required that "every officer or agent engaged in making disbursements on account of the United States . . . shall make all payments in gold and silver coin, or in treasury notes, if the creditor agree to receive said notes in payment." Though a principled pragmatism might have allowed reading this language as not intended to apply to realizing on bank credits created by loans made to the United States, a stubborn fact of the situation was that a dogmatically fervent hard-money faith had supplied the political impetus to enacting the 1846 statute. Hepburn, 155; Krooss (1), 516; Trescott, 28, 43. The continuing vitality of this political pressure showed itself in the willingness of Congress to accept the fuzzy terms of the 1861 amendment, instead of insisting on a clear repudiation of the specie-only command insofar as might be necessary to float the extraordinary war loans of that time. 12 Stat. 313 (1861) "suspended" the 1846 act "so far as to allow the Secretary of the Treasury to deposit any of the moneys obtained on any of the loans now authorized by law, to the credit of the Treasurer of the United States, in such solvent, specie-paying banks as he may select; and the said moneys, so deposited, may be withdrawn from such deposit for deposit with the regular authorized depositories, or for the payment of public dues . . . as may seem expedient to, or be directed by, the Secretary of the Treasury." Dunbar, 162, 163; Hammond (3), 60-66, 68, 79, 80, 94, 98. A secretary with more practical sense in money management might have read the 1861 amendment to authorize him to decide that it was "expedient" in the interest of the United States to write checks against its bank loans so that the money might be "withdrawn . . . for the payment of public dues." Cf. Barrett, 6, 7, 8-9, 13, 50. On Chase's public and private rationalizations of his insistence on gold, see

Hammond (3), 80-82. Hammond, id., 90-92, believes that behind the scenes Chase manipulated the framing of the 1861 amendment to give an appearance of substantial change without the reality, in order to keep the door open to his long-term policy of supplanting state bank notes with some kind of currency provided by or under authority of the central government. The case for this analysis rests mainly on plausible inference from the tenacity of Chase's favor for a national currency; Hammond cites no direct, contemporary evidence for his thesis. Compare, however, id., 99-100.

194. 12 Stat. 259 (1861); Hammond (3), 46-47; Hepburn, 180-81. Cf. Knox v. Lee, 12 Wallace 457, 540 (U.S. 1871).

195. Hammond (3), 81, 82. Cf. Trescott, 18, 145.

196. Cagan, 15, 16; Hammond (3), 150-59; Nussbaum, 100. See Veazie Bank v. Fenno, 8 Wallace 533, 537 (U.S. 1869).

197. This first issue of Treasury notes was incorporated in the $250 million authorization act which provided the base for the government's approach to the private banks. 12 Stat. 259 (1861), secs. 1, 2, 6, in Dunbar, 161; Hammond (3), 47, 87, 88-89, 140; Hepburn, 181; Knox (1), 75, 78, 84; Myers, 150.

198. 12 Stat. 345 (1862), 532 (1862), 709 (1863), in Dunbar, 163, 167, 174; Part One, supra, notes 54, 139, 225.

199. Knox v. Lee, 12 Wallace 457, 529, 533, 540-42 (U.S. 1871). Cf. Bank v. Supervisors, 7 id. 26 (U.S. 1868) (greenbacks are "securities" of United States within protection against state taxes given by the 1862 act to "all United States bonds and other securities.")

200. Part One, supra, note 191. No serious question was raised but that, following McCulloch and Osborn, Congress had authority to charter national banks, as instruments of national policy. See Farmers' & Mechanics' National Bank v. Dearing, 91 U.S. 29, 33 (1875); note 236, infra. A secondary argument for the national banks was to make it possible for lenders to pay for the United States bonds in a more reliable currency, which would not—like the legal-tender notes—foster inflation by providing reserves on which state banks could increase their own issues. Cagan, 16; Hammond (3), 315.

201. Of course the pursuit of national government fiscal policy entailed the consequence of barring state action which discriminated against such a federal program. But the problem dealt with by McCulloch v. Maryland, 4 Wheaton 316 (U.S. 1819) was different from the question, whether Congress might take pre-emptive measures against state policy in the interests of national money-system goals. That the federal government's fiscal needs might be served through the state banks was indicated by the first proposals, in late 1861, for creating a national currency by permitting or requiring state banks to base their note issues on United States securities and to receive notes from a federal government agency. Hammond (3), 140-42, 293; Redlich, 2:102. Indeed, the first national bank act, in 1863, authorized issue of national currency by state banks, though the comptroller of the currency refused to comply with this provision and recommended its repeal, which the 1864 act silently accomplished. Redlich, 2:102. See 12 Stat. 665 (1863), sec. 62; 13 Stat. 99 (1864), secs. 21, 22, 62; Dunbar, 172, 181, 190; Knox (2), 233. It should also be noted that there was no necessary exclusion of continued state action in chartering state banks to contribute to the money supply, in decisions recognizing that Congress might pre-empt the field of policy concerning nationally chartered banks to the extent of barring their subjection to nondiscriminatory state laws not directly dealing with money supply; being empowered to create national banks as agents of national fiscal, monetary, and commercial policy, Congress was entitled itself to provide a complete pattern of law

for the governance of its agents, both to assure them necessary means of functioning and to provide desirable uniformity in the law applicable to them. Farmers' & Mechanics' National Bank v. Dearing, 91 U.S. 29, 33, 35 (uniformity), 34 (functional capacity) (1875); Davis v. Elmira Savings Bank, 161 U.S. 275, 284 (functional needs) (1896); Easton v. Iowa, 188 U.S. 220, 229, 232 (uniformity), 230, 238 (functional needs) (1903). Dunne (2), 51, treats such decisions—dealing with usury, distributions on insolvency, and fraud—as extending federal authority into areas "historically . . . considered the exclusive preserve of state police powers." But, on the Court's stated grounds, these rulings seem only to apply familiar doctrine allowing Congress to supersede state law in areas of policy ultimately open to federal control. Thus, Dearing significantly relied on Gilman v. Philadelphia, 3 Wallace 713 (U.S. 1866); see 91 U.S. 29, 33. And Davis (161 U.S. 275, 290), and Easton (188 U.S. 220, 239) take pains to observe that general, nondiscriminatory state law may govern matters involving national banks, so long as there is no conflict with federal law. Cf. Cooley v. Board of Wardens of the Port of Philadelphia, 12 Howard 299 (U.S. 1851).

202. Hammond (3), 212, 217-18, 220, 232, 233, 245, 246, 248.

203. Bogart, 488, 683; Hammond (3), 285, 286, 288, 290, 321, 337-39.

204. Hammond (3), 142, 146, 201, 202, 205, 206, 219, 220.

205. Bogart, 627; Cagan, 16, 17; Faulkner, 488, 683; Hammond (3), 326, 328, 332, 333-34. Cf. Chase, C.J., in Veazie Bank v. Fenno, 8 Wallace 533, 548, 549 (U.S. 1869); Tiffany v. National Bank of Missouri, 18 id. 409, 413 (U.S. 1874); Mercantile Bank v. New York, 121 U.S. 138, 154 (1887). The idea that the national government might properly, and should, act to control the whole money supply for its greater reliability and uniformity was not invented in 1861-64. The concept traced back through various suggestions to the first half of the nineteenth century. Redlich, 2:99, 100, 101, 103. Redlich, id., 102, observes that the emphasis on providing a national medium of exchange appeared in the designations of the 1863 and 1864 statutes, each of which was entitled, not a national bank act, but "an Act to provide a National Currency." 12 Stat. 665 (1863), 13 Stat. 99 (1864), in Dunbar, 171, 178. Two aspects of the 1863-64 acts pointed especially to the over-all goal of providing a workable national currency: the deposited-bonds security, and the requirement that all national bank notes be acceptable by member banks of the system at par. 13 Stat. 99 (1864), secs. 21, 32. Cf. Redlich, id., 103.

206. 13 Stat. 469 (1865), in Dunbar, 198; Bogart, 683; Cagan, 16, 18, 19; Faulkner, 627; Knox (2), 99; Hammond (3), 292, 315, 346, 347; Redlich, 2:113. The idea of a prohibitive tax on bank notes had antecedents reaching back to 1830 and the 1850s and was mentioned in consideration of the 1863 national bank act, Redlich, 2:113.

207. Friedman and Schwartz, 18, 19; Horvitz, 306; Knox (2), 99, 270. See Lionberger v. Rouse, 9 Wallace 468, 475 (U.S. 1870), reflecting the disappearance of state bank notes. Congress asserted authority to apportion the authorized total circulation of national bank notes by formulae related to population and the organization of credit in the states and territories. These formulae worked in fact to restrict the amount of national bank notes authorized in the less developed parts of the country. In this aspect the national bank acts, together with the 1865 prohibitive tax on state bank notes, might be deemed to assert central authority to discriminate among regional economies and hence to raise a distinct issue of federalism. However, the functional reality of this situation seems to derive from failure to see the proper relations of law and the market, rather than from conflicts of interest within federalism, and hence it is discussed later in a market context. See note 241, infra. See, generally, Redlich, 2:119, 120.

208. Veazie Bank v. Fenno, 8 Wallace 533, 548 (U.S. 1869). Compare the characterization of the 1865 tax in Tiffany v. National Bank of Missouri, 18 Wallace 409, 413 (U.S. 1874), where the Court observed that "a duty has been imposed upon [the state banks'] . . . issues so large as to manifest a purpose to compel a withdrawal of all such issues from circulation." In Veazie Bank v. Fenno the Court also ruled on a point relevant to Congress's authority over fiscal rather than monetary policy, in holding that the 1865 tax was not such a levy as fell under the Constitution's formula for apportioning "direct" taxes. On the point of monetary policy, the Court explicitly validated Congress's authority to provide for the issue of national currency either directly or by delegation to nationally chartered banks, apart from any question of driving out the circulating paper of state-chartered banks. "These powers, until recently, were only partially and occasionally exercised. Lately, however, they have been called into full activity, and Congress has undertaken to supply a currency for the entire country." Veazie Bank v. Fenno, 8 Wallace 533, 548 (U.S. 1869). Some contemporary opinion read Veazie Bank v. Fenno as forecasting that the Court would uphold Congress's power to confer legal-tender status on the Treasury notes it authorized. But, this reading confused issues; creation of legal tender involved tension between governmental and market decision-making capacity, while Veazie Bank v. Fenno focused on issues of the federal balance of power. Cf. Warren (3), 2:509. James M. Beck seemed to accept as valid Congress's use of its prohibitive tax to implement federal authority to provide a national currency. Beck, 441, 442. But, he also seemed to confuse the issue of federalism and public-private power affecting control of money, when he criticized the 1869 decision for allowing Congress, under guise of a revenue measure, to destroy a reserved power of the states to charter banks of circulation. This is the issue apparently drawn, and as much confused, in the dissent by Nelson, J. (Davis, J., concurring), Veazie Bank v. Fenno, 8 Wallace 533, 555. To put the matter thus, begged the question and ignored rather than disproved the basis of the Court's decision. The Constitution contemplated federal supremacy in setting a national money-supply policy. In this light such authority as was reserved to the states existed only so long as Congress did not pre-empt the field. The Briscoe dictum was that the naked force of the Constitution's ban on state bills of credit did not bar the states from chartering private, note-issuing banks. That proposition was consistent with Congress's authority to decide what kind of paper money should circulate. Moreover, the protection which the McCulloch and Osborn decisions gave to the second Bank of the United States against discriminatory state action indicated that, if Congress adopted a monetary policy, it was empowered to make its policy a nationally effective policy opposed to state law.

209. Friedman and Schwartz, 19; Hammond (3), 347. The contemporary understanding, that the 1865 tax on state bank notes would probably operate to drive state banks out of existence altogether, is reflected in Tiffany v. National Bank of Missouri, 18 Wallace 409, 413 (U.S. 1874). The Court there said that the general policy indicated by the national bank legislation should lead to interpretation of that legislation favorable to the powers of the national banks; hence it read the federal statute as allowing a national bank to charge interest which might be either the maximum interest allowed by state law to state banks, or the maximum interest allowed by state law to individual lenders, whichever were the higher. This reading, the Court thought, "accords with the spirit of all the legislation of Congress. National banks have been national favorites. They were established for the purpose, in part, of providing a currency for the whole country, and in part to create a market for the loans of the general government. It could not have been intended, therefore, to expose

them to the hazard of unfriendly legislation by the states or to ruinous competition with state banks. On the contrary, much has been done to insure their taking the place of state banks. The latter have been substantially taxed out of existence. A duty has been imposed upon their issues so large as to manifest a purpose to compel a withdrawal of all such issues from circulation." For contemporary state court opinions reflecting the substantial identification of note issues with banking, see Bolles, 1:3, note 6.

210. Veazie Bank v. Fenno, 8 Wallace 533, 548 (U.S. 1869), spoke simply of Congress's power to create a national *currency*; the term was not then or later an apt one to refer to deposit-check money. Lionberger v. Rouse, 9 id., 468, 474 (U.S. 1870) interpreted 13 Stat. 99 (1864), sec. 41, declaring that any state tax on shares in national banks should not exceed the tax on shares of state-chartered banks, as intended to apply only to state banks of issue. The Court felt that this interpretation accorded with the goal of the national bank act, which was to provide a national currency: "There was nothing to fear from banks of discount and deposit merely, for in no event could they work any displacement of National bank circulation." The observation showed how far the Court then was from regarding bank lending as a major source of the money supply. So, too, the matter quoted in note 209, supra, from Tiffany v. National Bank of Missouri, 18 id., 409, 413 (U.S. 1874), indicates that the Court viewed state bank lending as operations dependent on state banks' note issues, rather than as a distinct source for creating money and earning profit. Though the Court's remarks in Tiffany seem to accept the idea that Congress's control of the money supply might be pressed to a point destructive of state banks, its observations do not appear to contemplate that the federal government might regulate bank lending on the ground that such lending was itself a source of money.

In Veazie Bank v. Fenno the Court also responded to the contention that the challenged tax was "so excessive as to indicate a purpose on the part of Congress to destroy the franchise of the Bank, and is, therefore, beyond the constitutional power of Congress." The Court's answer was badly expressed. It seemed to say, in effect, that since the statute on its face was a taxing measure, the Court lacked power to invalidate the act on the ground that Congress was in fact seeking another objective than the raising of revenue. 8 Wallace 533, 548 (U.S. 1869). If this other objective were recognized as itself a valid head of congressional power—as would be the purpose to regulate the whole national money supply—obviously there would be no problem. Cf. Ely, 1302. That the Court in 1869 did not see this point is itself telling evidence that the Court did not recognize that regulation of lending by state banks might be essential to exercising national supremacy over the system of money as regulating state bank notes. In fact, the argument to which the Court was here responding seems to have been that the 1865 tax should be deemed beyond Congress's power because its effect would be to destroy private property rights, namely the profit-making possibilities existing under state bank charters. Cf. argument of counsel, 19 Lawyers Edition 483. Congress has no independent authority to decide what profit-making franchises a state may create. But Congress may regulate state franchises as a necessary and proper incident of fulfilling authority of the federal government. Cf. Farmers' & Mechanics' National Bank v. Dearing, 91 U.S. 29, 34 (1875). Again, the Court's failure to carry the analysis through to this point indicates that it did not think of the activities of state banks—notably their lending—apart from their note issues as falling within the regulation of the money supply. In this respect, the analysis in Veazie Bank v. Fenno seems like the narrow approach which Marshall, C.J., took in Osborn v. Bank of the United States, 9 Wheaton 739, 861-62 (U.S.

1824), when he protected the bank's lending operations against state attack, not because these operations were an instrument of national monetary policy, but because they furnished means out of which the bank could sustain itself to exist as the government's fiscal agent.

211. Apart from the absence in the original national bank acts of any direct attempt to limit the monetary roles of state banks, the federal statutes reflected their acceptance of a competitive relation between the two systems especially in the care taken to define the lending authority of national banks in terms calculated to put them at least on a parity with state banks in regard to lawful rates of interest, and in stipulations that state taxes on national banks or on their shares should not discriminate in favor of state institutions and that state banks might elect to take national charters in place of their state charters without requirement of state approval. 13 Stat. 99 (1864), secs. 30, 41, 44, in Dunbar, 183, 187, 188. See Tiffany v. National Bank of Missouri, 18 Wallace 409, 413 (U.S. 1874) (competitive capacity in interest rates); Lionberger v. Rouse, 9 id., 468, 474 (U.S. 1870), and Mercantile Bank v. New York, 121 U.S. 138, 155, 157 (1887) (state taxes may not put national banks at competitive disadvantage); Casey v. Galli, 94 U.S. 673, 678 (1877) (federal authorization alone suffices for state bank to take national charter); Rankin v. Barton, 199 U.S. 228, 232 (1905) (receiver suing on statutory liability of stockholder of national bank found insolvent by comptroller is not bound by state statute of limitations). Compare the clash of attitudes on the late-twentieth-century relevance of federal statutory protection of national banks as "national instrumentalities" against state taxes, in First Agricultural National Bank v. State Tax Commission, 392 U.S. 339, 344-46 (Black, J., for majority), 355-56 (T. Marshall, J., for three dissenters) (1968). Continued recognition of the basic federal policy as one accepting competitive coexistence of national and state banks is reflected in Des Moines National Bank v. Fairweather, 263 U.S. 103, 116 (1923); First National Bank of Guthrie Center v. Anderson, 269 U.S. 341, 347, 348 (1926); First National Bank of Hartford v. City of Hartford, 273 U.S. 548, 556, 558 (1927). Congress's endowment of national banks with capacity to do trust business to match that allowed to state institutions was a particularly pointed twentieth-century reaffirmation of the competitive policy. See First National Bank of Bay City v. Fellows, ex rel. Union Trust Co., 244 U.S. 416 (1917). Cf. Raymond P. Kent, 43, 49-51, 57.

212. Prelude, supra, notes 49-52, 55-57.

213. Notes 8, 9, supra.

214. Hammond (3), 176, 178, 179, 187, 189, 191, 192, 195, 215, 216, 218, 220. Treasury notes authorized by several early acts, 12 Stat. 178, 259, 313, 338 (1861, 1862), were such hasty responses to what was viewed as a short-term emergency, that they do not add much to legislative precedent preceding the legal-tender acts. See Dunbar, 158, 160-63; Barrett, 5; Hepburn, 181-82; Knox (1), 82-84. For concession by leading opponents, in 1862, that Congress had authority to issue circulating paper that was not made legal tender, see Hammond (3), 189, 215, 221. Cf. Knox (1), 122. Some opposition was voiced, that there was no need in fact to issue any kind of circulating paper in aid of financing the war, but so far as this plea was made, its presence serves mainly to underline the contrary judgment reached by the congressional majorities. Cf., Hammond (3), 188. For the prime focus on the legal-tender question, see, id., 181-82, 184, 185, 186, 189, 190, 191, 193, 194, 212, 214, 216-17, 219, 222; Myers, 153-55. Though his opinion deserves the respect owing to a careful scholar, if Hammond, id., 226, means to condemn as unconstitutional the issue of any circulating paper by the federal government, even in a borrowing emergency, he

seems to run counter to the dominant note in the federal convention discussion. Prelude, supra, notes 49-52.

215. The Court's words in Veazie Bank v. Fenno, 8 Wallace 533, 548 (U.S. 1869) seem properly rated as a holding, since they were spoken to establish the action of Congress to which it was held it might attach its ban on state bank notes as a necessary and proper auxiliary. See, further, Hepburn v. Griswold, id., 603, 616 (U.S. 1870); Knox v. Lee, 12 id., 457, 541, 542, and Field, J., dissenting, id., 635-37 (U.S. 1871). Cf. Dunne (2), 67; Fairman (1), 159, and (2), 713, 760.

216. 20 Stat. 87 (1878), in Dunbar, 217; Nugent, 249; Unger, 364-73, especially 372. Back of the 1878 act was a fluctuating controversy over continuation, expansion, or retirement of the greenbacks, stretching from 1866 up. Friedman and Schwartz, 24, 47-49.

217. Juilliard v. Greenman, 110 U.S. 421, 443-44 (constitutional convention), 444 (incidents of power to borrow), 446 (power to provide a national currency), 448 (commerce power), 450 (in war or in peace, for needs of government or of the people) (1884). Cf. Hepburn v. Griswold, 8 Wallace 603, 619 (U.S. 1870). See Dunne (2), 81, 82. Field, J., dissenting, focused wholly on the question of Congress's power to confer legal-tender status on its paper. In this connection, however, he found the 1884 decision simply to bear out his forebodings concerning the decision of 1871; though in 1871 stress had been on the peculiar war emergency under which the Treasury notes were issued, he felt that it was always implicit that if Congress had any authority at all of this character, Congress must enjoy discretion to use the authority in peace or in war, and according to its appraisal of the public need. Field thus pointed up the significant breadth of the 1878 statute and the Court's validation of it, but professed to find nothing here that was not already embodied in the earlier actions of Congress and the Court. Juilliard v. Greenman, 110 U.S. 421, 457 (1884). However, he conceded that his analysis, though sound in logic, was not true to the historic fact, which was that the earlier actions were taken with attention engrossed by the war emergency. Id., 458. Cf. Field, J., dissenting in Knox v. Lee, 12 Wallace 457, 649 (U.S. 1871). The breadth of Congress's power, "whether . . . exercised in course of war or in time of peace," as established by the 1871 and 1884 decisions together, is recognized for the Court by Hughes, C.J., in Norman v. Baltimore & Ohio Railroad Co., 294 U.S. 240, 302-3 (1935). See, also, Dawson, 666, 670. Ames, 266-67, notes that the Court's invocation of the commerce clause to bulwark congressional power over money evoked no adverse response by way of proposals for restrictive amendment of the Constitution.

218. From a somewhat different standpoint than that taken in the text, John C. Ropes in an unsigned (and, by Mark Howe's judgment, "devastating") criticism of Hepburn, in 4 *American Law Review* 604, 612 (1870), likewise assessed as an issue of broader meaning than the legal-tender question the ruling that Congress had authority directly to authorize a national currency. Ropes's point, however, was that there was "fair matter for argument . . . whether, under a reasonably strict interpretation of the Constitution, Congress is not prohibited, by fair implication, from issuing a note currency." In this view, the majority of the Court "left their strongest ground" when they conceded Congress's authority to do so, because the matter went to basic authority, while if the basic power be granted, then "the giving a legal tender character to that currency is merely a question for the discretion of Congress." Howe, 2:50, identifies this commentary as by Ropes. Cf. Barrett, 81; Fairman (3), 713, 760. That the focus in 1862 was on the legal-tender issue, see note 214, supra.

219. On the federal convention: Prelude, supra, notes 53, 54; Part One, supra,

notes 176, 230; Dunne (2), 11-14; cf. Hacker, 156-59. On the mingled fears of inflation and desires for expansion fostered by legal-tender issues in 1862: Hammond (3),
171, 177, 181-83, 188-89, 191, 195, 220, 222-23, 224, 227, 231, 234; Meyers, 150,
157; Unger, 15. Cf. Hepburn v. Griswold, 8 Wallace 603, 619 (U.S. 1870). Significantly, in his dissent in Juilliard v. Greenman, 110 U.S. 421, 470 (1884), Field, J.,
expressed his deepest fear not over legal tender as such, but over the freedom he saw
the decision giving to run the government printing presses at will.

220. Prelude, supra, notes 59-65; Boudin, 2:151; Dunne (2), 11, 13, 15; Nussbaum, 118; Thayer, 74, 80, 83, 85-87, 94, 95, 97. Hepburn, 74, goes far beyond
what the record supports when he claims that "unquestionably the convention intended to withhold from the federal government the power to create paper money
with legal tender attributes." See Juilliard v. Greenman, 110 U.S. 421, 443 (1884).
Cf., Hepburn v. Griswold, 8 Wallace 603, 614 (U.S. 1870), and Miller, J., dissenting,
id. 627, 628. O. W. Holmes, Jr., in 4 *American Law Review* 768 (1870), and in his
twelfth edition of James Kent, 1:254, note (1873), suggested that the Constitution's
authorization to Congress to coin money amounted to a ban on making paper legal
tender. In Knox v. Lee, Field, J., dissenting, restated the point, and the majority took
pains to answer it, 12 Wallace 457, 536, 544, 651 (U.S. 1871), as Holmes with proper
pride of authorship noted in 7 *American Law Review* 146 (1872). Thayer, 75, 83,
85-87, shows that coin and legal tender are not synonomous. Cf. Fairman (1), 160,
note 34; Howe, 2:55, note 68.

221. On the arguments over letting the market fix the terms of government borrowing, see Barrett, 19, 22, 33, 44-45, 61, 64-65; Hammond (3), 168, 169, 180, 192,
198, 212-13; Hepburn, 189, 194; Myers, 154; Redlich, 2:95; Sharkey, 29, 31, 32. Cf.
Miller, J., dissenting, in Hepburn v. Griswold, 8 Wallace 603, 634 (U.S. 1870). Compare the fact that a proposal to confer legal-tender status on Treasury notes issued in
1814 to help finance the war was rejected, probably in part on grounds of policy, as
unfair, and probably in part out of doubt as to Congress's constitutional authority.
Hepburn, 90, 177; Knox (1), 33. In 1862 another factor in the policy debate was the
fear that sale of fresh government bonds at large discounts would depreciate the value
of government securities already outstanding and so impair the financial position of
financial institutions. Hammond (3), 180, 192, 198, 201. There was substantial, if
rather muted, support by bankers for the 1862 law, because they felt that they must
have legal-tender paper, if they could no longer obtain gold, to satisfy their importunate creditors and meet the reserves requirements of some state laws. The bankers'
support shows that operational importance was put on the legal-tender feature at that
key point of the economy. More broadly, however, it shows awareness of a basic
issue between governing the money stock by law and by market judgments. Cf.
Hammond (3), 178, 184, 185, 194, 196, 212, 217-18, 232. The grant of legal-tender
status as symbolizing assertion of the supremacy of legal over market processes appeared plainly in Congressman Elbridge G. Spaulding's argument that issuing the
legal-tender notes would "bring into full exercise all the higher powers of government
under the Constitution" and would "assert the power and dignity of the government
by the issue of its own notes, pledging the faith, the honor, and property of the
whole loyal people." Id., 180. Cf. id., 190, 204, 216. That the total of judgments and
factors relating the money supply to the flow of resource allocations was the deeper
reality of the matter, see id., 227; Myers, 155; Schumpeter (2), 719. Cf. Hepburn v.
Griswold, 8 Wallace 603, 608, 620, 621 (U.S. 1870).

222. Hepburn v. Griswold, 8 Wallace 603, 622 (the "decisive" ground), 623 ("the
spirit [of the contract clause] . . . should pervade the entire body of legislation"),

624 (due process forbids disappointing prior contractors relying on specie values) (U.S. 1870). Miller, J., dissenting, id., 637, in effect said that values based on market customs of relying on specie must yield to measures otherwise necessary and proper to exercising the authority of the federal government, and such "indirect effect of a great public measure, in depreciating the value of lands, stocks, bonds, and other contracts" could not be deemed a taking of property without due process of law. Fairman (2), 1145, finds the analysis of retroactivity in the Hepburn case to exceed regular bounds of due process doctrine. See, also, Fairman (3), 687-8, 714, 761, 774. Thayer, 91, thought it illegitimate to argue that an implied power (to create legal-tender paper) should be more subject to limitation from the "spirit" of the Constitution than would be an express power, such as that over bankruptcy.

223. Knox v. Lee, 12 Wallace 457, 529 and 545 (decision of legal tender an attribute of sovereignty), 543 (government circulating notes, left to the play of the market without aid of legal-tender status, would depreciate), 546 (government must be able to make good possible deficiencies of market for gold and silver), 549 (contracts to pay money are subject to government's control of currency) (U.S. 1871). The Court properly analyzed the retroactivity issue as not the most basic one; the root question was whether Congress might in any circumstances declare tokens other than specie to be binding lawful money, and the answer to that question applied to the impact of the money powers of Congress over future as well as past contracts. Id., 530. Cf. Dunne (1), 548. In justifying the reasonableness of Congress's judgment of the means necessary to finance the war, the Court in effect spelled out the inadequacy of market processes to accomplish the needed allocations of resources: ". . . the credit of the government had been tried to its utmost endurance. Every new issue of notes which had nothing more to rest upon than government credit, must have paralyzed it more and more. . . . [M]any persons and institutions refused to receive and pay those notes that had been issued. . . . The government could not pay [the troops] . . . with ordinary treasury notes, nor could they discharge their debts with such a currency. Something more was needed, something that had all the uses of money. And as no one could be compelled to take common treasury notes in payment of debts, and as the prospect of ultimate redemption was remote and contingent, it is not too much to say that they must have depreciated in the market long before the war closed, as did the currency of the Confederate States. Making the notes legal tenders gave them a new use, and it needs no argument to show that the value of things is in proportion to the uses to which they may be applied." Knox v. Lee, 12 Wallace 457, 542-43 (U.S. 1871). The Court drew with particular confidence on the legislative precedent of the 1834 change in the gold content of the dollar. It was no true distinction of this instance, that (as was argued) the change "only brought the legal value of gold coin more nearly into correspondence with its actual value in the market"; the fact remained that under the act a creditor would receive a sum 6 percent less in weight and in market value than what he was entitled to receive the day before the statutory change was effective. Yet this had been accepted as a proper use of law in the face of contrary contract expectations. Id., 552. Compare, also, Bradley, J., concurring, id., 554, 558, 560 (sovereignty), 559 (constitutional convention record inconclusive), 563-64 (government power over currency may supply deficiencies of the market), 566 (government control of money is superior to contract). See Dunne (2), 78; Fairman (2), 1145, and (3), 687-8, 714, 761, 774.

224. Juilliard v. Greenman, 110 U.S. 421, 448 (1884). This was a test case. Fairman (3), 771-2. As in the 1871 decision, the Court here again underlined the supremacy of legal processes in determining the system of money by its emphasis that such

power was normally a prerogative of sovereignty. Id., 447. The attack which Field, J., dissenting, id., 467, leveled against this particular argument highlights the extended role which the majority was prepared to assign to government in this area. Cf. Boudin, 2:153, 158, 179, 181; Dunne (2), 79; Fairman (1), 175; Warren (3), 2:654.

225. On the United States notes: 12 Stat. 345 (1862), sec. 1, and 12 Stat. 709 (1863), sec. 3; 18 Stat. 123 (1874), sec. 6; 20 Stat. 87 (1878); Dunbar, 167, 175, 212 217. On national bank notes: 12 Stat. 665 (1863), secs. 17, 62; 13 Stat. 99 (1864), secs. 21, 22, and 13 Stat. 498 (1865); 16 Stat. 251 (1870), sec. 1; 18 Stat. 123 (1874), sec. 9, 18 Stat. 296 (1875), sec. 3, and 18 Stat. 302 (1875); 22 Stat. 162 (1882), sec. 8; Dunbar, 171, 172, 181, 199, 202, 212, 214, 216, 221. On silver: 19 Stat. 215 (1876), sec. 1; 20 Stat. 25 (1878), sec. 1; 26 Stat. 289 (1890), sec. 1; Dunbar, 245, 247, 250. On the Aldrich-Vreeland Act: 35 Stat. 546 (1908), secs. 1, 5. Indicative of the attitude underlying this consistent pattern of statutory ceilings on note issues was the emphasis put on this feature in the debate over the 1864 revision of the national banking system by Congressman Samuel Hooper. To him, this was a critical aspect of the legislation, distinguishing the national banks from the state banks. Knox (2), 253. The cautious Senator John Sherman is credited by Redlich, 2:105, with putting into the first national bank legislation an absolute limitation on the total of national bank notes, an idea perhaps borrowed from an English statute of 1844. The history of the ceiling provisions on national bank notes is sketched in Cagan, 18, 19; Friedman and Schwartz, 21; Knox (2), 155. Friedman and Schwartz, 21, 781, point out that when 18 Stat. 296 (1875), sec. 3, Dunbar, 214, repealed the flat statutory ceiling on the total of national bank notes, Congress in effect gave the Treasury power to control the amount outstanding by deciding on the volume of bonds bearing the circulation privilege and their interest rates. But the Treasury made only sporadic use of this potential power, and most notably as a means to offset government surpluses rather than as a direct instrument of money supply control. Cf. Friedman and Schwartz, 128. The ceilings put on greenbacks and on silver-based money plainly reflected distrust of the inflationary tendencies of legislative provision of money. See notes 219, supra, 233, 235, infra. Cagan, 18, thinks that jealousy to maintain the state banks, rather than fear of inflation, was the prime mover in opposition to creating the national bank system. Granted the influence of concern for the state banks, the ceilings set on national bank-note issues make so much a pattern with the ceilings put on the greenbacks as to indicate a common concern against overissue. Cf. Hammond (3), 304-5, 309, 311 (opponents of national bank system equate "free-banking" principle with irresponsible issues of currency). Some supporting evidence for this reading is in the link which the Resumption Act made between repeal of the ceiling on national bank notes and the stipulation that greenbacks be retired to the amount of 80 percent of national bank-notes issued, until the greenbacks should be reduced to $300 million. 18 Stat. 296 (1875), sec. 3, in Dunbar, 214. This aspect of the 1875 act was partly a concession to paper-money advocates. But its limits were also a concession to those who feared paper inflation. Cf. Barrett, 130, 189; Friedman and Schwartz, 48, 81; Nugent, 11, 221, 224, 225; Unger, 252-57, 262, 263-64.

226. Cf. Friedman and Schwartz, 127, 128, 145, 148, note 20, 149-52, 154, 155; Taus, 68, 69, 70, 76, 79, 80, 81, 83.

227. Bronson v. Rodes, 7 Wallace 229 (U.S. 1869); Butler v. Horwitz, id., 258 (U.S. 1869); Trebilcock v. Wilson, 12 id., 687 (U.S. 1872). Ropes, 605, finds "unanswerable" the position taken by Miller, J., in dissent in the first case, that since before 1862 there was only one kind of legal-tender money in the United States (gold and silver dollars), a contract made before 1862 specifying payment in "gold and

silver coin, lawful money of the United States" could not fairly be interpreted to mean an election of specie as against legal-tender paper, when no legal-tender paper existed. Ropes points out that Hepburn v. Griswold, 8 Wallace 603 (U.S. 1870) abandoned the rationale of Bronson v. Rodes, because the 1870 decision held the legal-tender act invalid in regard to prior contracts which concededly made no explicit stipulation of payment in any particular medium; abandoning the theory that the contractor had made an election in regard to medium of payment in pre-1862 contracts required that in 1870 the Court take its stand on the basic constitutional issue. Ropes, on the other hand, thought the Court correct in arguing that provisions of the 1862 and 1863 statutes requiring that customs duties be paid in gold, by implication sanctioned private contracts to obtain the needed gold, and that gold clauses were, therefore, enforceable consistent with the legal-tender acts. Ropes, 604. Norman v. Baltimore & Ohio Railroad Co., 294 U.S. 240, 300, 306 (1935) accepts this appraisal of the 1862 policy, yet the vigor with which the Court there states the value of uniformity in provision for money settlement of transactions (294 U.S. at 315) suggests that with a different bias of values the Court of 1869 might have read the 1862 policy differently; the legal-tender act provisions concerning customs duties seem a narrow base to sustain an argument against the promotion of a uniform frame of money calculation in the economy at large. Considerable weight is due the estimate of Bradley, J., who thought that Congress in 1862 meant to render unenforceable clauses calling for payments in specie. Bradley, J., concurring in Knox v. Lee, 12 Wallace 457, 566, 567 (U.S. 1871), and dissenting in Trebilcock v. Wilson, id., 699 (U.S. 1872). In contrast to these considerations, the core value which moved the majority in Bronson v. Rodes shows in Chief Justice Chase's explanation of the peculiar importance of precious-metals coin, derived from the fact that its material has "inherent" value—i.e., not value derived from political decision. 7 Wallace 229, 249 (U.S. 1869).

228. 18 Stat. 296 (1875), in Dunbar, 215; Friedman and Schwartz, 24, 48, 54, 81.

229. 14 Stat. 31 (1866); 15 Stat. 34 (1868); 18 Stat. 123 (1874), sec. 6; 18 Stat. 296 (1875), sec. 3; 18 Stat. 87 (1878); Dunbar, 200, 201, 212, 214, 217. On the Treasury's contraction effort of 1866-68; Barrett, 163-80; Nugent, 45, 92-96; Unger, 41-43.

230. The desire for an impersonal market check appeared clearly in the reiterated argument of Secretary of the Treasury Hugh McCulloch for contracting the greenback supply, that gold coin was the only true money. Nugent, 36, 93. McCulloch spoke for the general tendency through the first half of the century, to accept uncritically the idea of an automatic, market-type control on money. Cf. Mints, 176, 177. For the argument of the more conservative opponents of contraction, that government should allow the economy to grow up to the greenbacks, see Barrett, 172; Nugent, 95, 142, 143; Unger, 160, 165-69, 191. On conservative distrust of the Resumption Act of 1875, as a precedent for central money management, see Unger, 260-63. A ground of distrust was the ambiguity of the act concerning possible authority of the Treasury to reissue greenbacks retired in offset to new issues by the national banks. Id., 256, 257. See, also, Barrett, 187. Ironically, the conservative secretary of the treasury (Benjamin H. Bristow) so interpreted the 1875 act as to authorize greater retirement of greenbacks than contractionists could have expected. Unger, 263-65. Cf. 18 Stat. 296 (1875), sec. 3.

231. Field, J., for the Court, in Bronson v. Rodes, 7 Wallace 229, 249 (U.S. 1869). Compare Unger, 336, 338 on comparable popular attitudes. This attitude ran

back to the foundations of national monetary policy, in the federal convention's sharp distrust of (government-produced, government-manipulated) paper money, compared with gold and silver. Prelude, supra, notes 16, 25, 26. The contrasting interests of the silver-mining interest and the confirmed paper-money men are sketched by Unger, 332-33, 335-36.

232. Secretary of the Treasury, Annual Report of 1867, 40th Cong., 2nd sess., *House Executive Documents,* no. 2, vol. 5, p. ix; Krooss (3), 2:1468, 1472; Mints, 177; Nugent, 36-37, 272. Nugent, 191, points out that from the middle seventies on, bimetallism could attract conservative supporters because, resting still on a precious metals base, it could resist the dangerous appeal of paper-money men, through the same arguments pushed in favor of a gold base.

233. That a gold base was trusted by its proponents because the physical and market limitations on its supply meant a nonpolitical check on the expansion of the money stock, see Dorfman, 3:65, 74, 228; Nugent, 36-37, 146-47, 192, 239, 240, 272; Unger, 323, 347, 359-60, 388, 402. Those who steered to a quiet passage the subsequently controversial act of 1873 striking the silver dollar from the coinage pattern apparently foresaw a declining price (increasing supply) of silver and were moved in part at least by desire to avoid the larger element of discretion that a silver increase might inject into determining the supply of money. Nugent, 144, 146-47, 149, 158, 170. The trust in gold because it would not invite political decisions on money was in effect asserted by Senator John Sherman in January 1874 when he praised "a specie standard" (meaning, in practice, then a gold standard, since silver had not yet become a key issue) because "this axiom is as immutable as the law of gravitation or the laws of the planetary system, and every device to evade it or avoid it has, by its failure, only demonstrated the universal law that specie measures all values as certainly as the surface of the ocean measures the level of the earth." Nugent, 185. Unger, 333, points out that the more radical silverites highlighted the desire for an automatic check implicit or explicit in the gold position, by their support of free silver as likely to lead to ready expansion of paper money.

234. The law-market, separation-of-powers issue was plainly stated for the bimetallists by the Englishman, Ernest Seyd, who held that "the true cause of the abnormal depression of trade is the contraction of the bimetallic currency by 'human' law, the so-called 'demonetization of silver.' " Nugent, 192. Two leading, conservative bimetallists in the United States—S. Dana Horton and Francis Amasa Walker—expressed a similar view of the virtues of silver added to gold in the money base. Silver would desirably enlarge the money stock. Walker felt that "a moderate and gradual metallic inflation" would come from bimetallism and would be good for the productive growth of the economy. But, under bimetallism, this would be money growth disciplined by the market; as Walker saw the matter, the best money supply "is a money the supply of which is determined by the cost of its production." Likewise, "real money" to Horton "must be a commodity . . . like all other commodities, subject to fluctuations of supply and demand." Nugent, 196. Men of this stamp, however, would put the use of silver within a frame set by international treaty, that is, by law; thus their "market" talk was more limited by legal process than it clearly acknowledged. Id., 195, 196, 198, 199. Cf. Friedman and Schwartz, 49; Hepburn, 293, 295, 345-47, 364. But even these conservative bimetallists and those for whom they spoke objected to a gold-only base as an excessive use of law to fix the money supply. Cf. Unger, 337-38. The more radical, free-silver men likewise attacked the exclusive gold base as an artificial limit on economic growth by law, favorable only to narrow creditor interests. They were willing to let the money stock grow with an

expanding supply of silver, in the confidence that resulting growth in purchasing power would develop the real economy to a scale matching the silver-based money; this was the free-silverites' counterpart of the law-limiting argument made earlier to allow the economy to "grow up to" the greenbacks. Dorfman, 3:18-19, 100, 103-4, 115-16, 226, 229-30; Hepburn, 276-77, 363; Myers, 201; Nugent, 199-200, 234, 237, 239-40; Unger, 330-32. Cf. Barrett, 85-86. Moreover, when it was put in functional rather than emotional tones, the free silver case argued for substituting market inter-action between gold and silver for legislative stipulation of one metal only as the money base. Thus, as the majority report of the Monetary Commission of 1876-77 put the matter, if the law provided for free coinage of silver at a 16:1 ratio to gold, upon any divergence in market value between them the law's sanction would give scope for greater demand for the cheaper metal, while allowing the market to drive out the dearer one; this movement would supply more of the higher-priced metal to world markets, until supply and demand came again into balance between the two metals. Dorfman, 3:19; cf. Nugent, 239, 240. In 1896 Bryan invoked somewhat sim-ilar supply-and-demand analysis of the virtues of free silver as curbing legal manipula-tions by narrow interests. Dorfman, 3:229. There was a similar search for automatic processes, as against political ones, in the scheme for interconvertible public bonds and currency, of the National Labor Union, about 1867-70. See Sharkey, 171, 220.

235. On Chase's distrust of legislative creation of currency: Barrett, 5, 15, 18, 63, 66; Hammond (3), 168, 173, 178, 184-86, 201-2; Hepburn, 187; Knox (2), 224; Nussbaum, 102. For Hamilton's view of the superior insulation of a privately managed national bank from the inflationary interests that might press on Congress, see note 120, supra. Bryan's "Cross of Gold" speech (1896) contains a classic version of the criticism of national bank notes, on the ground that creation of currency was a nondelegable function of government. Krooss (3), 3:2009, 2012. Cf. Hepburn, 313, 321, 378; Knox (2), 141, 279-80; Nugent, 42; Unger, 74-75, 208-10. Bryan held to his nondelegable function argument when in 1913 he opposed issue of currency solely on the credit of regional federal reserve banks and insisted that federal reserve notes be obligations of the United States. Link, 213. Though initiative lay with the banks in issuing national bank notes, the government did not lack all involvement, because it guaranteed redemption of the notes; if an issuing bank failed, the Treasury would forthwith pay its notes and cancel the bonds which underpinned them. 13 Stat. 99 (1864), sec. 46. Cf. Cagan, 18, 19; Friedman and Schwartz, 21, 23; Redlich, 2:105.

236. A proposal for a federal central bank would probably have been politically impracticable, both because of the political inheritance from the 1830s and because of current opposition from state banks. Cf. Hammond (1), 724, and (3), 138, 333, 350, 359; Knox (2), 251; Myers, 163; Nussbaum, 108; Redlich, 2:99, 108; Robert-son, 36; Trescott, 47; Unger, 18, 74-75. On the other hand, despite agrarian arguments that creation of money was a nondelegable function of government (note 235, supra), no substantial effort was made to deny that the legislative and judicial precedents surrounding the two banks of the United States established the power of Congress to charter some kind of national banks, and proponents of the 1863-64 laws build on this base. See Farmers' & Mechanics' National Bank v. Deering, 91 U.S. 29 33 (1875); Hammond (1), 726; Hepburn, 306; Unger, 18. Cf. T. Marshall, J., dissent-ing, in First Agricultural National Bank v. State Tax Commission, 392 U.S. 339, 348 355-56 (1968). While the 1863 act was being shaped, the New York superintendent of banks threatened that he would sue to enjoin national banks from issuing their bank notes in that state, Hammond (3), 342. Redlich, 2:110, says that the federal

authorities discussed with a leader of the New York bar his retainer on behalf of the United States against such a challenge. No such suit was brought, perhaps because of a sober estimate of the precedent against it. General acceptance of Congress's authority to charter banks in aid of national policies may also be inferred from the fact that, amid considerable controversy over the policy aspects of establishing the national bank system, no proposals were made to amend the Constitution one way or the other on the matter. Cf. Ames, 257. In the seventies two amendments were proposed to bar Congress from chartering private corporations to do business within the states but these came to nothing. Ibid.

237. The national banking legislation drew both general policy and organization details from the precedents of the state free-banking laws, especially those of New York and Massachusetts. Hammond (1), 727, and (3), 290, 304; Hepburn, 306; Knox (2), 97, 221, 222, 226; Redlich, 2:99, 104; Robertson, 41; Trescott, 49. The free-banking character of the national banking system was noted in McCormick v. Market Bank, 165 U.S. 538, 551 (1897). Redlich, 2:104, suggests that the national bank acts drew from the New York law the idea of backing notes with government bonds deposited with a public office and the issue of bank notes from a public office; from the Massachusetts law of 1858 was drawn the idea of specie reserve requirements against both bank notes and deposits, along with provision for central reserve city banks (whose holding of deposits by correspondent banks might be counted as part of the latter's required reserves) and provision for curtailing bank lending until required reserve ratios were restored. For an outline of regulatory provisions of the national bank legislation aimed at assuring the functional integrity of banks as individual institutions, see Cagan, 39-42. The costly rigidities of the national bank system as a means of providing both currency and deposit-check money were noted as a basis for creating the Federal Reserve System in Raichle v. Federal Reserve Bank of New York, 34 Fed. (2d) 910, 912 (2d Cir. 1929).

238. For the focus on securing the soundness of individual banks, primarily for the benefit of their particular noteholders, creditors, or stockholders, see McCormick v. Market Bank, 165 U.S. 538, 551-52 (1897); cf. Hammond (1), 731; Knox (2), 227, 235, 237, 239, 257, 268; Krooss (1), 35, 39, 255; Robertson, 71, 87; Trescott, 49, 52, 56, 58, 60, 63. In the first years of the national banking system, the comptroller's supervision aimed chiefly to assure that banks would be in condition to redeem their notes, if these were presented; it was some time before bank examinations gave more emphasis to the condition of banks' lending, with a view to protecting deposit-check money. Robertson, 71-76, 79-81; Trescott, 56.

239. Deposits, which were over one-half of the money supply in 1860, grew to provide 90 percent of it by 1913. Cagan, 30. Redlich, 2:184 notes that there are no contemporary breakdowns between lodged and created deposits in the nineteenth century, but that circumstantial evidence indicates that by 1894 created deposits accounted for between 75 and 80 percent of all deposits. See Friedman and Schwartz, 4, 16, 58, 122. Another indicator is that the demand for currency compared to total money holdings declined by nearly one-half in twenty years, from 44 percent in 1867, to 33 percent in 1874, to 24 percent in 1886. Cagan, 19. That Congress's prime concern was with currency and not with deposits, see Cagan, 16, 17; Hammond (1), 731; cf. Mints, 176. The 1865 federal tax on state bank notes reflected the same concentration on currency to the exclusion of deposits. Friedman and Schwartz, 19; Hammond (1), 734; Trescott, 53, 92.

240. On legal reserve requirements in the states: Friedman and Schwartz, 56 and 56, note 62, 118, note 44, 123, note 48; Jacoby, 213. On reserve requirements in the

national bank system: 13 Stat. 99 (1864), secs. 31, 32; 18 Stat. 123 (1874), secs. 2, 3; 24 Stat. 559 (1887), secs. 1, 2; 32 Stat. 1223 (1903); Dunbar, 184-85, 210-11, 225; cf. Cagan, 29; Hammond (1), 731; Hepburn, 309, 317, 337. By affecting the quantity of banks' earning assets, legal reserve requirements inherently regulated bank earnings. Though this was not itself a monetary regulation, it was an impact which further shows that policy toward banks was not obedient to laissez-faire values. Cf. Barger, 209-11, 260, 316.

241. That legal reserve requirements originated in concern for the security of the depositor's expectations, rather than for creating a means to regulate the money supply was indicated when 18 Stat. 123 (1874), sec. 2, struck from the national bank statute the requirement of a cash reserve against national bank notes, because the deposited bond security was deemed to satisfy all relevant concerns. Cf. Clay J. Anderson, 54; Friedman and Schwartz, 21, 781; Redlich, 2:117. By their rigidity and want of means for positive control the new reserve requirements were rendered largely irrelevant to money management. Cagan, 16, 17, 29, 30, 32, 40; Cotter, 47-49; Friedman and Schwartz, 117, note 44. Runs on banks reflected the focus of public policy on currency and its inattention to controls on lending and deposits. Friedman and Schwartz, 20, 21, 22, note 8, 23, Nussbaum, 129, 139, 157. The statutory-sanctioned pyramiding of reserves worked in effect to create some private central organization of reserves, but without public accountability. Barger, 35-37; Cagan, 36, 37; Cotter, 49; Jacoby, 213; Krooss (1), 255; Redlich, 2:104-5; Trescott, 150-52; Warburg, 1:13, 15, 24, 64. Another reflection of the failure to treat currency and bank credit as related components of a total money system was the criticism of the formula by which Congress at first apportioned national bank note issues among the states, one-half according to population and one-half according to existing banking capital and area business and resources. The working effect of the formula was to allocate the bulk of national bank note circulation to areas where the notes were less needed because deposit-check money was the dominant medium of exchange and to allocate the lowest amount of the currency to regions where checks were not yet so much used and bank loans continued to be made by providing bank notes to borrowers. 13 Stat. 498 (1865), in Dunbar, 199; cf. 16 Stat. 251 (1870) and 18 Stat. 123 (1874), in Dunbar, 203, 213 (redistribution of bank notes to regions not having received their due share), and 18 Stat. 296 (1875), in Dunbar, 215 (ceiling removed; regional allocations no longer an issue). See Hepburn, 311, 315, 317, 319; Redlich, 2:118-20.

242. The absence of any sustained, considerable issue about the over-all regulation of bank credit through the second half of the nineteenth century finds some reflection in Friedman and Schwartz, 58, 81; Redlich, 2:214; Robertson, 71-75; Trescott, 157. The earlier state of the matter is thrown into relief by the sharpness with which contestants drew the issue of who should control the money supply, in shaping the Federal Reserve System. Cf. Morison and Commager, 2:433-34.

243. The prevailing attitudes before 1860 treated bank deposits simply as private creditor-debtor contracts and not relevant to legal regulation of money. Hammond (1), 80, 83, 139, note, 338, 364, 498, 564, 565, 595, 690; Redlich, 1:91, 132, 142, and 2:4, 10. Not surprisingly, this viewpoint continued on stubbornly into the last half of the century. Hammond (1), 731, 734, and (2), 5; Hepburn, 332; Redlich, 2:117, 216; cf. Culbertson, 159; Friedman and Schwartz, 55-56, 195. That there were more sophisticated appraisals which saw deposits as part of the money supply only highlighted the dominance of the general view to the contrary. Cf. Hammond (1), 50, 51, 367, 368; Mints, 127, 176; Redlich, 2:4, 9, 10. Those who framed and

pressed for some kind of central money management in 1912-13 were concerned about bank lending in relation to the money supply only as they sought to provide a lender of last resort, armed with a flexible currency, to overcome short-run defects in the quantity of credit and currency, and especially to prevent the financial panics that came when depositors or country banks fell into fear which caused them suddenly and massively to prefer currency over deposits. Clay J. Anderson, 169, 170; Chandler, 12, 13; Goldenweiser, 109, 110; Knipe, 4, 5; Mints, 281, 284; Myers, 127-28, 189, 209, 246; Polakoff, 190, 191.

244. Barger, 27-28, 30, 35; Hammond (1), 706; Hepburn, 162-63, 240, 316, 332, 333, 337, 351-52, 353, 390-93; Knox (2), 114, 183, 197-99, 202-3; Redlich, 2:3, 6, 47, 51, 54, 158, 161, 236-39, 242, 425. Attorney General Richard Olney contributed to upholding the crisis role of clearinghouse certificates by ruling in 1893 that they were not within the intent of the 10 percent federal tax on paper issued for circulation by others than national banks. Measured by function, the clearinghouse certificates could readily have been found subject to the tax. But the attorney general found that in the light of related revenue statutes Congress intended that taxable status be determined solely by form and not by function, that only completely negotiable promissory notes were intended to be covered by the 10 percent tax, and that the certificates did not meet this formal test, since they were not instruments on which the participating banks or the clearinghouse could be sued in an action at common law and a judgment obtained by proving the paper alone without further evidence. 20 *Opinions of the Attorney General* 681, 682, 683 (1893). Cf. United States v. Isham, 17 Wallace 496, 506 (U.S. 1874). The care with which the terse, cryptic opinion stayed within formal criteria, in a situation where the issuers of the paper plainly intended to create money equivalents, suggests that the attorney general was in fact much concerned with the functional issue involved and did not want to upset a procedure serving an important money-system need. Cf. Hepburn, 352; Nussbaum, 120.

245. Friedman and Schwartz, 159-61, 164; Myers, 246; Nussbaum, 139; Redlich, 2:53, 163, 166, 236, 237, 239, 242, 257, 270, 289. There was another localized, but official, response to tensions created by the increased importance of bank lending in the money supply. Reacting *ad hoc* to particular crises of business confidence, state legislatures sometimes explicitly suspended statutory requirements that state-chartered banks honor their obligations in cash, state executive officers sometimes accomplished the same result by not enforcing sanctions against banks in times of general restriction of cash payments, and the courts showed their acceptance of the idea that pervasive crisis constituted an implied—functional and equitable—exception to the statutory duty of banks to pay claims in currency. Friedman and Schwartz, 161, cf. notes 117, 118, supra.

246. The Aldrich-Vreeland Act is 35 Stat. 546 (1908). Cf. Cochran and Miller, 286; Cotter, 53; Friedman and Schwartz, 170; Hacker and Zahler (2), 72, 129; Myers, 258; Redlich, 2:166, 167; Warburg, 1:21-22, 27; Wiebe (1), 73, 74.

247. Barger, 17, 24, 27, 29-34; Cagan, 29, note 15, 31, 32; Clifford, 48-49, 51-53, 76; Friedman and Schwartz, 53-56, 127-28, 149-50; Redlich, 2:175; Taus, 22, 23 29, 31, 33, 35-37, 39-40, 47, 49, 50, 64, 63-64, 67, 69, 70, 76, 79, 80, 81, 83, 86, 87, 95, 98-100, 104-6, 111, 113, 114, 115-17, 119, 122-26; Timberlake, 168-71. Timberlake, 182, estimates that in the Shaw years of most active Treasury central-bank-style effort, its deposits of government moneys in national banks could affect existing reserves of all banks (including state banks which held part of their reserves in national banks) by about 10 percent. The deficiencies of the Treasury in central-

bank-style operations were noted as a basis for justifying the powers of the Federal Reserve System in Raichle v. Federal Reserve Bank of New York, 34 Fed. (2d) 910, 912 (2d Cir. 1929).

248. See notes 217, 218, 222-24, supra, and Dawson, 666. Compare the distinction taken between value judgments declared with governing specificity in the Constitution's text, and those stated as general standards, committing areas of discretionary judgment to Congress, in Home Building & Loan Association v. Blaisdell, 290 U.S. 398, 426 (1934); see Black, J., concurring, in Application of Gault, 387 U.S. 1, 63 (1967). Compare, also, the contrast between the Court's strong, mid-twentieth-century application of the presumption of constitutionality to state economic regulatory legislation to Fourteenth Amendment due process challenges, and its more distrustful handling of state statutes challenged as burdening interstate commerce. Nebbia v. New York, 291 U.S. 502 (1934); Bibb v. Navajo Freight Lines, Inc., 359 U.S. (1959).

The problems of the greenbacks produced a few proposals for constitutional amendments. In 1866 the House passed a resolution instructing its Judiciary Committee to inquire into the expediency of amending the Constitution to limit Congress's power to issue circulating paper; nothing more was heard of this proposal. After Hepburn there was a proposal in 1870 for an amendment to authorize Congress to issue legal-tender notes. After Knox v. Lee, in 1873 and again in 1874, amendments were introduced to forbid Congress to make anything but gold and silver legal tender to pay debts; both amendments were tabled. The Greenback party's opposition to resumption of specie payments was reflected in amendments offered in 1878, to authorize and regulate the amounts of issues of legal-tender notes; these were buried in committee. After Juilliard four amending proposals were made; three in various terms forbade Congress to make anything but gold and silver legal tender except after a declaration of war, with one proposal adding the further requirement that the public safety require the measure; one proposal would limit the issue of legal-tender notes to $350 million, unless a greater issue were voted by two-thirds of each house of Congress; all of these were buried in committee or tabled. Ames, 258-59; Warren (3), 2:659, 660, note 1.

Apart from these greenback-centered proposals, in the years from 1860 to 1912 there was no substantial interest shown in constitutional amendments regarding Congress's power to create money. A small flurry in 1892 reflected attitudes which contributed to Bryan's support. See *Proposed Amendments,* Item 79 (1892: Congress shall have sole power to coin and issue money, and this power shall not be delegated to any individual or corporation; reported adversely), and Items 103 and 104 (1892; for issue of a national currency on a per capita basis; neither brought to vote).

249. See, generally, Hurst (2), 70-78; cf. Lawrence H. Chamberlain, 307-12; Stimson, 2:572. Relevant to the leading role of legislation is the Court's emphasis on the scope of legislative discretion, in Veazie Bank v. Fenno, 8 Wallace 533, 548, 549 (U.S. 1869), and Juilliard v. Greenman, 110 U.S. 421, 450 (1884).

250. On the Civil War policy leadership of the Treasury: Hammond (3), 87-88, 135-36, 264-66, 348-50; Hepburn, 199-202; Myers, 150, 153-57, 162-63. On later defaults of lawmakers and other leaders of opinion in providing insight into the functions and determinants of monetary policy: Clifford, 48-49, 81-82, 115-17; Friedman and Schwartz, 133-34; Harrod, 31-33; Nugent, 36, 37, 57, 146, 147, 166, 170, 180, 181, 224; Sharkey, 60; Unger, 27-30, 36-37, 43, 73-76, 154-69, 171-72, 247, 255-56, 260, 263, 264, 316-20; White (4), 111. The only contribution of the executive branch in the states was the slow, uneven, usually inadequate development of admin-

istrative scrutiny of the soundness of individual banks. Andersen, 86-100; Fine, 355; Redlich, 2:285; Robertson, 69.

251. Friedman and Schwartz, 81, 83, 85, 133-34, 697, 698; Glass, 29, 60, 156; Nugent, 57, 155, 157; Unger, 5, 49, 61, 76, 108, 145, 149, 151, 255-57, 260, 263, 315-20, 330, 332. Carter Glass tersely summarized the record of inattention to the truly central area of money supply control when he observed that from 1863-64 to 1912 "not a single comprehensive attempt was made by Congress even to consider a reserve banking measure." Glass, 29. Cf. McAdoo, 213. The single most damning charge made against the legislative process as a procedure for adjusting monetary policy to public interest was that 17 Stat. 424 (1873), in Dunbar, 241, in striking the silver dollar from the roster of recognized coins accomplished the narrow self-interest of powerful men of wealth by a secret conspiracy against the Congress as well as against the common people. It is symbolic of the emptiness of so much of the politics of money through the late nineteenth century that responsible scholars have found this "Crime of '73" at best a product of political paranoia. The immediate purpose of thus far demonetizing silver was repeatedly and officially declared at the time; the step was known to the soft-money and silver interests of the time, and then evoked no objection from them; the action was a conservative, but at basis technically or functionally oriented, judgment concerning the formal requisites of a stable system of money values; and study fails to show it to have been either the product of, or of peculiar benefit to, any particular pocketbook interest. The contemporary crisscross-ing of positions among merchants, industrialists, and bankers on the issue of resuming specie payments produces such difficulty in aligning the partisans as further to blur the special-interest relevance of the 1873 statute. Given the fluctuating market rela-tions of gold and silver, the 1873 statute and its aftermath show the unwisdom of trying to regulate by statutory detail what should have been dealt with by delegation to administrators under standards set by Congress. But this lesson in the functional capacities and limitations of legislation, rather than condemnation of the integrity of the legislative process, seems to be the realistic conclusion to draw from the episode. Friedman and Schwartz, 113-15; Hepburn, 271-73; Knox (2), 150-51; Nugent, 140, 144, 148-49, 155, 157, 158, 167, 168, 170; Unger, 329, 331. Harrod, 17, does not upset this judgment when he concludes that "the act [of 1873] may have been sub-jectively innocent and yet objectively a crime."

252. Cf. Hurst (4), 137-67.

253. Jefferson, *Works,* 6:197, 204 (opinion against the constitutionality of a national bank, 15 February 1791); McCulloch v. Maryland, 4 Wheaton 316, 421, 423 (U.S. 1819); cf. Thayer, 89, 94.

254. 7 *American Law Review* 146 (1872), identified as Holmes's work in Frank-furter, 798. See Boudin, 2:168; Fairman (1), 162.

255. The presumption of constitutionality was invoked in Knox v. Lee, 12 Wal-lace 457, 531, 542 (U.S. 1871), though the Court majority also made plain that it felt affirmatively convinced of the constitutionality of Congress's action. Id., 540, 542-43. Contrast Hepburn v. Griswold, 8 id., 603, 619-21 (U.S. 1870). On the Brad-ley and Strong appointments, see Dunne (1), 539; Fairman (2), 1131-32, 1142; Warren (3), 2:517. Impropriety attached rather to the decision in the first legal-tender case, than to that in the second. The 1870 case was pressed to decision when all the other justices shared the opinion that Grier, J., one of the five making up the majority, was mentally incapacitated; the decision departed from the Court's rule announced in connection with early arguments of cases in 8 Peters 118, 122 (U.S. 1834), that a constitutional question should be decided only with the concurrence of

a majority of the whole Court, since when the 1870 judgment was entered on a five to three vote, the Court had a legal membership of nine; finally, Chase's turn of position as chief justice from that which he had taken—reluctantly, against his better policy opinion—as secretary of the treasury, was colored by his ambition for the presidency. Fairman (2), 1145, 1146, 1147.

Though he offers no evidence, Boudin, 2:44, 156, infers that the Court deliberately avoided the legal-tender issue when the question was presented under the urgency of wartime in Roosevelt v. Meyer, 1 Wallace 512 (U.S. 1863). That decision went on a ground of appellate jurisdiction which the Court ruled to have been wrongly taken in Trebilcock v. Wilson, 12 id., 687 (U.S. 1872). Warren (3), 2:387, 498, takes the Court's handling of the matter in 1863 at face value. Fairman (1), 152, observes that it was not until June 1865, when the Kentucky court held the legal-tender act unconstitutional, that a case existed appealable within the law laid down in Roosevelt v. Meyer. He further observes that the composition of the Court in 1863 "gives no encouragement to the idea that the justices were adopting an unwarrantably narrow view of their jurisdiction in order to spare the Legal Tender Act from the ordeal of scrutiny." See, also, Fairman (3), 697-8. In later years, but before Hepburn, the Court warily skirted the constitutional issue by restrictive interpretations of the legal-tender act, in Lane County v. Oregon, 7 id., 71 (U.S. 1869), and Bronson v. Rodes, and Butler v. Horwitz, id., 229, 258 (U.S. 1869), but at this point of time of course there can be no convincing imputation of concern to avoid a question of the legality of action taken under a present war emergency. Cf. Warren (3), 2:500-501.

256. Notes 224, 248, supra. Juilliard v. Greenman, 110 U.S. 421, 450 (1884) invoked the presumption of constitutionality specifically on the question of the grant of legal-tender status, and this use of the presumption seems appropriate to that issue. Cf. notes 217, 218, 222-24, 248, supra.

257. Norman v. Baltimore & Ohio Railroad Co., 294 U.S. 240, 303 ("Whatever power there is over the currency is vested in the Congress"), 306, 315 (decision applicable not only to private contracts, but also to contracts or obligations of states and their political subdivisions) (1935). The Court's summary dismissal of any Tenth Amendment question was not inadvertent; counsel for the private bondholder had pressed the assertion that Congress's action wrongly interfered with a domain of contract law left by the Constitution to the states. Id., 243, 246.

258. Federal Reserve Board regulatory authority in a matter ordinarily within state law—the legal terms of existence of bank trust departments—was upheld incident to the decision in First National Bank of Bay City v. Fellows, ex rel. Union Trust Co., 244 U.S. 416, 426, 427 (1917), but the Federal Reserve status was tangential there to the principal question, of Congress's authority to arm national banks with powers which would keep them competitive with state banks. Westfall v. United States, 274 U.S. 256, 258 (1927) held that Congress did not offend the Tenth Amendment when it made it a federal crime to obtain funds by fraud from a state member bank of the Federal Reserve System. But this is a limited ruling; the Court emphasized that the state bank entered the system by its own choice; thus the decision accepted the valid existence of the system in a context which posed minimum clash with states rights. Accord: Hiatt v. United States, 4 Fed. (2d) 374, 377 (7th Cir. 1924), cert. denied 268 U.S. 704 (1925).

259. Raichle v. Federal Reserve Bank of New York, 34 Fed. (2d) 910, 914 (2d Cir. 1929). This is doubly a dictum; the plaintiff's suit was dismissed for want of the Federal Reserve Board as a party defendant, since the board was deemed an indispensable party; moreover, the plaintiff sued primarily to raise Fifth-Amendment-type

property claims. However, weight may properly be attached to so deliberate a statement of the law from a bench consisting of circuit judges, Augustus Hand and Learned Swan. A similar view may fairly be taken as implicit in Bryan v. Federal Open Market Committee, 235 Fed. Supp. 877 (D. Montana, 1964), though the Tenth Amendment point was not dealt with there in terms. Claiming as taxpayers or as residents and citizens living under the sovereignty of the United States, plaintiffs in Horne v. Federal Reserve Bank of Minneapolis, 344 Fed. (2d) 725 (8th Cir. 1965) argued (1) that issue of federal reserve notes was unlawful coining of money by the banks, contrary to U.S. Constitution, Article 1, sec. 8, as well as an unlawful delegation of legislative authority; (2) that creation of book credits by the banks was unlawful coining of money; (3) that United States securities bought by banks with federal reserve notes were given without consideration and void. The court summarily rejected all these challenges, on the ground that plaintiffs presented no claim of right or infringement of right special to them as compared with the general body of taxpayers and persons under the sovereignty of the United States, and hence lacked standing. Accord: Koll v. Wayzata State Bank, 397 Fed. (2d) 124, 127 (8th Cir. 1968); United States v. Anderson, 433 Fed. (2d) 856, 858 (8th Cir. 1970). Several lower federal courts had no difficulty in finding the creation of the Federal Deposit Insurance Corporation and its attendant legislation valid exercises of Congress's power, in contrast to objections that deposit insurance was business simply for state law. This was held in cases involving federal criminal prosecutions for conduct harmful to state banks which were insured under FDIC. The decisions, therefore, are subject to the limitation observed in note 258, supra, concerning Westfall v. United States, that the situations did not involve supersession of state law. Weir v. United States, 92 Fed. (2d) 634, 636, 637 (7th Cir. 1937), cert. denied, 302 U.S. 761 (1937); United States v. Doherty, 18 Fed. Supp. 793, 794 (D. Neb. 1937), aff'd. 94 Fed. (2d) 495 (8th Cir. 1937), cert. denied, 303 U.S. 658 (1937); Curtis v. Hiatt, 169 Fed. (2d) 1019, 1021 (3rd Cir. 1948), cert. denied, 336 U.S. 921 (1949); Way v. United States, 268 Fed. (2d) 785, 786 (10th Cir. 1959). See Freeling v. FDIC, 221 Fed. Supp. 1955 (W.D. Okla. 1962), aff'd., 326 Fed. (2d) 971 (10th Cir. 1963).

260. On the importance of deposit-check money in the twentieth-century money supply: Commission on Money and Credit (2), 63; Culbertson, 151, 159, 166; Friedman and Schwartz, 195, 196, 434; Gordon W. McKinley, 204, 208, 210. That commercial banks had, through checks drawn on deposits, come to supply 80 percent of the money stock was cited as a key fact in the concern of antitrust law with mergers among such institutions, in United States v. Manufacturers Hanover Trust Co., 240 Fed. Supp. 867, 890 (S.D. N.Y. 1965).

261. On optional entry by state banks into the FRS, 38 Stat. 251 (1913), sec. 9; into the FDIC system, 48 Stat. 162 (1933), sec. 8, creating sec. 12B of the Federal Reserve Act, subsec. (y) (1933), and id., 969 (1934). Congress made a deliberate choice to leave optional state bank membership in the Federal Reserve System. Chandler, 9, 10; Goldenweiser, 30; Willis (1), 318. There was never a substantial effort to compel state banks into membership, though in 1961 the unofficial Commission on Money and Credit recommended that all insured banks be required to join. Commission on Money and Credit (1), 77, 91; cf. Chandler, 81, 82; Knipe, 9. Cf. *New York Times,* 10 September 1969, p. 59, col. 7 (Congressman Henry Reuss suggests federal deposit insurance be conditioned on all insured banks' compliance with Federal Reserve regulations). On the 1865 tax on circulating state bank notes, as a measure thought calculated to destroy the state banks, see notes 206-11, supra.

262. Knipe, 9. Probably the respect in which the co-existence of nonmember, state-chartered banks most pointedly limited the setting of Federal Reserve policy

was in fixing the height to which required reserves against deposits could be pushed. By diminishing banks' earning assets higher reserves had sharp bearing on bank profits; too much pressure here might induce state member banks to leave the system, or national banks to switch to state charters in order to put themselves outside the system. Cf. Barger, 209-11, 260, 316, 347; Commission on Money and Credit (1), 76; Goldenweiser, 33. In 1962, by a narrow majority, an advisory committee to the comptroller of the currency—its membership drawn wholly from the community of national banks—concluded that the Federal Reserve Act should continue to require that national banks be in the system. The principal opinion for making membership optional for all banks was among smaller banks, which apparently felt sharp cost burdens in the reserves required by Federal Reserve regulations; significantly, the same committee recommended lower reserve requirements on demand deposits and removal of reserve requirements against time and savings accounts as well as of interest rate ceilings. State bank supervisory officials and state bankers were critical of the report, as calculated to favor the competitive position of national banks. *New York Times,* 21 September 1962, p. 37, col. 1; 23 September 1962, sec. 3, p. 1, col. 1; 25 September 1962, p. 49, col. 1.

263. Bolles, 1:40; Commission on Money and Credit (2), 38; Robertson, 164, 166; Wille, 733, 735, 745.

264. Compare Hopkins Federal Savings & Loan Association v. Cleary, 296 U.S. 315 (1935), where the Court held that, under the limitation declared by the Tenth Amendment, Congress lacked authority to authorize a majority of voting stockholders of a state-chartered savings and loan association to convert the association to a federal savings and loan association without the consent and over the objection of the chartering state. The Court emphasized that provision for such associations within its boundaries was a valid object of a state's public policy: "No one would say with reference to the business conducted by these petitioners [state-chartered savings and loan associations] that Congress could prohibit the formation or continuance of such associations by the states, whatever may be its power to charter them itself." Id., 338. The Court underlined this point by noting that there was nothing to the contrary in the decision in First National Bank of Bay City v. Fellows, ex rel. Union Trust Co., 244 U.S. 416 (1917), that Congress might give national banks the same power as state banks to act as executors or administrators, to the end that national banks could effectively compete with state banks. "This is far from a holding that the function of acting as executors and administrators may be withdrawn from the state banks and lodged by the Congress in the national banks alone." Hopkins Federal Savings & Loan Association v. Cleary, 296 U.S. 315, 337, 338 (1935). With equal care the Court disclaimed intimating an opinion whether Congress might enjoy authority to supplant state-chartered banks whose operations contributed directly to the money supply. In Casey v. Galli, 94 U.S. 673 (1877), no question of constitutionality had been raised by the party challenging the legality of a conversion of a state-chartered bank to a national bank. "Distinctions may conceivably exist between the power of Congress in respect of banks of issue and deposit, and its power in respect of associations to encourage industry and thrift. Whether that be so or not, all that was said in *Casey* v. *Galli* as to the condition of consent was unnecessary to the decision if it was meant to do more than define the meaning of the statute" there involved. Hopkins Federal Savings & Loan Association v. Cleary, 296 U.S. 315, 343 (1935).

265. Trescott, 108, 161-62, notes the existence and failure of the early twentieth-century state deposit-insurance plans. This device was challenged, and upheld, on due process grounds, in Noble State Bank v. Haskell, 219 U.S. 104 (1911). Appar-

ently no case raised a challenge based on intrusion upon Congress's money powers. The inference from such decisions as Fox v. State of Ohio, 5 Howard 410 (U.S. 1847), and Westfall v. United States, 274 U.S. 256 (1927) (conduct may violate both state and federal criminal law, protecting the integrity of the money stock), is that, faced with the latter question, the Court would have held that state deposit-insurance legislation was constitutional until Congress affirmatively pre-empted the field.

266. Cf. Osborn v. Bank of the United States, 9 Wheaton 738, 859-63 (U.S. 1824) (Congress may constitutionally empower second bank to do general banking business, where such powers may be deemed reasonably necessary and proper to maintain an agency carrying out federal functions); Veazie Bank v. Fenno, 8 Wallace 533, 548 (U.S. 1869) (Congress has broad constitutional authority to provide a uniform national system of coin and currency); First National Bank of Bay City v. Fellows, ex rel. Union Trust Co., 244 U.S. 416, 420 (1917), Smith v. Kansas City Title & Trust Co., 255 U.S. 180, 208, 209 (1921), and Missouri ex rel. Burnes National Bank of St. Joseph v. Duncan, 265 U.S. 17, 24 (1924), as well as First Federal Savings & Loan Association of Wisconsin v. Loomis, 97 Fed. (2d) 831 (7th Cir. 1938) (Congress has broad authority to create financial institutions to perform federal functions, even though they are also empowered to do other banking or financial business not intrinsically subjects of federal concern). Two executive precedents incident to the economic crisis of 1933 seem pertinent. By Proclamation no. 2039, 6 March 1933, 48 Stat. Pt. 2, p. 1689, under 40 Stat. 41 (1917), the president closed all national and state banks and related financial institutions for a several-day emergency "holiday." See Norman v. Baltimore & Ohio Railroad Co., 294 U.S. 240, 295 (1935); Goldenweiser, 167-69; Redford, 769. In that year the general counsel of the Federal Reserve Board also gave his opinion that Congress had authority to impose uniform reserve requirements on all banks. Goldenweiser, 288, 289, noting opinion of Walter Wyatt, general counsel, Federal Reserve Board, 19 *Fed. Res. Bull.* 166 (1933). The Court consistently upheld Congress's authority to protect national banks against interference by state law, as in Mercantile National Bank at Dallas v. Langdeau, 371 U.S. 555 (1963). But these decisions may be distinguished as rendered within the frame of an assumption of co-existent banking systems. Various commentators can be found through the 1920s who assert that Congress lacks constitutional authority to nationalize banking, or even to require that all banks join the Federal Reserve System, and this opinion was stated in Annual Report of the Comptroller of the Currency (1924), p. 5. See Raymond P. Kent, 43, 57.

267. On the formal policy, see, e.g., First National Bank in St. Louis v. Missouri ex rel. Barrett, 263 U.S. 640, 656 (1924); Mercantile National Bank at Dallas v. Langdeau, 371 U.S. 555 (1963); First National Bank of Logan, Utah v. Walker Bank & Trust Co., 385 U.S. 252, 261 (1967). On complaints by national banks over their competitive disadvantages notwithstanding various pieces of federal legislation, see Raymond P. Kent, 43, 48-51. On the other hand, the care taken that national banks should meet state legal requirements so far as these did not impair federal functions reflected a sense of the practical power residing in institutions doing general banking business. Thus the much complained of congressional policy against branching by national banks—save within close limits related to state laws authorizing branching—was said to be peculiar to the national bank statutes and not to apply to savings institutions. North Arlington National Bank v. Kearney Federal Savings & Loan Association, 187 Fed. (2d) 564, 566 (3rd Cir. 1951), cert. denied, 342 U.S. 816 (1951); United States v. First Federal Savings & Loan Association, 151 Fed. Supp. 690, 697 (E.D. Wis. 1957). Cf. United States v. Manufacturers Hanover Trust Co.,

240 Fed. Supp. 867, 891 (S.D.N.Y. 1965). On the regime of Comptroller Saxon: Fischer, 70, 218-23, 229; Robertson, 149-54, 160. State banker concern that the Saxon policies might threaten the dual banking system mounted to a special pitch in 1963. See *New York Times,* 2 April 1963, p. 61, col. 2, 22 April, p. 35, col. 6, 2 May, p. 45, col. 1, 3 May, p. 30, col. 1, 4 May, p. 28, col. 6, 11 June, p. 47, col. 2, 8 October, p. 59, col. 3; cf. id., 6 November 1966, sec. 3, p. 1, col. 3. Fear that state banks might convert to federal charters gained urgency in New York when the Chase Manhattan Bank made the switch. Id., 13 February 1966, sec. 3, p. 1, col. 2, 6 November 1966, sec. 3, p. 1, col. 3.

268. Compare Cooley v. Board of Wardens of the Port of Philadelphia, 12 Howard 299 (U.S. 1851) with Hopkins Federal Savings & Loan Association v. Cleary, 296 U.S. 315 (1935). In an opinion dated 5 December 1932 Walter Wyatt, general counsel of the Federal Reserve Board, advised that Congress might validly impose uniform reserve requirements on all banks in the country as a necessary and proper incident of its general authority over the national money supply. 19 *Fed. Res. Bull.* 166 (1933). See Goldenweiser, 288, 289. Cf. notes 208 and 267, supra, and 279, infra. But compare Annual Report of the Comptroller of the Currency (1924), p. 5, dogmatically denying the authority of the United States to require that all banks be under national charters or become members of the Federal Reserve System. See Raymond P. Kent, 48, 57.

269. See note 262, supra.

270. Chandler, 9, 10; Commission on Money and Credit (2), 35; cf. Willis (1), 318, 398, 806-13. For the 1930s see 48 Stat. 162 (1933), sec. 8, creating Federal Reserve Act, Sec. 12B (f); 49 Stat. 684 (1935), sec. 101, creating Sec. 12B (y) (1); 53 Stat. 842 (1939), sec. 2, repealing (y) (1); Barger, 347; Robertson, 127; Welman, 15. In 1940 the Federal Reserve Board asked Congress to impose uniform reserve requirements on all banks, at a time when the board was worried about controlling excess reserves in the system; Congress did not act. Annual Report (1940), p. 69; see Barger, 348. In 1949 a subcommittee of the Joint Economic Committee made a comparable recommendation. Barger, ibid. In 1944 the board chairman (Eccles) proposed that the president use his statutory powers for executive reorganization to put in the board the regulatory jobs it shared with the comptroller and the FDIC, with the likelihood that the shift would lead to imposing uniform reserve requirements on all banks; the president doubted his power, or the need then of using it, and nothing was done. Ibid. In 1961 the Commission on Money and Credit, created by the private Committee for Economic Development, recommended that all insured commercial banks be required to become Federal Reserve members. Commission on Money and Credit (1), 77. A presidential Committee on Financial Institutions recommended in 1963 that nationally set reserve requirements be extended to all commercial banks and to some extent to savings institutions, but without requiring Federal Reserve membership; the committee later decided not to press the recommendation because of the breadth of policy issues it opened up. *New York Times,* 23 April 1963, p. 47, col. 1; 25 April 1963, p. 41, col. 2, 29 April 1963, p. 30, col. 1, 27 May 1963, p. 41, col. 5. The Federal Reserve Board in its Annual Report (1964), p. 202, recommended that all insured commercial banks be subject to nationally set reserve requirements but like the presidential committee the board did not suggest requiring membership in the system. *New York Times,* 23 March 1965, p. 51, col. 1.

271. Chandler, 81, 82; Culbertson, 166; Goldenweiser, 30, 31, 288. 289; Wallich and Wallich, 323, 324. For qualifying, or opposing views, see Raymond P. Kent 55-62; Sproul, 78.

272. Proclamation no. 2039, 6 March 1933, 48 Stat., Pt. 2, p. 1689. See Friedman and Schwartz, 11, 299, 328, 421. In a context as much political as legal, President Hoover's attorney general was of the opinion that the president lacked statutory authority to close all banks, or at least that there was such doubt on the matter that the action should be taken only with approval of the incoming president; Roosevelt was unwilling to give his approval before he took office. Goldenweiser, 166, 167.

273. 48 Stat. 886 (1934), sec. 78g. For application of the statute in cases involving state banks, see Cooper v. North Jersey Trust Co., 226 Fed. Supp. 972 (S.D.N.Y. 1964); Serzysko v. Chase Manhattan Bank, 290 Fed. Supp. 74 (S.D.N.Y. 1968), aff'd., 409 Fed. (2d) 1360 (2d Cir. 1969), cert. denied, 396 U.S. 904 (1969). Cf. Loss, 2:1241, 1242. See, also, Collateral Lenders Committee v. Board of Governors of the Federal Reserve System, 281 Fed. Supp. 899, 906-7 (S.D.N.Y. 1968). There seems to be no reported decision raising a Tenth Amendment issue as to sec. 78g.

274. 70 Stat. 133 (1956), 80 Stat. 236 (1966). The 1956 act applied by its terms to "any national banking institution or any state bank, savings bank or trust company"; the 1966 formulation plainly included all of these institutions, and more. The scope left for state regulation, even of state banks, in this respect was only to adopt more stringent limitations. Braeburn Securities Corporation v. Smith, 15 Ill. (3d) 55, 61-62, 153 N.E. (2d) 806, 810 (1958), appeal dismissed, 359 U.S. 311 (1959). Cf. Whitney National Bank in Jefferson Parish v. Bank of New Orleans & Trust Co., 379 U.S. 411, 424-25 (1965). Application of the federal statute to state-chartered banks may be seen in First Wisconsin Bankshares Corporation v. Board of Governors of the Federal Reserve System, 325 Fed. (2d) 946 (7th Cir. 1963), and Marine Corporation v. Board of Governors of the Federal Reserve System, id. 960 (7th Cir. 1963).

275. 74 Stat. 129 (1960), 80 Stat. 7 (1966). Application of this legislation to a state-chartered bank may be seen in United States v. Manufacturers Hanover Trust Co., 240 Fed. Supp. 867, 893 (S.D.N.Y. 1965). The statutes require premerger approval by the comptroller of the currency in regard to national banks, by the Federal Reserve Board in regard to state member banks, and by the FDIC in regard to state, nonmember, insured banks. These categories account for about 95 percent of all banks in the country. Lifland, 15, 18.

276. On the policy of competitive coexistence and the hopes originally pinned on it, see notes 203, 205, 206, 207, 209, 211, supra. In 1900 out of 12,427 banks, 3,731 were national and 8,696 were state. After sharp increases in both categories, soon after establishment of the Federal Reserve System, in 1915 of 27,390 banks, 7,597 were national and 19,793 were state. After many casualties of the depression, in 1940 of 14,534 banks, 5,164 were national and 9,370 were state. In 1960 of 13,503 banks, 4,542 were national and 8,961 were state. Commission on Money and Credit (2), 34.

277. On concentration of bank deposits in FRS members: Knipe, 9. Thus, Friedman and Schwartz, 196, estimate the distinction between member and nonmember banks as more important by mid-twentieth century than the distinction between national and state banks. On FDIC membership: Friedman and Schwartz, 437; Treiber, 250. New York experience bore witness to the strong functional pressures for all-inclusive FDIC membership. New York banks withdrew from the starting federal insurance plan in June 1934 in favor of their own insurance fund. They abandoned their plan, to enter the FDIC scheme in 1943, out of concern that a state-wide plan would not be strong enough to withstand a major emergency. Friedman and Schwartz, 437, note 17.

278. Cf. Culbertson, 159, 166; David C. Elliott, 200, 310, 311; Friedman and

Schwartz, 436. See *New York Times,* 28 October 1963, p. 41, col. 8 (state banks sensitive to appointments to board of FDIC).

279. American Bank & Trust Co. v. Federal Reserve Bank of Atlanta, Georgia, 256 U.S. 350 (1921), on a motion to dismiss, held that plaintiff stated a cause of action for an injunction, on allegations that defendant was accumulating checks drawn on plaintiff for presentation for cash solely to compel plaintiff's compliance with defendant's par clearance policy. "[T]he United States did not intend by [the Federal Reserve Act] . . . to sanction this sort of warfare upon legitimate creations of the States." Cf. Brookings State Bank v. Federal Reserve Bank of San Francisco, 277 Fed. 430 (D. Ore. 1921), s.c. 281 Fed. 222 (D. Ore. 1922), s.c. 291 Fed. 659 (D. Ore. 1923); Farmers & Merchants Bank of Catlettsburg, Ky. v. Federal Reserve Bank of Cleveland, 286 Fed. 610 (E.D. Ky. 1922). But, in the same case after a hearing on evidence, 262 U.S. 643 (1923), the Court found sufficient evidence to uphold the determinations by the courts below, that the federal reserve bank was not acting for the alleged purpose of sheer duress, but was presenting checks which came to it in the ordinary course of business, and which under the statutory ban on payment of exchange fees by federal reserve banks, it had no option but to present over the counter for cash when the drawee bank demanded a fee for a remittance. "Country banks are not entitled to protection against legitimate competition. Their loss here shown is of the kind to which business concerns are commonly subjected when improved facilities are introduced by others, or a more efficient competitor enters the field. It is *damnum absque injuria.*" Id., 648. Accord: First State Bank of Hugo v. Federal Reserve Bank of Minneapolis, 174 Minn. 535, 219 N.W. 908 (1928). Though it did not mention the point, the Court thus interpreted the Federal Reserve legislation as continuing the congressional policy of competitive coexistence determined upon in the national bank acts of 1863 and 1864. Also, though the Court mentioned no constitutional issue, the decision seems implicitly to rule that Congress may constitutionally sanction business competition of federal with state monetary institutions, where the arrangement is reasonably calculated to fulfill national policy on money. The vigor with which country banks pressed for protection of their exchange fees, both in opposition to enacting the Federal Reserve legislation and in opposition to its administration to foster clearance on other than a par basis, is shown in Willis (1), 398, 401, 406. On the reasonable, national grounds of a par clearance policy, see David C. Elliott, 300; Nussbaum, 168; Sproul, 74; Treiber, 249, note 9. 254, note 2, 262; Willis (1), 401, 413-14, 1054, 1061-63. In Farmers and Merchants Bank of Monroe, North Carolina v. Federal Reserve Bank of Richmond, Virginia, 262 U.S. 649 (1923), on the other hand, the Court said that the Federal Reserve legislation simply authorized the banks to offer clearing service and did not command establishment of universal par clearance; thus there was no conflict with federal policy where a state statute provided that, absent contrary explicit stipulation between the parties, the contract between a bank and its depositor should be taken to give the depositor's consent that the bank at its option pay checks drawn on it by drafts on its correspondent bank, when the check was presented by any federal reserve bank, post office, or express company or by the agent of any of these, thus so far relieving the bank of its common law obligation to pay cash on presentation over the counter. Id., 659. Of course, in the face of the statutory ban on paying exchange fees, the federal reserve bank was not obliged to collect checks for its depositors, wherever the drawee bank refused to remit funds except on allowance of an exchange charge. Id., 663, 665. Again, the Court in effect recognized a policy of competitive coexistence analogous to that set in 1863-64: Congress's purpose in the Federal Reserve Act provisions re-

garding check clearance "was to enable the Board to offer to non-member banks the use of its facilities which it was hoped would prove a sufficient inducement to them to forego exchange charges; but to preserve in non-member banks the right to reject such offer; and to protect the interests of member and affiliated non-member banks (in competition with the non-affiliated state banks) by allowing those also connected with the federal system to make a reasonable exchange charge to others than the reserve banks." Id., 666. The Court noted that eight states, including North Carolina, had passed comparable legislation which the Court characterized as intended "to protect . . . state banks from this threatened loss, which might disable them." Id., 658. The North Carolina act was entitled "an Act to promote the solvency of state banks" and provided as it did "in order to prevent accumulation of unnecessary amounts of currency in the vaults of" state banks. The Court's opinion does not mention constitutional issues. But, in this context, it seems fair to assume that the Court gave weight to the indicated concern of the North Carolina legislature to promote a legitimate purpose of the state economy; on its face, therefore, the state statute did not suggest an effort discriminatory against or nakedly hostile to legitimate federal policy, such as might have given occasion to bring McCulloch v. Maryland into play. Cf. Hopkins Federal Savings & Loan Association v. Cleary, 296 U.S. 315, 338 (1935), note 264, supra. Through mid-twentieth century the Federal Reserve System did not achieve universal par clearance, it settled down finally to the practice of not accepting for collection checks drawn on nonpar banks. Sproul, 74; Waage, 229. In 1957 the Federal Reserve handled about one-third of the approximately ten billion checks written in the country; many checks were, of course, cleared simply among banks within the same city; correspondent banks continued important in the process, however. Waage, 226, 228.

280. Note 259, supra. On the wide reach and dominating importance of open-market operations: Chandler, 234; David C. Elliott, 310, 311; Goldenweiser, 87; Knipe, 28-30, 151; Youngdahl, 139-40.

281. Chandler, 9, 41; Glass, 71; McAdoo, 218, 227, 242-43; Rowe 55; Warburg, 1:18, 19, 29, 34-35, 38, 46, 57, 410; Willis (1), 40, 84, 121, 146, 147, 278, 364, 436, 437. Warburg, 1:12, 38, 57-58, 67, 68, 99, points up the emotion with which contemporary opinion tended to see the issue as one simply between Wall Street control or agrarian political control. Symptomatic of the prevailing recognition that a central bank on the Biddle model would be unacceptable was the fact that the Aldrich Plan, produced in connection with the work of the National Monetary Commission (1911-12) and reflecting preferences of conservative, big-city bankers, provided for a central, national organization, but one which would preserve the autonomy of member banks, which would directly and indirectly have a large part in selecting the management. Dunne (3), 46; Hepburn, 396; Warburg, 1:374, 573, 575; Willis (1), 80-82. Symptomatic, too, was the fact that the kind of bill early put forward by Glass, before Wilson's decisive intervention, contemplated substantial autonomy in regional banks and was vague in regard to the strength to be put in whatever central supervisory office might be included. Cf. Glass, 223, 252; Link, 204; McAdoo, 220, 221; Warburg, 1:489-91; Willis (1), 143, 145. At one point in maneuvers over the proposals which eventuated in the Federal Reserve Act, Secretary of the Treasury McAdoo suggested that money control be lodged in a bureau of the Treasury. He later disclaimed serious intent for this idea and characterized it as a bargaining tactic to break banker resistance to providing for a substantial number of regional banks. McAdoo, 242-45; cf. Glass, 100, 109-10, 172, 223; Rowe, 87. The Federal Reserve Act allowed the regional banks to create branches, but this was simply for adminis-

trative convenience and by institutions not designed themselves directly to engage in commercial banking business, in contrast to Biddle's bank. Cf. Chandler, 9. The operations of a branch are reflected in Anderson v. Federal Reserve Bank of Boston, 69 Fed. (2d) 319 (5th Cir. 1934), cert. denied, 293 U.S. 562 (1934). In 1965 there were twenty-four branches among the twelve regional banks. Knipe, 8; Treiber, 249.

282. Glass, 223; Hepburn, 402, 404; Link, 203-4; McAdoo, 220, 221; Warburg, 1:18, 36, 82-84, 87, 101, 164, 170, 442, 423; Willis (1), 143, 145.

283. 38 Stat. 251 (1913), sec. 2. Cf. Chandler, 9, 10; David C. Elliott, 300; Glass, 191-92, 252-54; Link, 203, 204; Warburg, 1:422; Willis (1), 124-25, 134, 142, 146, 173, 278, 284, 286-87, 307, 308. Despite conflict, a unifying thread ran through the shaping of the Federal Reserve legislation, combining pressure for centralized facilities (especially reserves) and supervision and for substantial decentralization in control. Warburg, 1:67, 85, 88, 91, 97, 105, 113-14, 122, 410, 422, 423, 488. The intent that the regional organization of the system have working reality was in effect acknowledged in American Bank & Trust Co. v. Federal Reserve Bank of Atlanta, Georgia, 256 U.S. 350, 357 (1921). A bill brought by Georgia-incorporated banks to enjoin conduct of the Federal Reserve Bank of Atlanta was held to present a case properly removed to federal court on the defendant's motion, despite the provision of the Judicial Code that for purpose of suits against them national banking associations should be deemed citizens of the states in which they are located. The Court ruled that this provision did not apply to federal reserve banks, because "the reasons for localizing ordinary commercial banks do not apply to the Federal Reserve Banks created after the Judicial Code was enacted."

284. 30 *Opinions of the Attorney General* 497, 502 (1915); id., 517 (1916). The attorney general argued with some plausibility that, taken in their ordinary meaning, the statutory words authorizing the board to "readjust" district lines did not authorize abolishing a district, and that there was an implication of institutional continuity when the statute granted each bank, when organized, capacity to have succession for twenty years, unless it was dissolved sooner by an act of Congress, or forfeited its franchise for some violation of law. So, too, he reasonably argued that the statutory grant of authority to the banks to set up branches would provide–short of further action by Congress–for meeting any inconvenience in a bank's location which might arise from change in currents of regional business. Id., 504, 507, 522. On the other hand, the attorney general seems to betray sheer bias of policy–and probably to reflect the distrust of centralized, banker power which spurred opposition to the idea of reducing districts–when he argued, also, that to concede any authority in the board to reduce the districts below the original twelve must require conceding its authority to reduce the number "not only to eight but to six, four, or even one, if in the judgment of the Board 'due regard to the convenience and customary course of business' dictates that policy." Id., 506. Nothing is clearer in the legislative history of the Federal Reserve Act than the strong distrust of centralization which underlay its favor for regionalism. Notes 281, 282, supra. In particular, there had been sharp differences between those who wanted few (two or three) and those who wanted many (twenty or more) regional banks. Warburg, 1:93, 108, 112, 121-24, 423. Viewed in this light, the act's stipulation that the original organization committee might create no less than eight, nor more than twelve districts should properly be taken to strike a compromise, providing a framework likewise binding on the board in any authority it might be deemed given to change the number of districts. Cf. Warburg, 1:439. President Wilson strongly opposed any reduction in the number of districts, out of his belief that wise policy called for maintaining a larger rather than smaller number of

points of community contact for the system. Id., 452. See Bogen, 338; Clifford, 89-92; David C. Elliott, 300; Knipe, 8; Treiber, 249; Warburg, 1:429-37; Willis (1), 727-35.

285. Barger, 45; Clifford, 370-72, 380; Goldenweiser, 294; Treiber, 249, 251; Cf. Warburg, 1:94, 411. See, also, Peoples Bank v. Federal Reserve Bank of San Francisco, 58 Fed. Supp. 25, 31 (N.D. Cal. 1944), declaring that conditions imposed by the Federal Reserve Board on a state bank's membership in the system may not be litigated on the theory that the conditions constitute a cloud on the member bank's title to its stock in the Federal Reserve Bank, because such "shares are a mere incident to its membership" in the system, and as nontransferable and non-negotiable instruments have no market value and are redeemed upon termination of membership. Suspicious of banker influence, Congressman Wright Patman urged abolishing member-bank stock ownership in the Federal Reserve Banks. New York Times, 20 January 1964, p. 28, col. 8; 21 December 1964, p. 49, col. 7. The board's chairman was opposed; the step might drive some smaller banks out of the system, if they lost this attractive investment. Id., 22 January 1964, p. 50, col. 4. The New York Times editorially supported retiring member-banks' stock ownership, to emphasize the public character of the banks. Id., 30 June 1964, p. 32, col. 1. See Barger, 135-36.

286. On calculated ambiguities in the statute's demarcation of roles between the board and the banks, see Warburg, 1:473, 489-91, 496-97. On the banks' development of their supervisory role over individual members' credit operations, financial condition, and management quality: Barger, 279; Board of Governors, 132, 138, 195-99; Chapin, 23-25; Commission on Money and Credit (2), 89; Goldenweiser, 85, 86, 239, 294; Isbell, 29-32; Wallich and Wallich, 330, 331; Wyrick, 3, 5. Note the caution in Wyrick, 4, that bank supervision has only indirect relation to monetary policy and is not used as an instrument of monetary policy. Cf. Barger, 350. The board strengthened the hand of the regional banks by its usual practice of referring to the appropriate bank for initial disposition inquiries about the meaning or application of the governing statutes and regulations, submitted by others than the banks themselves. Attorney General's Committee (1), 48, 49. The board further enhanced the banks' supervisory roles by enlarging the matters over which it formally delegated power to the banks. New York Times, 12 June 1967, p. 67, col. 5. The banks' right to refuse to rediscount for their members was recognized, obiter, in Raichle v. Federal Reserve Bank of New York, 34 Fed. (2d) 912, 914, 915 (2d Cir. 1929). Congress confirmed this authority in 48 Stat. 162 (1933), sec. 3(a). The original act simply authorized the banks to extend such credit to their member banks as might be offered with due regard for the claims of other member banks. The 1933 act added that such extensions of credit must also be with due regard to "the maintenance of sound credit conditions, and the accommodation of commerce, industry, and agriculture." In terms that contrast sharply with the typical nineteenth-century focus simply on the soundness of banks vis à vis their creditors, the 1933 act went on to emphasize that the supervisory responsibility of the federal reserve banks should be directed, also, to the steadiness of the general monetary situation: "Each Federal Reserve Bank shall keep itself informed of the general character and amount of the loans and investments of its member banks with a view to ascertaining whether undue use is being made of bank credit for the speculative carrying of or trading in securities, real estate, or commodities, or for any other purpose inconsistent with the maintenance of sound credit conditions; and, in determining whether to grant or refuse advances, rediscounts or other credit accommodation, the Federal reserve banks shall give consideration to such information."

287. Chandler, 12, 66-67; Eccles, 168, 179; Rowe, 69, 82; Warburg, 1:171-73.

288. Chandler, 73, 74, 215, 216, 222; Rowe, 70, 71; Warburg, 1:141-42, 174-75.

289. 49 Stat. 684 (1935), sec. 201. Cf. Barger, 120.

290. 49 Stat. 684 (1935) sec. 205. Cf. note 297, infra. The creation of the FOMC was said to be not an invalid delegation of legislative power, in a dictum in Bryan v. FOMC, 235 Fed. Supp. 877, 882, note 2 (D. Montana 1964). There had been two intermediate steps toward the centralizing action taken in 1935. In 1930, after some friction among the regional banks, the board established an Open Market Policy Conference, with its governor as the representative from each bank, and an executive committee; all of the decisions of this body must be submitted to the board for approval, and without that approval the body might not act. Clifford, 111; Eccles, 169; Youngdahl, 121. The Banking Act of 1933, 48 Stat. 162, sec. 8 first put a statutory base under the open-market apparatus. Much like the board's 1930 action, the 1933 act created a Federal Open Market Committee of one representative from each bank; the members of the board might attend the committee's meetings, no bank might engage in open-market operations except within board regulations; if a bank did not wish to join in operations as decided upon by the committee, the bank might on due notice elect not to participate. Cf. Rowe, 88. Barger, 118, 120, attributes the 1935 change largely to the insistence of Marriner Eccles, as part of the terms on which he accepted appointment as governor of the Federal Reserve Board. On the position of the New York Federal Reserve Bank vis à vis the board in policy making, see Barger, 277-78, 360, and note 293, infra.

291. Goldenweiser, 280; Wallich and Wallich, 330; cf. Barger, 278, 279. But cf. New York Times, 24 January 1964, p. 37, col. 7 (three board members testify that they have never known bank president members of FOMC to line up solidly against board members, and that both groups often split among themselves); id., 10 February 1967, p. 51, col. 2 (examples of mixed voting patterns). Senator Glass strongly opposed putting control of open-market operations solely in the board and supported the view bitterly urged by the banks, that control over the banks' resources should not be put in a government agency which had no ownership in those assets. Inclusion of a minority of bank presidents in the FOMC was a compromise which probably saved this part of the legislation. Eccles, 181; Goldenweiser, 280. Later, Congressman Wright Patman—distrustful of banker influence—suggested abolishing the FOMC and putting its functions wholly in the board; though he continued to press his proposal, it won no material support in the Congress as a whole. New York Times, 20 January 1964, p. 28, col. 8; 24 January 1964, p. 37, col. 7; 9 March 1964, p. 45, col. 6; 30 June 1964, p. 32, col. 1; 21 December 1964, p. 49, col. 7. See Barger, 135-36.

292. Clifford, 132, 221; Friedman and Schwartz, 446, note 26. An analogous development was the creation of a board-controlled committee to supplant a committee directed by the regional banks in developing legislative programs for the system. So, too, the board insisted that the Federal Reserve Advisory Council should consult the board before issuing public statements. Eccles, 188-93.

293. 40 Stat. 232 (1917), secs. 5, 6; 48 Stat. 162 (1933), sec. 10. The 1933 act declared that the board "shall exercise special supervision over all relationships and transactions of any kind entered into by any Federal reserve bank with any foreign bank or banker" and that all such dealings be subject to the board's rules. Further, "no officer or other representative of any Federal reserve bank shall conduct negotiations of any kind with the officers or representatives of any foreign bank or banker without first obtaining the permission of the Federal Reserve Board." Compare, on the New York bank's leadership in foreign monetary relations in the 1920s, Chandler,

96-98, 255-57, 314-15, 319, 443; Goldenweiser, 277, 278. Because of its position at the country's key money market, the New York bank tended to play a large role in the conduct of domestic open-market operations before and after the events of 1923 and 1935. This was especially so because, in addition, the Treasury put much reliance on the New York bank for executing the fiscal-agent services which the government wanted from the system. Though the creation of the FOMC formally dispossessed the New York bank of title to a leading role in open-market policy, that bank was still used by the committee as prime agent to effectuate committee decisions. 56 Stat. 647, sec. 1 (1942) recognized the situation by providing that a representative of the New York Federal Reserve Bank should always sit on the FOMC. Cf. Clifford, 131; Knipe, 14; Rowe, 91. Moreover, the public records of the committee's decisions were cast in terms vague enough, and sometimes contradictory enough, to suggest that the operating desk at the New York bank still enjoyed a large discretion to influence what was done. Clifford, 98, 99, 101-3, 126, 279; Friedman and Schwartz, 190, 364, 366, Knipe, 116. Warburg, 1:122, suggests that the influence of the New York Federal Reserve Bank would have been relatively less in the system, had there been fewer regional banks and, as he views it, greater consequent financial weight in each of them.

294. 38 Stat. 251 (1913), sec. 14(d); Goldenweiser, 83, 147, 148. Warburg, 1:489-91, points out that some earlier versions of the Glass bill clearly put the fixing of discount rates in a central commission or board and that even as introduced in the House the Glass bill in effect put command in the board by requiring the regional banks to establish discount rates "each week, or as much oftener as required, subject to review and determination of the Federal Reserve Board." The terms of final compromise substituted in the banks authority to establish discount rates "from time to time, subject to review and determination" of the board. Despite its calculated ambiguity, this language, in the context of the legislative history, seems to show a prevailing intent to assign a greater decision-making role to the banks. Cf. id., 127-28, 174, 418. However, the board's assertion of control fitted the working facts of the credit market. Contrary to 1913 expectations, rediscount rates did not tend to vary by districts, but tended to conform to open-market rates in New York. This was because member banks, by custom as well as by the regional banks' discipline, borrowed from the banks not to make profit by lending to their customers at higher rates, but rather just to maintain their reserve positions. For this latter purpose the immediate determining factor tended to be the comparative cost to member banks of selling their holdings of government securities or of borrowing from the system; since rates on government securities were set in the New York money market, Federal Reserve rediscount rates tended to come to rest on a nationally uniform basis in comparison. Id., 86, 116, 117.

295. 32 *Opinions of the Attorney General* 81 (1919). The attorney general emphasized particularly that in the course of passage, sec. 14(d) was changed from declaring the power of Federal Reserve Banks to fix rediscount rates "subject to review" by the board to a power "subject to review and determination" by the board. Id., 83. The attorney general viewed the policy of the act as being to establish distinct roles for the banks and the board, with the board ultimately in control of general direction: "The scheme of the entire Act is to have Federal reserve banks in different parts of the country, so that their operations may be accommodated to the business needs of each section, and to vest final power in the Federal Reserve Board, so as to insure a conduct of business by each bank which will not be detrimental to the carrying out of the entire plan." Id., 83-84. See Link, 217; Warburg, 1:496. On

the controversy with the New York Bank: Barger, 57; Chandler, 163-65; Clifford, 115, 116. On the Chicago episode: Barger, 84; Goldenweiser, 83, 147, 148; Warburg, 1:488. Though as secretary of the treasury in 1919 Glass had sought the attorney general's opinion strengthening the board's hand, in 1927 as a senator he criticized the board for acting against the Chicago bank's judgment and indicated regret at the pressure he had earlier exerted for central authority. Goldenweiser, 147.

296. 49 Stat. 684 (1935), sec. 206(b). Cf. Goldenweiser, 147, 148.

297. 49 Stat. 684 (1935), sec. 205. Earlier, Raichle v. Federal Reserve Bank of New York, 34 Fed. (2d) 910, 916 (2d Cir. 1929), had in effect recognized the decisive power of the Federal Reserve Board in setting open-market policy as well as rediscount rates, by dismissing the bill brought by a private investor to enjoin the Federal Reserve Bank of New York from open-market operations, on the ground that the direct and supervisory authority given the board by the statute made the board an indispensable party. The Federal Reserve Act, said the court, was a recognition that the national bank system was defective because "it provided no central regulating force, and furnished no adequate means for controlling interest rates, or preventing or lessening financial stringencies and panics." Conversely, the court took note of "the wide powers of supervision and control given to the Federal Reserve Board over the whole Reserve System." Id., 912, 913. See, also, Geery v. Minnesota Tax Commission, 202 Minn. 366, 373, 375, 278 N.W. 594, 598 (1938). See, generally, Barger, 121; Clifford, 106; Friedman and Schwartz, 251, 445-47; Goldenweiser, 87. There was a policy precedent or analogy for the central authority created in 1935 over open-market operations in 38 Stat. 251 (1913), sec. 11(b), empowering the Federal Reserve Board on vote of at least five of its seven members to require a federal reserve bank to rediscount paper of another federal reserve bank at rates fixed by the board. There was a contest at the drafting stage over including this central authority, but it was finally inserted as a power desirable for the effectiveness of the new organization as a system. Glass, 151. Inclusion of this authority and omission of a comparable provision connected with the authority given the regional banks to trade in government securities on the open market make a consistent pattern in terms of the thinking of 1913, in which rediscounting was to be the system's key money-supply control instrument, and open-market operations were regarded as a minor auxiliary. See notes 341, 342, infra. The authority conferred on the board in 1913 thereafter stayed in the Federal Reserve legislation, but does not seem ever to have been of critical importance in actual operations—an outcome which fits the general experience of the system, that rediscounting did not prove the decisive power it was forecast to be. Cf. Willis (2), 83. Barger, 121, suggests that the background availability of the board's authority to require any reserve bank to rediscount for another was what permitted effective open-market operations before 1933-35, even though the prior law allowed any regional bank to decline to participate in open-market dealings. He offers no evidence in support, however.

298. Goldenweiser, 87. Cf. note 280, supra.

299. 49 Stat. 684 (1935), sec. 207. Member bank reserve ratios had stood fixed in the statutes from 1917 to 1933. Barger, 55, finds in the 1917 reduction of reserve requirements from the 1913 level evidence of the failure to see bank reserves as an instrument to regulate credit; the failure is the more striking in view of the fact that in 1906 Secretary of the Treasury Shaw suggested this control technique. Id., 119. Congress first gave the board authority to alter reserve requirements in the Thomas Amendment to the Agricultural Adjustment Act of 1933, 48 Stat. 31, sec. 46, but subject to the approval of the president. In dropping this requirement of presidential

approval, while making the authority permanent, the 1935 act underlined Congress's acceptance of a dominant role for the board—probably from conservatives' fear of inflation—though the act did set a ceiling on the board's increase of reserve requirements at double the reserve levels set in the 1917 amendments to the Federal Reserve Act. Barger, 119; Friedman and Schwartz, 447, 448; Jacoby, 213; Treiber, 256, 260; Wallich and Wallich, 329, 334, 335.

300. Note 273, supra. This authority was implemented in Federal Reserve Regulation T in 1934, in regard to brokers and dealers, and by Regulation U in 1936, in regard to banks. Bogen, 345, 350; Grove, 141, 155; Friedman and Schwartz 448; Wallich and Wallich, 330. Friedman and Schwartz, 516, estimate that the grant of this power and its use "had negligible monetary consequences"; the fact of the grant is, nonetheless, relevant as an indicator of congressional policy on the general power position of the board. In 1963 an SEC special study of the stock exchanges felt that such limited evidence as was available indicated that unregulated lending sources could still pour an unsettling amount of speculative money into the stock market. *New York Times,* 12 August 1963, p. 29, col. 2. Another loophole was indicated when the Federal Reserve Board proposed that regulation be extended to affect over-the-counter as well as listed stocks. Id., 23 March 1965, p. 51, col. 1.

301. 48 Stat. 162 (1933), sec. 11(b); 49 Stat. 684 (1935), sec. 324(c); Wallich and Wallich, 328, 329.

302. Consumer credit controls were first given the board by Executive Order No. 8843, 9 August 1941, were ended by Congress as of 1 November 1947, were reauthorized by Congress from August 1948 to 30 June 1949 only in regard to installment credit, were restored by Congress under the pressures of the Korean War in September 1950 (with Regulation W issued under this act), were relaxed on Congress's direction in midsummer of 1951 (with Regulation W suspended by the board in May 1952), and Congress allowed the authority to lapse with the repeal of certain Defense Production Act amendments in 1952, though the board had recommended continuance of the authority. 61 Stat. 921 (1947); 62 Stat. 1291 (1948); 64 Stat. 798 (1950), sec. 601; 65 Stat. 131 (1951), sec. 106(a); 66 Stat. 296 (1952), sec. 116(a). See Bogen, 345, 346; Friedman and Schwartz, 448, 555, 580, 604, 611, note 8. Friedman and Schwartz, 577-78, do not estimate such controls as having major effect on the money stock as a whole. In 1950 Congress also gave the president temporary authority over real estate credit, and he delegated this authority to the board over new construction only; the authority was suspended pursuant to Congress's indicated policy of relaxation in September 1952 and Congress ended it in June 1953. 64 Stat. 798 (1950), sec. 602; 66 Stat. 296 (1952), sec. 116(a), (b); 67 Stat. 129 (1953), sec. 11(a); Bogen, 346; Grove, 163-68.

303. Note 293, supra.

304. Cf. Warburg, 1:169-70, 410. So, Raichle v. Federal Reserve Bank of New York, 34 Fed. (2d) 910, 912, 913 (2d Cir. 1929), noting that the key defect of the old national banking system was that "it provided no central regulating force," emphasized that a prime feature of the 1913 act was "the wide powers of supervision and control given to the Federal Reserve Board over the whole Reserve System."

305. Part One, supra, notes 211, 212, 243. See Friedman and Schwartz, 462 ("the most far-reaching alteration in [the] . . . legal structure [of the money system] since the departure from gold during the Civil War and subsequent resumption in 1879"), 463 (law-declared government monopoly on possession of monetary gold a "step . . . unprecedented in the United States"), 474 ("it is clearly a fiduciary rather than a commodity standard, but it is not possible to specify briefly who manages its

quantity and on what principles"). Cf. Dawson, 649, 651, 653, 665-66, 674; Drucker, 61, 62; Sutton, et al., 239-45.

306. Norman v. Baltimore and Ohio Railroad Co., 294 U.S. 240, 303, 304 (ready acceptance of sweeping congressional authority over the system of money in general), 306 (retroactivity the distinctive issue here) (1935). See notes 218-23, supra. Cf. Dawson, 665, 666, 669; Hart, 1062, 1066. How firm set was the doctrine—retroactively apart—was indicated in Horne v. Federal Reserve Bank of Minneapolis, 344 Fed. (2d) 725, 729 (8th Cir. 1965), when for want of a substantial constitutional question the court sustained entry of a summary judgment against plaintiffs who refused to accept Federal Reserve notes as legal tender offered them in exchange for Canadian dollars.

307. Part One, supra, notes 211-13, 241-43. Cf. Post and Willard, 1227.

308. Cf. United States v. Darby, 312 U.S. 100, 115, 116 (1941); Dawson, 666, note 36, 667, note 38. Veazie Bank v. Fenno, 8 Wallace 533, 548 (U.S. 1869) apparently ruled out consideration of Congress's "motive" (i.e., the presence of an illegitimate purpose collateral with a legitimate one) in the exercise of power over the currency. See note 210, supra, and compare Ely, 1210, 1212, 1281, 1302-6.

309. Hacker, 175; Handlin and Handlin, 10, 14, 22-23; Hartz, 7-9, 206, 291; Myers, 29; Morison and Commager, 1:207-8.

310. Hepburn, 89-92; Myers, 78-82; North (1), 70-71. The Mexican War was too short and demanded too little of a buoyant economy to occasion problems over the value of money. Cf. Myers, 136-37; North (1), 66.

311. Hammond (3), 231, 249, 307; Morison and Commager, 1:710-11; Myers, 171-72; Nussbaum, 102-4. Like the Mexican War, the Spanish-American War was too limited in its demands on the economy to produce any significant problem of monetary policy. Hepburn, 375; Nussbaum, 148.

312. George P. Adams, Jr., 5-6, 100, 107, 130, 132, 138; Backman, 10, 17-19; Hardy, 4-9, 10, 11, 15, 23, 32-35, 37-38, 67; Krooss (1), 466, 467; Myers, 285-87; Nussbaum, 168-69; Stein (1), 89, 90, 123, 124.

313. Friedman and Schwartz, 557; Harris (1), 6, 7, 9, 15; Krooss (1), 469; Myers, 356-59.

314. Prelude, supra, notes 43-46.

315. United States v. L. Cohen Grocery Co., 255 U.S. 81, 83 (1921). The solicitor general cites, notably, Munn v. Illinois, 94 U.S. 113 (1876), and German Alliance Insurance Co. v. Lewis, 233 U.S. 389 (1914).

316. United States v. L. Cohen Grocery Co., 255 U.S. 81, 88-89 (1921). The Court there says that the existence or nonexistence of a state of war is "negligible, and we put it out of view," but this must be read as applied to the vagueness issue, and without reference to the grounds of Congress's substantive power.

317. Yakus v. United States, 321 U.S. 414, 422 (1944) ("That Congress has constitutional authority to prescribe commodity prices as a war emergency measure, and that the Act was adopted by Congress in the exercise of that power, are not questioned here, and need not now be considered save as they have a bearing on the procedural features of the Act.") See Case v. Bowles, 327 U.S. 92, 101 (1946).

318. The Court's focus was sharply on the war-needs basis of the legislation. Cf. Bowles v. Willingham, 321 U.S. 503, 519 (1944); Woods v. Miller, 333 U.S. 138, 141, 143-44 (1948). So in Case v. Bowles, 327 U.S. 92, 102 (1946), in construing the federal price control act to apply to sales of timber by a state from land owned by the state under grant from the United States for support of public schools, and in holding the act so construed to be constitutional, the Court stressed solely the fact

that the regulation was "in order to carry on war." To exempt state transactions here would make the constitutional power of the United States to make war "inadequate for its full purpose. And this result would impair a prime purpose of the Federal Government's establishment."

319. A. L. A. Schechter Poultry Corp. v. United States, 295 U.S. 495, 537 (unlawful delegation), 542 (act exceeds commerce power) (1935). The Court treated the delegation point first and at vigorous length. Id., 529-42. In its discussion of the commerce clause point, id., 542-50, the Court seemed particularly troubled by the wages-hours regulations under the code; its condemnation, thus, was not addressed to general price-fixing regulations as such. Compare the like focus in Carter v. Carter Coal Co., 298 U.S. 238 (1936). The force of these decisions is thrown into much doubt by later rulings more ready to recognize that a whole pattern of economic relations may be subject to federal regulation as affecting interstate commerce, though the particular incidents of the patterns involve local dealings such as Congress might not ordinarily regulate. NLRB v. Friedman-Harry Marks Clothing Co., 301 U.S. 58 (1937); United States v. Darby, 312 U.S. 100 (1941); Wickard v. Filburn, 317 U.S. 111 (1942).

320. 60 Stat. 23 (1946).

321. Auerbach, 193; Bailey, 9-11, 45, 47, 105, 130-32, 161, 171, 224-25; Burns and Samuelson, 46; Nourse, 70-74, 335, 338; Rostow, 128; Stark, 322; Stein (2), 201, 214; cf. Condliffe, 255, 260; Flash, 287. Auerbach, ibid., suggests that sec. 2 of the act, in directing the federal government to pursue the statutory goals by means which are "consistent with . . . other essential considerations of national policy," might be taken to warrant weighing the value of price stability in the policy mix.

322. Barger, 78-81; Chandler, 13-14; Friedman and Schwartz, 163-408, 626; Nourse, 51; Raskind, 300, 303, 304-10; Rostow, 145. In 1931-32 bills were proposed to charge the Federal Reserve to re-flate prices of commodities and then to stabilize them; the bills did not pass. Barger, 109-12. To say that the system was slow to avow clear responsibility for steadying the purchasing power of money is not to say that concern for the price level was not on occasion a factor in its policies. Barger, 232, notes 1923, 1936-37, 1950-53, 1955-57, and 1958-59 as times in which the system tightened credit partly under the influence of rising prices. Its bias was usually for deflation; much less often did it act to promote price rises, though it seems to have had this aim in cheap-money periods in the 1930s.

323. Friedman and Schwartz, 596, 628-29; Raskind, 311-12; Stark, 324; cf. Clifford, 33, 34.

324. Auerbach, 193, 251; Flash, 287, 288; Sheahan, 13, 15, 16. On the council's relative emphasis on private power in the market as a prime source of concern, see Auerbach, 195, 197, 204, 212, 216, 220-21, 251; Condliffe, 254, 257, 258, 266; Sheahan, 16. There was earlier worry over inflation, and this found expression in connection with council reports, but without such clear-cut drawing upon the policy found in the 1946 act as a warrant for restrictive government action. Cf. Nourse, 210-11, 214, 238, 316. Dewald and Johnson, 187, find that 1952-61 monetary policy objectives stressed high employment and growth over price stability; they find that public concern over price stability and the international balance of payments developed only toward the end of this span.

325. In the fall of 1947 President Truman asked Congress to reinstate lapsed authority for price and wage controls; the proposal never had a chance of success in a hostile Republican Congress. Barger, 149. President John F. Kennedy's Council of Economic Advisers rejected mandatory price controls as "neither desirable in the

American tradition nor practical in a diffuse and decentralized continental economy." Auerbach, 213, 251; cf. id., 195, 207, 209, 212, 245, 251. See Sheahan, 185-86. Cf. Burns and Samuelson, 37. Even the "guideposts" were attacked by Republican members of the Joint Committee on the Economic Report in 1964 and 1966, as representing undesirable, cloaked official control of the private economy. Auerbach, 244. Government, indeed, was not without means of compulsion, though it did not accept a formal scheme of compulsory price controls. Thus it might threaten to invoke the antitrust laws, to withdraw government contracts, or to sell commodities out of government stockpiles. Auerbach, 213, 216-18, 220, 226, 250; Sheahan, 174, 175.

326. Cf. Arthur S. Miller, 174. Of particularly persuasive relevance to sustaining general price controls by the federal government in peacetime would be Nebbia v. New York, 291 U.S. 502, 531, 536-37 (1934) (under due process of law, there is nothing peculiarly sacrosanct against public regulation about prices; price regulation is not limited to public utilities, but may apply wherever reasonable grounds in public interest exist); Wickard v. Filburn, 317 U.S. 111 (1942), emphasizing (id., 120) "the embracing and penetrating nature" of the commerce power, and that "it is well established by decisions of this Court that the power to regulate commerce includes the power to regulate the prices at which commodities in that commerce are dealt in and practices affecting such prices," id., 128, as well as ruling that wheat acreage quotas did not offend due process of law, though the particular quotas burdened individuals in the interest of a general program, for "control of total supply upon which the whole statutory plan is based, depends upon control of individual supply." Id., 130.

327. On the public character of the central board: David C. Elliott, 297, 298; Glass, 82, 112-16, 178 (cf., id., 54, 80, 86, 151, 162, 165, 166, 171-74, 194, 205, 223, 241); Link, 204, 217; Warburg, 1:55, 100, 126, 412, 422; Willis (1), 250-52, 256-56, 496. Warburg, 1:422, notes that Wilson's first appointees included three bankers. For comparison with the Aldrich Plan, see Glass, 681; Link, 204; Warburg, 1:22, 50, 59, 99, 108, 412; cf. Willis (1), 389-90, 393, 398, 404, 430. On the government's share in creating regional bank boards: Hepburn, 412; Land, 19, 20; Myers, 261. The 1935 act's treatment of the office of chief executive of the regional banks was a compromise. The House proposed that the former office of governor be merged with that of chairman of the bank's board and that this official be named by the regional bank's board, but that his continuance in office must be approved every three years by the Federal Reserve Board and that he become one of the government-appointed members of the regional bank board. The Senate responded to objections that this arrangement would put the management of each regional bank in a chief executive basically responsible to the government, and the Senate prevailed. Rowe, 81, 83, 84; cf. Clifford, 71, note 8.

328. Chandler, 9, 10; Hepburn, 411, 412; Land, 19, 20, 24, 30; Treiber, 250; Trescott, 158-59. But cf. notes 262, 269, supra.

329. Clifford, 371, 372, 373, 378, 379, 388; Knipe, 10, 207; Mints, 281-82; Treiber, 248, 250, 251; Warburg, 1:94, 170, 411; Willis (1), 173, 250-52, 256-57, 496.

330. Commission on Money and Credit (1), 84, 89; Glass, 116, 118; Myers, 261. Cf. Eccles, 188-91.

331. Clifford, 133, 332; Commission on Money and Credit (1), 90; Knipe, 15; Wallich and Wallich, 330.

332. Barger, 45; Chandler, 12, 14-15, 195-98, 216, 235; Clifford, 370, 380, 381; Eccles, 168, 179; Goldenweiser, 276, 294, 296; Knipe, 10, 32-33. Of symbolic as well

as practical significance for subordinating the market freedom of member banks to the requirements of the system is Continental Bank & Trust Co. of Salt Lake City, Utah v. Woodall, 239 Fed. (2d) 707, 710 (10th Cir. 1957), cert. denied, 353 U.S. 909 (1957), holding that under 38 Stat. 258 (1913), sec. 9, the Federal Reserve Board may exercise continuing as well as initial authority to determine the adequacy of a member bank's capital structure. Compare *Barron's,* 25 July 1960, p. 1, where this conservative journal approves such Federal Reserve supervision on the ground that the alternative—to protect the security of the money system—would be bail-outs by the Federal Reserve Board or the FDIC, which would lead toward "hand[ing] over all decision-making to an omnipotent Washington."

333. Commission on Money and Credit (2), 35, 36; Knipe, 9; Trescott, 270, 271; Treiber, 250.

334. Clifford, 370, 375, 380, 381, 389; Eccles, 166, 168, 169; Friedman and Schwartz, 190, 241, 447; Goldenweiser, 277-78, 281, 282, 292, 293, 295; Knipe, 11, 14, 16; Treiber, 253.

335. Goldenweiser, 280; Knipe, 15.

336. David C. Elliott, 300; Friedman and Schwartz, 342, 346, 351; Knipe, 18-20; Sproul, 74; cf. Warburg, 1:24; Willis (1), 74, 80. Prophetically, big-city bankers opposed the 1913 legislation particularly because they disliked the centralization of reserves under it. In part their opposition was from fear of losing profitable business with their correspondent banks, but also because they feared the leverage for public (to them, "political") controls that centralized reserves would offer. Glass, 63, 83, 151; Warburg, 1:12, 16, 19, 45; Willis (1), 394, 396, 398, 401, 406.

337. Early expectation was that the discount rate would be the Federal Reserve's prime control instrument. Chandler, 235; Friedman and Schwartz, 193; Goldenweiser, 83; Polakoff, 191, 192. The statutory embodiments of the real bills faith in semiautomatic regulation of the money supply were in 38 Stat. 251 (1913), secs. 13 (Federal Reserve lending to member banks on eligible paper), 14 (issue of Federal Reserve notes against 100 percent eligible paper pledge, plus 40 percent gold reserve); 40 Stat. 232 (1917), sec. 7 (60 percent eligible paper suffices, with 40 percent gold reserve continued). 39 Stat. 752, 753 (1916) authorized federal reserve banks to lend to their members on the members' own notes, thus making it unnecessary that the member banks rediscount their customers' paper. The change forecast the end of rediscounting as the standard form for member-bank borrowing at the reserve. The 1916 act continued to pay tribute to the real-bills criterion to govern the process, insofar as it stipulated that member banks' notes be secured by eligible paper. But it signalled a move toward more flexible money-management authority in the Federal Reserve by authorizing pledge of government obligations as alternative security. The statute implied uneasiness about this relaxation, however, when it limited members to borrowing on their own notes for only fifteen days at a time. 48 Stat. 162 (1933), sec. 9 distinguished between borrowing on pledge of government securities for fifteen days and on pledge of eligible commercial paper for ninety days. Cf. Barger, 45, 54, 65, 119.

Real-bills dogma partly reflected exaggerated attention to liquidity in the sense of convertibility of deposits to cash, at the expense of attention to adjusting total money supply to the needs and timing of a productive economy. Cf. Barger, 48-49; Friedman and Schwartz, 192. But the doctrine was attractive to conservatives because it promised to minimize official intervention in the market. Clay J. Anderson, 169, 170; Berle and Pederson, 16, 119-21; Chandler, 14, 133, 134; Eccles, 171, 172; Friedman and Schwartz, 169, 191, 253; Goldenweiser, 125, 126; Mints, 260, 264-65,

284; Polakoff, 192. The doctrine was illusory as a promise of functional adjustment of money and the economy, however. In essence it meant passive response to market swings to which it offered no resistance and on which it offered no basis for judgment. Chandler, 187, 235; Friedman and Schwartz, 191; Knipe, 32-33. Though it seemed to hold bank credit to "sound" uses, it did not in fact do so, because it provided no check on the end uses to which banks put the credit they obtained by pledging eligible paper, and ignored the interchangeable effects of other factors which might affect the creation of deposit-check money, notably gold inflows and member banks' open-market sales of government securities. Clay J. Anderson, 169; Chandler, 187, 194, 195, 197, 198; Friedman and Schwartz, 193, 253; Goldenweiser, 111, 126, 149, 150, 153, 154; Polakoff, 191, 192. Even as "security," eligible paper was a feeble resource; it might not be available as a pledge base for Federal Reserve lending when business was bad and such rescue credit was most needed; under pressure, lending federal reserve banks probably could not realize on the security without bringing on the disaster they wished to avert; in any case the requirement of special security seems irrelevant in regard to notes which by statute were from the start declared obligations of the United States and a first lien on all assets of the federal reserve bank to which they were issued. Friedman and Schwartz, 191, 253; Goldenweiser, 125, 128; Mints, 264-65; Polakoff, 191, 192; Timberlake, 198, 200, 201. The statutory insistence on the real-bills formula to govern Federal Reserve lending and note issues was ended, first temporarily, and ultimately on a permanent basis, in 47 Stat. 56 (1932), secs. 1, 2, 3 (the Glass-Steagall Act); 49 Stat. 684 (1935), sec. 204; 59 Stat. 237 (1945), sec. 1. See Wallich and Wallich, 319-20, 330. The initial step was taken in 1932 because of fears in Congress and in the White House that the Federal Reserve would not be able to service its member banks, for want of suitable collateral for loans, and would itself be brought to a financial crisis if it must issue increasing amounts of Federal Reserve notes simply against gold. Friedman and Schwartz, 400, 404-6, and Timberlake, 161, 198, do not think that the evidence shows that a crisis existed in fact; in their appraisal, eligible paper was sufficiently available, and a properly bold use of open-market purchases by the Federal Reserve could have enabled member banks to foster business borrowing which would have provided more eligible paper. But they do not deny that a crisis was envisaged in congressional and White House circles, if not within the Federal Reserve itself. Cf. Friedman and Schwartz, 321, 404. Other commentators, though without making the specific case which Friedman and Schwartz spell out from the record, apparently make a contrary estimate, concluding that the statutory limits and the business situation did join to create a crisis in fact. Clay J. Anderson, 165; Barger, 101-3, 115; Eccles, 171, 172, 181; Goldenweiser, 123, 124, 128, 159-60, 161. Cf. Chandler, 185 (fear for Federal Reserve gold position in 1920-21). The requirement of a gold reserve for deposits was abolished by 79 Stat. 5 (1965), sec. 1; that for Federal Reserve notes by 82 Stat. 50 (1968), sec. 3.

Another sign of official concern for the Federal Reserve gold position in the crisis atmosphere in which the New Deal was launched, as well as of the reluctant yielding to the need for more scope for Federal Reserve money-supply control, was 48 Stat. 1 (1933), sec. 401, authorizing issue of federal reserve bank notes to regional banks on their own notes, secured by direct obligations of the United States or other suitable security, in lieu of federal reserve notes. A few such federal reserve bank notes were issued as a token in 1933. But the reopening of the commercial banks brought a return flow of regular currency from the hoarding public which removed the need for this reborn, Aldrich-Vreeland-type emergency paper. The federal reserve bank notes which had been printed were issued in World War II to save labor and materials. Authority for their continuance was withdrawn by 59 Stat. 237 (1945), sec. 3. Cf. Friedman and Schwartz, 328, 421-22; Goldenweiser, 168, 172.

An issue related to the note-issuing power of federal reserve banks loomed large enough in the 1913 debates over monetary reform to appear, at one point, as sufficient to block any central-bank-style change. Bryan—representing a still vigorous agrarian distrust of bankers—insisted dogmatically that only the government might legitimately create money. He saw this principle offended by provision for federal reserve notes issued by federal reserve banks two-thirds of whose directors would be private persons chosen by private constituencies of member banks, and backed by pledge of private commercial paper. In a move critical to the negotiations with the Bryan Democrats, the administration persuaded Bryan that his principle of government issue of all money was satisfied by the declaration—the authorship of which we do not know—written into the Federal Reserve Act, that federal reserve notes were obligations of the United States. Dorfman, 3:339; Dunne (3), 49-50; Glass, 122-25, 137, 190, 199; Link, 206-13; Warburg, 1:20, 78, 82, 105, 110, 126, 422; Willis (1), 53, 196, 247-50, 429, 456, 467. Along with the provision for a board of "public" members, the obligations-of-the-United-States clause became, on the other side, a point of opposition from bankers who saw it as another forecast of politically inspired fiat money. Nonetheless, the provision stayed in. Chandler, 35, 36; Glass, 190, 199; Link, 218, 225, 229, 236; Willis (1), 429. Important as the matter had been to bargaining through the legislation, it never emerged as operationally significant. Barger, 44; Bradford, 24; Chandler, 39; Harrod, 42. Indeed, Carter Glass quotes Wilson's contemporary estimate, that the "obligations" clause was a "shadow," the concession of which would save the substance of the bill, to give the Federal Reserve capacity to provide a flexible currency. Glass, 125. The declaration lost any substance it ever had as a distinct security when Congress made federal reserve notes legal tender for all public as well as private debts and concurrently forbade private circulation of gold. 48 Stat. 31, 52, 113 (1933); 79 Stat. 255 (1965). See Bernstein, 104, Rostow, 49. Bryan's original objection was in substance involved in contentions that the issue of federal reserve notes was unlawful coining of money by the banks, as was also creation of book credits by the banks, in alleged violation of U.S. Constitution, art. I, sec. 8. But the contenders were held to lack standing—claiming simply as taxpayers or citizens, without showing infringement of any right distinctive to them—in Horne v. Federal Reserve Bank of Minneapolis, 344 Fed. (2d) 725, 728 729 (8th Cir. 1965), and Koll v. Wayzata State Bank, 397 Fed. (2d) 124, 126, 127 (8th Cir. 1968). Cf. United States v. Anderson, 433 Fed. (2d) 856, 858 (8th Cir. 1970).

338. On establishment of the full statutory control of the federal reserve banks and board over lending to member banks, see note 286, supra. The board's Regulation A set out the restrictive policy on member bank borrowing from the system. Access to Federal Reserve discount facilities, it declared, "is granted as a privilege." In what became its settled form Regulation A further said that "Federal Reserve credit is generally extended on a short-term basis," that long-term credit would be available for "unusual situations," but that "under ordinary conditions the continuous use of Federal Reserve credit by a member bank over a considerable period of time is not regarded as appropriate." 12 C.F.R. 201.0 (1971); see Polakoff, 197, note 13; Wilson, 251, 255. On official administrative practice as implementing these declared attitudes: Clay J. Anderson, 47; Goldenweiser, 86; David H. McKinley, 93; Treiber, 257, 259; Youngdahl, 115. The administrative practice dated from the mid-1920s, Barger, 59. It was reaffirmed by the board in 1955, when member bor-

rowing increased after years of abeyance. 54 *Fed. Res. Bull.* 545, 546 (1968); Friedman and Schwartz, 233, 268-69; *New York Times,* 30 July 1968, p. 49, col. 6. Member bank custom tended to reinforce the official pressure from the mid-1920s. Friedman and Schwartz, 233; Goldenweiser, 86, 116; David H. McKinley, 90, 92, 93, 106, 107; Polakoff, 193, 205; Youngdahl, 115, 124, 139.

Youngdahl, 124, observes that member banks tended to feel pressure more from the level of their free reserves—or, conversely, the level of their borrowings from the Federal Reserve—than from the discount rate. This phenomenon appeared in a different guise in the effectiveness of Federal Reserve open-market operations. Chandler, 222-29, 233, 234; Knipe, 283, 284, 295; Polakoff, 194; Treiber, 253, 256, 258. On the clumsiness and doubtful effect of discount rate changes within the pattern set by Federal Reserve policy and member bank custom: Clay J. Anderson, 23, 24, 44, 46; Goldenweiser, 136, 137; Knipe, 122, 281, 283, 294; David H. McKinley, 111; Treiber, 256. However, some opinion assigned a higher effect to use of the discount rate, at least at some points in Federal Reserve history. Cf. Clay J. Anderson, 45, 46; Goldenweiser, 26, 27; Knipe, 281; Polakoff, 196-98. The Federal Reserve committee suggestions for more flexible use of discounting were set out in 54 *Fed. Res. Bull.* 545 (1968). See, also, George W. Mitchell statement to the Joint Economic Committee, 11 September 1968, id., 743. Cf. Berle and Pederson, 124, 125; *New York Times,* 20 November 1965, p. 43, col. 3, 12 November 1966, p. 37, col. 3, 30 July 1968, p. 49, col. 6, 22 July 1968, p. 1, col. 6, 29 October 1968, p. 63, col. 5. The Joint Economic Committee seems not to have objected to the general pattern suggested, but the suggestions were not implemented at any time through 1970. See *New York Times,* 24 September 1968, p. 63, col. 5, 6 February 1969, p. 51, col. 5. Contrasting with the 1968 suggestion was the conservatism of the Commission on Money and Credit, created by the Committee for Economic Development, which in 1961 advocated retaining the discount facility as a source of temporary credit with relatively infrequent changes in the discount rate. Commission on Money and Credit (1), 64, 65.

339. Barger, 252-56, and Goldenweiser, 53, 56, comment on twentieth-century monetary theorists who suggested the desirability of a 100 percent reserve requirement against demand deposits. The implications of a fractional reserve requirement situation for the allocation of money control between the law and the market are indicated in Barger, 253, and Tobin, 414-18. Tobin points up the discipline imposed by market risks on commercial banks, as well as the opportunity for discretion in allocating resources and the flexibility in response to general business and consumer demands for money, involved in a regime of commercial banks operating against fractional reserves. Cf. Barger, 255. On the other hand, legally required, fractional reserves—and legal limits on interest—make the law a limiting factor on market operations, by changing banks' calculations of the profitability of lending, from what those calculations would be without the law's restrictions. Tobin, 416. Cf. Barger, 209-11, 260, 316. Moreover, central-bank open-market purchases, as a technique of effecting legal regulation of reserves, may inject another law-created factor different from market influence, by tending to lower interest rates and thus make lending less attractive to the banks than it might otherwise be. Tobin, 417, 418. Thus, though experience shows no tight or automatic relation between reserves and bank deposits, the bank discretion thus indicated is not without substantial subjection to the law. Id., 417. Barger, 316, suggests that open-market operations be judged a superior money-supply regulatory technique because they do not raise the issue of the level of member banks' earnings, as this is inherently presented by decisions on the level of

required reserves; thus open-market operations may keep an extraneous issue from intruding on monetary policy. Cf. *New York Times,* 21 September 1962, p. 37, col. 1 (bankers' advisory committee to Comptroller of the Currency recommends less imposition of reserve requirements by law, in order to improve banks' earnings).

340. The board's new authority applied to demand or time deposits or both. 49 Stat. 684 (1935), sec. 207. Note 299, supra, provides the background of the act. On the sharp impact of formal changes in required reserves: Barger, 315, 320; Commission on Money and Credit (1), 67; Friedman and Schwartz, 517, 689; Goldenweiser, 92; Jacoby, 228. But see Jacoby, 233, rating reserves questions as a relatively minor part of the course of monetary policy. By statute or by administrative practice, changes in reserve requirements might conceivably be made a more flexible device, Jacoby, 227, 228; *New York Times,* 20 October 1962, p. 24, col. 1, 21 October 1962, sec. 3, p. 1, col. 1, 1 March 1967, p. 55, col. 1. As it was used it was generally a rather blunt instrument. Cf. Goldenweiser, 49, 50, 93, 177, 179, 227; Jacoby, 220, 221; Mints, 282; Treiber, 260. The rapid, full use of its new authority by the board in 1936-37 was taken by critics to show the hazards of weight and timing special to this device. Culbertson, 159; Friedman and Schwartz, 517, 688-89; Goldenweiser, 179, 180, 182; Jacoby, 227. Barger, 133, and Goldenweiser, 179, however, question that reserve requirement increases were the cause of the recession then experienced. Over the span of 1952-64 the board used its new authority to make five reductions in reserve requirements. Knipe, 209. In this context, Knipe warns that, for want of sufficiently frank and informative reporting on its use, the authority to vary reserves was likely to foster distrust of its employment for banker profits. Ibid. A somewhat similar policy view was taken by those who argued that the Federal Reserve should increase member bank reserves by buying government securities over a wider range of maturities, instead of by lowering legal reserve requirements; the purchased securities would add to the income of the federal reserve banks, and in turn to receipts of the Treasury; lower reserve requirements, on the other hand, spelled more profit for the banks, and the legitimacy of this profit was challenged, since it flowed from measures presumably taken simply for the public interest. Barger, 208-12; *New York Times,* 7 August 1959, p. 29, col. 1; 9 August 1959, sec. 3, p. 1, col. 6; 15 March 1960, p. 55, col. 1.

341. On the early, limited perception of the uses of open-market operations: Clay J. Anderson, 48; Barger, 62, 69-71; Chandler, 205, 206, 209, 214; David H. McKinley, 111; Youngdahl, 116, 117. Youngdahl, ibid, notes the need to wait upon the availability of federal securities in volume. Cf. Chandler, 116, 206; Warburg, 1:13. That administrative initiative developed the instrument, see Clay J. Anderson, 47, 48; Chandler, 203, 234; Eccles, 170; David C. Elliott, 311; cf. Wilson, 271. Administrative decision making continued to figure large in putting content into the open-market technique. Though the Federal Reserve Act limited the system's long-term dealings to United States securities, it was administrative action which determined, further, that open-market operations should center on short-term Treasury issues and should not at all venture into state or local government securities. Barger, 310-12; Goldenweiser, 87, 89, 90; Youngdahl, 137, 18. It was on administrative initiative that experiment was made in using open-market dealings to affect the structure of interest rates as well as the supply of money and credit. Bogen, 339, 346; Wallich and Wallich, 337. The administrators themselves created an executive committee within the FOMC in 1935 and ended it in 1957. Youngdahl, 121, 122.

342. The growth in perception of uses of the open-market technique is noted by Barger, 308; Chandler, 208, 210, 216, 234; Eccles, 169; Friedman and Schwartz, 296, 297; Youngdahl, 119, 120. The 1923 advance in formulated doctrine is dis-

cussed by Chandler, 188, 222-29, 233; Clifford, 111, 131-33; Friedman and Schwartz, 251-53; Youngdahl, 120, 121. On centralization of open-market operations: Chandler, 222, 233, 234; Clifford, 106, 108, 110, 111, 131-33, 22; Eccles, 168, 169, 170, 174; Friedman and Schwartz, 251, 445, 446; Mints, 281, 282. See notes 287, 288, 290-92, 298, supra.

343. The prevailing tone of commentators outside the system on the use of open-market operations over the span from the mid-1920s into the 1960s tends to be skeptical that the technique can be proved to have had determining effect for better or worse during most of that time. Commentators vary in assessing responsibility for this record. Analyses sometimes emphasize the sharp constraints which general political and economic circumstances put on the system during many years, especially in World Wars I and II and the Korean War and in the depression of the 1930s. Bogen, 344, 347; Friedman and Schwartz, 515; Knipe, 122; Wallich and Wallich, 319-20, 334-36. But critics also find considerable clumsiness and poor judgment in the system's management. Barger, 99, 101, 104, 107; Bogen, 348-54; Culbertson, 159; Friedman and Schwartz, 254-66, 298, 365-66, 515; Knipe, 136, 141. Observers also find a root cause for both limited impact and mistaken use of the control instrument in what they see as a disappointing record of the Federal Reserve Board and the regional banks in creating monetary theory adequate to the system's potential or its responsibilities. Clay J. Anderson, 170, 178; Barger, 75; Culbertson, 164, 165; Knipe, 28; Sproul, 65-67. Cf. *New York Times,* 3 February 1969, p. 47, col. 4, 4 February 1969 p. 47, col. 5, 3 March 1969, p. 47, col. 8, 12 March 1969, p. 61, col. 3, 23 August 1969, p. 35, col. 6. Mann, 803, gives a more sympathetic reading of the difficulties of finding workable monetary policy theory, but by his moderation underlines all the more the limited means with which the money controllers were working.

344. Board of Governors of the Federal Reserve System, Annual Report (1953), p. 88; 47 *Fed. Res. Bull.* 165 (1961); Barger, 182, 184, 186-87; Friedman and Schwartz, 632-35; Rostow, 196-97; Youngdahl, 137-38; *New York Times,* 21 February 1961, p. 49, col. 1, 10 March 1961, p. 37, col. 6, 9 March 1962, p. 39, col. 2. The 1961 change accorded with a recommendation by the Commission on Money and Credit, created by the (privately organized) Committee for Economic Development. Commission on Money and Credit (1), 64.

345. Clay J. Anderson, 169; Chandler, 235; Friedman and Schwartz, 191, 266-67, 297. Had the Federal Reserve dealt freely in United States securities of considerable difference in maturity dates, it might have turned open-market dealing into an instrument of some selective control, but this was not a sustained policy of the board. Cf. Barger, 309-10.

346. Barger, 85-96; Chandler, 124-32, 153-63; David C. Elliott, 313, 314; Friedman and Schwartz, 255, 298; Goldenweiser, 152, 153.

347. Notes 273, 300, supra. There was sharp but ultimately decisive controversy through 1929 preceding the stock market crash, as the board urged qualitative controls through pressure by the federal reserve banks on members believed to be lending for market speculation, and the New York Federal Reserve Bank argued for quantitative control through substantial increase in the discount rate. The difference rested in part on the New York bank's objection that qualitative controls improperly invaded member banks' market discretion, but also largely on the New York bank's more pragmatic objection that qualitative controls such as the board urged were impractical of administration. The 1934 legislation went a good way to meet the pragmatic objection, by directing enforcement at broker borrowers more than at lending banks. Cf. Barger, 117; Friedman and Schwartz, 257, 265.

348. Note 302, supra. On the limited impact of the board's use of its special powers, see Friedman and Schwartz, 516, 577-78. Cf. Bogen, 345, 346, 350; Grove, 141, 155-68. Diverse currents of opinion and interest swirled about the idea of using Federal Reserve money-supply powers to influence the allocation of credit among different end uses. The CED's Commission on Money and Credit was unfriendly to selective controls on credit, but on pragmatic rather than doctrinaire grounds, emphasizing problems of evasion, administrative complexity, and the range of discretion involved in setting goals in many fields. Commission on Money and Credit (1), 71-76. For expressions against selective controls, as unwise invasions of banks' market freedom, see *New York Times,* 10 November 1958, p. 45, col. 2; 24 September 1963, p. 51, col. 5 (comptroller of currency); 22 July 1968, p. 51, col. 8 (bankers' distrust of suggested Federal Reserve line-of-credit plan, lest it veil effort at closer control of bank portfolios); 17 February 1971, p. 51, col. 5, and 1 April 1971, p. 59, col. 1 (Federal Reserve opposition to grant of power to influence credit allocations according to social priorities), and 23 May 1971, sec. 3, p. 14, col. 3 (banker opposition to like proposal). See Barger, 306, 333. Cf. Stein (2), 278. For favoring views toward using existing Federal Reserve powers, or granting new powers, to effect credit according to specific end uses, see *New York Times,* 29 December 1959, p. 1, col. 2 (staff report of Joint Economic Committee of Congress: general controls tend to constrain wrong sectors, restricting desirable economic growth); 6 February 1964, p. 37, col. 5; 20 November 1965, p. 45, col. 3, and 2 March 1970, p. 55, col. 1 (board members urge that reserve requirements be set against assets instead of against deposits, to this end); 29 August 1966, p. 41, col. 8, and 28 December 1966, p. 1, col. 8 (reserve requirements changed to influence particular credit uses); 2 July 1969, p. 51, col. 4, and 31 December 1969, p. 35, col. 5 (interest rate ceilings to prevent run-off of funds from savings banks and savings and loan associations, to disadvantage of funds for housing); 23 April 1971, p. 49, col. 3 (Senate subcommittee favors Federal Reserve authority to set reserve requirements to influence credit allocations). A generalized expression of favor for maintaining substantial market discretion in member banks was the board's view that, using its statutory power to make rules and regulations affecting member banks, it should keep its regulations as flexible as was consistent with effectiveness. In the board's view, regulations should be designed to interfere no more than absolutely necessary with the ordinary operations of the banks. Attorney General's Committee (1), 28.

349. Part One, supra, notes 203-5 (focus on 1907-type crisis in shaping Federal Reserve); supra, notes 305 (1933-34 gold policy), 318, 325 (coolness toward peacetime price controls), 337 (rediscounting limits), 339 (limited concept of reserves), 341-43 (slow development of open-market operations), 346-48 (caution toward qualitative controls). The bias toward maintaining broad scope for bankers' market freedom usually found expression in such general lines of policy as the text mentions. The bias came to more pointed reflection in two instances. (1) The Federal Reserve Board seems to have been inhibited from a needed, more effective response to the liquidity crisis of 1932-33 by the market-oriented insistence of the statutes on a substantial gold reserve to back Federal Reserve notes. The board may have erred in estimating the situation, but the concern seems to have been real and of real impact on policy. See note 337, supra. (2) The board rejected arguments from the Joint Economic Committee of Congress in 1959-60 for increasing reserves by open-market operations (including abandonment of the bills-only policy and purchases of long-term bonds) instead of by reducing reserve requirements. To the committee open-market operations made sense, because the securities bought by the system would

earn money for the government, while also accomplishing the desired increase of bank reserves; reduced reserve requirements spelled more earnings for the member banks. For the board, Chairman William McChesney Martin resisted this emphasis; it would be "undermining our private enterprise system" by running the banking system for government profit and by government dictate, Barger, 208-12, especially at 211. Cf. *New York Times,* 21 September 1962, p. 37, col. 1 (bankers' advisory committee to comptroller of the currency recommends few legal reserve requirements, in order to improve banks' earnings).

350. Part One, supra, notes 21-24, 125-27; notes 84, 87, supra. See, generally, Dunne (4), 9-10.

351. Berle, 27, 29, and Berle and Pederson, 61-68, 73, 85-90, 100-7, 136, 141, 153 (growth of liquidity, in general); Barger, 327-30, Berle and Pederson, 31, 37-38, 70, 100-101, 112, Commission on Money and Credit (1), 78, 80, Krooss (1), 268, Gordon W. McKinley, 208, 210-15, and Tobin, 410, 415 (development of nonbanking financial intermediaries, in general); *New York Times,* 28 June 1959, sec. 3, p. 1, col. 1, 20 June 1961, p. 4, col. 6, 21 January 1962, sec. 3, p. 1, col. 2 (nonfinancial corporations as buyers of short-term paper of nonbank financial houses); id., 10 September 1969, p. 19, col. 1, 13 November 1969, p. 65, col. 4, and 18 January 1970, sec. 3, p. 1, col. 5 (credit cards). A skeptical view of the effect of nonbank financial intermediaries on the demand for money balances, and hence on money's velocity, with a recommendation against direct federal controls over all such institutions, appears in the report of the CED's Commission on Money and Credit, in 1961. Commission on Money and Credit (1), 78-81. An instance of contract flexibility within the frame of Federal Reserve regulation was the development of the "federal funds" market, in which member banks loaned one another their excess reserve balances with the federal reserve banks. Cf. Barger, 309; Friedman and Schwartz, 278; Rostow, 167. But "federal funds" were lent on such very short term as not to compete with Federal Reserve monetary control.

352. Gordon W. McKinley, 210, 216. Cf. Barger, 328, 329 (central-bank-influenced interest rates will affect how far other financial institutions than banks put funds in play). Government regulation sought to bulwark the financial integrity of some of these nonbanking financial institutions, notably insurance companies and savings and loan associations. Such regulation reduced potential crisis pressure on the money supply from this quarter, but did not amount to including such institutions within the frame of monetary regulation as such. Cf. Tobin, 410, 411.

353. *New York Times,* 28 June 1959, sec. 3, p. 1, col. 1, 16 July 1961, sec. 3, p. 1, col. 4, 21 January 1962, sec. 3, p. 1, col. 2, 20 October 1962, p. 24, col. 1, 21 October 1962, sec. 3, p. 1, col. 1, 1 March 1967, p. 1, col. 5. Cf. id., 22 April 1962, sec. 3, p. 1, col. 1, 12 August 1963, p. 29, col. 2 (concern whether unregulated lenders for security trading should be brought under Federal Reserve control). In 1961 the CED's Commission on Monday and Credit recommended continuing the ban on interest on demand deposits, but converting power over time deposit interest to a standby authority; it would extend regulatory power over savings institutions, also. Commission on Money and Credit (1), 167.

354. *New York Times,* 28 June 1959, sec. 3, p. 1, col. 1, and 16 July 1961, sec. 3, p. 1, col. 4 (volatility of short-term industrial lending to financial markets); id., 20 June 1971, sec. 3, p. 1, col. 7 (Federal Reserve as lender of last resort in crisis threat from Penn Central default).

355. Cf. Commission on Monday and Credit (1), 81, 158-60; Gordon W. McKinley, 216, 219, 223; Tobin, 410, 411, 415.

356. 48 Stat. 162 (1933), sec. 11 (b); 49 Stat. 684 (1935), secs. 101 (v) (8), 324 (c); 12 C.F.R. 217.2, 217.3, 217.7; Commission on Money and Credit (1), 167; id. (2), 66, 72-73, 81-83; Friedman and Schwartz, 443-45; Trescott, 207; *New York Times,* 21 January 1962, sec. 3, p. 1, col. 2, 11 March 1962, sec. 3, p. 1, col. 6, 21 September 1962, p. 37, col. 1, 21 January 1966, p. 36, col. 8, 10 June 1969, p. 63, col. 3. For particularly sharp expressions by bankers of the claims for market freedom as opposed to official interventions, see *New York Times,* 21 September 1962, p. 37, col. 1, 23 September 1962, sec. 3, p. 1, col. 1, with which compare, generally, Sutton, et al., 233-39.

357. When the Federal Reserve Board became concerned that issues of negotiable, short-term notes by member banks might bring into the banks fresh money on a scale that might imperil Federal Reserve control of the money supply, the board brought member banks' issue of such notes under interest-ceiling and reserve requirements by amending the definition of *deposits* in its regulations on those subjects. 12 C.F.R. 204.1 (f), 217.1 (f) (1971); cf. *New York Times,* 21 January 1962, sec. 3, p. 1, col. 2, 10 September 1964, p. 47, col. 1, 21 January 1966, p. 36, col. 8, 20 June 1971, sec. 3, p. 1, col. 7. The board had no statutory authority to regulate the commercial paper issued by nonbanking financial or industrial corporations. See, id., 2 July 1969, p. 51, col. 4. The threat then arose that member banks owned by a holding company would obtain funds through the latter's borrowing on its own short-term paper. The board's authority to regulate issue of such bank holding company paper was challenged by the bankers. The president of the First Pennsylvania Company put the challenge squarely in terms of the effect of a proposed board regulation upon the value of market freedom: "Such a proposal carries with it the strong implication that the commercial banking system is to be routinely denied each competitive innovation of a free market and thereby excluded from even the most elementary means of corporate finance. . . . The precedent which this proposal would establish raises sharp questions about the ability of commercial banks to survive within our economic framework." Id., 2 December 1969, p. 77, col. 4; cf. id., 30 October 1969, p. 67, col. 4. Congress settled the point by broadening the board's authority by 83 Stat. 374 (1969), implemented by the board in 12 C.F.R. 204.115 (1971). A related phenomenon was the growth of dollar holdings by banks chartered in the United States, in their foreign branches, and the movement of such "Eurodollars" into the domestic lending facilities of the parent banks. Under the same broadened authority given by 83 Stat. 374 (1969), the board subjected such Eurodollar balances to a stiff reserve requirement. 12 C.F.R. 204.112 (1971); cf. *New York Times,* 2 July 1969, p. 51, col. 4.

358. Cf. Barger, 347; Chandler, 9, 10; Culbertson, 166; Goldenweiser, 30; Robertson, 149; Rostow, 145; Sutton, et al., 239.

359. Notes 281-83 (federalism), 284, 285 (regional federalism), 327 (public board), 328-31 (private control elements), 336 (centralization of reserves), 337-48 (particular powers of board), supra. Cf. Barger, 40-46; James M. Burns, 176; Joseph P. Chamberlain, 169-74; Lawrence H. Chamberlain, 313-21; Dorfman, 3:339; Glass, 112-16, 178; Link, 203-22, 225, 229, 236; Myers, 260-63; Warburg, 1:55, 100, 126, 412, 422; Willis (1), 83, 173, 247-50, 364, 456, 467.

360. 38 Stat. 251 (1913), title and sec. 13. That the 1913 act's contribution was in creating a decision-making apparatus rather than in defining policy goals: Attorney General's Committee (1), 19-20; Barger, 286; Chandler, 12-14, Clifford, 86, 347; Eccles, 212; Friedman and Schwartz, 171, 193; Mints, 283, 284; Raskind, 300, 303, 304; Sproul, 65, 66. Compare Chandler, 5, 449, on the likely practical wisdom of so

limiting the initial legislative effort, with the observations on lack of pre-1913 theory for elaborating goals of monetary policy, in Barger, 40-41; Mints, 281, 284; Willis (1), 12-13, 16, 18, 25, 32, 42, 46, 92. Schumpeter (2), 1078, 1081, 1088, 1110-12, cautions that we not underestimate the amount of penetrating monetary analysis in the development of economic theory from about the mid-nineteenth century on, but he notes also that the best insights did not make their way into the common textbooks or into the common currents of talk among policy makers. On the practical significance of the 1913 act in setting administrative activity in motion, whatever the want of legislatively declared goals: Barger, 242; Chandler, 46, 54; Friedman and Schwartz, 296; Knipe, 5, 6; Rowe, 67; Sproul, 65, 68; Wilson, 271; Youngdahl, 139-40.

361. The summary in the text may be deemed too limited, yet at most there could be few additions to a list of major legislation relevant to the Federal Reserve System after 1913. One addition might be 40 Stat. 556 (1918), which authorized the president, for national defense purposes, to redistribute functions among "executive agencies"; argument was made that the Federal Reserve fell within Congress's meaning here, and hence when the board complained that the Treasury was meeting too much of World War I expenses from borrowing and too little from taxes, the secretary of the treasury threatened an executive order putting all the federal reserve banks' funds at Treasury disposition—a threat which did not have to be implemented. Cf. Chandler, 120-21; Clifford, 100.

362. Part One, supra, notes 211, 212, 243; note 305, supra.

363. 48 Stat. 162 (1933), sec. 8, put on a permanent basis by 49 Stat. 684 (1935), sec. 101, as amended by 53 Stat. 842 (1939). See Part One, supra, notes 114-16; note 270, supra.

364. 49 Stat. 684 (1935). On the limited creativity of the act compare Barger, 134; Knipe, 7-8; Mints, 284; Treiber, 262, 263; Wright, 630. Eccles, 212. 228, comments on his desire for a bolder definition of Federal Reserve objectives in the bill which he pressed. Cf. Lawrence H. Chamberlain, 347; Friedman and Schwartz, 534, 447-48.

365. 60 Stat. 23 (1946); Barger, 232; Clifford, 278; Commission on Money and Credit (1), 263; Friedman, 596; Knipe, 7, 197-200; Rostow, 128-29, 145, 251; Stein (2), 186, 201-2, 214. That the presence of the 1946 act helped spur concern with broader economic objectives among particular congressmen and within executive and administrative circles, while Congress as a whole showed little enthusiasm for taking responsibility for basic redefinitions of monetary policy, compare Auerbach, 193; Commission on Money and Credit (1), 263-64.

366. 38 Stat. 251 (1913), sec. 10; 42 Stat. 620 (1922); Barger, 355; David C. Elliott, 309, 311; Mints, 283; Rowe, 74. In shaping the first Federal Reserve legislation an early proposal was for a central board of four appointive members plus the secretary of the treasury, the secretary of agriculture, and the comptroller general. Warburg, 1:99, 127, 418, criticized this as proposing "a hopelessly political board" and found it a definite improvement when, in the bill as passed, the ex officio members omitted the secretary of agriculture. In 1959 the executive council of the AFL-CIO asked that the Federal Reserve Act be amended "to provide for adequate representation of labor, the consumer and small business interests" on the board. The existing biased membership of the board, said the executive council, produced "misguided anti-inflation measures" which brought unemployment and stifled economic growth, while increasing bank profits. "The insistence on 'independence' is really a masked effort to insure a self-centered bankers' approach to interest rates and mone-

tary policy." Nothing came of the plea. *New York Times,* 25 February 1959, p. 34, col. 1, and 6 March 1959, p. 24, col. 7. When the board was, at Wilson's insistence, made a public board, the bankers were given a Federal Advisory Council, as a consolation. Note 330, supra. This was a gesture toward a particular interest representation, but an interest which—unlike commerce or agriculture—was immediately involved in the administration of the system of money. This distinction was not convincing to Congressman Wright Patman—long distrustful of banker influence on general economic policy—who in a 1938 bill and hearings unsuccessfully pressed to abolish the advisory council as part of several items for reducing bankers' influence within the Federal Reserve System. Barger, 135-36. The advisory council was not merely available to initiate advice, but was also consulted by the board relative to proposed Federal Reserve regulations. Attorney General's Committee (1), 32 33. A more weighty inclusion of interest representation in the top decision-making machinery might be seen in the presence of five federal reserve bank presidents as voting members among the twelve members of the Federal Open Market Committee. In 1938 hearings board chairman Eccles criticized the presence of these officials on the FOMC, because they were selected by private bankers and businessmen and hence, Eccles thought, less plainly represented the public interest than did the board members. Clifford, 332; cf. Eccles, 168, 169.

367. Barger, 78, 79, 108-11, 135, 136; Clifford, 222, 348; Mints, 284. Instructive of the kind of stalemate that was likely to block a fresh statutory directive to the board was the episode of 1959. Democrats on the House Ways and Means Committee proposed to attach to a bill approving temporary increase in the interest the Treasury might pay to market savings bonds and long-term bonds a "sense of Congress" declaration, that the Federal Reserve System, while pursuing its primary mission of administering a sound monetary policy, should to the maximum extent consistent with such policy use such means as would aid the economical and efficient management of the public debt and should, where practicable, bring about needed future money expansion by buying United States securities of varying maturities. The declaration was opposed by the board chairman, the secretary of the treasury, and Republican congressmen, as inviting government-sponsored inflation. *New York Times,* 11 July 1959, p. 1, col. 1; 12 July, sec. 3, p. 1, col. 8; 24 July, p. 1, col. 3; 25 July, p. 15, col. 8; 24 July, p. 1, col. 3. Speaker Rayburn complained bitterly of what he viewed as the Federal Reserve's intransigence. Id., 24 July 1959, p. 1, col. 3; see note 380, infra. The proposed amendment was also criticized, however, because it did not state policy on the reserve's use of its authority regarding the discount rate or bank reserves, and because on the other hand it was unnecessary to legitimize Federal Reserve dealings in long-term securities, since the system already asserted that prerogative; thus, its suspicious opponents argued, the amendment might have the hidden purpose of pegging interest rates on government securities for expansionist ends, and if so, that had better be an openly declared goal. Id., 2 August 1959, sec. 3, p. 1, col. 8; cf. 3 August, p. 35, col. 2. The amendment's sponsor answered that, to the contrary, its aim was to urge the Federal Reserve, when it felt that credit expansion was desirable, to accomplish it by open-market purchases rather than by reducing member bank reserve requirements, so that the Federal Reserve might get more earnings, part of which would go back to the Treasury. Id., 7 August 1959, p. 29, col. 1, and 9 August, sec. 3, p. 1, col. 6; cf. 15 March 1960, p. 55, col. 1. Nothing further came of the proposal.

368. See note 388, infra.

369. Cf. James M. Burns, 41, 100, 171; Kenneth Culp Davis, 44-45, 49-50; Landis, 56-59, 75, 87.

370. Cf. Barger, 313; Clifford, 86; Friedman and Schwartz, 103, 266-67, 297.

371. Blakey and Blakey, 60-70; Blum and Kalven, 7-12; Dorfman, 3:218-19, 483; Groves, 444-45; Myers, 218, 240-41, 266; Ratner, 280-87, 298-307; Wiebe (2), 92-93, 219.

372. United States v. Philadelphia National Bank, 374 U.S. 321, 324, 337 (1963) (Court notes this is first case before it regarding application of the antitrust laws to the commercial banking industry), and id., 324, note 2 (for economic and historical materials cited); see Lifland, 15-19; Rostow, 213, 259, 368. Kaysen and Turner, 42, list commercial banking as a sector "exempt" from the antitrust laws. However, the "exemption" was not one declared in the basic statutes or spelled out plainly in legislative history. It was constituted, rather, by the practice for many years of not invoking the antitrust laws in the field, partly perhaps from a now out-moded, limited view of what activities were in or affected interstate commerce, partly perhaps because the national bank system was still regarded as largely an instrument of government monetary policy, partly from ill-defined assumptions that the many specialized legal regulations of banks should be deemed sufficient to police their market behavior. Cf. United States v. Philadelphia National Bank, supra, 327-30; Berle (1), 591; (Note) 75 *Harv. L. Rev.* 756, 759-60. The result, in any case, was that for years antitrust administration paid little or no attention to banking. Speaking with reference to investment as well as commercial banking, Berle (2), 434, observes that "[in 1932] there was no question whatever where the chiefs of the American economic power resided. They were the dominant figures in the banks and banking houses clustered near the corner of Broad and Wall Streets, and a few counterparts in Chicago. Their rule was then nearly absolute. They had no respect at all for the 'free market.' They could only be challenged by politics; they were, in the event, challenged by Franklin Roosevelt." Compare *New York Times*, 11 November 1969, p. 61, col. 3 (Walter Heller, economist and former CEA chairman, notes that failure to enforce the antitrust laws or lift governmental restrictions on market competition limit the effectiveness of both fiscal and monetary policy); Knipe, 28-30 (Federal Reserve influence decreases as impact moves from bank reserves, to bank assets, to volume of demand and time deposits, to general conditions of the economy), 201 (most cost-of-living increases of fifties and early sixties flowed from the exercise of power by economic blocs almost immune to any Federal Reserve actions). The handling of antitrust policy may have reached directly into the Federal Reserve Board in one instance. Eccles, 450-53, indicates that he believes that he was not reappointed as board chairman in 1948 because of pressure exerted through political channels by California banking interests concerned to halt antitrust action against a bank holding company in that state, the Transamerica Corporation. Though no longer chairman, Eccles did stay on the board, to play an influential role there. Cf. Barger, 355; Dana, 162-64.

373. Chapter I, note 243.

374. Lawrence H. Chamberlain, 324-33.

375. Barger, 118-21, 363, 364; Lawrence H. Chamberlain, 346-51; Eccles, 181.

376. Bailey, 106, 161-64, 173, 181, 237.

377. On the audit situation before 1933, and the 1933 change: Clifford, 78, 84, 140, 355; Commission on Money and Credit (1), 86; Raskind, 302; *New York Times*, 4 April 1967, p. 40, col. 6. Cf. Robertson, 177 (analogous exemption of comptroller of the currency from GAO audit). Clifford, 355, note 23, suggests that the 1933 change was made to offset the assessment Congress had put on the regional banks, of one half their surplus, to launch the FDIC. Note, however, Eccles's caution against exaggerating the significance of budgetary independence, in light of other pressures on the system to fit its policies into the government's general economic policies.

Clifford, 140, 141. Functionally analogous to the formal budgetary independence given by freedom from GAO audit was the contribution to practical independence given the banks by their earnings from open-market operations. Cf. Barger, 209-10, 316. Bryan v. FOMC, 235 Fed. Supp. 877, 879, note 1 (D. Montana 1964) declared, *obiter,* that FOMC operations were not in violation of U.S. Constitution, art. I, sec. 9 (7), that no money shall be drawn from the Treasury but in consequence of appropriations made by law, and that a regular statement and account of the receipts and expenditures of all public money shall be published from time to time. In the court's opinion, this clause refers only to dealings in funds arising from taxes and excises required by law to be deposited in the Treasury; funds are not "public money" within that clause of the Constitution simply because they are received by a federal agency in the lawful exercise of its public functions. The court cites Varney v. Warehimer, 147 Fed. (2d) 238, 245 (6th Cir. 1945), cert. denied, 325 U.S. 882 (1945)—not a case involving regulation of money—where the point was held, dogmatically, without analysis. The Federal Reserve System was omitted from audit provisions of the Government Corporation Control Act of 1945 on recommendation of the comptroller general, because he deemed Federal Reserve internal audit procedures satisfactory and because the banks were owned by their member banks; the FDIC was put under qualified jurisdiction of the GAO. 59 Stat. 597 (1945), secs. 201, 202; Clifford, 356. Over the years various suggestions came to nothing, to put the system under external audit, or—more drastically—to require that it obtain its operating funds from Congress and to abolish member bank stockholding in the regional banks. Clifford, 356, 361-67; Raskind, 302; Rowe, 136-58. The board elaborated internal audit procedures to conciliate congressional critics who wanted external audit and went so far as to suggest amending the Federal Reserve Act to require joining private, independent accountants in auditing the board, and to ratify this practice as already applied by the board to the regional banks. These actions did not satisfy the leading critic, Congressman Wright Patman. Clifford, 354, 366.

378. Congress held hearings in response to criticism that unduly restrictive action by the Federal Reserve produced a pronounced drop in farm products prices in 1920. This criticism was all after the event and the congressional committee in 1922 acquitted the board, though criticizing it for not earlier braking the general price rises of the time, while recognizing that the board had been under Treasury pressure to support the 1919 "war" loan. David C. Elliott, 309, 311; Goldenweiser, 136, 137; Raskind, 304. Friedman and Schwartz, 255, hypothesize that the criticisms made of the tight policy in the 1920-22 episode may have made the board less vigorous in curbing credit expansion on the even of the 1929 collapse. They attribute a modest enlargement of open-market operations in 1932 to congressional pressure and to the legitimizing force of the Glass-Steagall Act, broadening the collateral on which federal reserve banks might advance funds to their members. 47 Stat. 56 (1932); Friedman and Schwartz, 191, note 4, and 363.

379. Knipe, 197, 198, 199, 200, generalizes for the span from about 1952-65 on the combination in the board and FOMC of favor for price restraint and avoidance of plain statement of that prevailing criterion. On particular episodes, see Barger, 187 (1961 shift from bills-only policy); Clifford, 255 (1951 Senate activity may have stiffened board for its stand for independence of the Treasury); Knipe, 85 (1952 move against inflationary trend), 88, 89, 90, 220 (Federal Reserve tactical shifts in spring of 1953 accompanying congressional criticism), 114, 115, 119, 122 (separate episodes of credit easing in May 1956 and October 1957 in context of congressional and White House criticisms), 141, 142 (March 1960 easing of credit following criti-

cism by some senators and by candidate John F. Kennedy). See, also, note 380, infra.

380. *New York Times,* 24 July 1959, p. 1, col. 3. See note 367, supra.

381. 49 Stat. 684 (1935), sec. 203 (d). Eccles opposed these enlarged reporting requirements, as encroaching on Federal Reserve independence. Clifford, 136, 137. The years 1961-64 saw skirmishes between the Joint Economic Committee, or some of its members, and the board over the adequacy of the reporting done by the board and the FOMC. *New York Times,* 7 December 1962, p. 59, col. 2; 18 March 1963, p. 13, col. 2; 23 September 1963, p. 43, col. 1; 6 February 1964, p. 37, col. 5. The board resisted publicizing details of decision making by it or the FOMC, as likely to create misleading impressions in the public and to sensitize the market unduly to Federal Reserve actions as compared with market response to the general business situation. Congressman Wright Patman successfully pressed the board to more revelations, however, when he claimed that the new "freedom of information" act, 80 Stat. 250 (1966), required that FOMC records be made available to the public forthwith. The board responded by deciding that FOMC decisions would be published three months after each FOMC meeting and that unpublished records of the board and the FOMC would be made available on request, unless they fell within stated statutory exceptions. *New York Times,* 15 August 1966, p. 39, col. 7. Congressman Patman complained that still not enough information was made available. Id., 30 June 1967, p. 51, col. 3. Knipe, 116, found the published data of limited use, because it was belated and often couched in Delphic terms. Even so, publication of FOMC records revealed matters theretofore reserved for distant historians. Cf. *New York Times,* 28 January 1970, p. 1, col. 6. Senator William Proxmire later successfully pressed the board for expansion of information furnished to Congress. See note 382, infra.

382. 60 Stat. 23 (1946), secs. 3 (Economic Report of the President), 4 (c) and (d) (CEA), 5 (b) (Joint Committee of Congress on the Economic Report); Barger, 378; Clifford, 326. Though the committee provided more continuity and expertness in inquiry, the board had as great assets of the same kind of its own, and a stubborn and adroit board chairman could battle the committee to a draw on a particular issue, as Chairman Martin did in 1961 over the issue of enlarging open-market operations rather than reducing member bank reserves to expand credit. Barger, 208-12. Compare the hearings called by the committee in reaction to the board's December 1965 increase in the discount rate, with the Joint Committee's eventual mild recommendations for more consultation between the board, the secretary of the treasury, and the CEA. *New York Times,* 8 December 1965, p. 1, col. 3; 14 December 1965, p. 1, col. 1; 11 February 1966, p. 30, col. 3. Cf. id., 28 January 1970, p. 1, col. 6. Having made the signal it desired, the board did not immediately press hard, but rather for some six months used open-market operations to keep credit easy, after which it began a sharp tightening. Meanwhile, though the administration did not seek the tax increases that the Federal Reserve staff wanted, administration spending was curbed, the investment tax credit was suspended, and government borrowing was curtailed. The pattern was that of give and take, rather than of sharply drawn lines of superiority and subordination. See *New York Times,* 14 September 1966, p. 63, col. 6; 21 September 1966, p. 61, col. 2; 4 December 1966, sec. 3, p. 1, col. 8. More indicative of the constructive possibilities in interplay between board and committee were events of 1968 concerning congressional directives and system response. The Joint Economic Committee proposed guidelines for the FOMC, whereby the system would increase the money supply according to the growth rate of the economy, with an annual growth rate from 2-6 percent, though the directive would not deprive the system of all discretion. The Joint Committee was critical of the extent of swings in

Federal Reserve policy and expressed its wish for more information on Federal Reserve decision making. Id., 10 July 1968, p. 49, col. 5. The board said that it would give more information and would also furnish an annual estimate of desirable monetary policy early in each year. Id., 7 August 1968, p. 57, col. 1. Later, however, the board hedged apparently on the question whether it would respond to the committee request for explanations when in any quarter the money supply might exceed the committee's suggested bounds. Id., 9 August 1968, p. 47, col. 2. Then the board agreed, and Senator William Proxmire accepted for the committee, that there be quarterly reports to the committee from the board on monetary and financial developments, including but not limited to the money supply, and hence avoiding a sharp focus on the movement of the money supply within the suggested 2-6 percent range. Id., 10 September 1968, p. 59, col. 2, and 12 September, p. 71, col. 2.

383. See, e.g., Federal Reserve Bank of Richmond v. Kalin, 77 Fed. (2d) 50 (4th Cir. 1935) (bank as noteholder); Federal Reserve Bank of Atlanta for use of American Surety Co. of New York v. Atlanta Trust Co., 91 Fed. (2d) 283 (5th Cir. 1937), cert. denied, 302 U.S. 738 (1937) (bank as endorser).

384. Norman v. Baltimore & Ohio Railroad Co., 294 U.S. 240 (1935); Perry v. United States, id., 330 (1935).

385. Cf. Knipe, 3.

386. On competitive equality: First National Bank of Bay City v. Fellows, ex rel. Union Trust Co., 244 U.S. 416 (1917). On par collections: note 279, supra.

387. Raichle v. Federal Reserve Bank of New York, 34 Fed. (2d) 910, 916 (2d Cir. 1929). Cf. Attorney General's Committee (1), 45.

388. Raichle v. Federal Reserve Bank of New York, 34 Fed. (2d), 910, 914 (2d Cir. 1929); see Bryan v. FOMC, 235 Fed. Supp. 877, 882, note 2 (D. Montana, 1964). Cf. First National Bank of Bay City v. Fellows, ex rel. Union Trust Co., 244 U.S. 416, 427 (1917) (Congress may delegate to board power to determine what operating authority a national bank must have to be functional competitor of state bank); Hampton & Co. v. United States, 276 U.S. 394, 404-5 (1928) (necessity of effective handling of detailed economic judgments warrants delegation to commission of power to adjust tariff rates in light of foreign costs of production); Yakus v. United States, 321 U.S. 414, 423, 424 (1944) (to protect dollar's purchasing power in wartime Congress may give administrators broad powers to regulate prices in market). But cf. Wright, 629.

389. Horne v. Federal Reserve Bank of Minneapolis, 344 Fed. (2d) 725 (8th Cir. 1965); Koll v. Wayzata State Bank, 397 Fed. (2d) 124 (8th Cir. 1968); cf. United States v. Anderson 433 Fed. (2d) 856 (8th Cir. 1970).

390. These authorities over de jure and de facto access to the commercial banking business originated with 13 Stat. 99 (1864), sec. 17 (comptroller of currency), and 48 Stat. 162 (1933), sec. 8, creating sec. 12B (e) of the Federal Reserve Act. From 1864 into the mid-1870s, the comptroller asserted some discretion in granting or denying national bank charters; from about 1875 until the middle 1920s the comptroller's office treated the national bank legislation as in substance a free-banking law, with little except formal check on charters; in particular, the Banking Act of 1933 set stiffer terms for charters, though policy varied in tightness of application under particular comptrollers. Attorney General's Committee (2), 16, 17; Commission on Money and Credit (2), 40; Robertson, 59-61, 66-69, 126, 128-31, 149, 153-54; Trescott, 269. On FDIC influence on the creation of banks: Attorney General's Committee (2), 37, 38; Commission on Money and Credit (2), 41; Friedman and Schwartz, 436-37; Raymond P. Kent, 62, 63; Trescott, 207, 266. There was

occasional friction through the mid-1920s, when the comptroller chartered national banks which the board had rejected as state-chartered institutions to be system members. Clifford 77, 78. FDIC practice included a facet analogous to the corporation's role in affecting the number of banks in operation, in that agency's policy to foster consolidations or reorganizations to absorb a weak institution and to keep its assets available to its community. Cf. Goldenweiser, 172. The Federal Reserve Board recognized the overlap of regulatory jobs among it and other agencies by its practice of submitting draft Federal Reserve regulations not only to the American Bankers Association and the Federal Advisory Council, but also to the comptroller of the currency, the FDIC, and the SEC. Attorney General's Committee (1), 32, 33, 34-36.

391. The RFC originated in 47 Stat. 5 (1932). Essential to its assistance to banks embarrassed by frozen assets was the provision for fresh stock issues by national banks, and for RFC subscriptions to banks' preferred stock, in 48 Stat. 1 (1933), Title III. See Friedman and Schwartz, 427, 428; Goldenweiser, 167-69; Hacker and Zahler (2), 379; Jones and Angly, 17, 19-20, 25-26, 32, 33-37, 39-40; Myers, 323; Taus, 191; Wallich and Wallich, 329, 331. Before 1933 the RFC was hampered by statutory limitations; it lacked statutory authority to contribute to banks' capital, and it was believed to be under requirement to publish the names of all borrowing banks, a publicity which banks wished to avoid. Conceivably it might have pumped funds into the banks before 1933 by vigorous open-market purchases of government securities, but it did not see that its function was to move this far into the role of central bank as lender of last resort. Cf. Berle and Pederson, 126, 127; Friedman and Schwartz, 325, 330, 331; Goldenweiser, 165; Trescott, 205. See the discussion in Berle and Pederson, 192, 195, 199, of the question whether Congress should create a lender of last resort for investment capital. The RFC was involved, but only as instrument and not as seat of policy making, in President Roosevelt's moves to devalue the dollar as a device to raise depressed commodity price levels. With the Treasury then under legal obligation to pay $20.67 per ounce for gold, the RFC—under White House direction—undertook to pay increasing prices for gold, paying in its own debentures, which the Treasury was obligated to buy from their holders on tender at face value. Undersecretary of the Treasury Dean Acheson firmly opposed this measure, as one without authority in law; his opposition was the basis for his subsequent resignation. Acheson, 186-92.

392. Commission on Money and Credit (2), 36-38; Culbertson, 166; Hepburn, 322-23; Robertson, 69-81, 107-12, 134-38; Sproul, 64; Treiber, 249; Trescott, 208; Wallich and Wallich, 329, 331.

393. Cf. Friedman and Schwartz, 434, 440, 441, 684. True, in 1932 some of the opposition to creating federal deposit insurance came from Federal Reserve officials, who in some ill-defined way saw such a program as an undesirable competitor with the system in regulating money. Id., 321 and 321, notes 27, 28, 435, note 13.

394. Berle and Pederson, 126, 127; Friedman and Schwartz, 330, 331; cf. Jones and Angly, 19, 20, 33.

395. It was significant that controversy over increased chartering of national banks as well as over national bank branching in the controversial regime of Comptroller James J. Saxon (1961-66) centered on the comptroller's declared policy of promoting more competition in banking. Fischer, 218-22; Robertson, 154, 162; Smith and Greenspun, 44; New York Times, 5 November 1966, sec. 3, p. 1, col. 3.

396. Barger, 35; Commission on Money and Credit (2), 97; Robertson, 137, 166-67; Wyrick, 4. But cf. Eccles, 267, 283.

397. Board of Governors, Annual Report, 1938, 89; Barger, 326, 349; Eccles, 276, 277; Robertson, 135-37; Trescott, 203.

398. Critics of overlapping examination assignments differed over whether examination should be concentrated in one agency, or divided between the comptroller of the currency and the FDIC, but the prevailing judgment was that the task should be removed from the Federal Reserve Board in order to help the board center its energies on monetary policy. Barger, 350; Clifford, 161, 189; Sproul, 76, 77; *New York Times,* 21 September 1962, p. 37, col. 1 (bankers committee advisory to comptroller), and 12 April 1965, p. 53, col. 8 (banker opinion distrusts consolidating examinations in but one agency, favors coordination by secretary of the treasury). On particular frictions among agencies all holding examination authority, see (Note) 65 *Colum. L. Rev.* 660 (1965). But cf. Attorney General's Committee (2), 40, 41. Various statutes also charged the Federal Reserve Board with regulation primarily directed to the fostering or preservation of competitive markets, or to promotion of sound lending practices. Thus it had responsibility (1) under 41 Stat. 378 (1919) to pass on applications to create foreign branches and subsidiaries of member banks; (2) under 44 Stat. 1224 (1927), sec. 9, to pass on applications of state-chartered member banks to establish branches; (3) under 47 Stat. 162 (1933), sec. 18, 48 Stat. 684 (1935), sec. 311, and 70 Stat. 133 (1956), sec. 3, to engage in certain regulation of bank holding companies; and (4) under 64 Stat. 873 (1950), sec. 2 (amending Federal Reserve Act, section 18(c)) to pass on mergers involving a state-chartered member bank. There was substantial opinion that these functions should be removed from the board, to allow it to focus better on monetary policy, especially since there were confusing overlaps of authority under some of these statutes among the board, the comptroller, and the FDIC as well as state supervisory bodies. Barger, 351; Knipe, 13, 14; *New York Times,* 28 May 1962, p. 28, col. 3 (board member recommends putting all competitive-market regulations in a new federal banking commission); *New York Times,* 21 September 1962, p. 37, col. 1 (similar recommendation of bankers advisory committee to comptroller) as well as id., 25 September 1962, p. 49, col. 1 and 8 October 1962, p. 35, col. 1 (advisory committee's recommendation distrusted by those fearing more liberality toward branch banking); id., 27 March 1964, p. 26, col. 3; id., 15 September 1969, p. 69, col. 8 (talk of White House executive order to put all regulation in protection of banking competition in FDIC and comptroller). Congress partly responded to such criticism by 80 Stat. 1314 (1966), authorizing the board to delegate "any of its functions, other than those relating to rulemaking or pertaining principally to monetary and credit policies," to hearing examiners, board members, or employees of the board or the regional banks. The board took its first step under this new authority by delegating various functions, for example the approval of domestic branches of state-chartered member banks, to regional banks or to members of its own staff, especially division heads. The board declared that it retained power to review its delegates' actions and authorized any of its delegates to certify to the board any question deemed of high importance. 53 *Fed. Res. Bull.* 1965 (1967); *New York Times,* 12 June 1967, p. 67, col. 5.

399. See, supra, notes 361-64, 366 (congressional action and inaction on policy directives and on system structure), 378-82 (board relations with congressional critics and committees). One proposal in 1913 would have made the secretary of agriculture an ex officio member of the Federal Reserve Board. Conservatives saw this as embodying their worst fears of "political" influence on money and counted it a gain that the ex officio members were finally limited to two who might be deemed more responsive to "sound" money values. Note 366, supra. Bryan Democrats, on the other hand, regarded the presence of the two Treasury officers with distrust, as opening central policy making to Wall Street influence. Cf. Glass, 100-110. On the 1935 act changes: Barger, 119-20; Commission on Money and Credit (1), 86; Rowe,

83, 84; Wallich and Wallich, 330. The comptroller of the currency was taken off the board less from objection to his presence as such than from the fact the secretary of the treasury in 1935 was offended by the idea that his subordinate might stay while the secretary had to leave. Clifford, 139; Eccles, 222. Senator Glass was a strong advocate of removing the secretary from the board, arguing from his own experience as secretary of the treasury that that official was thus positioned to exert undue influence on the board, for the treasury's interests, Clifford, 138. For an earlier opinion to like effect, see Warburg, 1:476-77. In 1919 Secretary Glass exerted himself to get an attorney general's opinion that the board might overrule discount rate changes proposed by a regional bank and threatened to have Benjamin Strong removed as governor of the New York bank. Chandler, 163-64. The record shows no other instance of such stark pressure by the secretary, however. Barger, 50, 64, argues that the secretary's influence was exaggerated in the debate; in the twenty years in which they sat, the ex officio members attended the board meetings irregularly, and the appointive members shaped most policy. Wallich and Wallich, 330, are likewise skeptical that the change practically enlarged the board's freedom, and suggest, rather, that it may have weakened liaison between the Federal Reserve and the Treasury when the growth of the public debt called for closer collaboration. If this latter effect operated, it was reduced by the growing activity of the Council of Economic Advisers under the Employment Act of 1946. Note 414, infra. Chronically suspicious of banker-minded favor on the Federal Reserve Board for price stability at the expense of economic activity and employment, Congressman Wright Patman in 1938 and again in 1964 proposed that the board be enlarged, made removable by Congress, or limited to four year terms, and that the Secretary of the Treasury again sit ex officio. The board's chairman opposed the 1964 proposal, as unwieldy and as unwisely putting the government's chief officer to pay the government's bills in a position to create the money with which to pay them. Nothing came of the proposals. Barger, 135-36; *New York Times,* 20 January 1964, p. 28, col. 8; *New York Times,* 22 January 1964, p. 50, col. 4; id., 9 March 1964, p. 45, col. 6.

400. Cf. Auerbach, 235; Eccles, 460-62; Friedman and Schwartz, 474; Knipe, 218. See also *New York Times,* 7 January 1963, p. 13, col. 3, and 9 March 1964, p. 45, col. 6 (board chairman Martin recognizes that Federal Reserve "independence" depends on cooperation with White House); id., 2 March 1966, sec. 3, p. 1, col. 5 (president of Federal Reserve Bank of New York observes that the system "is not independent *of* the Government, but independent *within* the Government"). Of course this realism was not inconsistent with recognizing that legislative history showed that in a measure the Federal Reserve Board was intended to be "an independent board or Government Establishment," not merely a supervisory body but rather "a distinctly administrative board with extensive powers." Opinion of the Attorney General (T. W. Gregory) to the Secretary of the Treasury, 16 November 1914, 30 *Opinions of the Attorney General* 308, 311, 314 (Washington, D.C., 1919). On the other hand, Mints, 285, 286, argues that Congress, with authority to delegate all monetary policy making to the Treasury, should probably do so because Treasury surpluses and deficits so unavoidably affect the money supply, especially since federal government operations have become as large as they have. The record showed that even in peacetime government borrowing was sometimes of such extent that Federal Reserve support had to be on a scale affecting the monetary situation. See *New York Times,* 19 February 1969, p. 61, col. 3; 13 May 1970, p. 61, col. 6; cf. id., 18 May 1970, p. 47, col. 7 (possibilities of Treasury seeking funds by auction or by investing trust funds).

401. 49 Stat. 684 (1935), sec. 203 (b). The 1913 act had put board terms at ten years, and the Banking Act of 1933 had lengthened them to twelve. The 1933 act had stricken the stipulation of the 1913 statute that board members be removable only for cause, but the 1935 act restored that safeguard. The 1935 act reduced the board from eight to seven members, now all appointive. By the accidents of history the new four-year terms of the chairman and vice chairman of the board fell in the middle of a presidential term, and the matter thus stood, in contravention of the original intention. The (unofficial) CED Commission on Money and Credit recommended in 1961, as did President Kennedy and Chairman Martin, that the terms be adjusted to be coterminus with presidential terms, but the idea now stirred opposition in the name of the board's independence. Commission on Money and Credit (1), 87; Knipe, 12; Rowe, 83, 84; Wallich and Wallich, 330; *New York Times,* 13 June 1962, p. 38, col. 3; id., 30 June 1964, p. 32, col. 1; id., 29 October 1964, p. 18, col. 3. The Commission on Money and Credit also recommended that the president be assured of one opportunity to make an appointment to the board soon after his inauguration, by putting the board at five members, with terms overlapping so that one would expire every odd year, with members eligible for reappointment. In a somewhat odd alliance, Congressman Wright Patman also favored such overlapping short terms, but would limit each appointee to one term. Commission on Money and Credit (1), 86-87; *New York Times,* 21 December 1964, p. 49, col. 7.

402. On World War I: Barger, 54-56; Clifford, 198, 199, 101-3; David C. Elliott, 301-4; Friedman and Schwartz, 239; Goldenweiser, 133, 134. On World War II: Barger, 143-46, 166; Bogen, 339, 341-46; Clifford, 164, 165, 180, 183, 186, 188, 195; Friedman and Schwartz, 552, 553, 563, 568; Goldenweiser, 185-87, 192-95; Wallich and Wallich, 337. On Korea: Barger, 161-62; Clifford, 230, 231, 233-35; Friedman and Schwartz, 610-11. Even under the pressures of war, there were incidents of controversy between Federal Reserve desires to curb inflation and Treasury desires for ready financing at favorable rates. But always, under such circumstances, the board felt compelled to act to support Treasury flotations, as the Treasury wanted them supported. See note 361, supra (Treasury threat of invoking Overman Act in World War I); Barger, 142, 144 (World War II arguments of Federal Reserve for higher short-term interest rates); Barger, 162, and Clifford, 234-35 (Federal Reserve support of low-yield Korean-period Treasury issue made in face of Federal Reserve increase in discount rate).

403. Indicative of the leeway afforded in peacetime for quite sharp differences between the board and the White House is the handling of the board's December 1965 increase in the discount rate, cited in note 382, supra. Compare the text accompanying notes 378-380, supra. One might expect that the urgency for government response to the 1930s depression would have produced some clear-cut example of the board's yielding to White House or strong congressional leadership under a peacetime emergency. But the board never asserted itself to draw such an issue; in most of that period it was relatively passive, in part, at the outset, for want of a strong leader within its own membership (before Marriner Eccles became chairman in 1935), partly because it feared that bold use of its new open-market tool might bring Federal Reserve note issues perilously close to the statutory gold reserve requirement, and largely because it seemed to despair of the efficacy of monetary measures in the face of so great a decline in business will to venture. Cf. Clay J. Anderson, 158, 160; Friedman and Schwartz, 407-19, 511-15, 517-20, 532-34; Goldenweiser, 161, 162, 175; Timberlake, 204. Though it must ultimately bow to determined use of their law-making powers by the president or Congress, the board was not precluded from a

leading role in debating the formulation of policy affecting the system of money, yet it was not heard or was not a significant participant in shaping such key decisions as those over gold, or expansion of the lender-of-last-resort functions of the Reconstruction Finance Corporation, or Congress's creation of the Thomas Amendment threat of inflating the national currency. The minor consultative role of the Federal Reserve authorities when the president launched his gold policy is reflected in Acheson, 189-90, while Jones and Angly, 20-22, implicitly indicate the similar situation in the RFC leadership in the banking crisis of 1933. Cf. Wallich and Wallich, 329, 331-32. Invocation of Federal Reserve opinion is conspicuously lacking in the controversy in Congress over the Thomas Amendment. Cf. Lawrence H. Chamberlain, 336-38. Indicative of the modesty with which the board was habituated to using its powers, even before it was under wartime Treasury pressure, was the haste with which it sold off large purchases of government securities it made to cushion the immediate impact of the outbreak of war in Europe in 1939 and of this country's involvement at Pearl Harbor. Bogen, 339, 342, 343.

404. Clifford, 253, 254, 255, 261-63, 349; Goldenweiser, 179, 180; cf. Barger, 275; Stein (2), 278. The practical freedom of the Federal Reserve was hedged about by recurrent criticism that its actions had been often erratic, ill-timed, or ill-informed, and that hence it should use its powers sparingly. See, for example, the current of criticism in the *New York Times* in 1969: 26 February, p. 61, cols. 4, 5; 27 February, p. 1, col. 6; 7 April, p. 61, col. 1; 9 September, p. 59, col. 2; 22 October, p. 57, col. 1; 1 December, p. 73, col. 5.

405. Cf. Barger, 337, 338, 343, 375-79; Heller, 17, 26-36; Lekachman, 219-25, 270-85; Tobin, 415; *New York Times,* 8 November 1964, sec. 3, p. 1, col. 4 (President Alfred Hayes of the Federal Reserve Bank of New York); id., 13 April 1964, p. 41, col. 2; id., 2 February 1966, p. 43, col. 2. See, also, Raichle v. Federal Reserve Bank of New York, 34 Fed. (2d) 910, 912 (2d Cir. 1927).

406. See notes 401 (subordination of Federal Reserve in active war years) and 403 (relative passivity of Board in 1930s depression), supra. Chandler, 133, 206-7, 208-15, discusses the Treasury's World War I bond issues as providing the unplanned base for open-market operations and charts the board's development of the new control technique without Treasury opposition and, indeed, with Treasury approval. Barger, 129, 138, notes the 1937 bond-support episode. For over-all judgments that, otherwise, through the years of the Federal Reserve System's existence, there have been few occasions of pronounced Treasury or White House pressure on the board's freedom to conduct money-supply policy, see Clay J. Anderson, 158, 160; Knipe, 219; *New York Times,* 22 October 1969, p. 57, col. 1; id., 8 January 1970, p. 17, col. 7.

407. Barger, 161-66; Bogen, 344, 346, 347; Clifford, 204, 205, 222, 230-35, 242-55, 259, 261-63, 265; Culbertson, 159; Eccles, 460-62; Goldenweiser, 199, 201-2, 206, 208, 211, 214; Youngdahl, 129-33. The board asked Congress to grant it authority further to raise required reserves for member banks and to impose supplementary reserve requirements on holdings of Treasury bills and certificates of indebtedness, to restore some of the Reserve's monetary control power foregone by its pegging of long-term government securities. But Congress granted only temporary authority for modest increases in reserve requirements, under 62 Stat. 1291 (1948), sec. 2 (limited to 30 June 1949). In 1956 the board made a different assessment of what would be a desirable division of authority with the Treasury and proposed that the Federal Reserve Act be amended to give the board full power to decide how it should render fiscal-agent service to the Treasury. Nothing came of the proposal. Clifford, 297.

408. Cf. Barger, 231; Clifford, 33, 34, 248, 253-54, 255-57, 259, 275-78; Heller, 66, 86; Knipe, 233; Lekachman, 175, 222; Tobin, 415; *New York Times,* 12 June 1961, p. 43, col. 1; id., 29 July 1970, p. 51, col. 1.

409. Note 405, supra. Indeed, economist James Tobin, former Council Economic Advisers member, in a letter to the *New York Times,* 15 December 1965, p. 46, col. 5, thought that those who saw Federal Reserve independence under regular and dangerous attack were drawing a false issue. In his observation, the Federal Reserve participated widely in policy-making processes of the executive branch, and the president regularly received the counsel of the board chairman and other high economic officials. The truth was, rather, he felt, that other relevant agencies did not participate enough in Federal Reserve deliberations "because of the paranoiac mania for Federal Reserve independence. The Federal Open Market Committee, the real high court of monetary policy in this country, does not even let the Secretary of the Treasury and the chairman of the Council of Economic Advisers inside the door to explain the Administration's economic and fiscal outlook and strategy."

410. On the sterilizing of gold imports in 1936: Barger, 126, 129; Friedman and Schwartz, 473, 504-6, 511, 519; Goldenweiser, 178; Taus, 225-29; Wallich and Wallich, 334, 335. Friedman and Schwartz, 519, suggest that a frustrating complex of factors constrained Federal Reserve open-market sales from coping with the late 1930s gold inflow. Such tactics might be interpreted as tightening credit when the economy was still depressed, with the Thomas Amendment still on the books with its threat of fiat currency, and with the Treasury's "stabilization fund" from the dollar devaluation available to allow the Treasury to counter Federal Reserve action that it did not like; moreover, sales large enough to be effective would deprive the Federal Reserve of needed earnings. On the interest "twist" of 1961-64: Knipe, 278, 280; cf. *New York Times,* 21 January 1962, sec. 3, p. 1, col. 8; id., 1 December 1971, p. 1, col. 8. The White House-determined dollar devaluation in 1934 was an initial impetus to the inflow of gold which threatened to overwhelm Federal Reserve money controls. Barger, 122, 123. The Stabilization Fund created by Congress from the bulk of the paper profit of the United States from the devaluation move was declared by Congress as available to adjust foreign exchange ratios and constituted a great increase in potential capacity of the Treasury for monetary maneuver. The Treasury did not choose to use this potential for its expansive possibilities on the domestic economy, but rather devoted the bulk of it to the United States contribution to the International Monetary Fund. Cf. Attorney General's Committee (1), 10, 11; Friedman and Schwartz, 470, 471; Goldenweiser, 16. The precedents represented by the events of 1936 and 1961-64 do not seem qualified by the leadership of the Federal Reserve Bank of New York from about 1924-27, in bringing the system to act for lower interest rates in the United States in order to help England and countries on the Continent attract and hold gold at a time when they were trying to restore a working international gold standard. Governor Benjamin Strong's initiatives in dealing to this effect with foreign central banks met no test of opposition from the Treasury or White House, which at this point in time took the view that government should not be active in affairs better left to processes somewhat resembling market operations. Barger, 75, 83-84; Chandler, 248, 249, 255, 256. Indicative of a later view, that the Treasury should lead in international monetary arrangements, was the designation of the secretary of the treasury as chairman of the National Advisory Council on International Monetary and Financial Problems (on which the chairman of the Federal Reserve Board sat as one member), as this body was created by the Bretton Woods Agreement Act, authorizing United States participation in the Inter-

national Monetary Fund. 59 Stat. 512 (1945), sec. 4(a). Cf. Barger, 226, 231; *New York Times,* 24 March 1962, p. 28, col. 8.

411. 38 Stat. 251 (1913), sec. 10 (as later amended in technical detail: "Nothing in this chapter shall be construed as taking away any powers heretofore vested by law in the Secretary of the Treasury which relate to the supervision, management, and control of the Treasury Department and bureaus under such department, and wherever any power vested by this chapter in the Board of Governors of the Federal Reserve System or the Federal Reserve agent appears to conflict with the powers of the Secretary of the Treasury, such powers shall be exercised subject to the supervision and control of the secretary"). Willis (1), 672, 835, 838, speaking with the knowledgeableness of a key inside draftsman of the 1913 legislation, comments on the important issues of Treasury-Federal Reserve relations left unresolved by the terms of the 1913 act. 38 Stat. 251 (1913), sec. 15 said that the federal reserve banks should act as fiscal agents for the government "when required" by the Treasury and said nothing about board supervision of the banks in that role, though sec. 11 gave the board general powers to examine the books and supervise the conduct of the regional banks. Cf. Clifford, 297. In this context, plainly sec. 10 meant that the Federal Reserve might not interfere with the immediate conduct of federal fiscal operations. United States v. Manufacturers Trust Co., 198 Fed. (2d) 366, 368 (2d Cir. 1952) (a Federal Reserve regulation may not abrogate statutory powers of Treasury to enforce collection of taxes). Plain on the legislative record, on the other hand, was rejection of an early suggestion of Secretary of the Treasury McAdoo that Congress simply create a bank of issue, with other central-bank-type powers, as a bureau of the Treasury. Congress did make the Federal Reserve System a separate administrative establishment of government, with its own responsibilities and its own capacities to fulfill those responsibilities. See Opinion of the Attorney General to the Secretary of the Treasury, 16 November 1914, 30 *Opinions of the Attorney General,* 308, note 400, supra. But cf. note 377, supra (board's accounts audited by Treasury to 1921, thence by comptroller of the currency to 1933). On the significance of rejection of the McAdoo proposal (which may have been only a tactical maneuver), see Glass, 100-10; Harding, 7-13; note 281, supra. But after one takes due account of these aspects of the record, still unresolved were the questions, how far the Treasury might use its fiscal powers to pursue monetary goals and how far for fiscal—primarily, debt-management—reasons it might override Federal Reserve monetary objectives.

412. On the monetary impacts of Treasury debt handling: Commission on Money and Credit (1), 194; Goldenweiser, 266; Mints, 285, 286. On the likely primacy of debt-management over monetary goals in Treasury calculations: Barger, 154; Clifford, 200, 207, 216, 278; Commission on Money and Credit (1), 100-101, 103-4, 108-10, Friedman and Schwartz, 553. On the 1919 bond flotation: Barger, 56; David C. Elliott, 309; Friedman and Schwartz, 224. See, further, supra, notes 406 (1937 episode), 407 (1946-51), 410 (1936, 1961-64). Because of its position in the key New York money market, the Federal Reserve Bank of New York early grew to be the Federal Reserve office primarily used by the Treasury for the fiscal-agent services it desired from the system. The New York bank took the initiative to harmonize its fiscal-agent role with system monetary policy, requesting and ordinarily obtaining Treasury cooperation in adjusting the government's money flows to avoid disturbing the general money market. But the New York bank regarded itself in these respects as responsible primarily to the Treasury. Clifford, 295-97; *New York Times,* 12 June 1961, p. 43, col. 1. Friedman and Schwartz, 635, suggest that, insofar as the FOMC at times limited its dealings to the shortest-term Treasury securities (the bills-only

policy), in effect it conceded to the Treasury responsibility for the maturity distribution of federal debt. 42 *Fed. Res. Bull.* 1181, 1182, 1184 (1956) brought the allocation of functions into sharper relief, with the board's suggestions for statutory revision of the provisions touching Federal Reserve-Treasury relations.

Three other aspects of the statutes of potential importance for Treasury effects on the money supply proved in fact of no great practical importance.

(1) Since 13 Stat. 104 (1864), sec. 16, national banks had been entitled to issue circulating notes secured by deposit of qualified United States bonds. Insofar as Congress authorized the Treasury from time to time to issue bonds carrying this privilege, inherently it empowered the Treasury to affect the money stock by its decisions to issue bonds of this character. In fact, the Treasury never undertook to use such statutory discretion as it had in this respect as a money control device. The provision for Federal Reserve notes reduced the importance of national bank notes, by providing a more flexible, competing currency. On 1 November 1924 the Treasury announced its intent to redeem all circulation-privilege bonds, but in the face of banks' opposition it did not carry through; the bonds were not yet callable and were selling above par, which made retirement look too expensive. In a gesture toward expanding the money supply against depression deflation, 47 Stat. 725 (1932), sec. 29, authorized national banks to issue for three years national bank notes secured by all government bonds of 3 3/8 percent yield or less. The 1932 act had the potential of a $900 million bank-note issue, but less than $200 million notes were issued. Before that act expired, the Treasury in 1935 began retiring all national bank notes by calling the last circulation-privilege bonds, making charges therefor to the credit of the federal reserve banks against the Treasury account, which it replenished by depositing with the banks gold certificate credits from part of the government's "profit" obtained by reducing the gold value of the dollar; about $645 million of the $2.8 billion devaluation profit was used to this purpose. Friedman and Schwartz, 442, including notes 19 and 20; Goldenweiser, 16; Taus, 147, 177, 193; Wallich and Wallich, 327.

(2) Under 38 Stat. 251 (1913), sec. 14 (b) there was no statutory bar to the federal reserve banks' buying securities directly from the Treasury, but except in the first days of the system the banks in practice bought only one-day bills by direct purchase. Goldenweiser, 89, 90. 49 Stat. 684 (1935), sec. 206 (a) amended sec. 14 (b) to stipulate that federal reserve banks might buy or sell direct obligations of the United States "only in the open market." 56 Stat. 176 (1942), sec. 401, authorized the banks to deal in such securities either in open market or directly from or to the United States, subject to FOMC direction and subject to an aggregate limit of $5 billion on securities acquired directly from the United States at any one time by the twelve federal reserve banks. Goldenweiser, op. cit. supra, finds this a hollow limitation against inflation, because the Treasury may always sell its securities to dealers from whom the banks may then buy them without legal limit.

(3) The Federal Reserve Act contained no direct authorization to the system to deal in government securities for the purpose of supporting the government bond market. Goldenweiser, 224, suggests that 49 Stat. 684 (1935), sec. 205, creating Federal Reserve Act, sec. 12A (c), in the course of legitimizing the FOMC, indirectly authorized such support action when it directed that system open-market operations "be governed with a view to accommodating commerce and business and with regard to their bearing upon the general credit situation of the country." This declaration might be taken to authorize support, if disturbances in the government bond market were so great as to threaten to disorganize the money or capital markets as a whole. In any case, the Federal Reserve Board seems never to have raised an issue of legality,

but only issues of policy judgment, when it was under Treasury pressure to support the government bond market. Thus in congressional hearings in 1948 Marriner Eccles, speaking for the board, took the position that "with the public debt the size it is, so much larger than the entire private debt, in fact equal to about 60% of all the debt— we must maintain the stability of the government securities market and confidence in it," and observed, further, "at no time have we tried to force a rate on the Treasury that they were unwilling to accept. I do not think it would be practical to do so. I think the central bank has certainly got to recognize the responsibility of the Treasury and to advise and work with Treasury officials in that regard. . . . [T]he Treasury and the Federal Reserve have cooperated pretty fully in connection with the management of the public debt." Barger, 170, 171. Cf. Friedman and Schwartz, 620-21, 625; Myers, 378; Rostow, 198. Of course, the fact that the Federal Reserve had authority to support the government bond market did not mean that it was necessarily good public policy to do so. Goldenweiser, 218, 219, 223, 224 presents considerations indicating both that the Treasury has typically possessed substantial means through investment in trust funds under its management and through its discretion to issue short-term debt, to act on its own to support the market, and that the factual need of market support is not beyond debate.

413. 38 Stat. 251 (1913), secs. 13 (authorizes Federal Reserve Banks to receive government deposits) and 15 (authorizes Treasury to require fiscal-agent and depository services from the banks). The subtreasury-depositories were ended by 41 Stat. 654 (1920), effective no later than 1 July 1921. Chandler, 105; Clifford 76; David C. Elliott, 297; Taus, 135, note 5, 176. On earlier policy regarding government deposits, see notes 175, 247, supra. Except for the hazards of political patronage, deposit of government funds in banks rather than in subtreasuries was in the interest of desirable flexibility in the general economy, since it put the funds where they could contribute to the lending reserves of the banking system; this value was enhanced by the greater centralization involved in putting them in the federal reserve banks. Chandler and David C. Elliott, op. cit. supra. At first hesitating to end the patronage connected with the old subtreasuries or with deposits in commercial banks and to lose interest paid by the latter, as well as fearful of disrupting the commercial banks by rapid withdrawals, the Treasury began after 1920 to concentrate its deposits more and more in the federal reserve banks. Taus, 137, 160-61, 175. However, the Treasury continued to hold authority to deposit government funds in commercial banks, if it so chose. See 13 Stat. 113 (1864), sec. 45, 12 U.S.C.A. sec. 90; Inland Waterways Corporation v. Young, 309 U.S. 517, 520-24 (1940). This continued discretion to use commercial banks was consistent with the fact that, confronted with the demand of some that the Treasury be required to keep all its deposits with federal reserve banks, Congress was probably moved more by Treasury desire to have options and by the fear of Bryan Democrats' fears that the new system would come under the particular control of Wall Street. Cf. Clifford, 76. Willis (1), 1111-12, comments on the deliberate change of the 1913 bill, to leave the secretary of the treasury discretion in placing government deposits. See, also, Warburg, 1:262, 263. Goldenweiser, 266, comments on the neutrality of Treasury deposit policy after the Treasury began to put substantially all government funds in the federal reserve banks. Secretary Andrew Mellon wrote *finis* to the older, if episodic, Treasury policy of shifting deposits in order to ease credit, when he refused to do so to alleviate tight credit in the agricultural regions of the country; instead, at the secretary's request, by Joint Resolution, 41 Stat. 1084 (1921), Congress directed the secretary to revive activities of the War Finance Corporation, whose loans made under the secretary's direction then helped

relieve the blows which agriculture felt from falling prices soon after World War I. Taus, 173.

414. Cf. Auerbach, 235, 248; Barger, 276, 282, 284; Commission on Money and Credit (1), 267-69, 276-77; Condliffe, 261; Flash, 291-93; Knipe, 234; Nourse, 294, 296, 357-58, 361, 399-402, 410-16; Nussbaum, 214; Rostow, 13-14, 175-76; *New York Times,* 2 February 1966, p. 43, col. 2; id., 29 July 1970, p. 51, col. 1. CEA-White House leadership was posed most explicitly by two policy recommendations in the early 1960s. The 1961 (unofficial) report of the CED's Commission on Money and Credit recommended amending the Employment Act of 1946 to provide that when the president's advices showed a tendency in the current economic situation significantly counter to the 1946 act's objectives, the president should supplement his annual economic report by statements at quarterly intervals so long as necessary, detailing steps taken by him and by government agencies "including the Federal Reserve System," to rectify the deficiencies, or explanations for any apparently inconsistent use being made "of any of these instruments." Commission on Money and Credit (1), 273. In 1964 the Democratic majority of the Domestic Finance Subcommittee of the House Banking and Currency Committee suggested that the Federal Reserve Board be put under statutory direction to pursue such credit policies as might be outlined by the president each January in his economic report to Congress. *New York Times,* 5 July 1964, sec. 3, p. 1, col. 8; id., 21 December 1964, p. 49, col. 7. Of course Federal Reserve-CEA-White House liaison did not work automatically; it sometimes broke down, and always the influence of both the CEA and the board depended critically on the attitude toward their roles taken by the president. See Barger, 163, Flash, 249, 296; Nourse, 378, 386.

Sources Cited

Sources Cited
[Official action documents are cited in full in the footnotes]

Abel, Albert S. "The Commerce Clause in the Constitutional Convention and in Contemporary Comment." 25 *Minn. L. Rev.* 432 (1941).

Acheson, Dean. *Morning and Noon.* Boston: Houghton Mifflin Co., 1965.

Adams, E. Sherman. "Effects of Federal Reserve Policy on Commercial Banks." In *The Federal Reserve System,* edited by Herbert V. Prochnow, p. 177. New York: Harper & Brothers, 1960.

Adams, George P., Jr. *Wartime Price Control.* Washington, D.C.: American Council on Public Affairs, 1942.

Adams, Henry. *History of the United States during the Administrations of Thomas Jefferson and James Madison.* 9 vols. New York: Albert and Charles Boni, 1930.

Adler, Edward A. "Business Jurisprudence." 28 *Harv. L. Rev.* 135 (1914). Reprinted in Association of American Law Schools, *Selected Essays on Constitutional Law.* 2:436. 3 vols. Chicago: Foundation Press, 1938.

Ames, Herman V. *The Proposed Amendments to the Constitution of the United States during the First Century of Its History.* Brooklyn, N.Y.: Central Book Co., 1969. Originally in *Annual Report of the American Historical Association,* 1896, Vol. II. Washington, D.C.: Government Printing Office, 1897.

Andersen, Theodore A. *A Century of Banking in Wisconsin.* Madison: State Historical Society of Wisconsin, 1954.

Anderson, Clay J. *A Half-Century of Federal Reserve Policy Making, 1914-1964.* Philadelphia: Federal Reserve Bank of Philadelphia, 1965.

Anderson, Ronald A. *Anderson's Uniform Commercial Code.* 2 vols. Rochester, N.Y.: Lawyers' Co-operative Publishing Co., 1961.

Angly, Edward. See Jones and Angly.

Attorney General's Committee on Administrative Procedure

(1) *The Federal Reserve System.* Staff Monograph no. 9. Washington, D.C.: Department of Justice, 1940.

(2) *Federal Control of Banking: Comptroller of the Currency, and Federal Deposit Insurance Corporation.* Staff Monograph no. 14. Washington, D.C.: Department of Justice, 1940.

Auerbach, Carl A. "Presidential Administration of Prices and Wages." 35 *Geo. Wash. L. Rev.* 191 (1966).

Backman, Jules. *Government Price-Fixing.* New York: Pitman Publishing Corporation, 1938.

Bailey, Stephen Kemp. *Congress Makes a Law.* New York: Vintage Books, no date. Original ed. New York: Columbia University Press, 1950.

Bankers Manual on the Uniform Commercial Code. Rochester, N.Y.: Massachusetts Bankers' Association, assisted by Lawyers' Co-operative Publishing Co., 1958.

Barger, Harold. *The Management of Money.* Chicago: Rand, McNally & Co., 1964.

Barrett, Don C. *The Greenbacks and Resumption of Specie Payments, 1862-1879.* Gloucester, Mass.: Peter Smith, 1965. Original ed. Cambridge, Mass.: Harvard University Press, 1931.

Beard, Charles, and Beard, Mary. *The Rise of American Civilization.* 2 vols. New York: Macmillan Co., 1927.

Beck, James M. "Nullification by Indirection." 23 *Harv. L. Rev.* 441 (1910).

Beer, Thomas. *The Mauve Decade: American Life at the End of the Nineteenth Century.* Garden City, N.Y.: Garden City Publishing Co., 1926.

Benedict, Murray R. *Farm Policies of the United States, 1790-1950.* New York: Twentieth Century Fund, 1953.

Benson, Lee. *The Concept of Jacksonian Democracy.* New York: Atheneum, 1964.

Berle, A. A.

(1) "Banking under the Anti-Trust Laws." 49 *Colum. L. Rev. 589 (1949).*

(2) "Modern Functions of the Corporate System." 62 Colum. L. Rev. 433 (1962).

(3) *The American Economic Republic.* New York: Harcourt, Brace & World, Inc., 1963.

Berle, A. A., and Pederson, Victoria J. *Liquid Claims and National Wealth.* New York: Macmillan Co., 1934.

Bernstein, Peter L. *A Primer on Money, Banking, and Gold.* New York: Vintage Books, 1965.

Beveridge, Albert J. *The Life of John Marshall.* 4 vols. Boston: Houghton Mifflin Co., 1919.

Black, Henry Campbell. *A Treatise on the Law of Judgments.* 2 vols. 2d ed. St. Paul, Minnesota: West Publishing Co., 1902.

Blakey, Roy G., and Blakey, Gladys C. *The Federal Income Tax.* New York: Longmans Green & Co., 1940.

Blum, Walter J., and Kalven, Harry, Jr. *The Uneasy Case for Progressive Taxation.* Chicago: University of Chicago Press, Phoenix Books, 1953.

Board of Governors of the Federal Reserve System, and the United States Treasury. *The Federal Reserve and the Treasury: Answers to Questions from the Commission on Money and Credit.* Englewood Cliffs, N.J.: Prentice-Hall, Inc., 1963.

Bogart, Ernest L. *Economic History of the American People.* 2d ed. New York: Longmans, Green & Co., 1938.

Bogen, Jules I. "The Federal Reserve System Since 1940." In *The Federal Reserve System,* edited by Herbert V. Prochnow, p. 338. New York: Harper & Brothers, 1960.

Bolles, Albert S. *Modern Law of Banking.* 2 vols. Philadelphia: George T. Bisel Co., 1907.

Boudin, Louis B. *Government by Judiciary.* 2 vols. New York: William Godwin, Inc., 1932.

Bowers, Claude G. *Jefferson and Hamilton.* Boston: Houghton Mifflin Co., 1925.

Bradford, Frederick A. "A Proper Monetary System." In *A Proper Monetary and Banking System for the United States,* edited by James W. Bell and Walter E. Spahr, p. 1. New York: Ronald Press, 1960.

Braucher, Robert, and Sutherland, Arthur E., Jr. *Commercial Transactions.* 2d ed. Brooklyn, N.Y.: Foundation Press, Inc., 1958.

Brown, Ray Andrews. "The Making of the Wisconsin Constitution." 1949 *Wis. L. Rev.* 648 1952 id., 23.

Bruchey, Stuart. *The Roots of American Economic Growth, 1607-1861.* New York: Harper & Row, Harper Torchbooks, 1968.

Burkhead, Jesse. *Government Budgeting.* New York: John Wiley & Sons, Inc., 1956.

Burns, Arthur F., and Samuelson, Paul A. *Full Employment Guideposts and Economic Stability.* Washington, D.C.: American Enterprise Institute for Public Policy Research, 1967.

Burns, James M. *Congress on Trial.* New York: Harper & Brothers, 1949.

Cadman, John W., Jr. *The Corporation in New Jersey: Business and Politics, 1791-1875.* Cambridge, Mass.: Harvard University Press, 1949.

Cagan, Phillip. "The First Fifty Years of the National Banking System—An

Historical Appraisal." In *Banking and Monetary Studies,* edited by Deane Carson. Homewood, Ill.: Richard D. Irwin, Inc., 1963.

Caine, M. R. See Shultz and Caine.

Catterall, Ralph C. H. *The Second Bank of the United States.* Chicago: University of Chicago Press, 1903.

Chafee, Zechariah, Jr., and Simpson, Sidney Post. *Cases on Equity.* 2 vols. Cambridge, Mass.: Published by the editors, 1934.

Chamberlain, Joseph P. *Legislative Processes, National and State.* New York: D. Appleton-Century Co., 1936.

Chamberlain, Lawrence H. *The President, Congress and Legislation.* New York: Columbia University Press, 1947.

Chandler, Lester V. *Benjamin Strong, Central Banker.* Washington, D.C.: Brookings Institution, 1958.

Chapin, Earl H. "Techniques of Bank Examination." In Federal Reserve Bank of St. Louis, *Bank Supervision,* p. 21. St. Louis: Federal Reserve Bank of St. Louis, 1963.

Ciriacy-Wantrup, S. V. *Resource Conservation: Economics and Policies.* Berkeley: University of California Press, 1952.

Clark, John Maurice. *Economic Institutions and Human Welfare.* New York: Alfred A. Knopf, 1957.

Clarke, M. St. Clair, and Hall, D. A. *Legislative and Documentary History of the Bank of the United States.* Washington, D.C.: Gale and Seaton, 1832.

Clifford, Albert J. *The Independence of the Federal Reserve System.* Philadelphia: University of Pennsylvania Press, 1965.

Cochran, Thomas C. "The Entrepreneur in American Capital Formation." In National Bureau of Economic Research, *Capital Formation and Economic Growth,* p. 339. Princeton, N.J.: Princeton University Press, 1955.

Cochran, Thomas C., and Miller, William. *The Age of Enterprise.* New York: Macmillan Co., 1943.

Coit, Margaret L. *John C. Calhoun, American Portrait.* Boston: Houghton Mifflin Co., 1950.

Coleman, George W. "Legal Reserve Requirements." In *The Federal Reserve System,* edited by Herbert V. Prochnow, p. 75. New York: Harper & Brothers, 1960.

Commission on Money and Credit
  (1) *Money and Credit: Their Influence on Jobs, Prices, and Growth.* Englewood Cliffs, N.J.: Prentice-Hall, Inc., 1961.
  (2) *The Commercial Banking Industry.* Englewood Cliffs, N.J.: Prentice-Hall, Inc., 1962.

Condliffe, J. E. "The Guideline Economy." 35 *Geo. Wash. L. Rev.* 253 (1966).

Cooper, Frank E. See Dawson and Cooper.

Corbin, Arthur L. *Corbin on Contracts.* 7 vols. St. Paul, Minn.: West Publishing Co., 1964.

Cotter, Cornelius P. *Government and Private Enterprise.* New York: Holt, Rinehart & Winston, 1960.

Crosskey, William W. *Politics and the Constitution in the History of the United States.* 2 vols. Chicago: University of Chicago Press, 1953.

Culbertson, J. M. "Government Financial Policy in the Effective Market Economy." In *Banking and Monetary Studies,* edited by Deane Carson. Homewood, Ill.: Richard D. Irwin, Inc., 1963.

Dana, Julian. *A. P. Giannini, Giant in the West.* New York: Prentice-Hall, Inc., 1947.

Daniel, John W. *A Treatise on the Law of Negotiable Instruments.* 7th ed., edited by Thomas H. Calvert. 3 vols. New York: Baker, Voorhis & Co., 1933.

Davis, Joseph S. *Essays in the Earlier History of American Corporations.* 2 vols. Cambridge, Mass.: Harvard University Press, 1917.

Davis, Kenneth Culp. *Discretionary Justice.* Baton Rouge, La.: Louisiana State University Press, 1969.

Dawson, John P. "The Gold Clause Decisions." 33 *Mich. L. Rev.* 647 (1935).

Dawson, John P., and Cooper, Frank E. "The Effect of Inflation on Private Contracts: United States, 1861-1879." 33 *Mich. L. Rev.* 706, 852 (1935).

Dewald, William G., and Johnson, Harry G. "An Objective Analysis of the Objectives of American Monetary Policy, 1952-61." In *Banking and Monetary Studies,* edited by Deane Carson, p. 171. Homewood, Ill.: Richard D. Irwin, Inc., 1963.

Dewey, Davis R. *Financial History of the United States.* 7th ed. New York: Longmans, Green & Co., 1920.

Dodd, E. Merrick, Jr. *American Business Corporations until 1860.* Cambridge, Mass.: Harvard University Press, 1954.

Dorfman, Joseph. *The Economic Mind in American Civilization.* 5 vols. New York: Viking Press, 1949.

Drucker, Peter. *The Future of Industrial Man.* New York: John Day Co. 1942.

Dunbar, Charles F. *Laws of the United States Relating to Currency, Finance, and Banking.* New York: Greenwood Publishers, 1968. Original ed. New York: Ginn & Co., 1893.

Dunne, Gerald T.
> (1) "President Grant and Chief Justice Chase: A Footnote to the Legal Tender Cases." 5 *St. Louis Univ. L. Jour.* 539 (1959).
>
> (2) *Monetary Decisions of the Supreme Court.* New Brunswick, N.J.: Rutgers University Press, 1960.
>
> (3) "A Christmas Present for the President." *Business Horizons* (Winter, 1963), p. 43. Bloomington, Ind.: Graduate School of Business, Indiana University.
>
> (4) "The Legal Basis of Bank Supervision." In Federal Reserve Bank of St. Louis, *Bank Supervision,* p. 6. St. Louis: Federal Reserve Bank of St. Louis, 1963.

Eccles, Marriner S. *Beckoning Frontiers.* Edited by Sidney Hyman. New York: Alfred A. Knopf, 1951.

Ederer, Rupert J. *The Evolution of Money.* Washington, D.C.: Public Affairs Press, 1964.

Elliott, David C. "The Federal Reserve System 1914-1929." In *The Federal Reserve System,* edited by Herbert V. Prochnow, p. 295. New York: Harper & Brothers, 1960.

Elliott, Jonathan. *Debates in the Several State Conventions on the Adoption of the Federal Constitution.* 5 vols. Philadelphia: J. B. Lippincott & Co., 1863.

Ely, John Hart. "Legislative and Administrative Motivation in Constitutional Law." 79 *Yale L. Jour.* 1205 (1970).

Evans, George H., Jr.
> (1) *Business Incorporations in the United States, 1800-1943.* New York: National Bureau of Economic Research, Inc., 1948.
>
> (2) *Basic Economics: A Macro- and Micro-Analysis.* New York: Alfred A. Knopf, 1950.

Fairman, Charles
> (1) *Mr. Justice Miller and the Supreme Court, 1862-1890.* Cambridge, Mass.: Harvard University Press, 1939.
>
> (2) "Mr. Justice Bradley's Appointment to the Supreme Court and the Legal Tender Cases." 54 *Harv. L. Rev.* 977 (1941).
>
> (3) *Reconstruction and Reunion, 1864-88: Part One.* New York: Macmillan Co., 1971.

Farrand, Max. *The Records of the Federal Convention of 1787.* 4 vols. Rev. ed. New Haven: Yale University Press, 1937.

Faulkner, Harold U. *American Economic History.* 4th ed. New York: Harper & Brothers, 1938.

Federalist, The. Edited by Henry Cabot Lodge. New York: G. P. Putnam's Sons, 1907.

Fine, Sidney. *Laissez Faire and the General-Welfare State: A Study of Conflict In American Thought, 1865-1901.* Ann Arbor: University of Michigan Press, 1956.

Fischer, Gerald C. *American Banking Structure.* New York: Columbia University Press, 1968.

Flash, Edward S., Jr. "The Broadening Scope of the President's Economic Advice." 35 *Geo. Wash. L. Rev.* 286 (1966).

Frankfurter, Felix. "The Early Writings of O. W. Holmes, Jr." 44 *Harv. L. Rev.* 717 (1931).

Freeman, Abraham Clark. *A Treatise of the Law of Judgments.* 3 vols. San Francisco: Bancroft-Whitney Co., 1925.

Freund, Ernst. *Standards of American Legislation.* Chicago: University of Chicago Press, 1917.

Friedman, Milton. *Capitalism and Freedom.* Chicago: University of Chicago Press, Phoenix Books, 1962.

Friedman, Milton, and Schwartz, Anna Jacobson. *A Monetary History of the United States, 1867-1960.* Princeton, N.J.: Princeton University Press, 1963.

Gates, Paul Wallace. "The Role of the Land Speculator in Western Development." In *The Public Lands,* edited by Vernon Carstensen, p. 349. Madison: University of Wisconsin Press, 1963.

Glass, Carter. *An Adventure in Constructive Finance.* New York: Doubleday, Page & Co., 1927.

Goldenweiser, E. A. *American Monetary Policy.* New York: McGraw-Hill Book Co., Inc., 1951.

Gouge, William. *Short History of Paper Money and Banking in the United States.* 2d ed. New York: B. & S. Collins, 1835.

Gould, John M. *The National Bank Acts.* Boston: Little, Brown & Co., 1904.

Govan, Thomas P. *Nicholas Biddle: Nationalist and Public Banker, 1786-1844.* Chicago: University of Chicago Press, 1959.

Greenspun, Nathaniel. See Smith and Greenspun.

Grove, David L. "Selective Credit Controls." In *The Federal Reserve System,* edited by Herbert V. Prochnow, p. 141. New York: Harper & Brothers, 1960.

Groves, Harold M. *Financing Government.* New York: Henry Holt and Co., 1939.

Gunther, Gerald. *John Marshall's Defense of McCulloch v. Maryland.* Stanford, Calif.: Stanford University Press, 1969.

Hacker, Louis M. *The Triumph of American Capitalism.* New York: Simon & Schuster, 1940.

Hacker, Louis M., and Kendrick, Benjamin B. *The United States Since 1865.* New York: F. S. Crofts & Co., 1936.

Hacker, Louis M., and Zahler, Helene S.
(1) *The Shaping of the American Tradition.* 2 vols. New York: Columbia University Press, 1947.
(2) *The United States in the 20th Century.* New York: Appleton-Century-Crofts, Inc., 1952.

Hale, Robert L. *Freedom through Law: Public Control of Private Governing Power.* New York: Columbia University Press, 1952.

Hamilton, Alexander. *The Works of Alexander Hamilton.* Edited by Henry Cabot Lodge. 12 vols. New York: G. P. Putnam's Sons, 1904.

Hammond, Bray
(1) *Banks and Politics in America: From the Revolution to the Civil War.* Princeton, N.J.: Princeton University Press, 1957.
(2) "Banking before the Civil War." In *Banking and Monetary Studies,* edited by Deane Carson, p. 1. Homewood, Ill.: Richard D. Irwin, Inc., 1963.
(3) *Sovereignty and an Empty Purse: Banks and Politics in the Civil War.* Princeton, N.J.: Princeton University Press, 1970.

Handlin, Oscar, and Handlin, Mary Flug. *Commonwealth: A Study of the Role of Government in the American Economy: Massachusetts, 1774-1861.* Rev. ed. Cambridge, Mass.: Belknap Press of Harvard University Press, 1969.

Hansen, Alvin H. *The American Economy.* New York: McGraw-Hill Book Co., Inc., 1957.

Harding, W. P. G. *The Formative Period of the Federal Reserve System.* Cambridge, Mass.: Houghton Mifflin Co., 1925.

Hardy, Charles O. *Wartime Control of Prices.* Washington, D.C.: Brookings Institution, 1940.

Harl, M. T. "Federal Deposit Insurance Corporation." A 6 *Corporate Reorganization and American Bankruptcy Review* 253 (1947).

Harris, Seymour E.
(1) *Price and Related Controls in the United States.* New York: McGraw-Hill Book Co., Inc., 1945.
(2) *John Maynard Keynes, Economist and Policy Maker.* New York: Charles Scribner's Sons, 1955.
See Sutton, Francis X., et al.

Harrod, Roy. *The Dollar.* 2d ed. New York: W. W. Norton & Co., Inc., 1963.

Hart, Henry L., Jr. "The Gold Clause in United States Bonds." 48 *Harv. L. Rev.* 1057 (1935).

Hartz, Louis. *Economic Policy and Democratic Thought: Pennsylvania, 1776-1860.* Cambridge, Mass.: Harvard University Press, 1948.

Heath, Milton S. *Constructive Liberalism: The Role of the State in Economic Development in Georgia to 1860.* Cambridge, Mass.: Harvard University Press, 1954.

Heller, Walter W. *New Dimensions of Political Economy.* Cambridge, Mass.: Harvard University Press, 1966.

Henderson, Gerard C. *The Position of Foreign Corporations in American Constitutional Law.* Cambridge, Mass.: Harvard University Press, 1918.

Hepburn, A. Barton. *A History of Currency in the United States.* Rev. ed. 1924. New York: Augustus M. Kelley, Publishers, 1967.

Hibbard, Benjamin H. *A History of the Public Land Policies.* New York: Peter Smith, 1939.

Hockett, Homer Carey. *The Constitutional History of the United States.* 2 vols. New York: Macmillan Co., 1939.

Hofstadter, Richard
(1) *The American Political Tradition and the Men Who Made It.* New York: Alfred A. Knopf, 1948.
(2) *The Age of Reform: From Bryan to F.D.R.* New York: Alfred A. Knopf, 1955.

Horvitz, Paul M. "Branch Banking, Mergers, and Competition." In *Banking and Monetary Studies,* edited by Deane Carson. Homewood, Ill.: Richard D. Irwin, Inc., 1963.

Howe, Mark DeWolfe. *Justice Oliver Wendell Holmes.* 2 vols. Cambridge, Mass.: Belknap Press of Harvard University Press, 1963.

Hunt, Alva R. *A Treatise on the Law of Tender.* St. Paul, Minn.: Frank P. Dufresne, 1903.

Hurst, James Willard
(1) "Treason in the United States." 58 *Harv. L. Rev.* 226 (1944).
(2) *The Growth of American Law: The Law Makers.* Boston: Little, Brown & Co., 1950.
(3) *Law and the Conditions of Freedom in the Nineteenth-Century United States.* Madison: University of Wisconsin Press, 1956.
(4) *Law and Social Process in United States History.* Ann Arbor, Mich.: University of Michigan Law School, 1960.
(5) *Law and Economic Growth: The Legal History of the Lumber Industry in Wisconsin, 1836-1915.* Cambridge, Mass.: Belknap Press of Harvard University, 1964.
(6) *The Legitimacy of the Business Corporation.* Charlottesville, Va.: University Press of Virginia, 1970.

Hyneman, Charles S. *Bureaucracy in a Democracy.* New York: Harper & Brothers, 1950.

Isbell, Wilbur H. "Review and Appraisal." In Federal Reserve Bank of St. Louis, *Bank Supervision,* p. 27. St. Louis: Federal Reserve Bank of St. Louis, 1963.

Jacoby, Neil. "The Structure and Use of Variable Bank Reserve Requirements." In *Banking and Monetary Studies,* edited by Deane Carson, p. 213. Homewood, Ill.: Richard D. Irwin, Inc., 1963.

Jefferson, Thomas. *Works.* Edited by Paul Leicester Ford. 12 vols. New York: G. P. Putnam's Sons, 1905.

———. *Writings.* Edited by H. A. Washington. 9 vols. Washington, D.C.: Taylor & Maury, 1853-54.

Johnson, F. A. J., and Krooss, Herman L. *The Origins and Development of the American Economy.* New York: Prentice-Hall, Inc., 1953.

Jones, Jesse H., and Angly, Edward. *Fifty Billion Dollars.* New York: Macmillan Co., 1951.

Journals of the Continental Congress, 1774-1789. 31 vols. Washington, D.C.: Government Printing Office, 1906.

Kalven, Harry. See Blum and Kalven.

Kapp, K. William. *The Social Costs of Private Enterprise.* Cambridge, Mass.: Harvard University Press, 1950.

Kaysen, Carl. See Sutton, Francis X., et al.

Kaysen, Carl, and Turner, Donald F. *Antitrust Policy, An Economic and Legal Analysis.* Cambridge, Mass.: Harvard University Press, 1965.

Kendrick, Benjamin B. See Hacker and Kendrick.

Kent, James. *Commentaries on American Law.* 4 vols. 12th ed. Edited by O. W. Holmes, Jr. Boston: Little, Brown & Co., 1873.

Kent, Raymond P. "Dual Banking Between the Two World Wars." In *Banking and Monetary Studies,* edited by Deane Carson, p. 43. Homewood, Ill.: Richard D. Irwin, Inc., 1963.

Knipe, James L. *The Federal Reserve and the American Dollar: Problems and Policies, 1946-1964.* Chapel Hill: University of North Carolina Press, 1965.

Knox, John Jay
  (1) *United States Notes.* 2d ed., rev. New York: Charles Scribner's Sons, 1885.
  (2) *A History of Banking in the United States.* New York: Augustus M. Kelley, Publishers, 1969. Original ed. New York: Bradford, Rhodes & Co., 1900.

Krooss, Herman E.
  (1) *American Economic Development.* Englewood Cliffs, N.J.: Prentice-Hall, Inc., 1955.
  (2) "The Historical Background of the American Banking System." In *The Federal Reserve System,* edited by Herbert V. Prochnow, p. 1.

New York: Harper & Brothers, 1960.

(3) Ed., *Documentary History of Banks and Currency in the United States.* 4 vols. New York: Chelsea House Publishers, 1969.

See Studenski and Krooss.

Kuehnl, George J. *The Wisconsin Business Corporation.* Madison: University of Wisconsin Press, 1959.

Land, James N. "The Federal Reserve Act." In *The Federal Reserve System,* edited by Herbert V. Prochnow, p. 19. New York: Harper & Brothers, 1960.

Landis, James M. *The Administrative Process.* New Haven: Yale University Press, 1938.

Laughlin, J. Laurence. *The History of Bimetallism in the United States.* New York: Appleton, 1901.

Lekachman, Robert. *The Age of Keynes.* New York: Random House, 1966.

Lerner, Eugene M. "Money, Prices, and Wages in the Confederacy, 1861-65." In *The Economic Impact of the American Civil War,* edited by Ralph Andreano. Cambridge, Mass.: Schenkman Publishing Co., 1962.

Lewis, Lawrence, Jr. *A History of the Bank of North America.* Philadelphia: J. B. Lippincott & Co., 1882.

Lifland, William T. "The Supreme Court, Congress, and Bank Mergers." 32 *Law and Contemporary Problems* 15 (1967).

Link, Arthur S. *Wilson: The New Freedom.* Princeton, N.J.: Princeton University Press, 1956.

Livermore, Shaw. *Early American Land Companies.* New York: Commonwealth Fund, 1939.

Loss, Louis. *Securities Regulation.* 3 vols. 2d ed. Boston: Little, Brown & Co., 1961.

Lynd, Robert S., and Lynd, Helen Merrell

(1) *Middletown: A Study in Contemporary American Culture.* New York: Harcourt, Brace & Co., 1929.

(2) *Middletown in Transition: A Study in Cultural Conflicts.* New York: Harcourt, Brace & Co., 1937.

McAdoo, William G. *Crowded Years.* Boston: Houghton Mifflin Co., 1931.

McKinley, David H. "The Discount Rate and Rediscount Policy." In *The Federal Reserve System,* edited by Herbert V. Prochnow, p. 90. New York: Harper & Bros., 1960.

McKinley, Gordon W. "Effects of Federal Reserve Policy on Nonmonetary Financial Institutions." In *The Federal Reserve System,* edited by Herbert V. Prochnow, p. 204. New York: Harper & Bros., 1960.

McLaughlin, Andrew C. *A Constitutional History of the United States.* New York: D. Appleton-Century Co., 1936.

Malone, Dumas. *Jefferson and the Rights of Man.* Boston: Little, Brown & Co., 1951.

Mann, Maurice. "How Does Monetary Policy Affect the Economy?" 54 Fed. Res. Bull. 803 (1968).

Marshall, Lynn L. "The Authorship of Jackson's Bank Veto Message." 50 Miss. Valley Hist. Rev. 466 (1963).

Mayo, Bernard
    (1) *Henry Clay: Spokesman of the New West.* Boston: Houghton Mifflin Co., 1937.
    (2) *Jefferson Himself.* Boston: Houghton Mifflin Co., 1942.

Meyers, Marvin. *The Jacksonian Persuasion: Politics and Belief.* Stanford, Calif.: Stanford University Press, 1957.

Miller, Arthur S. "Constitutional Revolution Consolidated: The Rise of the Positive State." 35 *Geo. Wash. L. Rev.* 172 (1966).

Miller, Charles A. *The Supreme Court and the Uses of History.* Cambridge, Mass.: Belknap Press of Harvard University Press, 1969.

Miller, John C. *Alexander Hamilton: Portrait in Paradox.* New York: Harper & Brothers, 1959.

Miller, William. See Cochran and Miller.

Mints, Lloyd W. *A History of Banking Theory in Great Britain and the United States.* Chicago: University of Chicago Press, 1945.

Mitchell, Broadus. *Alexander Hamilton: Youth to Maturity, 1755-1788.* New York: Macmillan Co., 1957.

Mitchell, Wesley C. *A History of the Greenbacks, 1862-1865.* Chicago: University of Chicago Press, 1903.

Morgan, Donald G. *Justice William Johnson, The First Dissenter.* Columbia: University of South Carolina Press, 1954.

Morison, Samuel Eliot, and Commager, Henry Steele. *The Growth of the American Republic.* 2 vols. 3d ed. New York: Oxford University Press, 1942.

Morris, Richard B., ed. *The Basic Ideas of Alexander Hamilton.* New York: Pocket Books, Inc., The Pocket Library, 1956.

Morse, John T., Jr. *A Treatise on the Law of Banks and Banking.* Edited by Harvey C. Voorhees. 2 vols. Boston: Little, Brown & Co., 1928.

Munn, Glenn G. *Encyclopedia of Banking and Finance.* 6th ed. Boston: Bankers Publishing Co., 1962.

Myers, Margaret G. *A Financial History of the United States.* New York: Columbia University Press, 1970.

Myrdal, Gunnar. *An International Economy.* New York: Harper & Brothers, 1956.

Nevins, Allan, and Commager, Henry Steele. *A Pocket History of the United States.* 5th ed. New York: Washington Square Press, 1967.

North, Douglass C.

    (1) *The Economic Growth of the United States, 1790-1860.* Englewood Cliffs, N.J.: Prentice-Hall, Inc., 1961.

    (2) *Growth and Welfare in the American Past.* Englewood Cliffs, N.J.: Prentice-Hall, Inc., 1966.

Nourse, Edwin G. *Economics in the Public Service: Administrative Aspects of the Employment Act.* New York: Harcourt, Brace & Co., 1953.

Nugent, Walter T. K. *Money and American Society, 1865-1880.* New York: Free Press, 1968.

Nussbaum, Arthur. *A History of the Dollar.* New York: Columbia University Press, 1957.

Page, William Herbert. *The Law of Contracts.* 7 vols. 2d ed. Cincinnati: W. H. Anderson Co., 1921.

Paris, James D. *Monetary Policies of the United States, 1932-1938.* New York: Columbia University Press, 1938.

Parsons, Theophilus. *The Law of Contracts.* Edited by John M. Gould. 3 vols. 9th ed. Boston: Little, Brown & Co., 1904.

Pederson, Victoria. See Berle and Pederson

Peterson, Merrill D. *The Jeffersonian Image in the American Mind.* New York: Oxford University Press, 1960.

Pfiffner, John M., and Presthus, Robert V. *Public Administration.* 4th ed. New York: Ronald Press Co., 1960.

Polakoff, Murray E. "Federal Reserve Discount Policy and Its Critics." In *Banking and Monetary Studies,* edited by Deane Carson, p. 190. Homewood, Ill.: Richard D. Irwin, Inc., 1963.

Post, Russell L., and Willard, Charles H. "The Power of Congress to Nullify Gold Clauses." 46 *Harv. L. Rev.* 1225 (1933).

Potter, David M. *People of Plenty: Economic Abundance and the American Character.* Chicago: University of Chicago Press, 1954.

Pound, Roscoe

    (1) "Visitatorial Jurisdiction over Corporations in Equity." 49 *Harv. L. Rev.* 369 (1936).

    (2) "The Economic Interpretation and the Law of Torts." 53 *Harv. L. Rev.* 365 (1940).

    (3) *Jurisprudence.* 5 vols. St. Paul, Minn.: West Publishing Co., 1959.

Powell, Ellis T. *The Evolution of the Money Market, 1385-1915.* London: Financial News, 1915.

Pratt, Lester A. *Bank Frauds.* New York: Ronald Press Co., 1965.

Presthus, Robert V. See Pfiffner and Presthus.

Primm, James Neal. *Economic Policy in the Development of a Western State: Missouri, 1820-1860.* Cambridge, Mass.: Harvard University Press, 1954.

Pritchard, Leland J. "Profit or Loss from Time Deposit Banking." In *Banking and Monetary Studies,* edited by Deane Carson, p. 369. Homewood, Ill.: Richard D. Irwin, Inc., 1963.

Proposed Amendments to the Constitution of the United States Introduced in Congress from December 4, 1889 to July 2, 1926. Senate Document no. 93, 69th Cong., 1st sess. Washington, D.C.: Government Printing Office, 1926.

Radin, Max. *Manners and Morals of Business.* Indianapolis: Bobbs-Merrill Co., 1939.

Randall, K. A. "The Federal Deposit Insurance Corporation: Regulatory Functions and Philosophy." 31 *Law and Contemporary Problems* 696 (1966).

Raney, William F. *Wisconsin, A Story of Progress.* New York: Prentice-Hall, Inc., 1940.

Raskind, Leo J. "The Federal Reserve System: An Administrative Agency for Contemporary Monetary Policy?" 35 *Geo. Wash. L. Rev.* 299 (1966).

Ratner, Sidney. *American Taxation: Its History as a Social Force in Democracy.* New York: W. W. Norton & Co., Inc., 1942.

Redford, Emmett S. "Dual Banking: A Case Study in Federalism." 31 *Law and Contemporary Problems* 749 (1966).

Redlich, Fritz. *The Molding of American Banking: Men and Ideas.* 2 vols. New York: Hafner Publishing Co., 1947.

Reynolds, A. R. *The Daniel Shaw Lumber Co.: A Case Study of the Wisconsin Lumbering Frontier.* New York: New York University Press, 1957.

Richardson, James D., ed. *A Compilation of the Messages and Papers of the Presidents, 1789-1897.* 10 vols. Washington, D.C.: Government Printing Office, 1896.

Robertson, Ross M. *The Comptroller and Bank Supervision: A Historical Appraisal.* Washington, D.C.: Office of the Comptroller of the Currency, 1968.

Rodkey, Robert G. *Legal Reserves in American Banking.* Michigan Business Studies, Vol. VI, no. 5. Ann Arbor: University of Michigan, 1934.

Rohrbough, Malcolm J. *The Land Office Business: The Settlement and Administration of American Public Lands, 1789-1837.* New York: Oxford University Press, 1968.

Ropes, John C. "Unsigned comment on Hepburn v. Griswold." 4 *Am. L. Rev.* 604 (1870).

Rostow, Eugene V. *Planning for Freedom.* New Haven: Yale University Press, 1959.

Rowe, J. Z. *The Public-Private Character of United States Central Banking.*

New Brunswick, N.J.: Rutgers University Press, 1965.

Samuelson, Paul A. See Burns and Samuelson.

Schachner, Nathan. *Alexander Hamilton.* New York: D. Appleton-Century Co., Inc. 1946.

Schlesinger, Arthur M., Jr. *The Coming of the New Deal.* Boston: Houghton Mifflin Co., 1958.

Schumpeter, Joseph A.

(1) Business Cycles. 2 vols. 1st ed. New York: McGraw-Hill Book Co., Inc., 1939.

(2) *History of Economic Analysis.* Edited by Elizabeth Boody Schumpeter. New York: Oxford University Press, 1954.

Sharkey, Robert P. *Money, Class and Party: An Economic Study of Civil War and Reconstruction.* Baltimore: Johns Hopkins Press, 1959.

Sheahan, John. *The Wage-Price Guideposts.* Washington, D.C.: Brookings Institution, 1967.

Shulman, Harry. "The Demise of Swift v. Tyson." 47 *Yale L. Jour.* 1336 (1938).

Shultz, William J., and Caine, M. R. *Financial Development of the United States.* New York: Prentice-Hall, Inc., 1937.

Simpson, Sidney Post. See Chafee and Simpson.

Skilton, Robert H. *Government and the Mortgage Debtor (1929 to 1939).* Philadelphia: University of Pennsylvania, 1944.

Smith, Adam. *An Inquiry into the Nature and Causes of the Wealth of Nations.* 2 vols. New York: E. P. Dutton & Co., 1926.

Smith, Charles W., Jr. *Roger B. Taney: Jacksonian Jurist.* Chapel Hill: University of North Carolina Press, 1936.

Smith, Tynan, and Greenspun, Nathaniel. "Structural Limitations on Bank Competition." 32 *Law and Contemporary Problems* 40 (1967).

Smith, Walter B. *Economic Aspects of the Second Bank of the United States.* Cambridge, Mass.: Harvard University Press, 1953.

Sproul, Allan. "The Federal Reserve System—Working Partner of the National Banking System for Half a Century." In *Banking and Monetary Studies,* edited by Deane Carson, p. 64. Homewood, Ill.: Richard D. Irwin, Inc., 1963.

Stark, John R. "Coordination of Monetary Policy: Unfinished Business." 35 *Geo. Wash. L. Rev.* 318 (1966).

Steffens, Roscoe. *Cases on Commercial and Investment Paper.* 3d ed. Brooklyn, N.Y.: Foundation Press, Inc., 1964.

Stein, Herbert

(1) *Government Price Policy in the United States during the World War.* Williamstown, Mass.: Williams College, 1939.

(2) *The Fiscal Revolution in America.* Chicago: University of Chicago Press, 1969.

Stern, Robert L. "That Commerce Which Concerns More States Than One." 47 *Harv. L. Rev.* 1335 (1934).

Stimson, Frederic J. *American Statute Law.* 2 vols. Boston: Boston Book Co., 1886, 1892.

Story, Joseph. *Commentaries on the Constitution of the United States.* 3 vols. Boston: Hilliard, Gray & Co., 1833.

Story, William W. *Life and Letters of Joseph Story.* 2 vols. Boston: Charles C. Little and James Brown, 1851.

Studenski, Paul, and Krooss, Herman. *Financial History of the United States.* New York: McGraw Hill Book Co., Inc., 1952.

Sutherland, Arthur E. See Braucher and Sutherland.

Sutton, Francis X.; Harris, Seymour E.; Kaysen, Carl; and Tobin, James. *The American Business Creed.* Cambridge, Mass.: Harvard University Press, 1956.

Swisher, Carl Brent. *Roger B. Taney.* New York: Macmillan Co. 1935.

Taus, Esther Rogoff. *Central Banking Functions of the United States Treasury, 1789-1941.* New York: Columbia University Press, 1943.

Taxay, Don. *The U.S. Mint and Coinage.* New York: Arco Publishing Co. Inc., 1966.

Thayer, James B. "Legal Tender." 1 *Harv. L. Rev.* 73 (1887).

Tiffany, Francis B. *Handbook of the Law of Banks and Banking.* St. Paul, Minn.: West Publishing Co., 1912.

Timberlake, Richard H., Jr. *Money, Banking, and Central Banking.* New York: Harper & Row, 1965.

Tobin, James. "Commercial Banks as Creators of 'Money.' " In *Banking and Monetary Studies,* edited by Deane Carson, p. 408. Homewood, Ill.: Richard D. Irwin, Inc., 1963.

See: Sutton, Francis X., et al.

Treiber, William F. "The Federal Reserve System After Fifty Years." 20 *The Business Lawyer* 247 (1965).

Trescott, Paul B. *Financing American Enterprise: The Story of Commercial Banking.* New York: Harper & Row, 1963.

Triffin, Robert. *Gold and the Dollar Crisis.* New Haven: Yale University Press, 1960.

Turner, Donald F. See Kaysen and Turner.

Unger, Irwin. *The Greenback Era: A Social and Political History of American Finance, 1865-1879.* Princeton, N.J.: Princeton University Press, 1964.

United States Bureau of the Census. *Historical Statistics of the United*

States, 1789-1945. Washington, D.C.: Government Printing Office, 1949.

Vattel, Emmerich de. *The Law of Nations.* Edited by Joseph Chitty. 4th Am. ed. Philadelphia: P. H. Nicklin & T. Johnson, 1835.

Ver Steeg, Clarence L. *Robert Morris: Revolutionary Financier.* Philadelphia: University of Pennsylvania Press, 1954.

Wagge, Thomas O. "Service and Supervisory Functions of the Federal Reserve System." In *The Federal Reserve System,* edited by Herbert V. Prochnow, p. 226. New York: Harper & Brothers, 1960.

Wallich, Mable T., and Wallich, Henry C. "The Federal Reserve System during the 1930's." In *The Federal Reserve System,* edited by Herbert V. Prochnow, p. 317. New York: Harper & Brothers, 1960.

Walters, Raymond, Jr. *Albert Gallatin: Jeffersonian Financier and Diplomat.* New York: Macmillan Co., 1957.

Warburg, Paul M. *The Federal Reserve System: Its Origin and Growth.* 2 vols. New York: Macmillan Co., 1930.

Ward, John W. *Andrew Jackson: Symbol for an Age.* New York: Oxford University Press, 1962.

Warren, Charles
(1) *Bankrupty in United States History.* Cambridge, Mass.: Harvard University Press, 1935.
(2) *The Making of the Constitution.* Boston: Little, Brown & Co., 1928.
(3) *The Supreme Court in United States History.* 2 vols. Rev. ed. Boston: Little, Brown & Co., 1935.

Welman, Joseph C., Jr. "Allocation of Supervisory Responsibility Today." In Federal Reserve Bank of St. Louis, *Bank Supervision,* p. 11. St. Louis: Federal Reserve Bank of St. Louis, 1963.

White, Leonard D.
(1) *The Federalists: A Study in Administrative History.* New York: Macmillan Co., 1948.
(2) *The Jeffersonians: A Study in Administrative History, 1801-1829.* New York: Macmillan Co., 1956.
(3) *The Jacksonians: A Study in Administrative History, 1829-1861.* New York: Macmillan Co., 1954.
(4) *The Republican Era: 1869-1901.* New York: Macmillan Co., 1958.

Weibe, Robert H.
(1) *Businessmen and Reform.* Cambridge, Mass.: Harvard University Press, 1962.
(2) *The Search for Order, 1877-1920.* New York: Hill and Wang, 1967.

Wilburn, Jean Alexander. *Biddle's Bank: The Crucial Years.* New York: Columbia University Press, 1967.

Willard, Charles H. See Post and Willard.

Wille, Frank. "State Banking: A Study in Dual Regulation." 31 *Law and Contemporary Problems* 733 (1966).

Williams, T. Harry. *Huey Long.* New York: Alfred A. Knopf, 1969.

Willis, Henry Parker

    (1) *The Federal Reserve System.* New York: Ronald Press Co. 1923.

    (2) *The Theory and Practice of Central Banking.* New York: Harper & Brothers, 1936.

Williston, Samuel. *A Treatise on the Law of Contracts.* 8 vols. Rev. ed., by Samuel Williston and George J. Thompson. New York: Baker, Voorhis & Co., 1936.

Wilson, Christopher W. "Regulations of the Board of Governors." In *The Federal Reserve System,* edited by Herbert V. Prochnow, p. 251. New York: Harper & Brothers, 1960.

Wiltse, Charles M. *The New Nation, 1800-1845.* New York: Hill and Wang, 1961.

Wish, Harvey. *Contemporary America.* Rev. ed. New York: Harper & Brothers, 1955.

Wright, Benjamin F., Jr. *The Contract Clause of the Constitution.* Cambridge, Mass.: Harvard University Press, 1938.

Wright, David McCord. "Is the Amended Federal Reserve Act Constitutional—A Study in the Delegation of Power." 23 *Va. L. Rev.* 629 (1937).

Wyrick, Orville O. "The General Nature of Bank Supervision." In Federal Reserve Bank of St. Louis, *Bank Supervision,* p. 1. St. Louis: Federal Reserve Bank of St. Louis, 1963.

Youngdahl, C. Richard. "Open-Market Operations." In *The Federal Reserve System,* edited by Herbert V. Prochnow, p. 113. New York: Harper & Brothers, 1960.

Zahler, Helene S. See Hacker and Zahler.

Zollman, Carl. *The Law of Banks and Banking.* 12 vols. Kansas City, Mo.: Vernon Law Book Co., 1936.

Index